Sensors Expo and Conference 2024

Santa Clara, California, USA
18-20 June 2024

ISBN: 979-8-3313-0065-4

Printed from e-media with permission by:

Curran Associates, Inc.
57 Morehouse Lane
Red Hook, NY 12571

Some format issues inherent in the e-media version may also appear in this print version.

Questex Media Group, Inc.
275 Grove Street, Suite 2-130
Newton, Massachusetts 02466
USA

Phone: (617) 219-8300

info@questex.com

Additional copies of this publication are available from:

Curran Associates, Inc.
57 Morehouse Lane
Red Hook, NY 12571 USA
Phone: 845-758-0400
Fax: 845-758-2633
Email: curran@proceedings.com
Web: www.proceedings.com

TABLE OF CONTENTS

Sensors Converge

The Future of Electronic Design: AI-Driven Automation

June 24–26, 2024 | Santa Clara, CA

#SensorsConverge

Part 0:
Analog Design In Italy

#SensorsConverge

Sensors Converge

In Italy

Lucca

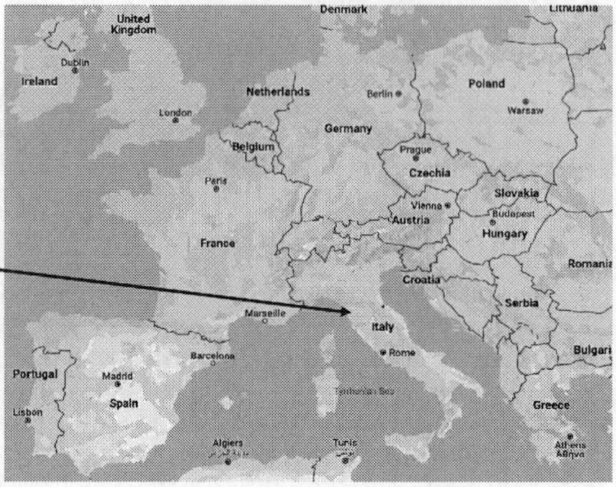

#SensorsConverge

Sensors Converge

In Italy

"Silicon"

#SensorsConverge

Sensors Converge

We Love Design

BCD

90nm 180nm

Low Power

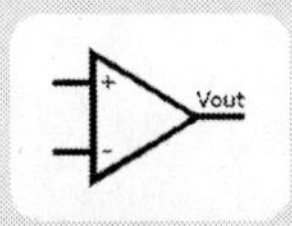

IPs

Advanced

Sensing

Switching

Focused

3D

Stack IC

Low Noise

Architectures

AI in Analog Design workflow

Part 1:
Problem in Analog Design

#SensorsConverge

Sensors Converge

Analog Designers

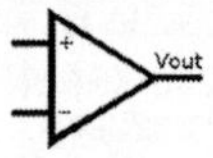

Digital Designers

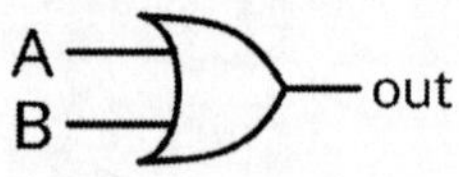

#SensorsConverge

Sensors Converge

Digital Designers

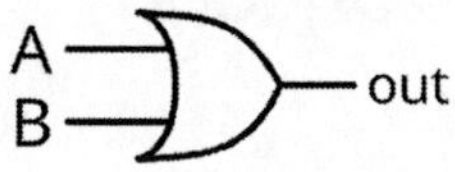

Massive Re-use of IPs

I/O IP | **MCU IP** | **DSP IP**

High Efficient Behavioral Model

#SensorsConverge

Sensors Converge

AI Ready

Digital Designers

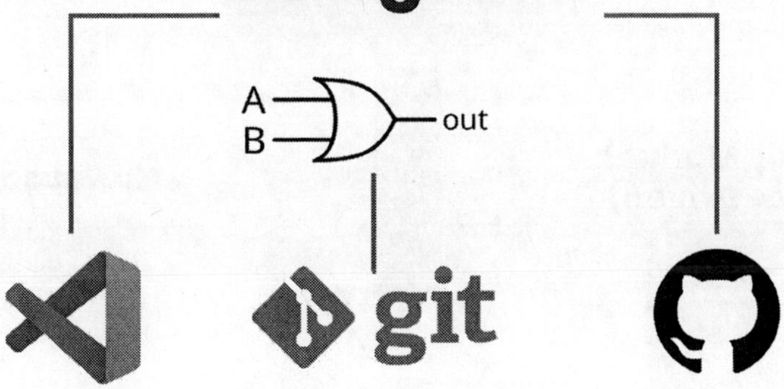

#SensorsConverge

Sensors Converge

Analog Designers

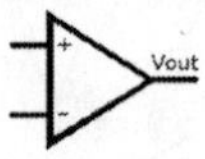

Analog Design in the early '00s

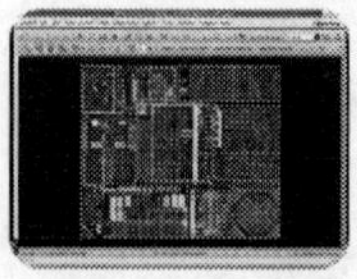

Analog Design today

#SensorsConverge

Sensors Converge

Analog Design Problems

Highly Manual (Spice Driven)

No Reuse

#SensorsConverge

Sensors Converge

Who to Blame?

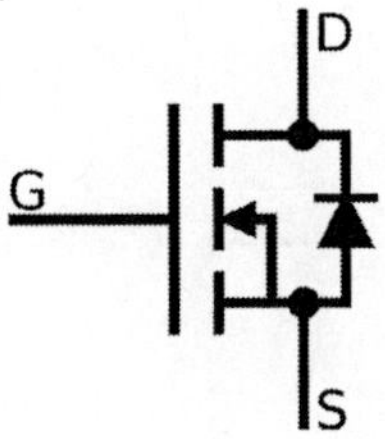

#SensorsConverge

Sensors Converge

Part 2:
AI for Analog Design

#SensorsConverge

Sensors Converge

Modelling IPs by AI

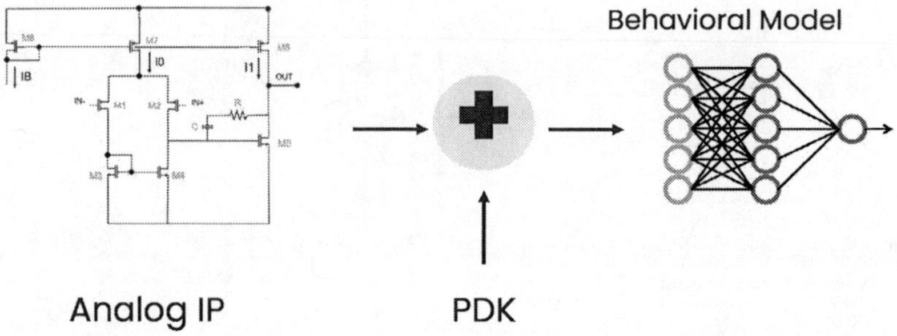

#SensorsConverge

Optimizing Analog IP

IP

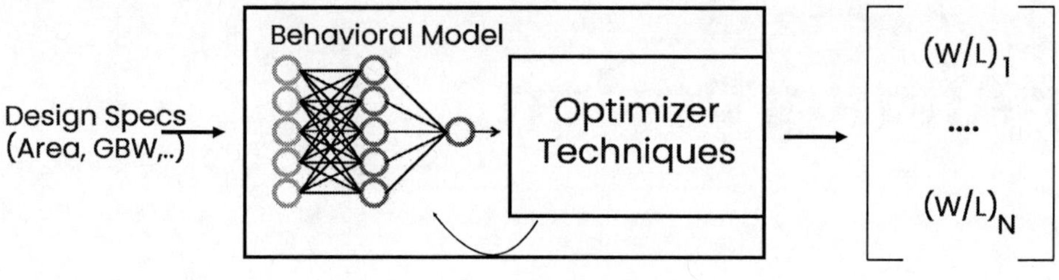

#SensorsConverge

Optimizing Analog IP

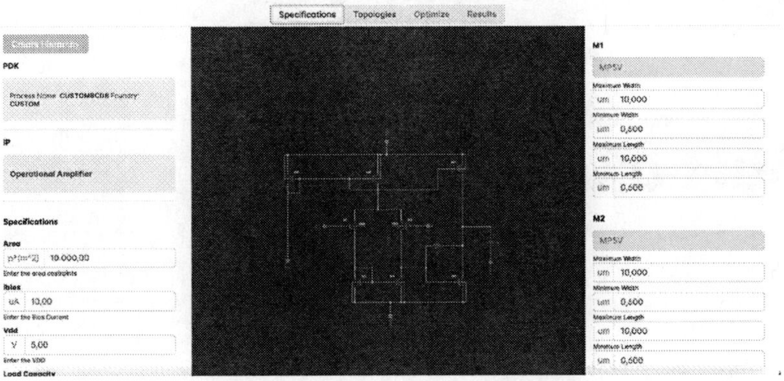

Evaluate
In 80s more
than 25'000
combinations

Specifications

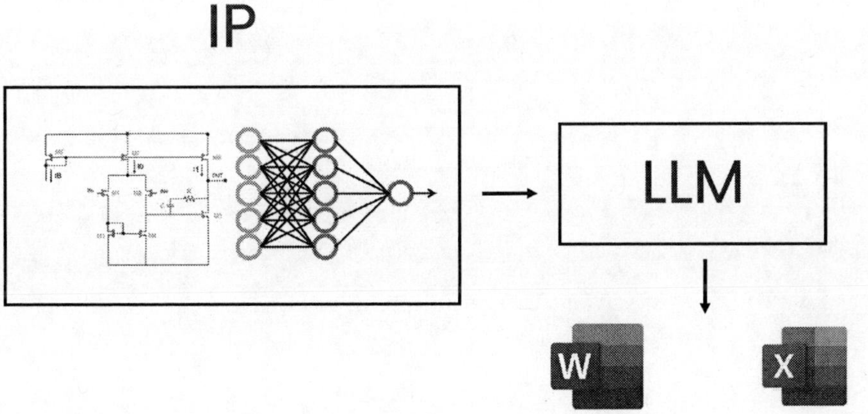

Final:
AI will be part of Analog Designer

#SensorsConverge

Sensors Converge

Pony.ai

Exploring the "End to End" use of Ai in automotive software

June 2024

Company Updates

6 Cities With Robotaxi testing & services, including drivered and driverless	**500+** Geographic coverage of ODDs in square miles	**500+** Vehicles in L4 fleet (300+ car, 200+ truck)	**20,000,000+** Autonomous Robotaxi miles
2,000+ Public facing rides provided on peak days	**0** Safety critical accidents	**1,300** Employees	**1,500,000+** Driverless Robotaxi miles

Global Landscape

Deeply-rooted in both United States and China markets, Pony.ai has been conducting road tests around the world since 2017. Our diverse experience operating *over 20 million autonomous miles* on public roads allows for the safe generalization of our technology into new environments.

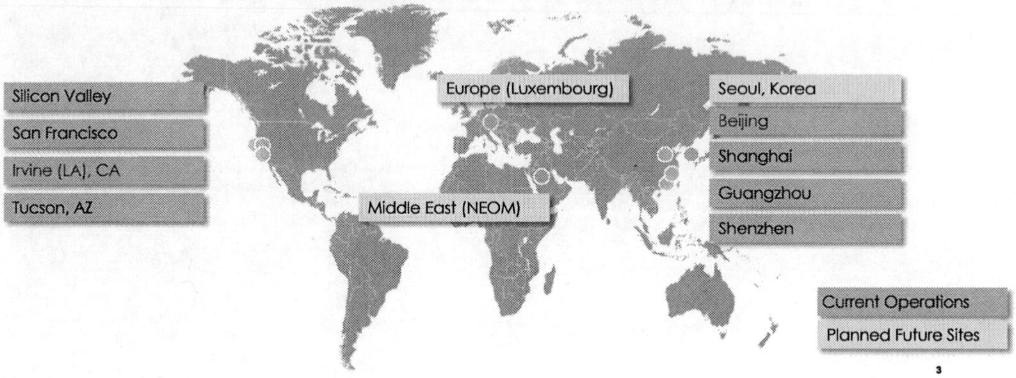

Pony.ai - Confidential material protected under NDA

3

Driverless Ride in China - Dec. 2022

Pony.ai - Confidential material protected under NDA

4

Where in the Stack AI used now?

Sensor fusion

The coordinated combination of data from numerous types of sensors as well as the input from a GPS or wheel encoder to solve for position. There are different types of fusion, but the end goal is to send the right data to the perception system.

Perception

Making sense of the fused data. Using sensor input to infer what the car is looking at and where it is. Lane marking, signage, pedestrians, cars, trucks, bikes, animals etc, etc. Traditionally this processes uses AI models develop using Deep Learning or other techniques.

Prediction

Now that we know what it is, what will it do ? Prediction is all about determining when a pedestrian might step into the path of traffic or when a car that is behaving erratically may weave into the lane of the ego vehicle.

Planning

How to safety interact with other cars , trucks and pedestrians. This is the process of instructing the car as to when to stop, go or change directions in concert with traffic.

Control

This is where the rubber meets the road and the vehicle steers, accelerates or brakes simulating how it would feel is a human was driving. This is critical step in delivering a good ADAS system,, it need to be very smooth and assertive at the same time.

End to End Example - Presented by OpenDriveLab @ CVPR 2023

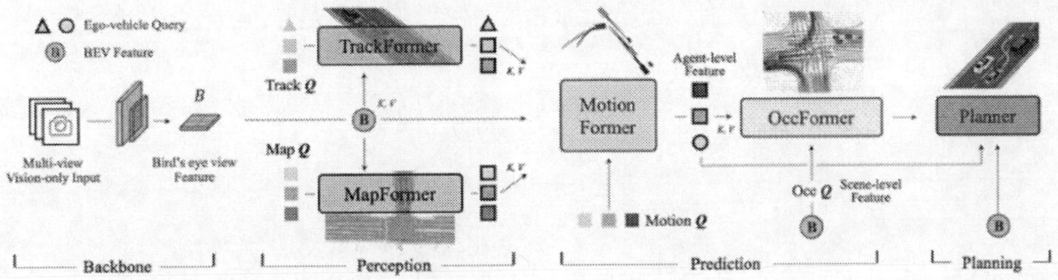

Figure 11: Pipeline of Unified Autonomous Driving (UniAD) [9].

https://github.com/OpenDriveLab/UniAD

Thank you!
pony.ai

Archetype AI

Newton, A Foundation Model For Physical AI

Sensors Converge
June 24, 2024

1

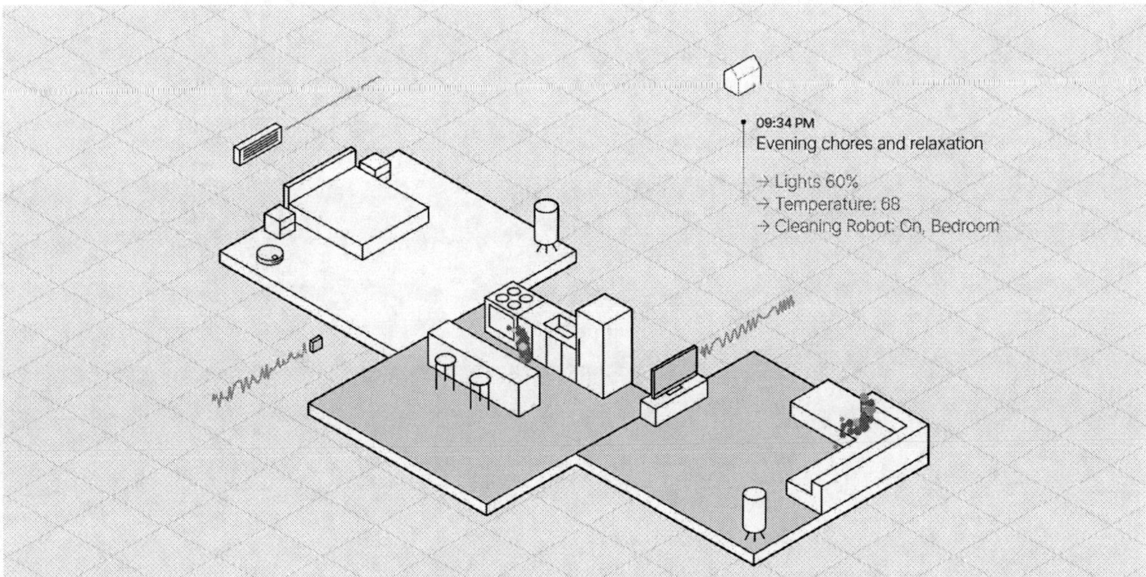

Archetype AI © 2024

3

Newton: One foundation model for the physical world to serve all use cases across all verticals and data types. A Large Behavior Model (LBM).

Fragmented solutions ⟶ General solution

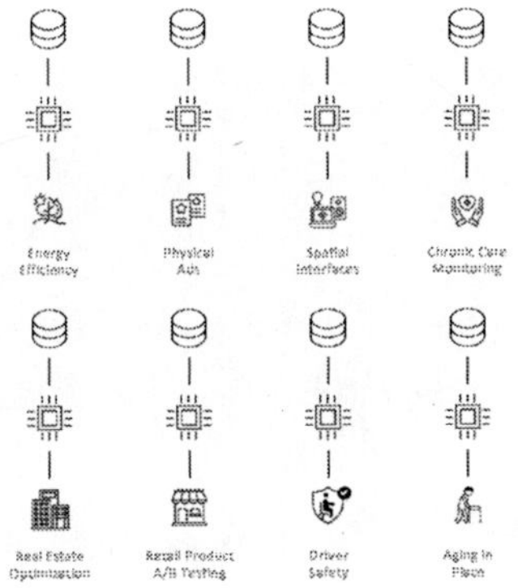

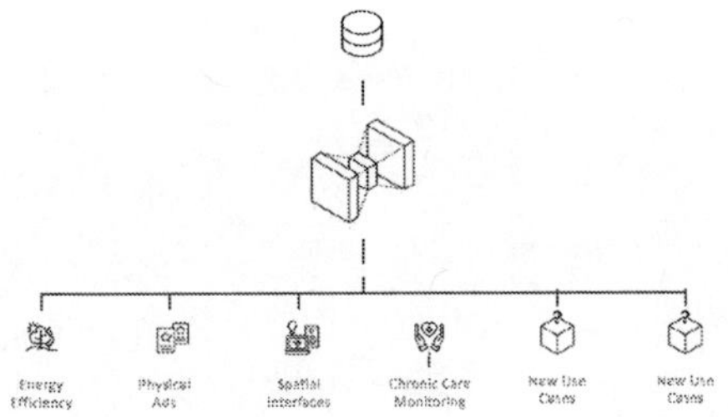

Newton: One foundation model for the physical world to serve all use cases across all verticals and data types. A Large Behavior Model (LBM).

Fragmented solutions ⟶ General solution

One model per use case

- High development cost
- Requires AI expertise
- Narrow and siloed
- Hardware specific
- Software updates difficult to maintain
- Difficult to integrate into existing systems and flows

One model for ALL use cases

- Foundation model gives economy of scale
- Low cost to fine tune (if needed)
- No AI expertise required
- Sensor fusion into a unified representation
- Hardware and sensor agnostic
- Simplified updates to one common model
- Integrates smoothly and usable by anyone

A foundation AI model that understands the physical world
by learning about it directly from sensor data

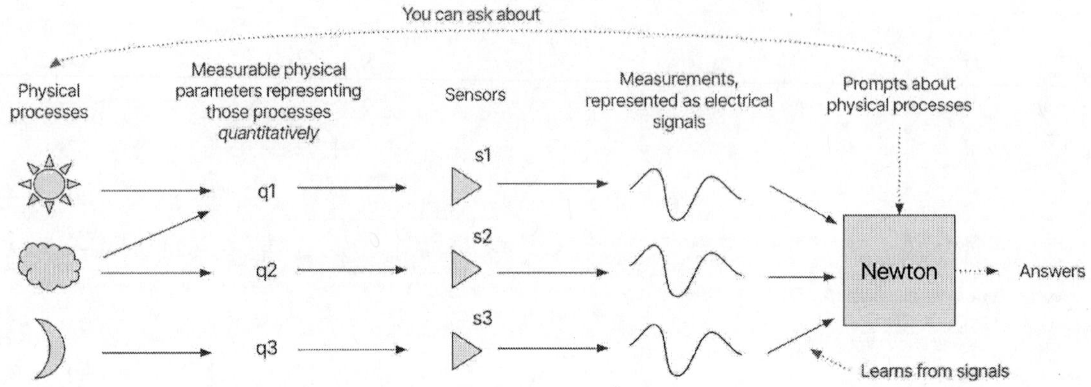

Pre-trained to understand all kinds of physical sensor data...

including sensor types and domains
It has never seen before

Newton architecture

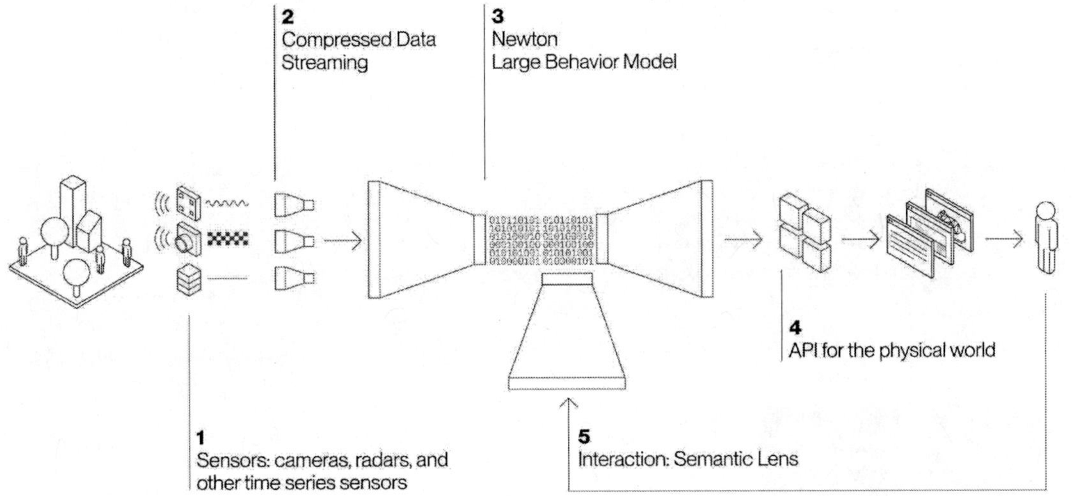

Newton's universal time series encoder learns directly from sensor data to understand the common underlying structures of time-varying physical signals.

We can apply the encoder to sensor types and domains it never saw in training.

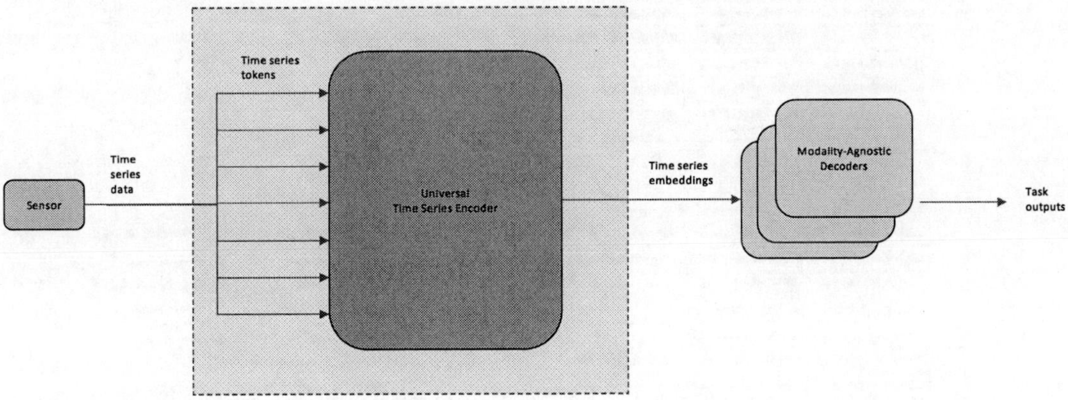

We have validated and applied the universal time series encoder to a broad variety of physical sensors and downstream tasks.

1. Compression & reconstruction

Training dataset: Accelerometer
Target dataset: Temperature

Training dataset: Accelerometer
Target dataset: Gyroscope

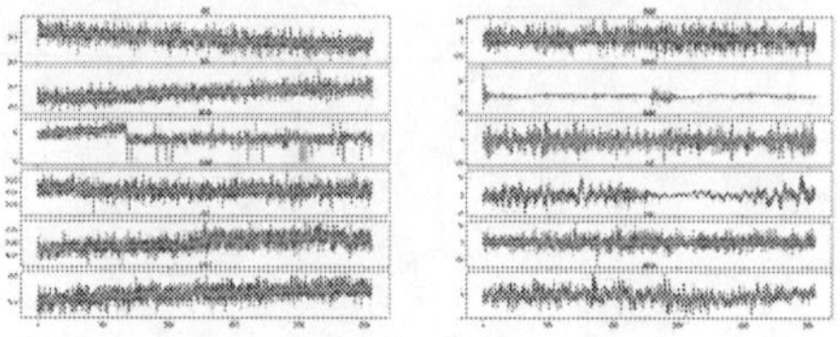

2. Classification

Target use case: Radar presence detection

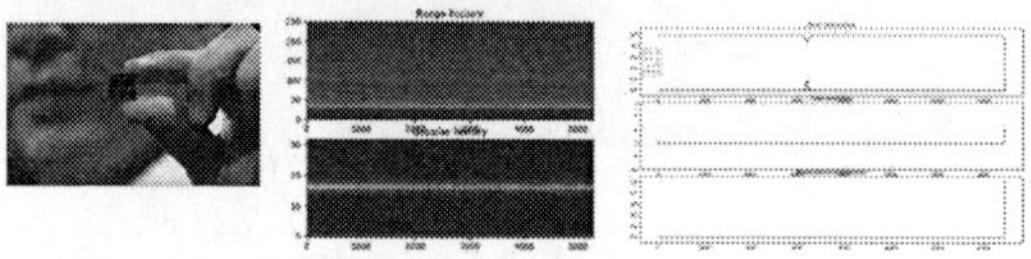

3. Forecasting

Training dataset: Cross-modal
Target dataset: Temperature (never seen in training)

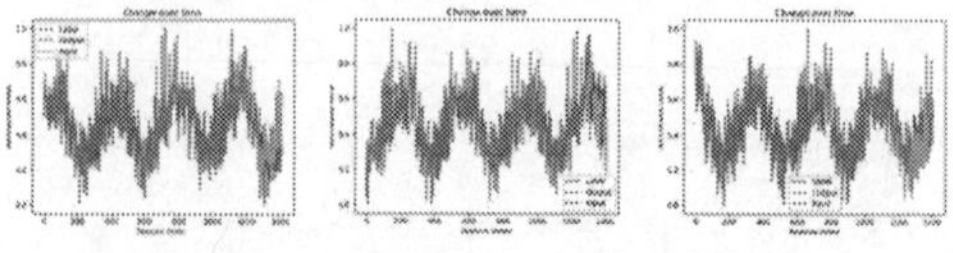

Training dataset: Cross-modal
Target dataset: Electricity (never seen in training)

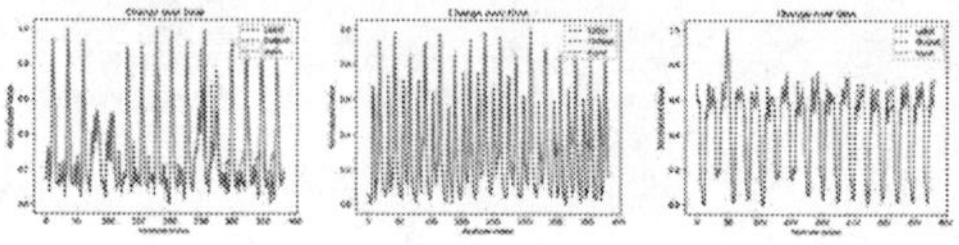

Archetype AI © 2024

1. Modality-Agnostic Compression and Reconstruction

UNE Application to Passive Vehicular Sensors Dataset

Accelerometer

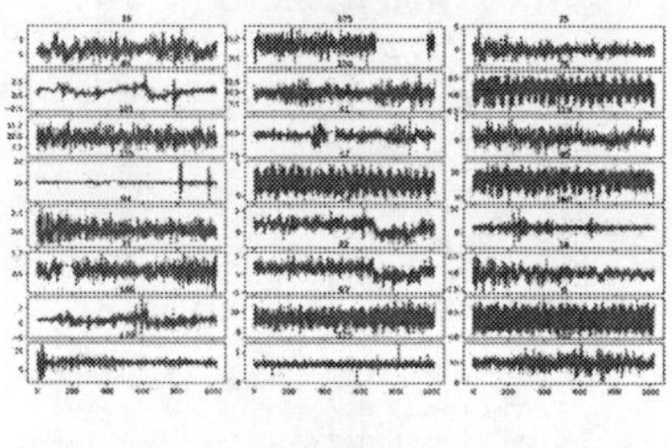

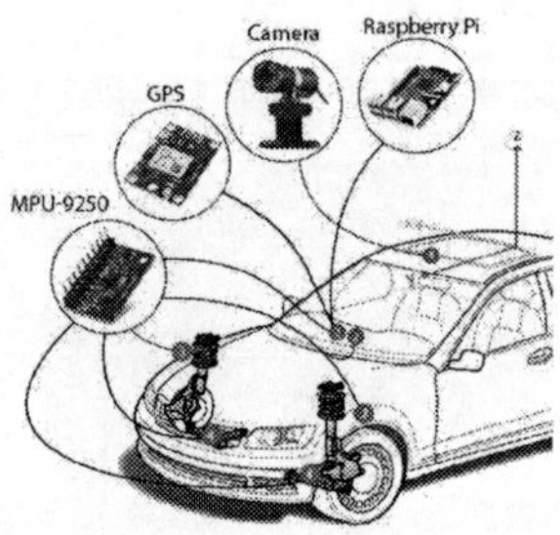

Gyroscope

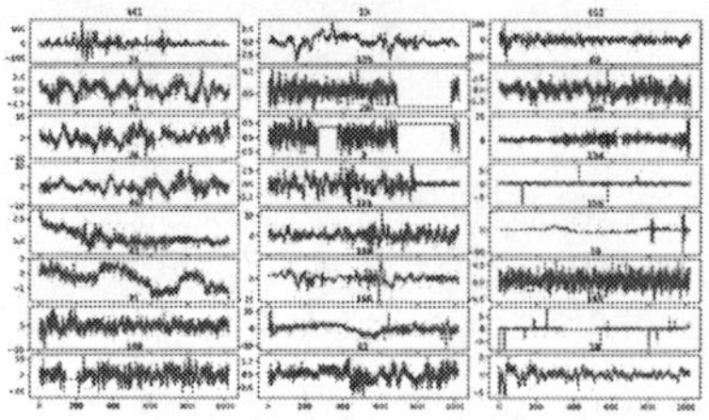

Temperature

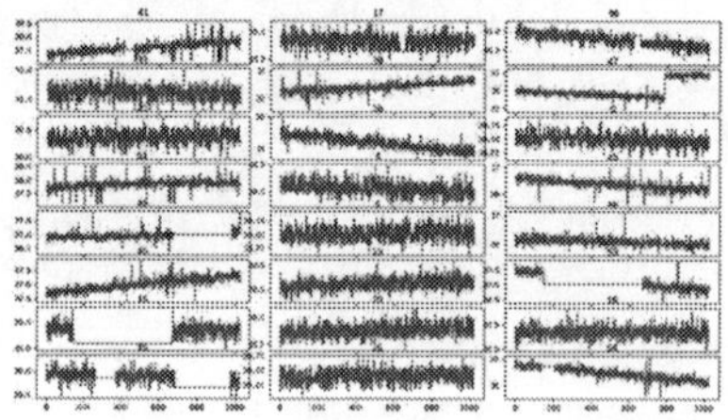

Archetype AI © 2024

How it was tested

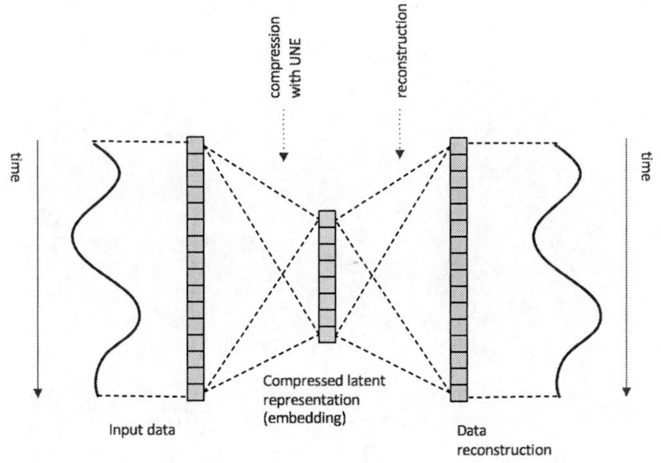

1. We trained Universal Neural Encoder (UNE) on accelerometer data.

2. We then used pre-trained UNE to compress and reconstruct different types of sensor data, including data that UNE never "saw" before

	Training	Validation	Testing
Accelerometer	X	X	X
Gyroscope			X
Temperature			X

01
Trained w/ accelerometer.
Accelerometer reconstruction task.

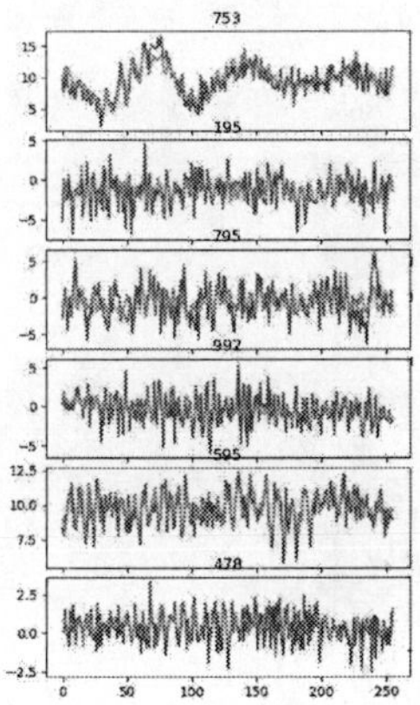

02
Trained w/ accelerometer.
Gyroscope reconstruction.

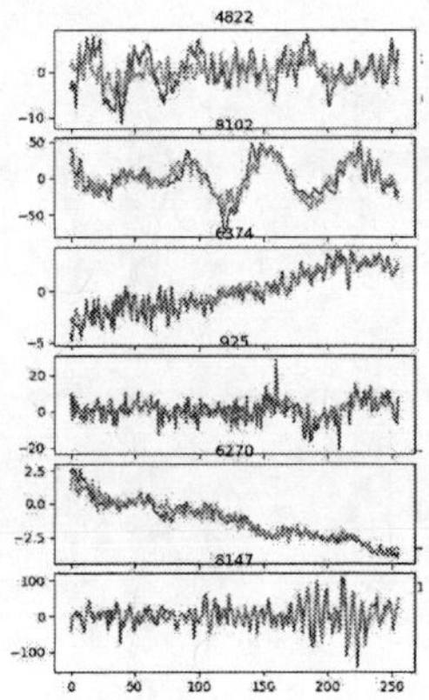

03
Trained w/ accelerometer.
Temperature reconstruction.

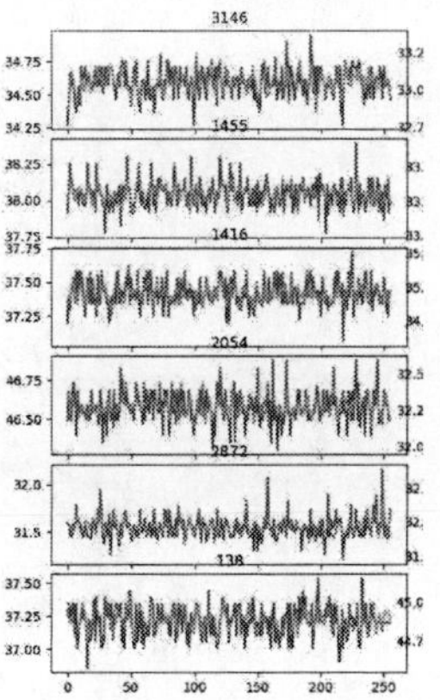

Ground Truth
Reconstruction

2. Modality-Agnostic Classification
Universal Neural Encoder application to radar data

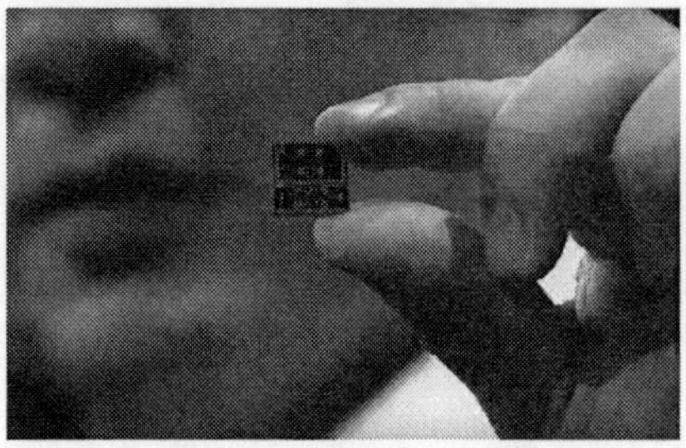

We trained UNE on radar data and built a Modality-Agnostic Decoder to cluster the data according to the classes.

We used 2 multi-label classes: human presence and moving object presence.

Reconstruction of multichannel I/Q radar data using UNE

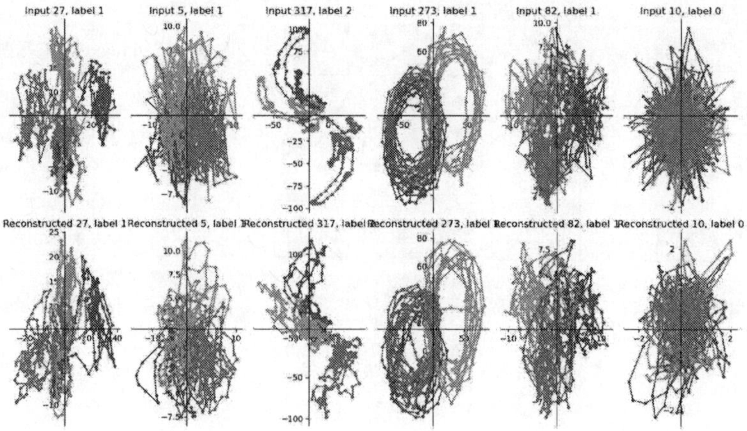

Radar classification with Universal Neural Encoder

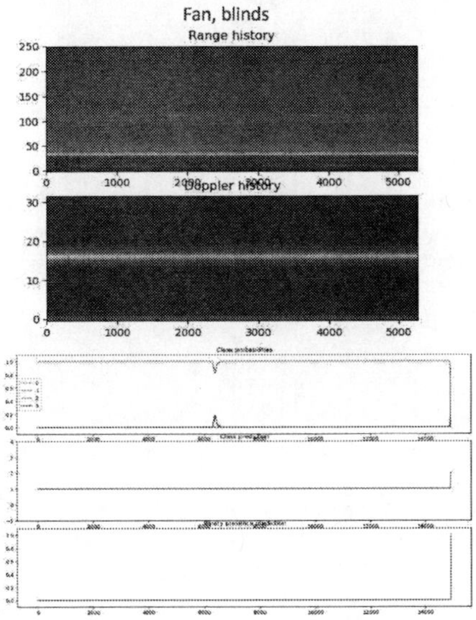

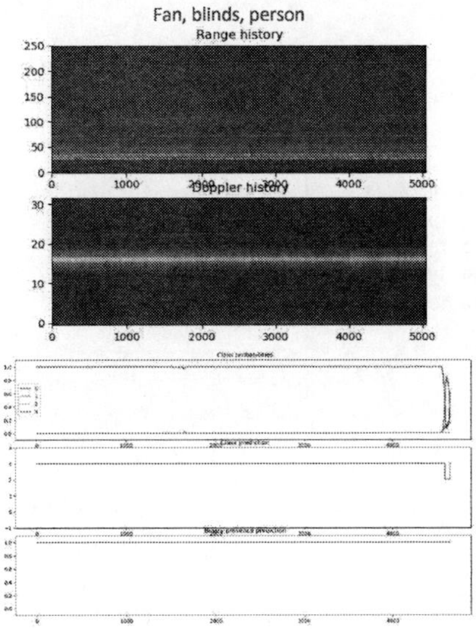

Archetype

3. Modality-Agnostic Forecasting

<u>Target dataset</u>: Temperature; <u>Pre-training datasets</u>: Traffic, Weather, Etth/Ettm, HAR, PAMAP2, PVS

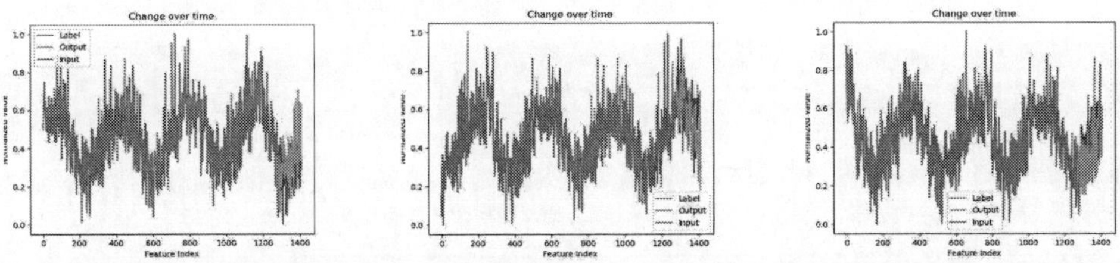

<u>Target dataset</u>: Electricity; <u>Pre-training datasets</u>: Traffic, Weather, Etth/Ettm, HAR, PAMAP2, PVS

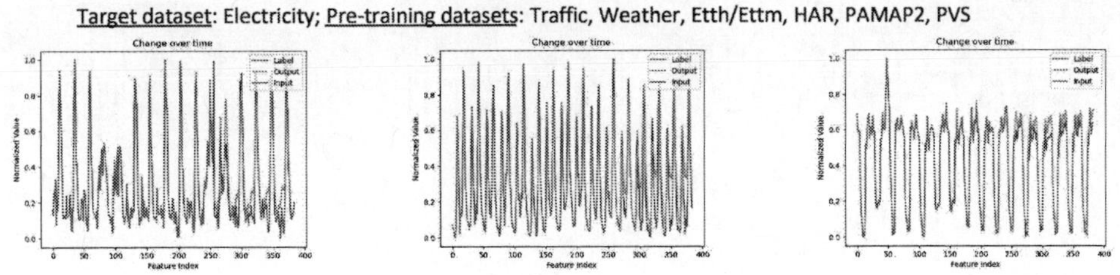

Ground Truth
Forecast

Forecasting
-> Comparison with SOTA

Newton Universal Sensor Encoder performs better than classic statistical techniques like ARIMA.

Target dataset: Traffic
Pre-training datasets: Electricity, Weather, Etth/Ettm, HAR, PAMAP2, PVS

Ground Truth
Forecast

Classic statistical technique	Newton, zero-shot	Newton, fine-tuned
Mean square error: 0.0231	Mean square error: 0.0201	Mean square error: 0.0111

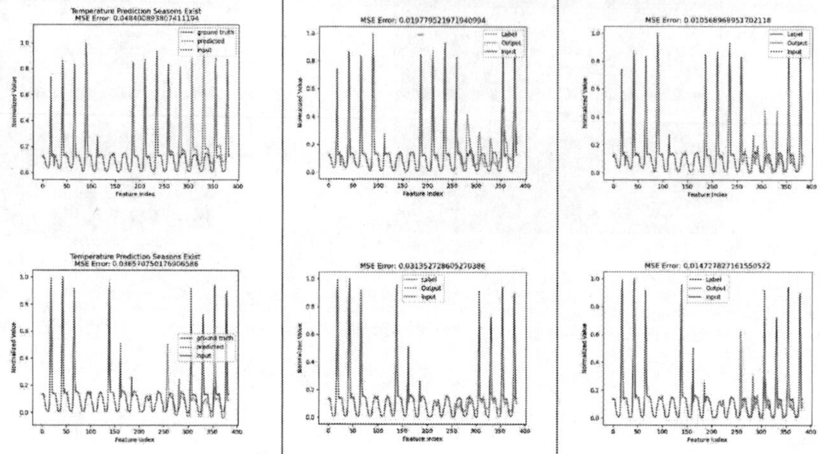

Archetype AI © 2024

26

Comparison of Newton fine-tuning vs zero-shot forecasting

Target dataset: Electricity

	Zero-shot	Fine-tuned decoder	Fully fine-tuned
MSE	0.0277	0.0178	0.0148

Zero-shot

Fine-tuned decoder

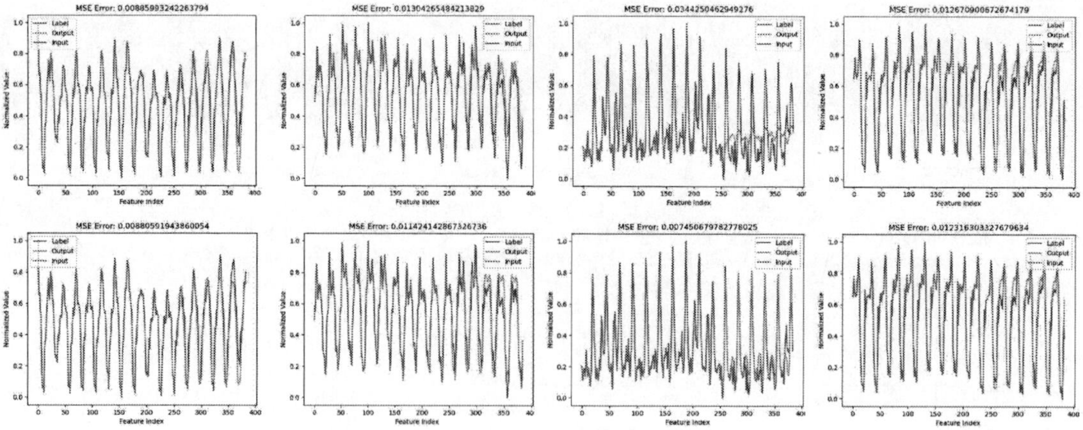

Archetype AI © 2024

Confidential. Do not distribute.

Pre-training datasets: Traffic, Weather, Etth/Ettm, HAR, PAMAP2, PVS

We are piloting Newton with design partners to deploy physical AI use cases.

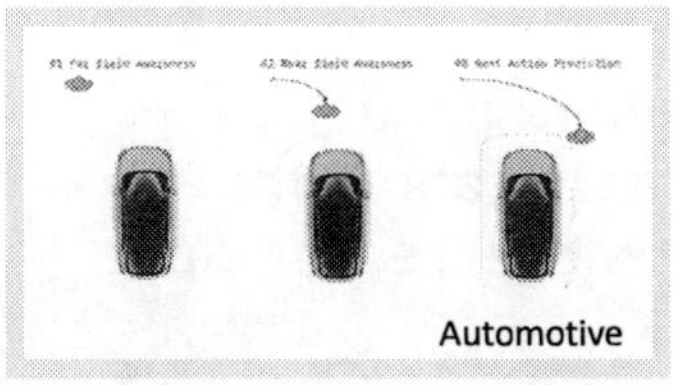

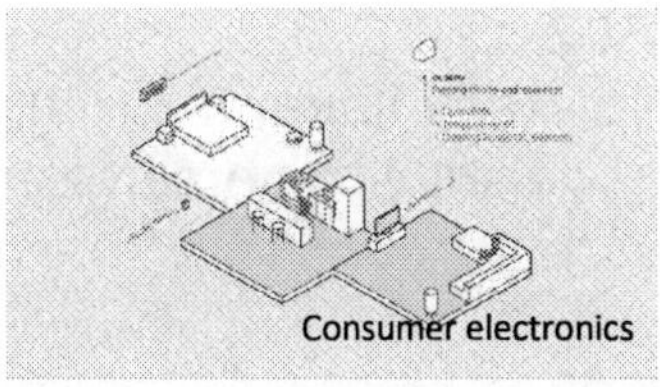

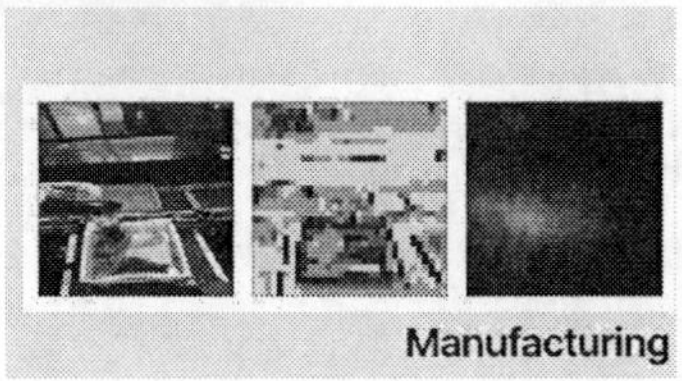

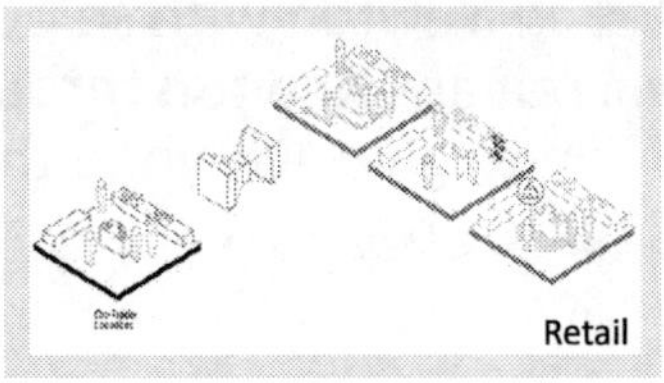

Manufacturing – Industrial Process Monitoring

-> Design partner problems

Monitoring hundreds and thousands of sensors on process lines is challenging due to limited AI and ML resources.

Each company has custom processes. Much data is underutilized, service overhead is high, reliability and precision are insufficient.

-> Newton Solution

Single model, Newton, replaces multiple narrow ML models to monitor all sensor data at the manufacturing site or machine.

Sensor fusion across multiple modalities and sensors provides new insights and recommendations to optimize performance.

Other use cases

- Fusion of video and time series sensor data for monitoring, training, and guidance.
- Predictive maintenance for equipment
- Natural language interaction with very large sensor data sets, e.g. semantic search

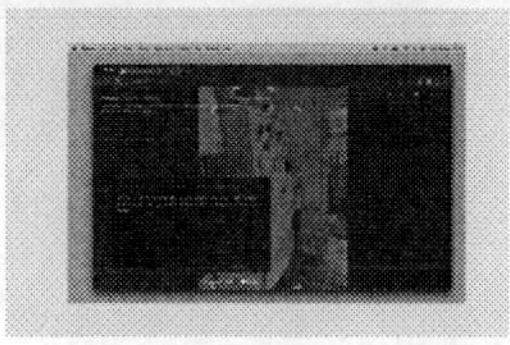

-> 01
Archetype AI is a physical AI company helping humanity make sense of the world.

-> 02
We are building Newton, the first foundation model able to perceive and reason about the world through real time multimodal sensor data.

-> 03
We are now piloting Newton with select design partners. We will release Newton through our developer platform to give everyone the power of AI to solve real world problems.

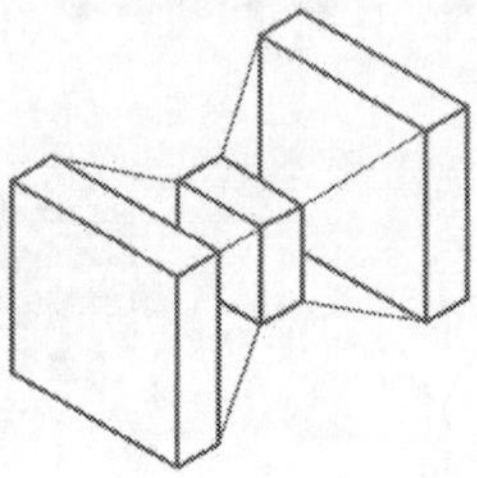

Thank you

Demo:
Equipment Maintenance

Real time understanding of unusual situations and anomalies.

Newton detects and investigates maintenance problems based on video and audio.

LINK ->

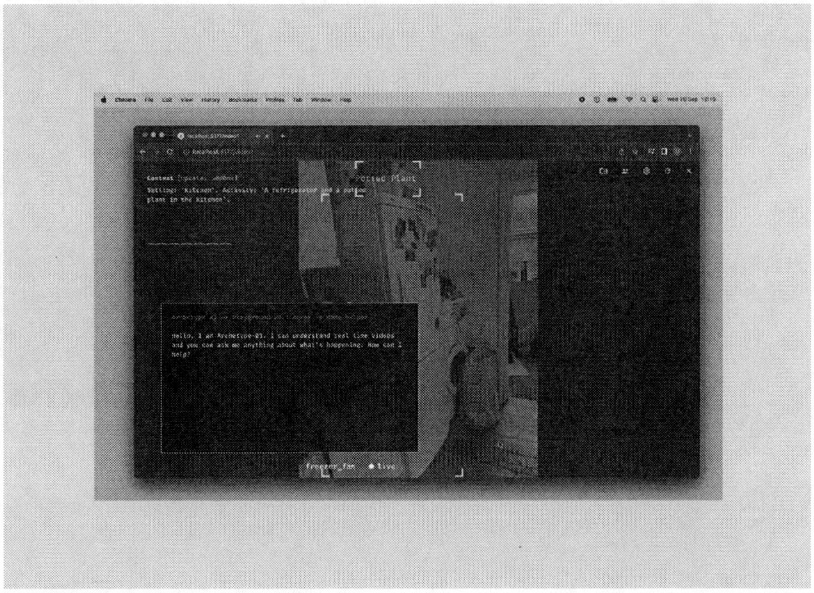

Demo:
Activity transcription

Step-by-step activity description in real time.

Demo:
Activity prediction

Next step prediction in real time.

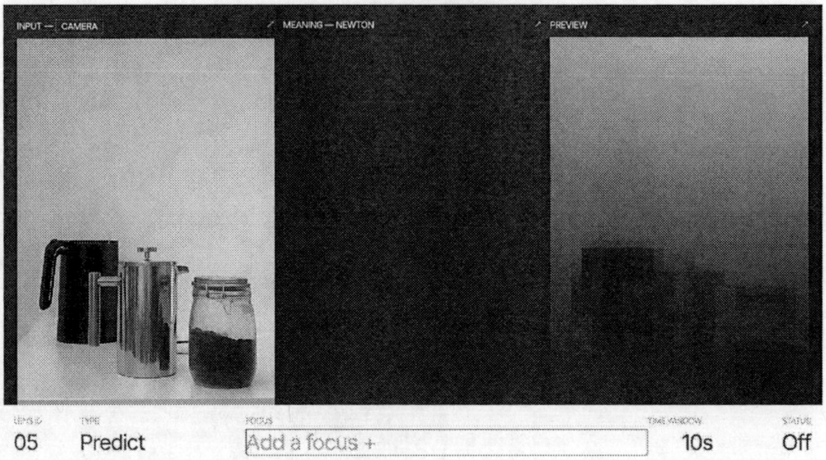

Sensors Converge
ATTEND CONFERENCE EXPO SCHEDULE HOTEL EXHIBIT AWARDS MANAGE REGISTRATION
REGISTER NOW
North America's Largest Electronics Event for Design Engineers
June 24-26, 2024
Santa Clara Convention Center, Santa Clara, CA
Register Now
Exhibit
Panel
Implementing AI: Best Practices, Workforce Considerations & Overcoming Obstacles
June 24th 2024 – 11:00-11:40 hrs PST - Grand Ballroom E
Moderator: Dr. Martin Serrano, Insight SFI Research Centre
Speakers: Mio Suzuki, Director, Advanced Technologies Trek Bicycle
Gaia Bellone, Chief Data Scientist, Prudential
Dr. Ivan Poupryev, CEO & Founder, Archetype AI
Sensors Converge
Connect
Advertise
Contact Us
Join Us
Newsletters
Our Brands
Fierce Electronics
Fierce Telecom
Fierce Wireless
Our Events
Electronics
Wireless & Telecom

Sensors Converge
PANEL:
Implementing AI: Best Practices, Workforce Considerations & Overcoming Obstacles
June 24th 2024 - 11am-11:40 hrs PST - Grand Ballroom E
Dr. Martin Serrano
Insight SFI Centre
Head Scientist of the Internet of Things (UIoT) Research Unit
Gaia Bellone
Prudential
Vice President, Head of Global Data and AI Enablement, CDAO Emerging Markets, Chief Data Office
Mio Suzuki
Trek Bicycle
Director, Advanced Technologies
Dr. Ivan Poupryev
Archetype AI
Founder & CEO
Sensors Converge
Connect
Advertise
Contact Us
Join Us
Newsletters
Our Brands
Fierce Electronics
Fierce Telecom
Fierce Wireless
Our Events
Electronics
Wireless & Telecom

Implementing AI: Best Practices, Workforce Considerations & Overcoming Obstacles
June 24th 2024 - 11am-11:40 hrs PST - Grand Ballroom E

Gaia is a dynamic and accomplished leader in the field of Data Science and Artificial Intelligence. In her current role at Prudential Financial, she leads Global Data and AI Enablement and serves as Chief Data and Analytics Officer (CDAO) for Emerging Markets.

Her contributions to Prudential Financial have been significant and impactful. As the former Chief Data Scientist at Prudential, she led the Data Science team in creating innovative solutions for Digital, Marketing, Sales, and Distribution, the AI/ML Platform team, and the GenAI Enterprise Program. Her leadership and strategic vision have been instrumental in driving business growth and enhancing operational efficiency.

Gaia Bellone
Prudential
Vice President,
Head of Global Data and AI Enablement,
CDAO Emerging Markets,
Chief Data Office

Prior to her tenure at Prudential, she held prominent positions at Key Bank and JPMorgan Chase. At Key Bank, she served as the Head of Data Science for the Community Bank. Her leadership and expertise in data science were crucial in optimizing the bank's operations and improving customer experience. At JPMorgan Chase, she led the data science teams for Home Lending and Auto Finance. Her strategic insights and data-driven solutions significantly improved the business performance in these sectors, contributing to the overall success of the enterprise.

Sensors Converge

Connect: Advertise, Contact Us | Join Us: Newsletters | Our Brands: Fierce Electronics, Fierce Telecom, Fierce Wireless | Our Events: Electronics, Wireless & Telecom

Implementing AI: Best Practices, Workforce Considerations & Overcoming Obstacles
June 24th 2024 - 11am-11:40 hrs PST - Grand Ballroom E

Mio Suzuki is a devoted technologist with a mission to introduce ground-breaking technologies to organizations, enabling transformation of visionary concepts into tangible realities.

Her core areas of expertise encompass AI/Data Science, pioneering use of spatial computing and advanced simulation on product development and operation applications and crafting embedded AI solutions for two-wheeler mobility products.

Mio Suzuki
Trek Bicycle
Director,
Advanced Technologies

She has been spearheading the establishment of Trek's AI Center of Excellence, collaborating seamlessly with various business units to harness the potential of AI in propelling progress throughout the company.

Sensors Converge

Connect: Advertise, Contact Us | Join Us: Newsletters | Our Brands: Fierce Electronics, Fierce Telecom, Fierce Wireless | Our Events: Electronics, Wireless & Telecom

Implementing AI: Best Practices, Workforce Considerations & Overcoming Obstacles

June 24th 2024 - 11am-11:40 hrs PST - Grand Ballroom E

Dr. Ivan Poupyrev is an award-winning inventor, scientist, and entrepreneur. Currently, he is the CEO and founder of Archetype AI, and deep tech AI start up which seeks to build a foundational model that can understand and reason about the physical world in real time, what he calls 'Physical AI.'

Dr. Ivan Poupryev
Archetype AI
Founder & CEO

A former technology executive at Google and a research scientist at Disney Imagineering and Sony before that. Dr. Poupyrev is an inventor with more than 100 issued patents and over 100 publications. TED speaker, and National Design Award winner. Ivan was named 'one of the best interaction designers in the world' by Fast Company.

Sensors Converge

Connect: Advertise, Contact Us
Join Us: Newsletters
Our Brands: Fierce Electronics, Fierce Telecom, Fierce Wireless
Our Events: Electronics, Wireless & Telecom

Implementing AI: Best Practices, Workforce Considerations & Overcoming Obstacles

June 24th 2024 - 11am-11:40 hrs PST - Grand Ballroom E

Obstacles & Challenges:

- The on-line data that is easily available is almost all used, we need to start looking at new kinds of data
- The on-line AI is siloed and not connected to the physical world

Workforce Considerations:

- Talk about lack of talent and how AI can help. The problem is not replacement, problem is making people more efficient

Best Practices:

- Large Behaviour Models versus Language models. LBM that understands behaviours of the people and machines.

Envisioning AI trends and Expectations

* Forward Looking General Comments on your own view?
* Differences on Innovation Management and methods to Include more innovation?
* How to Introduce business needs?
* Different types of AI. Physical AI
* Application Areas Vs Cross Domain Areas,

Sensors Converge

Connect: Advertise, Contact Us
Join Us: Newsletters
Our Brands: Fierce Electronics, Fierce Telecom, Fierce Wireless
Our Events: Electronics, Wireless & Telecom

Sensors Converge

How Advanced Driver Assistance Systems are changing the way we drive

Sneha Sudhir Shetiya | June 24–26, 2024 | Santa Clara, CA

#SensorsConverge

Agenda

- Significance of mobility:Industrial Revolution
- The need for self driving
- The first self driven car
- Examples today: Tesla Revolution, Cruise, Waymo
- OEMs competition
- Safety aspects
- Conclusion

#SensorsConverge

Sensors Converge

Car before the turn of the century

- Increased Mobility
- Industrial Revolution
- Personal Freedom
- Military Application
- Evolution of Technology

Cars today

- Reducing Human Error
- Improved Situational Awareness
- Efficiency and Convenience: Traffic Optimization, Automated Features, Real-Time Information
- Future of Autonomous Vehicles: Paving the Way for Self-Driving Cars, Infrastructure Preparation

Image Source:https://mercedes-benz-publicarchive.com/marsClassic/en/instance/ko/Mercedes-Knight-1030-hp---2565-hp-1910---1924.xhtml?oid=5943 https://hdqwalls.com/tesla-roadster-2020-wallpaper

First Self Driven Cars

- 1920s : In July 1925, Houdina Radio Control first demonstrated the radio-controlled "American Wonder" on New York City streets.
- 1930s: An early depiction of automated guided cars was Norman Bel Geddes's Futurama exhibit sponsored by General Motors at the 1939 World's Fair.
- 1950s: In 1953, RCA Labs successfully created a system with a miniature car guided and controlled by wires laid in a pattern on a laboratory floor.
- 1960s: In 1960, Ohio State University's Communication and Control Systems Laboratory launched a project to develop driverless cars which were activated by electronic devices embedded in the roadway.
- 1980s: Mercedes-Benz van with self-driving capabilities
- 1990s: in 1995, Carnegie Mellon's Navlab 5

Image Source:https://www.imeche.org/news/news-article/mercedes-benz-unveils-futuristic-'vision-van'
https://www.cs.cmu.edu/~tjochem/nhaa/navlab5_details.html

DARPA Challenge

- 2000s

Video Source: https://www.youtube.com/watch?v=2gQ3P5BpLjQ

#SensorsConverge

Sensors Converge

Some examples of ADAS features in vehicles on streets today

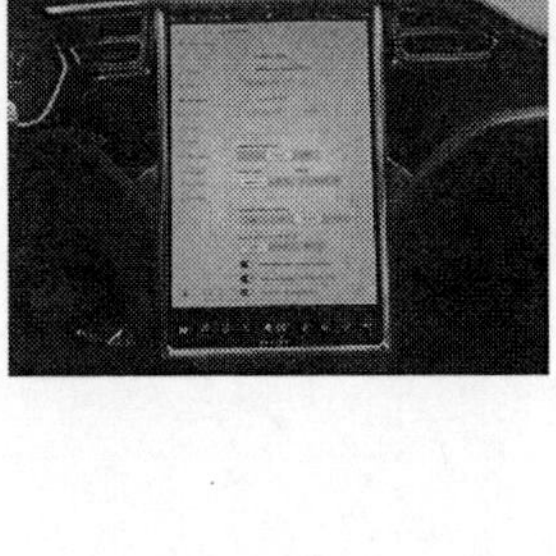

Image Source: https://teslamotorsclub.com/tmc/threads/can-you-tell-if-this-used-model-s-has-fsd.193646/
https://waymo.com/waymo-driver/
https://www.wired.com/story/gm-cruise-generation-3-self-driving-car/

#SensorsConverge

Sensors Converge

Autonomous Trucking is not behind

Image Source: https://torc.ai/trucking/
https://www.wfaa.com/article/news/local/insider-qa-aurora-ceo-chris-urmson-on-self-driving-trucks-autonomous/287-fe589d59-a52f-4269-9424-9531a24dcc87
https://www.ambarella.com/news/kodiak-robotics-selects-ambarella-ai-domain-controller-soc-for-next-generation-autonomous-trucks/

OEMs Competition

- Ford - Blue Cruise
- GM- Super Cruise
- Mercedes - Drive Pilot

Functional Safety and SOTIF importance

- FUSA(ISO26262)
- SOTIF-Safety Of The Intended Functionality(PAS-21448)

#SensorsConverge

Sensors Converge

CONCLUSION

- ADAS is an ever-evolving technology and it varies based on the usecase.
- Safety is critical and it is challenging to achieve 100% validation.
- System On Chip Designs will play a critical role in providing the computing power necessary for self driving capabilities
- GenAI capabilities in model building for mobile vehicles yet to be explored.
- Increased cost with add on features , cybersecurity requirements and government regulations are huge challenged posed to the Industry today.

#SensorsConverge

Sensors Converge

THANK YOU
QUESTIONS?

#SensorsConverge

Sensors Converge

Architectures for Safe Automated Driving

Chaitanya Shinde - System Safety Expert - AV
June 24–26, 2024 | Santa Clara, CA

#SensorsConverge

THE | AUTONOMOUS

Working Group Safety & Architecture

#SensorsConverge

Sensors Converge

Safety & Architecture Working Group

Mission & Vision

- Building a safe and failure-free AD system for complex driving tasks is a huge challenge. An AD system needs to tolerate faults and maintain safe operation (fail degraded and sometime fail operational).
- Many industry players start with concepts incrementally from legacy ADAS or pre-development projects.
- Our approach is to first think about a solid, high-level architecture for AD.
- Safety is not an area to compete or compromise on - it is highly beneficial to collaborate on this topic.

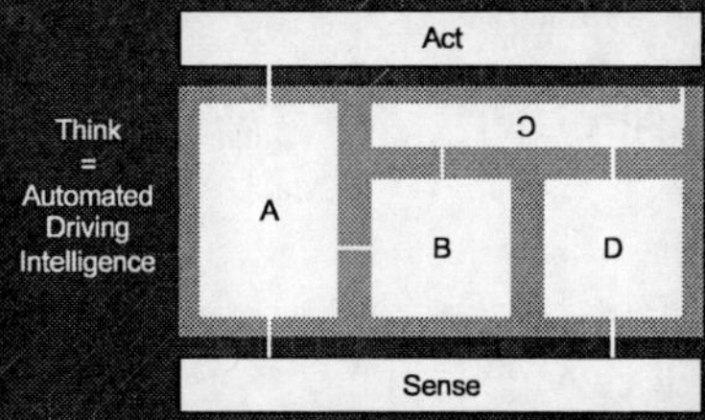

#SensorsConverge

Sensors Converge

Safety & Architecture Working Group

Meet our members

infineon
Udo Dannebaum
Jens Rosenbusch

KTH
Martin Törngren

BASELABS Data Fusion Results
Gabi Escuela

Private Contributors
Nahla Ben Mosbeh
Chaitanya Shinde

TTTechAuto
Christian Mangold
Moritz Antlanger
Georg Niedrist
Friedrich Reisenberger

CoreAVI INNOVATING A SAFER TOMORROW
Neil Stroud
Matthew

DENSO
DENSO AUTOMOTIVE Deutschland GmbH
Justin-Kiyoshi Tiele
Kazuhito Takenaka

#SensorsConverge

Sensors Converge

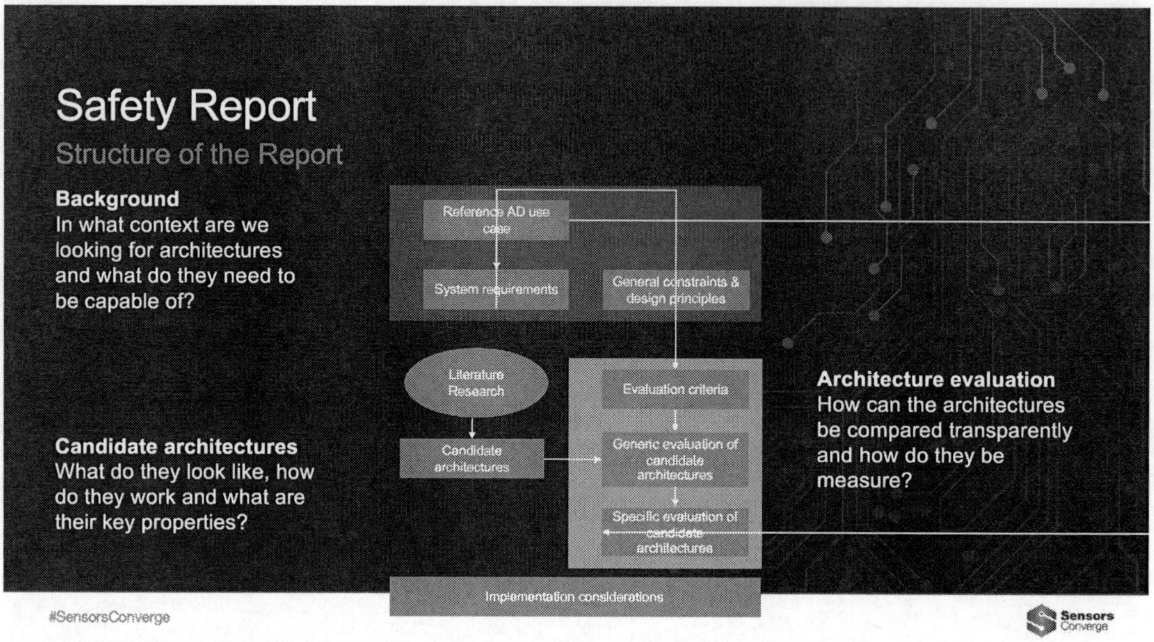
Safety Report
Structure of the Report
Background
In what context are we looking for architectures and what do they need to be capable of?
Candidate architectures
What do they look like, how do they work and what are their key properties?
Reference AD use case
System requirements
General constraints & design principles
Literature Research
Candidate architectures
Evaluation criteria
Generic evaluation of candidate architectures
Specific evaluation of candidate architectures
Implementation considerations
Architecture evaluation
How can the architectures be compared transparently and how do they be measure?
#SensorsConverge
Sensors Converge

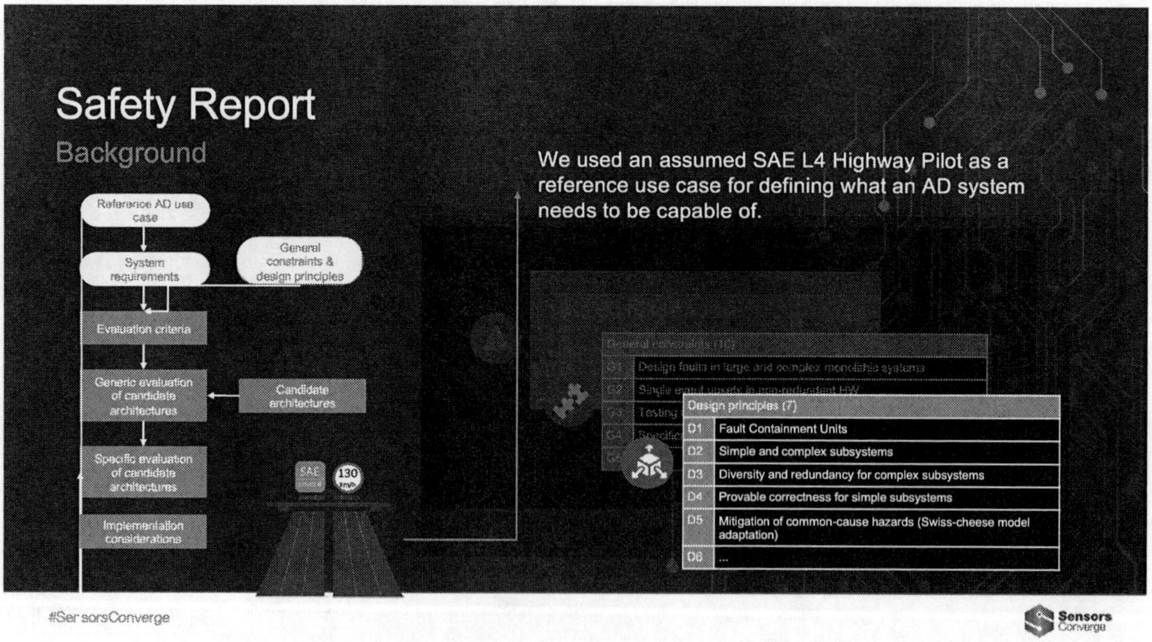
Safety Report
Background
Reference AD use case
System requirements
General constraints & design principles
Evaluation criteria
Generic evaluation of candidate architectures
Candidate architectures
Specific evaluation of candidate architectures
Implementation considerations
We used an assumed SAE L4 Highway Pilot as a reference use case for defining what an AD system needs to be capable of.
SAE
130
Design principles (7)
D1 Fault Containment Units
D2 Simple and complex subsystems
D3 Diversity and redundancy for complex subsystems
D4 Provable correctness for simple subsystems
D5 Mitigation of common-cause hazards (Swiss-cheese model adaptation)
D6 ...
#SensorsConverge
Sensors Converge

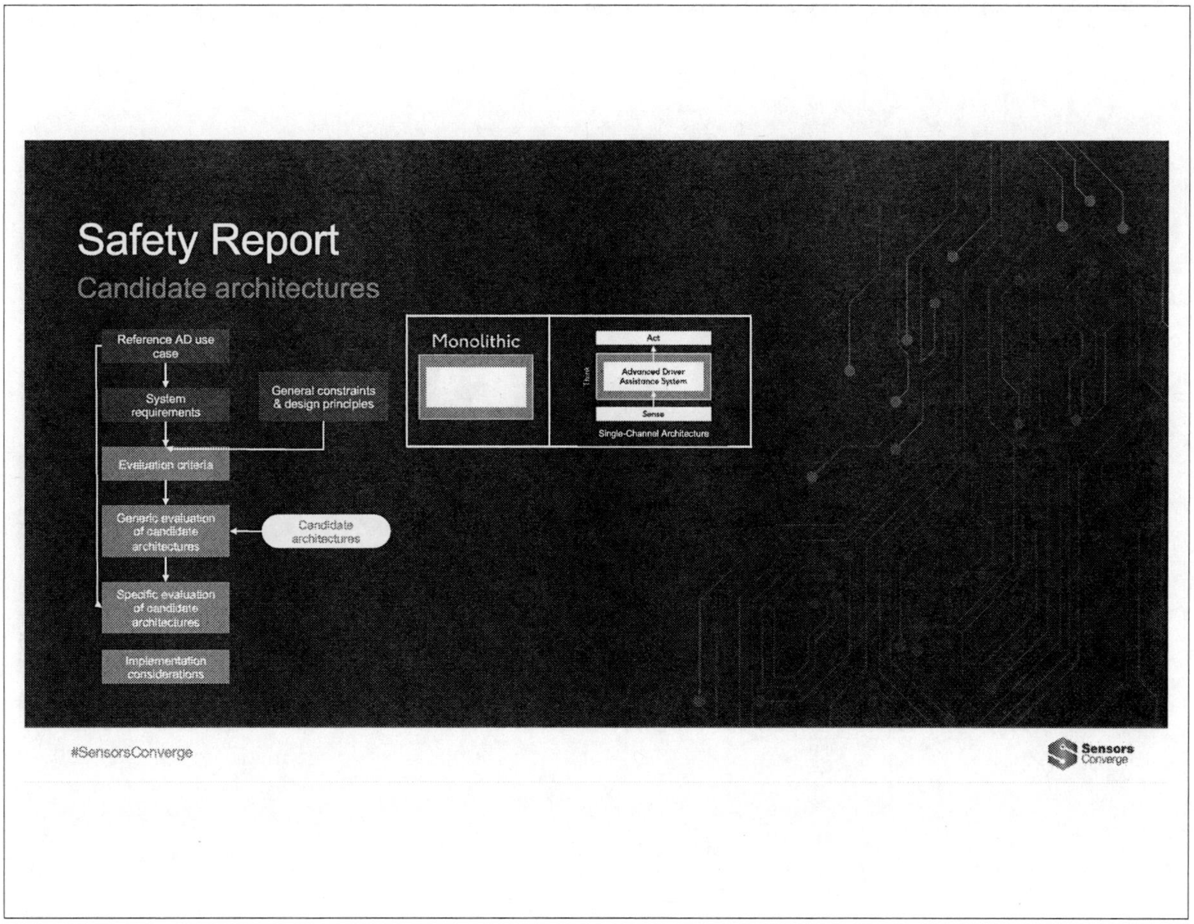
Safety Report
Candidate architectures
Reference AD use case
System requirements
General constraints & design principles
Evaluation criteria
Generic evaluation of candidate architectures
Candidate architectures
Specific evaluation of candidate architectures
Implementation considerations
Monolithic
Act
Think
Advanced Driver Assistance System
Sense
Single-Channel Architecture
#SensorsConverge
Sensors Converge

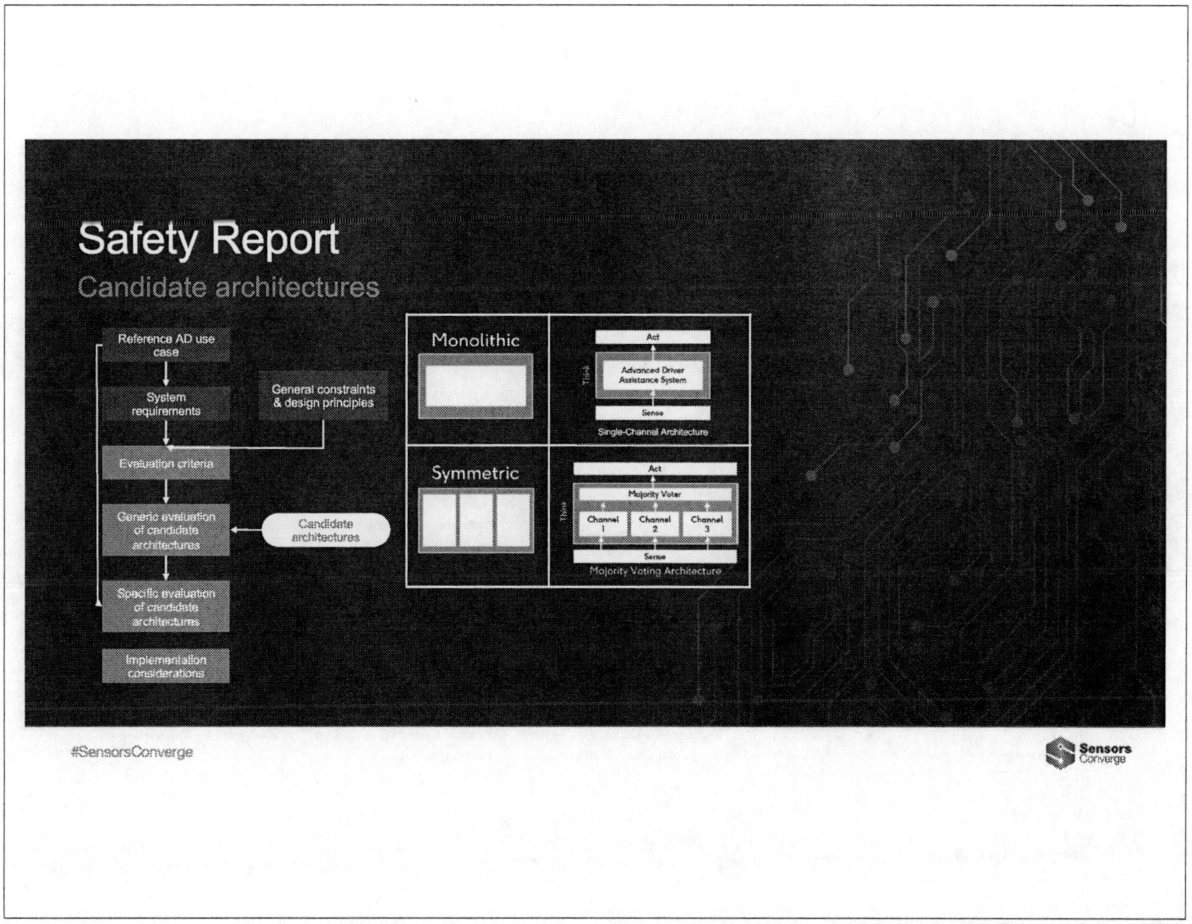
Safety Report
Candidate architectures
Reference AD use case
System requirements
General constraints & design principles
Evaluation criteria
Generic evaluation of candidate architectures
Candidate architectures
Specific evaluation of candidate architectures
Implementation considerations
Monolithic
Act
Think
Advanced Driver Assistance System
Sense
Single-Channel Architecture
Symmetric
Act
Majority Voter
Think
Channel 1
Channel 2
Channel 3
Sense
Majority Voting Architecture
#SensorsConverge
Sensors Converge

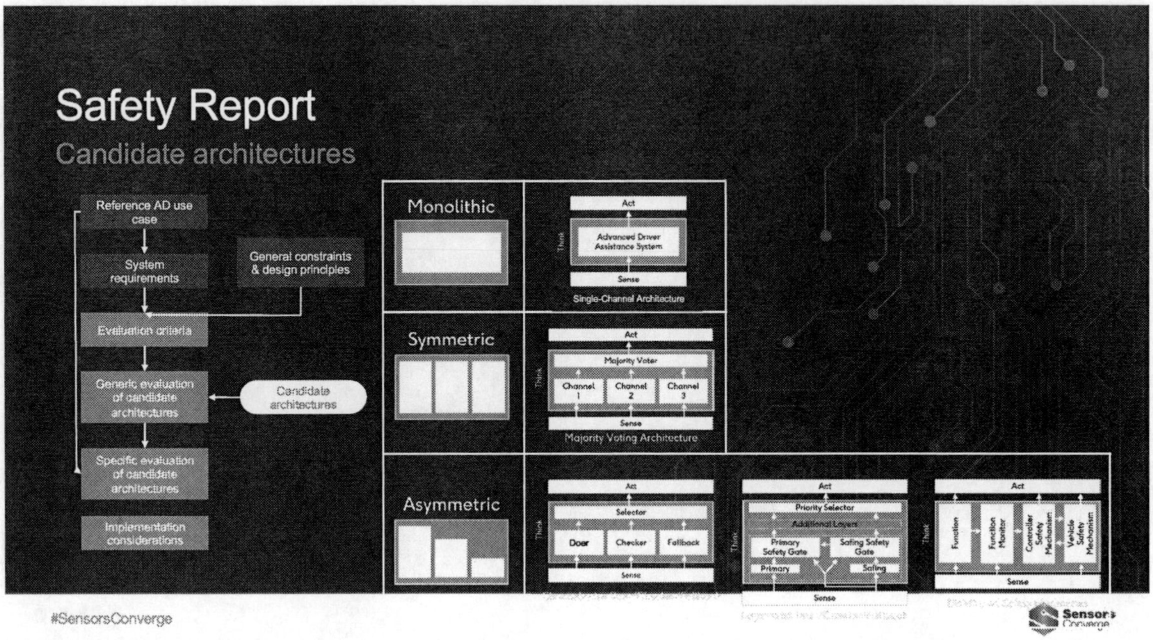
Safety Report
Candidate architectures
Reference AD use case
System requirements
General constraints & design principles
Evaluation criteria
Generic evaluation of candidate architectures
Candidate architectures
Specific evaluation of candidate architectures
Implementation considerations
Monolithic
Act
Think
Advanced Driver Assistance System
Sense
Single-Channel Architecture
Symmetric
Act
Majority Voter
Channel 1
Channel 2
Channel 3
Sense
Majority Voting Architecture
Asymmetric
Act
Selector
Doer
Checker
Fallback
Sense
Act
Priority Selector
Additional Layers
Primary Safety Gate
Safing Safety Gate
Primary
Safing
Sense
Act
Function
Function Monitor
Controller Safety Mechanism
Vehicle Safety Mechanism
Sense
#SensorsConverge
Sensors Converge

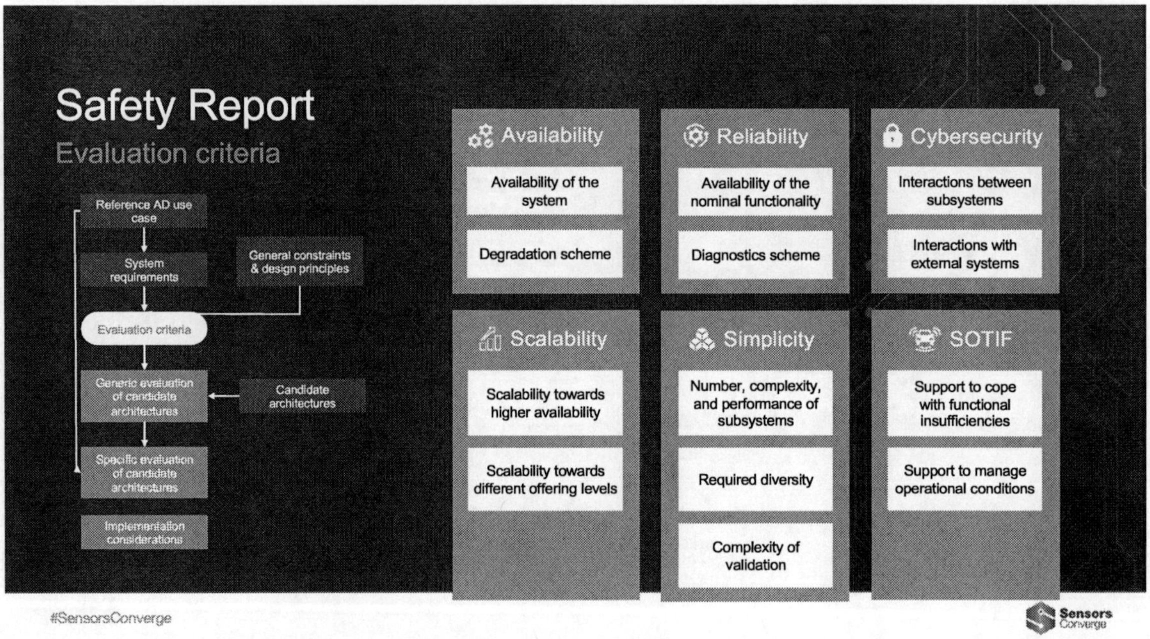
Safety Report
Evaluation criteria
Reference AD use case
System requirements
General constraints & design principles
Evaluation criteria
Generic evaluation of candidate architectures
Candidate architectures
Specific evaluation of candidate architectures
Implementation considerations
Availability
Availability of the system
Degradation scheme
Reliability
Availability of the nominal functionality
Diagnostics scheme
Cybersecurity
Interactions between subsystems
Interactions with external systems
Scalability
Scalability towards higher availability
Scalability towards different offering levels
Simplicity
Number, complexity, and performance of subsystems
Required diversity
Complexity of validation
SOTIF
Support to cope with functional insufficiencies
Support to manage operational conditions
#SensorsConverge
Sensors Converge

Safety Report

Evaluation Process

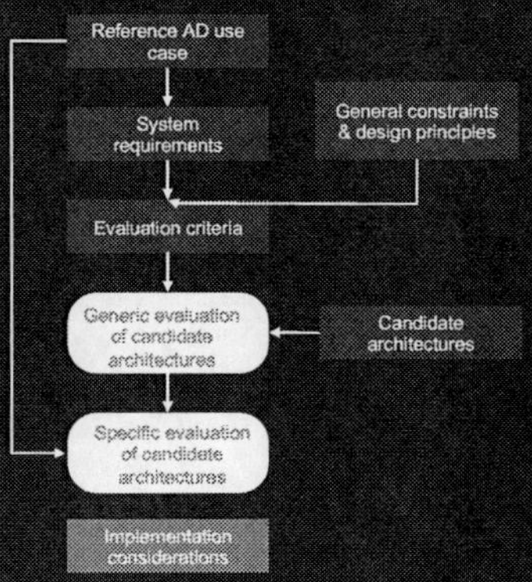

Step 1: Generic evaluation

Architecture 1	Architecture 2
Observation: …	Observation: …
Observation: …	Observation: …

Step 2: Specific evaluation

Architecture 1		Architecture 2	
Pros	...	Pros	…
Cons	...	Cons	…

#SensorsConverge

Architecture evaluation

Key findings

Asymmetric architectures are better suited than symmetric ones for the complexity in Automated Driving.

Independently developed, complementary channels can compensate for each other's weaknesses.

A combination of these patterns allows for:

- Sound partitioning with simple and purposeful interfaces.
- Predictable system states under nominal and off-nominal conditions.
- Solid and verifiable safety argumentation.

The considered asymmetric architectures share two **fundamental design patterns:**

- **Doer / Checker**: One channel performs the function, the other monitors it.
- **Active / Hot Stand-By**: One channel is active, and the other is stand-by; if the active is unavailable or unsafe, the stand-by takes over.

How to continue

Join us!

Starting from the current Safety & Architecture Report, we discuss to continue in different directions:

- Focus on design and validation principles for architectural concepts.
- Extend analysis to newly proposed architectures, around analyzing Sufficient Independence
- Holistic approach to Dependability i.e. combining Safety + Cybersecurity for L4 AD

#SensorsConverge

Thank you!

Chaitanya Shinde

System Safety Expert - AV

THE | AUTONOMOUS

info@the-autonomous.com

#SensorsConverge

Sensors Converge

Accelerating Automotive AI using open-source technologies

Aniket Saha
VP Product Strategy, Tenstorrent

tenstorrent

Confidential

Tenstorrent

- Founded in 2016
- $400M+ raised from Samsung, Hyundai, Fidelity, Eclipse, Jim Keller and others
- 450+ employees in 5 offices: Toronto, Santa Clara, Austin, Belgrade, Bangalore
- Delivering Silicon-proven IP (for RISC-V CPU and AI) and Accelerated Compute Systems

tenstorrent

2

Accelerating AI Everywhere

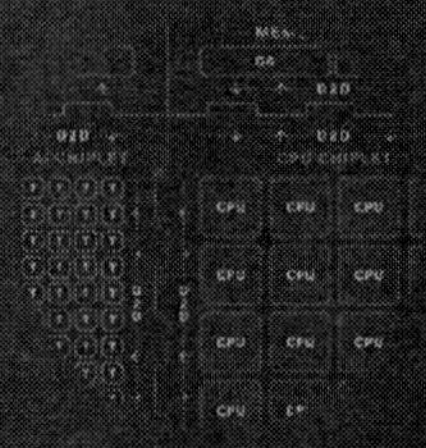

Provide Solutions

- Co-designed HW and SW
- Silicon-Proven IP
- IP → Chiplets → SoCs → Boards → Systems → Cloud

Market Scalable

- From Edge to Cloud
- For Inference and Training
- Flexible Product Options

Open Ecosystem

- Open-Source Technology
- Workload specific customizations
- No vendor lock-in

tenstorrent

Developing the compute fabrics for AI

RISC-V

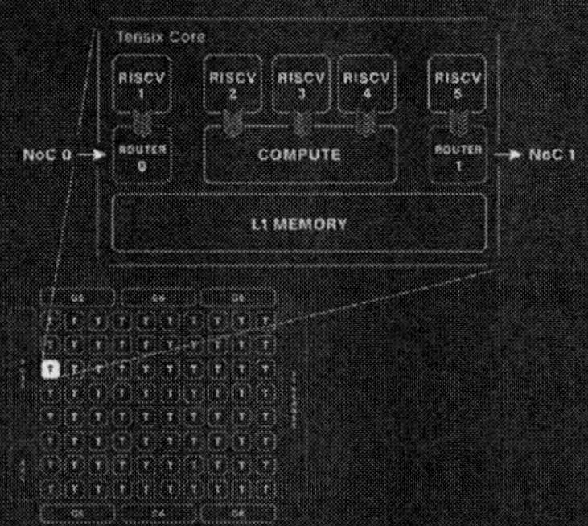

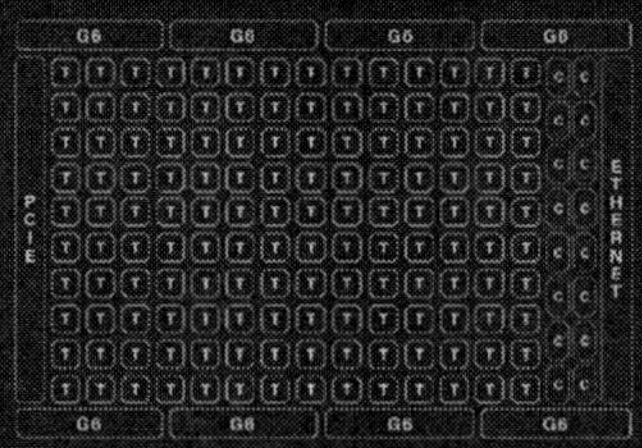

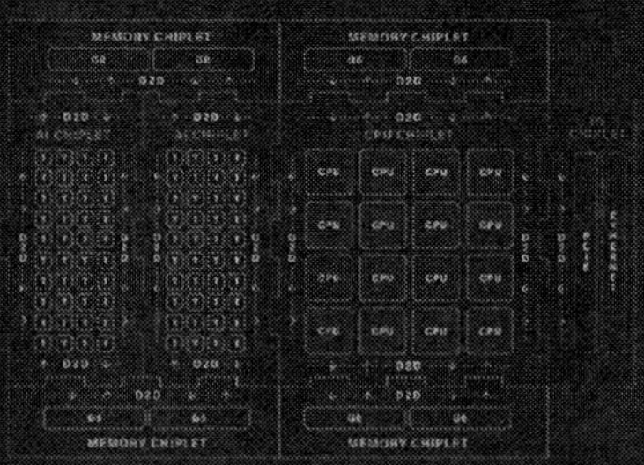

Today: Embedded RISC-V processors for AI

Tomorrow: Integrated RISC-V for high-performance AI

Future: Heterogenous high-performance RISC-V + AI chiplets

tenstorrent

4

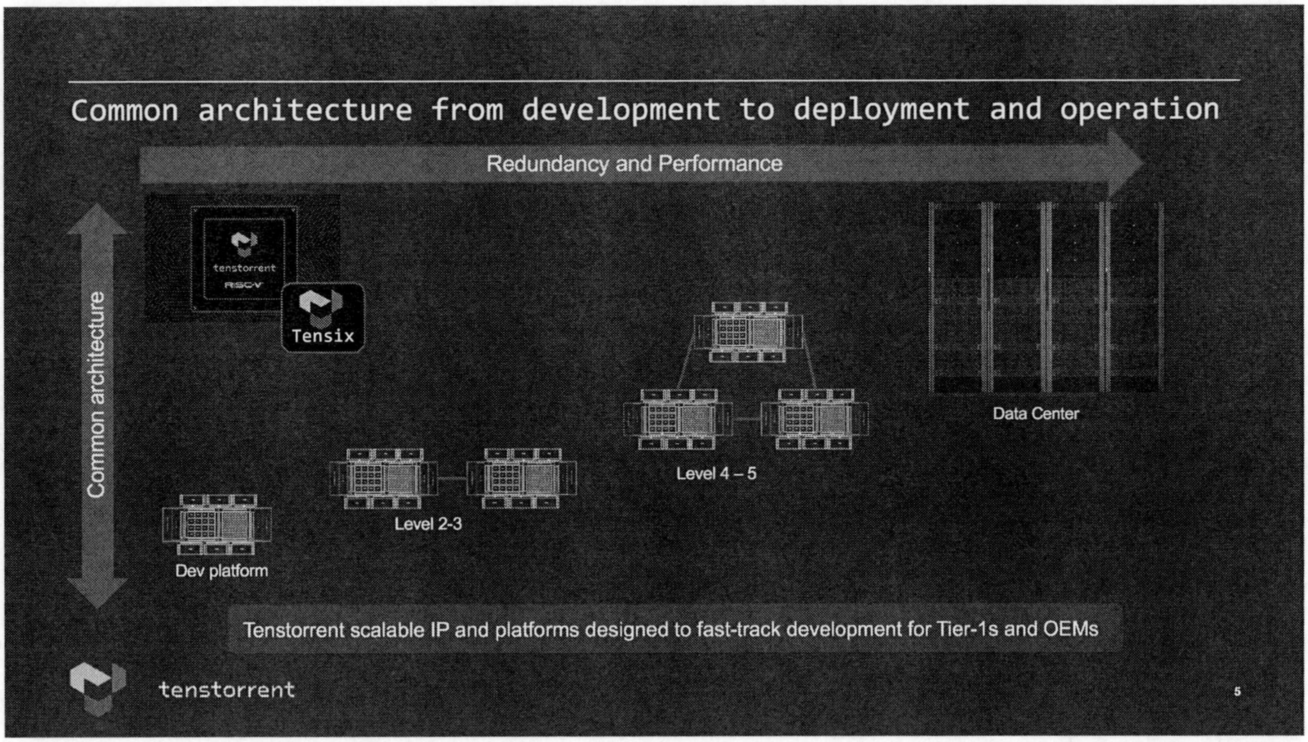
Common architecture from development to deployment and operation
Redundancy and Performance
Common architecture
tenstorrent
RISC-V
Tensix
Data Center
Level 4 – 5
Level 2-3
Dev platform
Tenstorrent scalable IP and platforms designed to fast-track development for Tier-1s and OEMs
tenstorrent
5

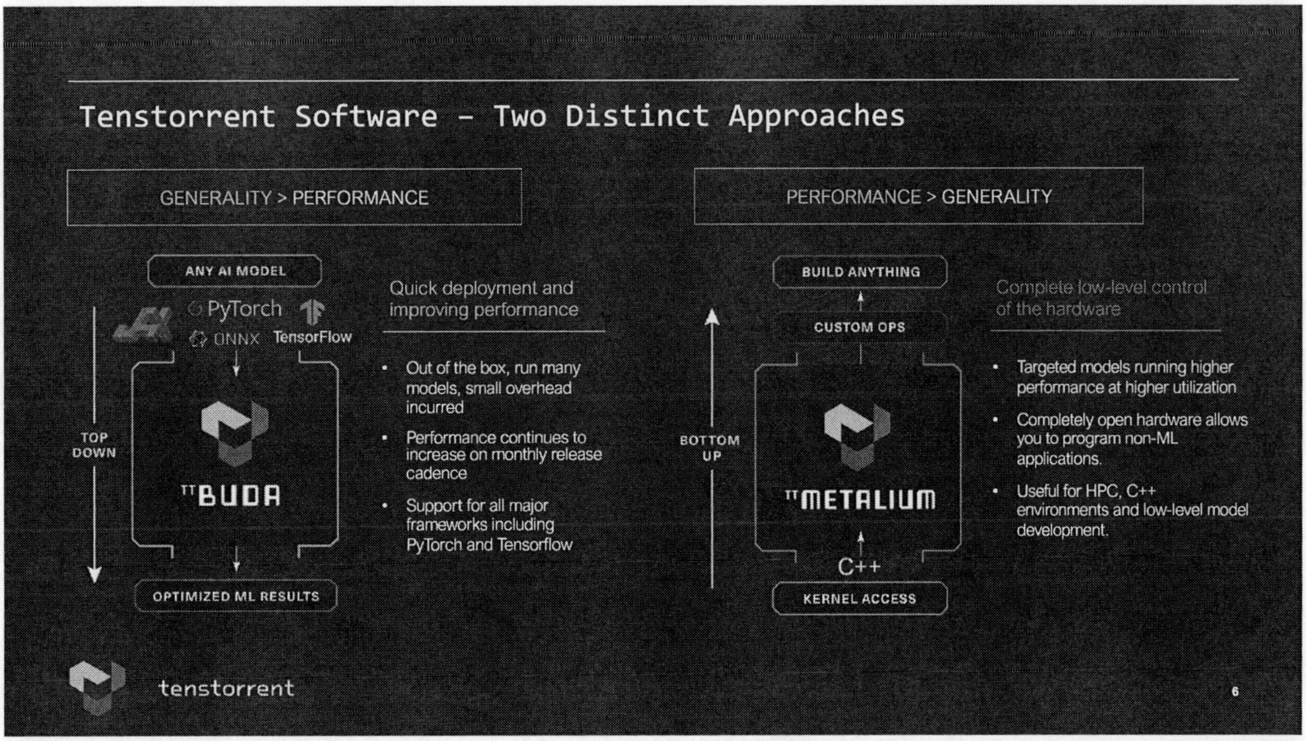
Tenstorrent Software – Two Distinct Approaches
GENERALITY > PERFORMANCE
PERFORMANCE > GENERALITY
ANY AI MODEL
PyTorch
ONNX
TensorFlow
TOP DOWN
TTBUDA
OPTIMIZED ML RESULTS
Quick deployment and improving performance
• Out of the box, run many models, small overhead incurred
• Performance continues to increase on monthly release cadence
• Support for all major frameworks including PyTorch and Tensorflow
BUILD ANYTHING
CUSTOM OPS
BOTTOM UP
TTMETALIUM
C++
KERNEL ACCESS
Complete low-level control of the hardware
• Targeted models running higher performance at higher utilization
• Completely open hardware allows you to program non-ML applications.
• Useful for HPC, C++ environments and low-level model development.
tenstorrent
6

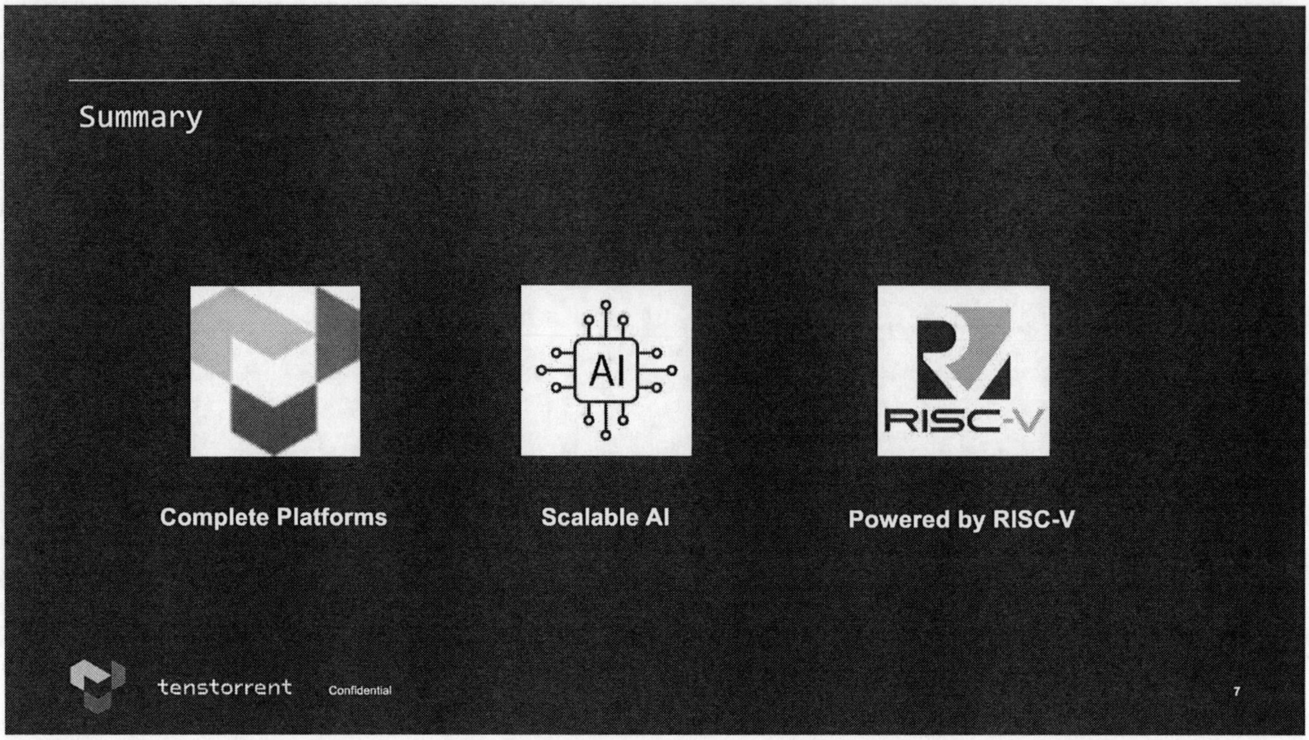
Summary
Complete Platforms
AI
Scalable AI
RISC-V
Powered by RISC-V
tenstorrent
Confidential
7

Opportunities for Multi-Functional Printed Sensors in Auto Tech

Dr Jack Howley – Technology Analyst, IDTechEx
research@IDTechEx.com

www.IDTechEx.com/FlexSensors

IDTechEx

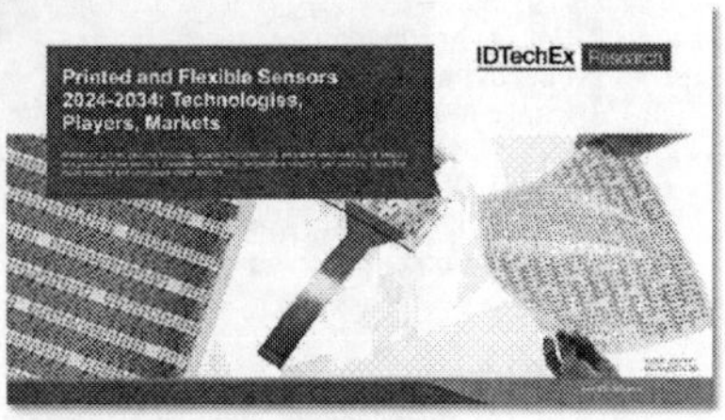

  IDTechEx

Printed sensor technology, market, and established auto tech applications

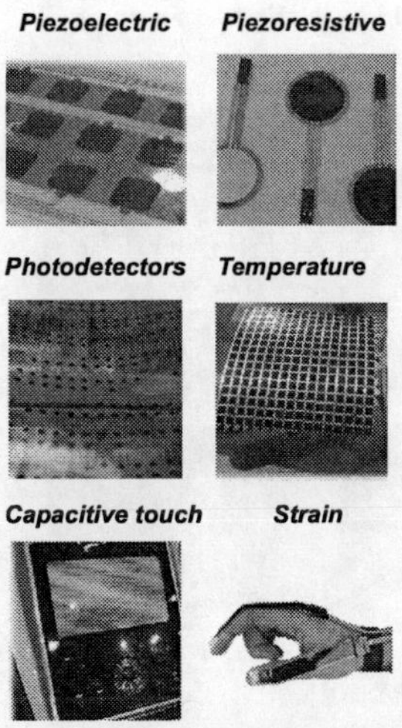

Key technology differentials

- Flexible
- Thin form factor
- Multiparametric
- Large area
- Scalable manufacturing
- Hybrid functionality

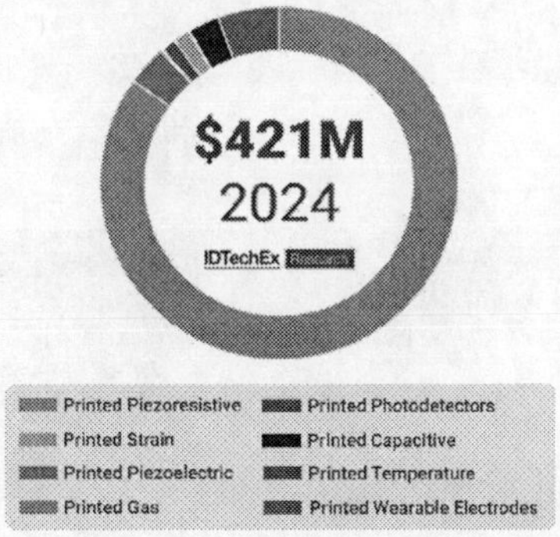

Force sensing resistor pioneered passenger safety in auto tech

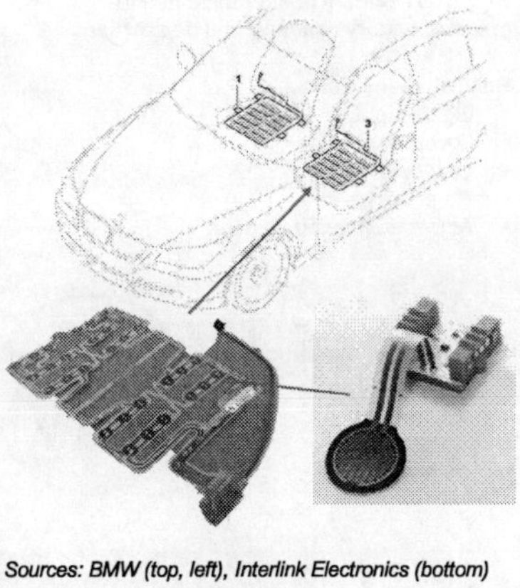

Sources: BMW (top, left), Interlink Electronics (bottom)

  IDTechEx

Automotive mega-trends and printed sensor opportunities

IDTechEx Research

Established	Emerging		Future	
User safety	Electrification	Vehicle ownership saturation	Vehicle autonomy	Hydrogen fuel cell vehicles

Printed sensor technologies

Piezoresistive / Force	Photodetectors
Piezoelectric	Temperature
Capacitive Touch	Strain

Battery health monitoring
Seat occupancy detection

Battery health monitoring
Fuel storage integrity monitoring
Haptic feedback

Infotainment systems
Human machine interfaces

Spatial mapping
Biometric authentication

Thermal management
Battery health monitoring
Low-power heating

Battery health monitoring
Human machine interfaces

Materials, performance, and benchmarking of printed sensor technologies can be found at www.idtechex.com/FlexSensors

Slide 3 Copyright © IDTechEx | www.IDTechEx.com IDTechEx

Battery health monitoring and optimization opportunities

Extending electric vehicle lifetime is a valuable problem to solve.

Solution - Battery heath monitoring to optimize battery charging and deployment.

Solution requirements:
- Lightweight
- Low power
- Low cost
- Relevant metrics
- Active monitoring solution

Key metrics: State of charge, Swelling, Temperature

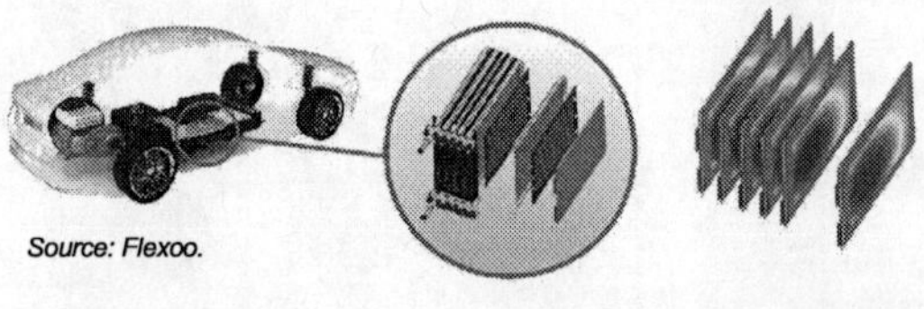

Source: Flexoo.

Value of solution = up to $3000 in savings per vehicle

Battery health monitoring with printed electronics

Slide 4 Copyright © IDTechEx | www.IDTechEx.com IDTechEx

Factors dictating when and if printed sensors for battery health monitoring will be required

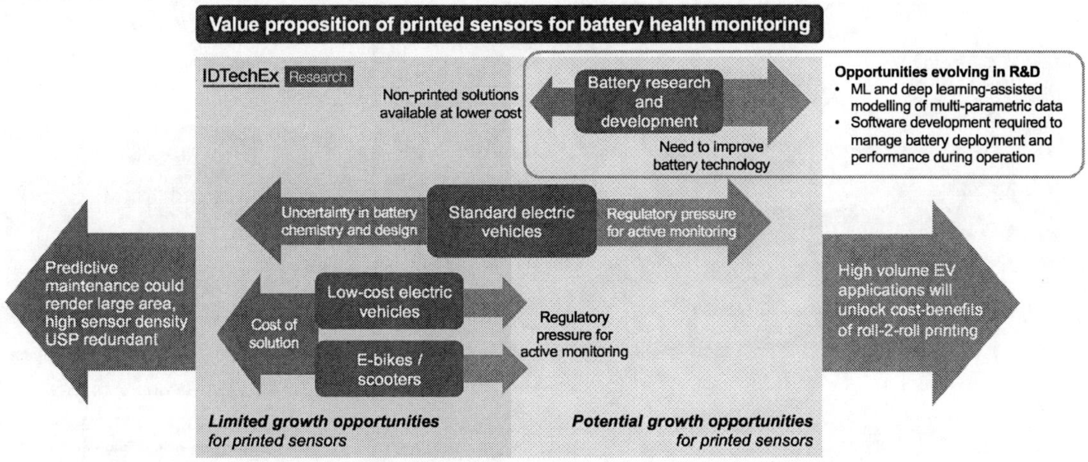

IDTechEx

Opportunity for printed photodetectors to supply low-cost LIDAR sensing

InGaAs image sensors are expensive and have associated supply risks

Solution – Low-cost printed organic photodetectors have the potential to displace InGaAs sensors for NIR and SWIR sensing.

Source: ISORG

isorg

RAYNERGY TEK
the inventive solution

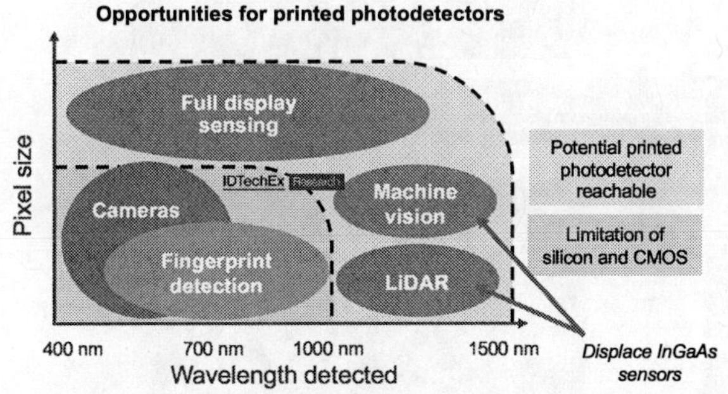

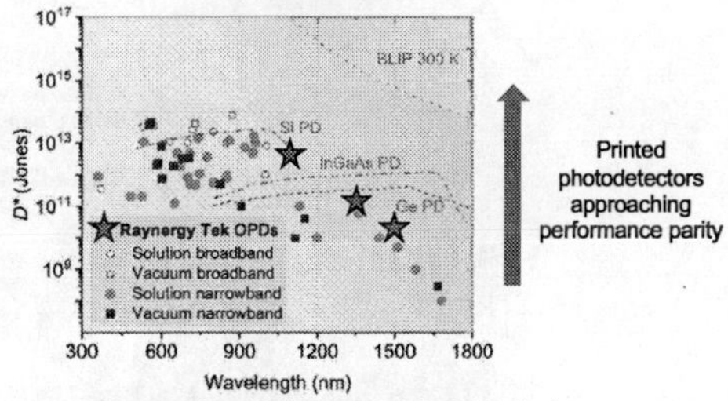

Source: Mater. Horiz., 2022,9, 220-251 (edited).

IDTechEx

Auto tech outlook and printed sensor growth opportunities

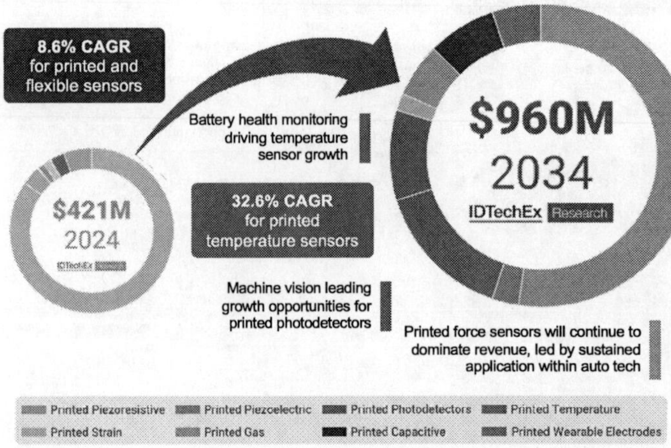

Find out more:

www.IDTechEx.com/FlexSensors

Printed and Flexible Sensors 2024-2034

Sample pages are available for all IDTechEx reports

linkedin.com/in/jackhowley

Thank you for listening – Q&A

IDTechEx.com/Sensors

Sample pages are available for all IDTechEx reports

MARVELL

Future of Automotive HPC

- Chiplets

Willard Tu
AVP, Automotive Compute
Jun 24, 2024

Customer want maximum benefits: scalability, reusability, TTM, lower development costs

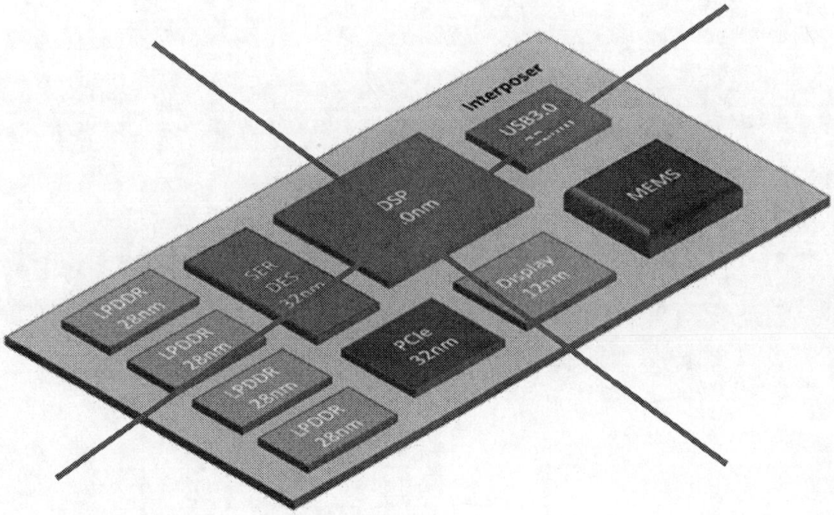

- Customer vision of chiplet is vastly different than reality today
- Building blocks need to big enough to justify the "beach head" of D2D interconnect.
- Single vendor solutions exist
- Multi-vendor is much more difficult

2

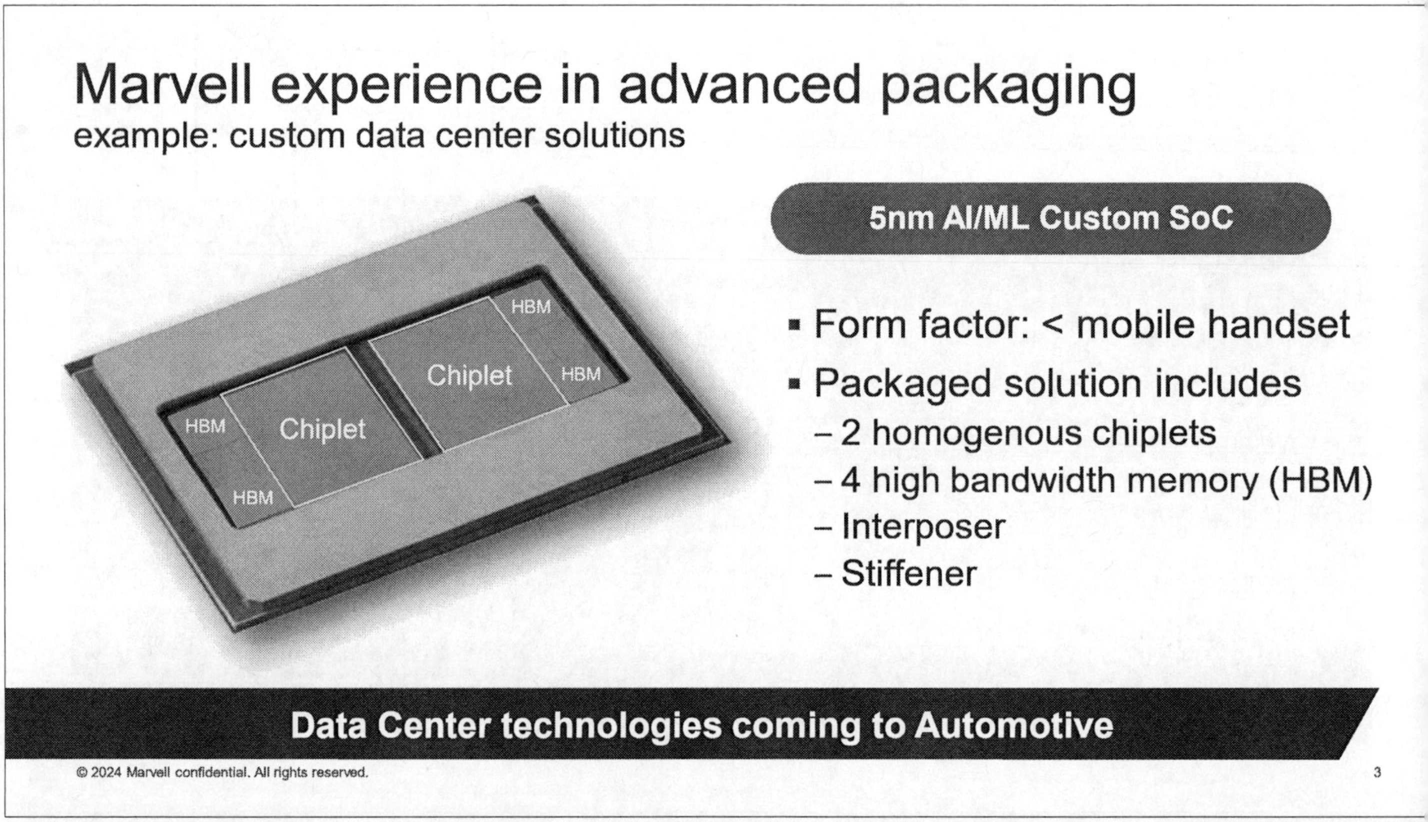
Marvell experience in advanced packaging
example: custom data center solutions
HBM
Chiplet
HBM
HBM
Chiplet
HBM
5nm AI/ML Custom SoC
▪ Form factor: < mobile handset
▪ Packaged solution includes
– 2 homogenous chiplets
– 4 high bandwidth memory (HBM)
– Interposer
– Stiffener
Data Center technologies coming to Automotive
© 2024 Marvell confidential. All rights reserved.
3

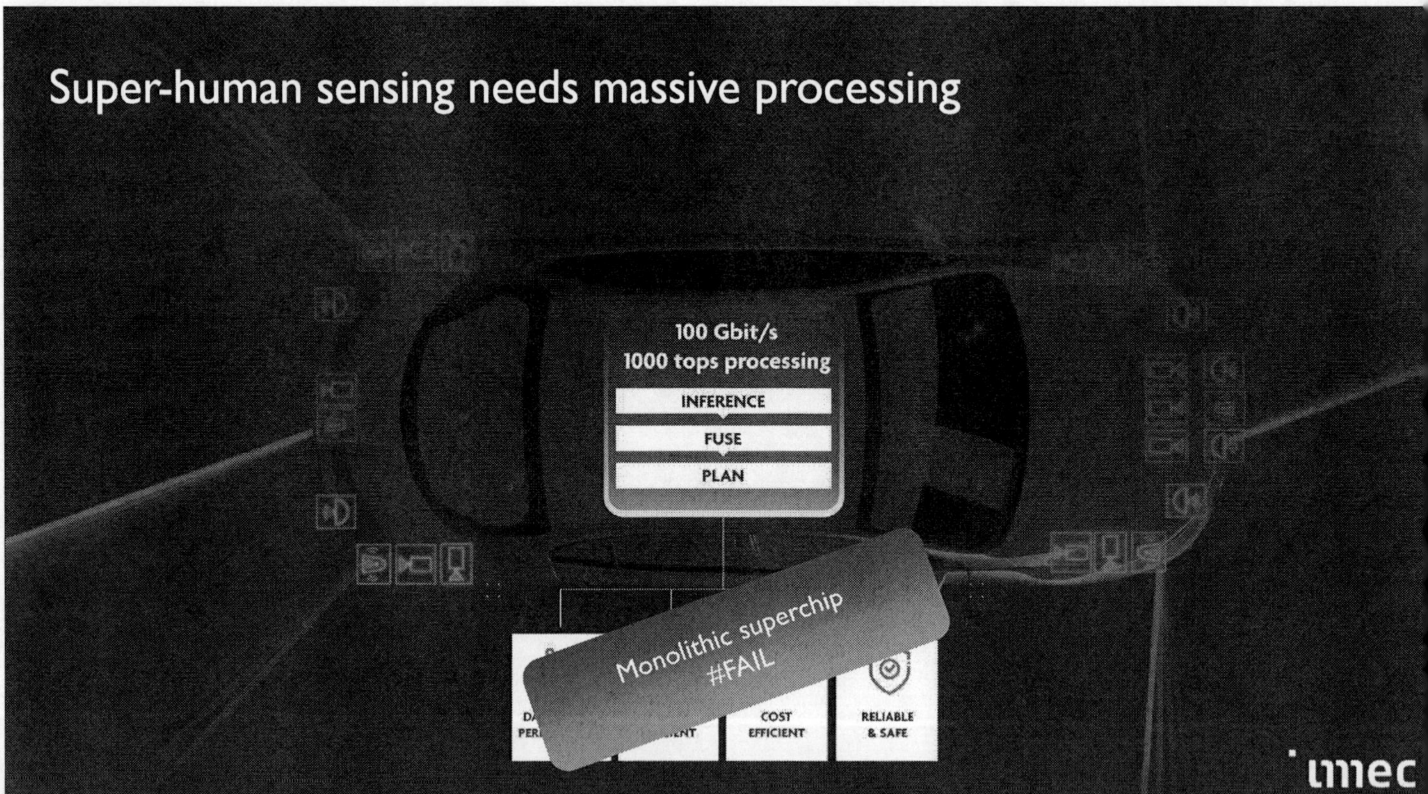
Super-human sensing needs massive processing
100 Gbit/s
1000 tops processing
INFERENCE
FUSE
PLAN
Monolithic superchip
#FAIL
COST
EFFICIENT
RELIABLE
& SAFE
imec

The increasing R&D cost challenge

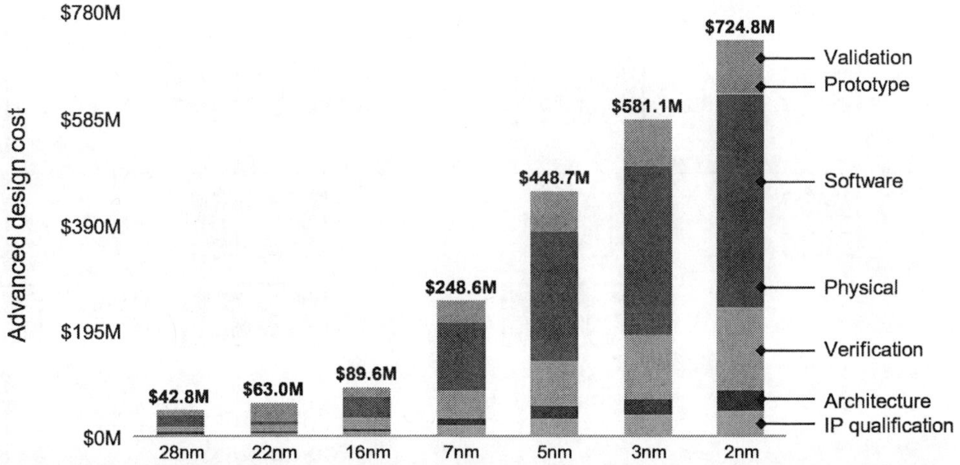

Source: IBS report, design activities and strategies implications, July 2022

Leading edge development costs significantly more expensive

SoC scalability using a “single” chiplets

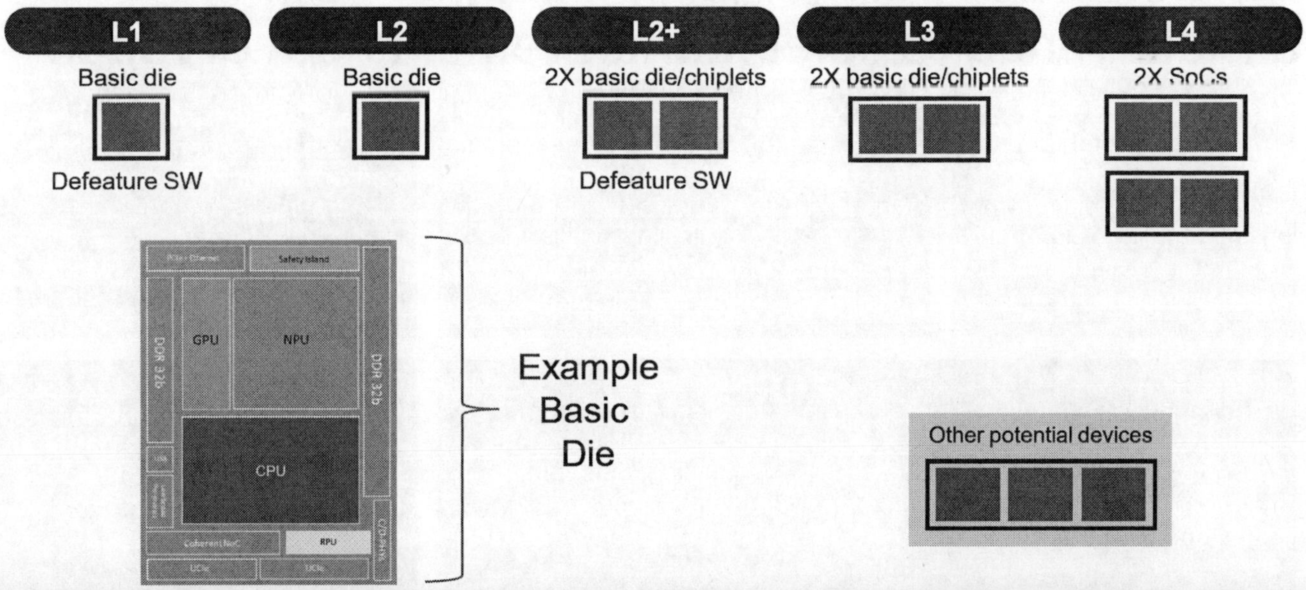

Different vehicle trims

More flexibility with more chiplets

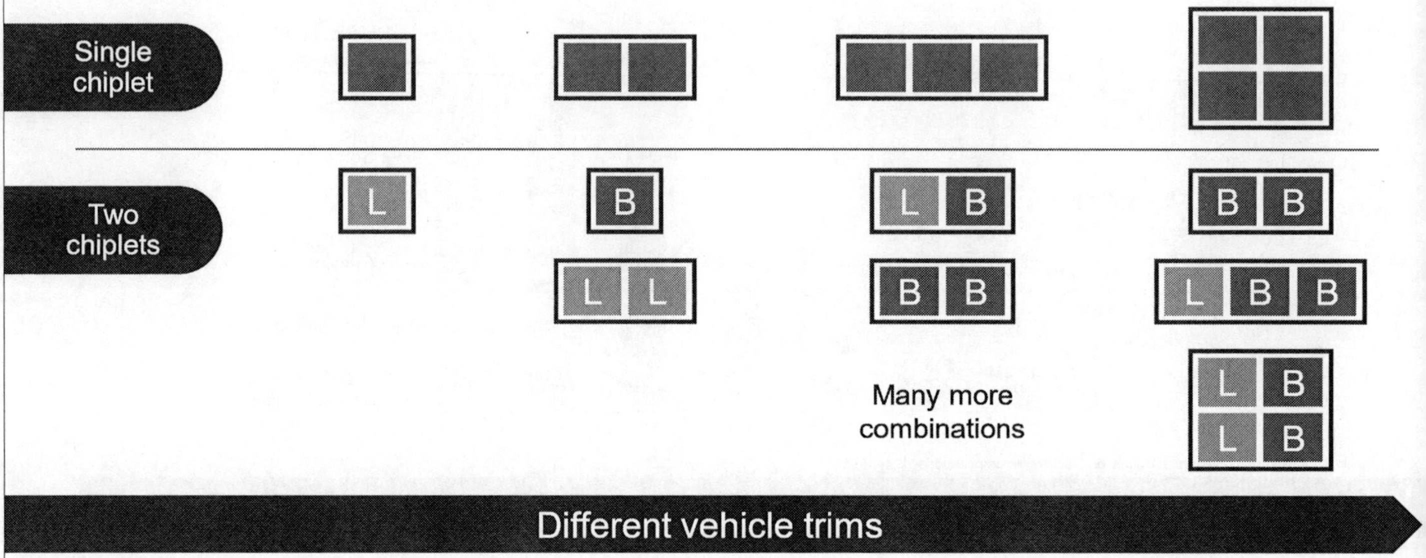

 7

Chiplets ease pain for large designs – but a multi-vendor chiplet market remains out of reach

"Leading-edge processors with large transistor counts will increasingly benefit from this technology, although most will be single-vendor designs."

"Most eyes have been on Intel and AMD, as they employ chiplets in their largest designs. Each has its own technology, with the former preferring silicon-based EMIB links while the latter stays mainly with organic substrates, which are far cheaper."

"Nearly all the new chiplet designs are expensive data-center products. Exceptions include Intel's Meteor Lake, which targets mainstream PCs, and the D-Matrix DLA, which targets the edge."

"The benefit of chopping a large chip into smaller pieces is that each piece yields better than the whole, reducing overall cost. Chiplets add packaging cost, however – especially if assembled on a silicon interposer instead of an organic substrate inside the package. Each smaller die also grows slightly to accommodate the die-to-die communication interface."

"These challenges mean, in the opinion of one panel at the conference, a viable multi-vendor chiplet ecosystem is 5-10 years away."

Tech Insights Microprocessor Report, Bryon Moyer, November 18, 2022

 8

Automotive Chiplet efforts

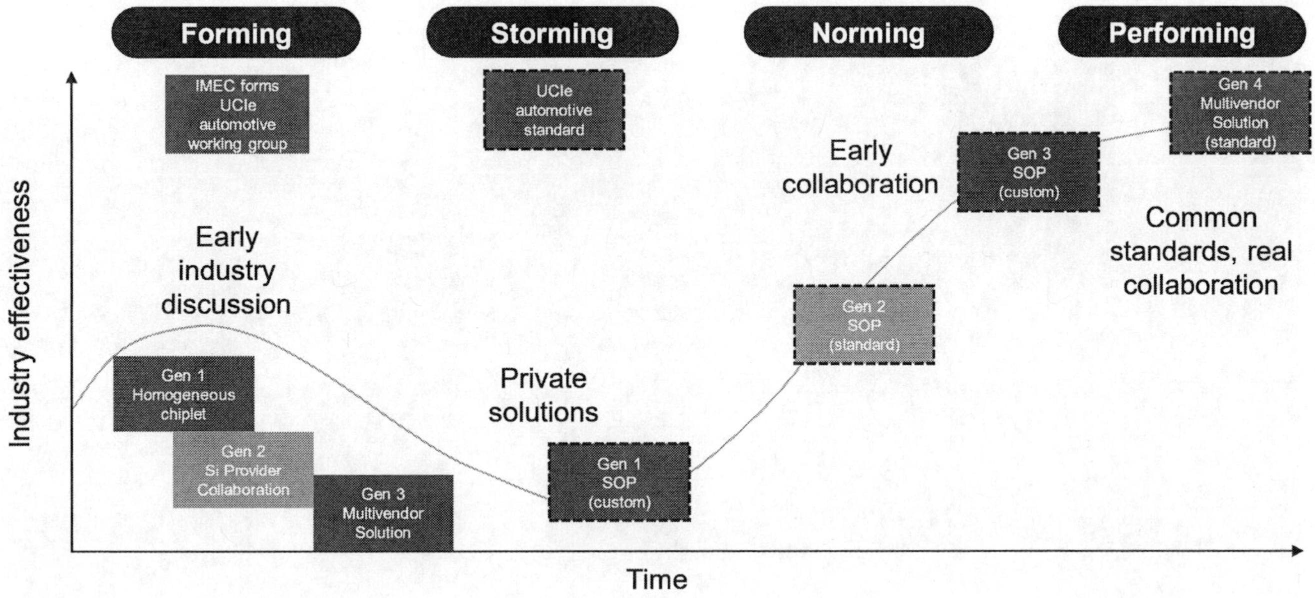

9

The final message

1. The OEM and Silicon market forces are pushing us into chiplets
2. Chiplets are happening NOW – there are bold companies paving the way

10

MARVELL

Thank You

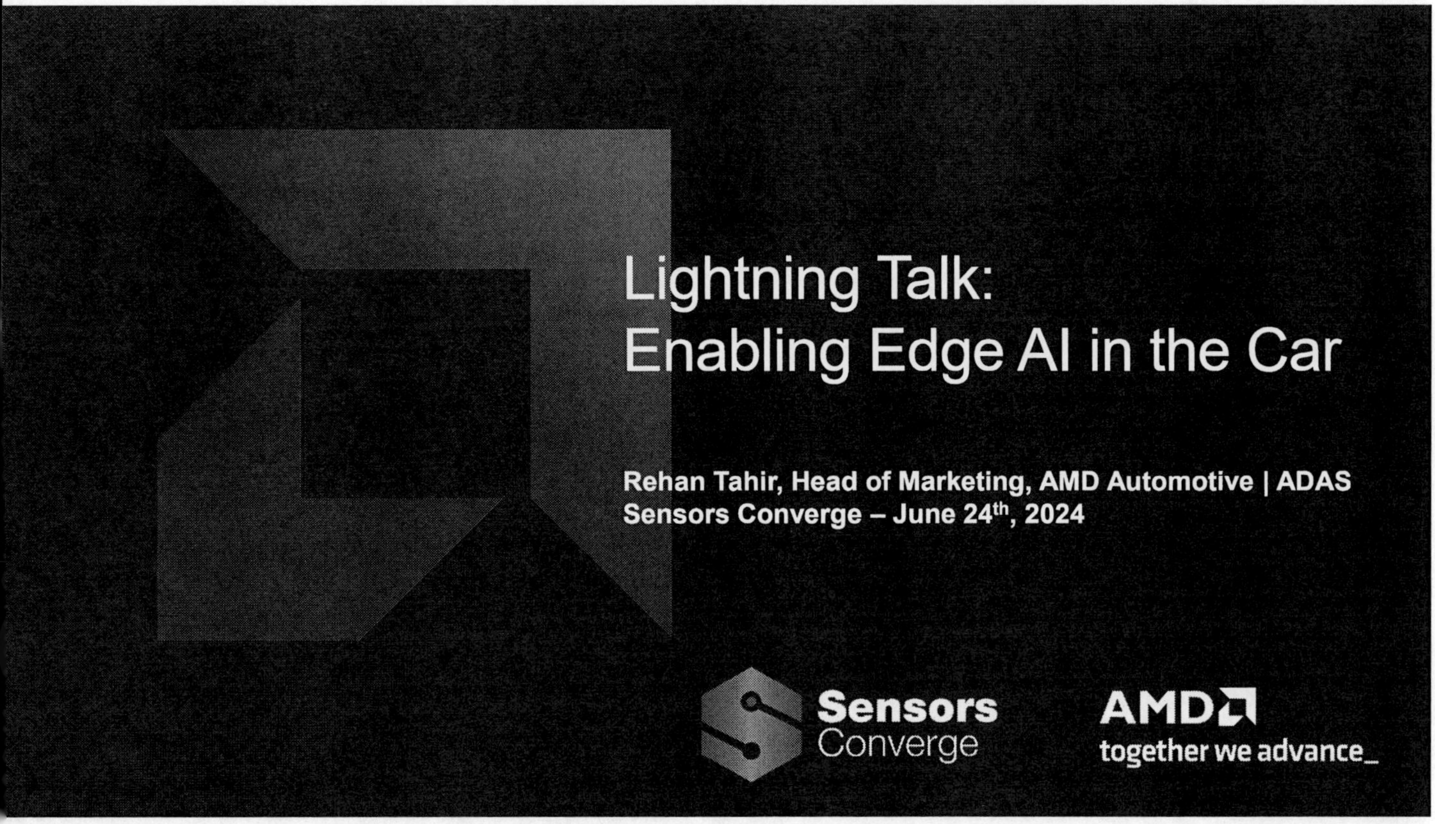
Lightning Talk:
Enabling Edge AI in the Car
Rehan Tahir, Head of Marketing, AMD Automotive | ADAS
Sensors Converge – June 24th, 2024
Sensors Converge
AMD
together we advance_

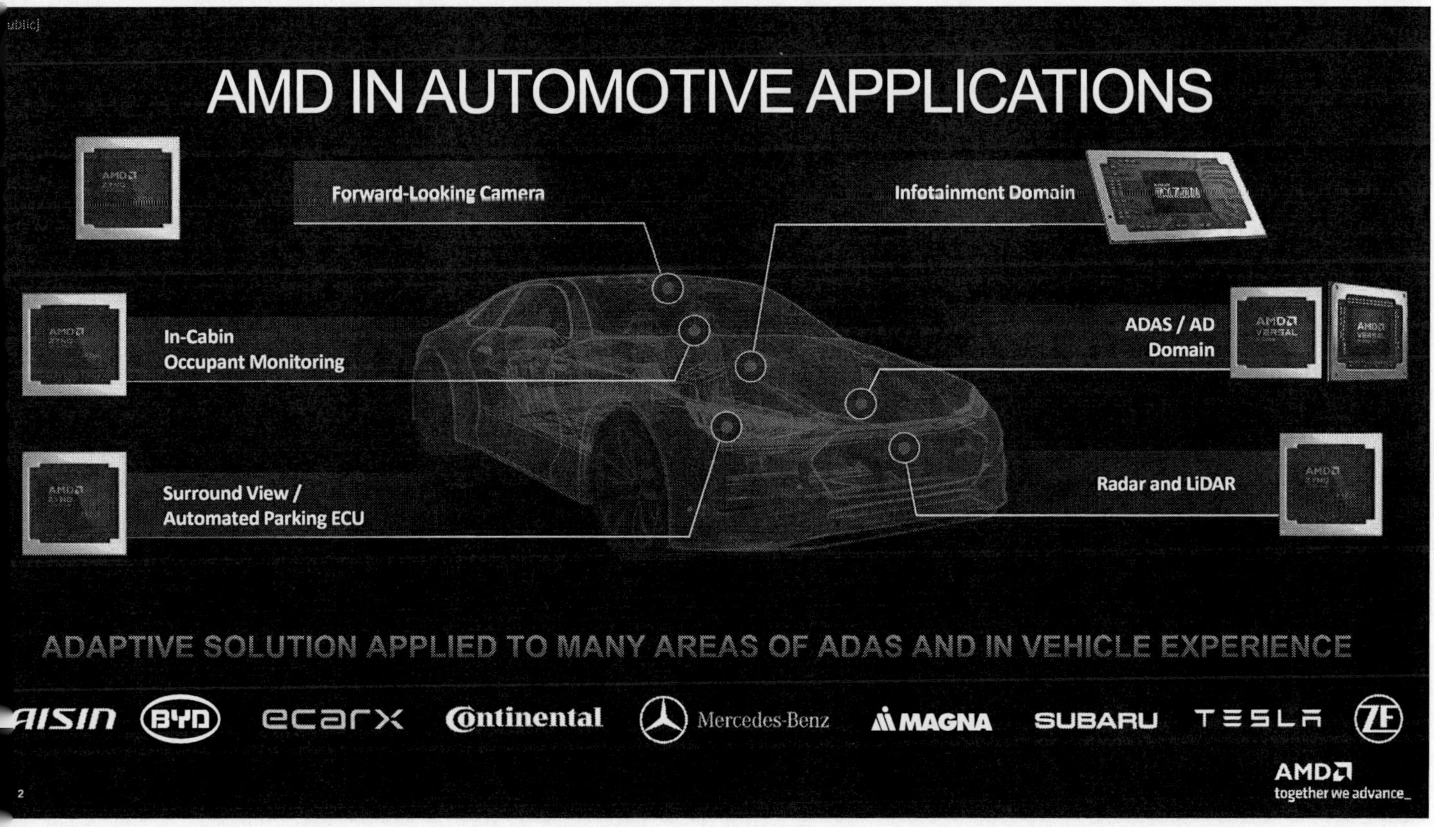
AMD IN AUTOMOTIVE APPLICATIONS
Forward-Looking Camera
Infotainment Domain
In-Cabin
Occupant Monitoring
ADAS / AD
Domain
Surround View /
Automated Parking ECU
Radar and LiDAR
ADAPTIVE SOLUTION APPLIED TO MANY AREAS OF ADAS AND IN VEHICLE EXPERIENCE
AISIN
BYD
ecarx
Continental
Mercedes-Benz
MAGNA
SUBARU
TESLA
ZF
AMD
together we advance_
2

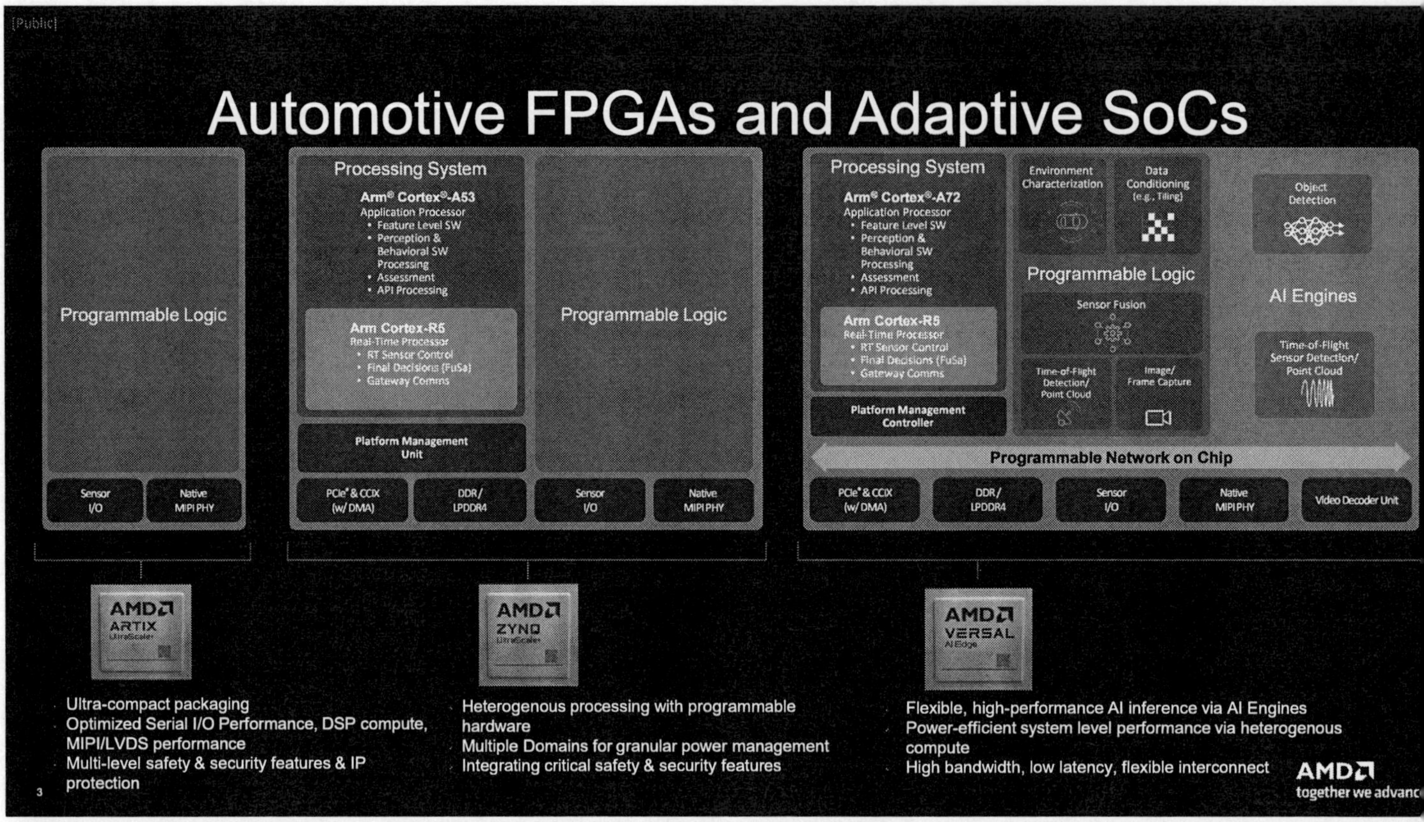
[Public]
Automotive FPGAs and Adaptive SoCs
Programmable Logic
Sensor I/O
Native MIPI PHY
Processing System
Arm® Cortex®-A53
Application Processor
• Feature Level SW
• Perception & Behavioral SW Processing
• Assessment
• API Processing
Arm Cortex-R5
Real-Time Processor
• RT Sensor Control
• Final Decisions (FuSa)
• Gateway Comms
Platform Management Unit
PCIe® & CCIX (w/ DMA)
DDR/ LPDDR4
Programmable Logic
Sensor I/O
Native MIPI PHY
Processing System
Arm® Cortex®-A72
Application Processor
• Feature Level SW
• Perception & Behavioral SW Processing
• Assessment
• API Processing
Arm Cortex-R5
Real-Time Processor
• RT Sensor Control
• Final Decisions (FuSa)
• Gateway Comms
Platform Management Controller
Environment Characterization
Data Conditioning (e.g., Tiling)
Programmable Logic
Sensor Fusion
Time-of-Flight Detection/ Point Cloud
Image/ Frame Capture
Object Detection
AI Engines
Time-of-Flight Sensor Detection/ Point Cloud
Programmable Network on Chip
PCIe® & CCIX (w/ DMA)
DDR/ LPDDR4
Sensor I/O
Native MIPI PHY
Video Decoder Unit
AMD ARTIX UltraScale+
AMD ZYNQ UltraScale+
AMD VERSAL AI Edge
Ultra-compact packaging
Optimized Serial I/O Performance, DSP compute, MIPI/LVDS performance
Multi-level safety & security features & IP protection
Heterogenous processing with programmable hardware
Multiple Domains for granular power management
Integrating critical safety & security features
Flexible, high-performance AI inference via AI Engines
Power-efficient system level performance via heterogenous compute
High bandwidth, low latency, flexible interconnect
3
AMD
together we advanc

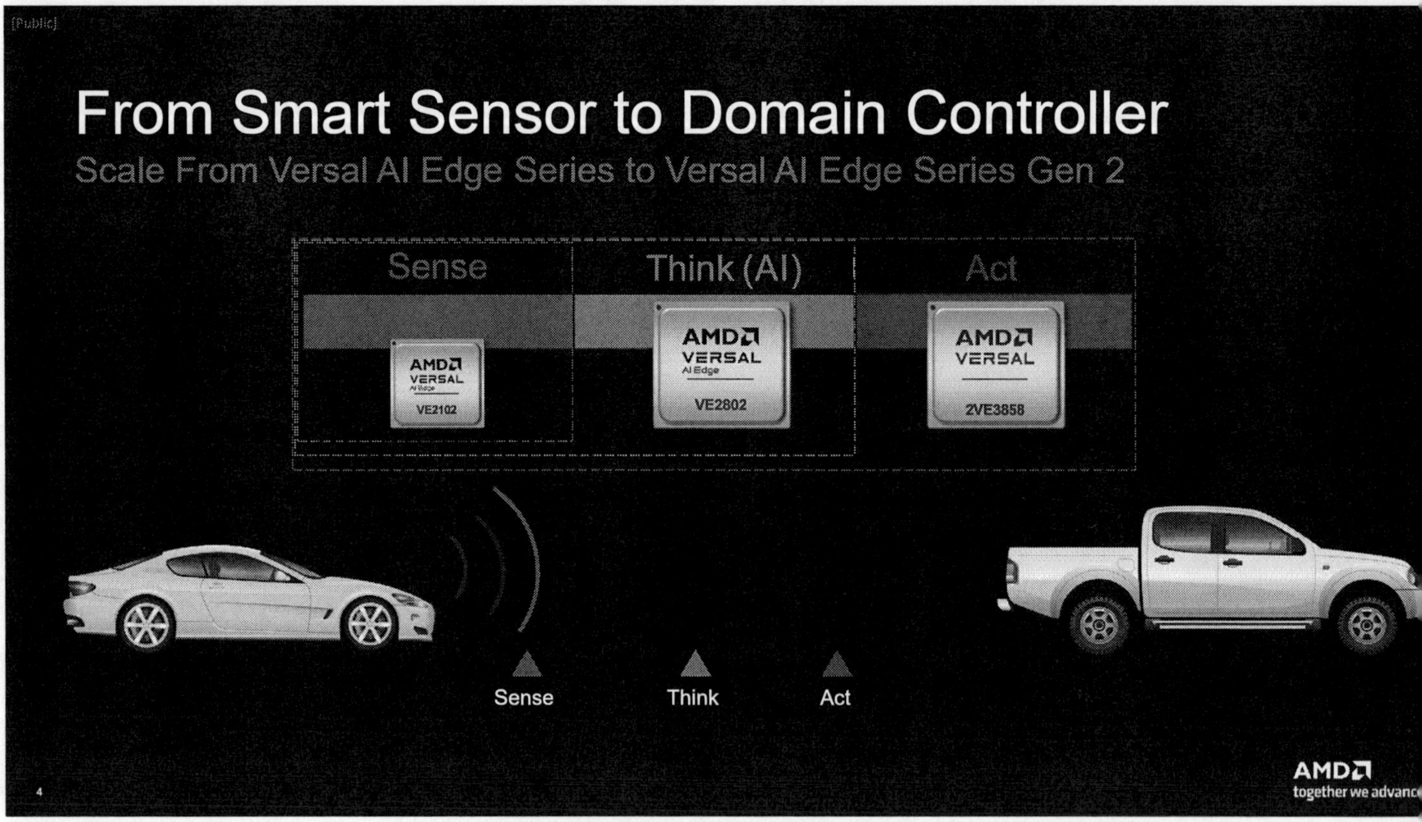
[Public]
From Smart Sensor to Domain Controller
Scale From Versal AI Edge Series to Versal AI Edge Series Gen 2
Sense
Think (AI)
Act
AMD VERSAL AI Edge VE2102
AMD VERSAL AI Edge VE2802
AMD VERSAL 2VE3858
Sense
Think
Act
4
AMD
together we advanc

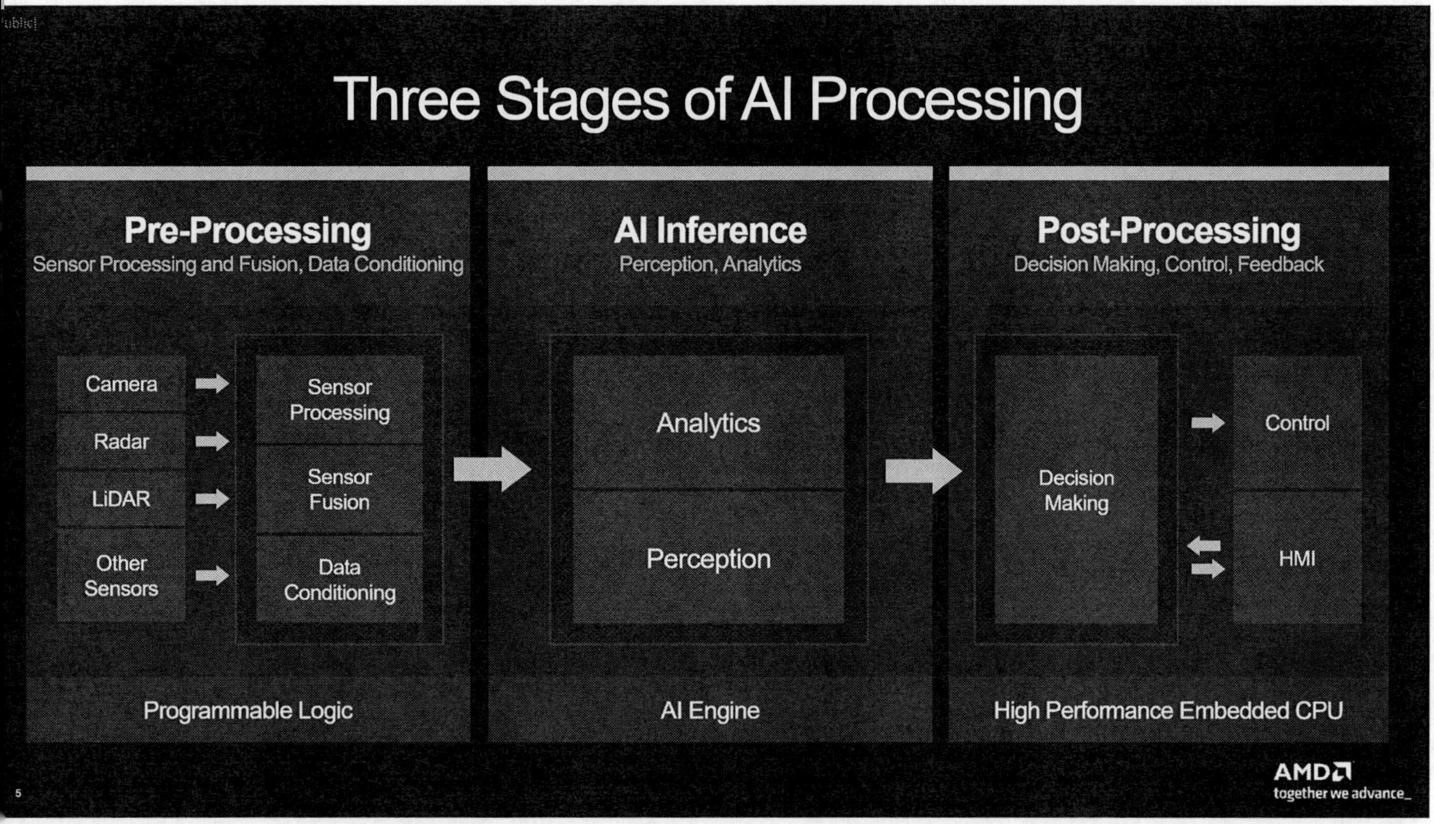
Three Stages of AI Processing
Pre-Processing
Sensor Processing and Fusion, Data Conditioning
Camera
Radar
LiDAR
Other Sensors
Sensor Processing
Sensor Fusion
Data Conditioning
Programmable Logic
AI Inference
Perception, Analytics
Analytics
Perception
AI Engine
Post-Processing
Decision Making, Control, Feedback
Decision Making
Control
HMI
High Performance Embedded CPU
5
AMD
together we advance_

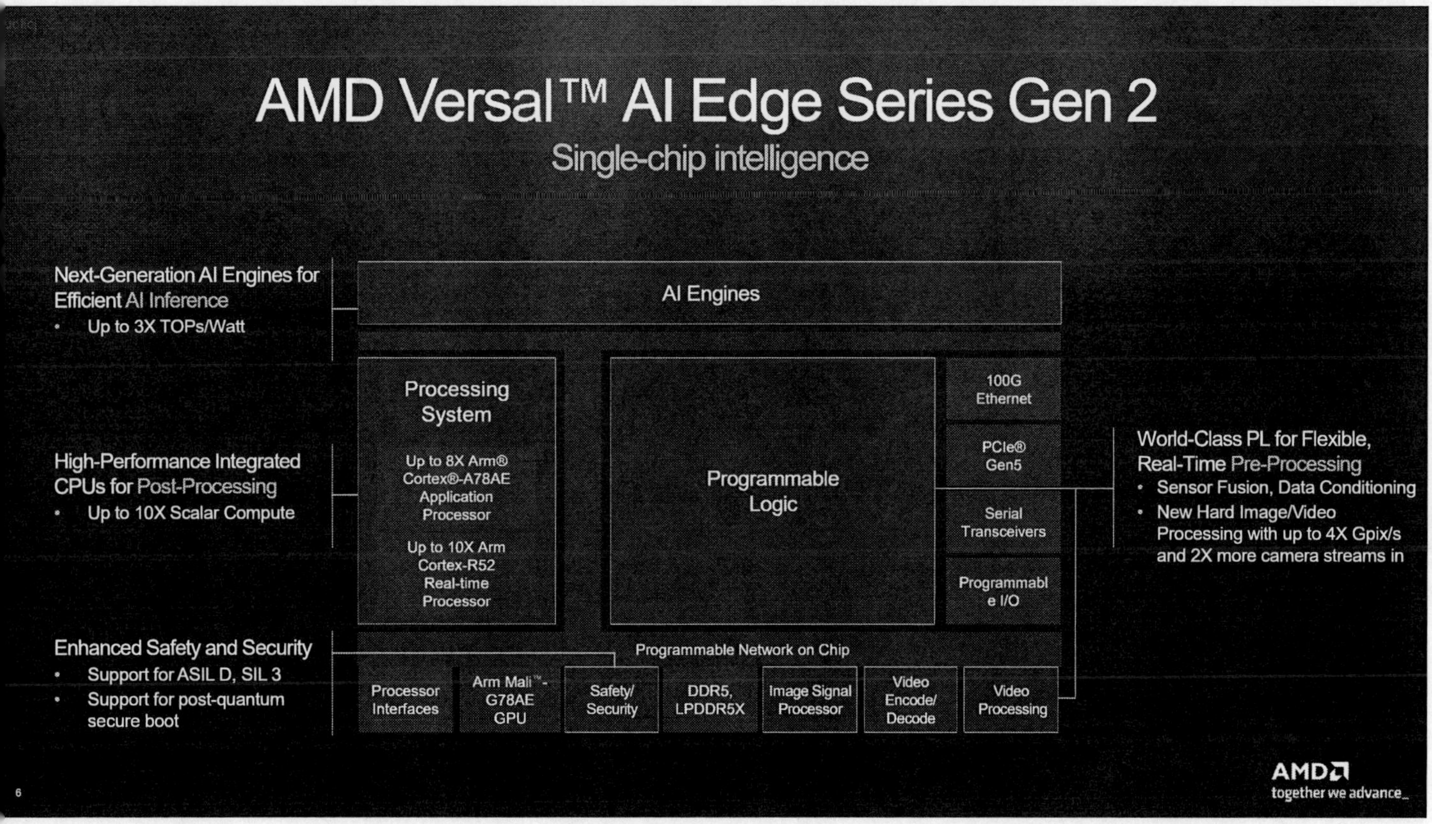
AMD Versal™ AI Edge Series Gen 2
Single-chip intelligence
Next-Generation AI Engines for Efficient AI Inference
• Up to 3X TOPs/Watt
High-Performance Integrated CPUs for Post-Processing
• Up to 10X Scalar Compute
Enhanced Safety and Security
• Support for ASIL D, SIL 3
• Support for post-quantum secure boot
AI Engines
Processing System
Up to 8X Arm® Cortex®-A78AE Application Processor
Up to 10X Arm Cortex-R52 Real-time Processor
Programmable Logic
100G Ethernet
PCIe® Gen5
Serial Transceivers
Programmable I/O
Programmable Network on Chip
Processor Interfaces
Arm Mali™-G78AE GPU
Safety/ Security
DDR5, LPDDR5X
Image Signal Processor
Video Encode/ Decode
Video Processing
World-Class PL for Flexible, Real-Time Pre-Processing
• Sensor Fusion, Data Conditioning
• New Hard Image/Video Processing with up to 4X Gpix/s and 2X more camera streams in
6
AMD
together we advance_

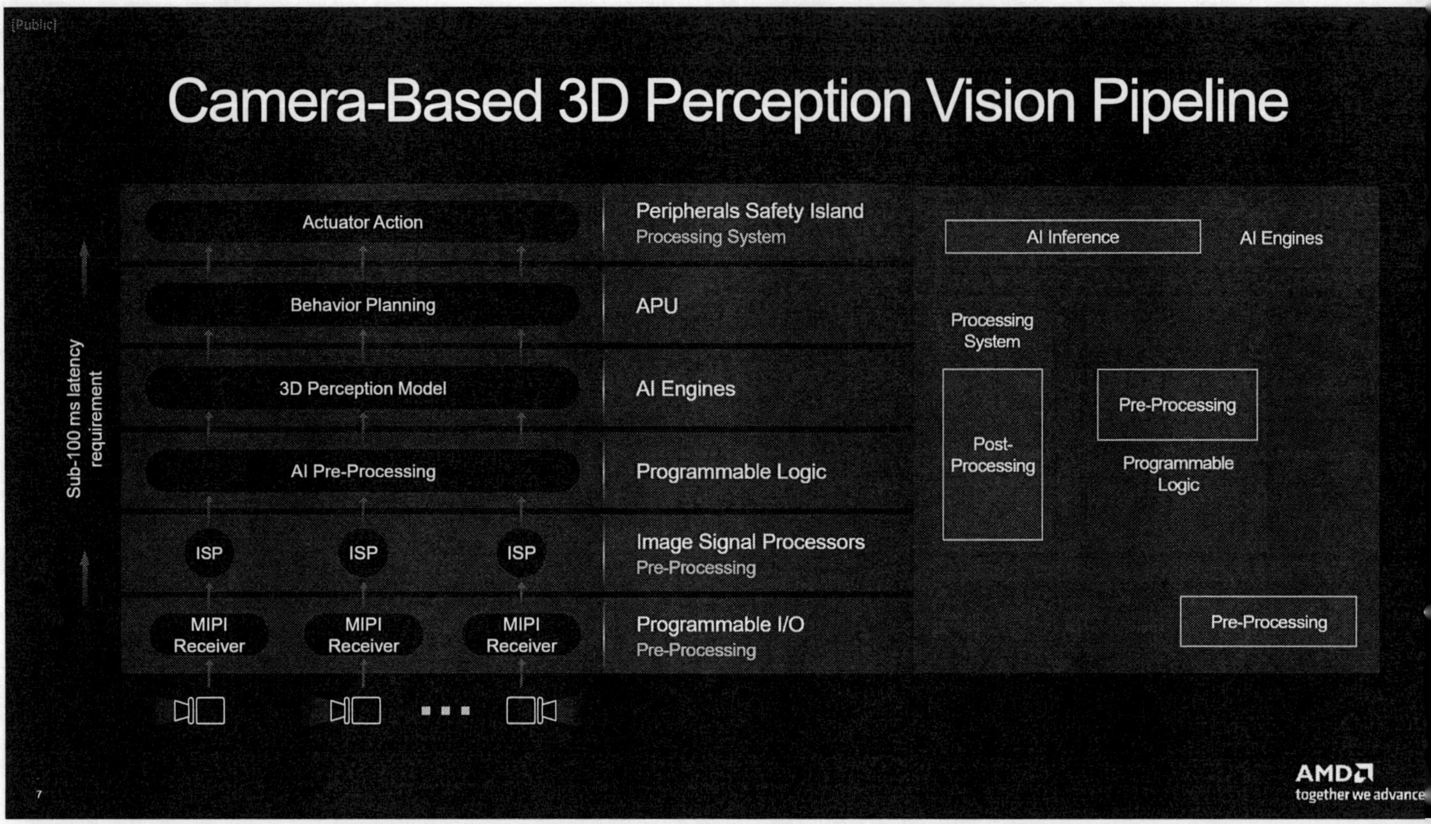
[Public]
Camera-Based 3D Perception Vision Pipeline
Sub-100 ms latency requirement
Actuator Action
Behavior Planning
3D Perception Model
AI Pre-Processing
ISP
ISP
ISP
MIPI Receiver
MIPI Receiver
MIPI Receiver
Peripherals Safety Island
Processing System
APU
AI Engines
Programmable Logic
Image Signal Processors
Pre-Processing
Programmable I/O
Pre-Processing
AI Inference
AI Engines
Processing System
Post-Processing
Pre-Processing
Programmable Logic
Pre-Processing
7
AMD
together we advance

AMD

CHALLENGES AND OPPORTUNITIES FOR PRINTED / FLEXIBLE /STRETCHABLE AND FUNCTIONAL FABRIC/ E-TEXTILE SENSORS AND SENSOR-BASED SYSTEMS: NEW PLATFORMS TO ENABLE WEARABLE AND IOT APPLICATIONS

Sensors Converge Precon
Santa Clara California Convention Center
June 24, 2024

Roger H. Grace
President, Roger Grace Associates
rgrace@rgrace.com
www.rgrace.com

ROGER GRACE ASSOCIATES
MARKETING COUNSEL

MEA CULPA

- My colleagues have oft-times accused me of making "text-rich" presentations…and while I agree…the rationale for this is that I wish to provide the attendee with information that they can "take home" and use…rather that trying to remember my rambling comments or taking copious notes to collect the data points.
- I trust that you can appreciate my position on this…and thank you for your kind understanding.

ROGER GRACE ASSOCIATES
MARKETING COUNSEL

PRESENTATION OUTLINE

- Definitions
- Why printable/flexible/stretchable and E-Textile/smart fabric sensors?
- Situational analysis
- Market analysis
- Technology status of printed/flexible system functionalities
- Manufacturing process
- Industry activities
  - Commercial
  - Research/Academic
- Critical Success Factors
- Monetizing
- Summary/Conclusions/Recommendations

ROGER GRACE BACKGROUND

- Education: BSEE, MSEE (Raytheon Graduate Fellow) Northeastern University, Boston, MA; MBA Program, California Berkeley
- Design Engineer with specialty in microwave and RF, 13 years…Raytheon, Avco
- Applications Engineer, RF semiconductors, 3 years, Avantek/HP
- Marketing Manager, MEMS, 3 years, Foxboro ICT
- Marketing Consultant, MEMS, Sensors and Semiconductors, 40 years
- Guest Lecturer, University of California Berkeley, 1990-2003
- Alumni Engineer of the Year, 2004, Northeastern University
- Co-Founder ,Past President and Board member of Micro ,Nano and Emerging Technology Commercialization Education Foundation (MANCEF)
- Published over 70 papers and articles on MEMS/Sensors/Commercialization
- Organized and Chaired over 30 technical sessions worldwide on MEMS/Sensors
- Board membership…Florida MEP, University of Michigan WIMSS, Northeastern University High Rate Nanomanufacturing Center
- Organizing committee includes IEEE Transducers 2009,COMS, Smart Systems Integration (EU), Advanced Microsystems for Automotive Applications (EU), Bestowed Inaugural "Sensor Industry Impact Award" by Sensors Expo/Sensors Magazine 2016

ROGER GRACE ASSOCIATES OVERVIEW

- Founded in 1982,a pioneer in the MEMS/Sensors strategic marketing and analysis sector www.rgrace.com
- Clients include the "who's who" of industrial and government organizations worldwide
- Headquartered in Bonita Springs, Florida / San Francisco, California
- Focus on MEMS/Sensors and Capital Equipment markets
- Capabilities include…refer to next PPT.
  - Custom market research…product definition, application opportunity assessment,
  - New product introductions
  - Market strategy development
  - Merger and Acquisition (M&A) due diligence
  - Sales and distribution channel development
  - Integrated marketing communications
    - Promotion
    - Public Relations
    - Positioning and Branding

ROGER GRACE ASSOCIATES
MARKETING COUNSEL

TECHNOLOGY COMMERCIALIZATION* PROCESS MODEL

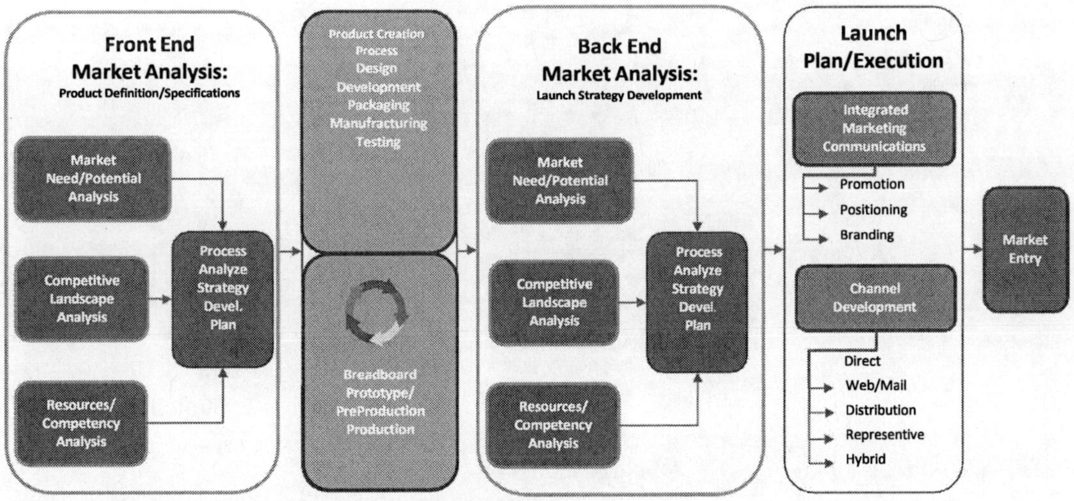

*Def: Process or cycle of introducing a new product or production method to the market

Roger Grace Associates supports its clients in front and back-end market analysis as well as in the product launch plan and execution

ROGER GRACE ASSOCIATES
MARKETING COUNSEL

MARKET RESEARCH METHODOLOGY

- PRIMARY: OVER 120 in-person, in-lab and telephone in-depth interviews with technology participants beginning in early 2015…and continuing
- SECONDARY: Data mining vis-à-vis the web …addressing the entire ecosystem of participants
- Attendance at several technical conferences and trade shows
- Participation in webinars

ROGER GRACE ASSOCIATES MARKETING COUNSEL

WHY PRINTED / FLEXIBLE / STRETCHABLE & E-TEXTILE / SMART FABRIC

Attribute	Benefit	
	Cost	Functionality
Printed	• Low Infrastructure • Low Unit (R-2-R)	• Large device size • Arraying capability • Low profile • Ease of hybrid integration • Reduced time to market
Flexible		• Application driven (especially human interface)
Stretchable		• Application driven (especially human interface)
E-Textile/ Smart Fabric	• Low Infrastructure • Low unit	• Application driven (especially human interface) • Large device size • Arraying capability • Low profile

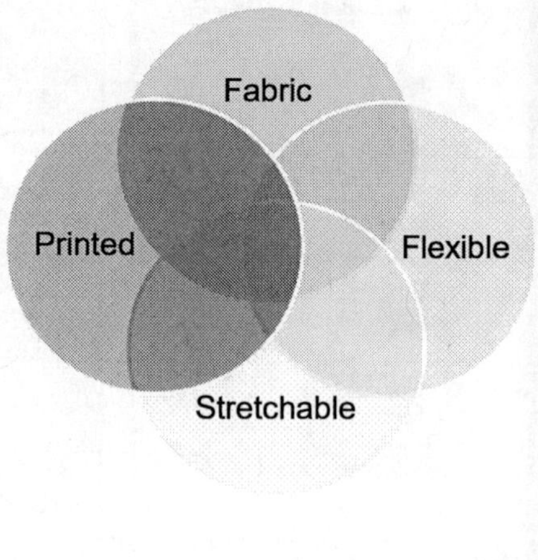

ROGER GRACE ASSOCIATES MARKETING COUNSEL

COMMERCIALIZATION DRIVING FUNCTIONS

- Small size / low profile / low weight
- Ability to conform to attaching surfaces…especially in bio applications
- Robust and highly reliable vis-à-vis judicious material selection
- Low manufacturing cost based on existing batch mode processing with the ability to be scaled to a uber- high volume / uber low cost roll-to-roll (R2R) or weaving manufacturing approach
- Enhanced performance over discrete 3-D solutions because of their size and geometry
- Device-to-device uniformity
- Low CAPEX requirements for manufacturing
- Ease for integration (including discrete) of other functionalities onto same or layered carriers…hybrid approaches
- Ability for arraying
- Large area coverage capability
- Expected to benefit from momentum of popularity of Flexible Hybrid Electronics (FHE) and associated manufacturing capabilities

SENSOR-BASED SYSTEM SOLUTIONS

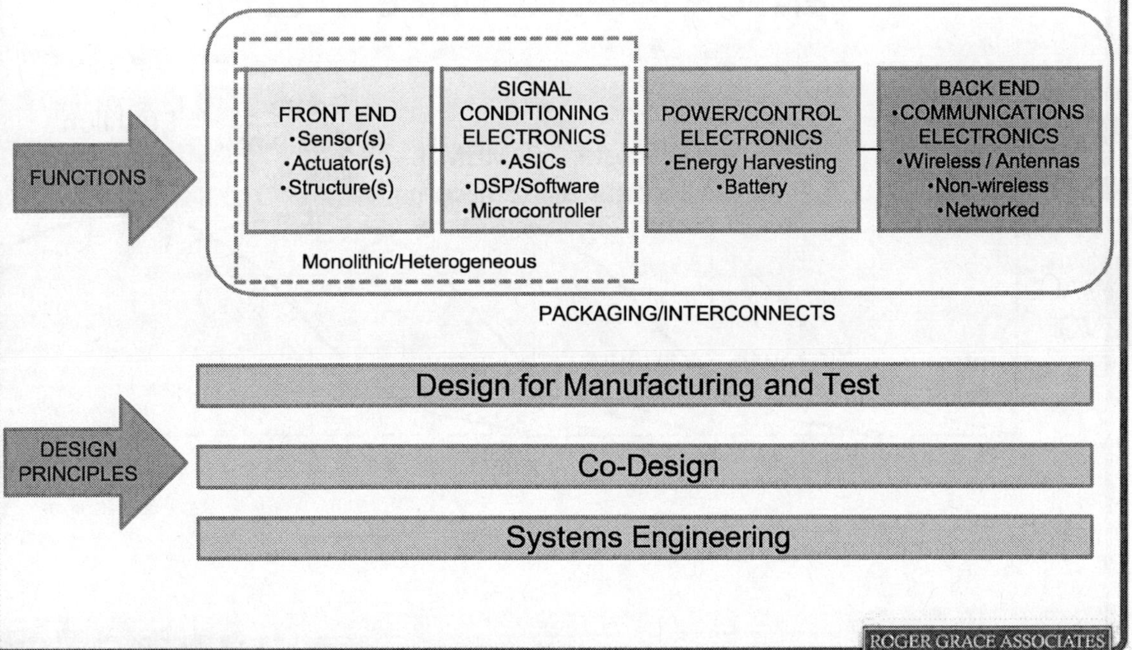

SITUATIONAL ANALYSIS

- Printed/flexible sensors are a logical extension of printed displays (OLED) and Flexible Hybrid Electronics (FHE) electronics…and are chemistry and materials (not electronically) driven and are truly a convergence of technologies
- First commercially success in 1985 by Interlink Electronics and followed by Tekscan …Force Sensing Resistors (FSR)
- To be considered as a compliment / not replacement to Silicon functionalities
- Use much the same infrastructure as printed electronics
- Sensors typically have simple structures and thus easy to manufacture
- Flexible / extensible manufacturing processes:
  - Batch mode for low-to-medium volume applications
  - Roll-to-Roll (R2R) for large volume applications
- Only a small number of companies currently in volume production
- Significant activity in agencies, research labs and universities worldwide
- Many possible application opportunities with a focus on major opportunities for wearables e.g. sports monitoring and home healthcare monitoring
- High volume application opportunities expected to fuel dramatic growth
- Adequate market research coverage to date…i.e. IDTechEx, Modor, Research and Markets
- Limited design and analysis tools currently available

ROGER GRACE ASSOCIATES
MARKETING COUNSEL

SENSOR PRODUCT LIFE CYCLES

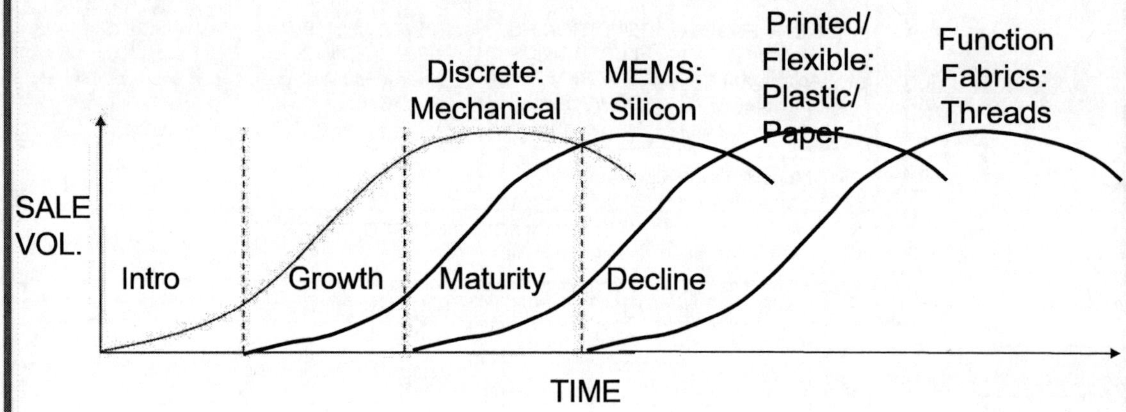

Copyright© 2024 Roger Grace Associates

ROGER GRACE ASSOCIATES
MARKETING COUNSEL

WHERE IT ALL BEGAN

Johannes Gutenberg; Mainz, Germany 1440

ROGER GRACE ASSOCIATES
MARKETING COUNSEL

ECOSYSTEM

- Broad and in-depth (many suppliers for each) ecosystem in place in the value chain
- Suppliers include:
  - Materials, chemicals
  - Equipment
  - Sensors
  - Interconnects
  - Integration
  - Packaging
  - End product design
  - Manufacturing
  - Design, layout and analysis tools
  - Sales and distribution of final product
- Collaboration up and down the value chain will be critical for participants success…one cannot successfully go it alone

ROGER GRACE ASSOCIATES
MARKETING COUNSEL

EMERGING HIGH VOLUME APPLICATION OPPORTUNITIES

- It is common knowledge that many high volume applications exists…however the big question is which are the most lucrative ones and when?
- Need to take into account the "Grace / Walsh 30 year development process for MEMS"
- Current acknowledged current application opportunities include:
  - Package tracking
  - International monitoring of the environment by chemical / gas sensors connected by mobile networks
  - Disposables….e.g. diapers
  - Wearables …Personal health / fitness monitoring e.g. "e-medical"/ military battlefield
  - Food, beverage and drug status monitoring…e.g. UCBerkeley
  - Patient activity monitoring

ROGER GRACE ASSOCIATES MARKETING COUNSEL

DEVICE MATERIAL COST COMPARISON

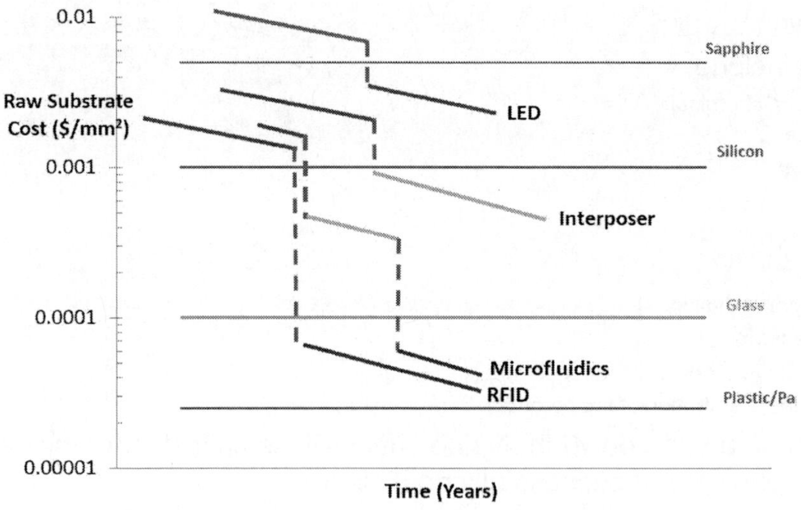

Source: AM Fitzgerald /adapted from P. Werbaneth

ROGER GRACE ASSOCIATES MARKETING COUNSEL

DESIGN & MANUFACTURING PROCESS

- Complex process flow…lots of "landmines" to avoid
- Critical to have design & manufacturing "kickoff" meeting to bring all aspects of the design & manufacturing involved and addressed from day 1
- Decision on printing process driven by several factors…Sheet fed or Roll-to-Roll
  - Volume
  - Specifications
- Scalability…start with sheet-fed for prototypes and low volumes…migrate to Roll-to-Roll for large volumes
- Selection of base materials and inks is critical to performance and manufacturability
- "Converters" or…packagers…integrate the sheets into the final products
  - Cutting
  - Lamination
  - Connection to the outside world

ROGER GRACE ASSOCIATES
MARKETING COUNSEL

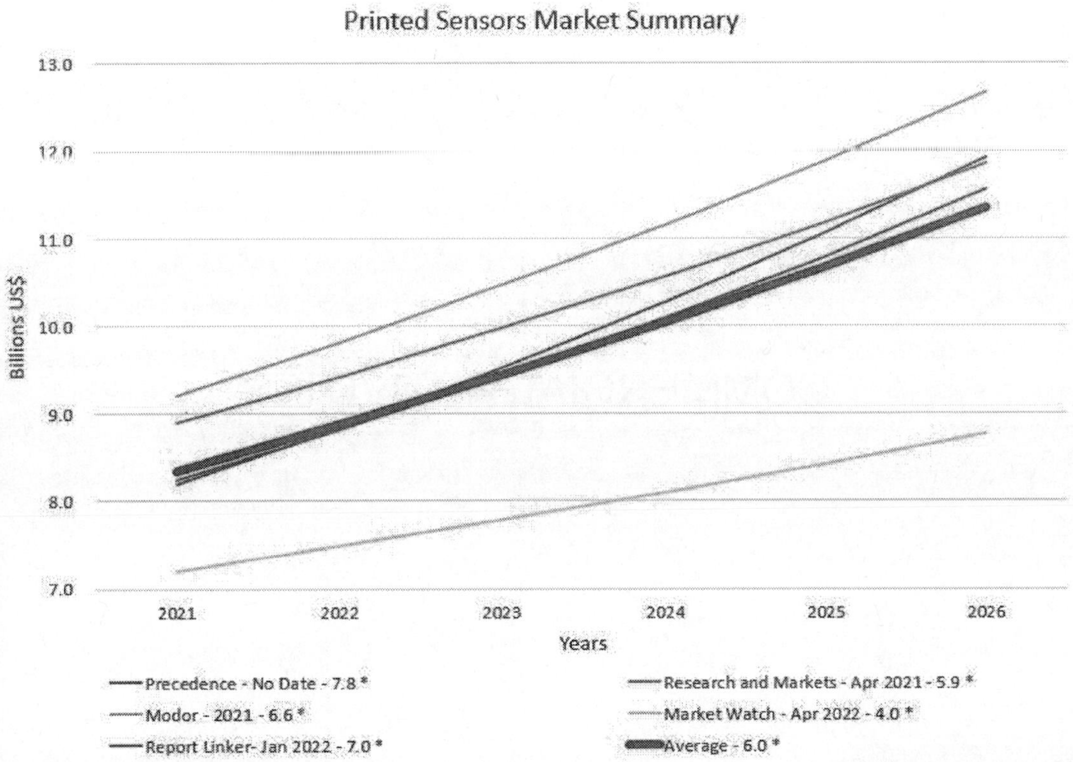

*CAGR – Compound Annual Growth Rate

ROGER GRACE ASSOCIATES
MARKETING COUNSEL

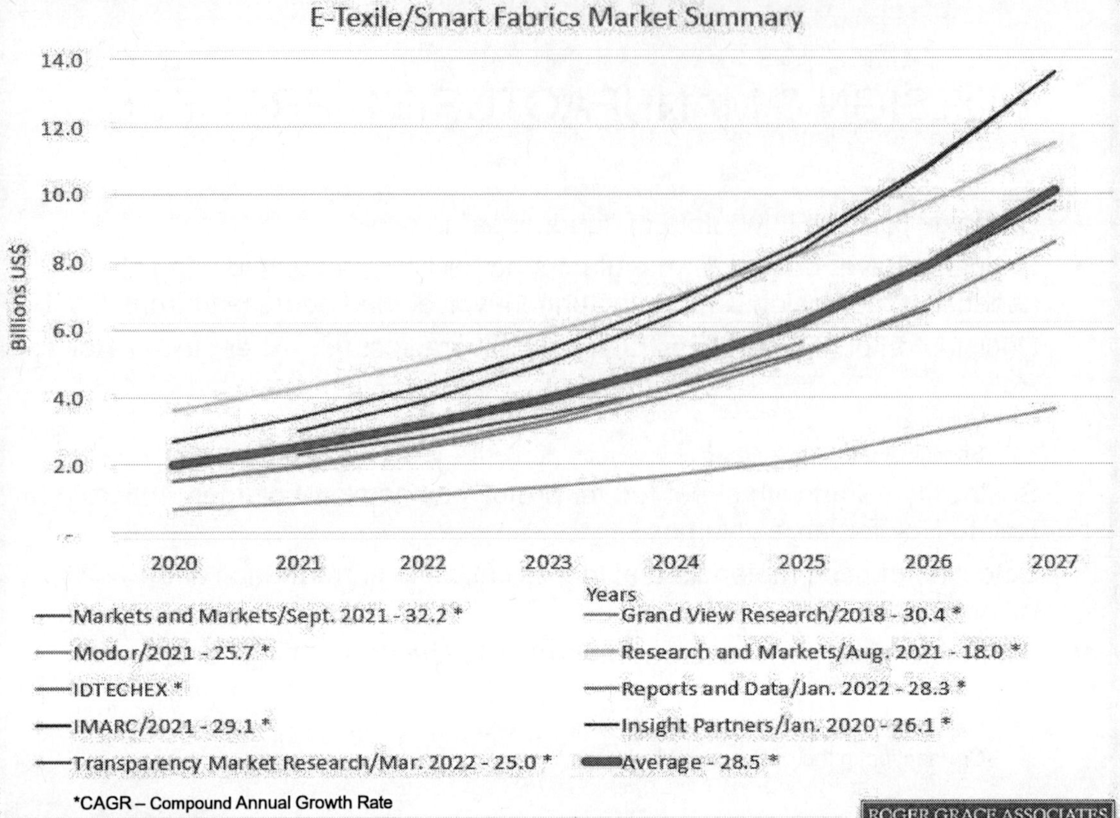

ROGER GRACE ASSOCIATES
MARKETING COUNSEL

.

COMMERCIAL ACTIVITIES

ROGER GRACE ASSOCIATES
MARKETING COUNSEL

CURRENT COMMERCIALIZATION PLAYERS

- Limited “reported” activity in sensors production
- No apparent large volume producers
- No apparent “big dogs” involved (yet)…e.g. Bosch, ST, ADI, Freescale …however we believe that “big dogs” are funding efforts in P/F and FF vis-à-vis subcontracts with research institutes and universities
- Over 100 smaller players worldwide addressing individual parameters
- Virtually all current participants not “traditional” sensor companies but rather materials / chemical companies e.g. Brewer Science
- Sensor parameters currently being addressed include:
  - Chemical/gas
  - Touch/force/pressure
  - Temperature
  - Humidity
  - Bio
  - Air flow
  - Imaging
  - Conducting electrodes

SUPPLIER LANDSCAPE

Company	Force/Touch	Temperature	Humidity	Gas	Electrodes	Bio-Chem	Imaging	Shock	Time of Flight	Flow	Other
BodiTrack/Vista Medical (Canada)	•										
Brewer Science		•	•								
Drop Sense (Spain)					•						
Electrozyme						•					
Flexpoint	•		•							•	
GSI Technologies					•						
Interlink Electronics	•										
ISORG (France)							•				
MC10						•					
Nikkoia (France)							•				
Peratech (UK)	•										
Piezotech (France)					•			•	•		
Plastic Electronics GmbH (Austria)	•										
PolyIC (Germany)	•										
PST (So. Africa)		•									
Sensitronics	•										
Spec Sensors				•							
Synkera				•							
Tactonic	•										
Tekscan	•										
Temptime		•									
T-Inc	•										

Not exhaustive
Alphabetical order

TEKSCAN

- Location: Norwood MA
- Introduced: Early 1990's
- Brand name: Flexiforce
- Parameter sensed: Force, rate of change of force, relative change in force, touch, contact
- Construction: Two layers of polyester substrates with printing of layer of conductive silver (connections) and layer of pressure sensitive ink attached by an adhesive bond
- Applications include sports/fitness consumer, medical devices, robotics, control and diagnostic

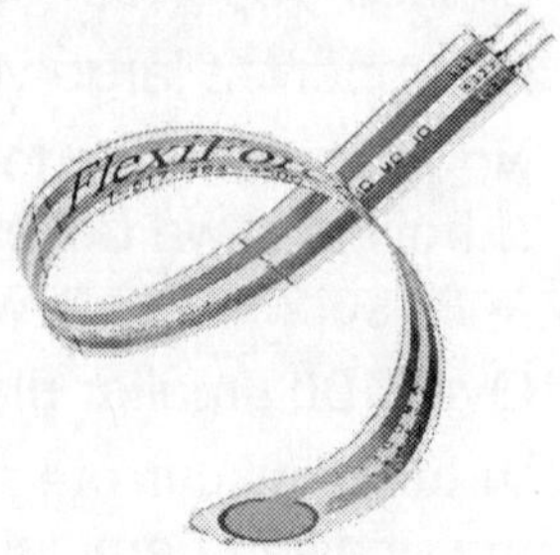

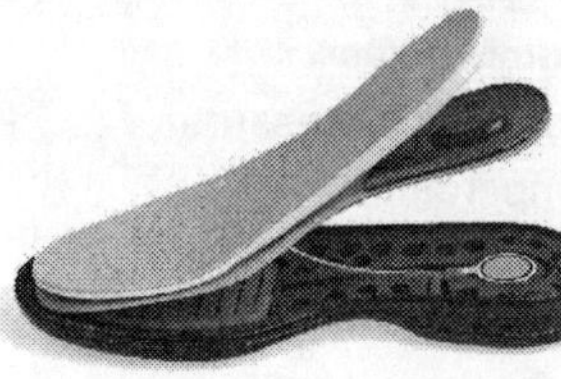

ISORG

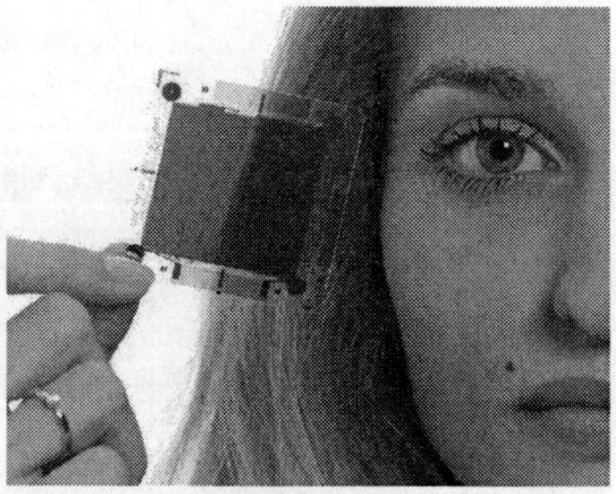

- Location: Grenoble, France
- Parameter sensed: imaging sensor
- Visible/NIR up to 900 nm.
- Low dark current
- Large dynamic range
- PET plastic foil: 32 x 32 cm. moving to 60 x 60 cm.; 5 x 5 cm. device
- PET backplane
- Applications: whole -hand fingerprint analysis/biometrics, medical x-ray imaging ,IoT inventory analysis
- CEA-Leti spinoff in 2009
- Received 28M Euro infusion

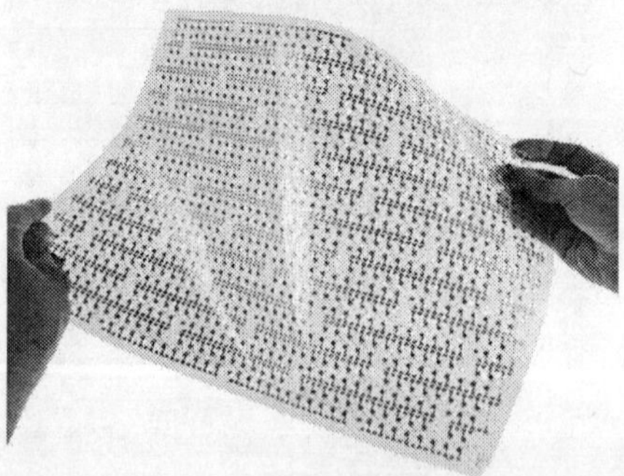

HOLOGENIX / CELLIANT

- Founded: 2017 in LA
- Works on principle of certain minerals plus 88 trace elements react to heat and emit full spectrum IR energy
- Proprietary minerals added to liquid phase of the polymeric thread extrusion process
- Currently EU Class 1 medical device
- FDA classified as medical device with no class determination
- Applications include apparel, medical/wound care, diabetes
- Products include T-shirts (UnderArmor), socks, sheets (Pure Care) Mattresses (Bear)

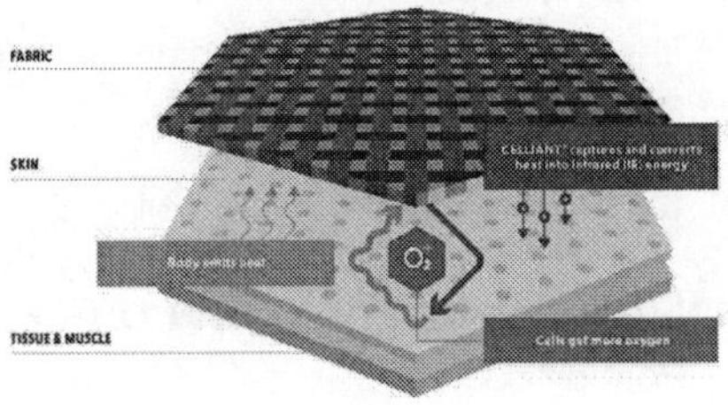

ROGER GRACE ASSOCIATES
MARKETING COUNSEL

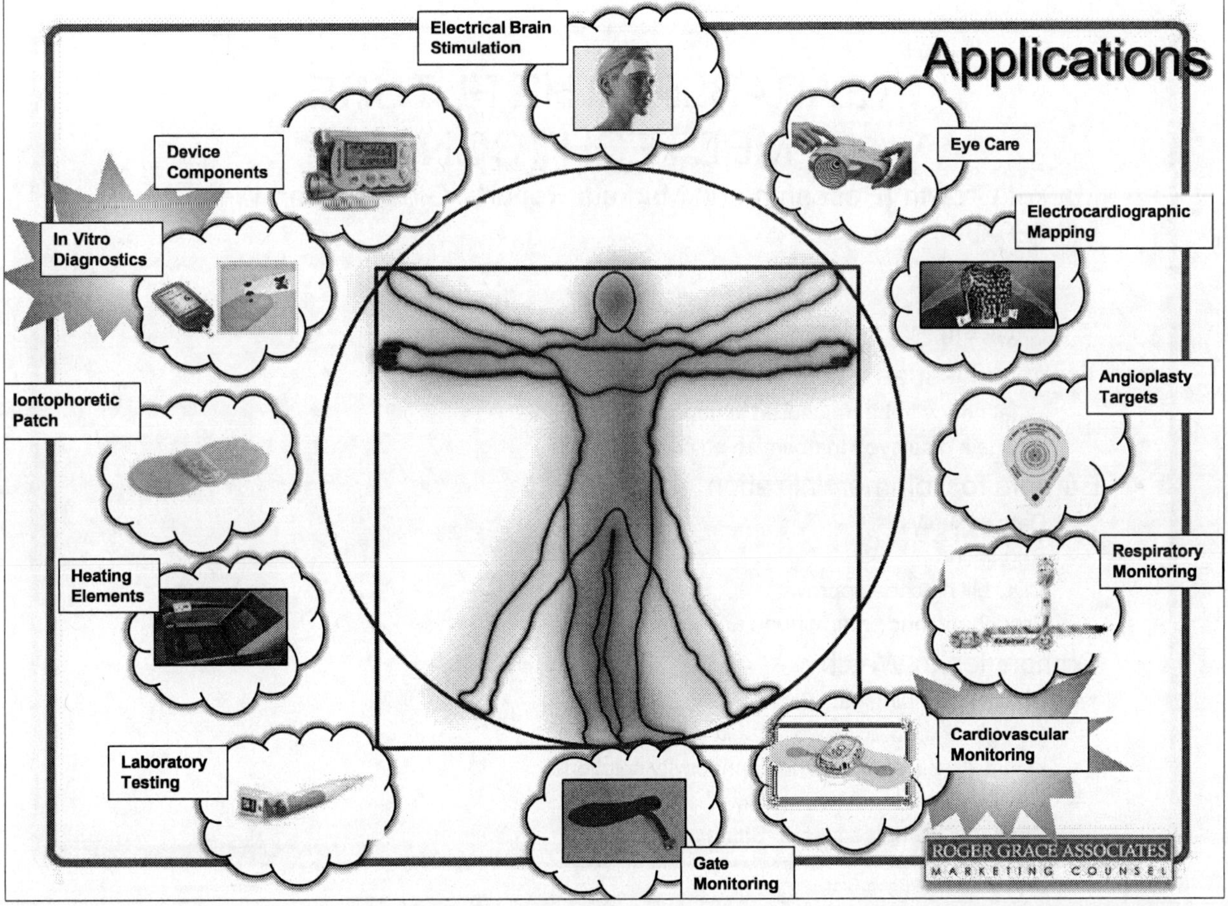

WEARABLES:THE FUTURE OF MEDTECH*

- Definition:
  - On-body vs. off-body
  - Apple watch vs. Sensoria T-Shirt
- Objective: provide "transparent computing"…Davide Vigano/CEO Sensoria
- Forcing Factors
  - "the pandemic transformed healthcare"…Alfred Poor, Editor, Heath Tech Insider
  - Rate of adoption acerated by
    - Aging-in-place
    - Adoption of telemedicine/telehealth
    - Recent developments in AI
- Applications…remote and on-person monitoring
  - Post-procedure
  - Physical therapy
  - Chronic illness
- Technical Issues…Hardware
  - Hybrid/"pod" approach for sensing, computation, communication, power
  - Packaging/interfacing sensor platforms to systems

*key take-aways from the WEAR Conference…June 7-9, 2022 Scottsdale, AZ

ROGER GRACE ASSOCIATES
MARKETING COUNSEL

WEARABLES:THE FUTURE OFMEDTECH*(CONT.)

- Market Growth (Research and Markets Report: "Global Smart Wearables" Feb. 2023)
  - $20.64 B(2022)
  - $34.39B(2027)
  - CAGR=10.2%
- Technical Issues…Software/Data
  - What needs to be measured to impact decisions
  - How is it displayed to optimize efficacy
- Barriers to Commercialization
  - Data security
  - Regulation
  - CDC billing code approval
  - Broadband and smart phone access
- Companies to Watch
  - Butler Technologies…Smart T-Shirt
  - Hologenix…Smart power T-shirt (Under Armor)
  - Liquid Wire…sensors and connectivity solutions
  - Nextiles…smart fabric sensors
  - Sensoria…Smart socks, T-Shirts and bras

ROGER GRACE ASSOCIATES
MARKETING COUNSEL

UNIVERSITIES / RESEARCH INSTITUTES ACTIVITIES

ROGER GRACE ASSOCIATES
MARKETING COUNSEL

R&D LANDSCAPE OVERVIEW

- Considerable R&D activity in sensor development (and their integration) into systems a.k.a. products in many research institutes and universities: Asia
  - ITRI-Taiwan
  - Sungkyonk wan University-Korea
- Europe
  - CEA-Leti France
  - CSEM Switzerland
  - Fraunhofer Europe (67 with approx. 10 involved in P/F Electronics including Chemnitz/ENAS, Munich/EMFT, Dresden/IPMS and Berlin/IZM)))
  - IMEC/ Holst Netherlands
  - VTT Finland
  - INESC Portugal
- US
  - Arizona State University
  - Northeastern University
  - Stanford
  - UC Berkeley
  - UC San Diego
  - GE Research
  - parc
  - UMASS Amherst
  - UMASS Lowell
  - UC Irvine
  - Western Michigan University
  - Ohio State
  - N.C. State

ROGER GRACE ASSOCIATES
MARKETING COUNSEL

PRINTOCENT CLUSTER

- Location: Oulu, Finland
- Started: 2008 www.Printocent.fi
- Facilities (shared):
  - VTT
  - OUAS
  - University of Oulu
- Funding: 40M Euros (EU and Regional)
- Turnover of companies (2019): 25M Euros
- Total number of companies in cluster: 40
- Number of companies catalyzed: 30
- Number of jobs created: 300
- Purpose: Provide open access to companies for scale-up of manufacturing capabilities for the creation and manufacturing of "printed intelligence"
- Created a six-part series of webinars in mid-2020 on "Printed Intelligence"
- Offers free…"Handbook of Printed Intelligence" as pdf download

ROGER GRACE ASSOCIATES
MARKETING COUNSEL

US PUBLIC / PRIVATE CONSORTIA

- AFFOA (Advanced Functional Fabrics of America) www.affoa.org.
  - Location: Cambridge, MA (MIT)
  - Founded in 2016
  - Funding:$75M (US DOD) with grants from governments, industry and academia totaling approximately $325M
  - Focus: Enabling manufacturing
- NEXT FLEX / SEMI www.nextflex.org.
  - Location: San Jose, CA
  - Founded in 2015
  - Funding:$75M (US DOD) with grants from governments, industry and academia totaling approximately $325M
  - Focus: Enabling manufacturing (flexible hybrid approach)

ROGER GRACE ASSOCIATES
MARKETING COUNSEL

INTEGRATION CHALLENGES

- The future success will reside in the ability of suppliers to judiciously select the required functionalities of the individual circuit functions and determine the optimum format/platform for their realization in specific applications
- Monolithic vs. heterogeneous vs. hybrid integration strategies…TBD
- Connectivity of individual devices
- Packaging/encapsulation of total solution
- Reliability issues…especially with wearables continuous washing/drying
- Modelling challenges
- Determination of the manufacturing method to minimize cost, maximize functionality and maximize reliability e.g. Flextronics, Jabil
- Major efforts underway in EU to address this issue…also with NextFlex in the US

ROGER GRACE ASSOCIATES
MARKETING COUNSEL

SYSTEM INTEGRATION

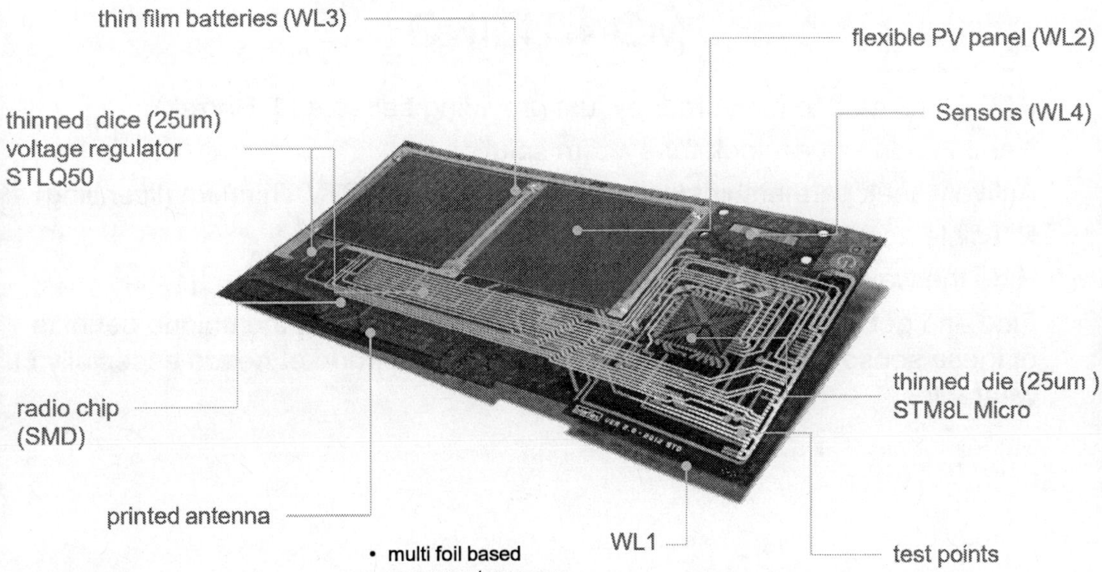

- multi foil based
- energy autonomous
- thin and flexible

INFOTECH automation, cea, BOSCH Invented for life, Henkel, ST, Fraunhofer EMFT

ROGER GRACE ASSOCIATES
MARKETING COUNSEL

CRITICAL SUCCESS FACTORS

- Ability to demonstrate value- add to critical applications
- Ability of to demonstrate equal- to -better performance vs. competitive approaches…and my market research say "yes"
- Growth of the wearables market uncertainty
- Ability of non-flexible/non-organic functional solutions to accommodate application requirements
- Entry of additional players (with big R&D Budgets) to help commercialize the technology
- Adoption of standard processes based on the broad availability of materials
- Continuation of robust funding of research activities by governments …e.g. Next Flex (US), AFFOA (US), PrintoCent (Finland)
- Ability of existing sensor companies to adopt a paradigm shift from a electromechanical technology mindset to that of a materials one
- Continuation of over-hyping of flexible electronics opportunities
- BOTTOM LINE….I believe there is lots of uncertainty at this time…"as goes flexible hybrid electronics so goes its sensors"…R. Grace

ROGER GRACE ASSOCIATES
MARKETING COUNSEL

MONITIZING

- FACT…Its hard to make money just providing sensors (J. Bryzek)
- Need to add value…look for system solutions
- Actively seek partnerships/collaborations … e.g. PST / ThinFilm (licensing)
- Possible acquisition strategy
- Ride the wave of the printed electronics (PE) growth
- Find and get designed into applications that can exploit the unique benefits of these sensor technologies and address unmet market needs especially in wearables

ROGER GRACE ASSOCIATES
MARKETING COUNSEL

SUMMARY / CONCLUSIONS

- Limited:
  - number of success stories to date
  - number of commercial companies in volume production
  - number of parameters currently being measured:
    - Pressure / force / touch
    - Gas analyses
    - Temperature
    - Humidity
- Solid growth foreseen by several market research groups
  - Printed: CAGR (average) =6% (2021-2026)?
  - Functional Fabric: CAGR (average)= 28% (2020-2027)
- Growth forcing functions
  - Replacement of existing solutions…lower cost, enhanced functionality
  - Creation of new solutions based on enabling nature of P/F/S and FF
- Will require a significant marketing/applications pull vs. technology push
- A "systems solution" approach will be required…not just a sensor!
- Wearables for military, sport fitness, disposables, package tracking, e-healthcare and environmental monitoring expected to propel market
- Ability to scale to R-2-R for large volume/low cost application opportunities

ROGER GRACE ASSOCIATES
MARKETING COUNSEL

SUMMARY / CONCLUSIONS (cont.)

- Low cost CAPEX makes commercialization by many organizations possible
- I believe that the success of Printed/Flexible/Stretchable and Functional Fabric/E-Textile sensors will weigh heavily on the success of flexible hybrid electronics (FHE) …the future will be interesting

ROGER GRACE ASSOCIATES
MARKETING COUNSEL

FURTHER READING

- Articles by Roger Grace on P/F/S and E-Textile/Smart Fabric sensors have appeared in:
  - Electronic Products-June, 2015 Electronic Products; July 2015
  - Sensors Magazine Newsletter-September 25, 2015
  - Sensor Magazin (Germany)-November 2015
  - Commercial Micromanufacturing Magazine (UK)-December 2015
  - Commercial Micromanufacturing Magazine (UK)-May/June 2018

…and all available on the Roger Grace Associates website www.rgrace.com in the drop down tab…"Articles"

ROGER GRACE ASSOCIATES
MARKETING COUNSEL

Since this was a shortened presentation due to time constraints…
the entire presentation will be available to attendees by kindly requesting it via email to me at …rgrace@rgrace.com

Please enter to win
a pair of Smart socks courtesy of Hologenix

ROGER GRACE ASSOCIATES
MARKETING COUNSEL

molex *creating connections for life*

Integration and Interconnects

Rob Irwin
Product Development Manager
June 2024

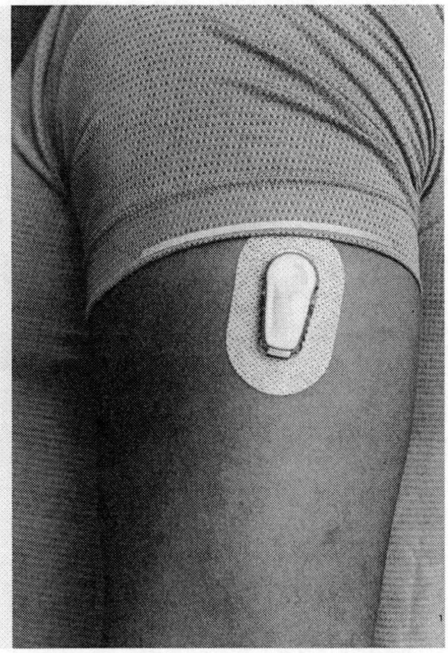

ROB IRWIN

Product Development Manager for Molex's Printed Circuit Solutions product family. Rob has a BS in Materials Science and Engineering from the University of Minnesota. Rob joined Molex during their acquisition of Soligie Printed Electronics in 2015 and has 18 years of experience in technology, product and program management related to integration of flexible electronics into systems and devices in diverse industry segments.

molex

Agenda

- Overview
- Introduction to Printed Hybrid Electronics (PHE)
- Critical Factors for Printed Hybrid Electronics
- Customization, Design and Development
- Designing with the End in Mind
- Case Studies
- Emerging Technologies and Trends
- Q&A

molex

Overview of Flexible Electronics

Integration of Components and Materials

DISPOSABLES

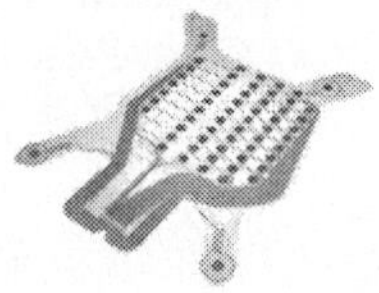

WEARABLES

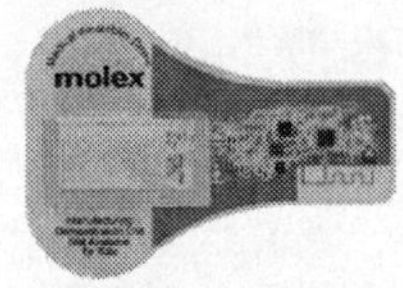

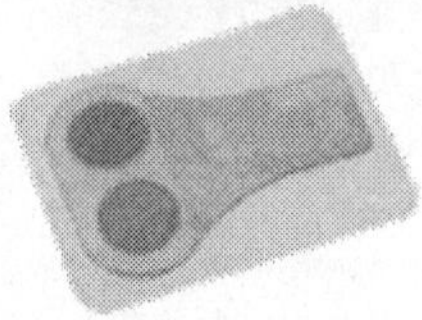

MONITORING

CIRCUITRY

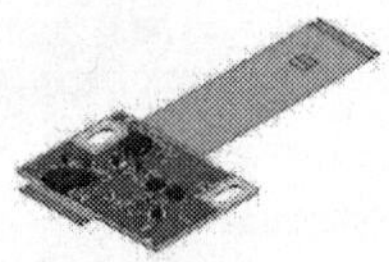

molex 4

What are Printed Hybrid Electronics

- Advanced printing techniques
  - Screen printing, flexography, gravure, inkjet, aerosol
- Electronic circuits on various substrates
  - Thin films, flexible or rigid
- Rigid, Printed or thin film sensors
  - Capacitive touch, force sensing, temperature sensing

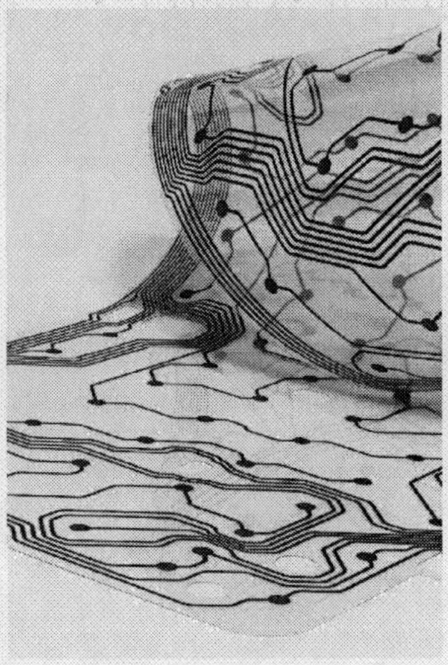

molex 5

Critical Success Factors for PHE

Key Capabilities for Hybrid Electronic Systems

- Early Engagement
- Goal Alignment
- Collaborative or Turnkey Development
- Technology Readiness and Analysis of Alternatives
- Product and Design Development
  - Material Selection
    - Choosing materials
    - Performance and cost
- Process Development
  - Configuring Existing Processes
  - Innovating

End-to-End Product Design
Close collaboration with our customers

Global Support
Design and manufacturing in Europe, Asia, and North America

Trusted Provider
Dedicated cross-functional team with customer-first approach

molex 6

Customization

Design and Development

- Application and Use Case
- Functionality
- Circuitry
  - Printed
  - Etched
- Electronic Component Integration
- Advanced Thin Film Converting Techniques
  - Sheet
  - Roll-to-roll

Molex demo: customization example

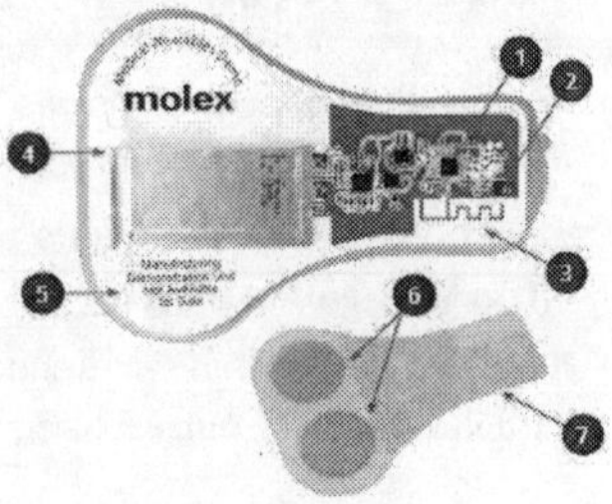

1. BLE connectivity to mobile app
2. On/off dome switch
3. Printed antenna
4. Thin-flex battery for one-time use
5. Flexible substrate
6. Hydrogel and electrodes
7. Adhesive layer and release liner

Designing with the End in Mind

Manufacturing Considerations for Final Use Case

- Printed Conductive Circuits
  - Silver, Copper, Carbon
  - Dielectrics
- Flexible Substrates
  - PET (Polyester), PC, Polyimide
  - Paper, Fabrics, Non-Woven Fabrics, Stretchable Substrates (Dev)
  - Various Thicknesses from 3mil+
- Electronic Component Attach and Test
  - SMT: Low Temp Solder, Epoxy Attachment
  - Component Encapsulation
- Films and Adhesives Converting
- Die Cutting, Laminating, Island Placement
- Functional Testing
- Final Product Packaging

Case Study

- Printed electrodes, hydrogel compatibility
- Long shelf life, short term use
- High volume, efficient manufacturing (R2R)
- Quality, delivery, sustain

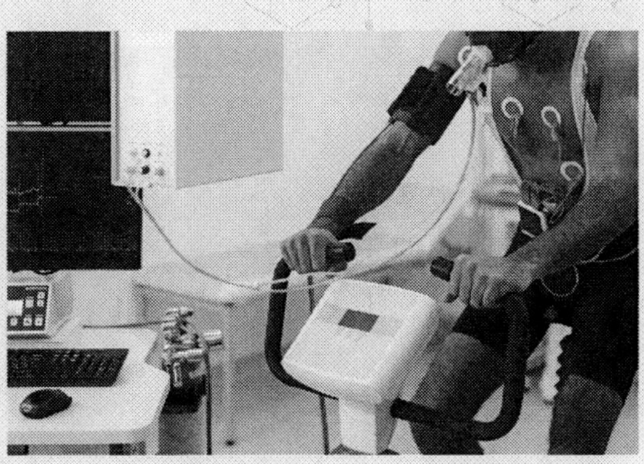

molex

Case Study

- Wireless asset label
- Hybrid print and etch solution
- Thin film battery
- High volume, high yield

molex

Emerging Technologies and Trends

Future Direction and Innovation

- Emerging Technologies
  - Alternative Electrode Interface Materials
  - Innovative Electronic Integration Materials
  - Alternative Substrates
  - Innovative Inks E.g., Copper
- Market Trends
  - AI and IoT
- Opportunities

Trends ⟶

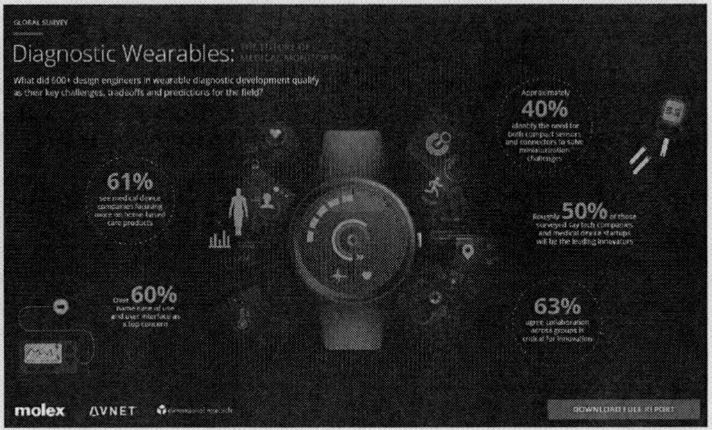

Questions?

Please ask questions you might have regarding integration and interconnect solutions

molex *creating connections for life*

Thank You

molex

creating connections for life

muRata
INNOVATOR IN ELECTRONICS

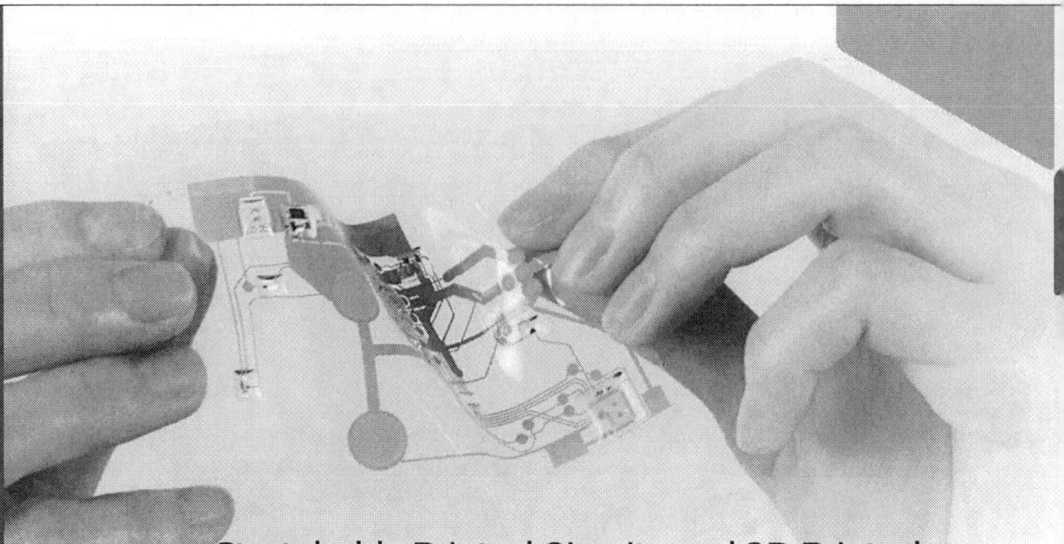

Stretchable Printed Circuits and 3D Printed Ceramics: Innovative Platform Technologies Enable Sensor Creation for Medical Wearable Applications

Murata Electronics North America: Mark Waugh

Murata Manufacturing Co., Ltd.: Nobuyasu Hori and Takumi Okashiro

About Murata

Murata Manufacturing is a comprehensive electronic component manufacturer that creates cutting-edge technologies and components. Under the slogan *Innovator in Electronics,* we contribute to a flourishing society.

Strengths

- Research and development of cutting-edge materials
- Extensive product lineup
- Global production and sales network

Profile

- Founded: 1994
- Sales: ~ $15 Bil USD
- Number of Companies: 87 (30 domestic companies and 57 overseas companies)
- Number of Employees: 73,164 (33,178 in Japan and 39,986 overseas)

Other Murata products for wellness

Miniature & high quality components

- Capacitors
- Thermistors
- Timing devices
- Bluetooth modules
- AMR sensors
- Micro batteries
- RFID tags
- Ionizers

muRata

Murata Core Technologies

Analytical technology	Materials characterization	Failure analysis				
Back-end processing technology	Packaging	Measurement	Automation	Industrial engineering		
Product design technology	High frequency design	Device design	Embedded design	High reliability design	Circuit design	Simulation
Front-end processing technology	Laminating & stacking	Printing	Sintering	Nano & thin-film fabrication	Surface finishing	Precision mechanical processing
Materials technology	Materials design	Materials processing				

3

Substrate Evolution

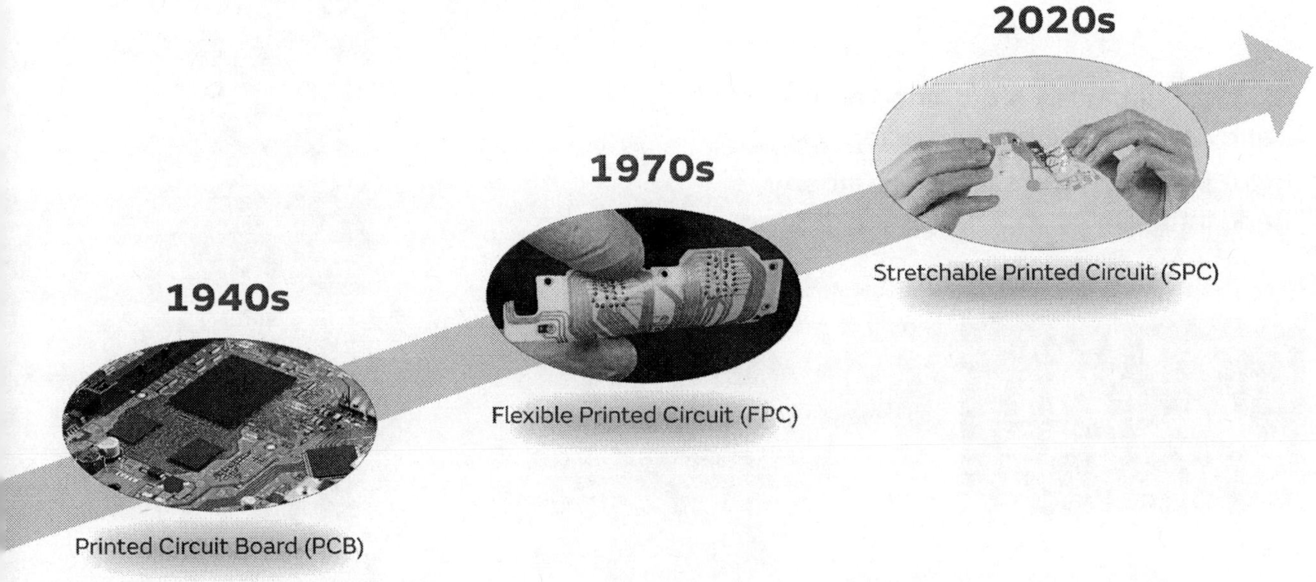

4

Data Driven Medicine/ IoMT

The era of healthcare monitoring devices is upon us, promising to achieve P4 Medicine* through IoMT

- Prediction
- Prevention
- Personalization
- Participation

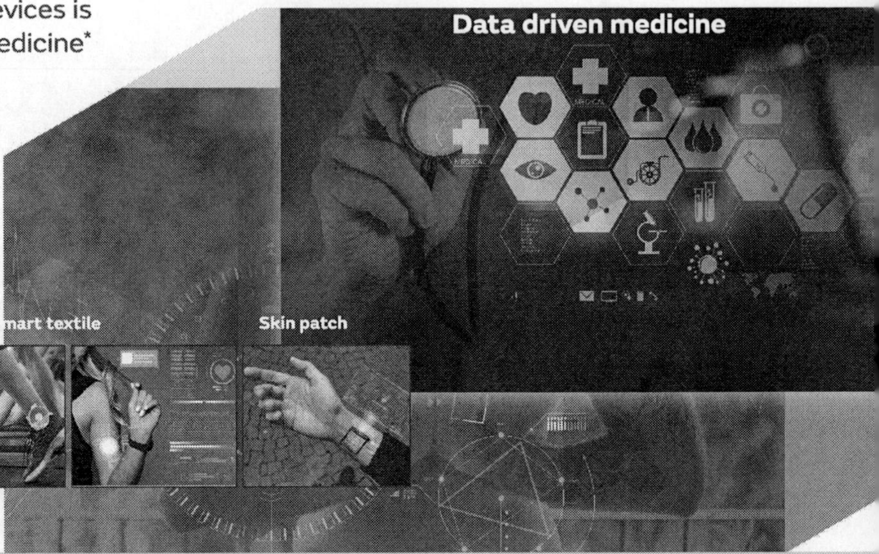

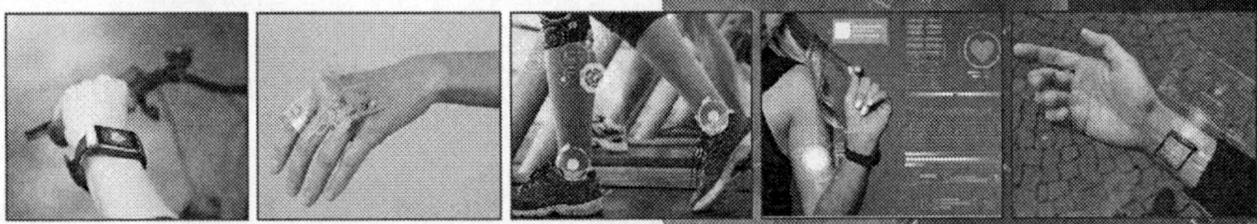

* Dr. Leroy Hood, President of Institute for Systems Biology

 * Dr. Leroy Hood, President of Institute for Systems Biology

Flexible Printed Circuit (FPC) Challenges

- Lack of elasticity is not good adhesion and conformability on bending body
- Not gentle on the skin of the elderly and infants

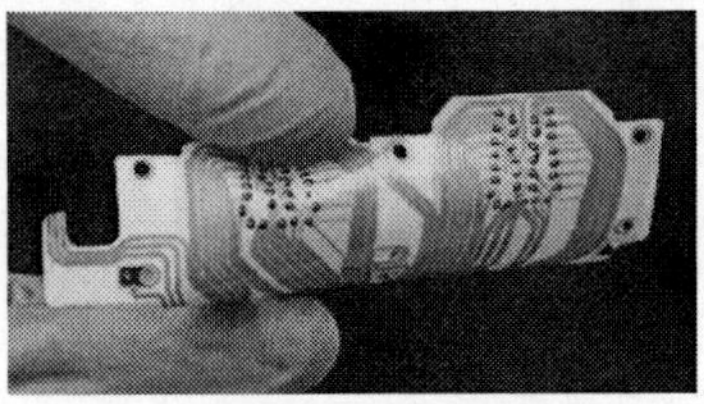

FPC

SPC

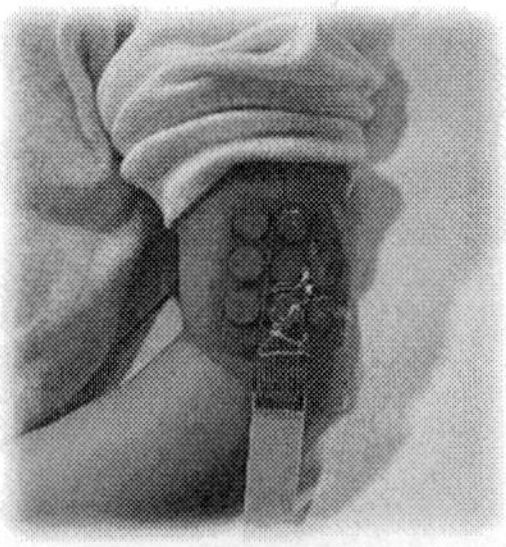

SPC

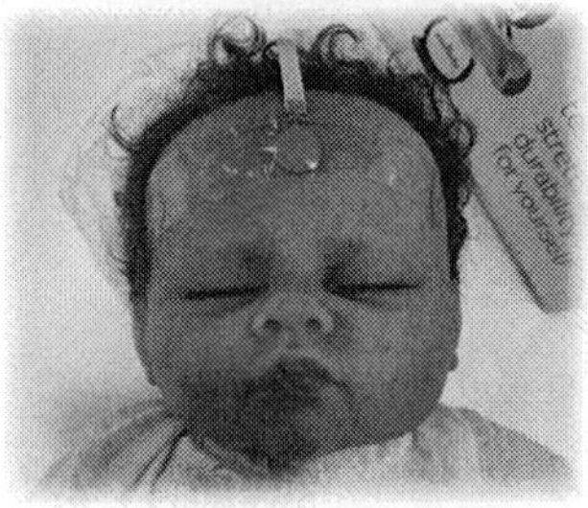

What is a Stretchable Printed Circuit (SPC)

What can be achieved: PCBs and FPCs function **on stretchable substrates.**

PCB

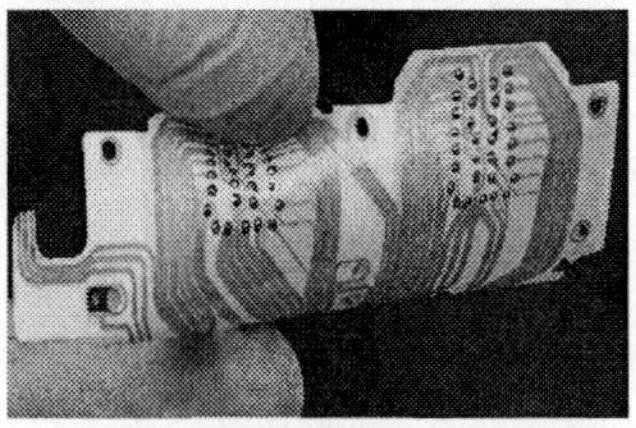

FPC

- Knowledge of stretchable substrates and stretchable conductive material
- Printing of stretchable sensor electrodes (EC12 Compliant)
- Component mounting and hybrid bonding technology between substrates
- Modeling and simulation based on stretching behavior
- Coating materials for patients' safety

Achieve on a stretchable substrate!

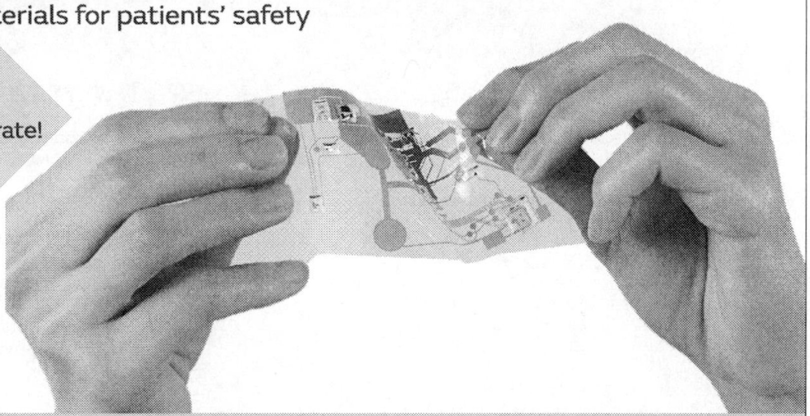

7

SPC Applications and Sensors

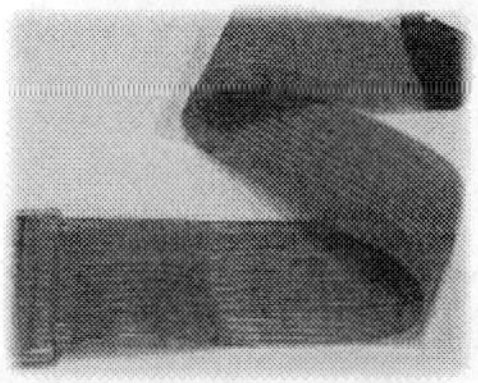

Soft-on-skin device connector

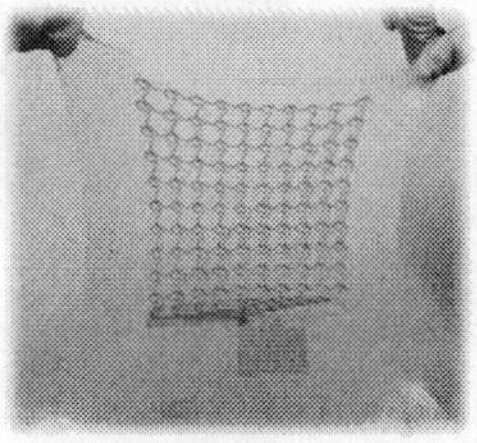

Body surface temperature distribution

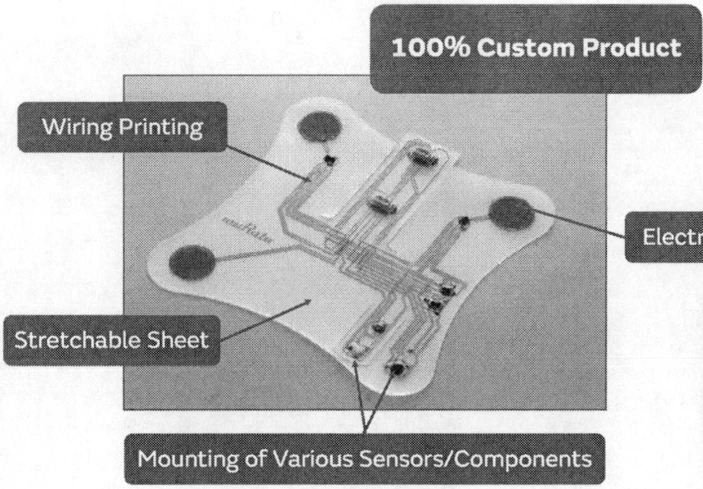

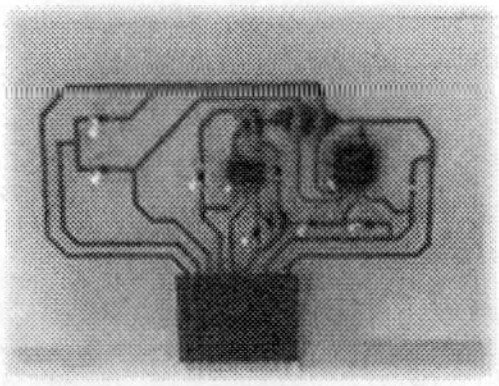

Mounted accelerometer

Wrapped around the body measure bioimpedance

8

Various Biopotential/Bioimpedance Sensors using SPC

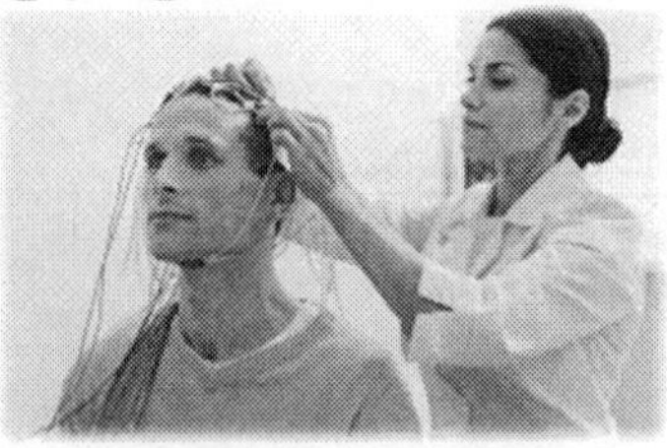

EEG

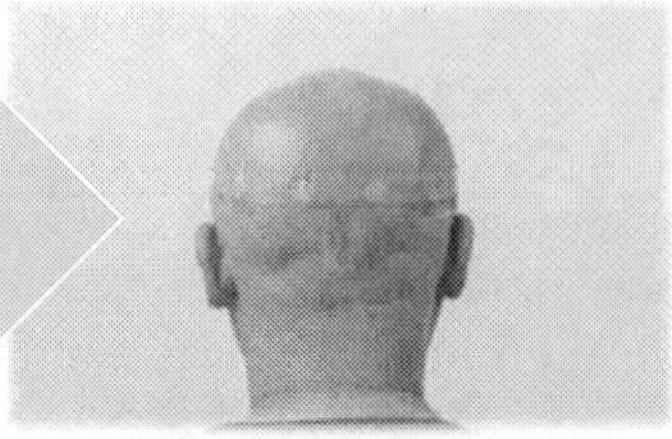

Traditional Technology

- Needed much wiring for each electrode
- Necessary to pull it around
- Time-consuming to install and remove each patch
- Difficult to catch small signal

SPC Technology

- All electrodes and wiring are placed on ONE sheet
- No need to pull it around
- One-touch installation and removal are possible
- Better data accuracy is achieved by mounting an amplifier right next to the electrodes

- **ECG** (Electrocardiogram) - Passive
- **EEG** (Electroencephalogram) - Passive
- **EMG** (Electromyograph) - Passive
- **EIT** (Electrical Impedance Tomography) - Active

9

SPC Biopotential/ Bioimpedance Sensor Examples

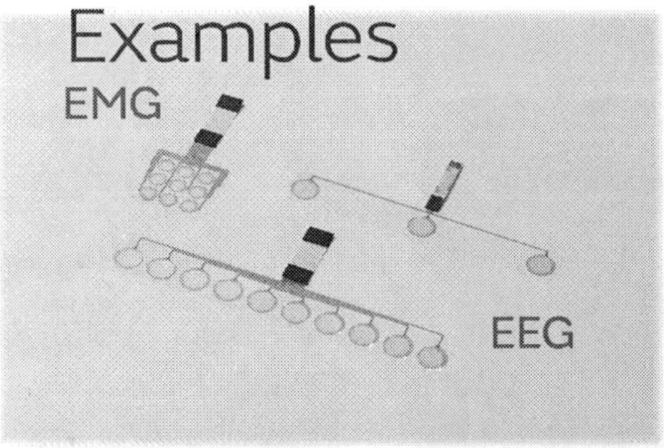

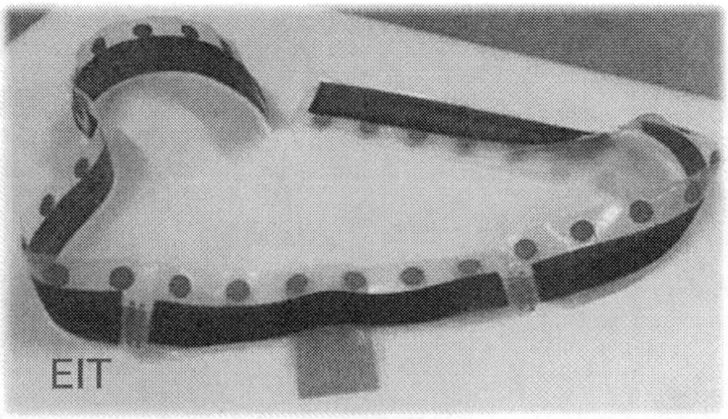

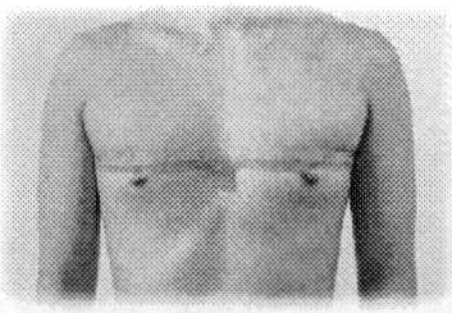

EIT

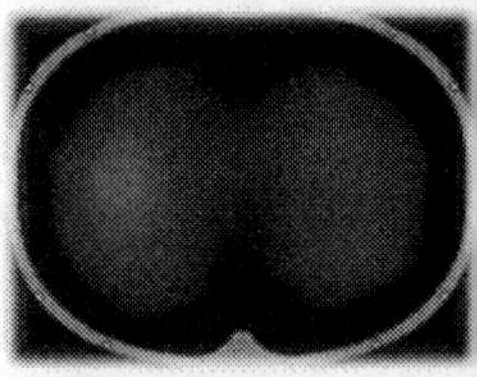

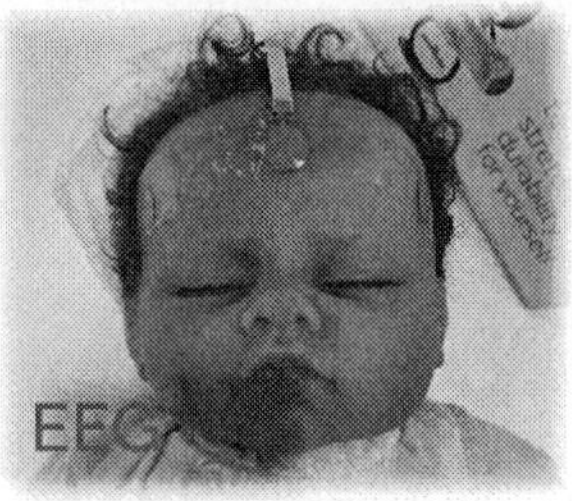

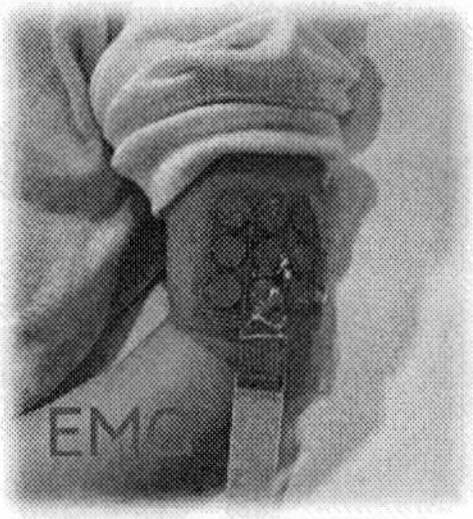

EEG

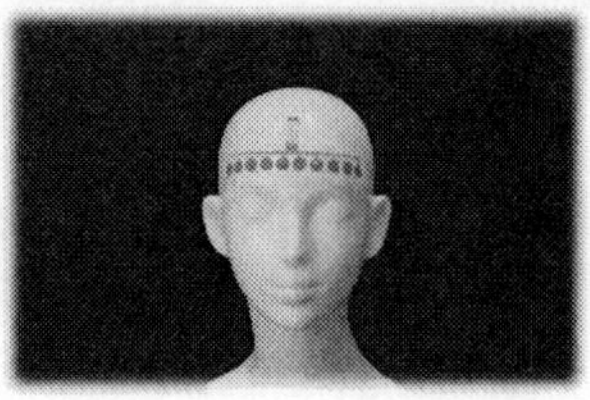

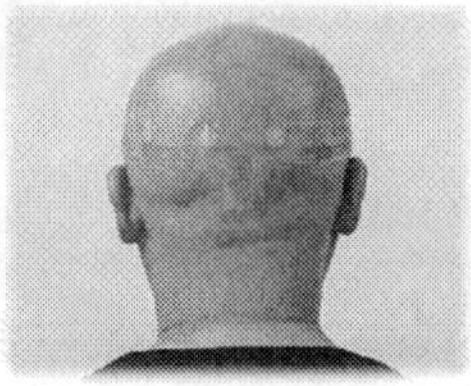

10

Active ECG Sensor Electrode

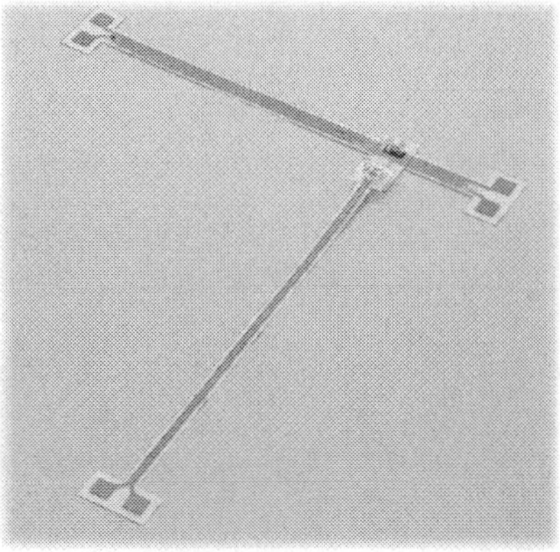

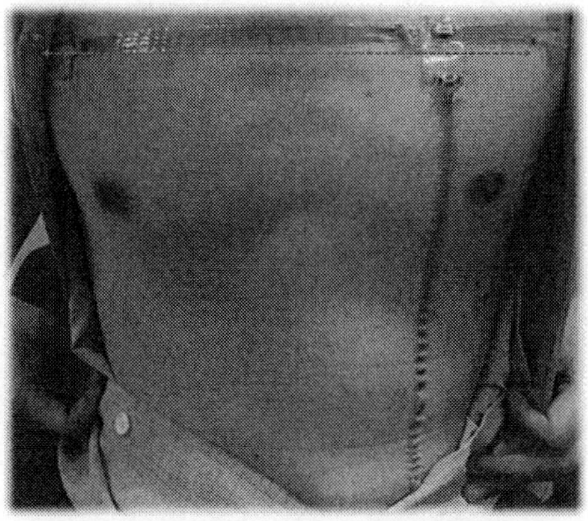

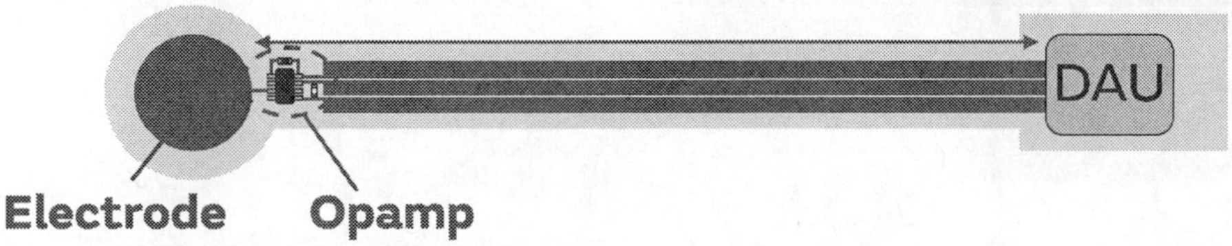

Biopotential Measurement

Appearance

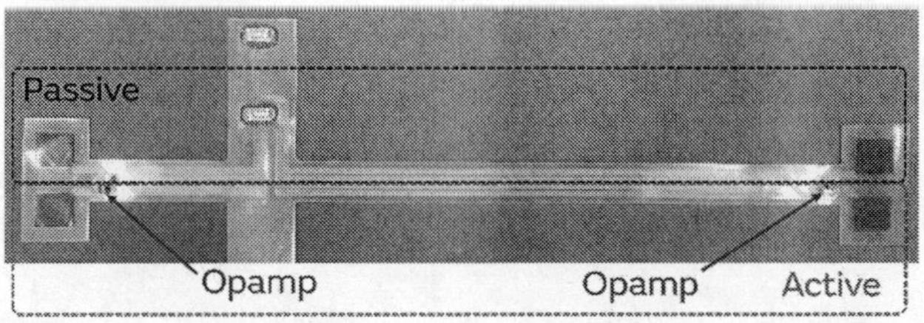

Cross-sectional image

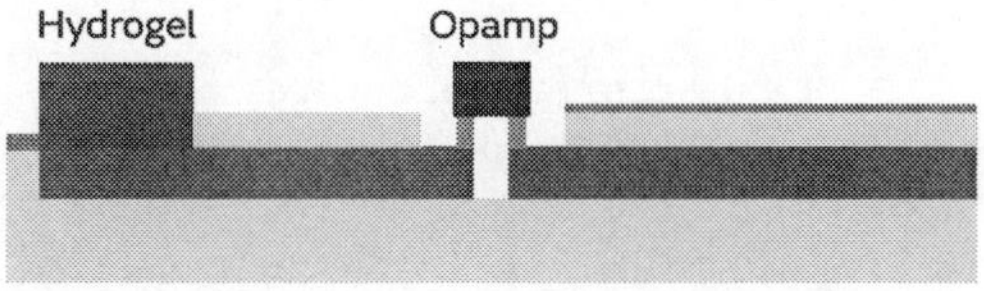

Electrical circuit / Active electrode

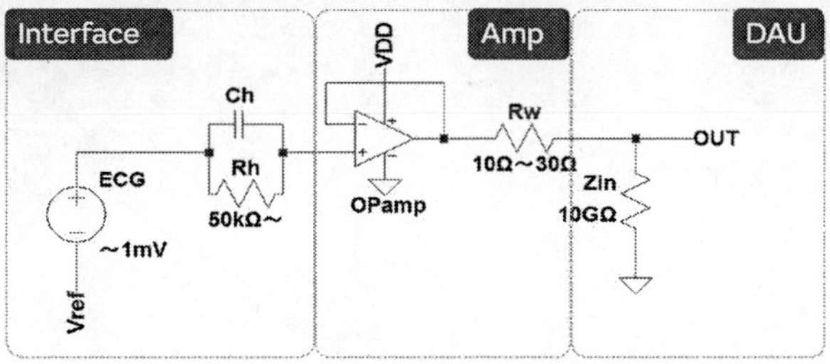

Noise Prevention by Active Electrode

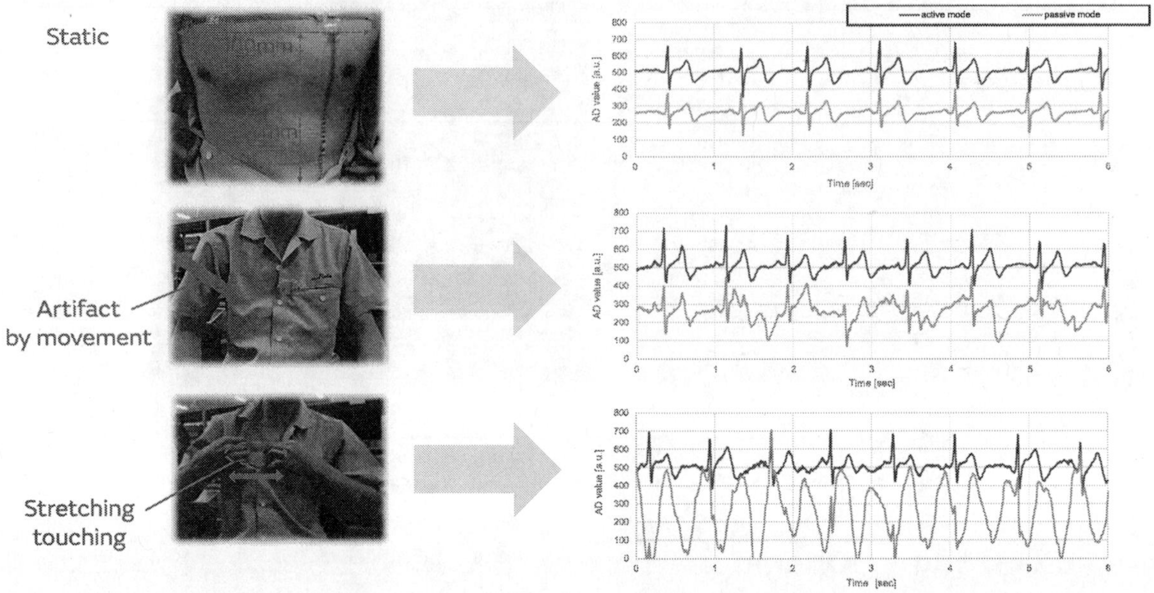

SPC Multilayer Stacking Technology

Multilayering blocks EM noise and maximizes bio-signals

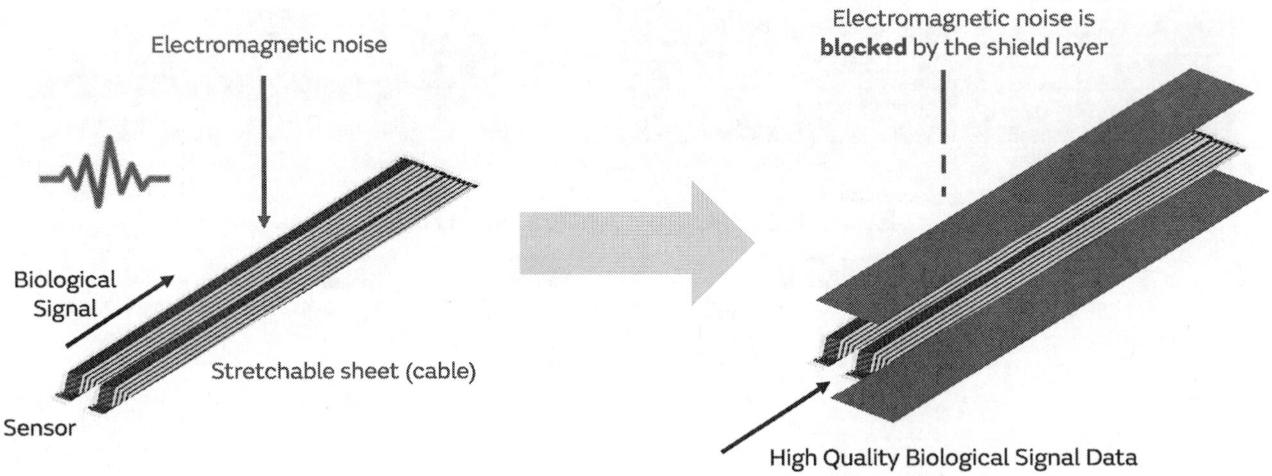

SPC Solves Conventional Technology Challenges

Challenge	Solution
Long-time use is not good/comfortable for patients	Very soft and light materials are comfortable for patients
Different Positions of Sensor Electrode on individual patients	Easy to adjust the size and positions by stretchability
Need many wirings for each sensor electrode	Achieve multi sensor electrodes and wirings onto one sheet Lead to easy set up!
Small signals	Amplify the signal by mounting amplifiers near electrodes
	Add sensors like temperature, accelerometer, etc.

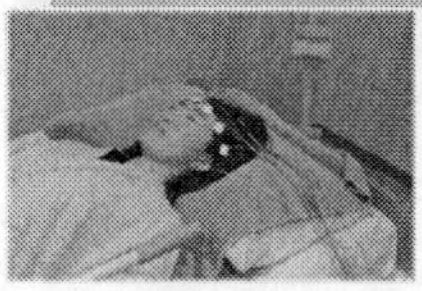

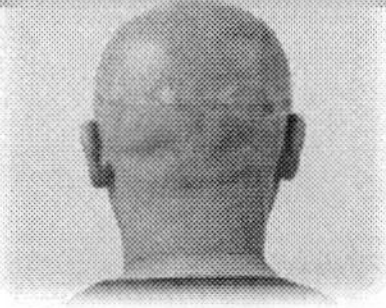

15

muRata

SPC Technology Readiness Level

Commercial deployment

Real world

- TRL 9 — SPC
- TRL 8
- TRL 7

Simulated world

- TRL 6
- TRL 5
- TRL 4

Research Lab

- TRL 3
- TRL 2
- TRL 1

Identified Idea

- Actual system proven in an operational environment (competitive manufacturing in the case of key enabling technologies, or in space)
- System completed and qualified
- System prototype demonstration in an operational environment
- Technology demonstrated in a relevant environment (industrially relevant environment in the case of enabling technologies)
- Technology is validated in a relevant environment (industrially relevant environment in the case of key enabling technologies
- Technology validated in a lab
- Experimental proof of concept
- Technology concept formulated
- Basic principles observed

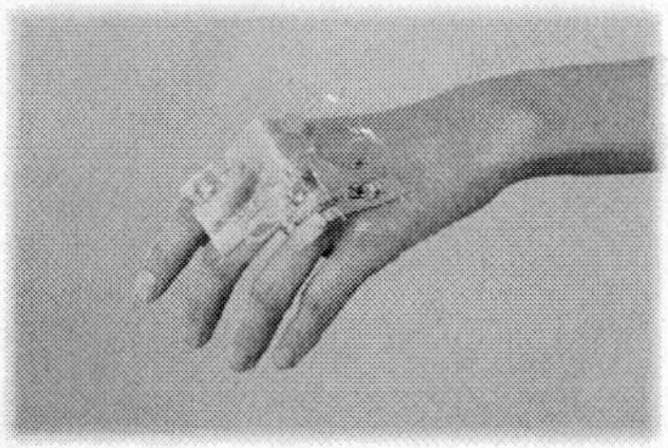

16

muRata

SPC Integration

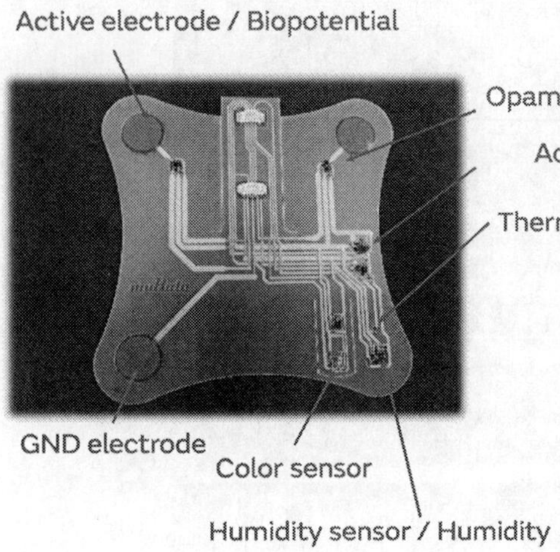

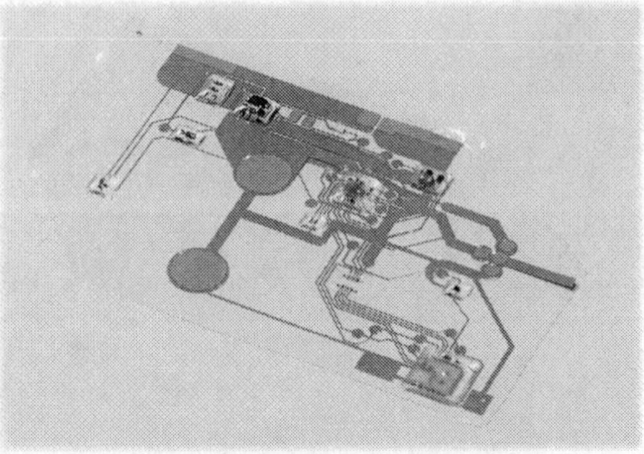

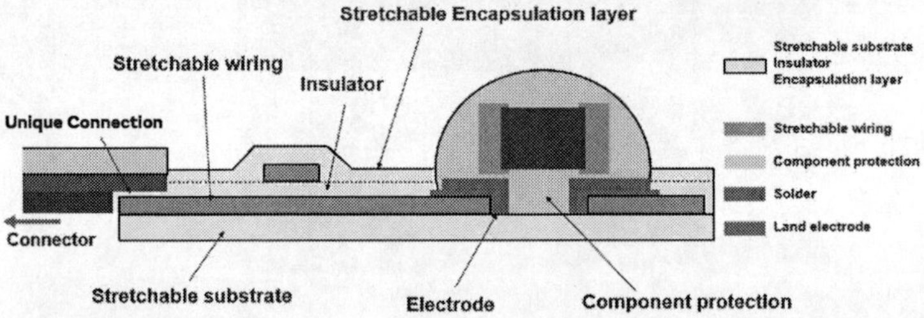

17

INNOVATOR IN ELECTRONICS

3D Printed Ceramic Technology

What is NeuroStone™

Neuron + Stone = NeuroStone™

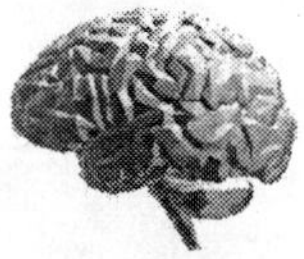
+

=

Freeform

Freeform:

Employs 3D inkjet printing with ceramic and copper particle suspension followed by co-firing

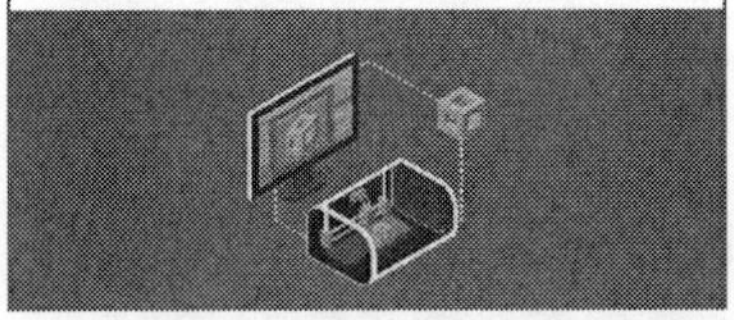

Interconnected

Interconnected:

NeuroStone™ technology provides both free-form and non-planar electrodes both internally and externally

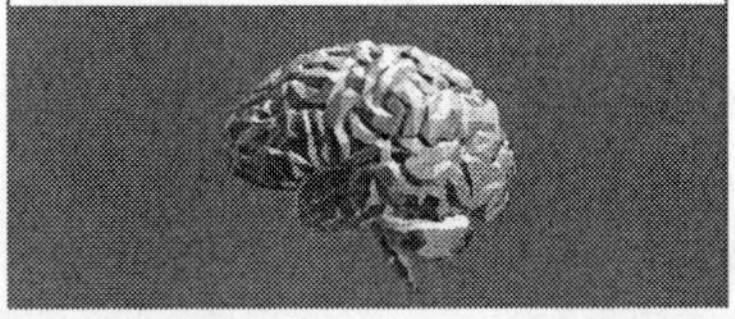

Ceramic device

Ceramic device:

Custom 3D fabricated devices based on Murata's low-temperature firing ceramic technology

NeuroStone™ Application: Electrode for Implants

Novel 3D-printed Electrodes for Implantable Biopotential Monitoring Applications

*2021 43rd Annual International Conference of the IEEE Engineering in Medicine & Biology Society (EMBC)

NeuroStone™ Application: Electrode for Implants

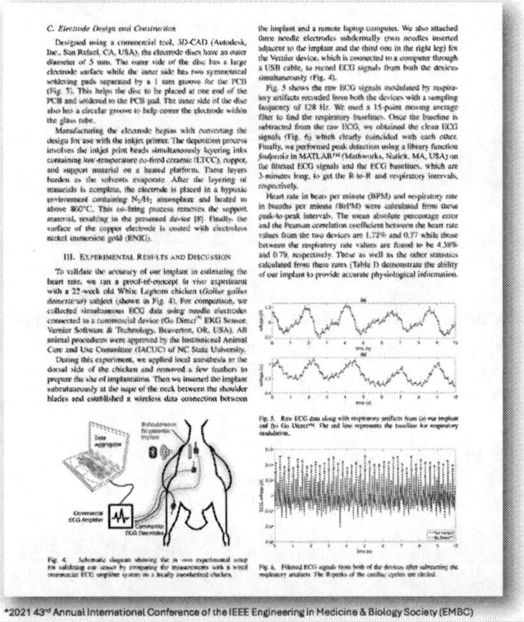

*2021 43rd Annual International Conference of the IEEE Engineering in Medicine & Biology Society (EMBC)

NeuroStone™ Application: Electrode for Implants

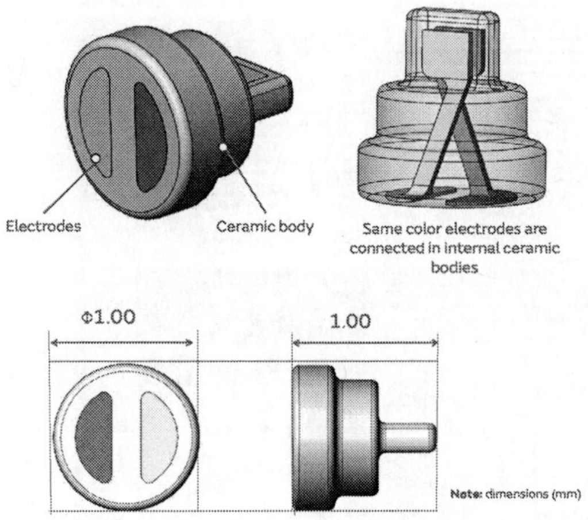

Mounting structure of implant electrodes

- Easy to assemble
- Miniaturizing structure
- High reliability

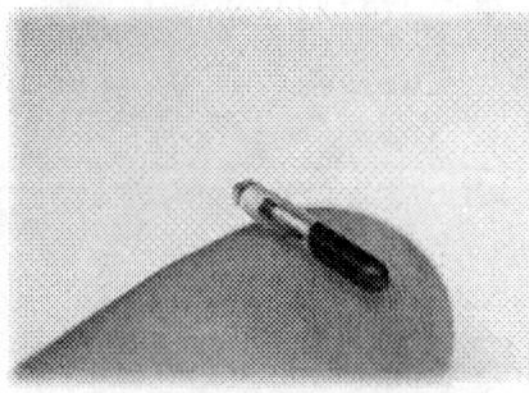

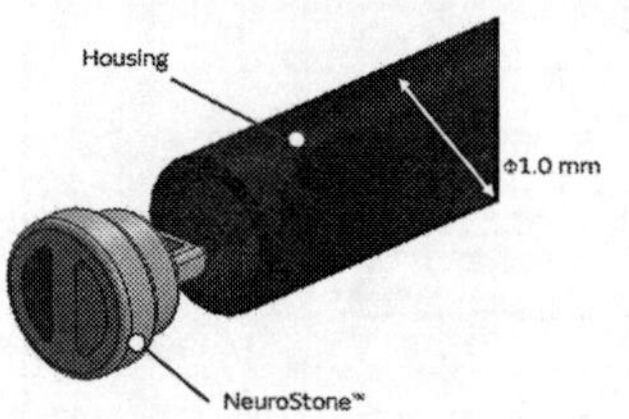

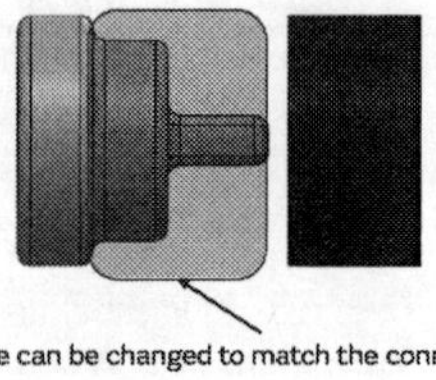

Shape can be changed to match the connector parts

muRata
INNOVATOR IN ELECTRONICS

Thank you!

Contact: mwaugh@murata.com

Visit us at booth #716

Sensors Converge

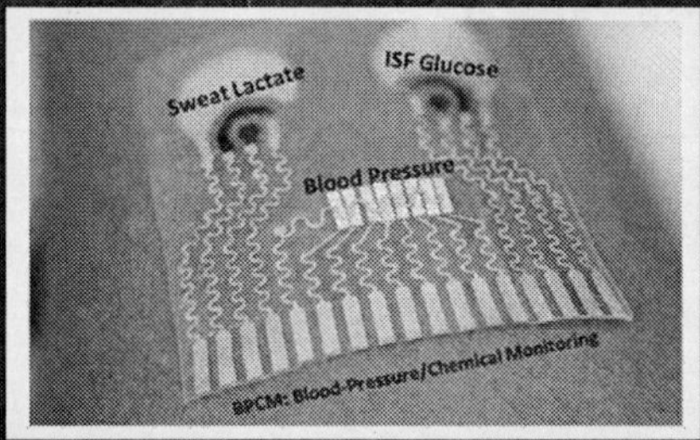

All-in-One: Multi-Modal Wearable Sensor Patches for Monitoring Chemistry and Vitals

Joseph Wang, UCSD
Director: UCSD Center for Wearable Sensors (CWS)

June 24–26, 2024 | Santa Clara, CA

#SensorsConverge

Center for Wearable Sensors

UC SAN DIEGO NANO BIOELECTRONICS LAB

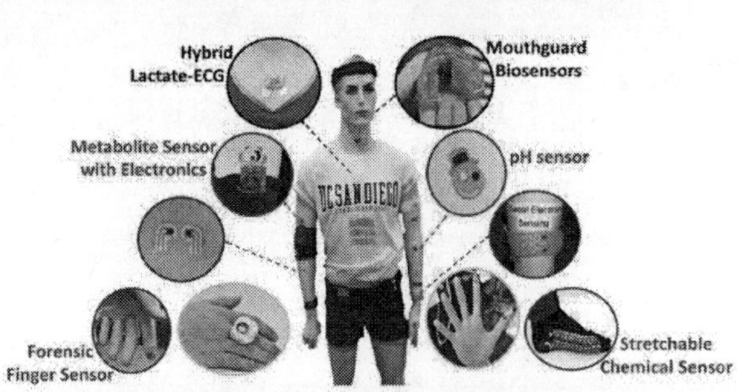

Sensors Converge 2024

NBE-Team: Printed Flexible Electrochemical Devices

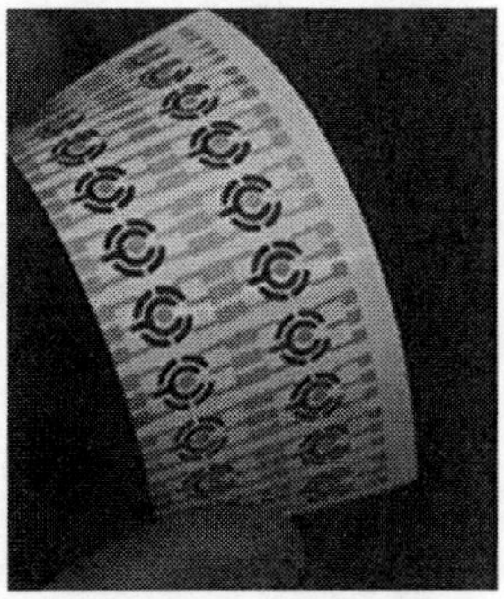

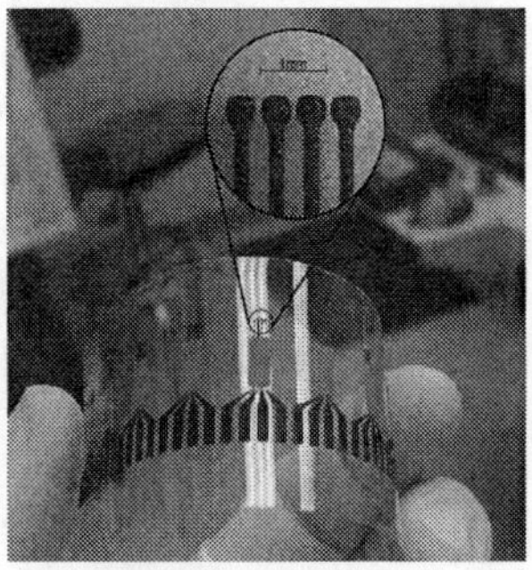

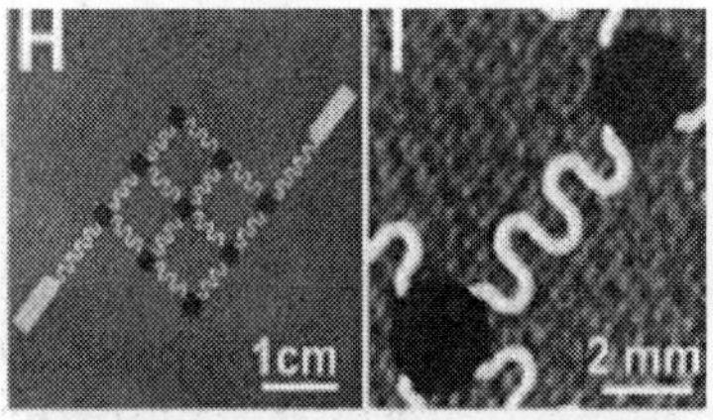

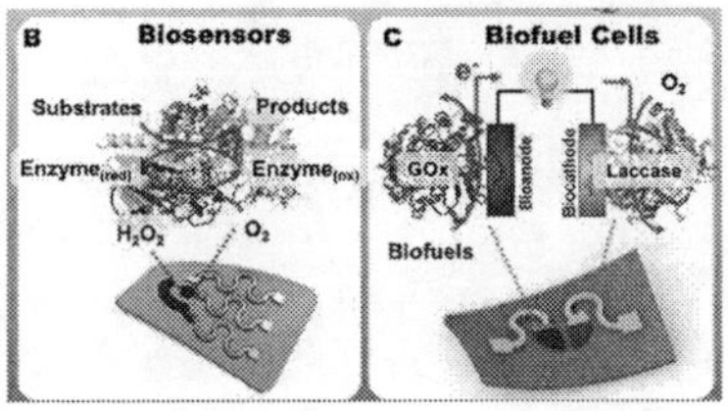

Coupling stretchable structures with stretchable materials:

1) Due to unwinding of free-standing serpentine or island-bridge **structures** (1st degree stretchability)

2) due to intrinsic stretchability of printable inks based on **ink formulation** (2nd degree stretchability).

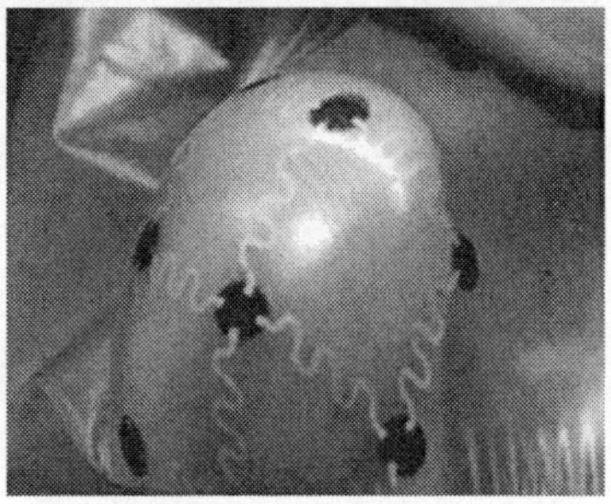

All Printed Highly Stretchable EC Devices printed device: Enduring extreme stress

Stretch-enduring inks with serpentine-patterned electrodes

Adv. Mater., 2015

IMAGINE

Imagine a future with a small skin-worn patches, capable of **performing multiple chemical and physical diagnostic tests** continuously and non-invasively (towards creating a 'lab-on-patch'), obviating the need for periodic lab testing, blood draws, and associated costs and delays.

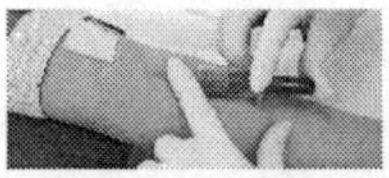

Lab-on-the-Skin
→

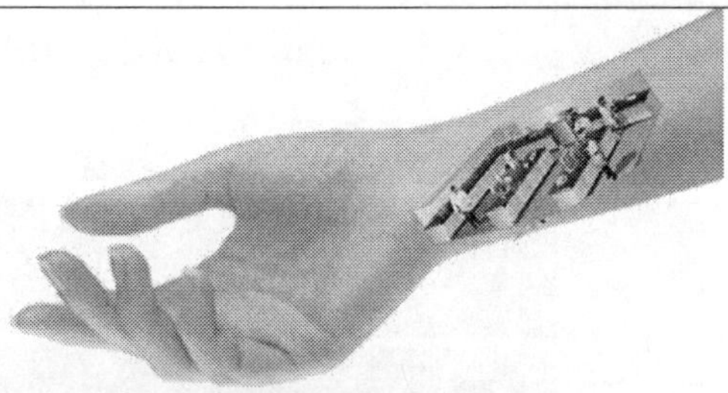

Future **Labs-on-the-Skin** would offer in real-time **summary of your health status** and **predict personalized disorders** and **abnormalities:**

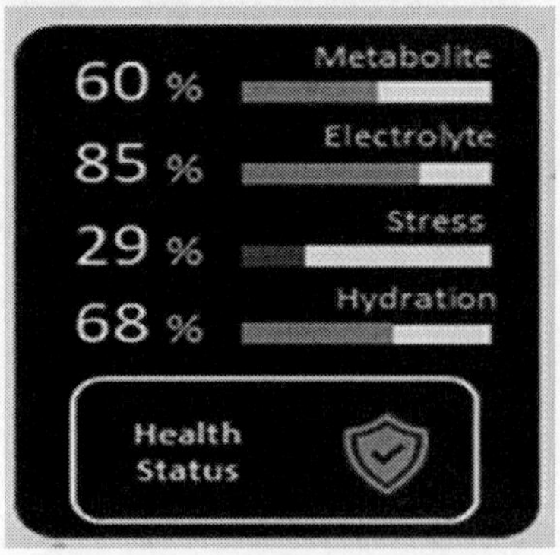

Summary of the **health status**

'Check Engine Light'.

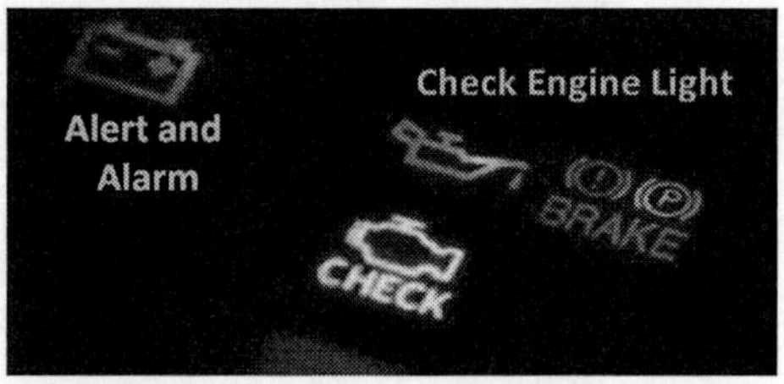

Early detection of health abnormalities

WEARABLE SENSORS

A comprehensive assessment of the wearer's **health** requires continuous information on dynamically-changing **chemical and physical** parameters.

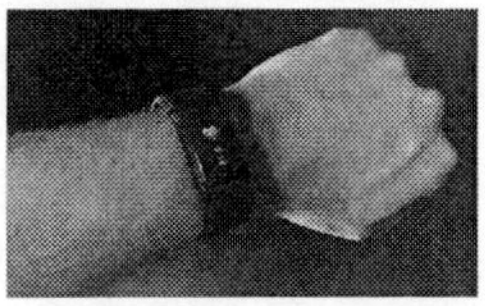

Early efforts (2 decades ago) focused on wearable physical sensors for tracking mobility or vital signs.

Beyond Vital and Mobility Signs

Molecular Information in Real Time

(UCSD 2009)

Bridging the gap between digital and biochemical analysis

Capture dynamic molecular data from the human body

Towards Personalized Healthcare

Center for Wearable Sensors UCSD

Wearable sensing opportunities

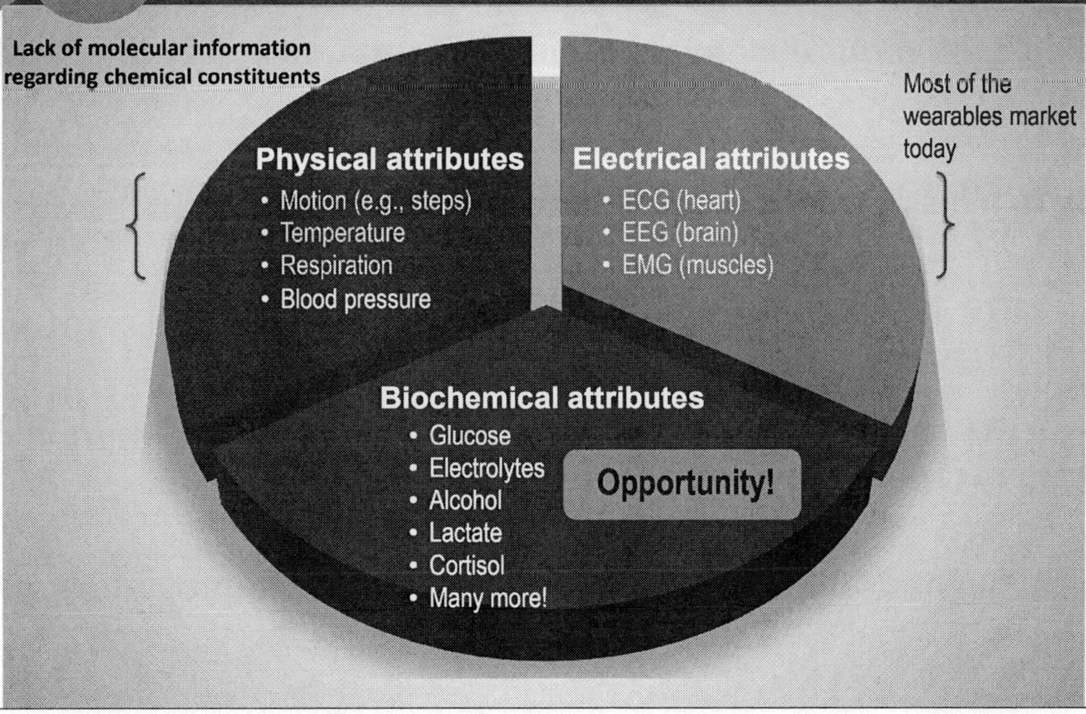

Center for Wearable Sensors | UCSD

Wearable sensing opportunities

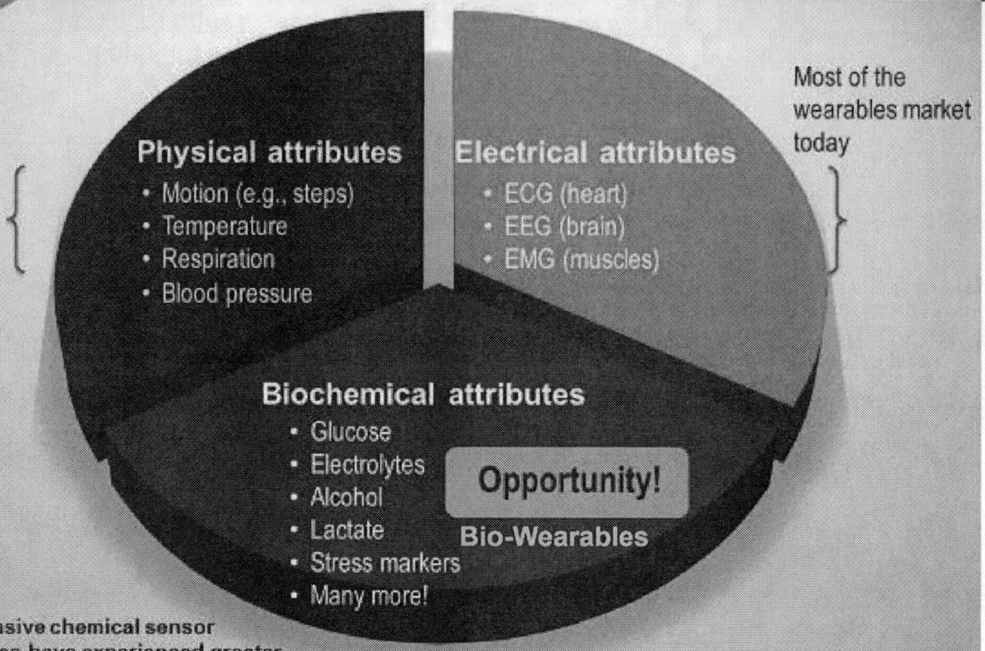

Non-invasive chemical sensor modalities have experienced greater challenges in commercial adoption that electrical/physical ones.

9

Wearable Chemical Sensors - Advantages

Center for Wearable Sensors

- **Providing continuous dynamic chemical information at any time and location.**
- **Gaining rich insights into temporal molecular trends**
- **Non-invasive assays without blood sampling**
- **Changing the way health is assessed and accesses towards improved compliance, care and equity.**
- **Distance diagnosis with lower healthcare costs and improved people life.**

UC San Diego
NanoEngineering
JACOBS SCHOOL OF ENGINEER

Wearable **Chemical** Sensing Devices - **Challenges:**

Center for Wearable Sensors

- Stability (biofouling, uncontrolled changing conditions)
- Accuracy requires large-scale validation (vs. blood gold standards)
- Safety (in mouth, on eyes, under skin)
- Compliance with the body movement and curvature
- Meeting the Energy demands
- Big data and data security
- Missing diagnostics info (on vital signs): Falling short of capturing the full spectrum of symptoms.

UC San Diego
NanoEngineering
JACOBS SCHOOL OF ENGINEERING

NBE
UC SAN DIEGO
NANO BIOELECTRONICS LAB

WEARABLE ELECTROCHEMICAL SENSING DEVICES

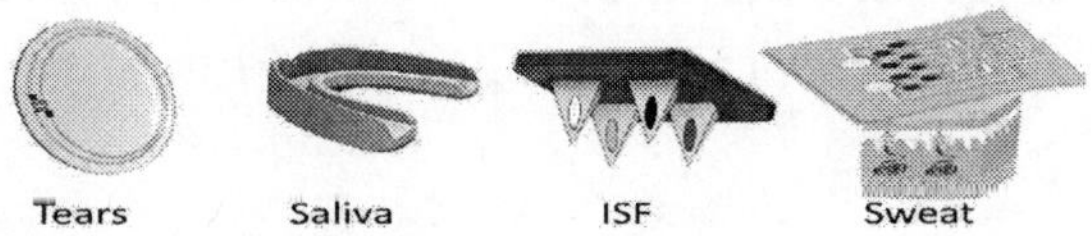

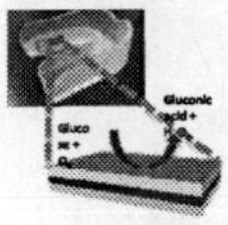

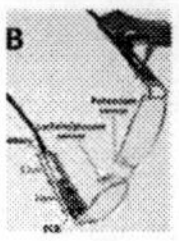

Non-Invasive analysis of:

1. **Sweat**
2. **Saliva**
3. **Tears**
4. **ISF**
5. **Surrounding Environment**

Monitoring of Molecular Biomarkers

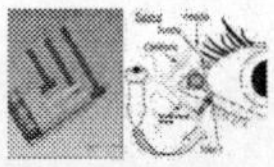

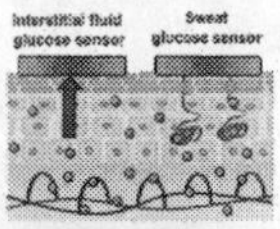

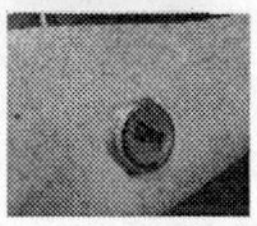

UC SAN DIEGO
NANO BIOELECTRONICS LAB

Center for Wearable Sensors

Wide Scope of Wearable Electrochemical Sensors
Molecular-level Health Monitoring

Real-Time Continuous Non-Invasive Monitoring of:

1. Metabolites
2. Electrolytes
3. Drugs (e.g., L-Dopa, Opioids)
4. Hormones
5. Stress markers
6. Disease markers
7. Vitamins
8. Cytokines
9. Neurotransmitters
10. Substances of Abuse
11. Chemical threats
12. Trace metals

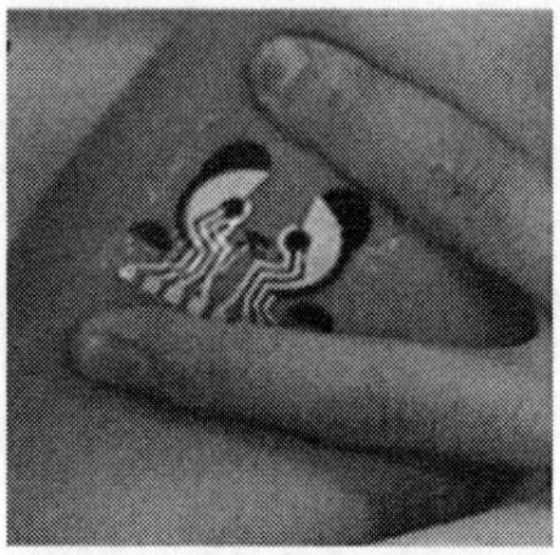

Assessing health, performance, safety and the environment anytime

Simultaneous Monitoring of both Sweat and ISF using a Single Wearable Biosensor Platform

For example, this Panda-like tattoo allows sampling and monitoring of the two epidermal biofluids at the same time (by combining iontophoretic sweat stimulation and ISF extraction).

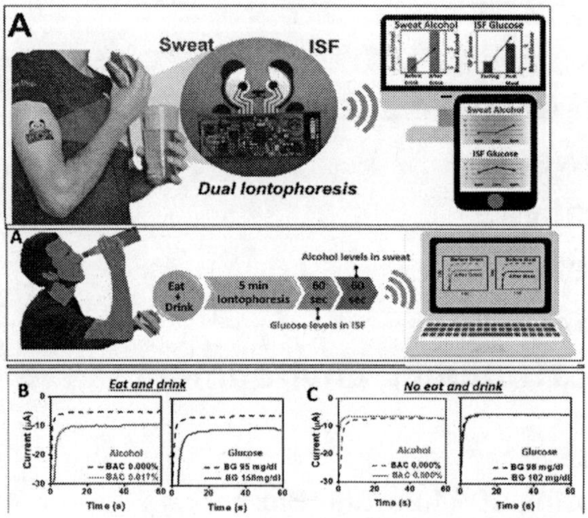

GlucoHol- Sweat Alcohol and ISF Glucose

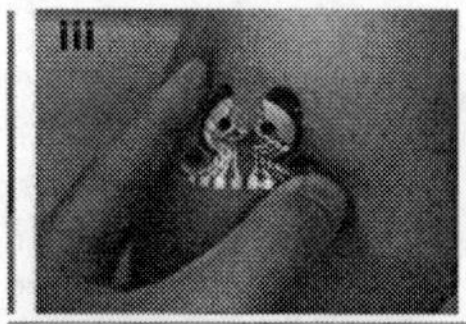

Advanced Science 2018

UC SAN DIEGO
NANO BIOELECTRONICS LAB

Our journey towards capturing dynamic molecular data from the human body (2009-present)

Center for Wearable Sensors

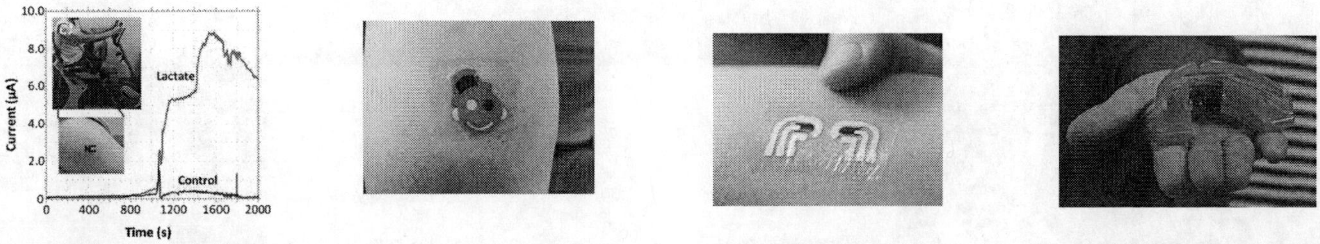

Sweat metabolites (2012) **pH (2011)** **ISF (2012 and 2015)** **Saliva (2014) and Tear (2016)**

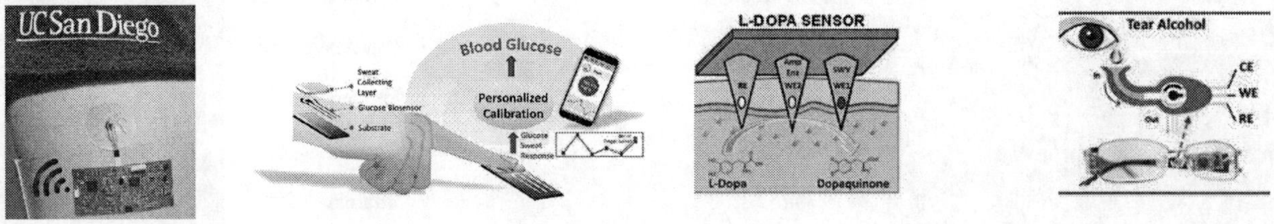

NBE Spinoffs: Persperion, Biolinq, Aquilx

UC SAN DIEGO
NANO BIOELECTRONICS LAB

Our UCSD Wearable Sensors: Whole Body ('head to toe') Sensors

Center for Wearable Sensors

Various form factors, based on different clothing and accessories

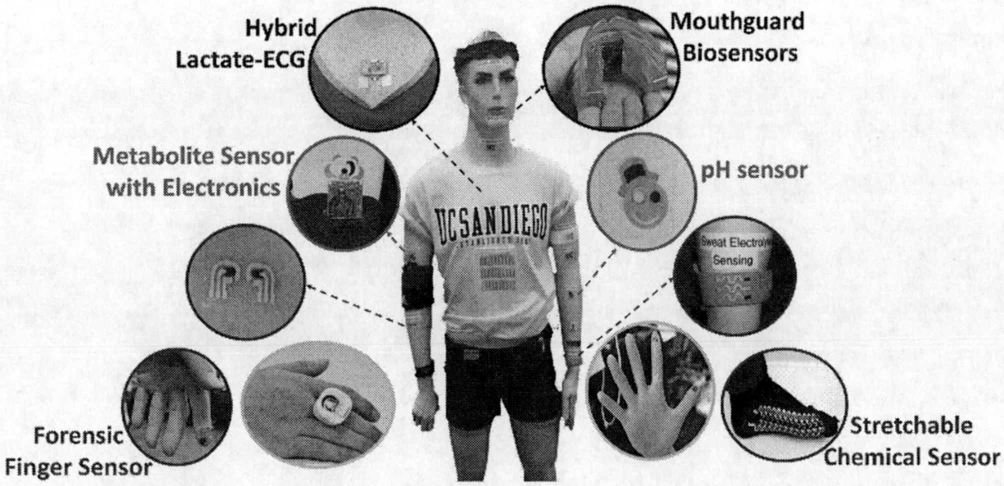

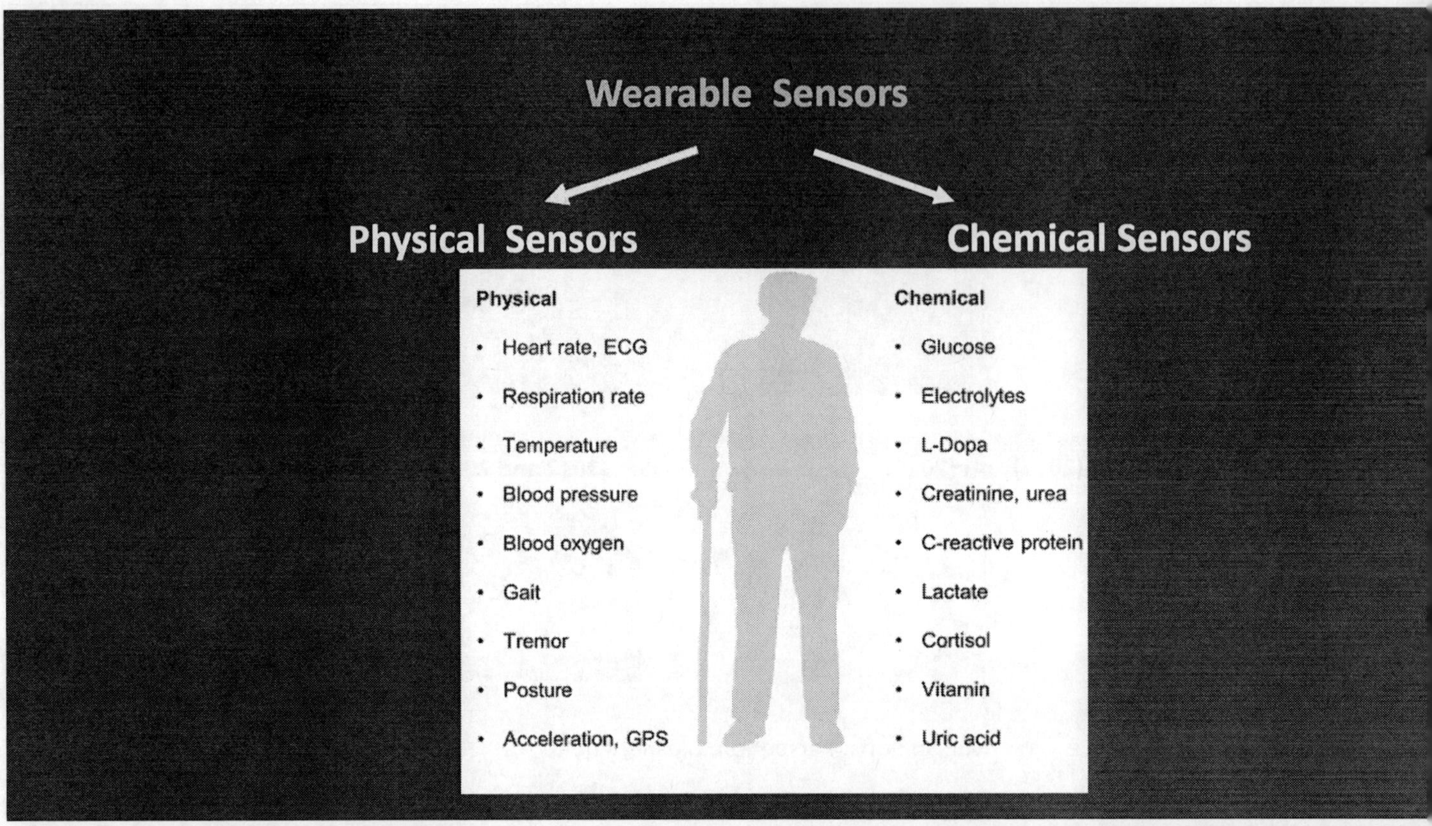
Wearable Sensors
Physical Sensors
Chemical Sensors
Physical
• Heart rate, ECG
• Respiration rate
• Temperature
• Blood pressure
• Blood oxygen
• Gait
• Tremor
• Posture
• Acceleration, GPS
Chemical
• Glucose
• Electrolytes
• L-Dopa
• Creatinine, urea
• C-reactive protein
• Lactate
• Cortisol
• Vitamin
• Uric acid

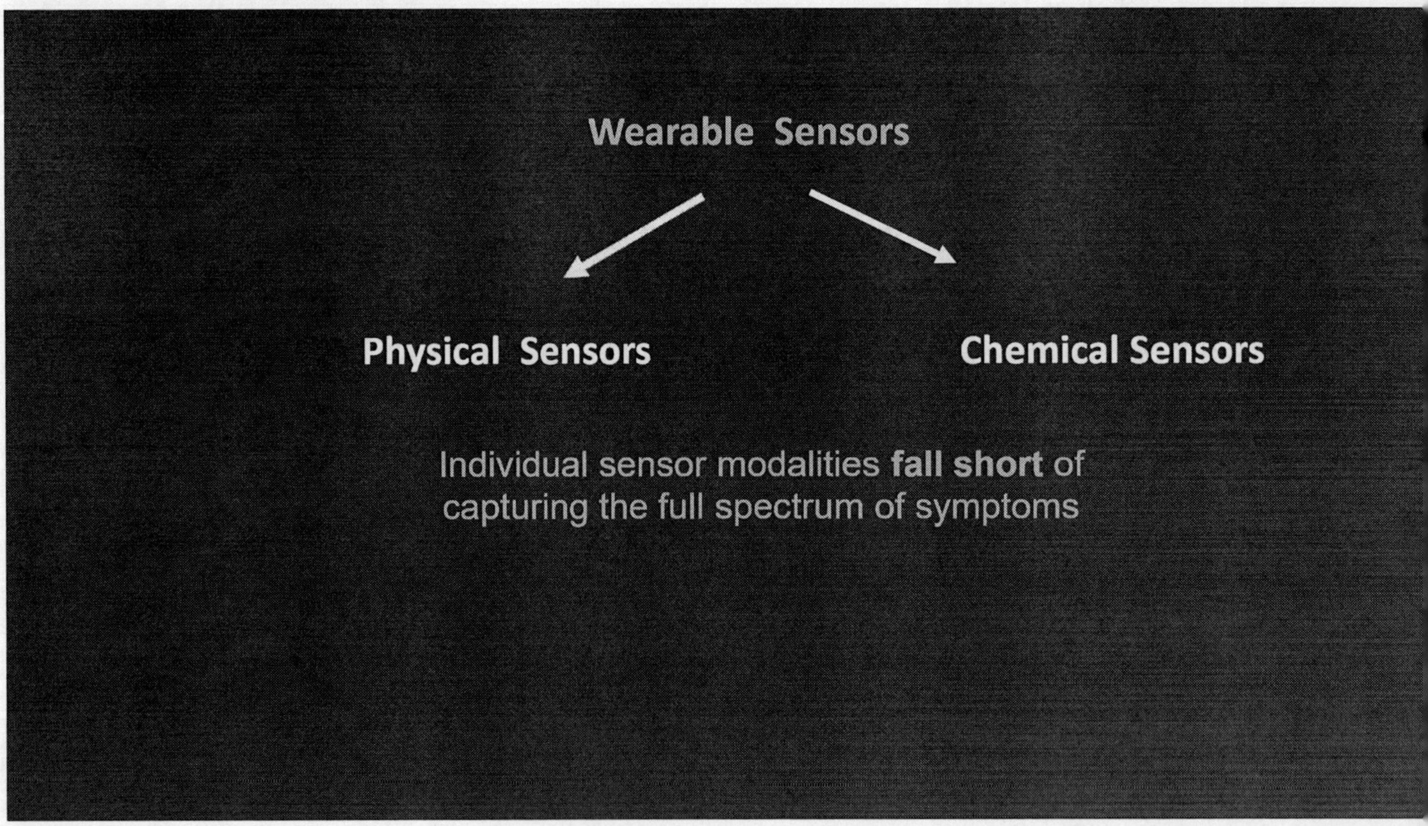
Wearable Sensors
Physical Sensors
Chemical Sensors
Individual sensor modalities **fall short** of capturing the full spectrum of symptoms

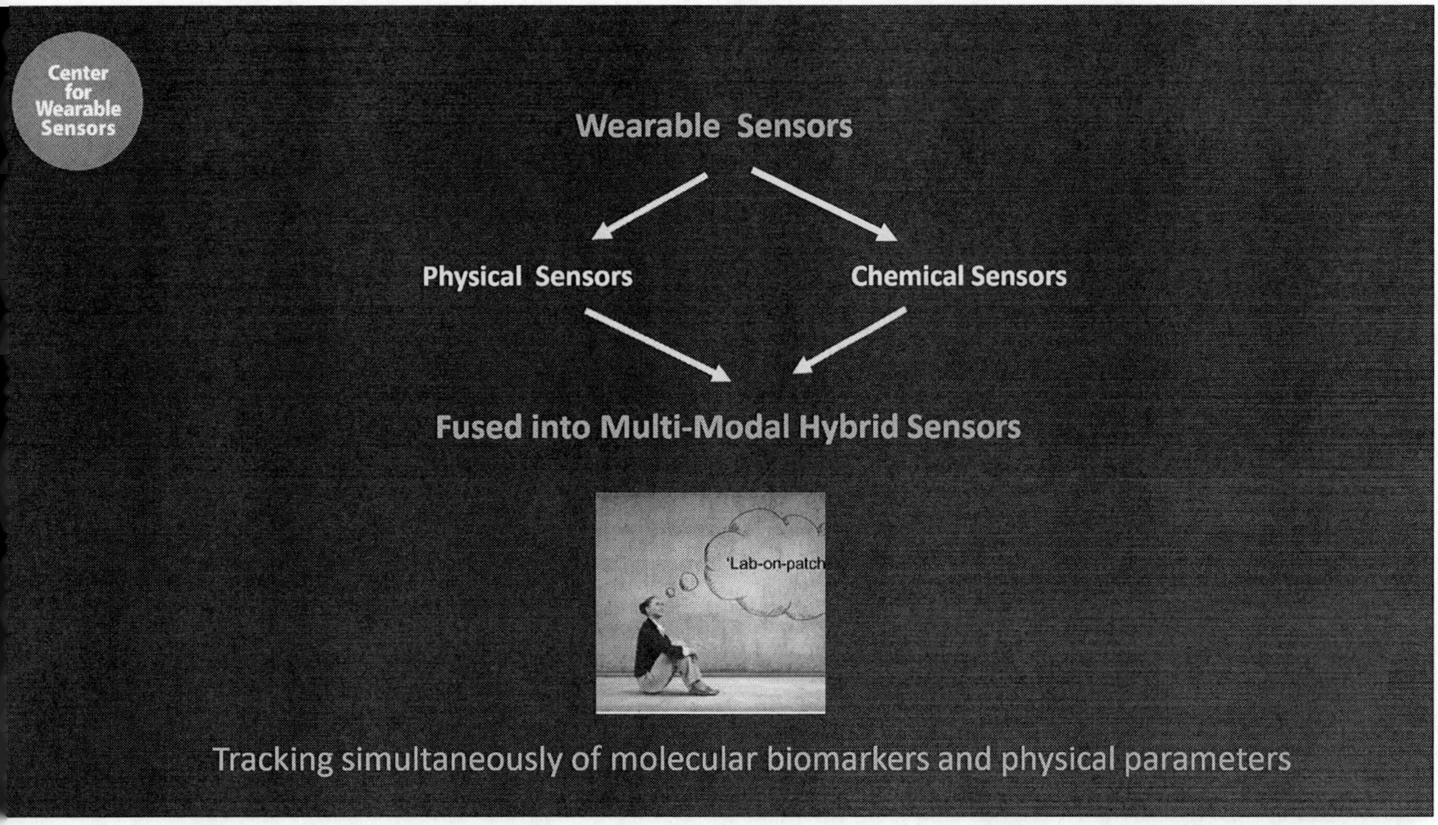
Center for Wearable Sensors
Wearable Sensors
Physical Sensors
Chemical Sensors
Fused into Multi-Modal Hybrid Sensors
'Lab-on-patch
Tracking simultaneously of molecular biomarkers and physical parameters

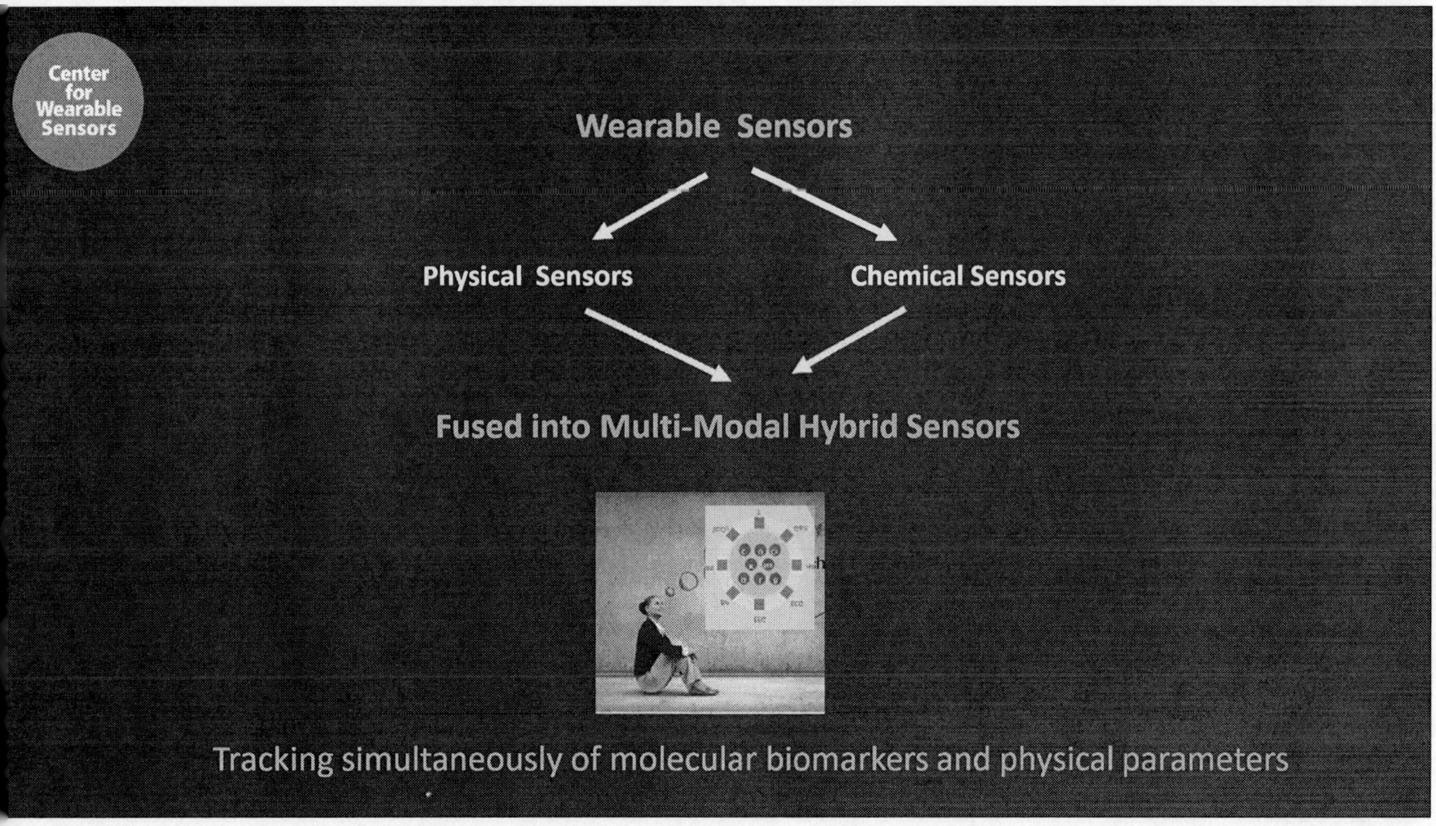
Center for Wearable Sensors
Wearable Sensors
Physical Sensors
Chemical Sensors
Fused into Multi-Modal Hybrid Sensors
Tracking simultaneously of molecular biomarkers and physical parameters

Wearable Sensors

Physical Sensors | **Chemical Sensors**

Fused into Multi-Modal Hybrid Sensors

Provide comprehensive understanding of a wearer's health status

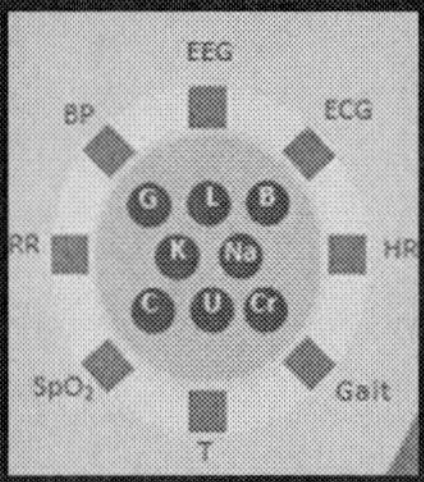

Tracking simultaneously of molecular biomarkers and physical parameters

Towards **simultaneous** recording of multiple vitals and biochemical temporal profiles

The combination of multiple **biochemical and biophysical sensors** on a single device will dramatically **increase personalized health information** and will improve the understanding of the human response to diverse activities.

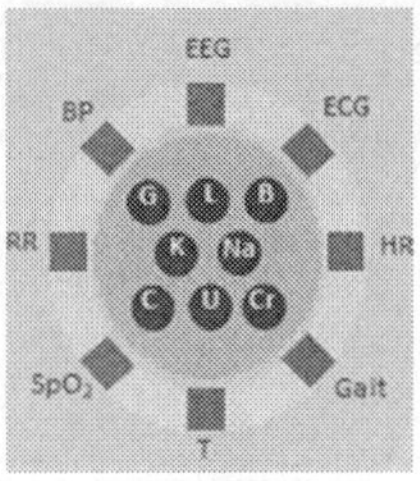

a Vitals

- ECG
- Heart rate
- Blood pressure
- SP_{O2}
- Respiration rate
- EEG
- Basal body temperature
- Galvanic skin response
- Gait
- Tremor

b Biochemicals

- Metabolites
- Electrolytes
- Drugs
- Vitamins
- pH
- Hormones
- Stress markers
- Inflammatory markers
- Host response biomarkers

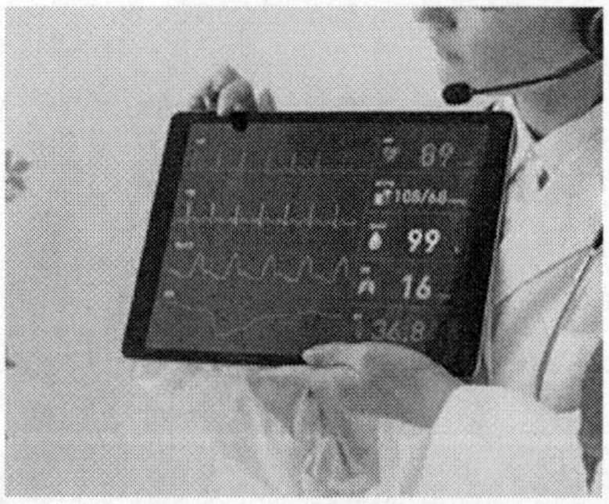

Delivering rich and timely information on the user's health status.

Hybrid Multi-Modal Sensing Systems

Simultaneous **chemical-physical measurements** offer a deeper understanding of the clinical conditions (vs physical or chemical sensing alone).

Rich multi-source information

Tracking of **biochemical and physical** parameters using the **same** device can increase the self-monitoring compliance of a patient, as it simplifies the complexity of using multiple devices for measuring these parameters.

Delivering rich and timely information on the user's health status.

Potential Applications (and related sensor pairing)

The **pairing of the specific chemical and physical sensors** into a **single wearable patch**, and hence the rational **selection of the specific sensing modules**, would **rely on the specific user case** and the corresponding **diagnostic requirements** (and settings).

- Multi-modal hybrid wearable bioelectronic modules will empower the simultaneous health tracking in users, **ranging from neonates to the elderly**, under **various settings** including:

- **Neonate** care settings
- Elderly care settings
- Ambulatory settings
- Intensive care settings
- Coexistence of **hypertension** and **diabetes**
- Rehabilitation care settings
- Dopa and gait in **Parkinson**

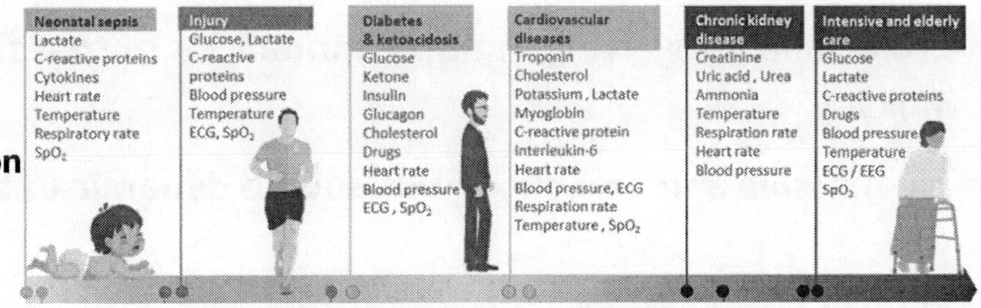

Different Target Groups and Sensing Needs

Early diagnoses for various settings

Wearable Chemical-Electrophysiological **Multi-Modal Sensing System**

Fusing the monitoring of electrophysiology and chemical markers into single epidermal non-invasive patch.

All in One:
Monitoring Chemistry and Vitals

Pairing of the specific chemical and physical sensors into a single wearable patch

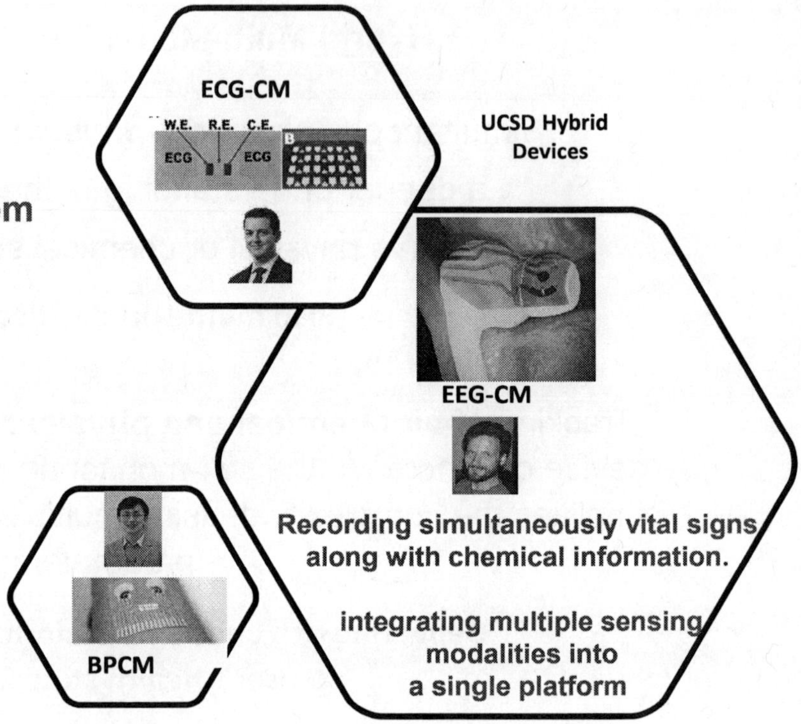

Challenges for Creating Reliable Multi-Modal Wearable Patches

Center for Wearable Sensors

- **Coupling of completely different transduction modalities and corresponding electronics onto small (stamp-size) footprint of an epidermal patch**
- **Maintaining the high clinical accuracy of the individual modalities**
- **Cross-talk: Integrating multiple modalities onto a single patch without Cross Talks**
- **Big massive and complex multi-source dynamic data**
- **Challenges in power management** (energy demands) **and hardware design**

UC San Diego
NanoEngineering
JACOBS SCHOOL OF ENGINEER

Wearable Hybrid Sensing Systems

Multi-modal wearable systems fusing seamlessly **different** chemical and physical **sensing modalities** on a **single** epidermal device.

Real-time multi-parameter electrophysiological and chemical health parameters. diagnostic information:

1. ECG/Chemical Sensing (*Nature Comm.* 2016)
2. Blood-Pressure/Chemical Sensing (*Nature Biomed. Eng.* 2021)
3. EEG/Chemical Sensing(*Nature Biomed. Eng.* 2023)

Capturing previously unavailable information in point-of-care conditions
Simultaneous recording of multiple vitals and biochemical temporal profiles

Center for Wearable Sensors

A Wearable **Chemical-Electrophysiological Hybrid Biosensing System** for Real-Time Health and Fitness Monitoring

Hybrid system **fusing** for the first time the monitoring of **electrophysiology with chemical sensing** into single fully patch.

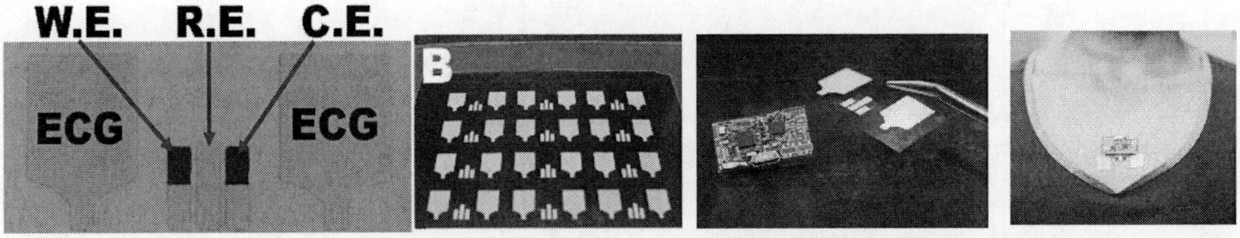

Images of the Chem-Phys printing stencil and of the array of printed Chem-Phys flexible patches.

Wearable Chemical-Electrophysiological Hybrid Biosensing **System**

Nature Comm., 2016

A Wearable **Chemical-Electrophysiological Hybrid Biosensing System**

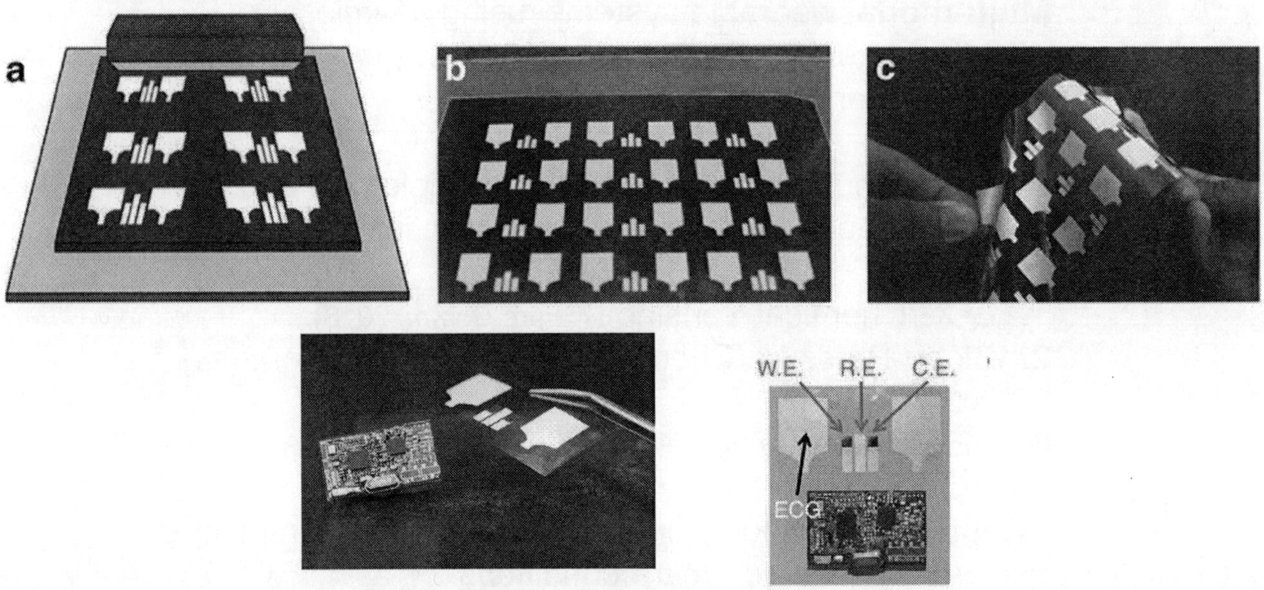

Hybrid system fusing the monitoring of electrophysiology with on-body chemical sensing into single fully patch.

Nature Comm 2016

Monitoring Chemistry and Vitals!

Hybrid system fusing the monitoring of electrophysiology with on-body chemical sensing into single fully patch.

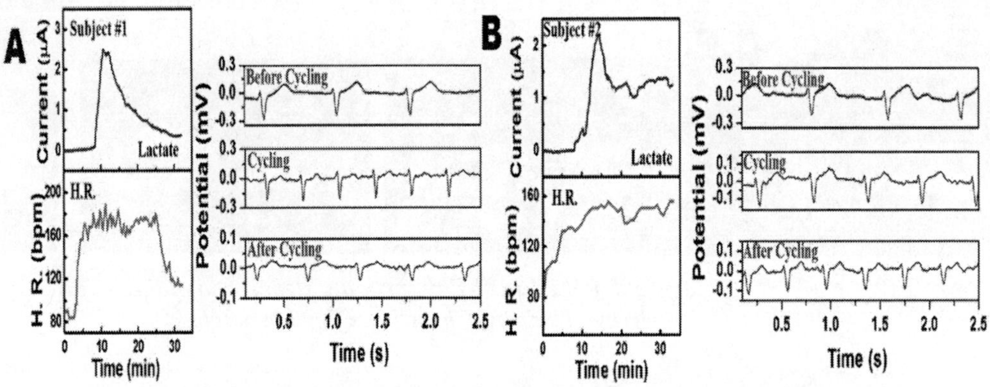

Dynamic changes in sweat-lactate levels and electrocardiogram signals were measured continuously during a bout of intense cycling.

Real-time on-body evaluation of the ***Chem-Phys hybrid patch*** *showing the lactate levels and Heart Rate for three human subjects.*

Nature Comm 2016

Integrated Blood Pressure-Chemical Sensing (BPCM) patch

Multimodal acoustic blood-pressure and electrochemical wearable biosensor within a single skin-conforming flexible patch.

BPCM

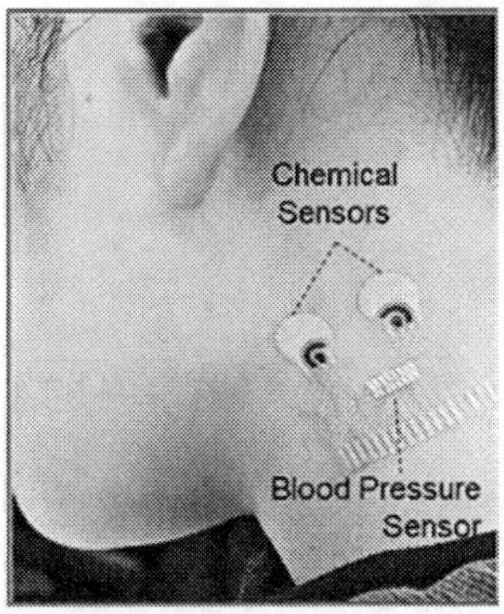

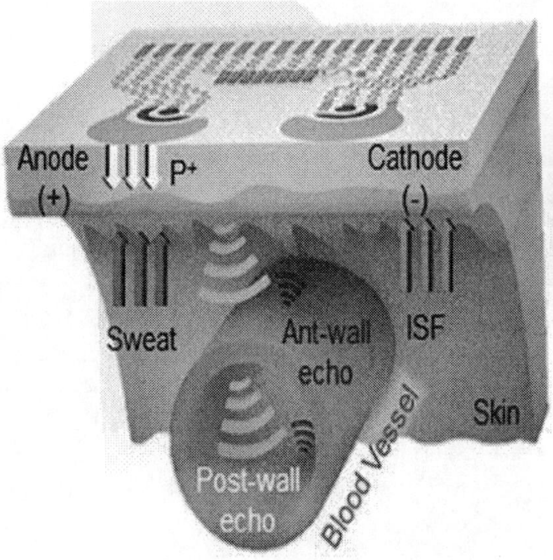

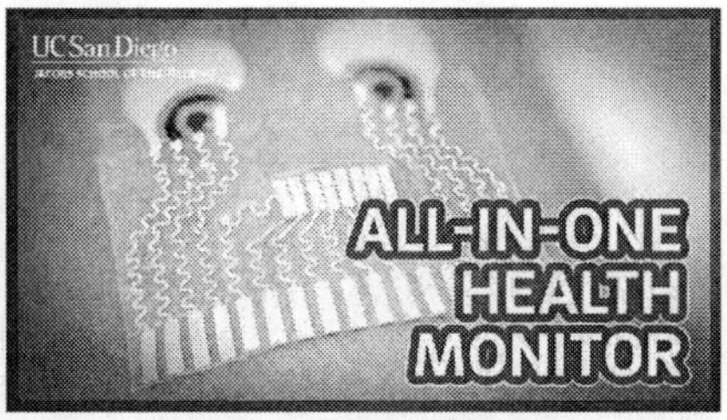

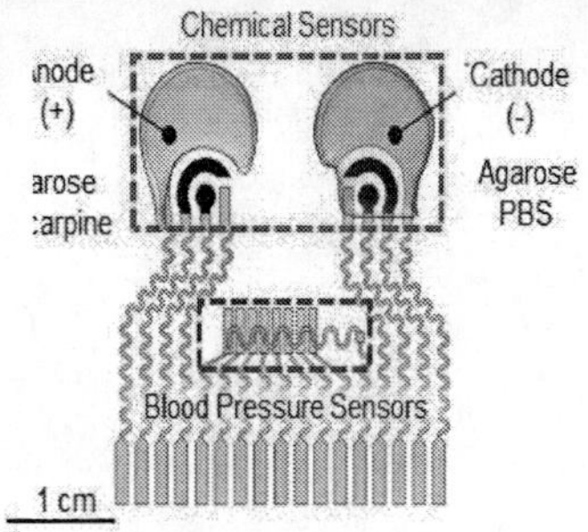

With Prof Sheng Xu

nature biomedical engineering

Soft wearable hybrid sensor patch with simultaneous BP and chemical sensing capability

Nature Biomedical Eng., 2021

Blood Pressure - Chemical Monitoring (BPCM)

Recording simultaneously BP along with chemical information.

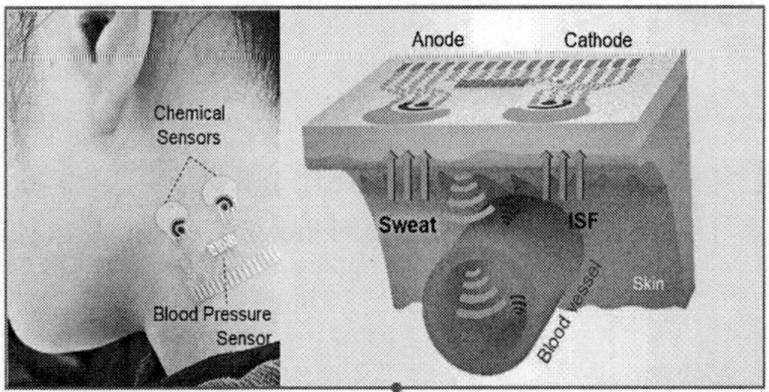

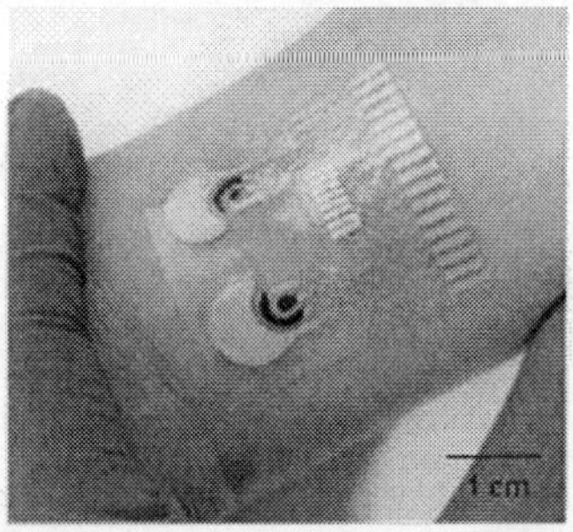

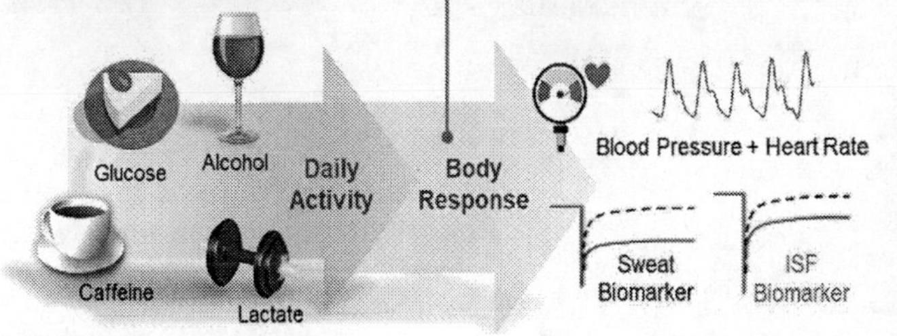

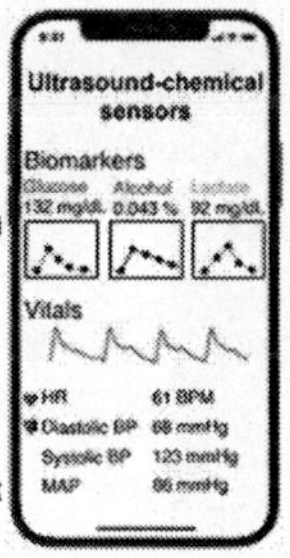

First example of a conformal skin-worn integrated device capable of **simultaneous monitoring of BP, HR, and multiple biomarkers** in ISF and sweat. We use ultrasonic transducers for monitoring the BP and HR, and electrochemical sensors for measuring the levels of sweat and ISF biomarkers.

nature biomedical engineering

All-In-One Health Monitor:
BPCM- Blood-Pressure/Chemical Monitoring

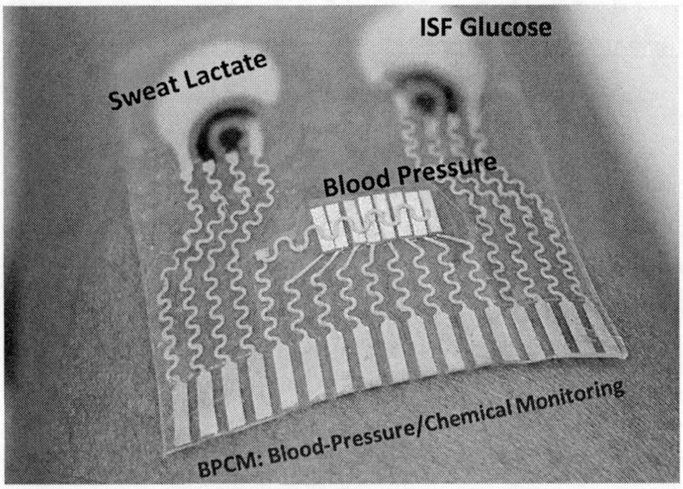

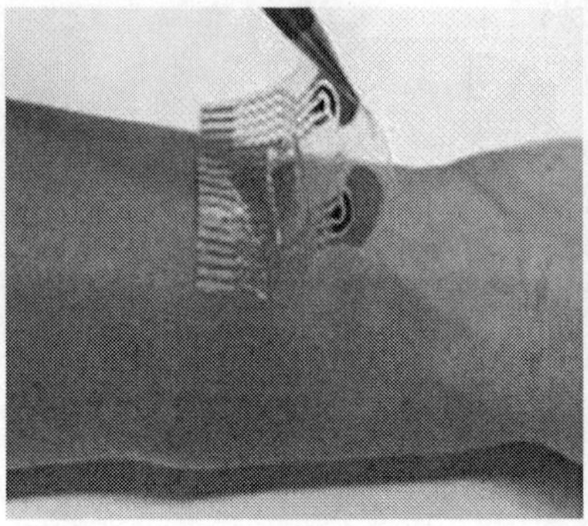

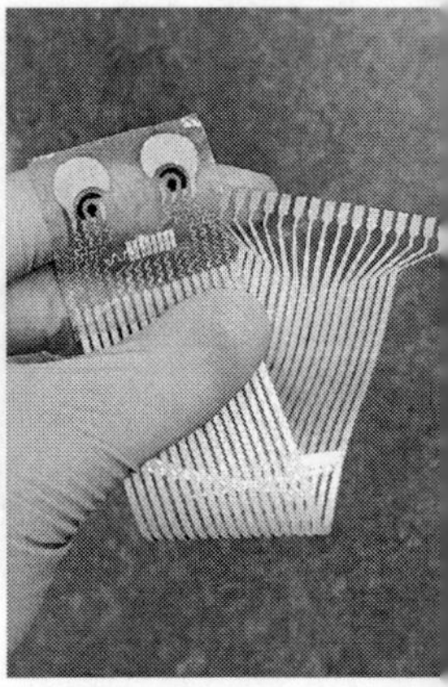

Nature Biomedical Eng., 2021

BPCM- Blood-Pressure/Chemical Monitoring

Leveraging novel **material selection** and **assembly processes** to ensure reliable BP and chemical sensing **without crosstalk**, along with **mechanical resiliency** and flexibility for conformal epidermal operation.

Crosstalk between the two sensing modalities.

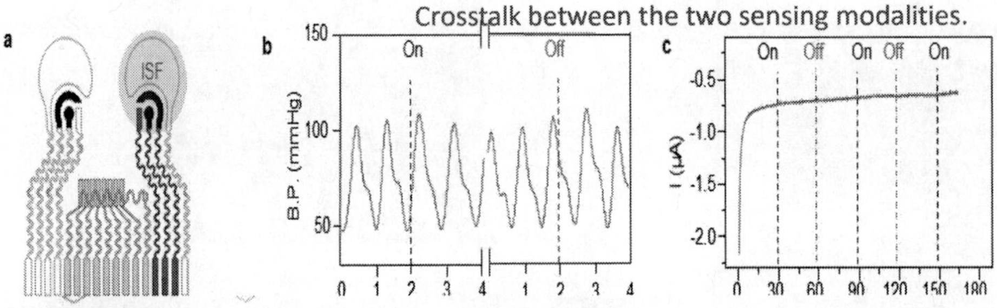

Signal interference **crosstalk** studies between the ISF electrochemical and the BP sensors

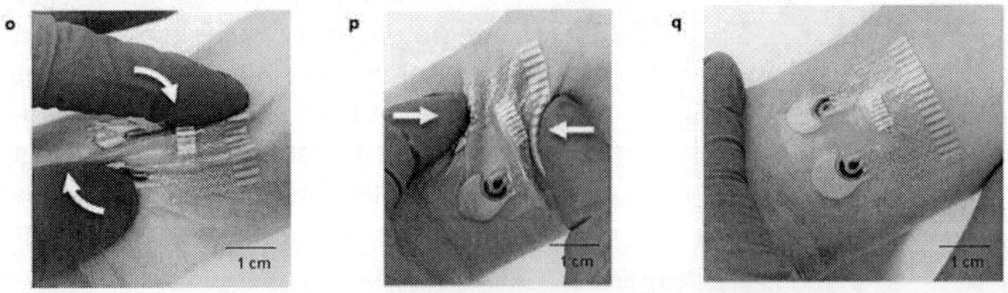

Skin conformability, and **mechanical integrity** of the device while twisting (**o**), bending (**p**), and after these deformations (**q**).

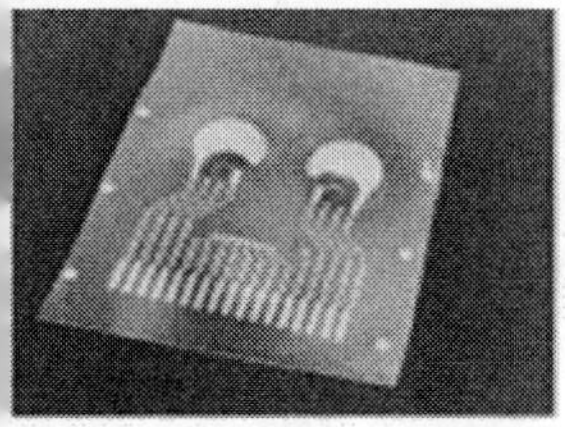

Continuous BP and Biomarker Monitoring

Exposure to multiple stimuli while monitoring cardiovascular parameters along with multiple biomarker levels

As expected, higher HR, BP, and sweat lactate levels during exercise

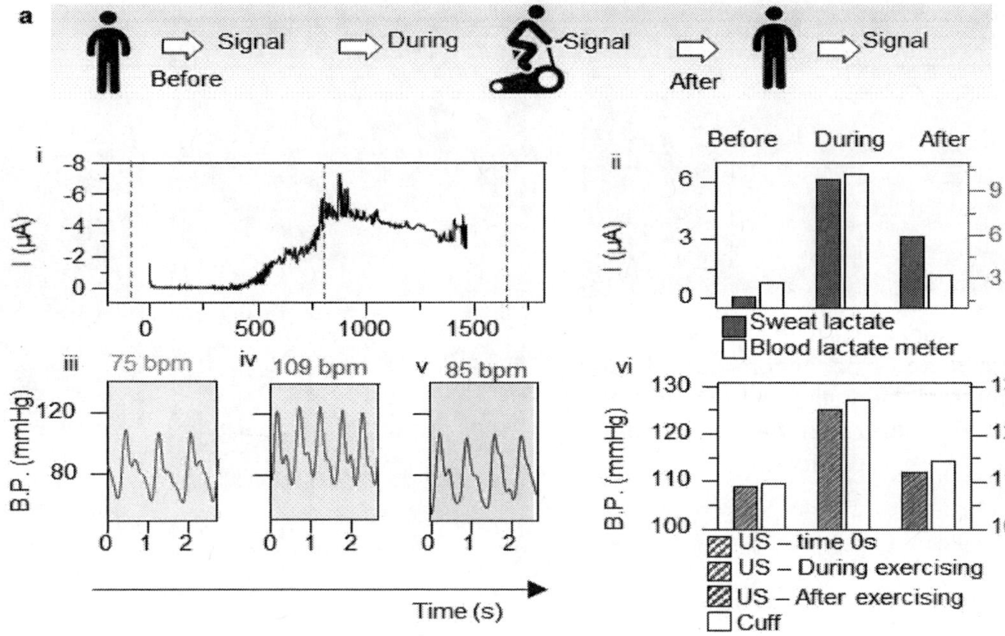

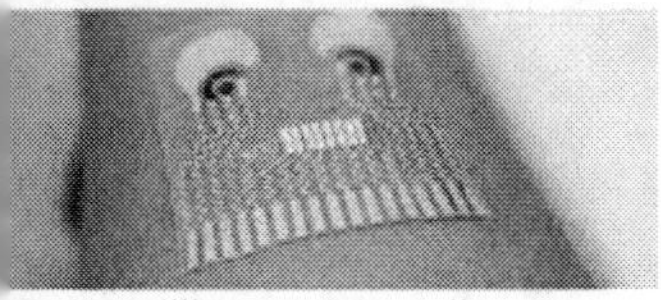

Nature Biomedical Eng., 2021

nature
biomedical engineering

Simultaneous monitoring of Brain states and the Tracking of Metabolites

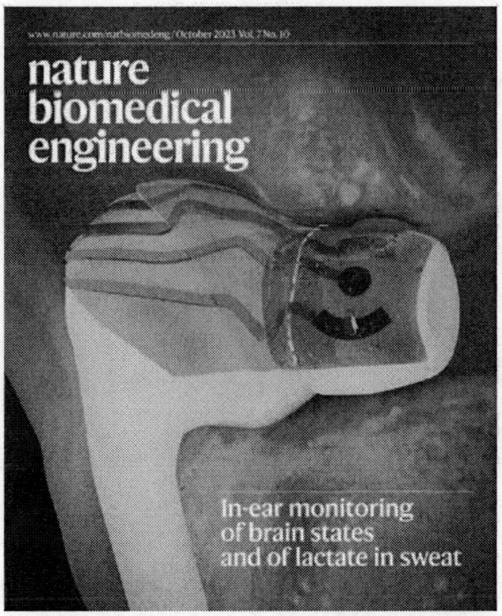

The cover illustrating the integration, on an earbud, of sensors for **brain activity** (via electroencephalography, electrooculography and electrodermal activity) and of **lactate levels** (electrochemically, in sweat).

In-ear integrated arrays of sensors

An integrated array of sensors, seamlessly incorporated into an earphone, for the simultaneous monitoring of electrophysiological and electrochemical signals.

First simultaneous recording of brain and biochemical signals in a single platform.

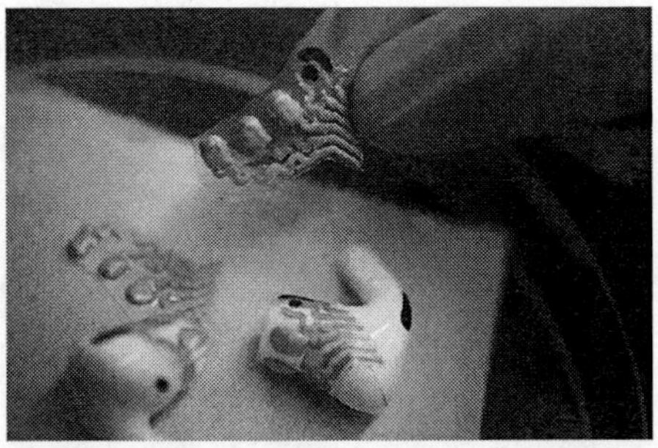

Integrated in-ear electrophysiological (ePhys) and electrochemical (eChem) system: Implementation of **both modalities** into a miniaturized non-invasive **in-ear platform.**

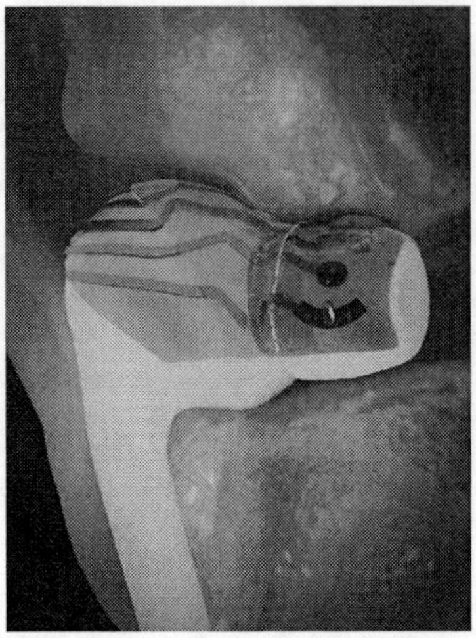

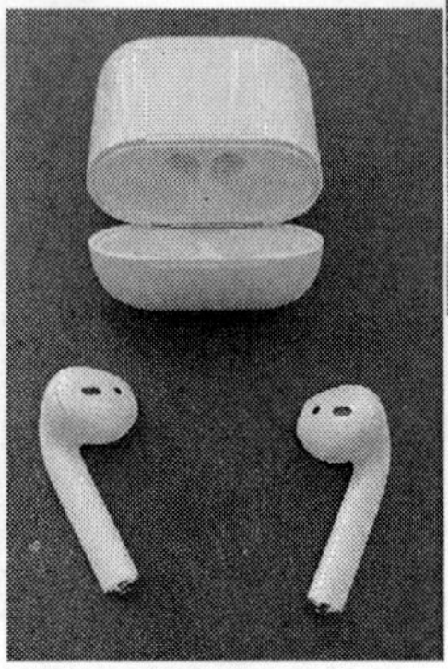

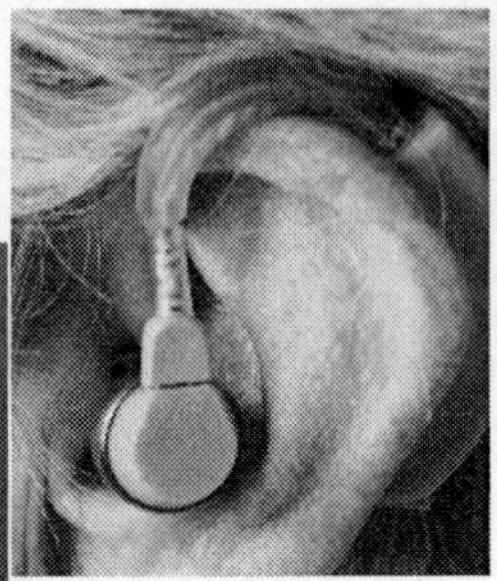

Earbuds: From listening pleasure to hearing aids for elderly people.

Nature Biomedical Engineering 2023

In-ear integrated sensor array for the continuous monitoring of brain activity and of lactate in sweat

Tracking continuously brain activity and exercise level

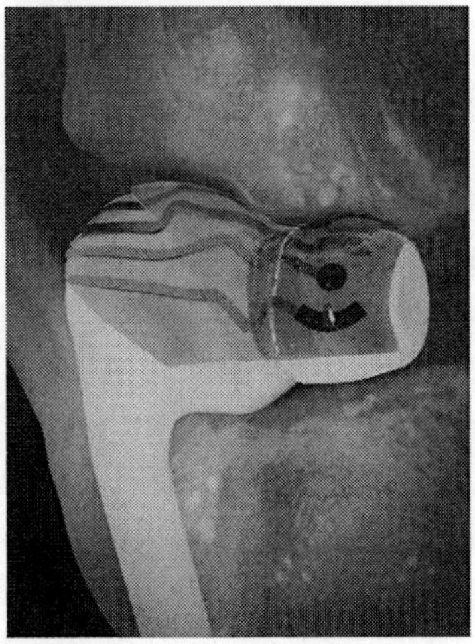

Multimodal in-ear electrophysiological and electrochemical sensors monitoring simultaneously the electroencephalogram (EEG), electrooculogram (EOG), electrodermal activity (EDA), and lactate concentration.

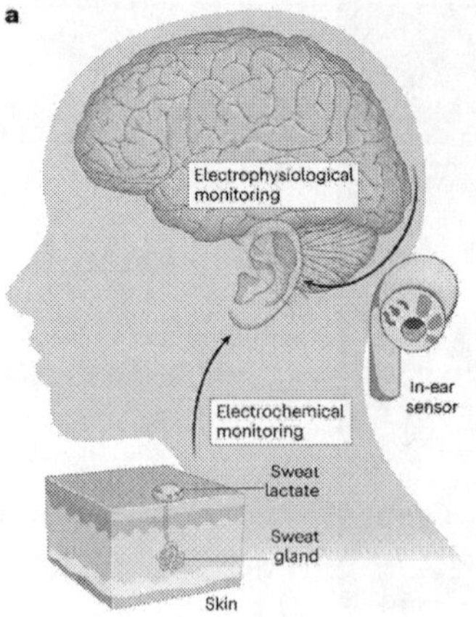

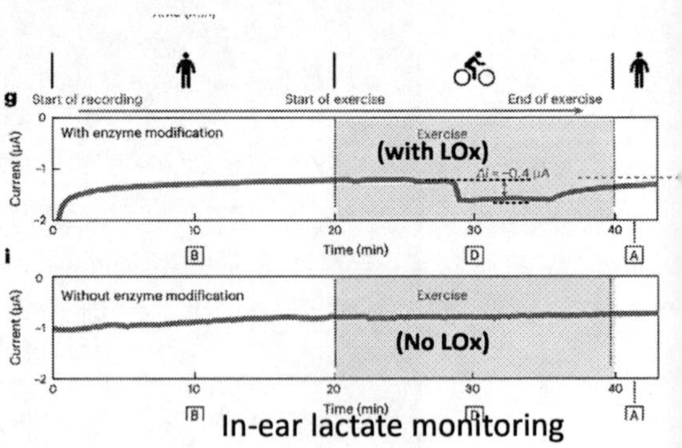

Nature Biomedical Engineering 2023

nature biomedical engineering

Brain and Metabolic signals in the Ear canal

Earbuds to Record Brain Activity and Exercise Levels

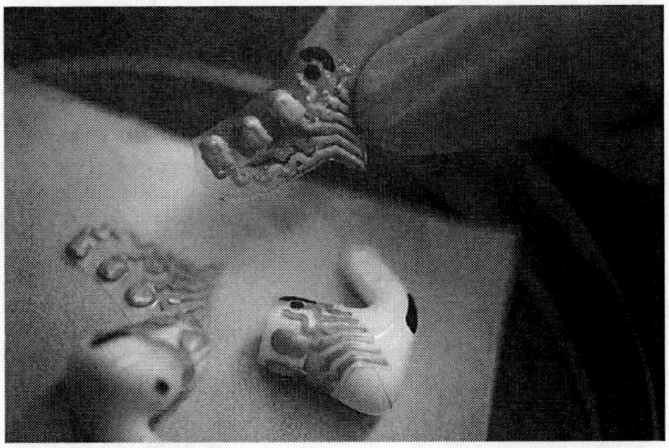

First simultaneous recording of brain electrophysiology and metabolic biomarkers

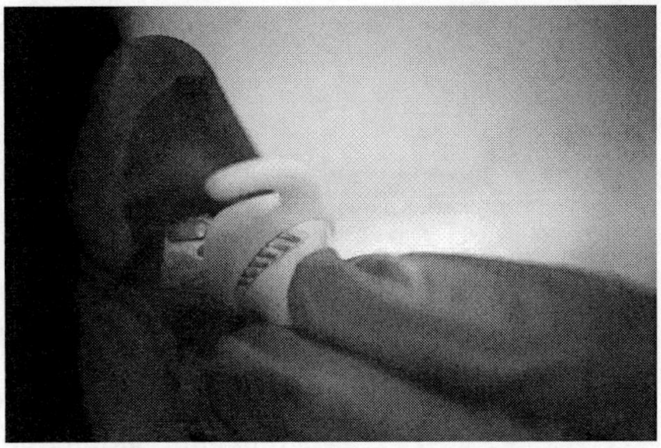

nature biomedical engineering

Earbuds for simultaneous tracking of brain activity and exercise levels

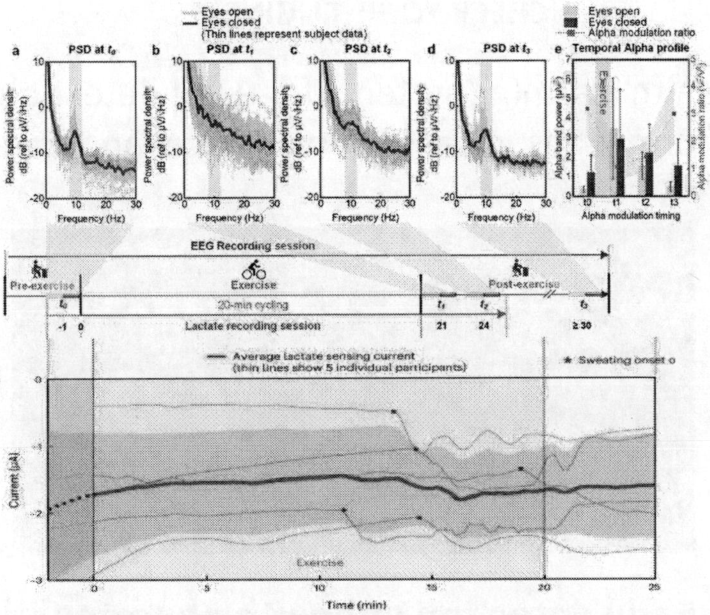

EEG and lactate integrated sensing across five subjections before, during, and after exercise.

nature Biomedical Engineering 2023

nature biomedical engineering

Multi-Sensor Data Fusion and Artificial Intelligence

The massive dynamic and complex multi-source data resulting from hybrid wearable sensor arrays requires strong **data fusing and mining** capabilities.

Integrating such cutting-edge multi-sensory wearable technology with big data processing (**ML-based fusing, mining, clustering, feature extraction**) will allow **prediction of health trends, disorders and outcomes** (and support timely medical interventions)

Extracting health-related features

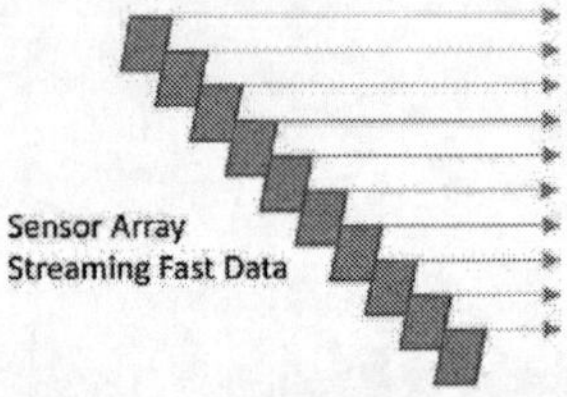

Predicting health trends, disorders and outcomes

Use advanced machine learning (ML) approaches to extract the maximum amount of information from the multi-sensory analytical response.

CHECK YOUR ENGINE

Establishing health alarming systems for early detection and prediction of health abnormalities, disease surveillance, and emergency alerts.

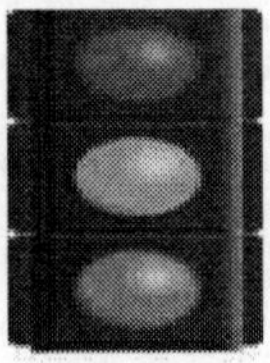

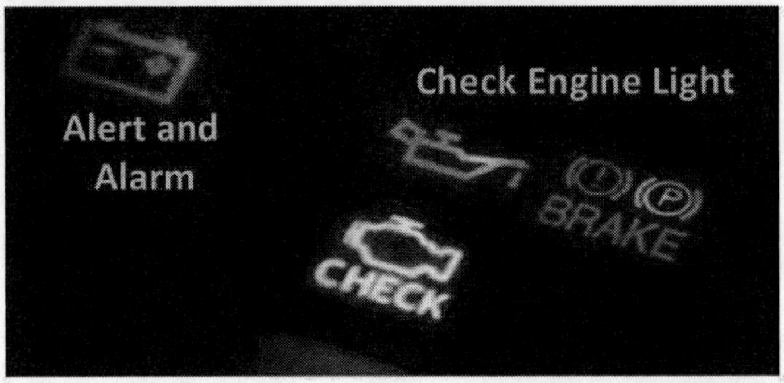

Early detection of health abnormalities

Multi-Modal Wearable Platforms

Expanding to additional physical and chemical sensing parameters
Towards comprehensive assessment of the wearer's overall health

Physical

- Heart rate, ECG
- Respiration rate
- Temperature
- Blood pressure
- Blood oxygen
- Gait
- Tremor
- Posture
- Acceleration, GPS

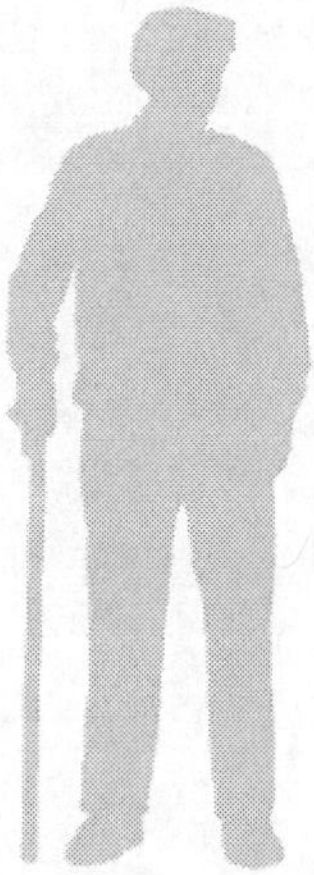

Chemical

- Glucose
- Electrolytes
- L-Dopa
- Creatinine, urea
- C-reactive protein
- Lactate
- Cortisol
- Vitamin
- Uric acid

a Vitals

ECG
Heart rate
Blood pressure
SP_{O2}
Respiration rate
EEG
Basal body temperature
Galvanic skin response
Gait
Tremor

b Biochemicals

Metabolites
Electrolytes
Drugs
Vitamins
pH
Hormones
Stress markers
Inflammatory markers
Host response biomarkers

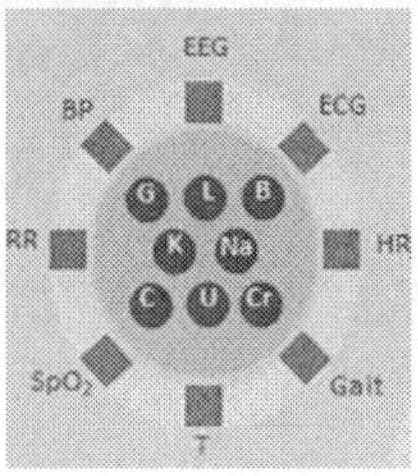

Center for Wearable Sensors

UCSD

Conclusions

Pairing of chemical and physical sensors on a single patch
towards rich multi-source information on the user's health status.

Multi-modal wearable systems offer comprehensive tracking of the wearer's health status (in connection to ML-based **feature extraction** and data classification).

Such continuous simultaneous tracking of molecular biomarkers and physical parameters opens up new opportunities for **personalized medicine, nutrition or wellness.**

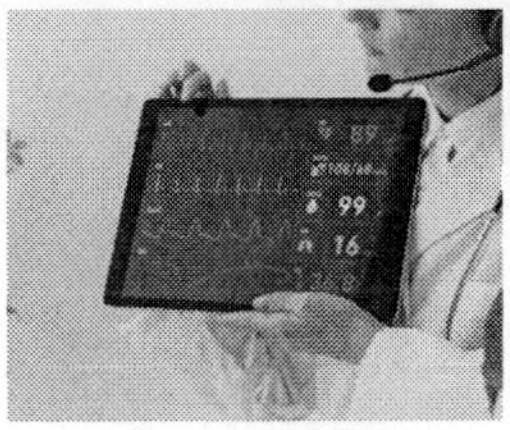

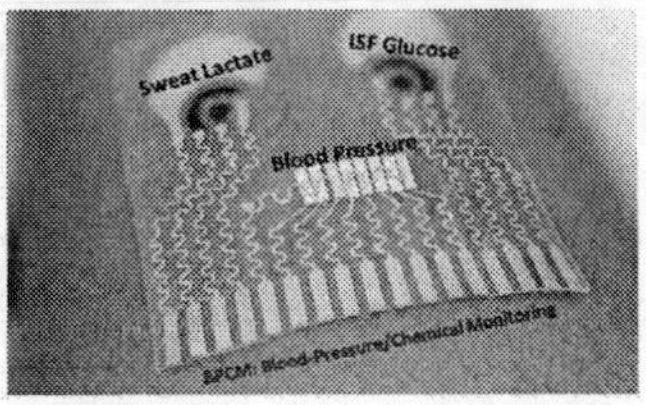

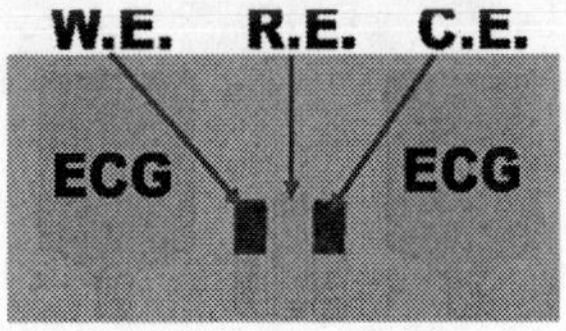

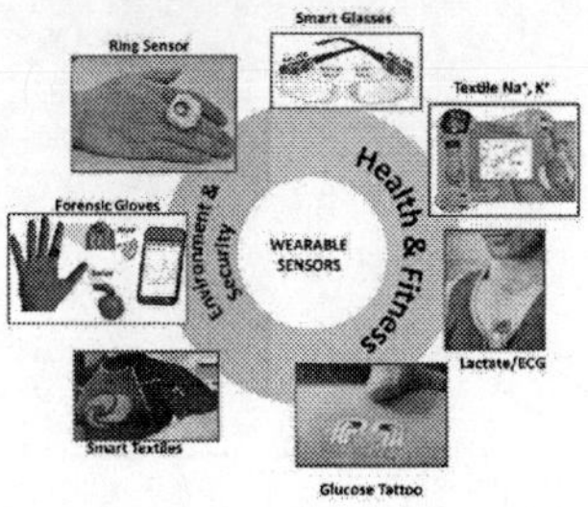

Special THANKS: NBE Team Members

December 2022

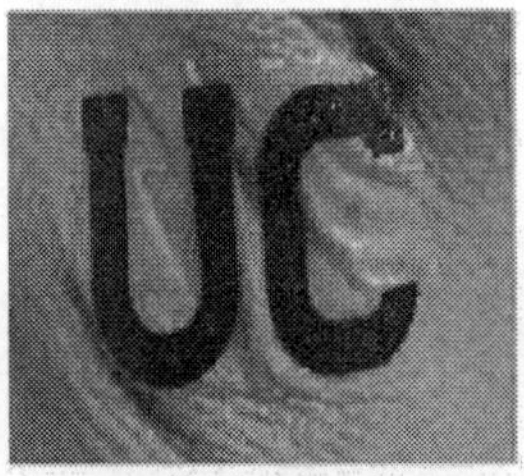

THANK YOU !

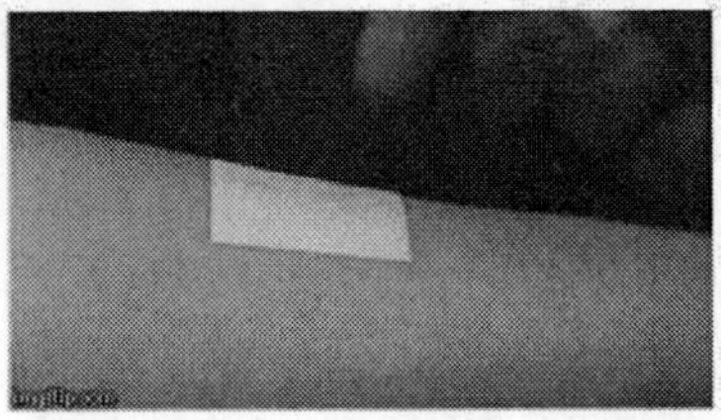

Funding:
NIH
ONR
Army
Nextflex
DOE
Samsung
Hamsley
JDRF
Honda
Nutromics
DSM
Pepsi

Students and Post-Docs:
Amay Bandodkar
Joshua Windmiller
Jayoung Kim
Wei Gao
Jinxing Li
Hazhir Teymourian
Rajan Kumar
Vinu Mohan
Julianne Sempionatto
Rupesh Mishra
Yugender Goud
Lee Hubble
Lu Yin
Farshad Tehrani
Ernesto De La Paz
Samar Sandhu
Tamo Saha
Shichao Ding
Kuldeep Mahato

NBE
UC SAN DIEGO
NANO BIOELECTRONICS LAB

Center for Wearable Sensors

Collaborators: P. Mercier, S. Xu, G. Cauwenberghs

#SensorsConverge

Sensors Converge

Sensors
Converge

Sensorizing With MEMS: the Latest in Products, Design, and Manufacturing

June 24, 2024 | Santa Clara, CA

#SensorsConverge

Live Polling

- Scan the QR code with your phone to join
- Leave the app open
- We'll do some polling throughout the session

#SensorsConverge

Sensors
Converge

Sensors Converge

Today's Agenda

Sensorizing With MEMS: the Latest in Products, Design, and Manufacturing					
Start	**End**	**Description**	**Speaker**	**Job Title**	**Company**
1:00 PM	1:15 PM	Moderator Welcome - SEMI MSIG Overview/Polling	Paul Carey, Ph.D.	Director MSIG	SEMI
1:15 PM	1:30 PM	MEMS market briefing – all eyes on innovation	Pierre Delbos	Technology & Market Analyst, MEMS & Sensing	YOLE
1:30 PM	1:50 PM	Challenges in Modeling and Simulation of MEMS	Jan Mehner	Managing Director	i-ROM
1:50 PM	2:10 PM	MEMS Product Development – Derisking the Transition to Production	Dr. Carolyn White	COO	A.M. Fitzgerald & Associates
2:10 PM	2:30 PM	Addressing High Volume Manufacturing Challenges and Technology Inflections in MEMS	Michelle Bourke	Managing Director | Specialty Technologies and Strategic Marketing	Lam Research
2:30 PM	2:40 PM	Break			
2:40 PM	3:00 PM	X-FAB's Microsystems: from MEMS to advanced packaging	Stijn Sampermans	Business Line Manager MEMS Sensors	X-Fab
3:00 PM	3:20 PM	Environmental Sensing: Making your Home, Building and City Smarter	Ryotaro Sakauchi	Sr. Manager, Business Development	Bosch
3:20 PM	3:40 PM	Latest advances in Piezo MEMS and the route to rapid volume production	Matteo Fusi	Product Marketing Manager - Sensors and Actuators	STMicro
3:40 PM	4:00 PM	MEMS & Sensors packaging innovation to accelerate AI everywhere	Scott Chen	Sr. VP of Engineering	ASE

#SensorsConverge

Sensors Converge

SEMI & MSIG Overview

#SensorsConverge

SEMI OVERVIEW

Your gateway to the ~$2.8T electronics supply chain

(Expected to grow to $4.5T+ by 2030)

SMART MANUFACTURING

SMART DATA-AI

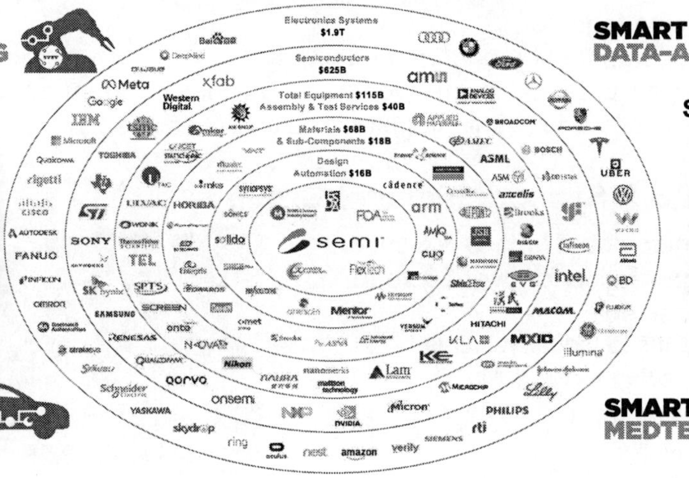

SEMI membership information:

www.semi.org

SMART MOBILITY

SMART MEDTECH

#SensorsConverge

2022 Market Data Estimates Sources: SEMI, IC Insights and TechInsights

Sensors Converge

One Membership → Many Technology Communities:

#SensorsConverge

Sensors Converge

Joining and Participating in Industry Groups is Important

- Build your network
- Fix problems together
- Good exposure for you and your company
- Leads to new personal, professional and business opportunities
- Amplifies your voice (within industry and to Government)

Chose MEMS & Sensors Industry Group !

- The premier global MEMS & Sensors trade organization for over 20 years
- Get Connected!
  - Start-ups to Industry Giants
  - Raw Materials to OEMs

#SensorsConverge

Sensors Converge

MSIG Goal | Help Member Companies Sensorize the World

Mission

– **Support member company growth with:**
1. **Education and Networking**
2. **Promotional opportunities**
3. **Collaborative problems solving**
4. **R&D Funding**
5. **New opportunities and markets**

Example vertical markets served

IoT | Automotive | Industrial Automation | Medical / Environmental

Visit our web site www.MSIG.org

#SensorsConverge 7/10/24

Sensors Converge

MSIG Has R&D Funding!

Funding Focus: Positioning, Navigation, and Timing (PNT)

Phase I (2020-2022): 10 Projects

- $6.1M ($15.2M with Cost Share) **[DONE]**

Phase II (2022-2027) [ON GOING]

- 5 years @$5M/year ($25M, $50M+ w/cost share)
- 2024 Activity:
  - **Year 1** (*started 2022*): 9 projects finishing up
  - **Year 2** (*started 2023*):
    - March: 10 new projects selected for funding
    - July: projects under contract
  - **Year 3** (*started this year*):
    - 4/30/24: Gap Analysis Workshop (MSTC@UCLA)
    - July: $5M PNT24 RFP to be announced

Dual use technology good for both private and public sectors

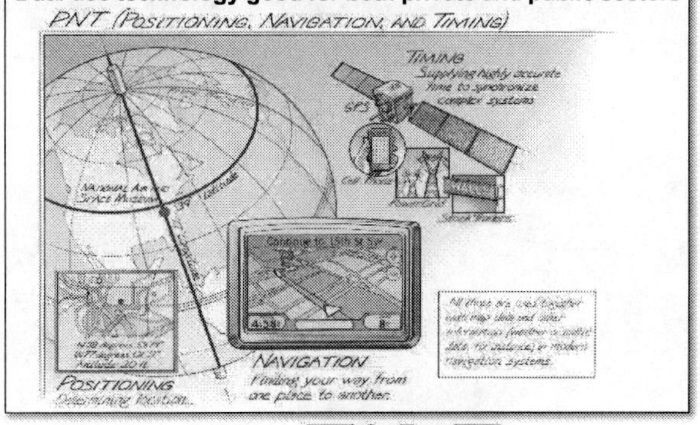

Topics: Intertial & Quantum Sensors, Chip Scale Atomic Clocks

Learn more: https://discover.semi.org/rd-program.html

SEMI MSIG Workgroups

1. Device

- Low SWAP-C gas sensor calibration methods and frequency to improve end use performance
- Activity: writing blog on sensor device characterization methods

2. Manufacturing

- MEMS Lab to Fab Document [1st draft done, still in revision as per SEMI Standards guidelines]

3. Reliability

- Working on a MEMS Mission Profile Survey to poll MEMS device users (customers)

4. Smart Cities Task Force

- Education (bring in experts) and Identifying New Markets
- Create web collateral (blogs, informative webinars, white papers)

Participating Companies

TDK InvenSense, BOSCH Invented for life, ST, SoftMEMS, eurofins, GE, ANALOG DEVICES, NXP, infineon, AMFITZGERALD, Lam RESEARCH, DRAPER, N5 Sensors, cea leti, menlomicro, hp, TELEDYNE DALSA Everywhereyoulook, Nordson SONOSCAN, RENESAS, OKMETIC

UPCOMING EVENTS
MOSCONE CENTER
SEMICON WEST
REGISTRATION
SEMICON® WEST
July 9–11, 2024
WWW.SEMICONWEST.ORG

semi
MEMS & SENSORS INDUSTRY GROUP
MEMS & SENSORS®
EXECUTIVE CONGRESS
OCTOBER 7–9, 2024 | CHÂTEAU-BROMONT HOTEL | QUEBEC, CANADA

MEMS & IMAGING
SENSORS SUMMIT
NOV 14-15, 2024
Munich, Germany
SAVE THE DATE!
MISS 2024
semi
MEMS & SENSORS
INDUSTRY GROUP

Sensors
Converge
Thank you! …
and now some
LIVE Polling!
#SensorsConverge

Sensors Converge

Challenges in Modeling & Simulation of MEMS

June 24–26, 2024 | Santa Clara, CA

#SensorsConverge

MEMS Inertial Sensors Products

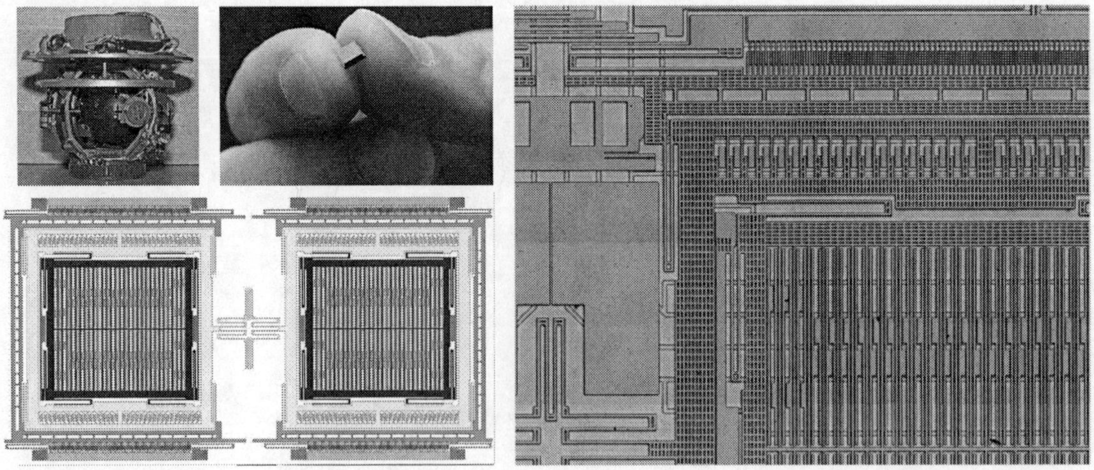

#SensorsConverge, i-ROM GmbH, Germany

iROM MAKING MEMS DESIGN EASY

Sensors Converge

3-Axis MEMS for Inertial Sensors Units

ADVANCED SURFACE MICROMACHINING PROCESS – A FIRST STEP TOWARDS 3D MEMS

ADVANCED SURFACE MICROMACHINING PROCESS – FOR INERTIAL SENSORS

J. Classen, A. Sorger, J. Mehner
Robert Bosch GmbH, Chemnitz University, GERMANY

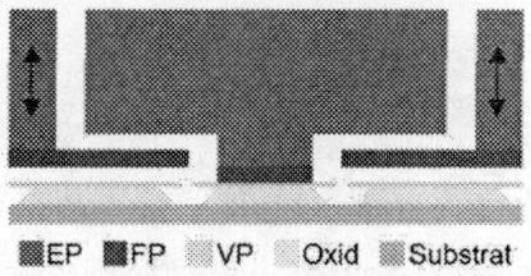

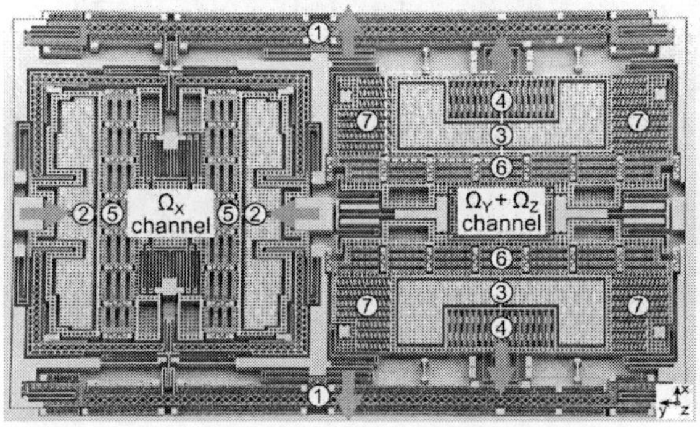

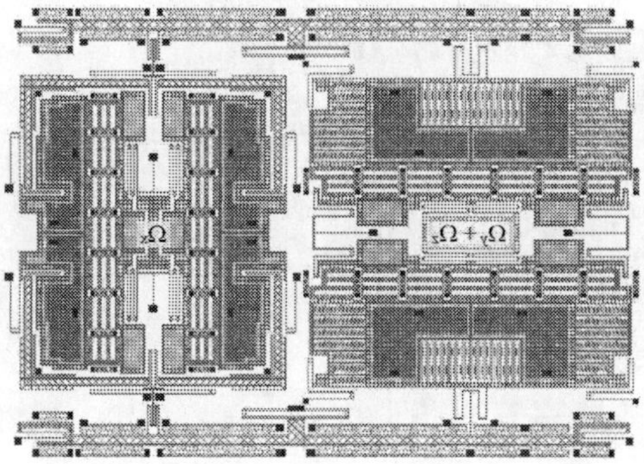

MEMS Micro Positioning System

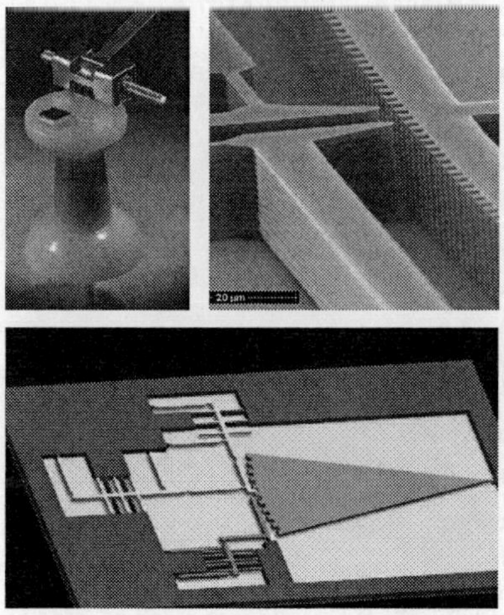

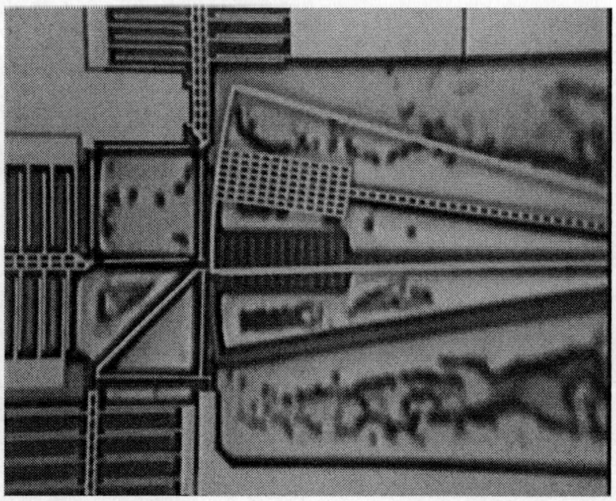

MEMS Micro Positioning System

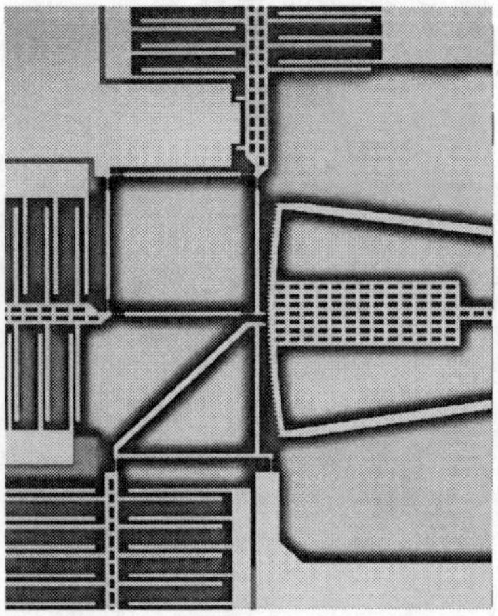

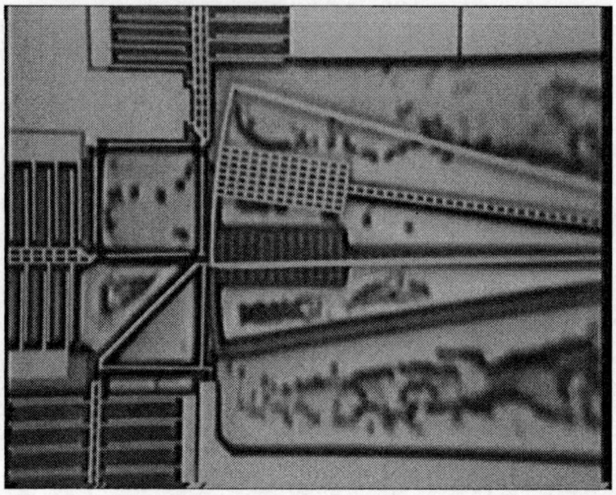

#SensorsConverge, i-ROM GmbH, Germany

MEMS Micro Switch

Optimized fluid-mechanical interactions enable the lowest switching time.

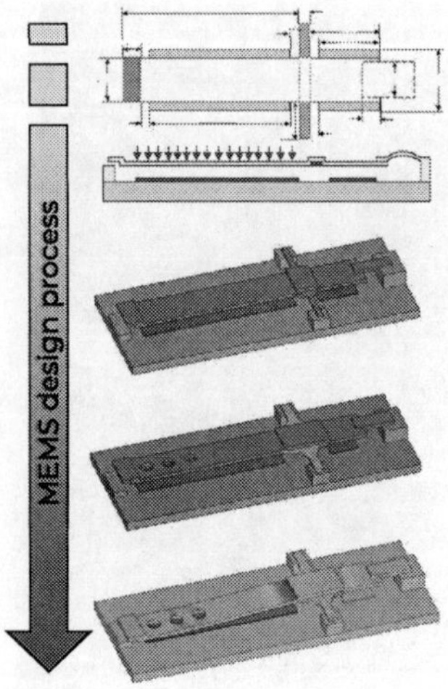

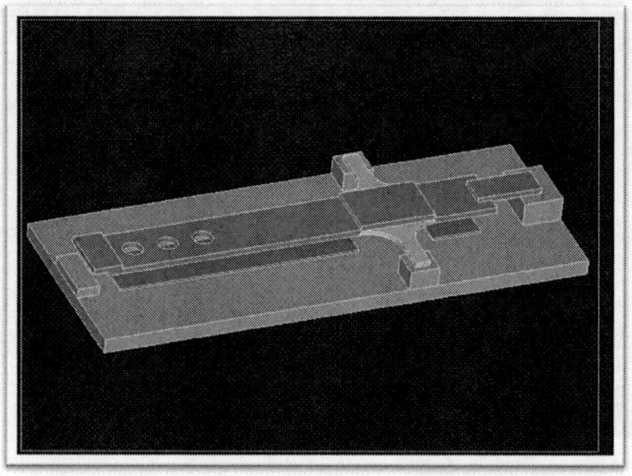

#SensorsConverge, i-ROM GmbH, Germany

Efficient Reduced Order Modeling

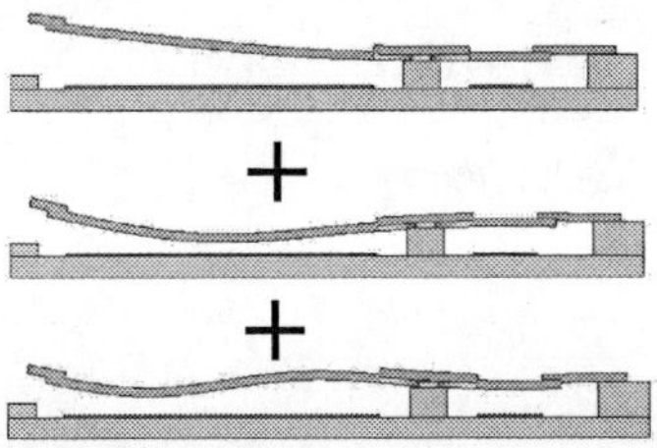

Reduced-Order-Modeling based on:

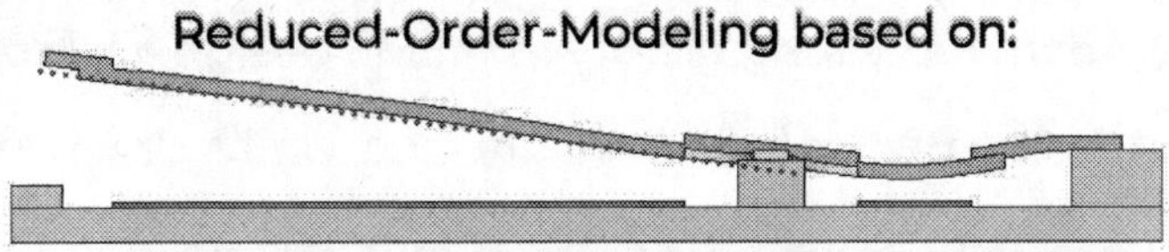

Modal Superposition using 3 modes only.

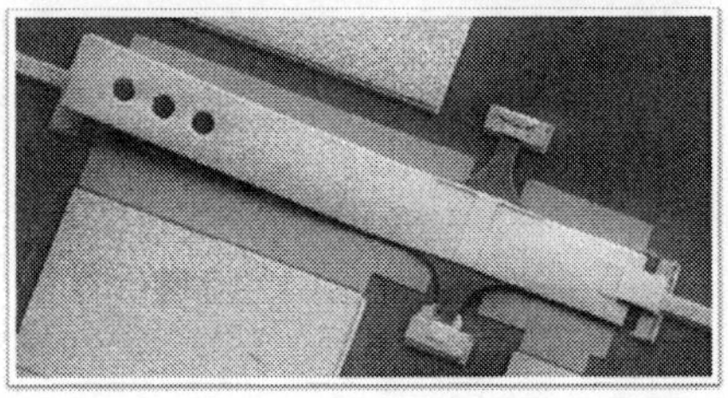

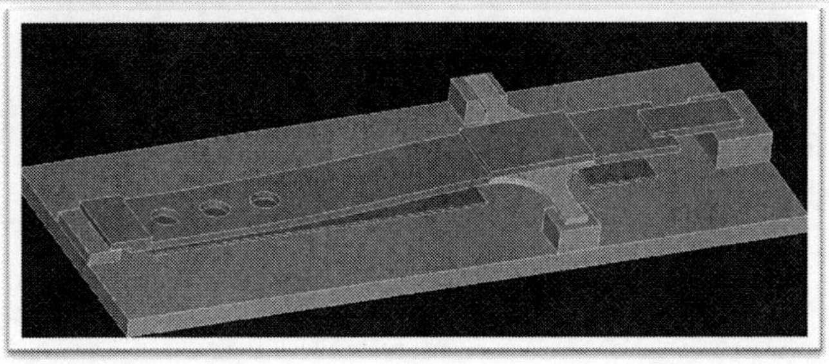

#SensorsConverge, i-ROM GmbH, Germany

iROM MAKING MEMS DESIGN EASY | Sensors Converge

Who is i-ROM?

i-ROM is a German company developing

SOFTWARE FOR MEMS DESIGN

i-ROM means

Intelligent - Reduced Order Modeling

≡ WIKIPEDIA The Free Encyclopedia — **Reduced order modeling (ROM)** is a technique for reducing the computational complexity of mathematical models in numerical simulations.

Our slogan

Making MEMS Design Easy

i-ROM MODELBUILDER®

Enables high speed and high accuracy in MEMS design and simulation.

#SensorsConverge, i-ROM GmbH, Germany

iROM MAKING MEMS DESIGN EASY | Sensors Converge

Who is i-ROM?

Our team has a long history in MEMS design and software development.

Academic background at the Chemnitz University, Germany:

- University degree program in MEMS started 1986
- International Master's degree program on MEMS
- Research in the MEMCAD-design team of Prof. Senturia at MIT (USA)

Industrial background:

- Finite element tool development for coupled-domain-simulations
- Reduced-order-modeling software and design support for MEMS

#SensorsConverge, i-ROM GmbH, Germany

Challenges of MEMS design

TDK InvenSense, MPU 6050

- ➤ Complicated shape elements
- ➤ Fast transient simulations
- ➤ Coupled physical domains
- ➤ Export to EDA-Tools

→ MEMS Design Automation
ANSYS COMSOL
COVENTOR SOFTMEMS INTELLISENSE
i-ROM MODELBUILDER®

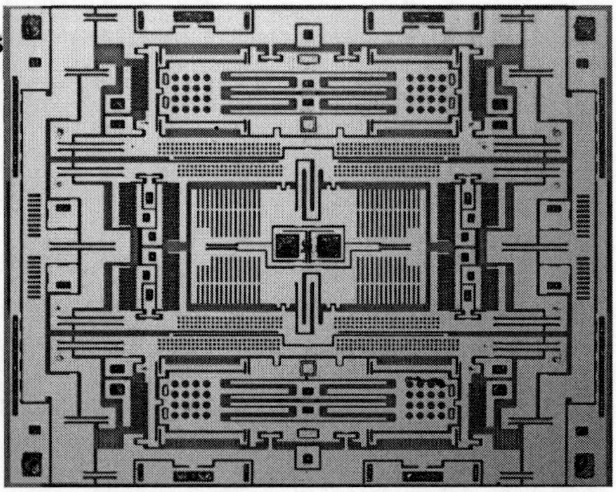

#SensorsConverge, i-ROM GmbH, Germany

Existing Design Flow for MEMS

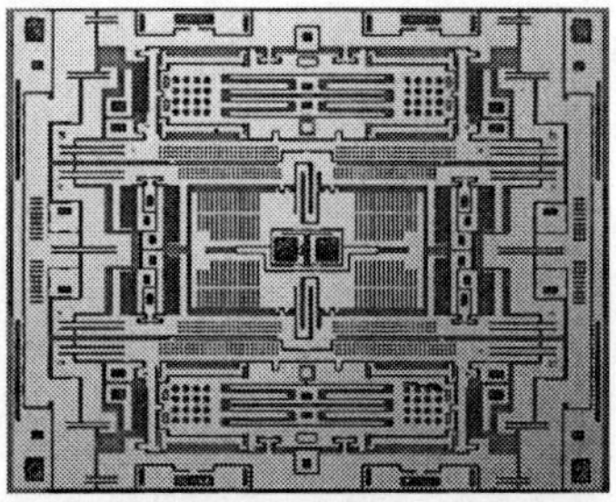

FAB process data (PDK) ➡ GDS layout ➡ Simulations based on mask layout
Manufactured prototype

Problems:
- It is difficult to optimize new designs (mask layouts are not parametric).
- It requires manual settings to identify shape elements (e.g. comb cells).

Design Flow of the MODELBUILDER

i-ROM MAKING MEMS DESIGN EASY

Process data (PDK):

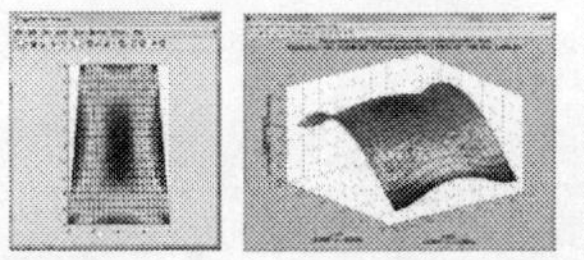

Model generation:
1) Command based
2) SKETCHER interface

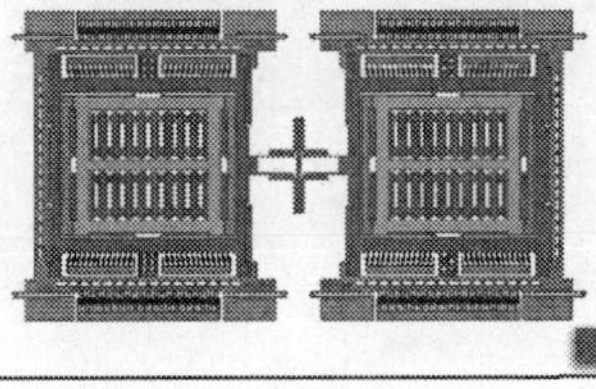

1) Conceptual design phase

2) Component design phase

i-ROM FEM core:

Experiments

Simulation features:
1) Rigid body models
2) FEM-based ROM

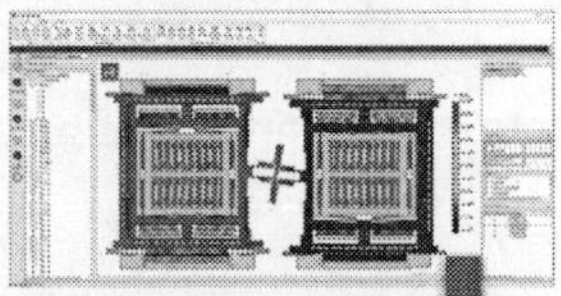

GDS mask layout:

Interfaces to:
Simulink, ANSYS, COMSOL

Reduced Order Modeling of MEMS

Conceptual design phase

i-ROM MODELBUILDER core

- Rigid mass bodies with 6 DOF
- Timoshenko beam elements
- Comb cells, plate capacitors, stopper... (analytical terms)

Component design phase

i-ROM FEM core

- FEM based data extraction for mechanical, electrostatic and fluidic domain elements
- Model order reduction (e.g. MSUP)

Modal Superposition

Mechanical domain (one equation for each mode):

$$\ddot{q}_i + 2\,\xi_i\,\omega_i\,\dot{q}_i + \omega_i^2\,q_i = \sum_r \frac{\partial C_{ij}}{2\,\partial q_i}\left(V_i - V_j\right)^2 + f_i\,S_i$$

Electrostatic forces

Electrostatic domain (one equation for each conductor):

$$I_i = \frac{\partial Q_i}{\partial t} = \sum_r \left(\frac{\partial C_{ij}}{\partial t}(V_i - V_j) + C_{ij}\left(\frac{\partial V_i}{\partial t} - \frac{\partial V_j}{\partial t} \right) \right)$$

Motion induced current — Current due to the voltage change

Transformation from modal to nodal displacements:

$$u(x,y,z,t) = \sum_{i=1}^{m} q_i(t)\,\varphi_i(x,y,z)$$

Modal amplitudes — Eigenvectors

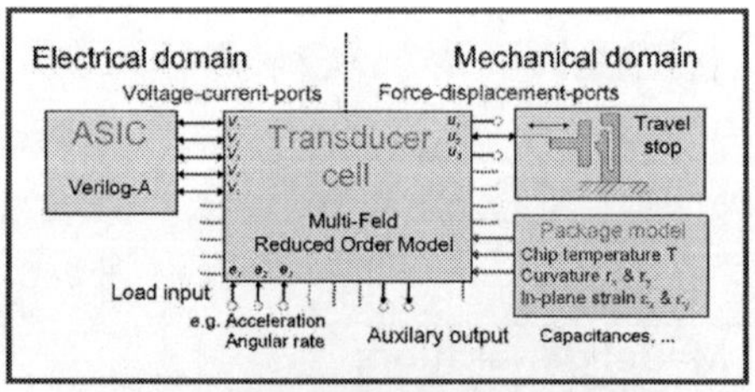

Flexible bending

$C_{ij} = f(q_m)$

Multivariable capacitance functions

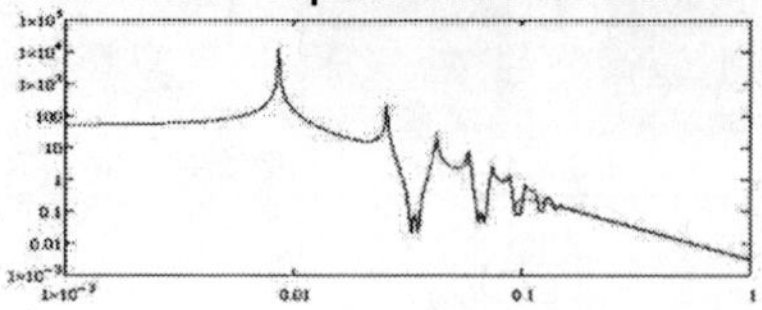

i-ROM MODELBUILDER core Command based approach

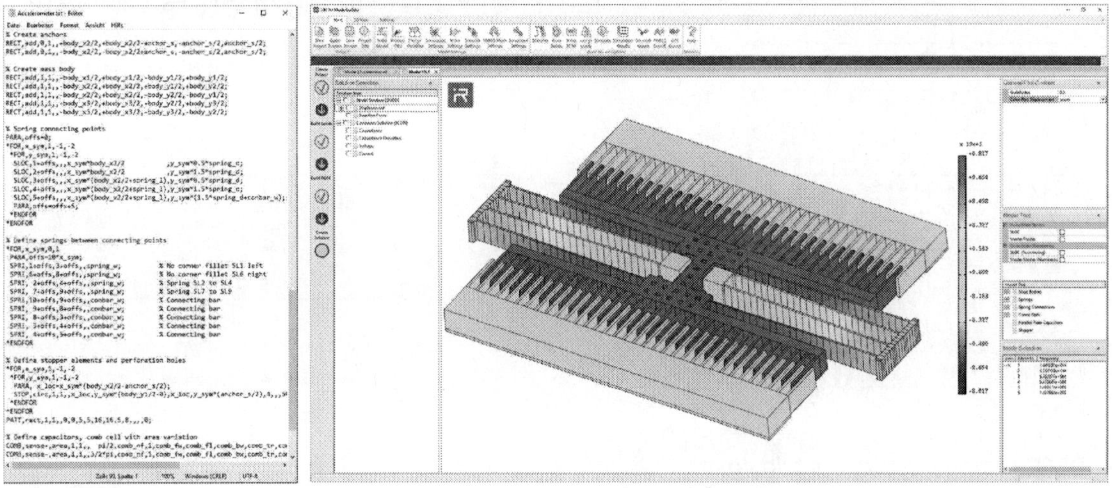

#SensorsConverge, i-ROM GmbH, Germany

Modeling example

i-ROM MODELBUILDER core: Command based approach

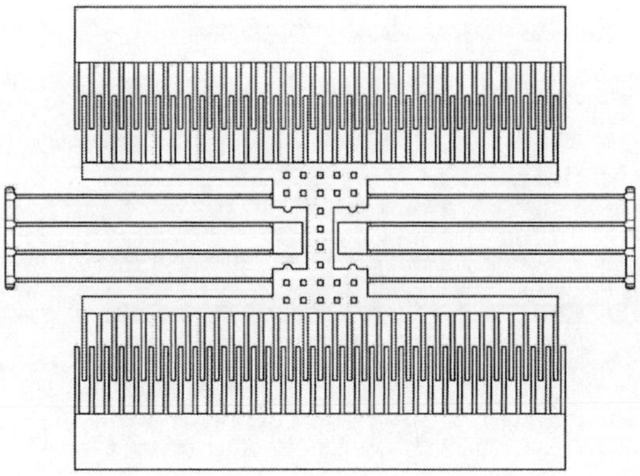

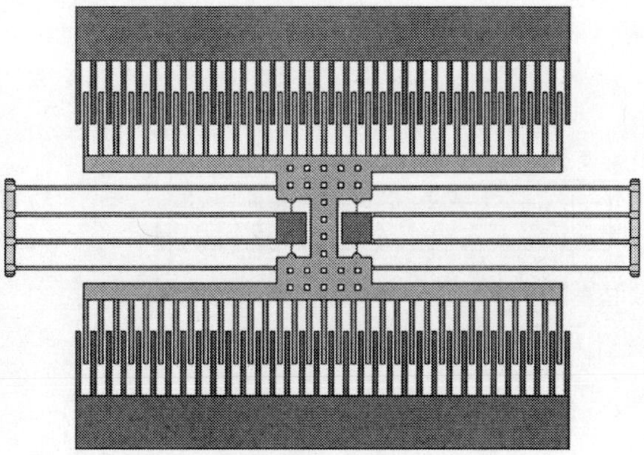

Fully parametric models are obtained by simple and intuitive commands

#SensorsConverge, i-ROM GmbH, Germany

Modeling example

Mass bodies: Primitives & Boolean operations
RECT, POLY, CIRC, ELPS, UDAR

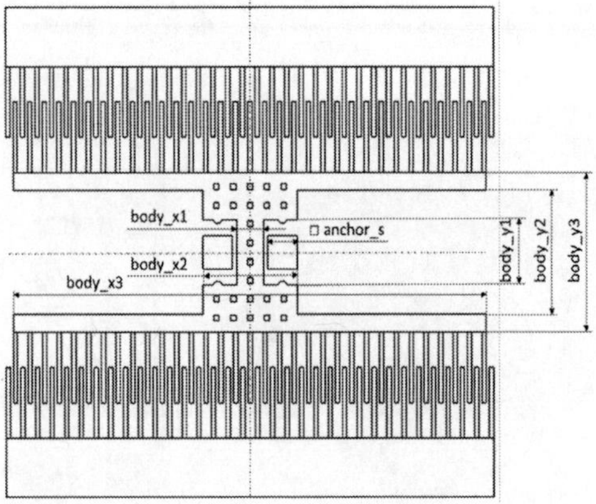

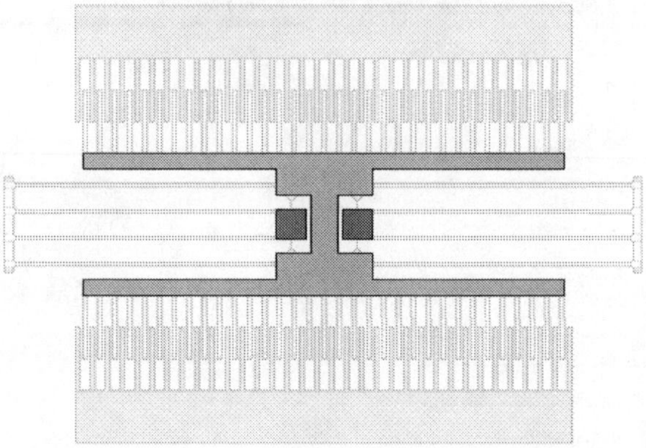

RECT, *add, body_id, mat_id, layer_id, x_left, x-right, y_lower, y_upper;*

Modeling example

Springs: Connecting points & Linking beams
SLOC, SPRI (straight, curved, tapered)

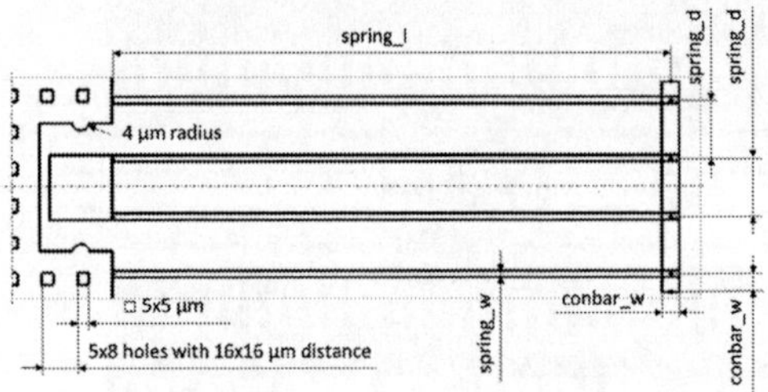

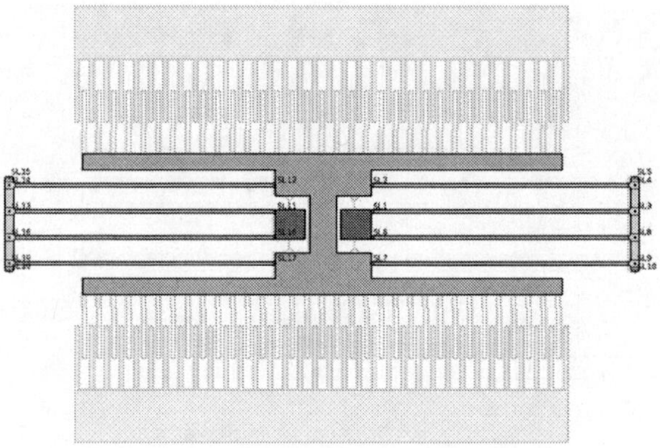

SLOC, *sloc_id, layer_id, x-pos, y_pos;*

SPRI, *sloc_b, sloc_e, sloc_cp, width1, width2;*

Modeling example

Capacitances: Comb cells & Plate capacitances
COMB, PCAP (default and user defined cells)

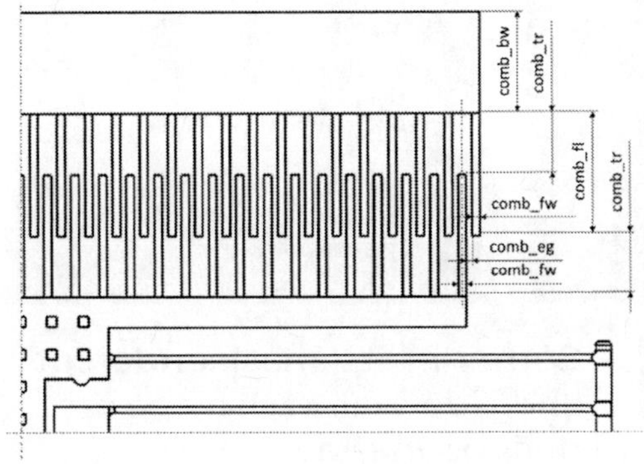

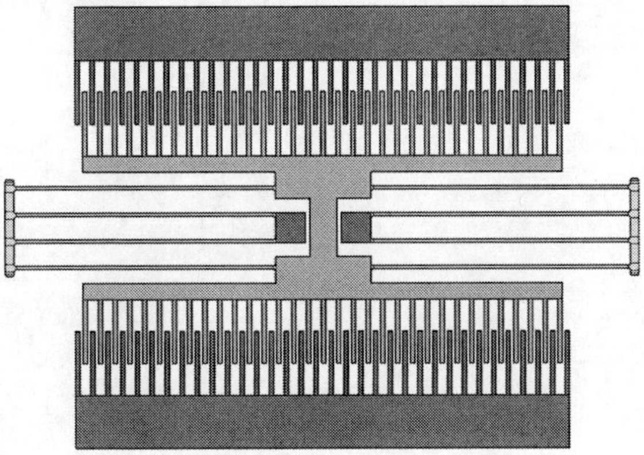

COMB, *sense+, type, layer_id, x-pos, y_pos, ...(dimensional parameters) ;*

Modeling example

Perforation patterns: PERF commands
Stopper elements: STOP, ZLIM (contact)

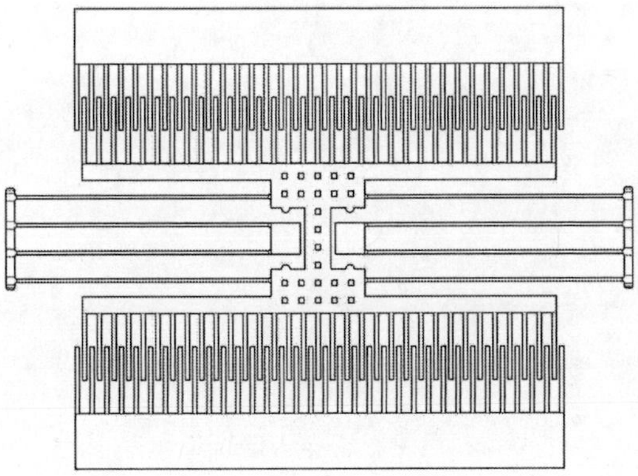

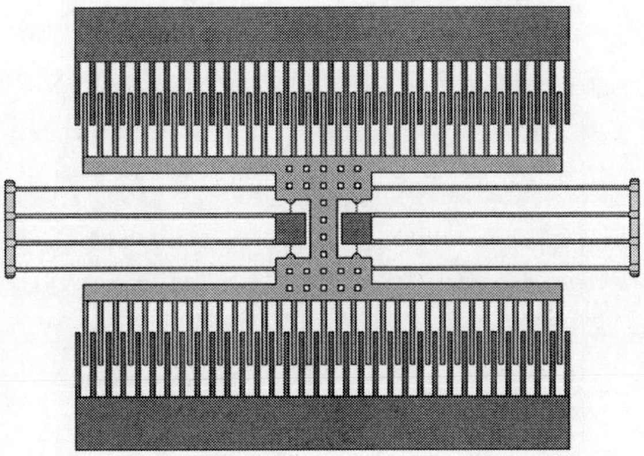

PERF, *type, layer_id, x-pos, y_pos, ...;*

STOP, *type, layer_id, x-c, y_c, x_t, y_t, ...;*

#SensorsConverge, i-ROM GmbH, Germany

Modeling example

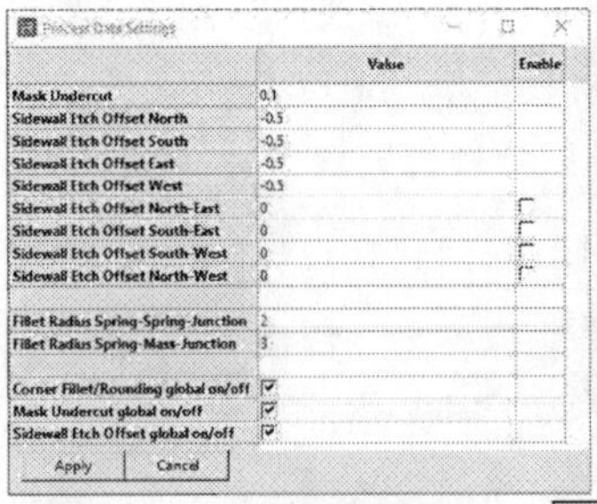

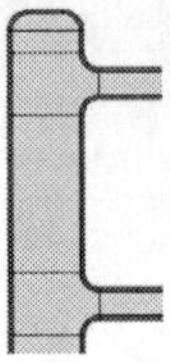

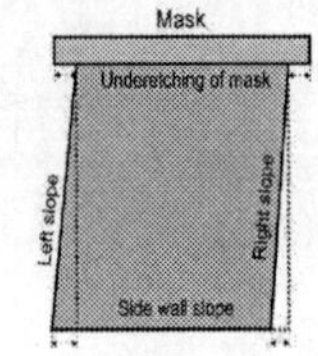

Corner fillets, mask undercut, and side-wall etch slope are defined in the

i-ROM MODELBUILDER-GUI

i-ROM SKETCHER **Graphical modeling approach**

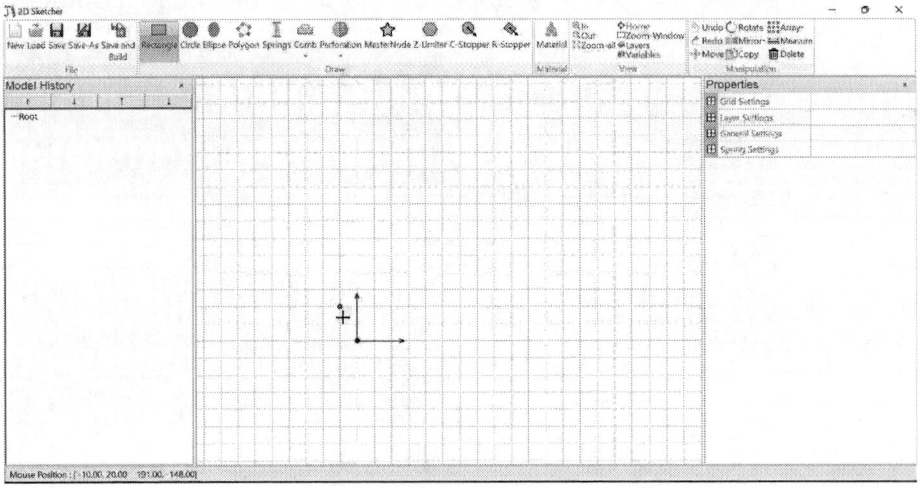

i-ROM SKETCHER Graphical modeling approach

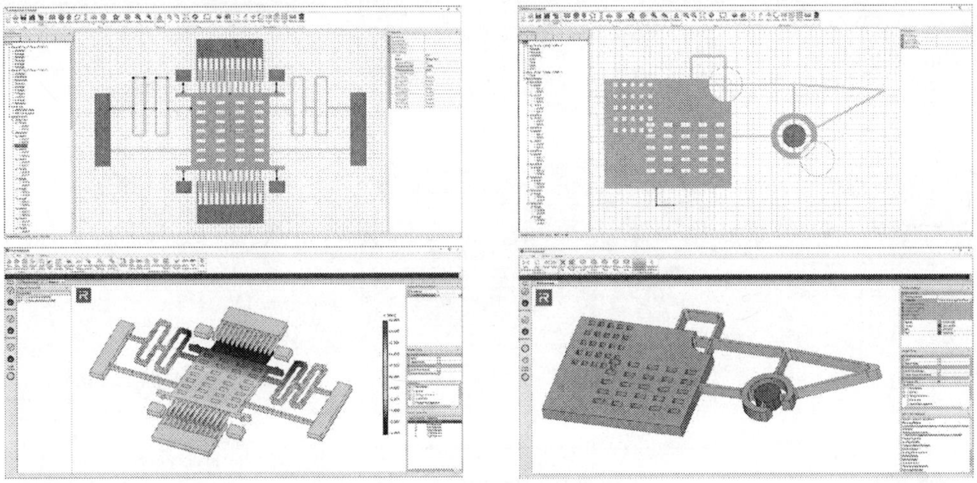

#SensorsConverge, i-ROM GmbH, Germany

i-ROM SKETCHER User defined areas and comb cells: Outer lines are straight, circular and Bezier curves

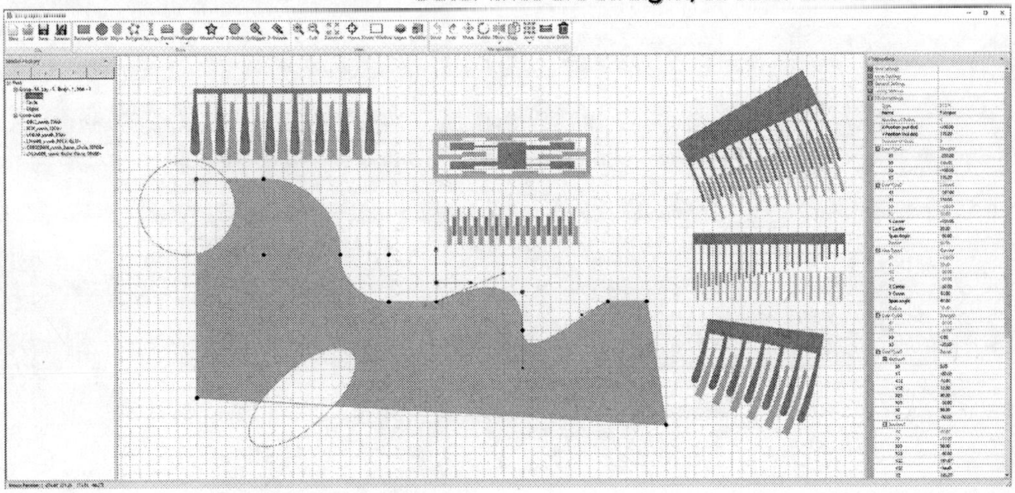

#SensorsConverge, i-ROM GmbH, Germany

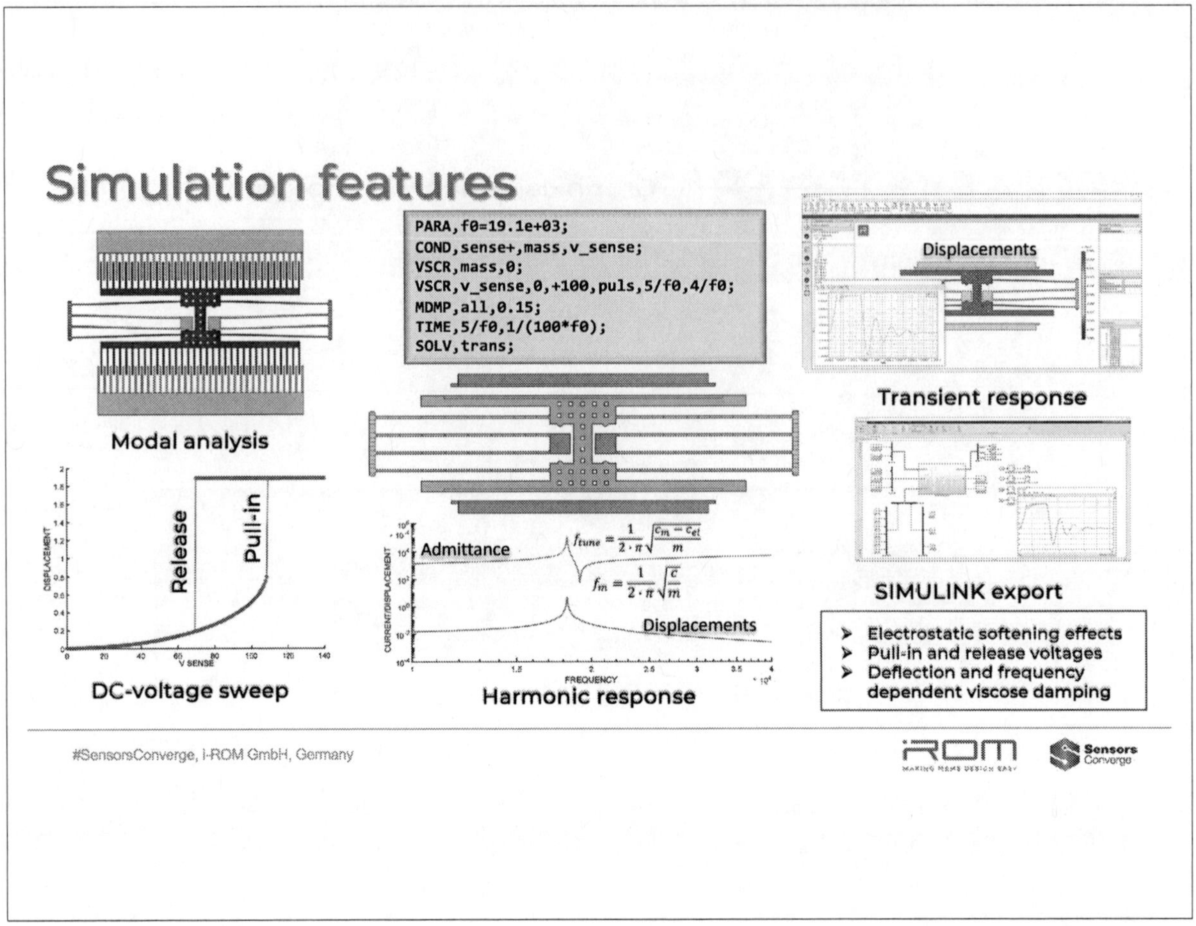
Simulation features
PARA,f0=19.1e+03;
COND,sense+,mass,v_sense;
VSCR,mass,0;
VSCR,v_sense,0,+100,puls,5/f0,4/f0;
MDMP,all,0.15;
TIME,5/f0,1/(100*f0);
SOLV,trans;
Displacements
Transient response
Modal analysis
SIMULINK export
Release
Pull-in
DISPLACEMENT
V SENSE
DC-voltage sweep
Admittance
$f_{tune} = \frac{1}{2 \cdot \pi}\sqrt{\frac{c_m - c_{el}}{m}}$
$f_m = \frac{1}{2 \cdot \pi}\sqrt{\frac{c}{m}}$
Displacements
CURRENT/DISPLACEMENT
FREQUENCY
Harmonic response
➤ Electrostatic softening effects
➤ Pull-in and release voltages
➤ Deflection and frequency dependent viscose damping
#SensorsConverge, i-ROM GmbH, Germany
iROM
MAKING MEMS DESIGN EASY
Sensors Converge

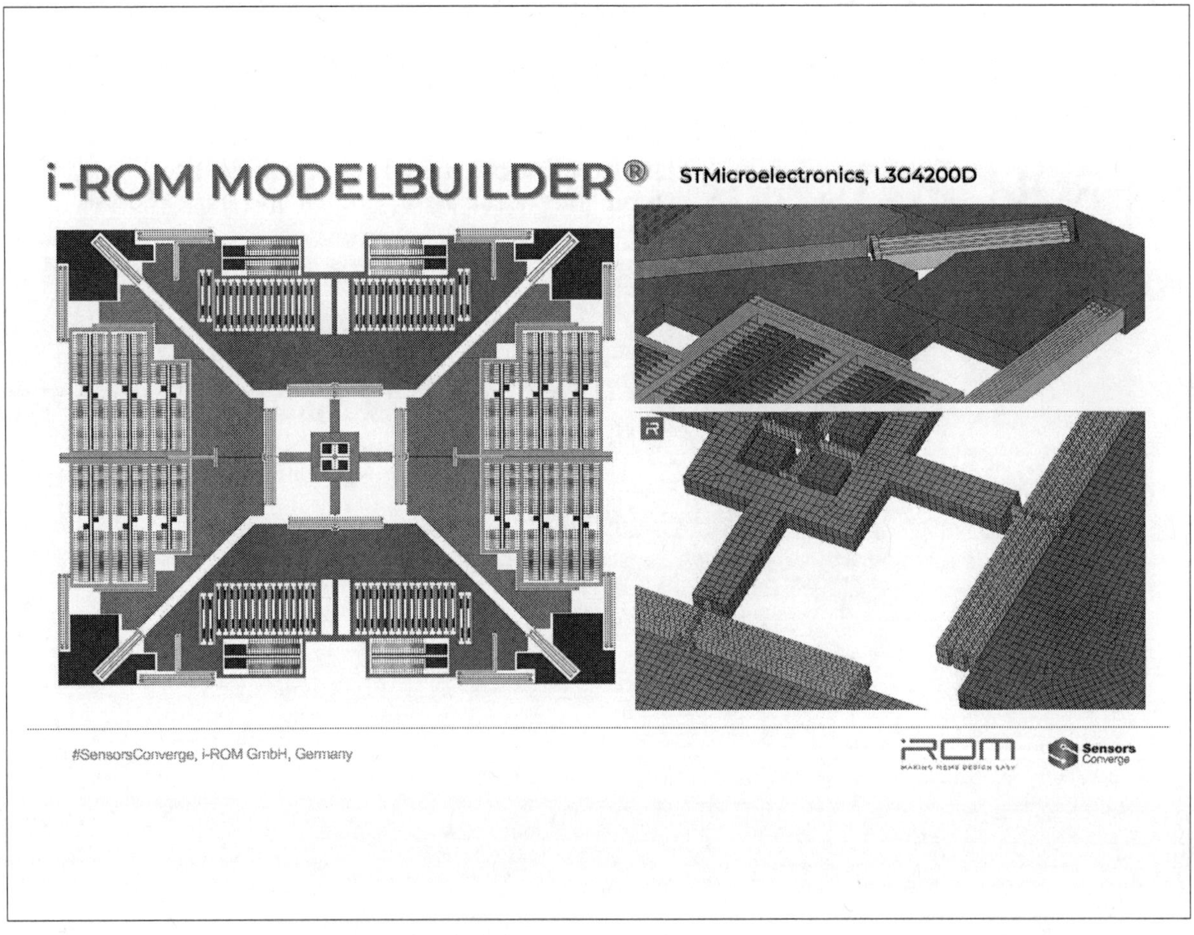
i-ROM MODELBUILDER ®
STMicroelectronics, L3G4200D
#SensorsConverge, i-ROM GmbH, Germany
iROM
MAKING MEMS DESIGN EASY
Sensors Converge

i-ROM FEM core ®

TDK InvenSense, MPU 6050

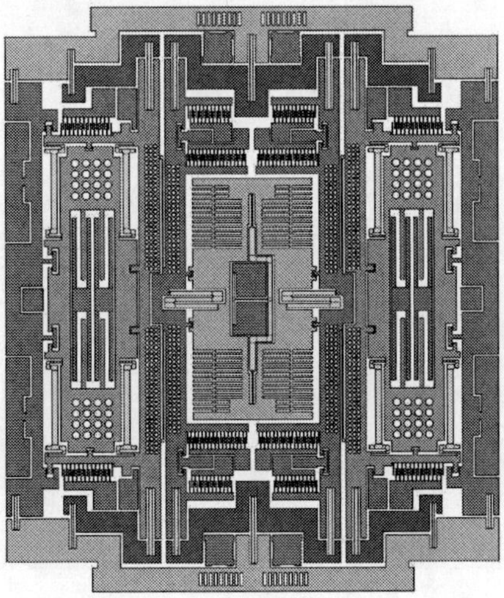

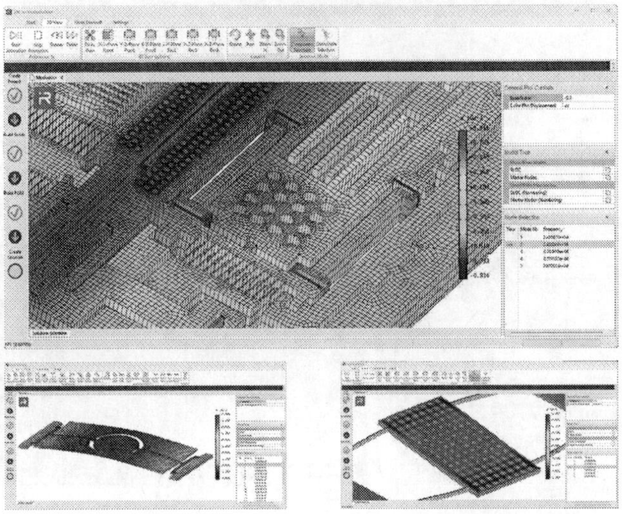

#SensorsConverge, i-ROM GmbH, Germany

iROM MAKING MEMS DESIGN EASY

Sensors Converge

Design rules, process data (PDK)

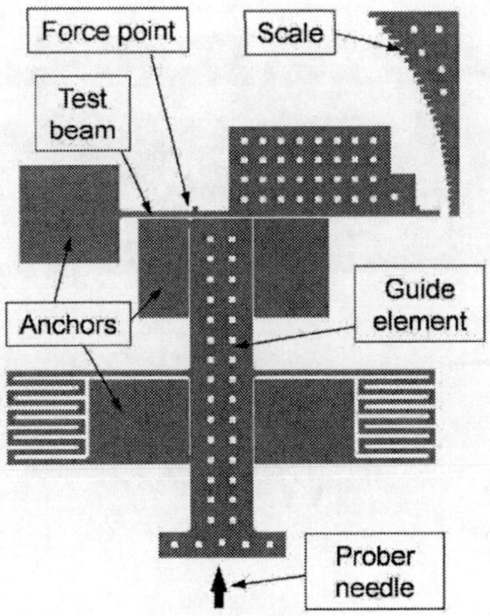

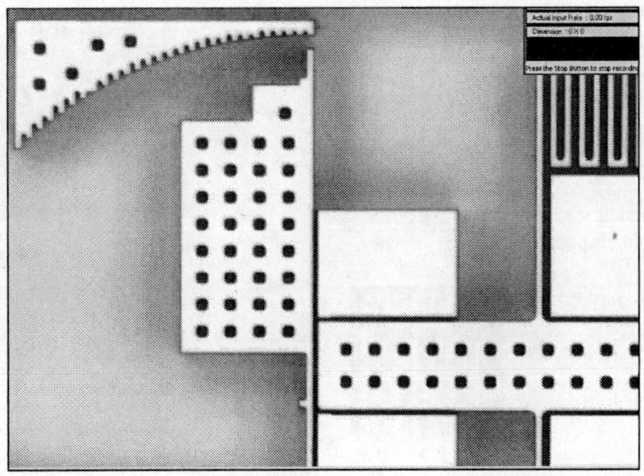

#SensorsConverge, i-ROM GmbH, Germany

iROM MAKING MEMS DESIGN EASY

Sensors Converge

Design rules, process data (PDK)

- Spring breakage
- Anchor breakage
- Adhesion at stopper

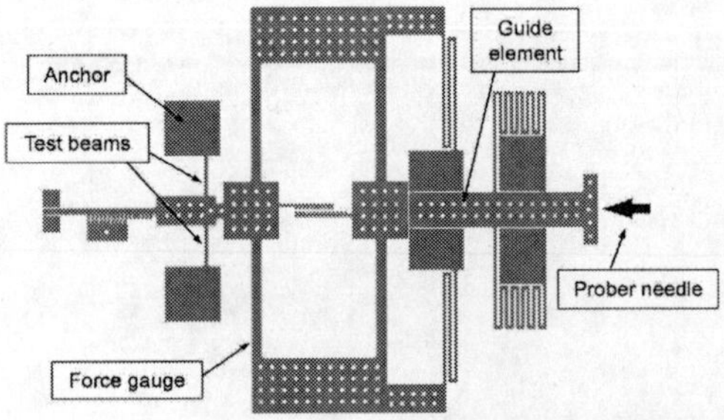

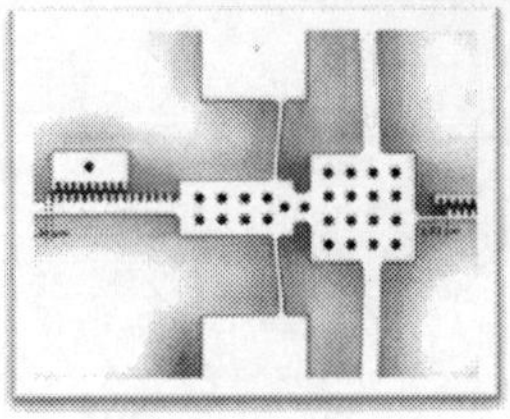

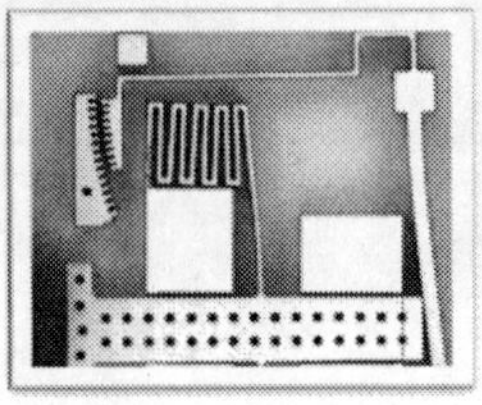

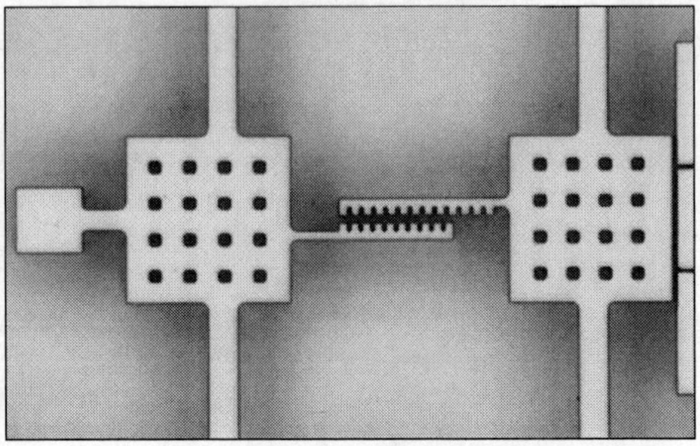

#SensorsConverge, I-ROM GmbH, Germany

Adhesion at stoppers

Pull-in:

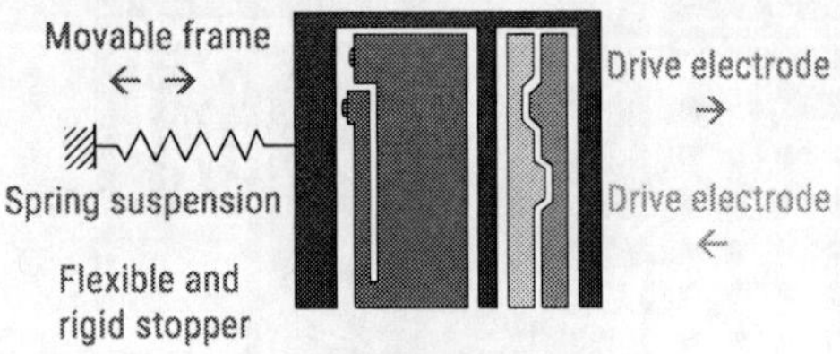

Pull-out test:

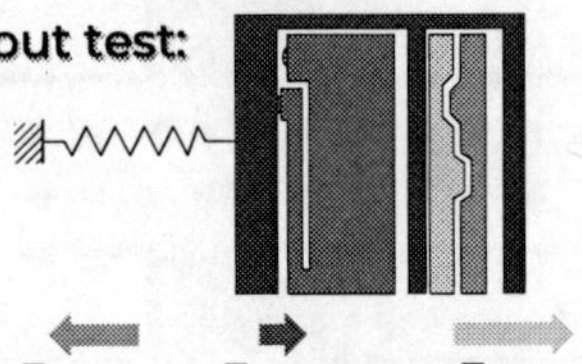

$$F_{Spring} = F_{Adhesion} + F_{Drive}(V)$$

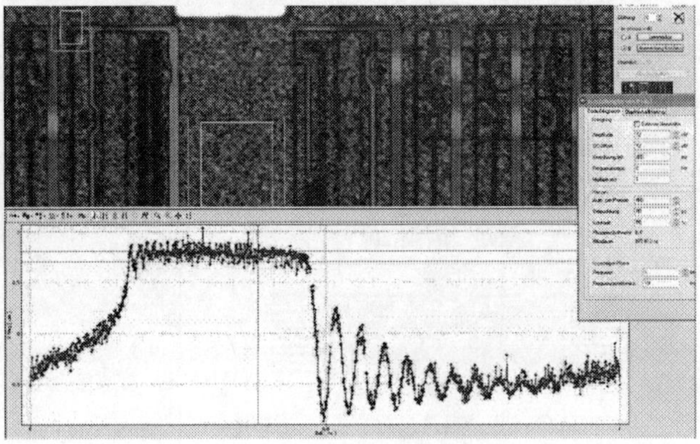

#SensorsConverge, I-ROM GmbH, Germany

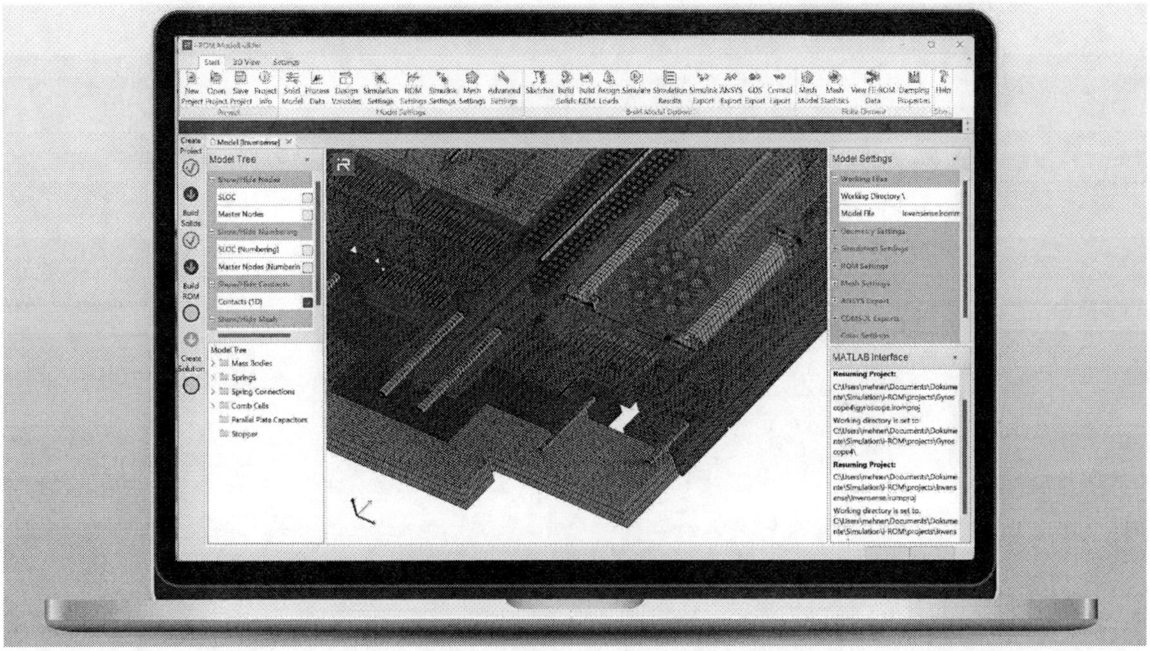
Model Tree
Model Settings
MATLAB Interface
Mass Bodies
Springs
Spring Connections
Comb Cells
Parallel Plate Capacitors
Stopper

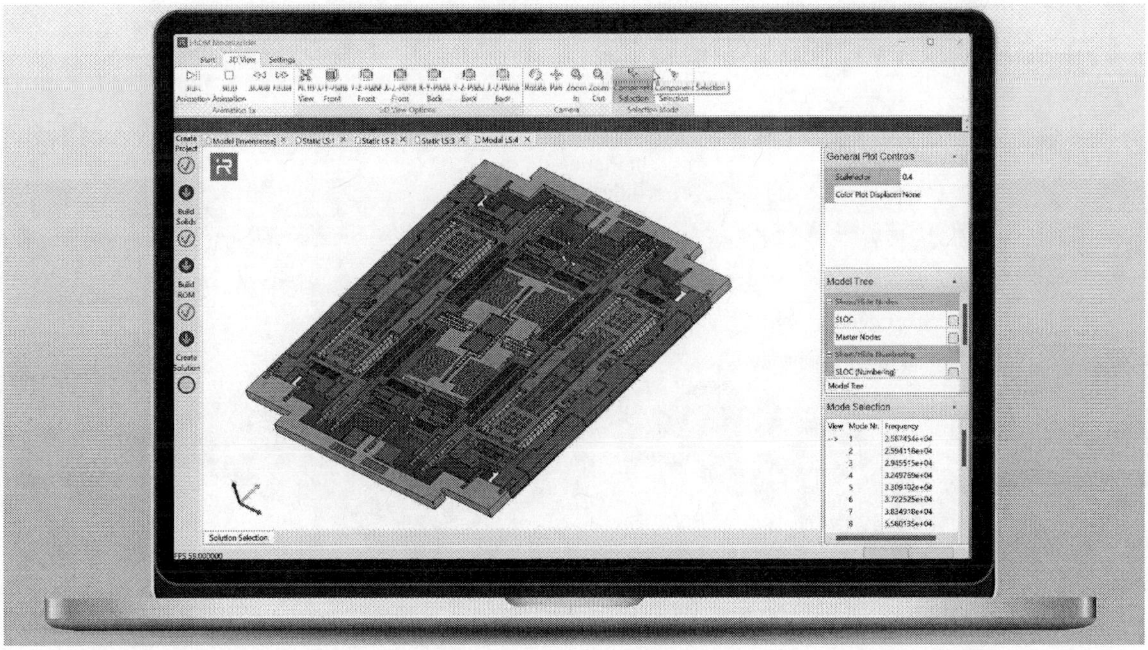
General Plot Controls
Model Tree
Mode Selection
Solution Selection

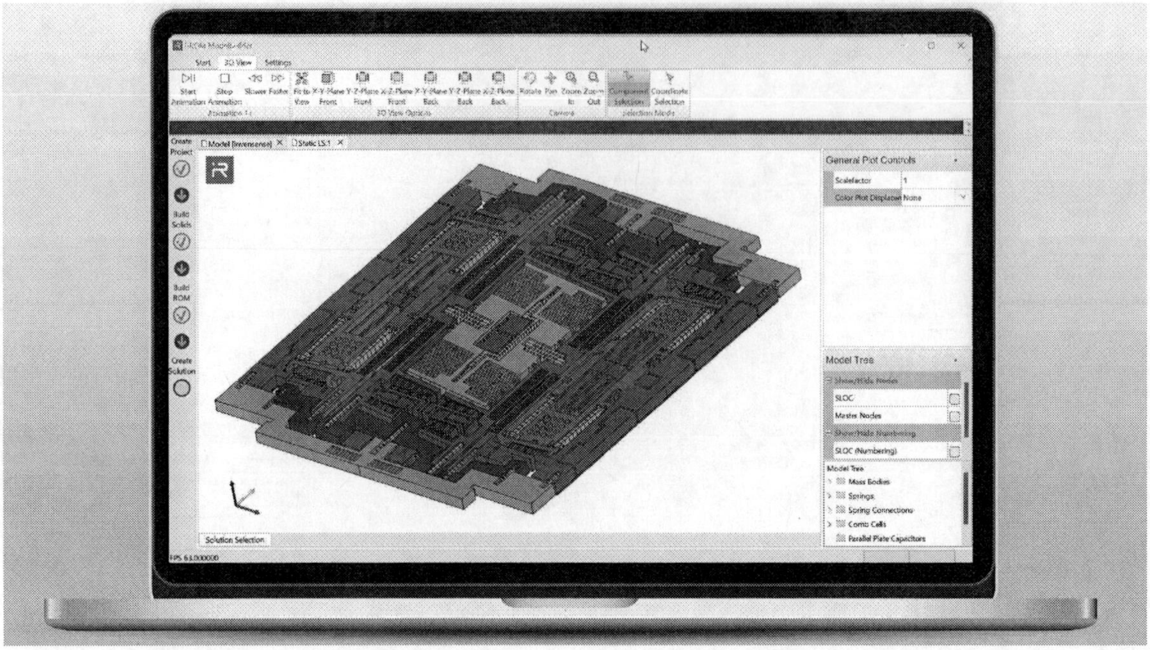

Latest Developments

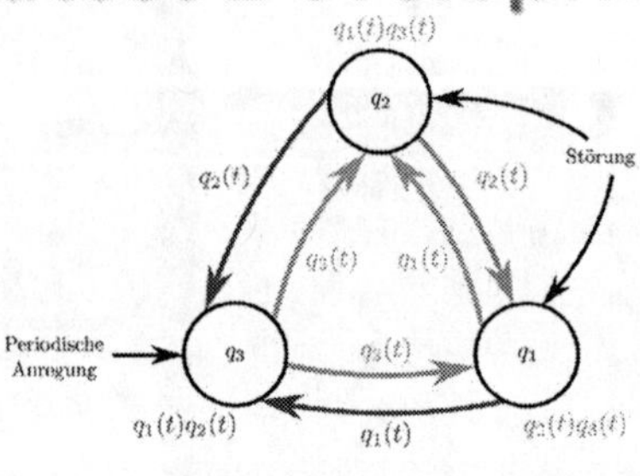

q_1 ... In-Plane
q_2 ... Out-Plane (Piston)
q_3 ... Drive

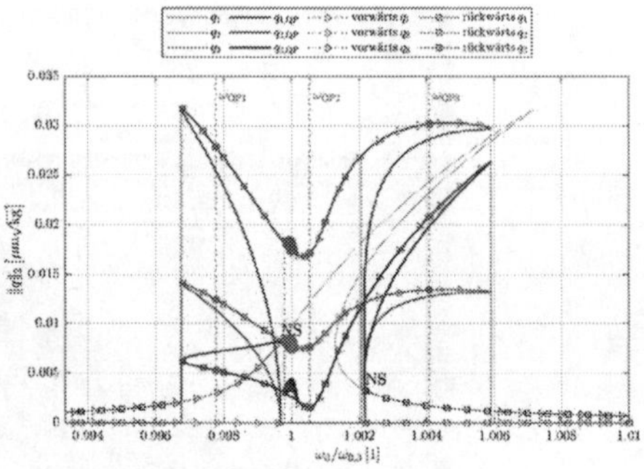

Without Mode-Coupling

With Mode-Coupling

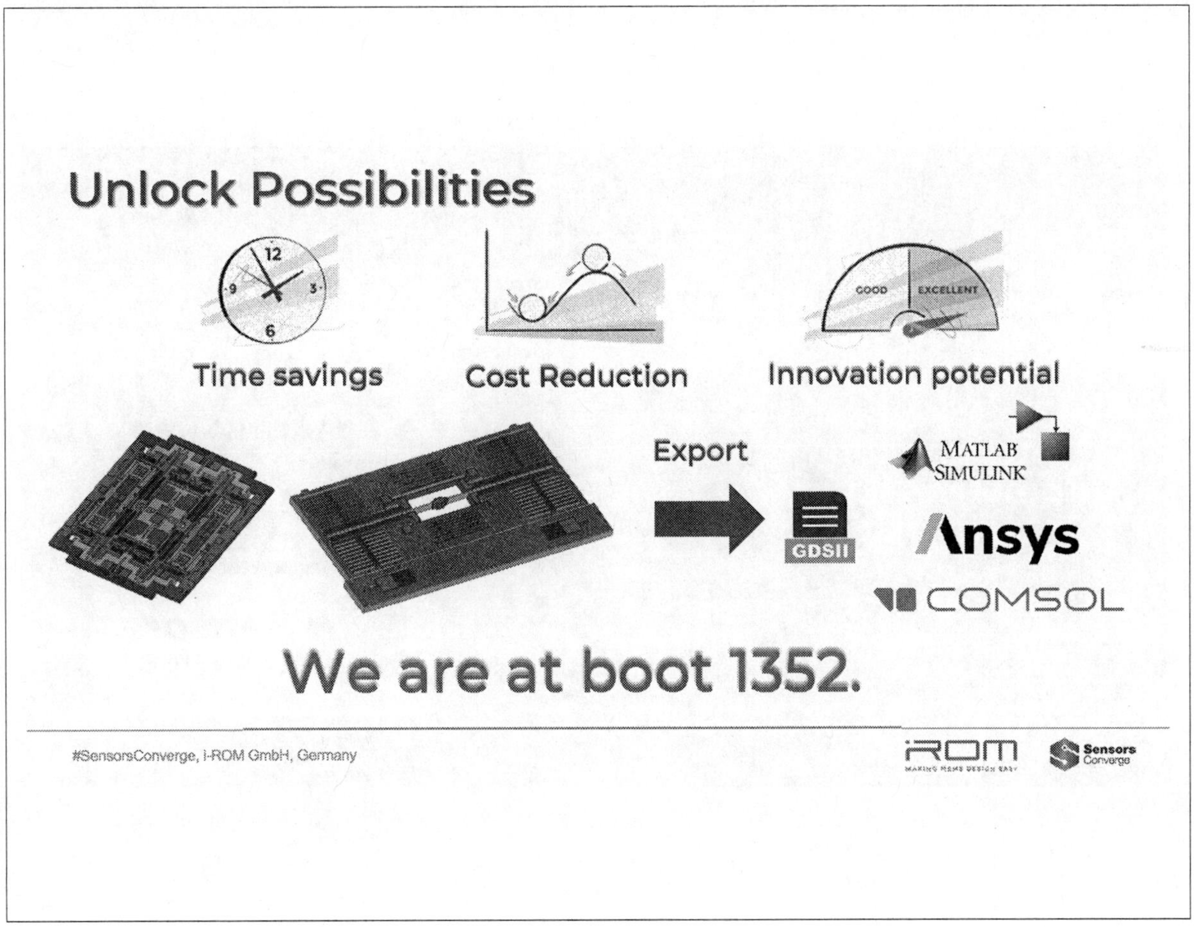
Unlock Possibilities
12
9
3
6
Time savings
Cost Reduction
GOOD
EXCELLENT
Innovation potential
Export
GDSII
MATLAB
SIMULINK
Ansys
COMSOL
We are at boot 1352.
#SensorsConverge, I-ROM GmbH, Germany
iROM
Sensors Converge

INTELLIGENCE TO SHAPE YOUR TOMORROW

MEMS & Sensors Steering the Automotive Industry Transformation

Sensors Converge

YOLE Intelligence

YINTR24407 | www.yolegroup.com | ©Yole Intelligence 2024

AGENDA

- Yole Group Presentation
- Context in the Automotive Sensors industry
- Update on Market data
- Sensors for Automotive – market shares
- Highlights of key ongoing transformations
    - The electrification of cars
    - Autonomous driving
    - Infotainment and Chassis sensorization
- Takeaway

YOLE Intelligence

MEMS & Sensors Steering the Automotive Industry Transformation | 2024 | 2

Yole Group Presentation

YOLE GROUP

We provide industrial companies, financial investors and R&D organizations, with market research and marketing analysis, technology, supply chain and cost analysis, as well as performance evaluation, to help our customers in their decision-making about their future business and manufacturing strategy in the semiconductor, photonic and electronic sectors.

3 CORE ACTIVITIES BASED ON DEEP SYNERGIES

Market & Technology

- Market, technology, and strategy consulting
- M&A, Due Diligence and evaluation of companies

Teardown Reverse engineering and costing

- Technology, process & cost analysis
- Teardown and reverse engineering
- Comparative analysis

Performance analysis

- Test of electric and electro-optical performance of devices
- Comparison of performances and related technical choice

OUR EXPERTISE

SEMICONDUCTOR INDUSTRY

• Imaging	• Memory
• Battery	• Photonics and Lighting
• Display	• Power Electronics
• Electronic Systems	• Radio Frequency
• Computing and Software	• Semiconductor Equipment
• Compound Semiconductor	• Semiconductor Packaging
• Global Semiconductor Trends	• Sensing and Actuating

YOLE Group

 5

Automotive Sensors Market

YOLE Intelligence

AUTOMOTIVE SENSORS MARKET

Which modules are included – Split by domain

Powertrain and Electrification

DC/DC converter, Main inverter, Onboard charger, Battery management system, Boost converter, Engine, peripheral, and exhaust control, Transmission, and hybrid control

Chassis and Others

Seat, alarm, Car access, Trunk, Window, Electronic park brake, Mirror, Wipers, Front lighting, Sunroof, Wheel, Suspension, Safety belt, Steering wheel, Brakes, Front bumper.

Infotainment and Telematics

Occupant monitoring, Telematics, HVAC, Viewing camera

ADAS and Safety

ADAS camera, Thermal camera, Radar, LiDAR, Ultrasonic, Airbag, ABS/ESP, Driver monitoring, Child detection

YOLE Intelligence

AUTOMOTIVE SENSORS MARKET

2023-29 Sensor market* for automotive applications by domain

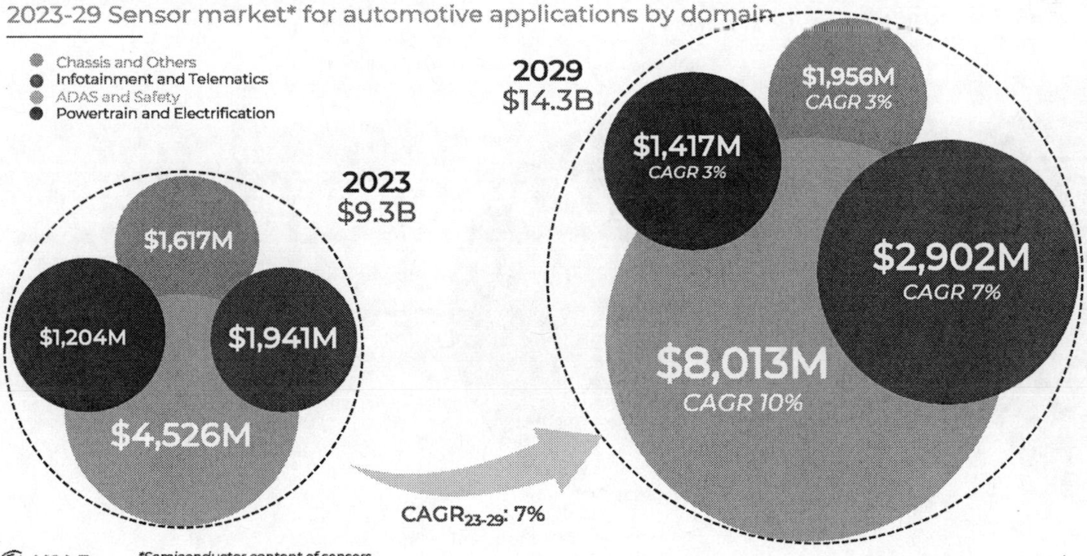

YOLE Intelligence

*Semiconductor content of sensors

AUTOMOTIVE SENSORS MARKET

2023-29 Sensor market* for automotive applications

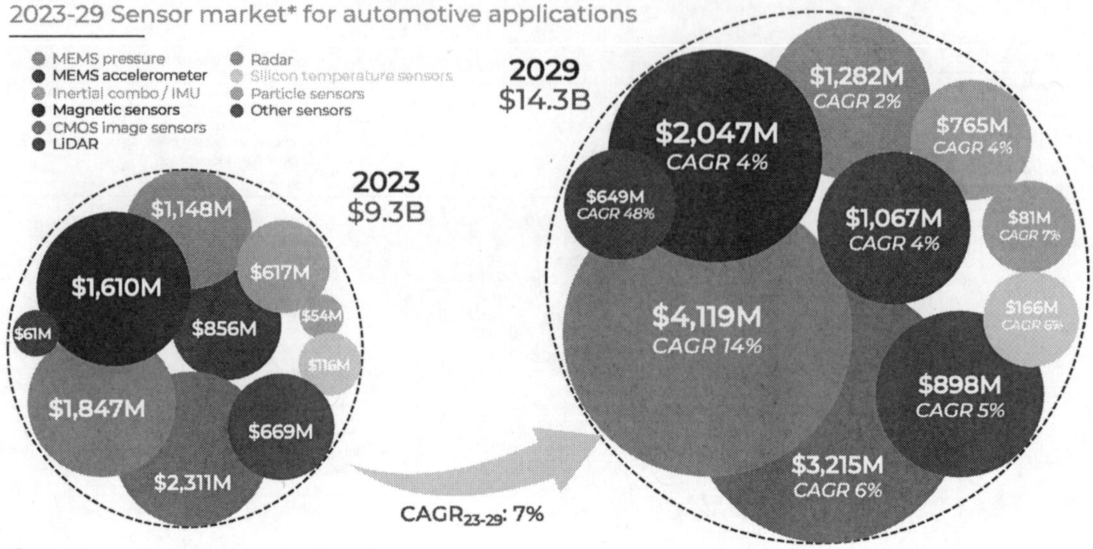

*Semiconductor content of sensors

AUTOMOTIVE SENSORS MARKET

Global semiconductor sensor market shares (1/2)

Bosch leads the market due to strong revenue in MEMS (pressure, accelerometer, IMU) and radar.

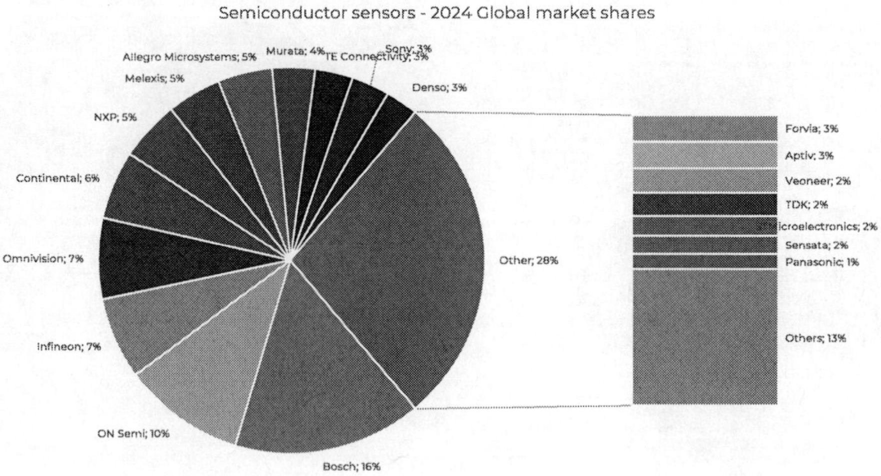

Electrification of cars

YOLE Intelligence

ELECTRIFICATION OF CARS

Engine evolution

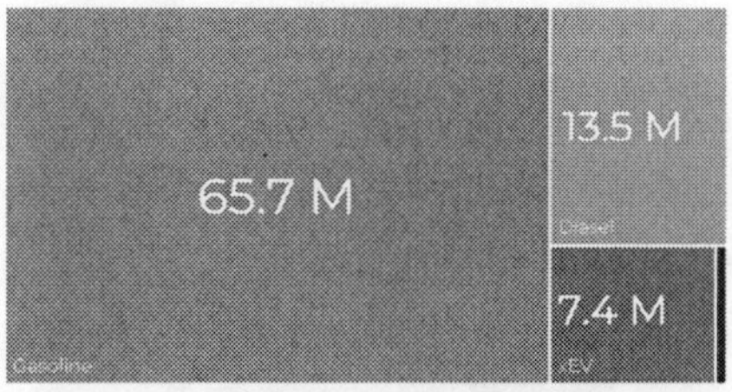

87.1 million vehicles in 2019

98 million vehicles in 2029

ICE (gasoline) | ICE (diesel) | xEV | Others

- The Automotive industry is transitioning from cars based on internal combustion engines (ICE), which represented 91% of the production in 2019, to electrified cars, which are expected to represent 43% of the production in 2029.
- Among these 42.4 million electrified vehicles, ~28 million are expected to be fully electric with no ICE at all.
- This is a massive change for OEMs and will significantly impact the components used inside the car. This implies much more semiconductor content and sensors to control each module of electric cars.

YOLE Intelligence

ELECTRIFICATION OF CARS

A broad number of applications for current sensors and position sensors

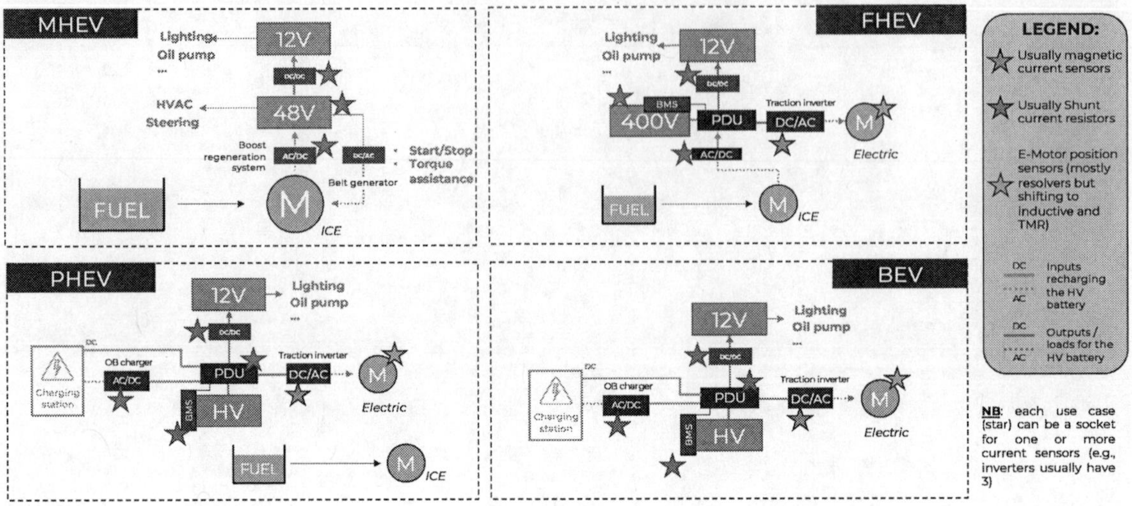

ELECTRIFICATION OF CARS

Thermal runaway detection

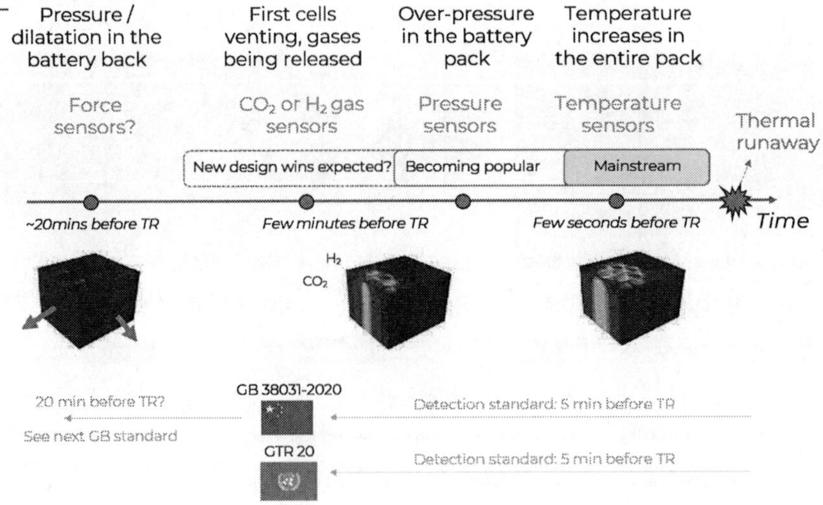

Autonomous Driving

YOLE Intelligence

MEMS & Sensors Steering the Automotive Industry Transformation | 2024 | 15

ADAS & SAFETY

Where are the modules in cars?

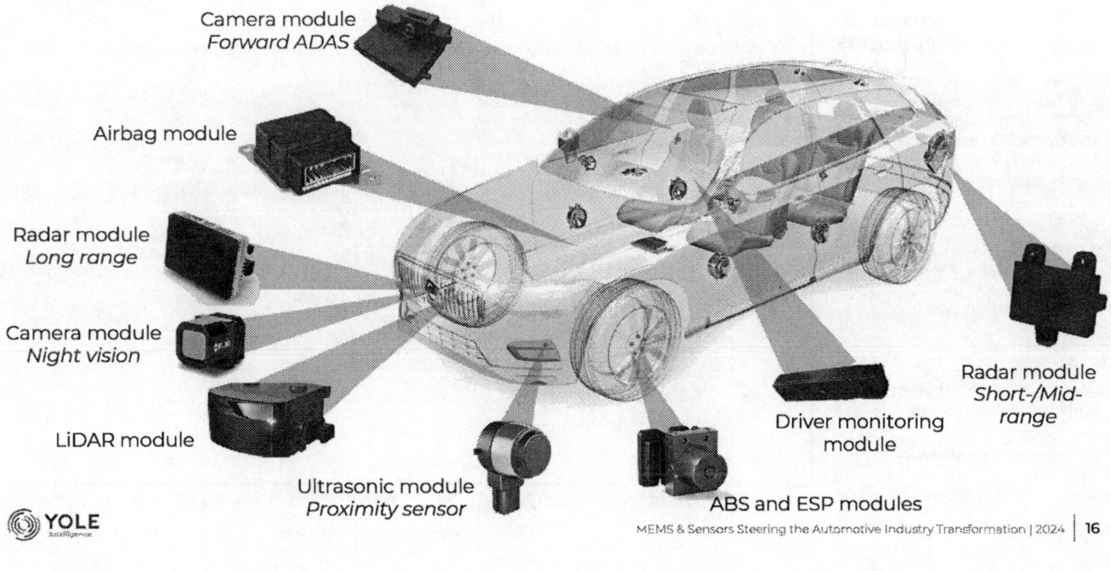

YOLE Intelligence

MEMS & Sensors Steering the Automotive Industry Transformation | 2024 | 16

ADAS & SAFETY

Sensing technology roadmaps

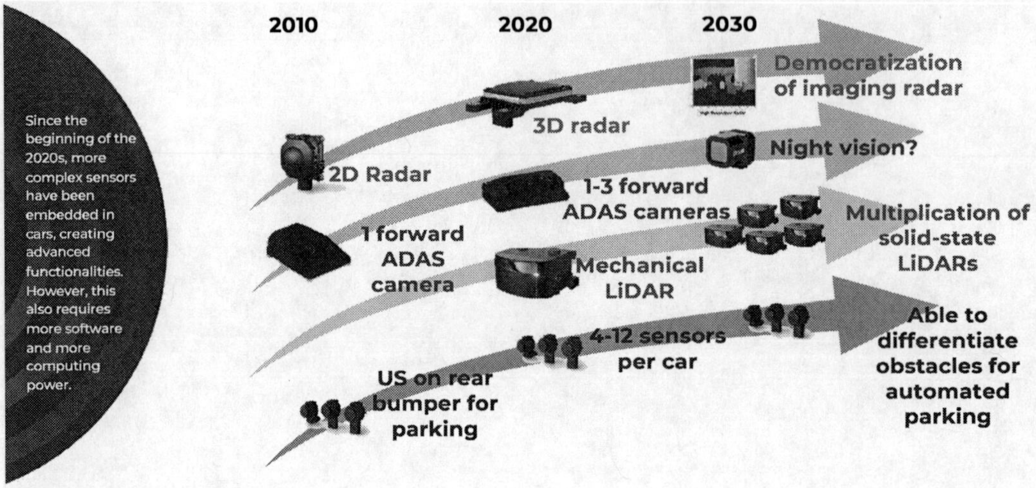

ADAS & SAFETY

Driver monitoring – Technology roadmap

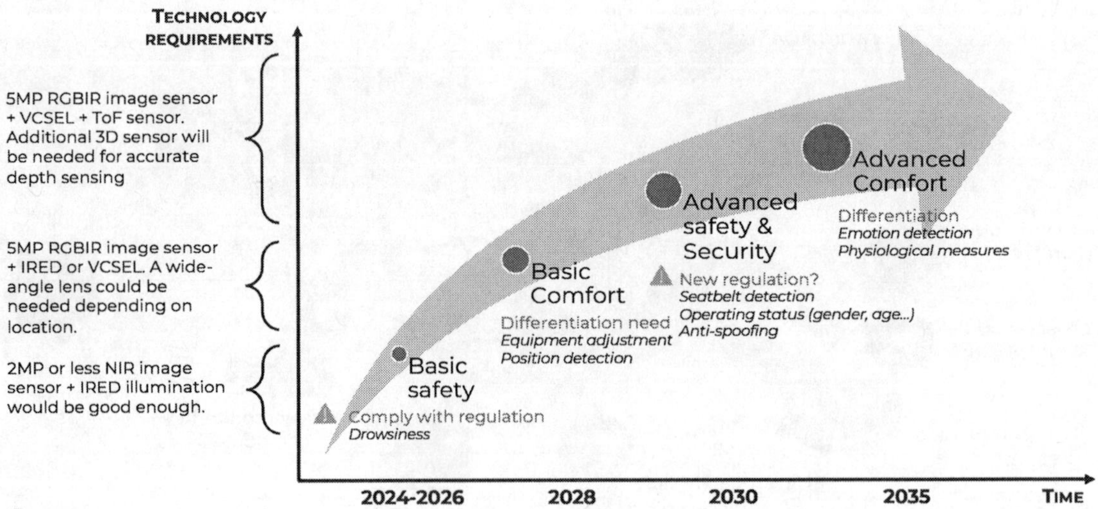

From infotainment to chassis...

A complete sensorization of cars!

SENSORIZATION OF CARS

Evolution of braking systems

We expect brake-by-wire technologies to become mandatory in the future, especially in xEVs. And for accurate braking management, position sensors will also be mandatory.

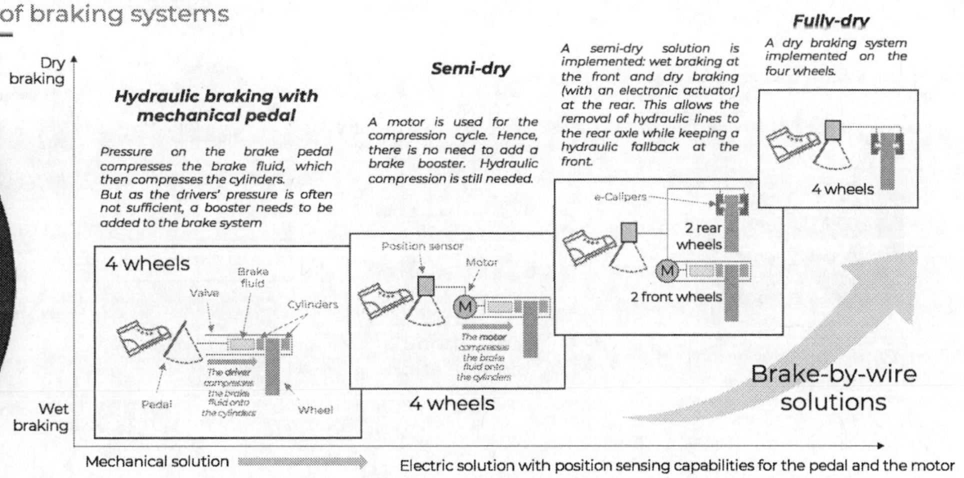

- Hydraulic fluid must be replaced regularly and needs bulky pumps, gears, etc., which is an inconvenience for car users (maintenance). Moreover, with autonomous driving mega-trends, it is becoming mandatory for cars to have electrically-driven braking systems.
- As with Electronic Parking Assist (now mainstream in current car models), we expect brake-by-wire solutions to increase their presence in the coming years.

SENSORIZATION OF CARS
HVAC and in-cabin ventilation: what's at stake

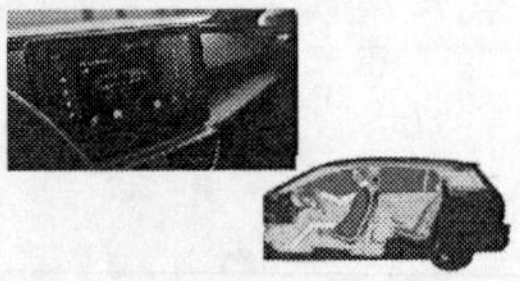

It has become mandatory to improve the comfort/driving conditions for car drivers and passengers as much as possible.
Hence, an enhanced air conditioning system with in-cabin/outdoor temperature and humidity sensors is needed.

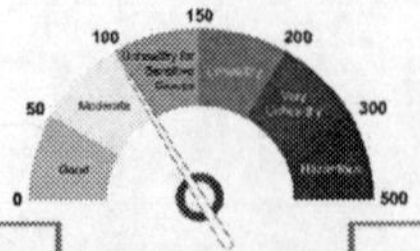

Comfort ⟷ Security

↑

Efficiency

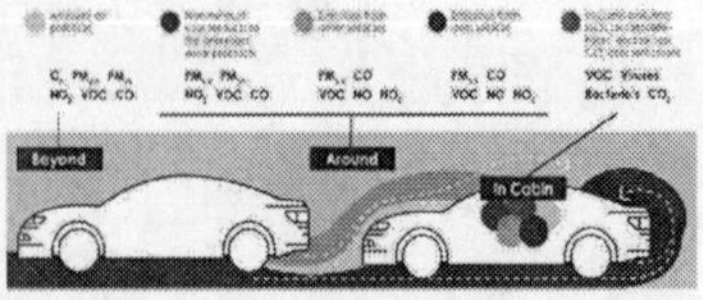

Air pollution is a significant risk factor for several health conditions, including respiratory infections, heart disease, stroke, and lung cancer.

As with the air quality at home or in the office, **in-cabin air quality has become a global concern** worldwide these last few years. A car driving ahead of you releases gases and particles that can enter your vehicle.

Ventilating car cabins is mandatory, as the driver's drowsiness is proportional to the CO_2 concentration in the air.
However, when it's cold, the incoming fresh air needs to be heated, which is power-hungry.
Hence, optimizing the ventilation process using air recirculation mechanisms and CO_2 sensors is essential.
→ Instead of constantly letting in fresh air that needs to be heated, the system recycles the in-cabin air while the level of CO_2 is low enough.

Additionally, by improving the power efficiency of the car (by reducing the power consumption of the air heater), xEV ranges can be increased.

IF: CO_2 level < threshold
→ recycle air
ELSE:
→ let new air enter the car
→ heat it
→ wait for the CO_2 level to drop below the threshold
→ back to first condition

YOLE Intelligence

SENSORIZATION OF CARS
From pressure monitoring to smart TPMS

By collecting the pressure sensor data and compensating for the temperature drift. Thanks to the accelerometer, the pressure is only measured when the car is moving.

One-time pressure measurement

Identifying which TPMS module is mounted on which wheel (no need to have a pairing process) based on the acceleration pattern of sensors

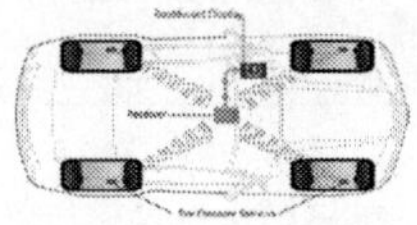

TPMS module identification

By analyzing the accelerometer data during each cycle

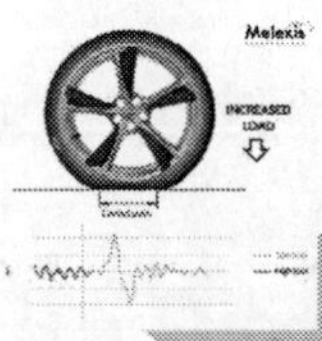

Load detection

By analyzing the evolution of the rolling characteristics of the tire

Tread depth

2030?

SMART TPMS: T° sensor, Pressure, High-end Accelerometer, + **software** (on edge or on car controllers) AI

Currently

Current TPMS: Basic Accelerometer, Pressure, T° sensor

2010+

YOLE Intelligence

Takeaway

CONCLUSION

- The automotive industry keeps flourishing, with the **electrification** of cars and **ADAS** pushing innovation further!

- Sensors are at the heart of these mega-trends.
  - 6.5 billion sensors for the automotive market were shipped in 2023 globally, generating **$9.3B** in revenue. And with a 7% revenue $CAGR_{23\text{-}29}$, we expect it will grow to **$14.3B** in 2029 with 8.8 billion sensors shipped worldwide.

- The upcoming years are poised to witness a dynamic transformation in automotive sensor technology driven by advancements in ADAS, autonomous driving, electrification, and the widespread adoption of sensors across global car fleets

→ Consequently, substantial reorganization within the industry and its supply chain is anticipated.

THANK YOU VERY MUCH!

Status of the MEMS Industry 2023
(2024 coming soon...)

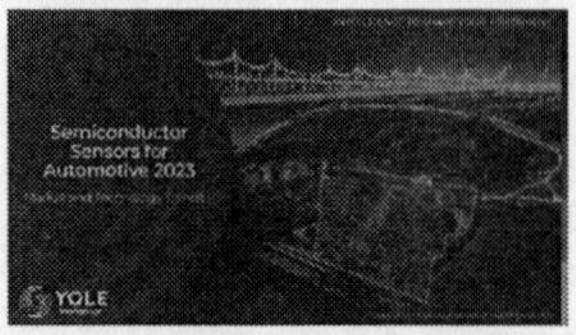

Semiconductor Sensors for Automotive 2024

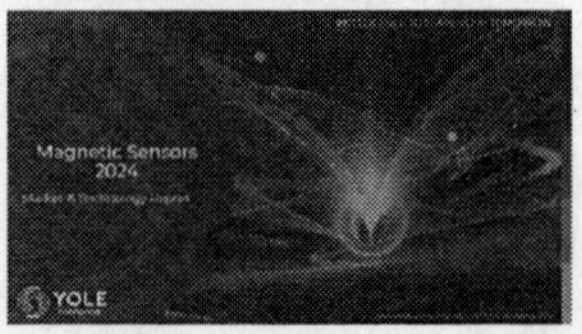

Magnetic Sensors 2024

If you have questions, please feel free to contact me by email

pierre.delbos@yolegroup.com

Sensors
Converge
X-FAB's Microsystems from MEMS to Advanced Packaging
June 24–26, 2024 | Santa Clara, CA
#SensorsConverge
Stijn.Sampermans@xfab.com

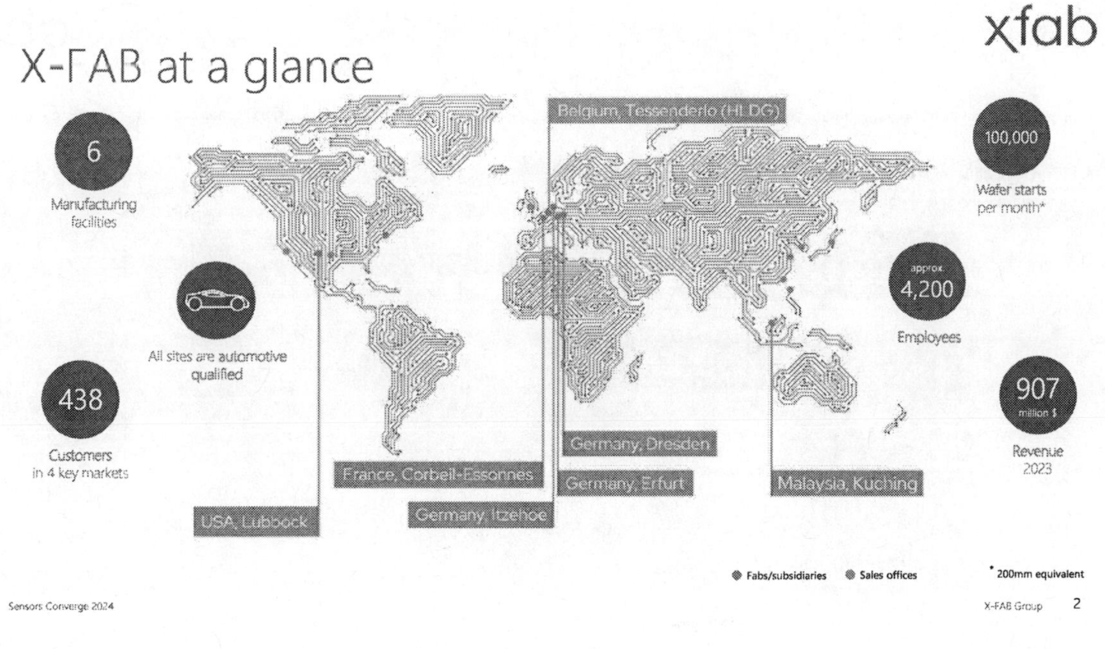
X-FAB at a glance
xfab
6
Manufacturing facilities
All sites are automotive qualified
438
Customers in 4 key markets
Belgium, Tessenderlo (HLDG)
USA, Lubbock
France, Corbeil-Essonnes
Germany, Itzehoe
Germany, Dresden
Germany, Erfurt
Malaysia, Kuching
100,000
Wafer starts per month*
approx.
4,200
Employees
907
million $
Revenue 2023
Fabs/subsidiaries
Sales offices
* 200mm equivalent
Sensors Converge 2024
X-FAB Group
2

xfab

Our comprehensive technology portfolio

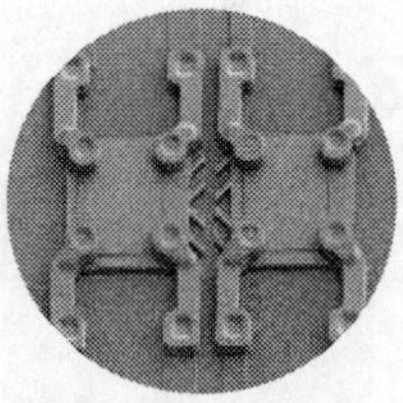

HV CMOS & SOI

- High voltage expertise with integration of various functionalities on one chip operating at high temperatures

MEMS/Microsystems

- MEMS with or without integrated CMOS
- Functional surfaces and Microfluidics
- Advanced Packaging and heterogeneous integration

SiC & GaN

- 6-inch silicon carbide
- 8-inch gallium nitride on silicon

MEMS – Micro-electromechanical system

Sensors Converge 2024 X-FAB Group 3

xfab

X-FAB is a Pure- Play Foundry

- Focus on complex technology, design support and manufacturing solutions.
- Provide open access to state-of-the-art semiconductor technologies for innovative electronic systems.
- X-FAB does not have own products, as it does not want to compete with its customers

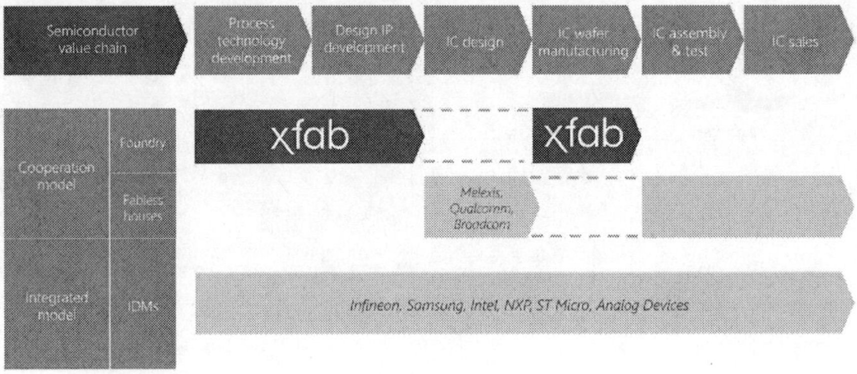

Sensors Converge 2024 X-FAB Group 4

X-FAB Microsystems business model

xfab

A company in the semiconductor industry specialized in the manufacture of microsystems

We are a pure-play **foundry**.

„Value add“ (AHSI) on X-FAB and alien-wafers on behalf of customers

Foundries create supply chains for customers! What are the expectations?

xfab

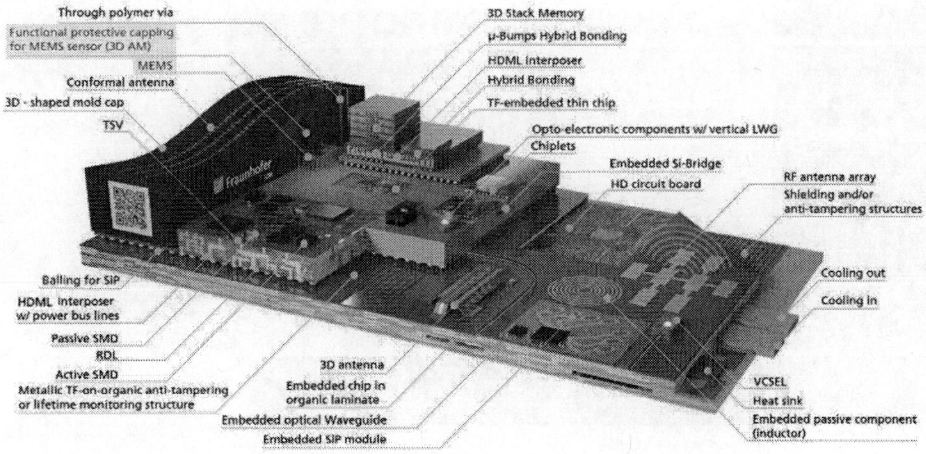

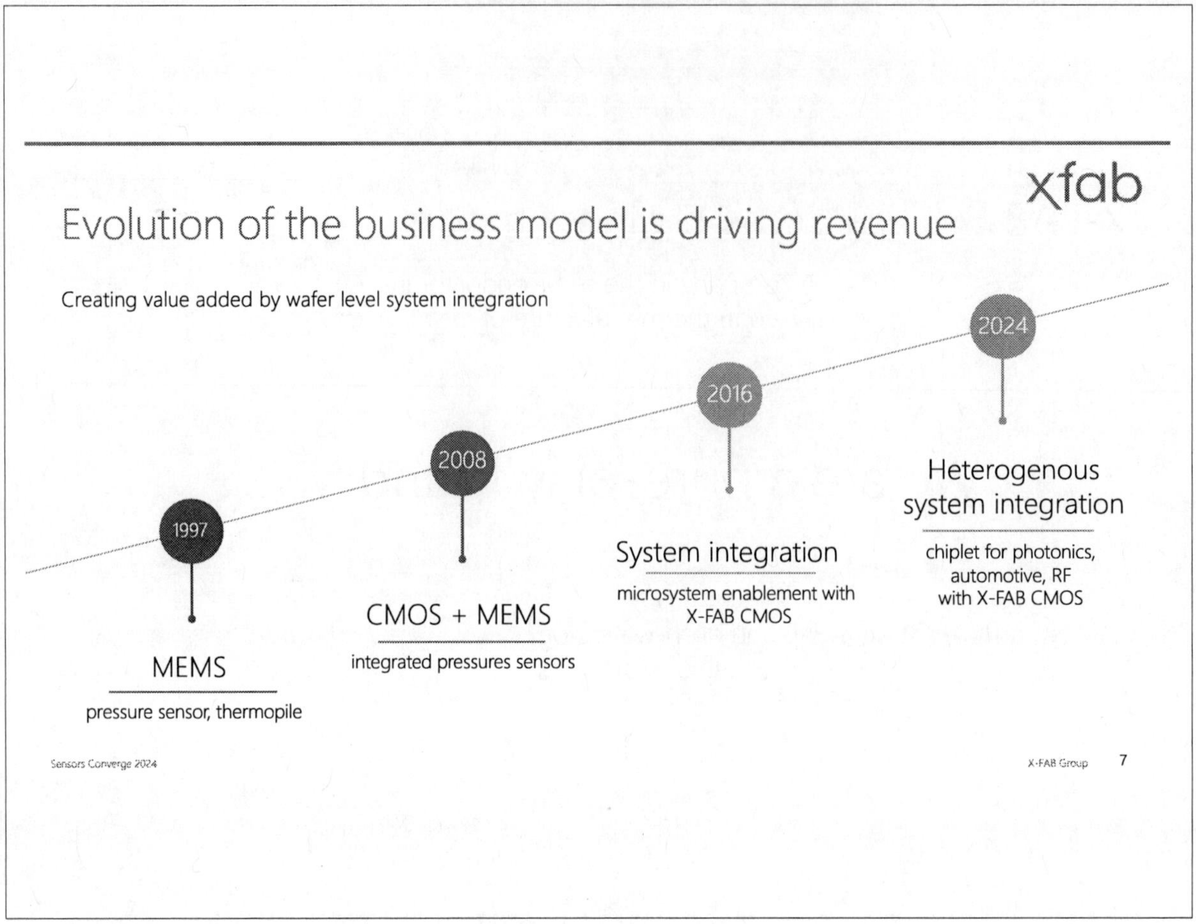
xfab
Evolution of the business model is driving revenue
Creating value added by wafer level system integration
1997
MEMS
pressure sensor, thermopile
2008
CMOS + MEMS
integrated pressures sensors
2016
System integration
microsystem enablement with X-FAB CMOS
2024
Heterogenous system integration
chiplet for photonics, automotive, RF with X-FAB CMOS
Sensors Converge 2024
X-FAB Group
7

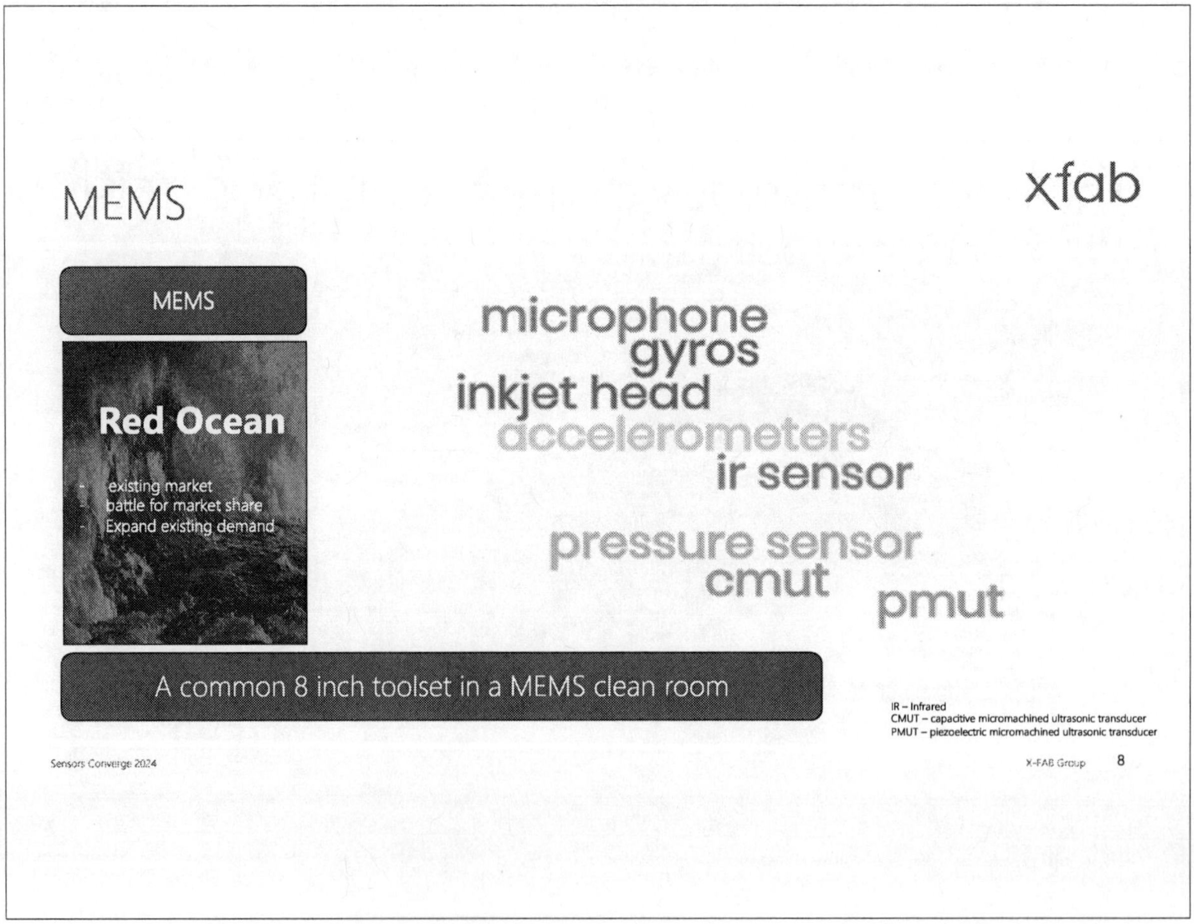
MEMS
xfab
MEMS
Red Ocean
- existing market
- battle for market share
- Expand existing demand
microphone
gyros
inkjet head
accelerometers
ir sensor
pressure sensor
cmut
pmut
A common 8 inch toolset in a MEMS clean room
IR – Infrared
CMUT – capacitive micromachined ultrasonic transducer
PMUT – piezoelectric micromachined ultrasonic transducer
Sensors Converge 2024
X-FAB Group
8

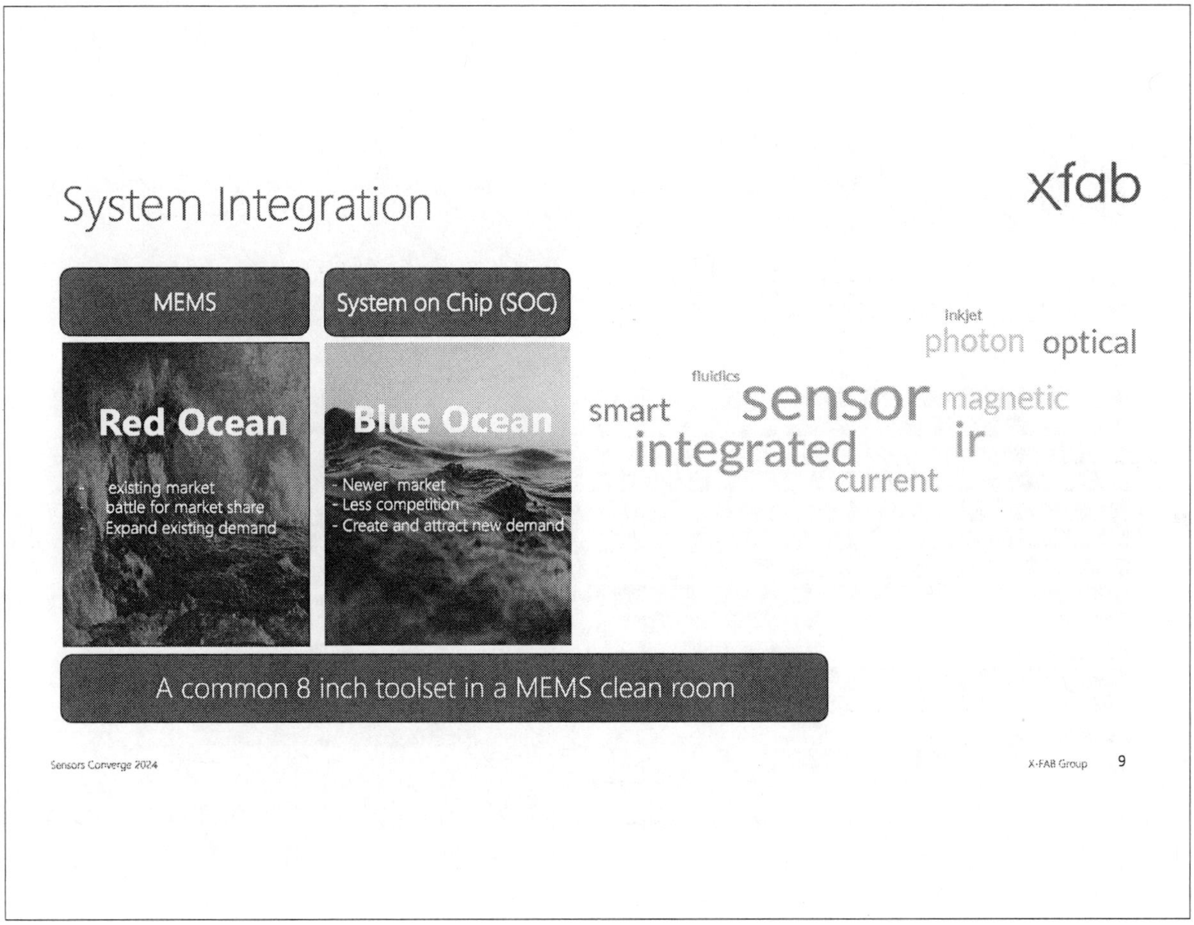
System Integration
xfab
MEMS
System on Chip (SOC)
Red Ocean
- existing market
- battle for market share
- Expand existing demand
Blue Ocean
- Newer market
- Less competition
- Create and attract new demand
inkjet
photon
optical
fluidics
smart
sensor
magnetic
integrated
ir
current
A common 8 inch toolset in a MEMS clean room
Sensors Converge 2024
X-FAB Group
9

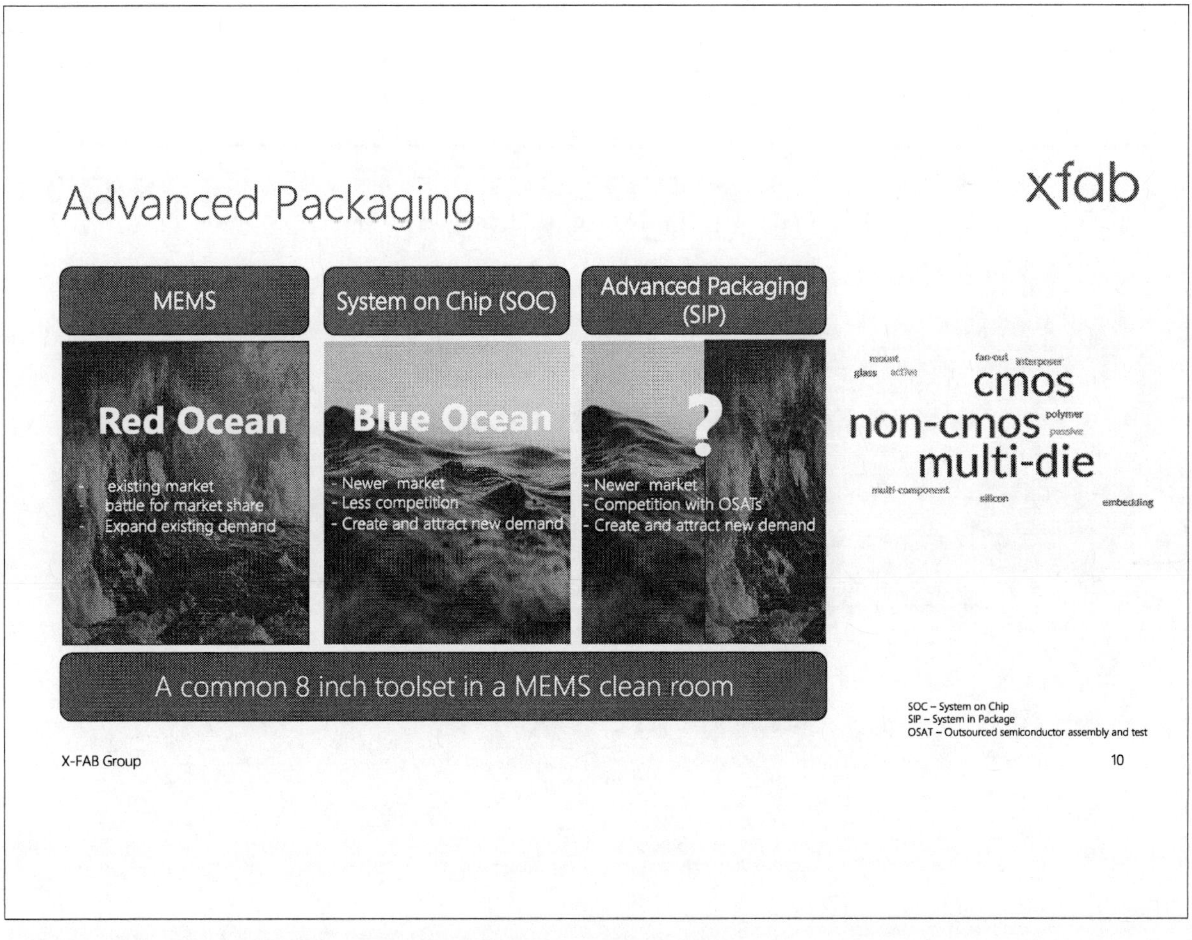
Advanced Packaging
xfab
MEMS
System on Chip (SOC)
Advanced Packaging (SIP)
Red Ocean
- existing market
- battle for market share
- Expand existing demand
Blue Ocean
- Newer market
- Less competition
- Create and attract new demand
?
- Newer market
- Competition with OSATs
- Create and attract new demand
mount
fan-out
interposer
glass
active
cmos
non-cmos
polymer
passive
multi-die
multi-component
silicon
embedding
A common 8 inch toolset in a MEMS clean room
SOC – System on Chip
SIP – System in Package
OSAT – Outsourced semiconductor assembly and test
X-FAB Group
10

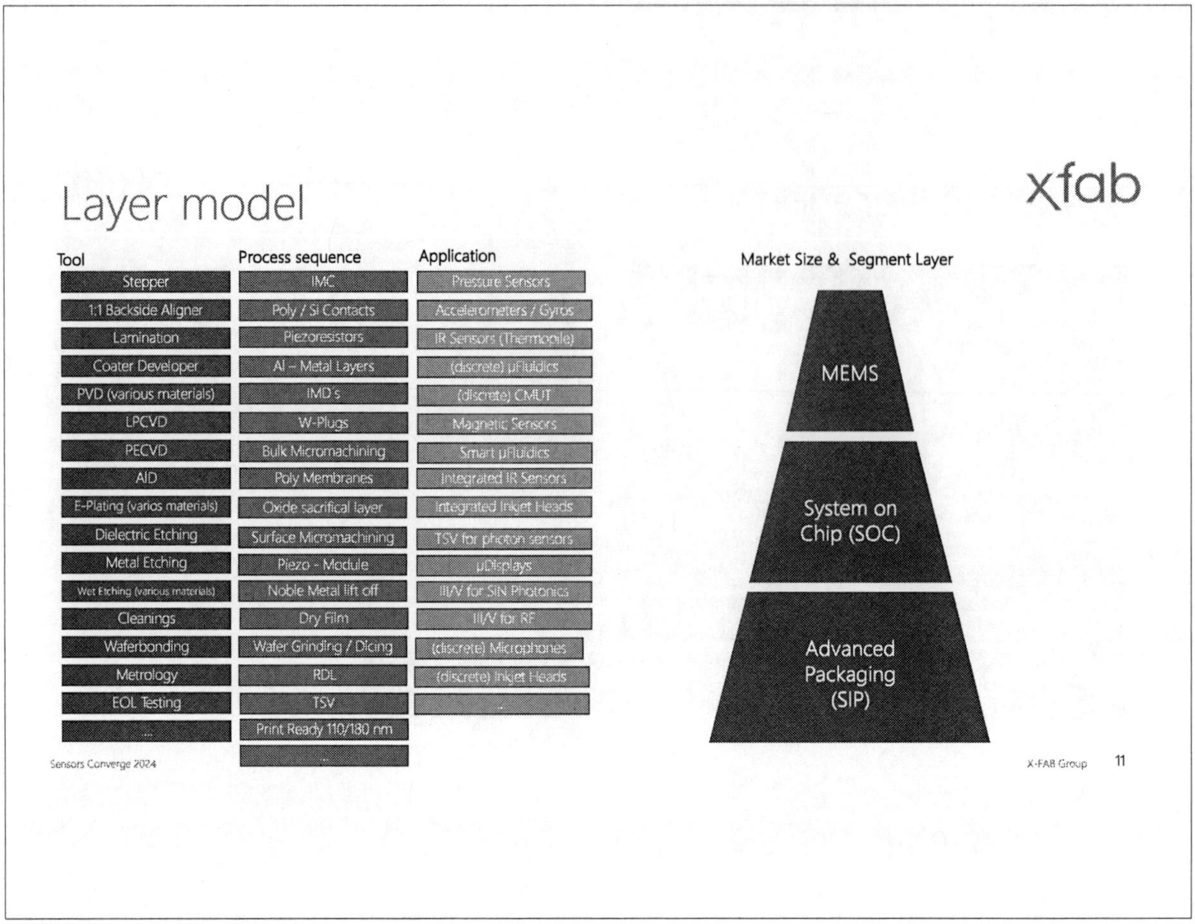
Layer model
xfab
Tool
Stepper
1:1 Backside Aligner
Lamination
Coater Developer
PVD (various materials)
LPCVD
PECVD
AlD
E-Plating (varios materials)
Dielectric Etching
Metal Etching
Wet Etching (various materials)
Cleanings
Waferbonding
Metrology
EOL Testing
...
Process sequence
IMC
Poly / Si Contacts
Piezoresistors
Al – Metal Layers
IMD's
W-Plugs
Bulk Micromachining
Poly Membranes
Oxide sacrifical layer
Surface Micromachining
Piezo - Module
Noble Metal lift off
Dry Film
Wafer Grinding / Dicing
RDL
TSV
Print Ready 110/180 nm
...
Application
Pressure Sensors
Accelerometers / Gyros
IR Sensors (Thermopile)
(discrete) µFluidics
(discrete) CMUT
Magnetic Sensors
Smart µFluidics
Integrated IR Sensors
Integrated Inkjet Heads
TSV for photon sensors
µDisplays
III/V for SiN Photonics
III/V for RF
(discrete) Microphones
(discrete) Inkjet Heads
...
Market Size & Segment Layer
MEMS
System on Chip (SOC)
Advanced Packaging (SIP)
Sensors Converge 2024
X-FAB Group
11

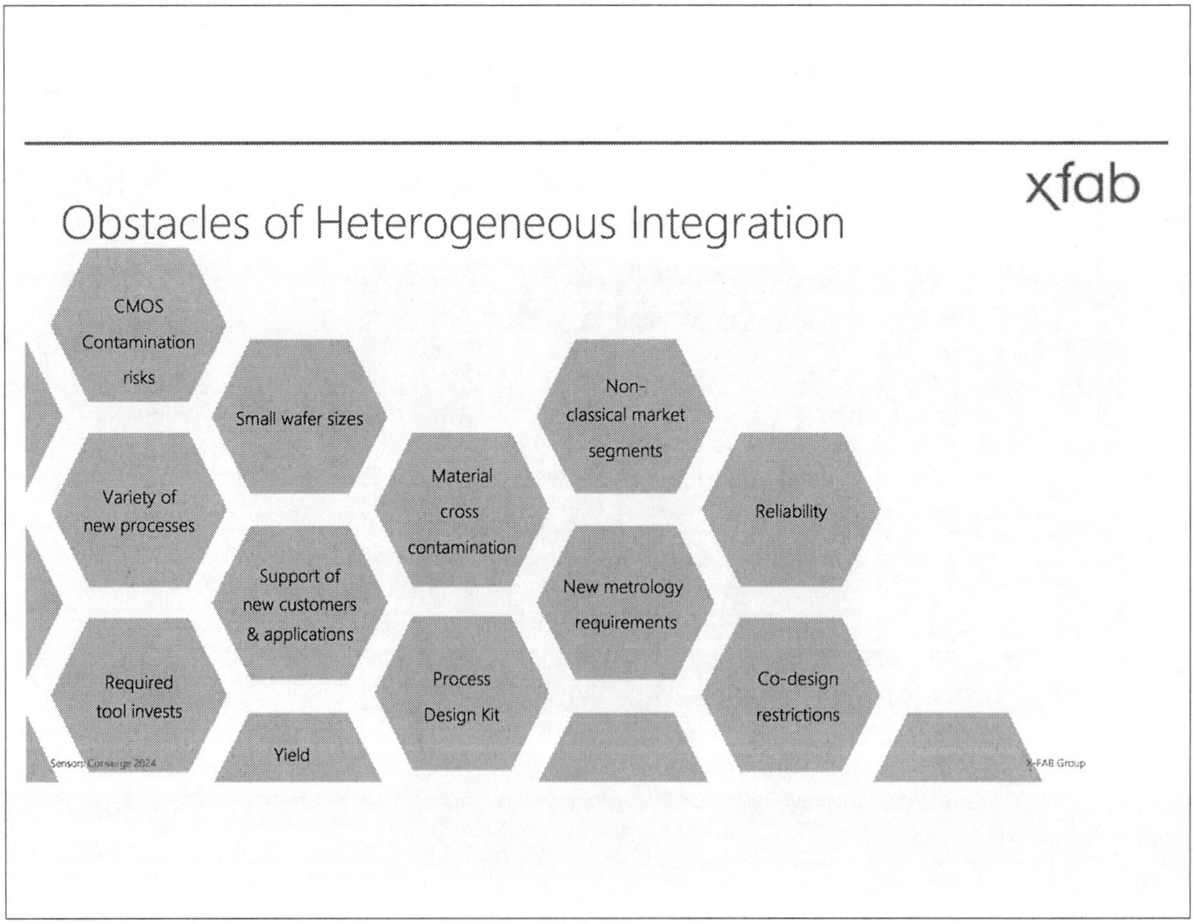
Obstacles of Heterogeneous Integration
xfab
CMOS Contamination risks
Small wafer sizes
Non-classical market segments
Material cross contamination
Reliability
Variety of new processes
Support of new customers & applications
New metrology requirements
Required tool invests
Process Design Kit
Co-design restrictions
Yield
Sensors Converge 2024
X-FAB Group

Process and Design Co-development is Key

xfab

Customer & X-FAB collaboration space

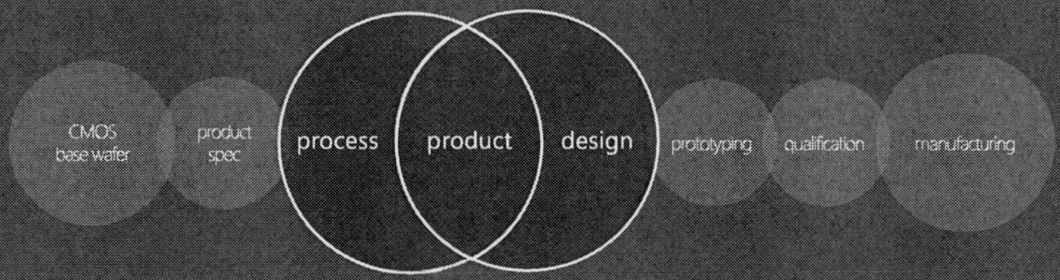

Innovation increases product **value**

Customised projects but with **higher** reward and substantial **customer commitment**

Scaling challenges

13

SIP and SOC foundry business model challenges

xfab

- Profitable growth in high fix cost environment
  - Non-CMOS clean room , tool / chamber dedications
  - Large, seldom fully utilized, tool set
- MEMS, HI and CMOS expertise
- Long time to market
  - Proof of concept at RTO + supply chain enablement by foundry
  - Fractured RTO landscape / FedEX approach
  - One of kind tool set
- High industrialization costs low volume environment
- Focus vs. reuse
  - Custom specific developments creates high opportunity cost environment

the Valley of Death

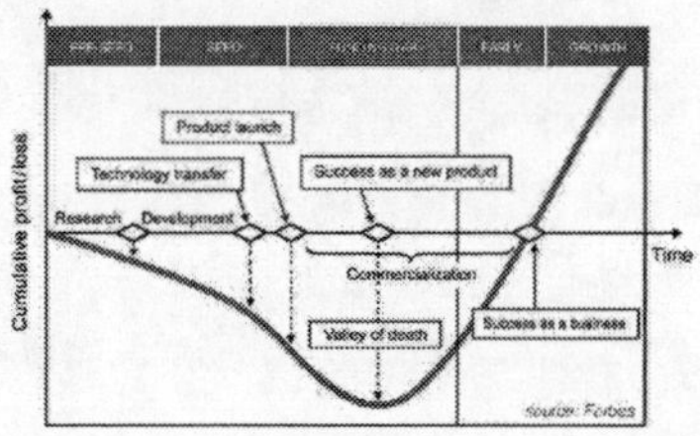

RTO- research and technology organization
HI-Heterogeneous Integration
SOC – System on Chip
SIP – System in Package

Sensors Converge 2024

X-FAB Group 14

Solutions to avoid / survive the valley of death

xfab

- Quick time to market and high volume
  - Select right opportunity & partner
- Support
  - EU or US Chips Act , China government, IPCEI
- RTO collaboration
  - IMEC , LETI , Fraunhofer / FMD
- Take your time
  - Focus & reuse

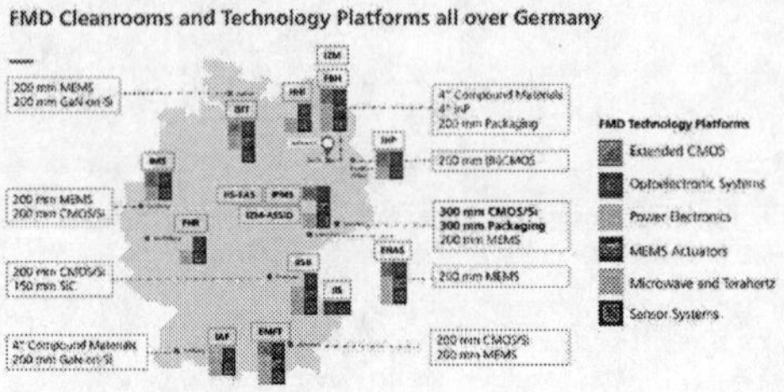

Market pull utilizing 3D / HI technologies

xfab

- Market pull
  - HPC
  - Automotive lighting
  - Photonics
  - Si µFluidic
  - FIR Sensors

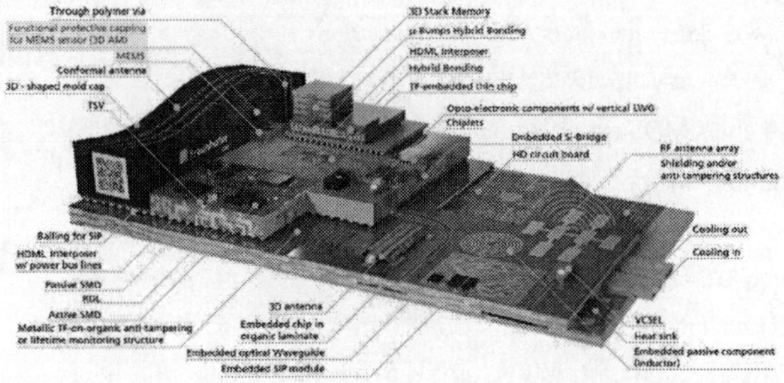

HPC –High Performance Computing

xfab

Application: Examples

X-FAB Group 17

xfab

Wireless Communication: Micro Transfer Printing

- GaAs offers higher electron mobility and improved sensitivity of Hall Plate sensors compared to standard Si.

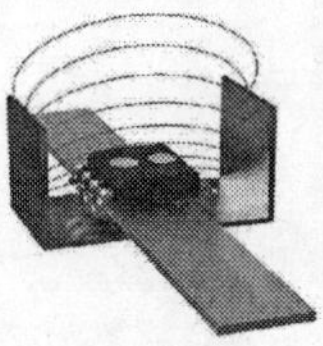

- GaN/GaAS HEMTs: fabrication as discrete devices and integration on Si ASICs as high power, high voltage or RF switches.

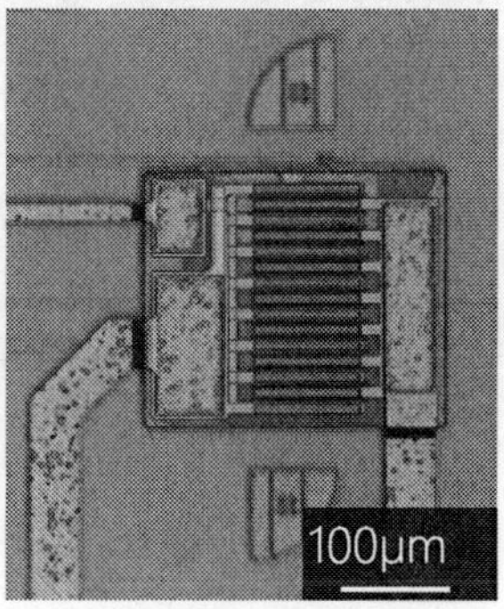

Sensors Converge 2024 X-FAB Group 18

Photonics: Micro Transfer Printing MicroLED

xfab

MicroLED displays are based on crystalline gallium nitride (GaN) and indium gallium aluminum phosphide (InGaAlP) semiconductors that are capable of new levels of brightness and efficiency unmatchable by OLED or LCD. Unlike OLED displays, microLED does not suffer from screen burn-in.

MicroLED displays offer:

- Perfect Blacks
- Excellent Color
- Near-Perfect Off-angle Viewing
- Brighter than OLED
- Slimmer than OLED
- Immune to Burn-in

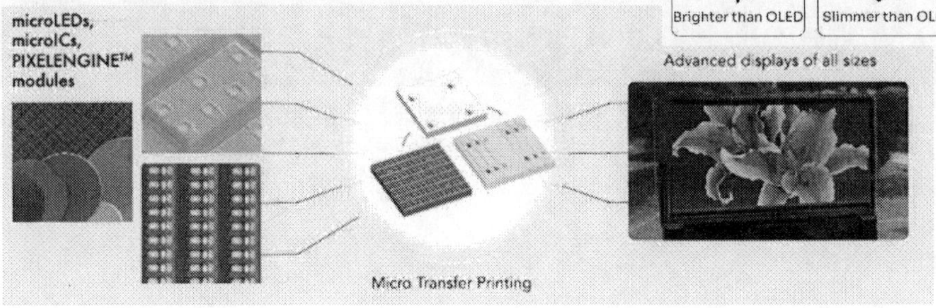

Xdisplay™

Automotive: MicroLED Headlights

xfab

ams OSRAM

xfab

Biomedical: DNA Sequencing

Fastest DNA sequencing technique done at Stanford with X-FAB Technology helps an undiagnosed patients find answers in 5 h and 2 min

› **Applications:**
- High throughput sequencing
- Larger genomes or projects
- Population-scale sequencing
- Highly multiplexed small genomes or targeted regions
- Whole transcriptomes (direct RNA or cDNA)

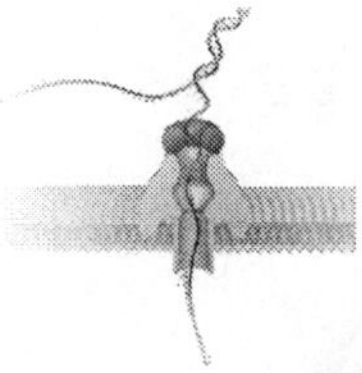

Researchers were able to quickly determine that Matthew Kunzman's heart failure was the result of a genetic condition — a finding that cleared the way for him to be placed on a heart transplant list immediately.
Courtesy of Jenny Kunzman

Oxford NANOPORE Technologies

https://med.stanford.edu/news/all-news/2022/01/dna-sequencing-technique.html

xfab

Medical/Personal Health care: FIR Sensor

› Main target market: Medical grade skin temperature & health monitoring wearables and mobile phones
- Continuous monitoring by non-contact measurement (more reliable)
- Use case: fertility tracking, infection detection, heat stress, sleep tracking

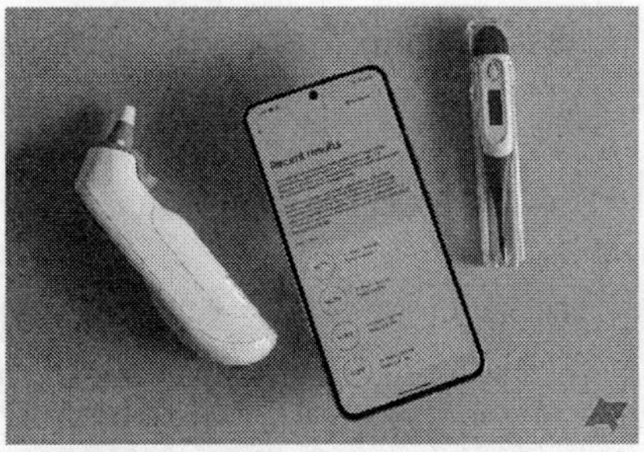

Melexis
INSPIRED ENGINEERING

Medical Micro Transfer Printing Stroke detection

xfab

- Application: *in-vivo* brain stroke sensor determining the provoking tissue by capacitative measurements.

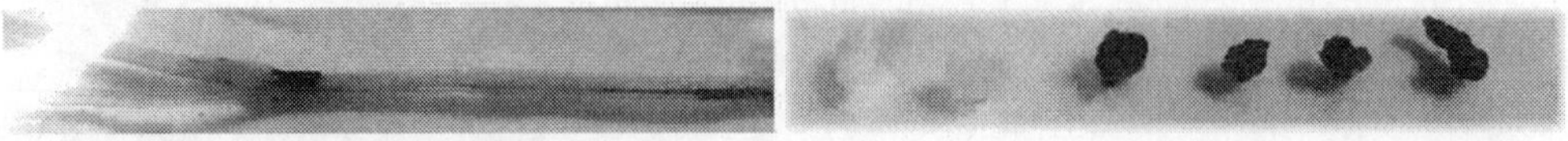

- Sensor ASICs (XT018) are transferred onto a thin polyimide layer that carries the metallization and enables a wrapping around the tip of a a guide wire.

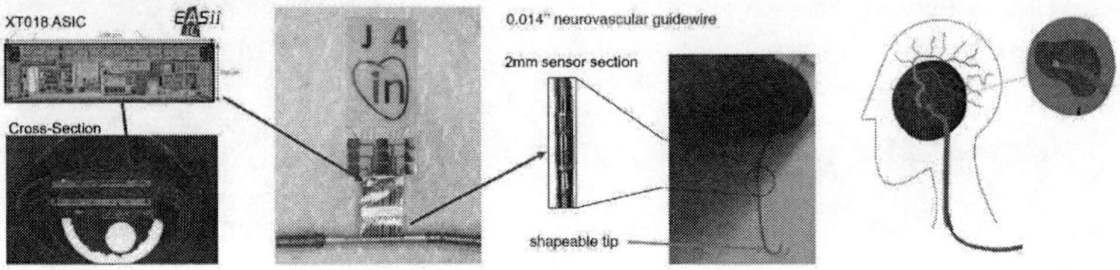

xfab

Thank you.

www.xfab.com

Sensors Converge

Environmental Sensors

Making your Home, Building and City Smarter

Ryotaro Sakauchi, Senior Manager Business Development

Robert Bosch LLC

June 24–26, 2024 | Santa Clara, CA

#SensorsConverge

Sensors in CE and IOT Applications

Smartphones

Hearables

Wearables

AR/VR Glasses & Headsets

Laptops & Tablets

Robots & Drones

Gaming & TV

IoT, Whitegoods, Smart Home

BOSCH

From Motion Sensing to Environmental Sensing

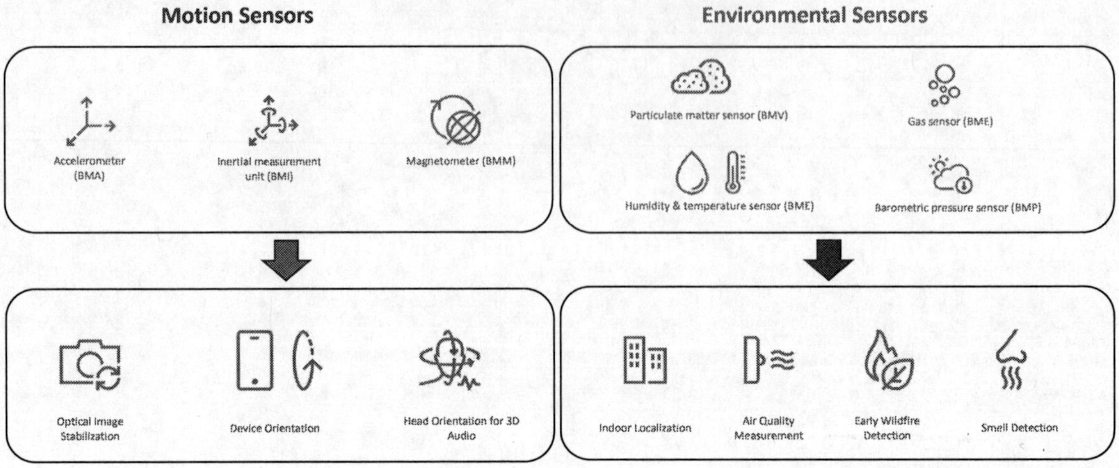

BOSCH

Impact of Sensors on our Everyday Lives

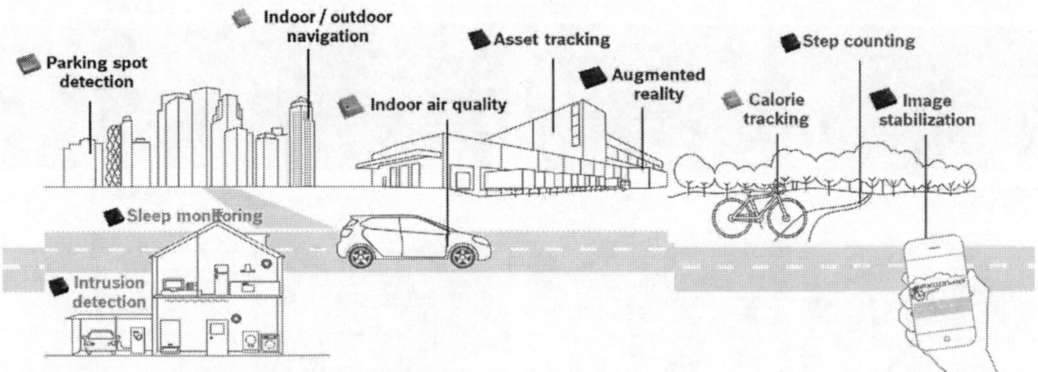

BOSCH

Indoor Localization with Pressure Sensors

- Accurate altitude detection helps to localize people where GPS signals are not available.
- Access to floor level information of smartphone users gives first responders crucial information to potentially save thousands of lives.
- Height information plays a crucial role for standard power Wi-Fi Access Points when transmitting in the 6 GHz spectrum.

5 BST/BUD-NA | 2024-06-05

BOSCH

Advancements in Pressure Sensor Technology

From piezo resistive sensing principle to capacitive sensing principle

Walking stairs

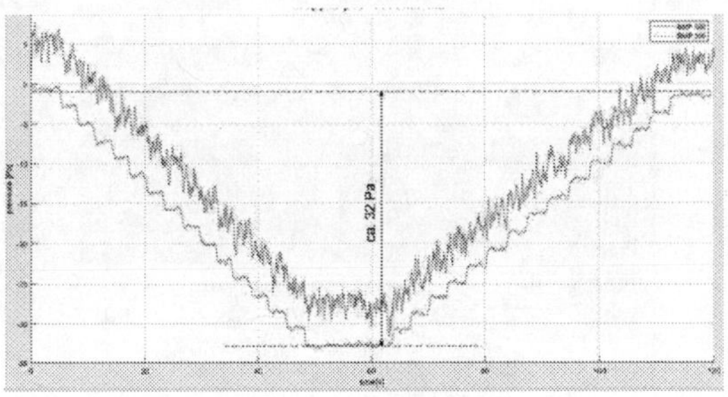

Floor detection

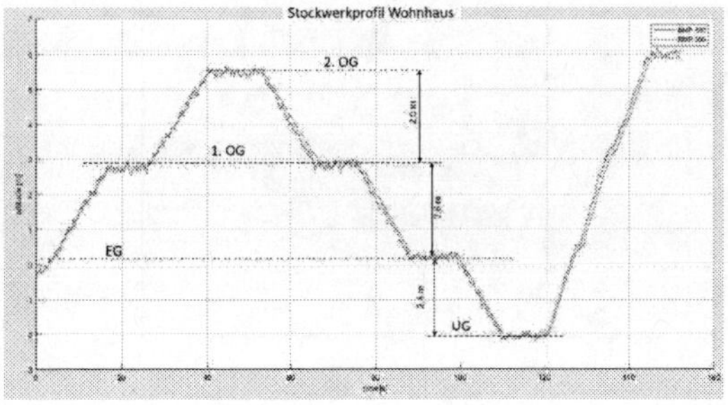

6 BST/BUD-NA | 2024-06-05

BOSCH

Air Quality Detection with Gas Sensors

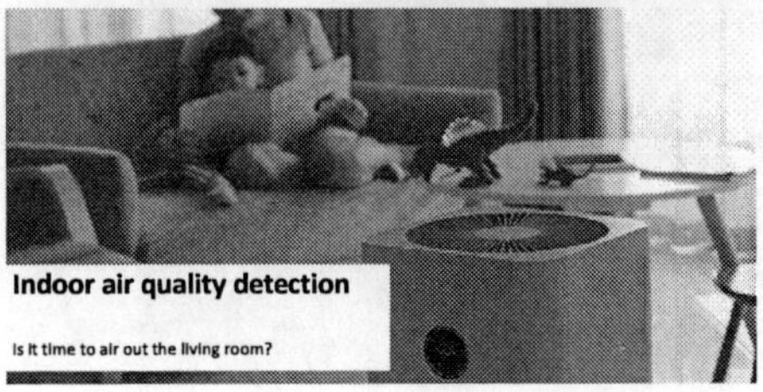

BOSCH

What's inside a Gas Sensor?

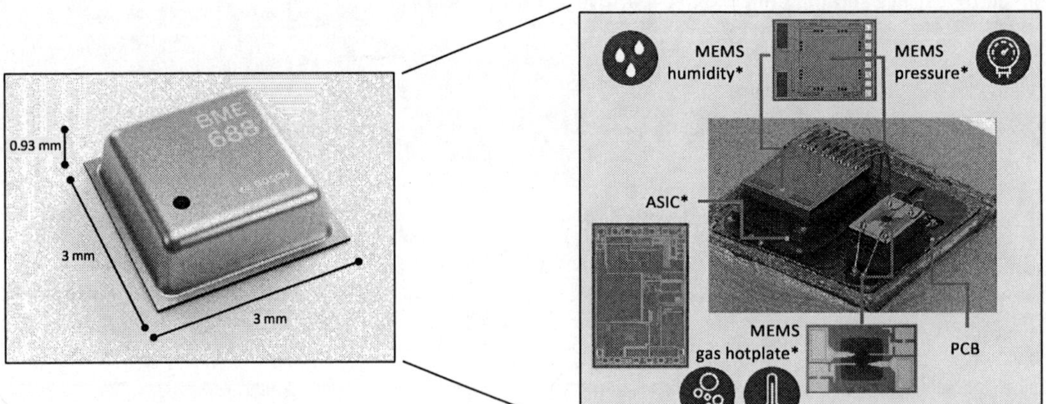

*Source: System Plus Consulting | BME680

BOSCH

Advances in Particle Sensing

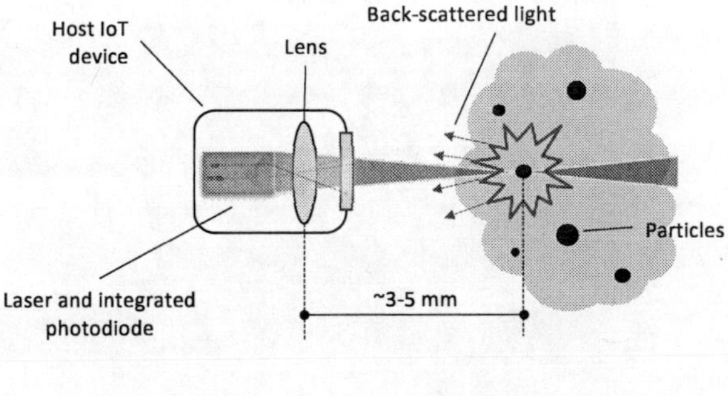

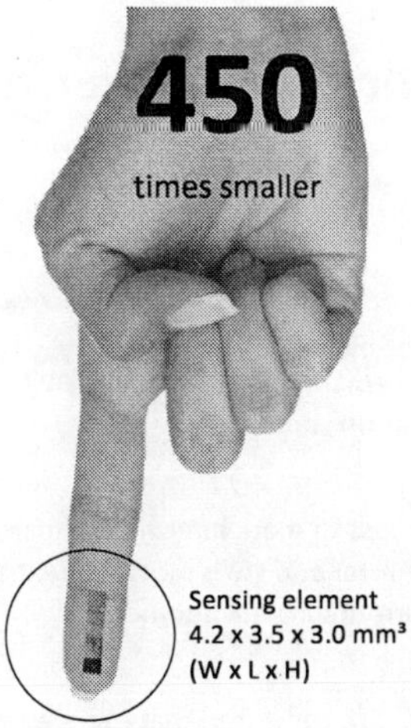

Sensor design with **integrated laser & photodiodes** projected to ambient air looking for particles and fine dust

Particles pass laser focus, **back-scattered light is measured** by the integrated photodiodes

PM concentration measured in µg/m³

BOSCH

Making your Home, Building and City smarter

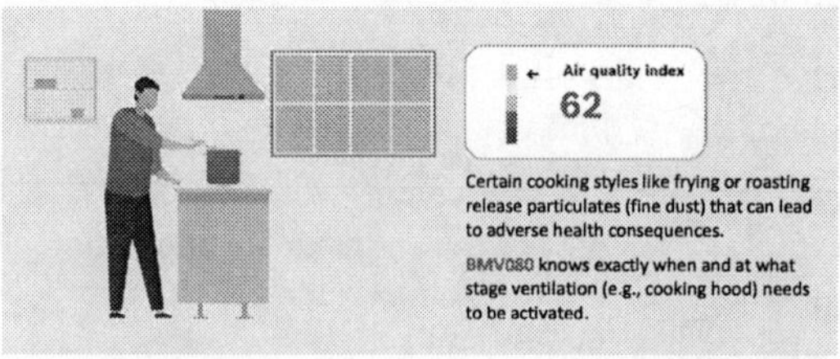

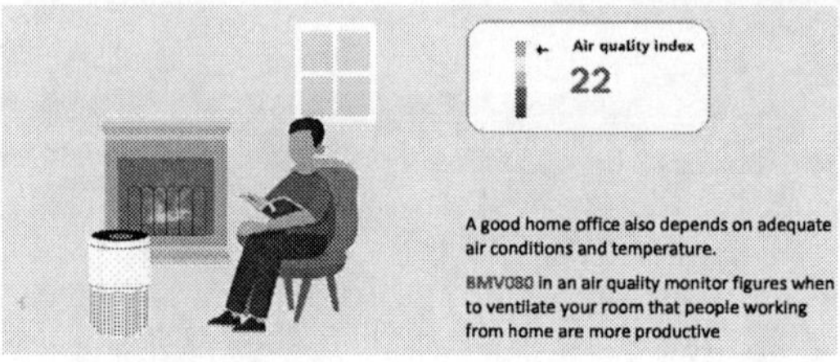

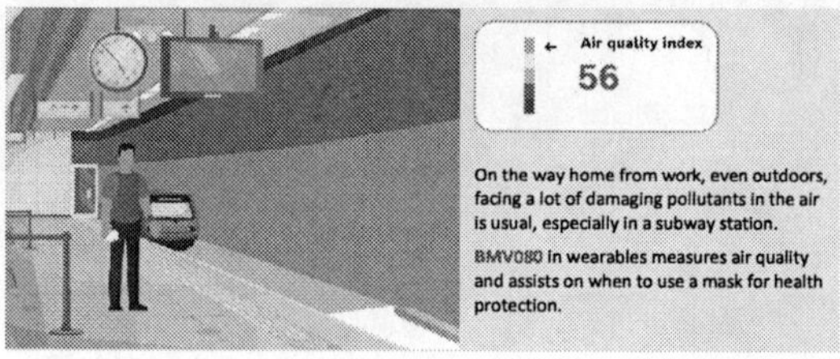

BOSCH

Connecting the Environment

- Environmental sensors add a new element to existing applications and gives it access to information that is not available through traditional motion sensors.
- Access to more information makes the application smarter and gives more context about the surrounding environment.
- We are convinced that more environmental context in consumer electronics will influence the health and safety of the end user.

BOSCH

GET IN TOUCH WITH US
@BoschMEMS
www.bosch-sensortec.com
community.bosch-sensortec.com
linkedin.com/company/bosch-sensortec
youtube.com/user/BoschSensortec
BOSCH

Sensors Converge

Latest advances in Piezo MEMS and the route to rapid volume production

June 24, 2024 | Santa Clara, CA

Matteo Fusi
Product Marketing Director
STMicroelectronics

#SensorsConverge

What do humans expect from technology today?

Sustainable | Technologies that **protect** and **help humans protect** the planet

Source: IEA

Two sides of the same coin

New MEMS products and applications able to **save energy** and improve **overall system efficiency**

New **sustainable technologies and materials**, which help humans to protect the planet

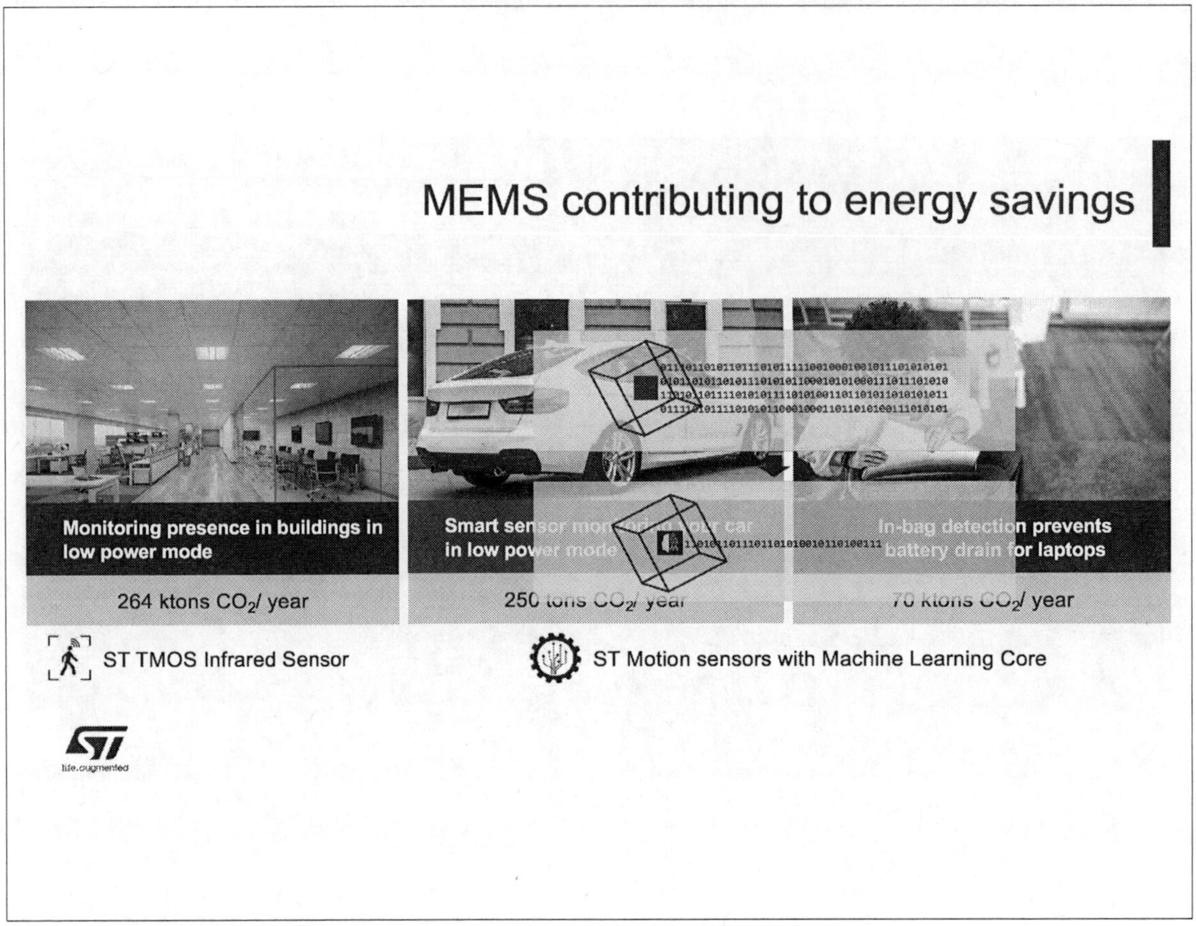
MEMS contributing to energy savings
Monitoring presence in buildings in low power mode
264 ktons CO_2/ year
Smart se
in low po
n prevents
for laptops
CO_2/ year
ST TMOS Infrared Sensor
ST Motion sensors with Machine Learning Core
life.augmented

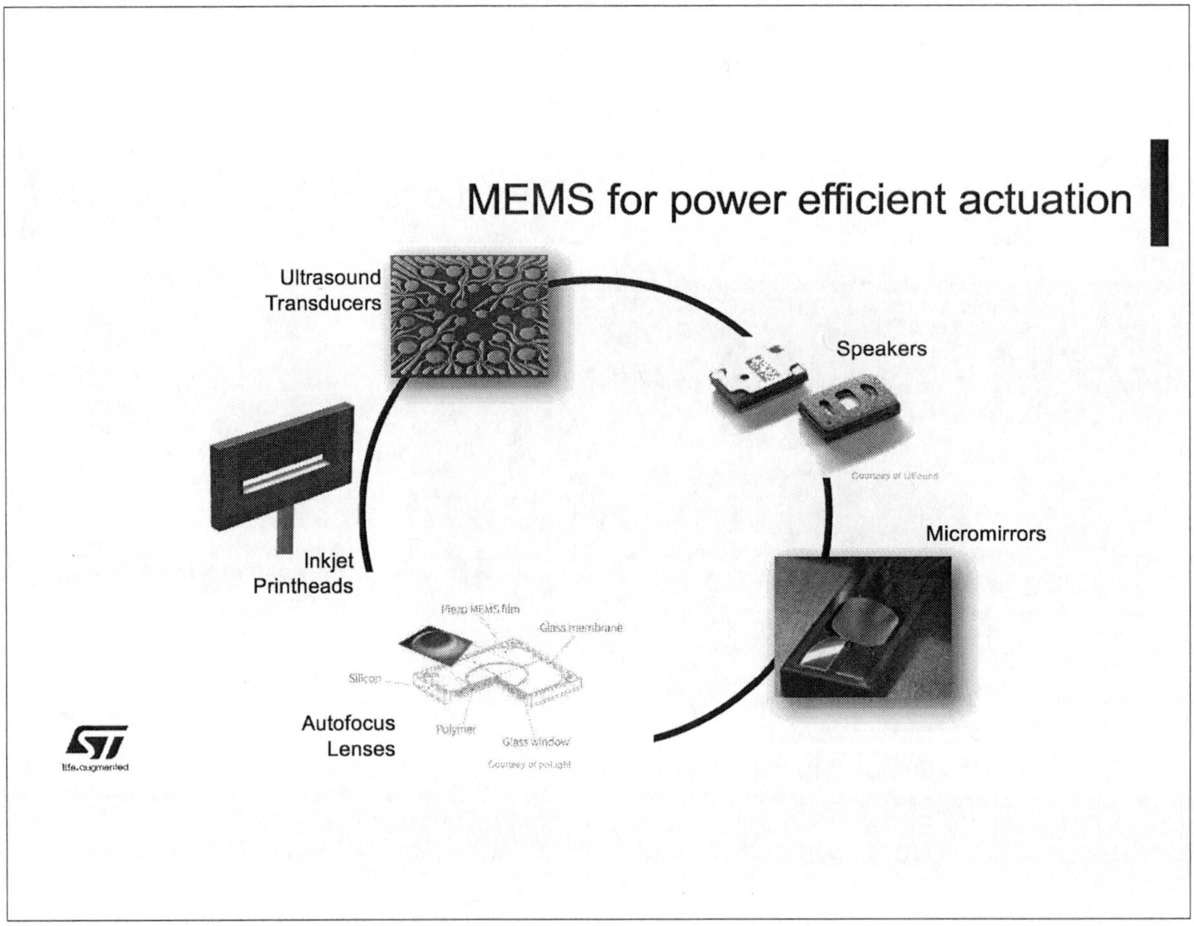
MEMS for power efficient actuation
Ultrasound Transducers
Speakers
Micromirrors
Inkjet Printheads
Autofocus Lenses
life.augmented

Piezo materials for MEMS actuators

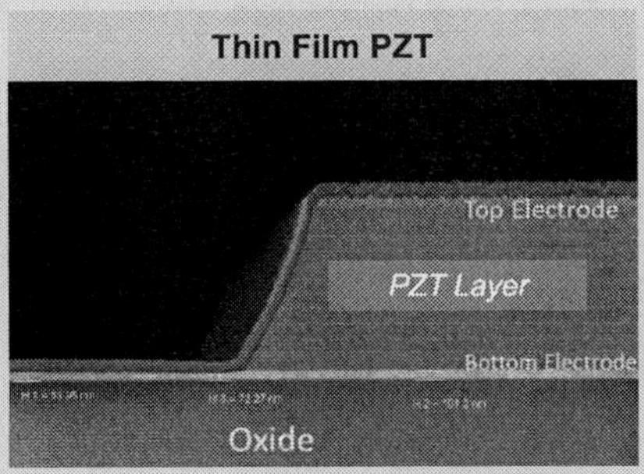

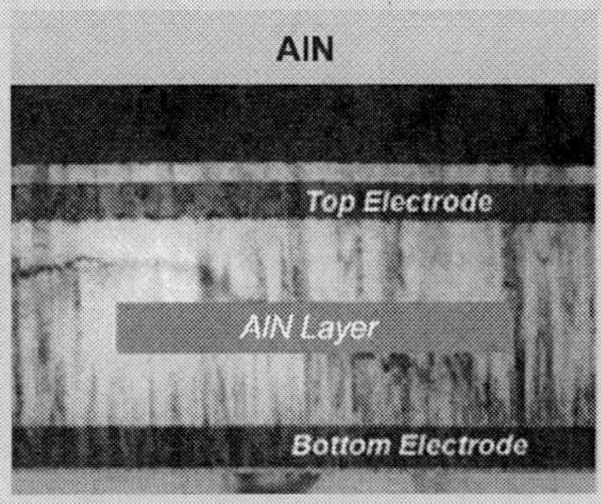

A sustainable path for piezo materials

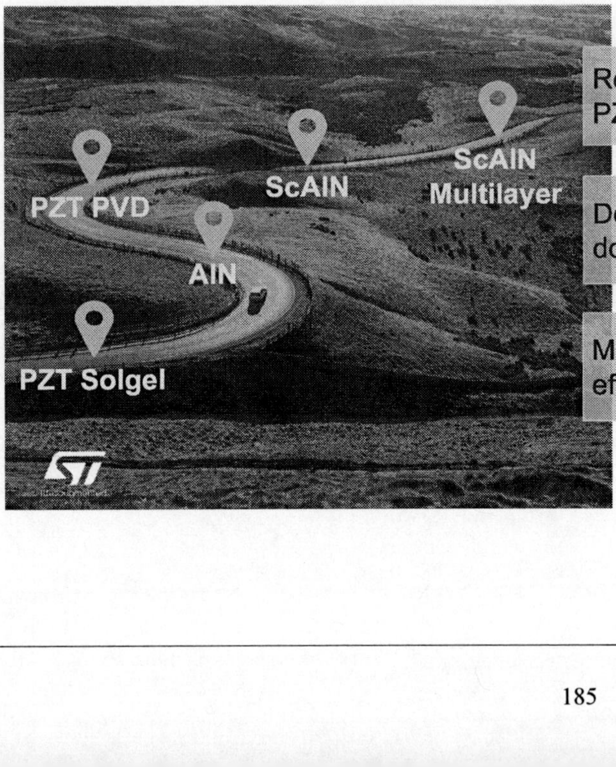

Replacing bulk PZT piezo with Thin Film PZT piezo (lead content reduction)

Development focus on higher % of Sc doped AlN to improve piezo coefficients

Multi-layer ScAlN for higher actuation efficiency and lead removal

What is the traditional development cycle of state-of-the-art MEMS products?

"MEMS development 101"

"Classical" development cycle
Working with multiple players slows down time-to-volume

Research → Development → Qualification → Low volume production → High volume production

Universities & Research Institutes often < 6"

$ →

Low-volume MEMS Fab 6-8"

$$ →

High-volume MEMS Fab 8"

Can we do better?
life.augmented

World's first Lab-in-Fab
for Piezoelectric MEMS
ST Techno Park in Ang Mo Kio
(Singapore)
life.augmented
Institute of Microelectronics
IME
ULVAC

Lab-in-Fab: accelerating time to volume

Lab-in-Fab model: all under one "roof"
Combining all phases in the same place

Research → Development → Qualification → Low volume production → High volume production

Lab-in-Fab

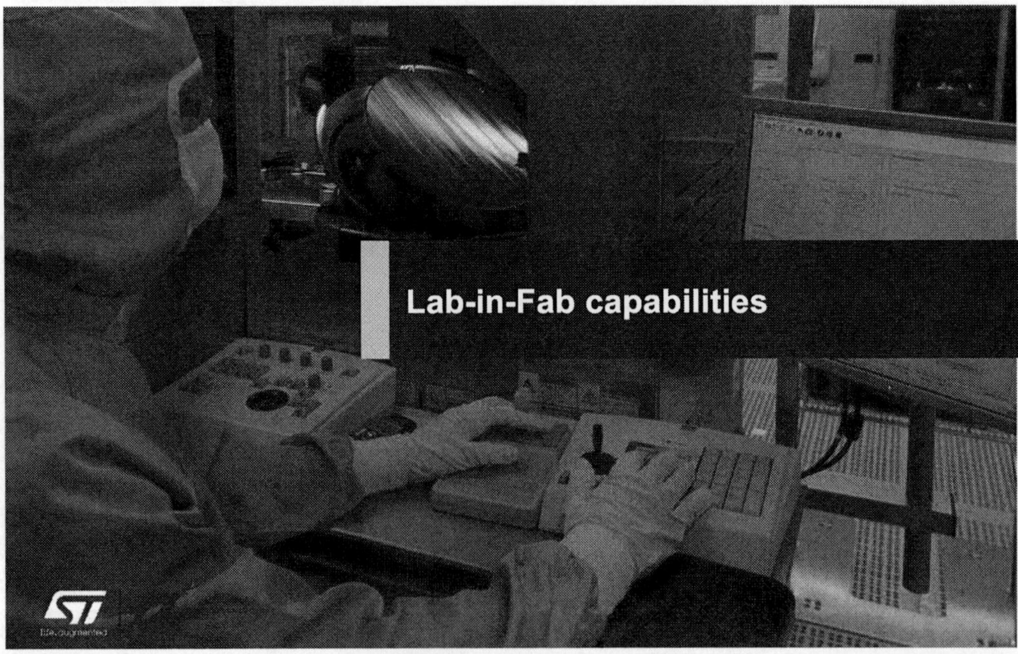

Lab-in-Fab capabilities

Key process modules

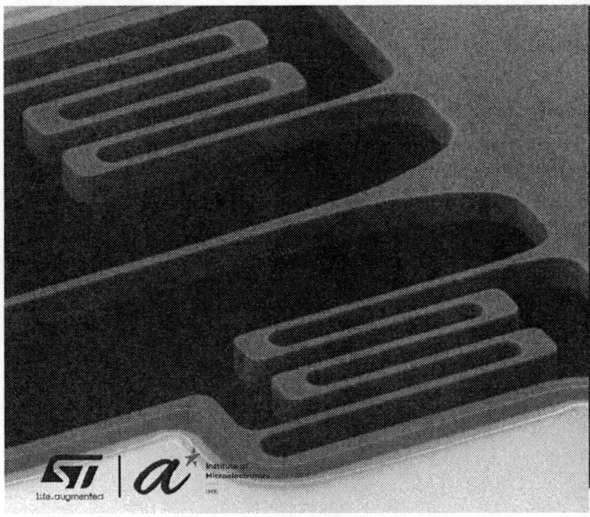

W2W bonding
Metallic, fusion, organic, temporary bonding

Dry etching
Silicon, silicon oxide, silicon nitride, metal, ….

Piezo materials
PZT and ScAlN

Metrology
Characterization & process control

Surface preparation
Wet etching & cleaning

Lab-in-Fab MPW Service

PVD PZT & ScAlN platforms

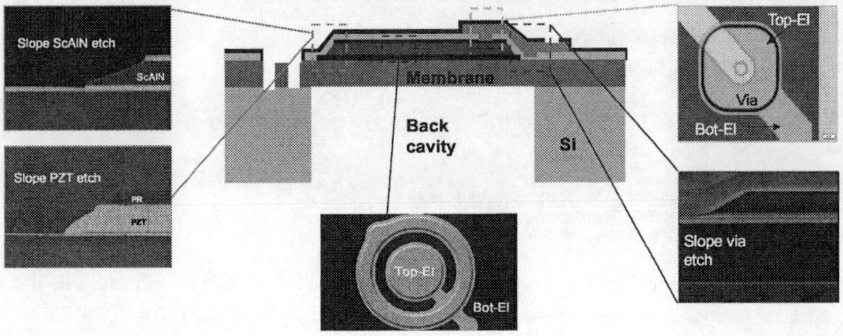

Key applications

- PMUT
- Microphone, micro-speaker
- RF resonators
- Other custom designs compatible with proposed process platforms

MPW: Multi Project Wafer

Multi-layer ScAlN MEMS

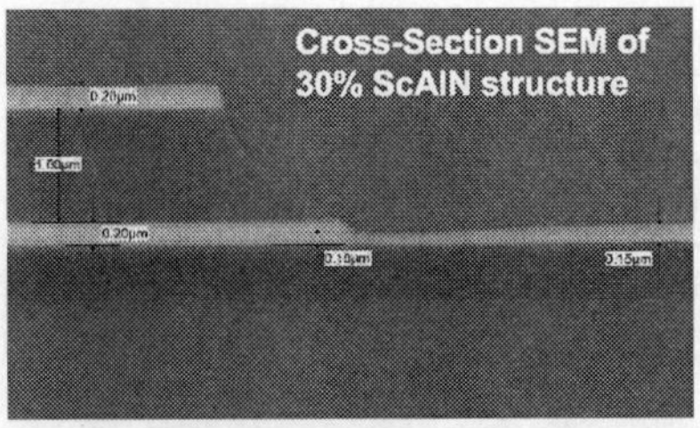

SEM Top Views

Schematic of 20% ScAlN bimorph structure

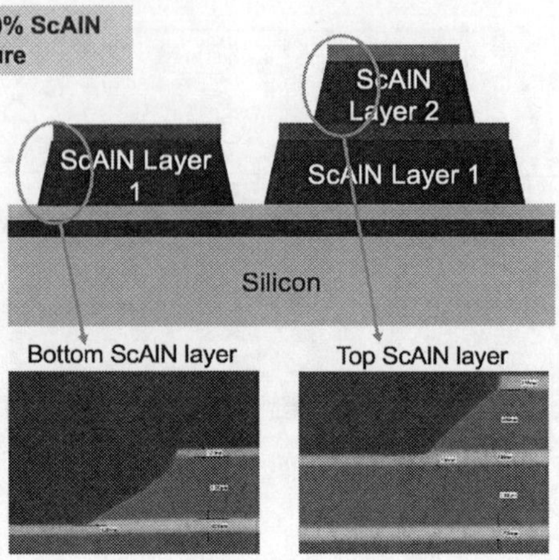

life.augmented
Institute of Microelectronics
IME

Takeaways

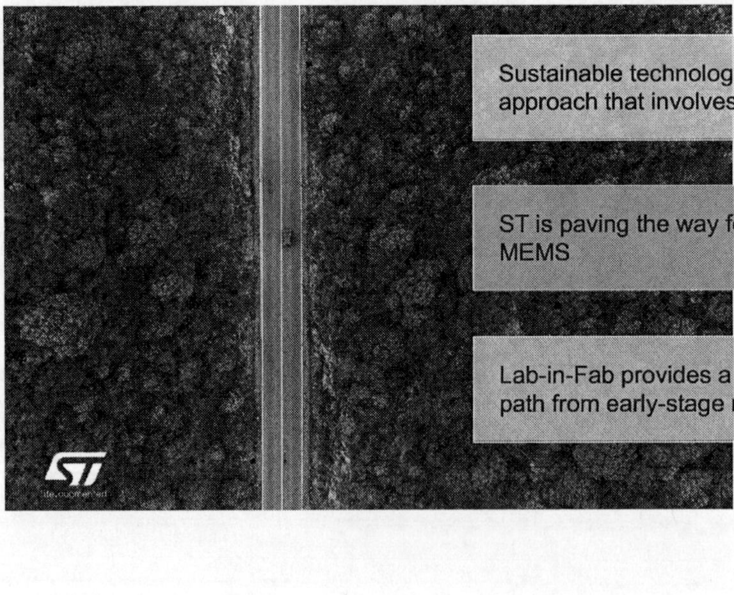

Sustainable technology requires a comprehensive approach that involves products, processes and materials

ST is paving the way for a sustainable evolution of piezo MEMS

Lab-in-Fab provides a unique framework to accelerate the path from early-stage research to high-volume production

life.augmented

Our technology starts with You

Find out more at www.st.com

life.augmented

Unlocking the
IoT with TinyML
and LoRaWAN
Rob Lauer & TJ VanToll
Developer Relations
blues
GPS
DIV
MAIN

blues
What to Expect
Today...

- Hands-On IoT/ML Workshop
- Functional Perspective ("How-To")
- High-Level Overview

- Deep Dive into any Topic
- "How do I do [x]?"
- Fluff ☺

Rob Lauer

Senior Director of DevRel

linkedin.com/in/rdlauer

TJ VanToll

Principal Developer Advocate

linkedin.com/in/tjvantoll

4

blues

Topics du Jour

- **IoT** – Wireless Connectivity with Blues
- **LoRaWAN** – The Things Stack
- **Machine Learning (TinyML)** – Edge Impulse

blues

THE THINGS STACK

EDGE IMPULSE

5

blues

Agenda

blues

Today's Agenda

- Wireless Connectivity with Blues and The Things Stack
- **Hands-On:** Getting Started with the Notecard and Notehub
- Break
- **Hands-On:** Getting Started with Swan
- TinyML with Edge Impulse
- Break
- **Hands-On:** Building an ML Solution with Blues and Edge Impulse

7

blues

Help!?!

blues

Software Installations

bit.ly/blues-tinyml-software

“

If we want to build a truly distributed Internet of Things with **BILLIONS** of sensors, then we’re going to need TinyML.

Stacey Higginbotham – Stacey on IoT

Wireless Connectivity with Blues

> “
>
> **Complexity kills.** It sucks the life out of developers, it makes products difficult to plan, build, and test.
>
> Ray Ozzie – Blues CEO

Easy for developers and **affordable** for all.

- **Securing** your data from device to cloud
- Building zero-config **low-power** hardware
- Providing an unmatched **developer experience**
- **Harmonizing the IoT** with interchangeable RATs

"Device-to-Cloud Data Pump"

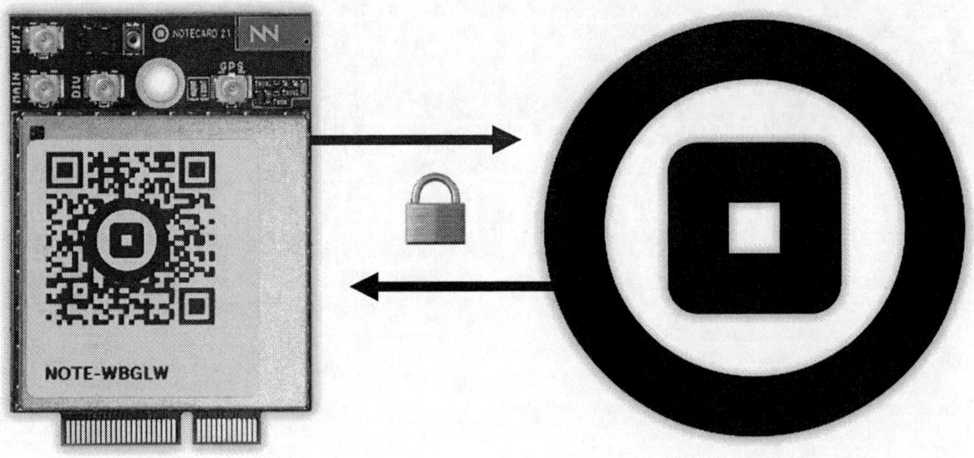

blues

The Notecard Options, Simplified

Cellular

LoRa

Wi-Fi

Cell + Wi-Fi

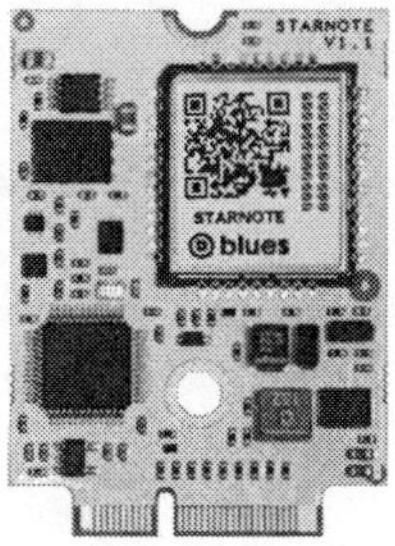

Satellite

15

blues

Notecard

- Low-power system-on-module
- Global Cellular/GPS, Wi-Fi, LoRa, Sat
- **Cellular:** 500MB cell data + 10 years service
- **Cellular:** Dual SIM support
- JSON-based API
- Python, Go, Arduino, C/C++, Zephyr

16

blues

Simple Example: *card.temp* API

Request

```
{ "req": "card.temp" }
```

Response

```
{
  "value": 27.625,
  "calibration": -3.0
}
```

17

blues

C Example: *card.temp* API

Request

```
J *req = NoteNewRequest("card.temp");
```

Response

```
J *rsp = NoteRequestResponse(req);
J *status = JGetString(rsp, "value");
…etc…
```

18

blues

Notecarrier

- Carrier boards for easy prototyping
- Notecarrier for every scenario:
  - **F** – Feather-compatible socket
  - **A** – Any MCU, onboard antennas
  - **B** – Small form factor
  - **Pi** – Raspberry Pi SBC
  - **R** – Arduino MKR and PRO
  - SparkFun MicroMod Cellular Function
  - Blues.ONE from RAKwireless

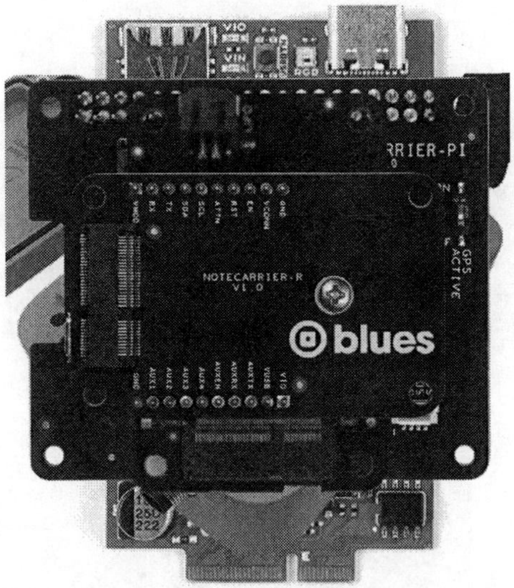

19

blues

Notehub

- **Secure cloud proxy** for Notecards
- Route data to **any cloud** app
- Manage **fleets** of devices
- OTA MCU/Notecard **firmware updates**
- **Secure** communications

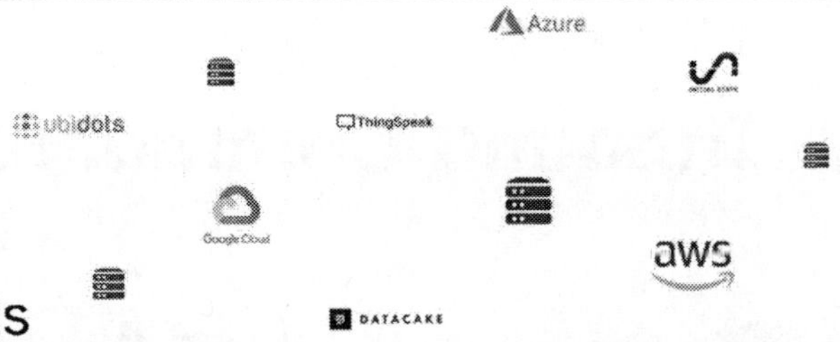

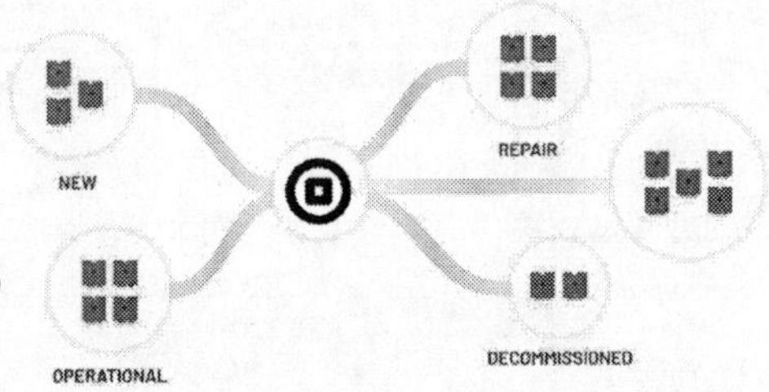

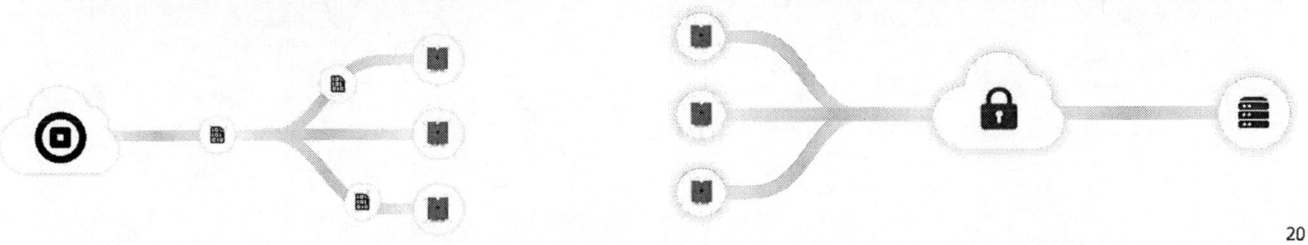

20

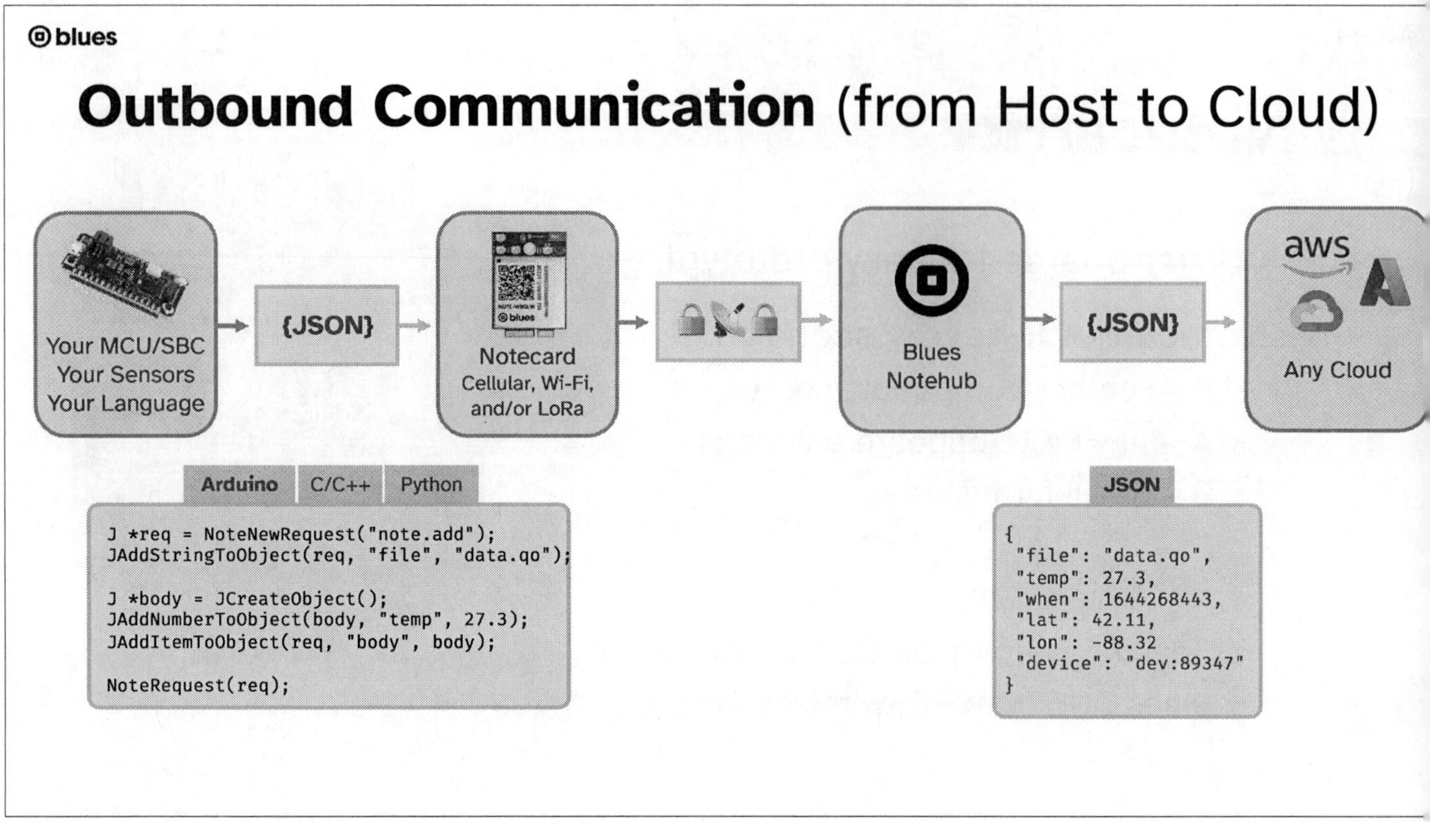
blues
Outbound Communication (from Host to Cloud)
Your MCU/SBC
Your Sensors
Your Language
{JSON}
Notecard
Cellular, Wi-Fi,
and/or LoRa
Blues
Notehub
{JSON}
aws
Any Cloud
Arduino
C/C++
Python
J *req = NoteNewRequest("note.add");
JAddStringToObject(req, "file", "data.qo");
J *body = JCreateObject();
JAddNumberToObject(body, "temp", 27.3);
JAddItemToObject(req, "body", body);
NoteRequest(req);
JSON
{
"file": "data.qo",
"temp": 27.3,
"when": 1644268443,
"lat": 42.11,
"lon": -88.32
"device": "dev:89347"
}

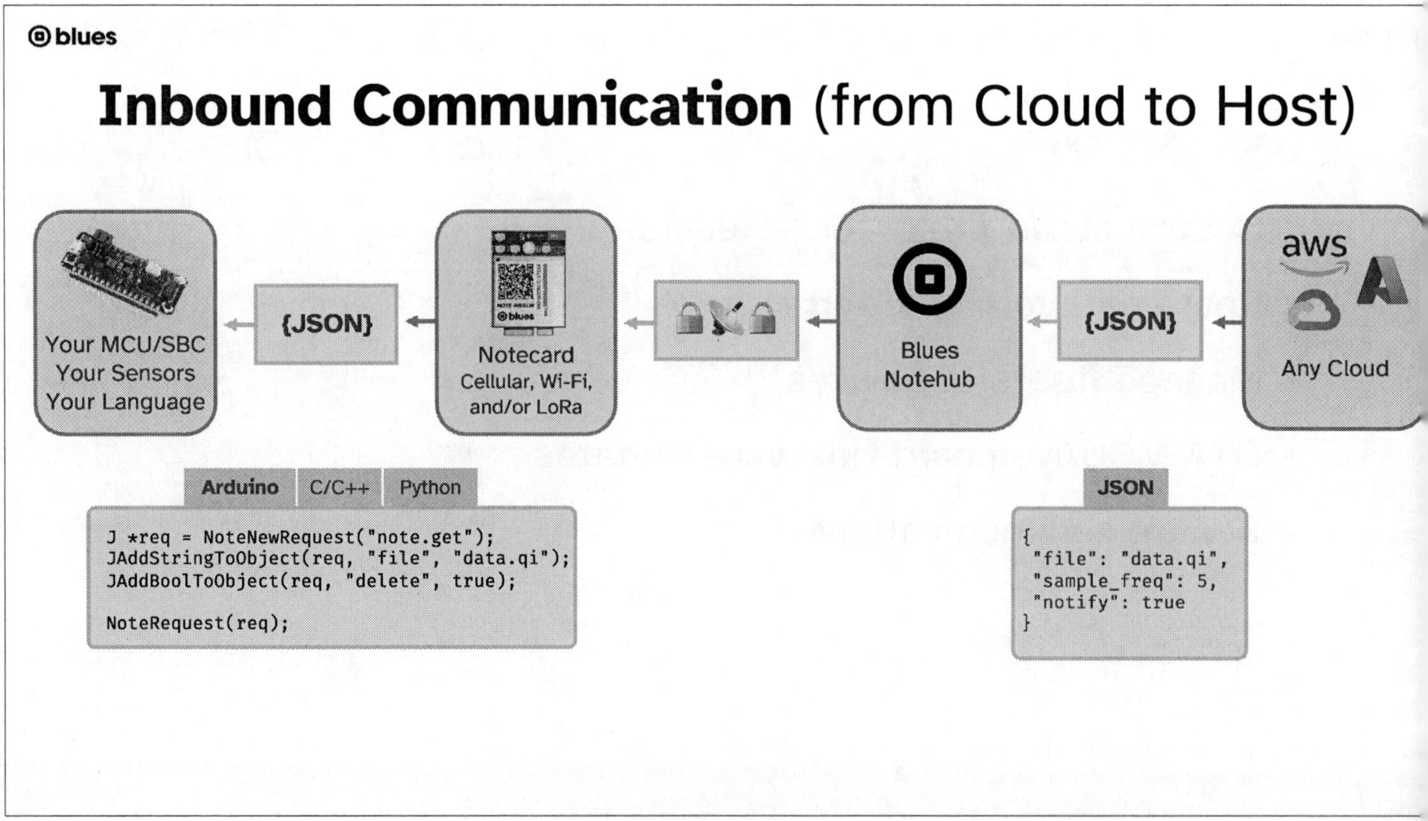
blues
Inbound Communication (from Cloud to Host)
Your MCU/SBC
Your Sensors
Your Language
{JSON}
Notecard
Cellular, Wi-Fi,
and/or LoRa
Blues
Notehub
{JSON}
aws
Any Cloud
Arduino
C/C++
Python
J *req = NoteNewRequest("note.get");
JAddStringToObject(req, "file", "data.qi");
JAddBoolToObject(req, "delete", true);
NoteRequest(req);
JSON
{
"file": "data.qi",
"sample_freq": 5,
"notify": true
}

blues

Wireless IoT the Blues Way

(It Just Works™)

```
{
 "file": "temp.qo",
 "temp": 27.3,
 "when": 1644268443
}
```


23

Wireless via LoRa and LoRaWAN

blues

LoRa LoRaWAN®

25

blues

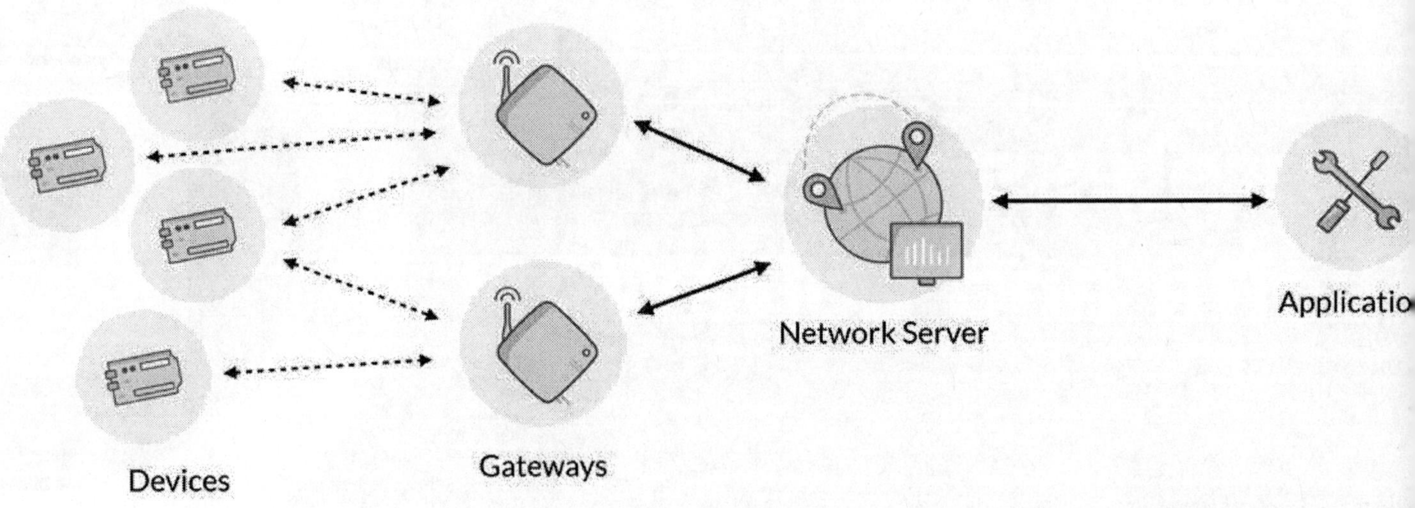

THE THINGS INDUSTRIES

26

blues

Advantages of LoRa/LoRaWAN

- Low-Cost
- Low-Power
- Long Range
- Security

27

THE THINGS INDUSTRIES

Where companies scale their LoRaWAN® solutions

We empower companies to unleash the power of LoRaWAN to build secure and scalable solutions.

→ 363M messages last week on The Things Stack

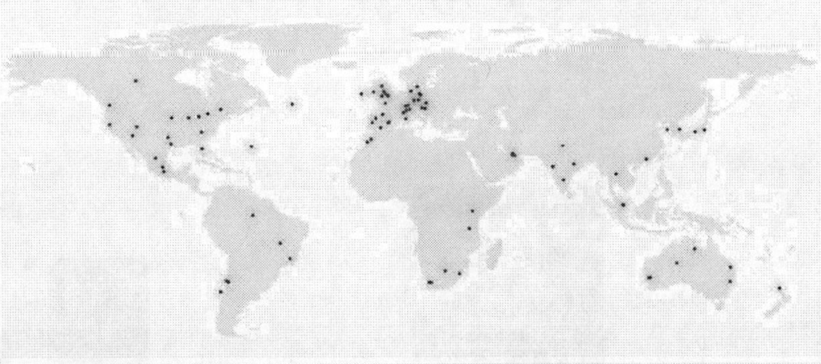

blues

Interchangeable RATs

1. Same Developer APIs `{ "req": "note.add" }`

2. Same Physical Footprint*

29

blues

Notecard LoRa and Blues Starter Kit for LoRaWAN

$10
US (915 MHz)
EU (868 MHz)

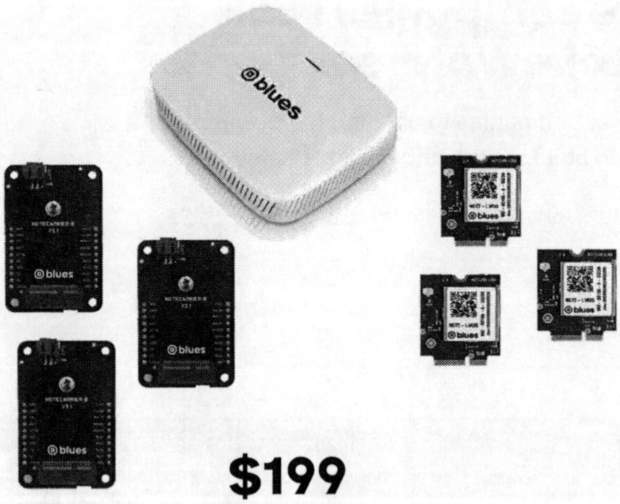

$199
US (915 MHz)
EU (868 MHz)

30

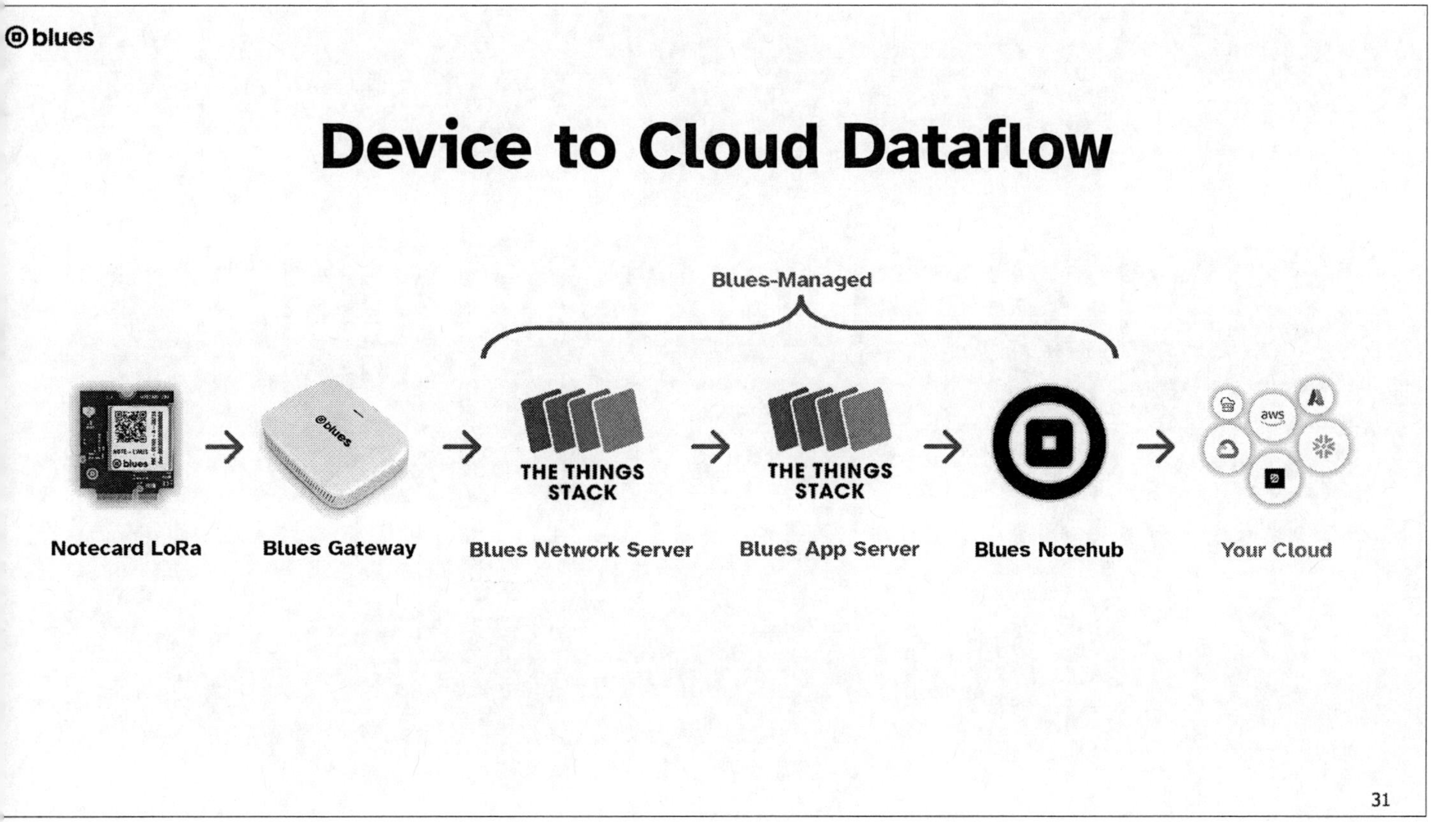
blues
Device to Cloud Dataflow
Blues-Managed
THE THINGS STACK
THE THINGS STACK
Notecard LoRa
Blues Gateway
Blues Network Server
Blues App Server
Blues Notehub
Your Cloud
31

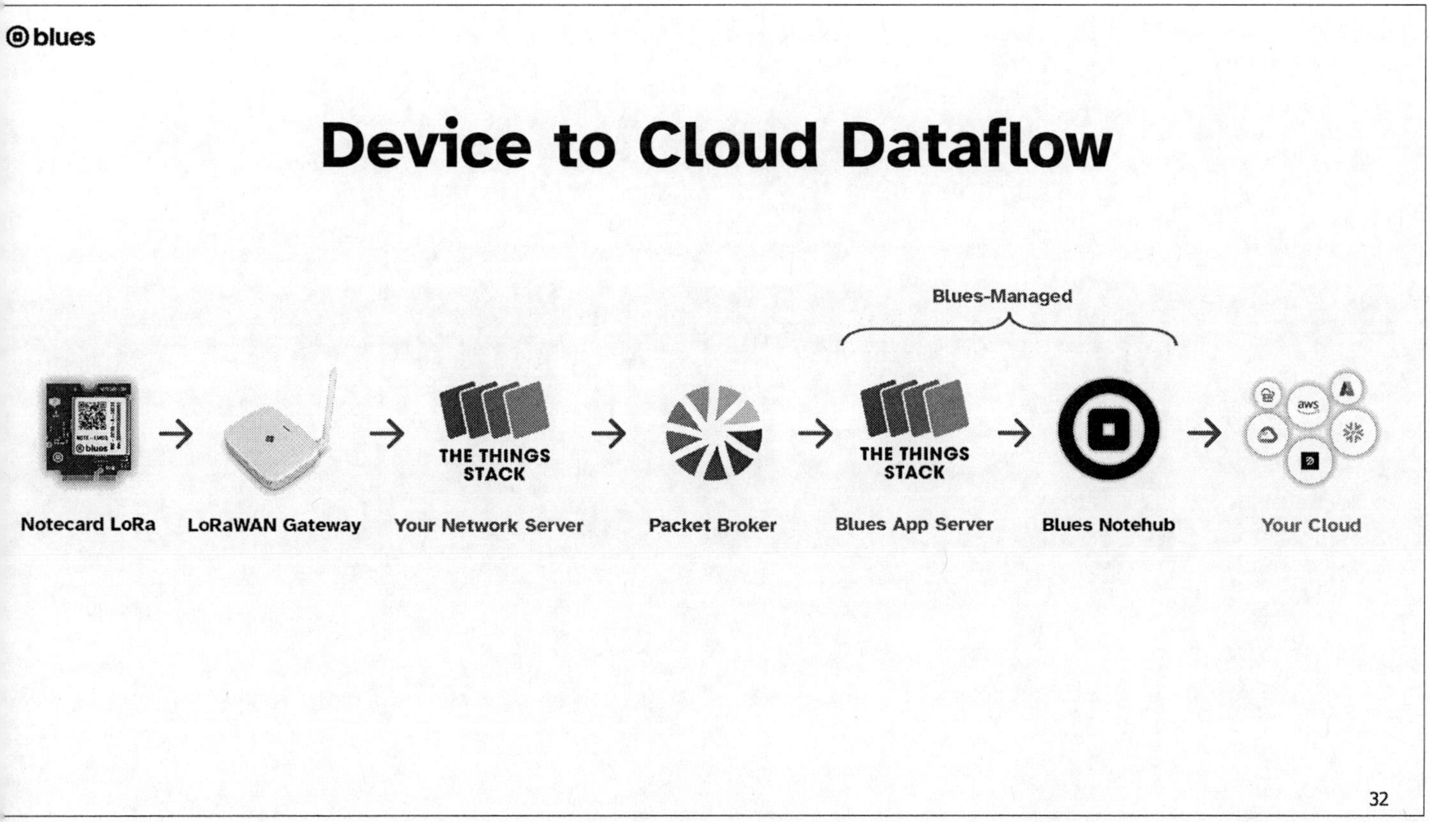
blues
Device to Cloud Dataflow
Blues-Managed
THE THINGS STACK
THE THINGS STACK
Notecard LoRa
LoRaWAN Gateway
Your Network Server
Packet Broker
Blues App Server
Blues Notehub
Your Cloud
32

blues
Lab #1: Notecard LoRa
bit.ly/blues-lora

blues
Break Time

blues

Lab #2: Blues Swan

bit.ly/blues-swan

TinyML with Edge Impulse

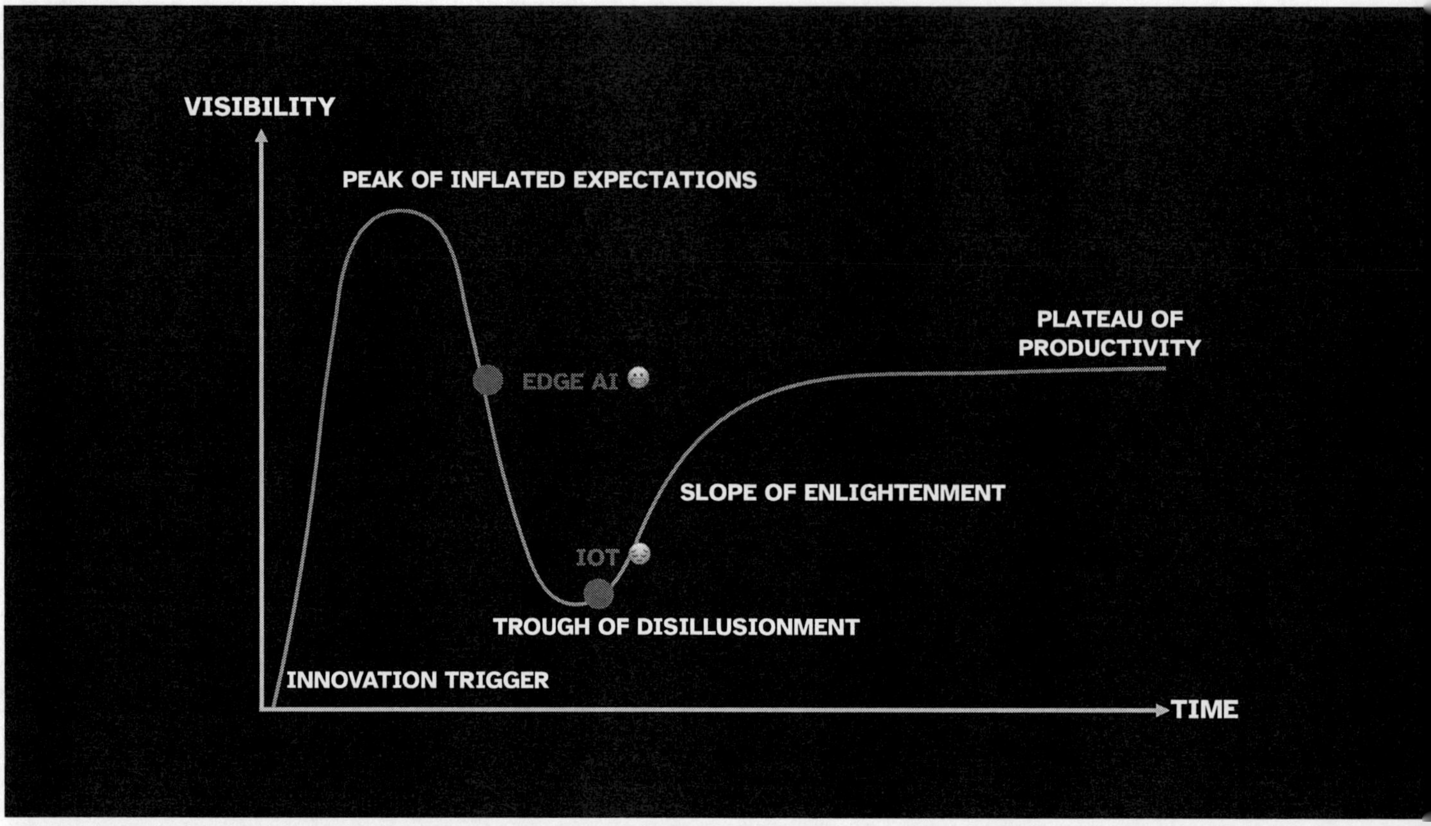

blues

What even *is* Machine Learning?

60% of the time, It works every time.

blues

cup: 53%
wine glass: 51%
cell phone: 51%

40

"

Machine learning is the study of computer algorithms that **improve automatically through experience** and by the **use of data**. It is seen as a part of AI.

"

Machine learning **lets computers learn from data**...versus being explicitly told what to do.

blues

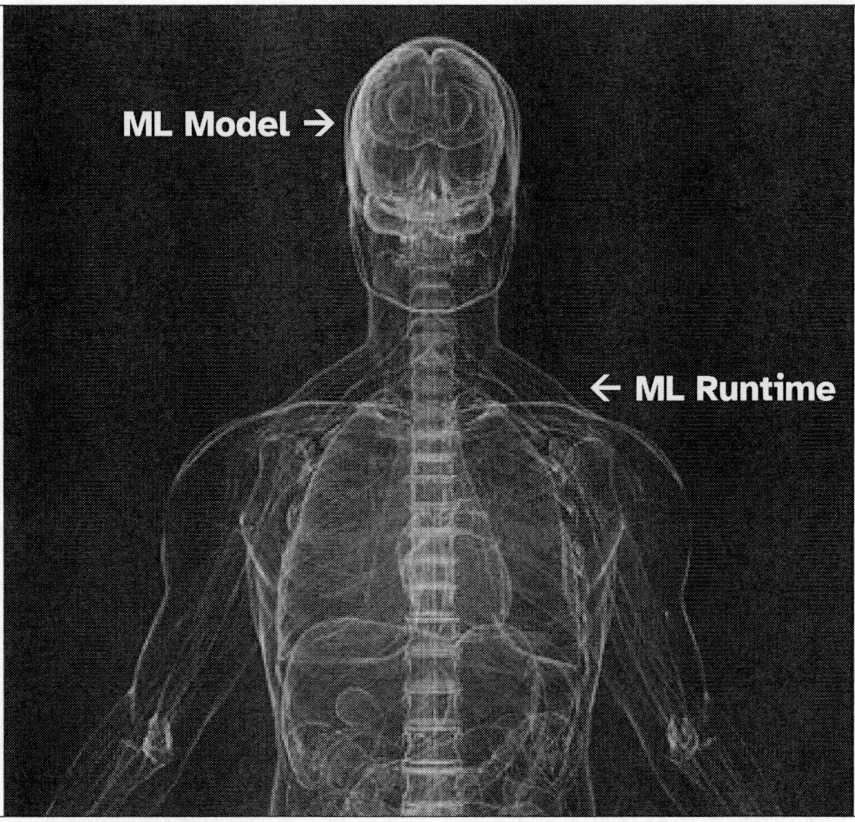

blues

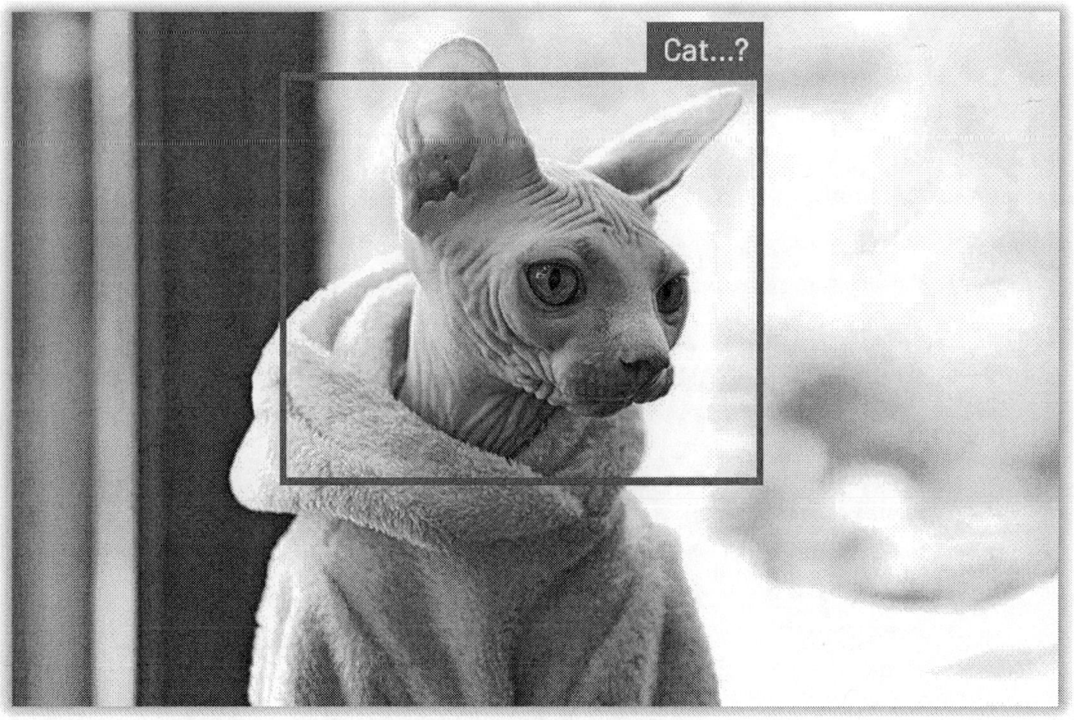

44

blues

What even *is* TinyML?

blues

TinyML in Practice

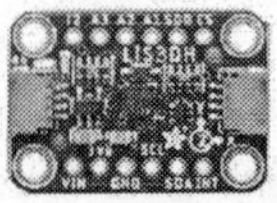

35.884	30.895	49.120
36.177	29.853	50.124
37.296	30.296	51.074
38.553	30.400	50.259
38.357	31.290	49.044
39.559	31.209	48.082
34.968	30.340	48.234
34.923	29.775	50.910
37.441	29.265	52.113
39.572	30.954	51.086
37.155	30.858	48.364
39.261	32.018	46.920

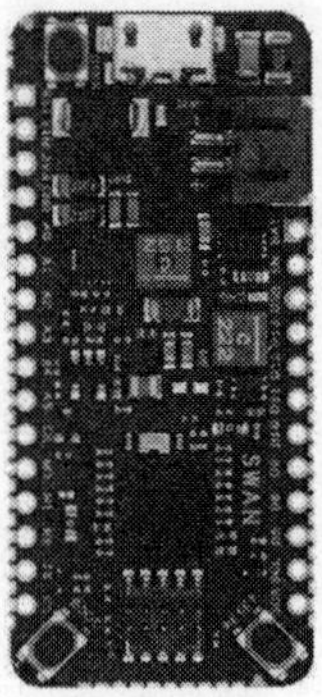

"Device is upside down!"

46

blues

ML for Preventative Maintenance

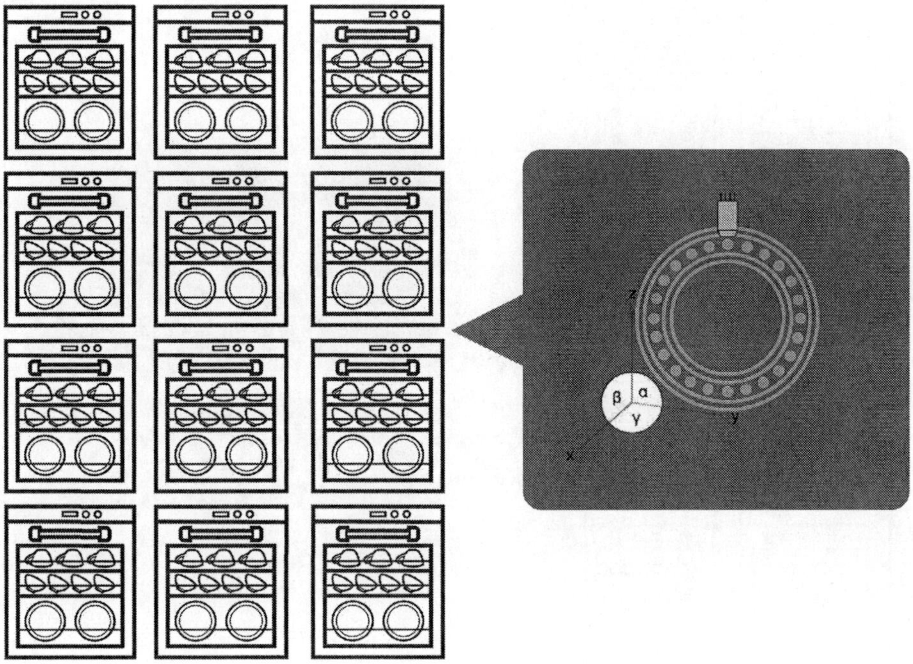

blues

ML for Preventative Maintenance

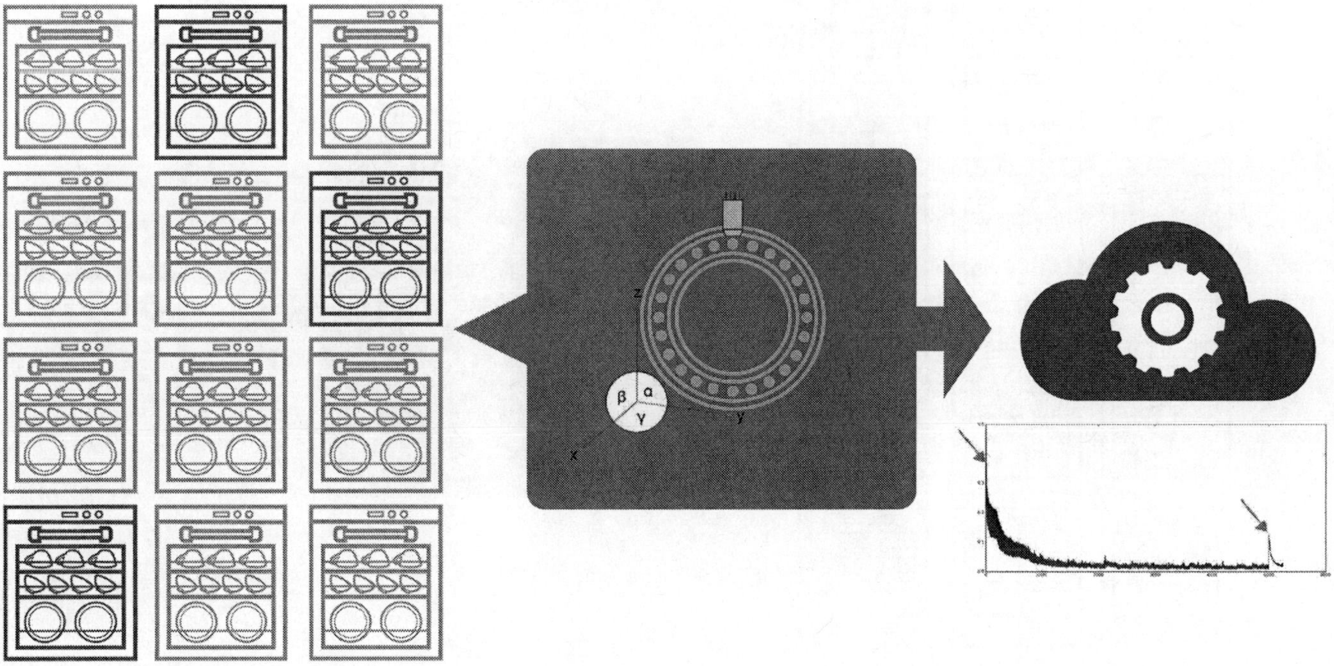

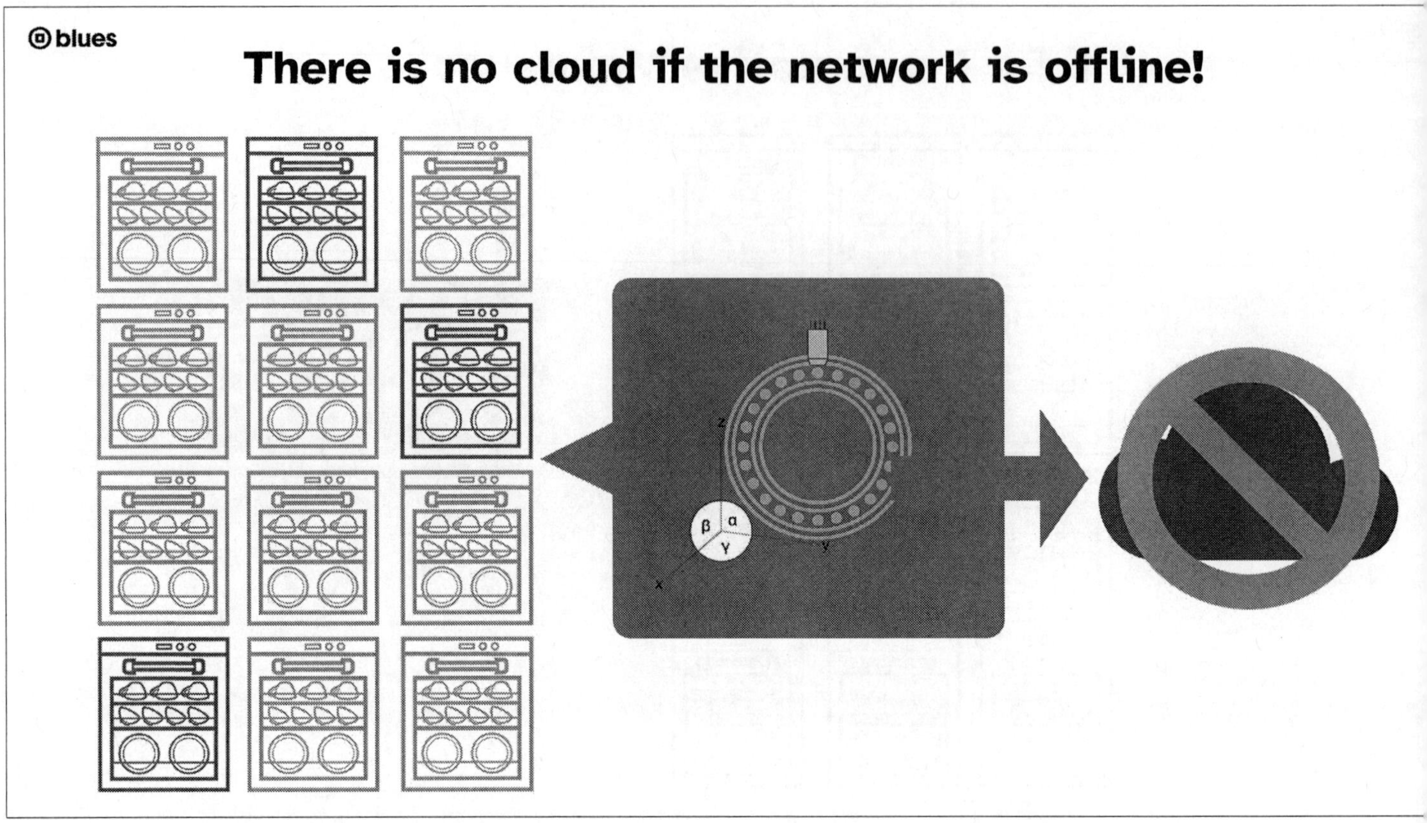
blues
There is no cloud if the network is offline!
z
β
α
γ
y
x

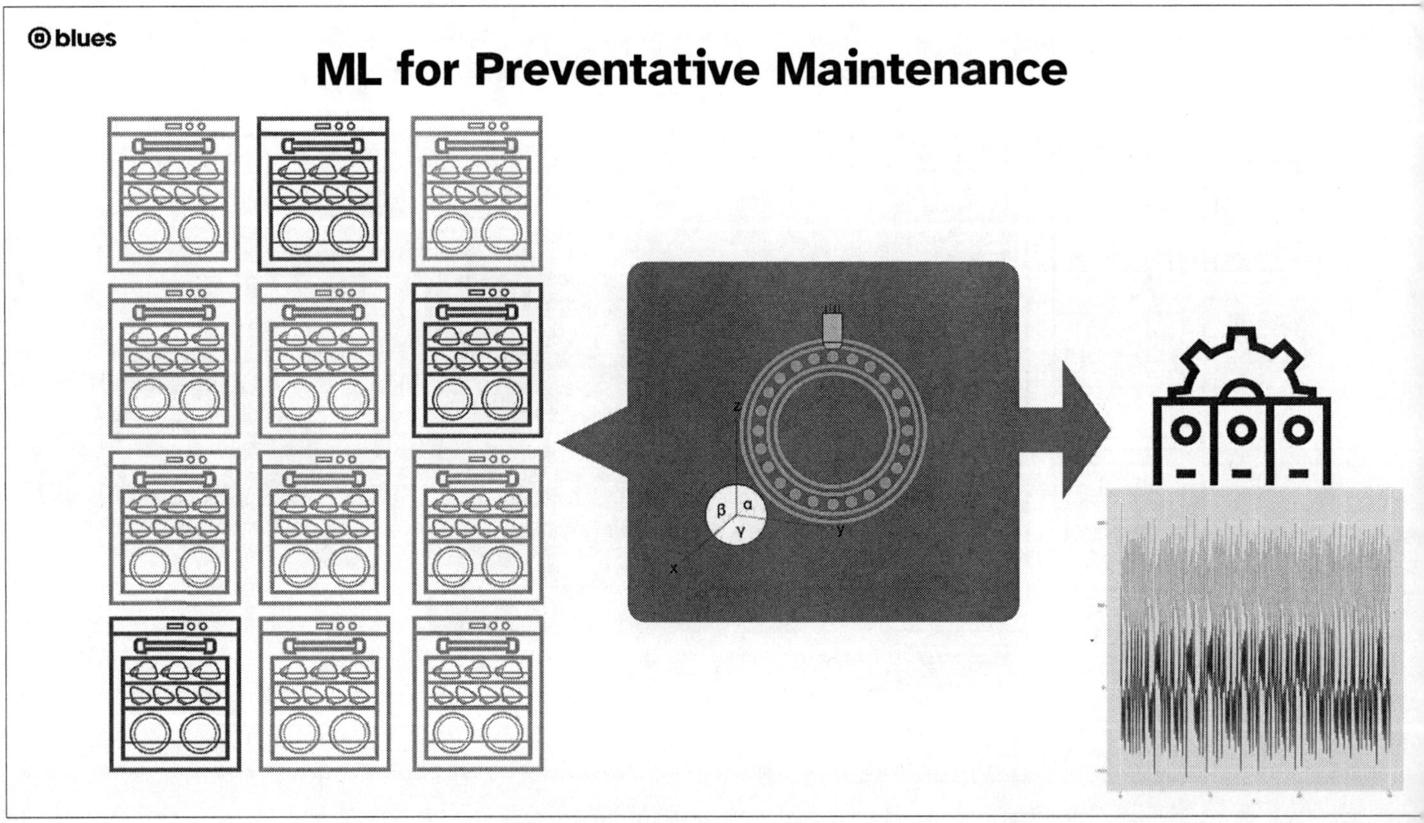
blues
ML for Preventative Maintenance
z
β
α
γ
y
x

blues

Benefits of Edge AI/ML

Innovation
Add new differentiating features, become a market leader by standing out from your competition

Privacy
Data stays on the device, gets processed locally and drives remote alerts, notifications, and actions

Power
Stay operational for longer periods of time

Cost
Save on storage and compute costs by not sending raw data constantly to the cloud

Reliability
Be operational in low connectivity environments

Latency
Process data real-time on the edge device, without having to wait for a response back from the cloud

blues

The "Edge" is the IoT

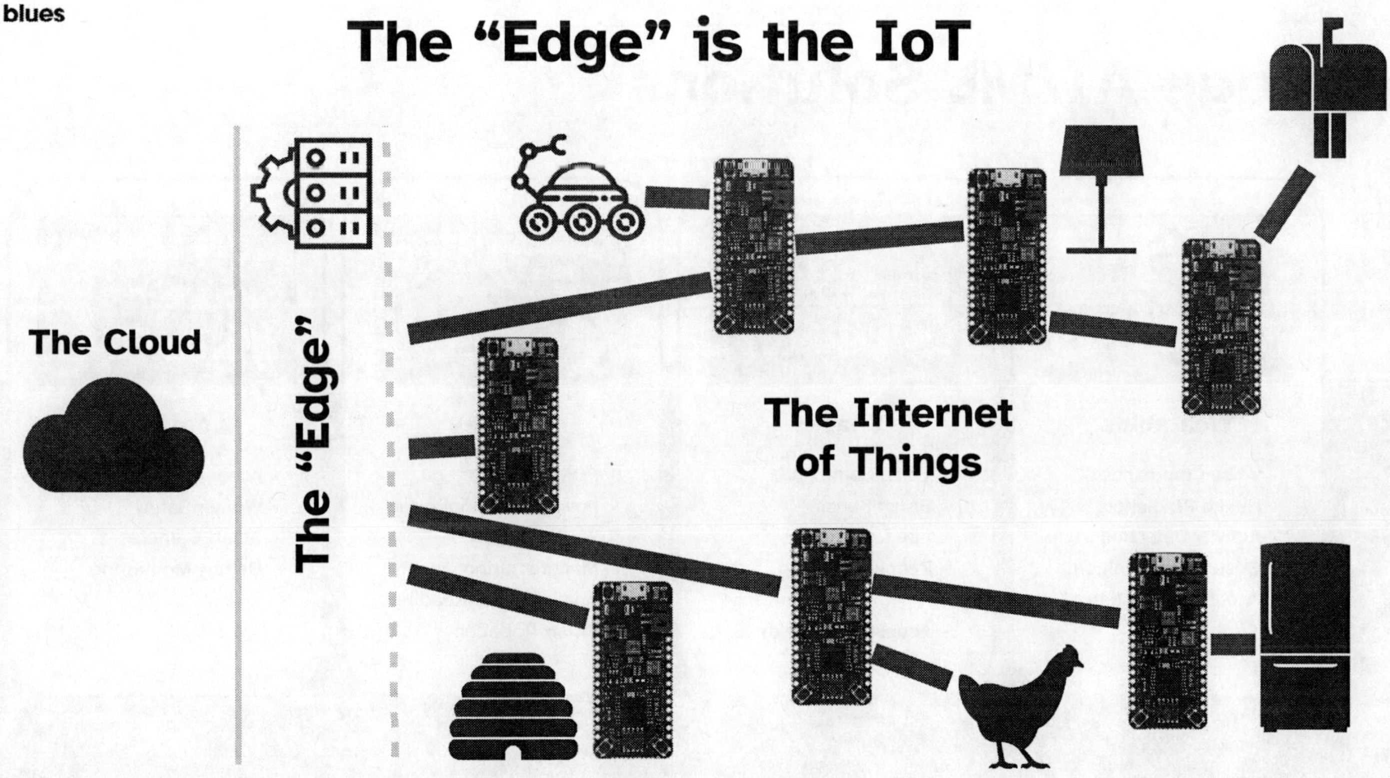

“

The cloud may be infinite, but your pipe to it is **not**.

I have no idea...

blues

Edge AI/ML Solutions

Wearables

- Voice Commands
- Health Prediction
- Activity Detection
- Gesture Recognition
- Acoustic Detection

Spaces

- Voice Commands
- Smart Sensing
- Fire Detection
- People Counting
- HVAC Maintenance
- Acoustic Detection

Industry

- PDM - Motors
- Power Grid Monitoring
- Worker Safety
- Manufacturing Quality
- Analog Meter Reading
- Smart Robotics

Logistics

- Asset Tracking
- Worker Safety
- Smart Cameras
- Battery Monitoring

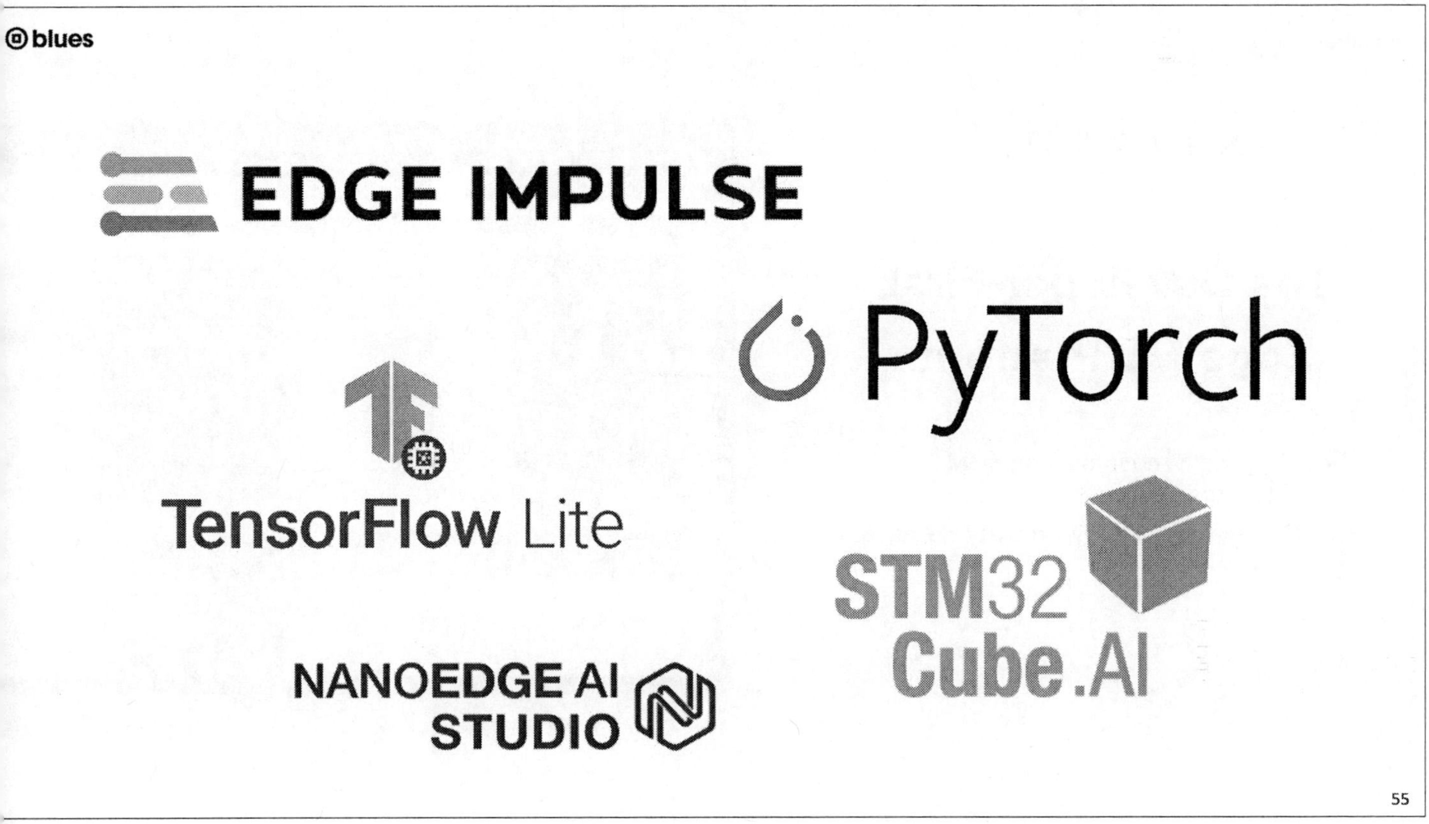
blues
EDGE IMPULSE
PyTorch
TensorFlow Lite
STM32
Cube.AI
NANOEDGE AI
STUDIO
55

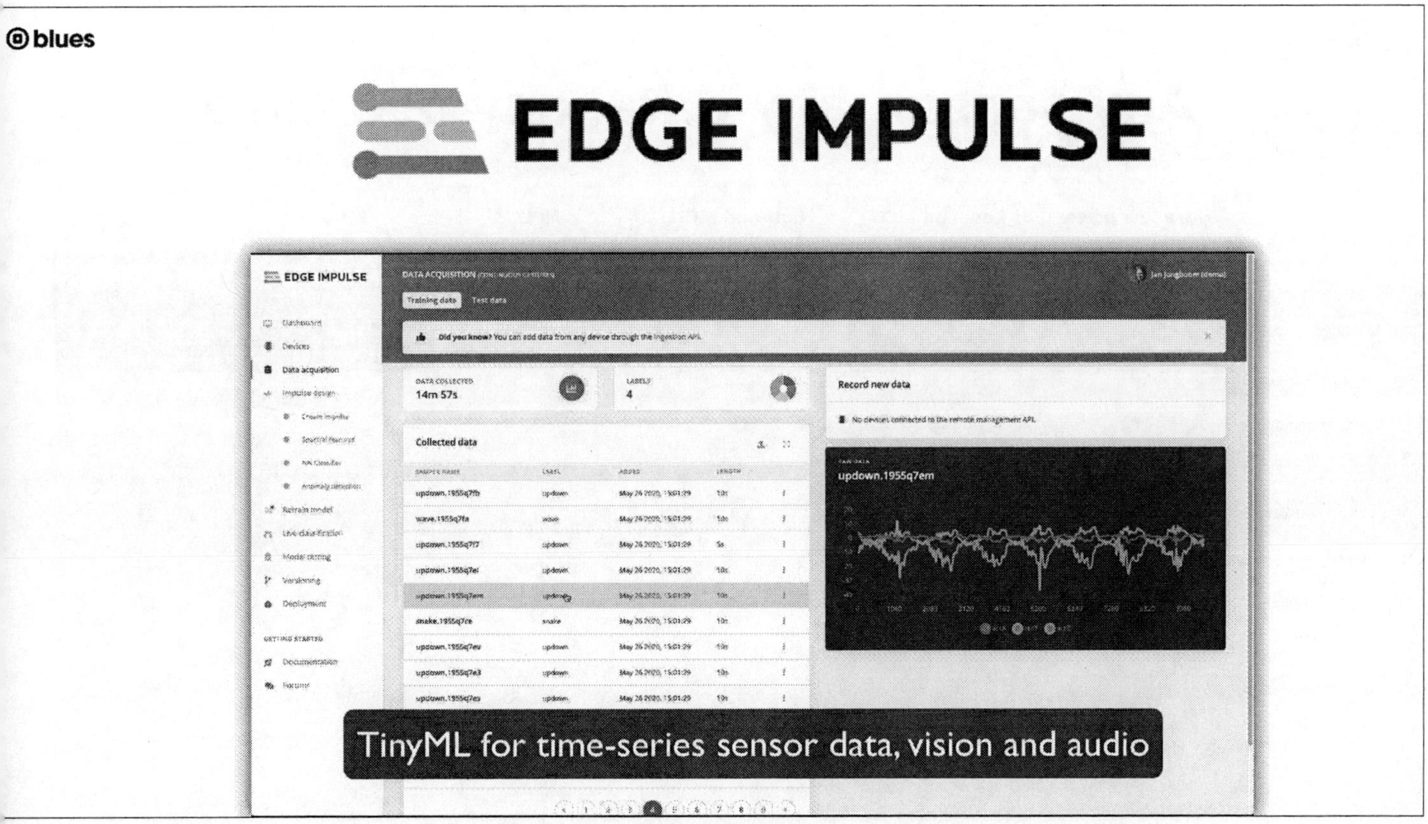
blues
EDGE IMPULSE
EDGE IMPULSE
DATA ACQUISITION
Training data
Test data
Data acquisition
14m 57s
4
Record new data
Collected data
updown.1955q7em
TinyML for time-series sensor data, vision and audio

blues

EDGE IMPULSE

The Developer-First Edge ML Platform

- No royalty, no impact on BOM
- Your IP, stays your IP
- Total explainability, no black boxes

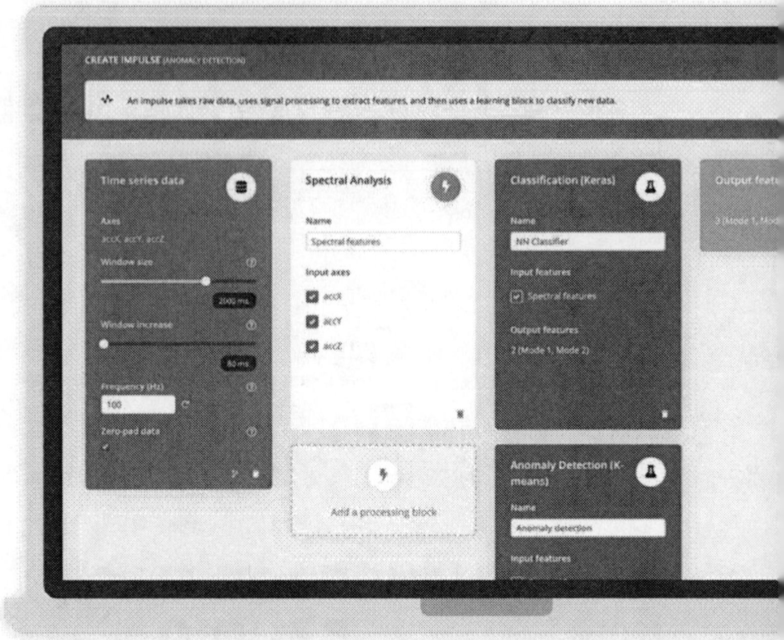

blues

Any sensor, any data, any use case

	Ultra low power	Low-end MCU	High-end MCU	NPU	MPU	GPU
Memory	Anomaly detection 10kB	Sensor data classification 18kB	Audio classification 50kB	Image classification 256kB	Object detection complex voice processing 1MB+	Video classification 1GB+
Sensor	✓	✓	✓	✓	✓	✓
Audio	✓	✓	✓	✓	✓	✓
Image			✓	✓	✓	✓
Video					✓	✓

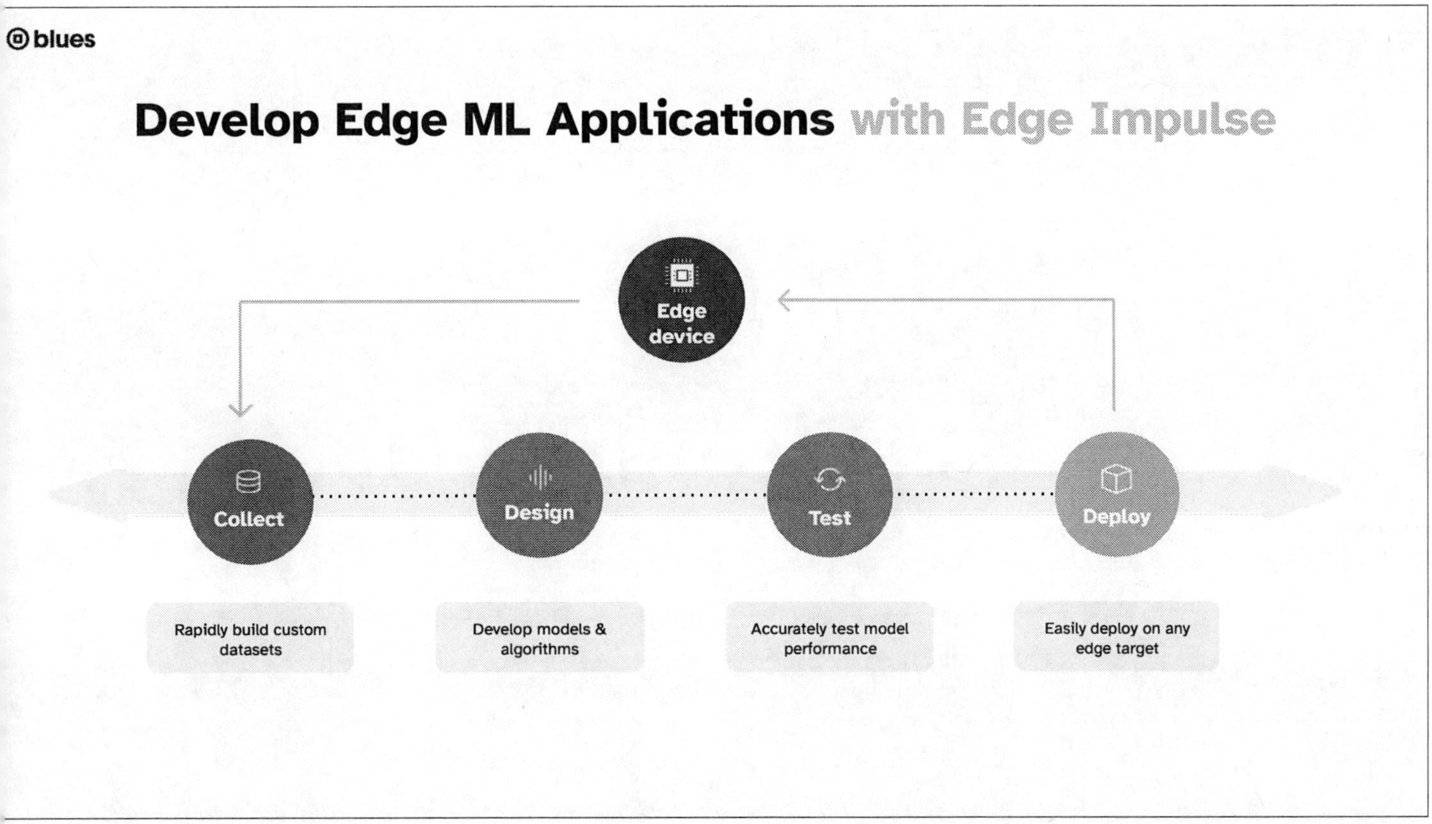
blues
Develop Edge ML Applications with Edge Impulse
Edge device
Collect
Design
Test
Deploy
Rapidly build custom datasets
Develop models & algorithms
Accurately test model performance
Easily deploy on any edge target

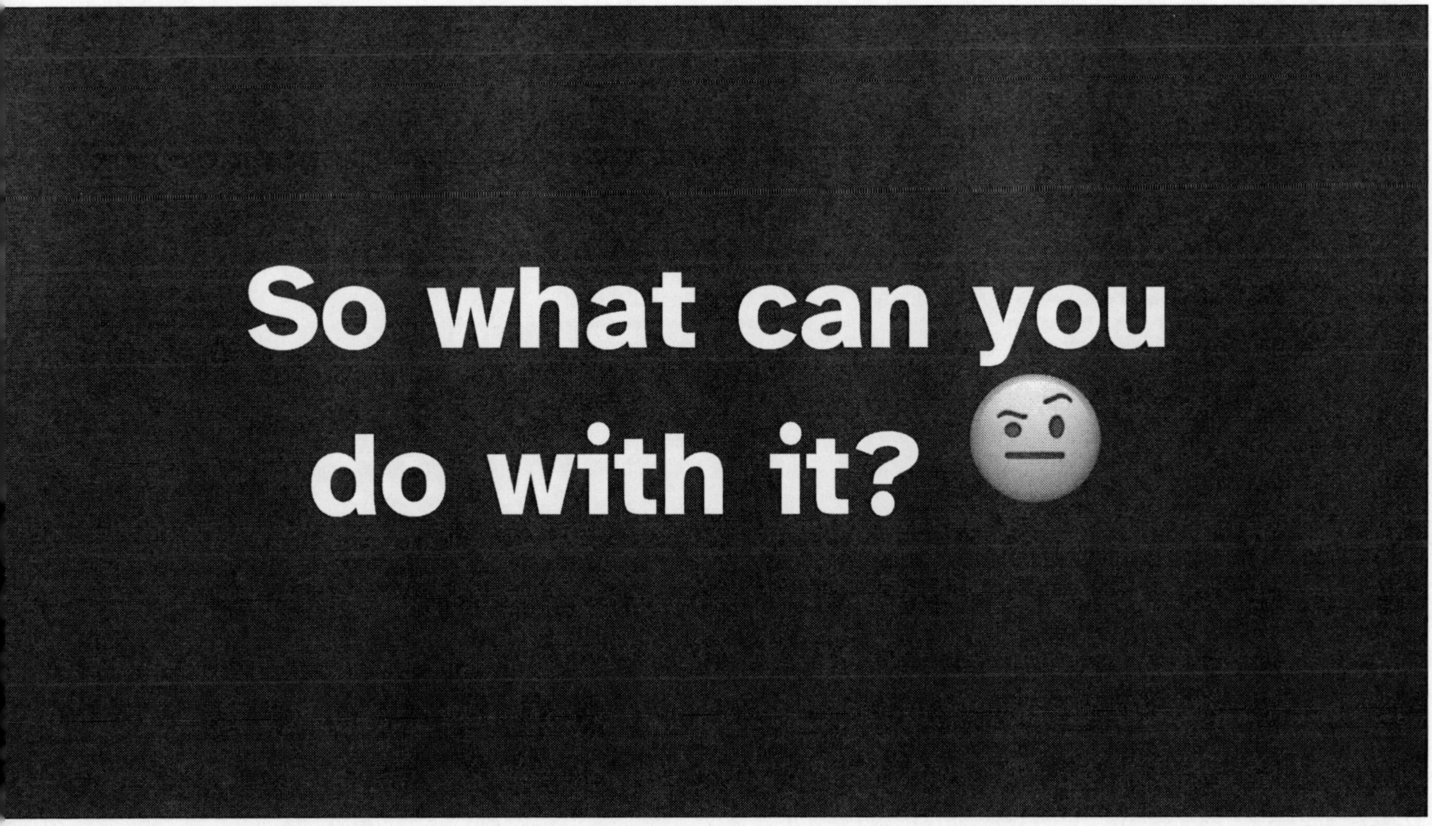
So what can you do with it?

Remote Birding
with the
Raspberry Pi

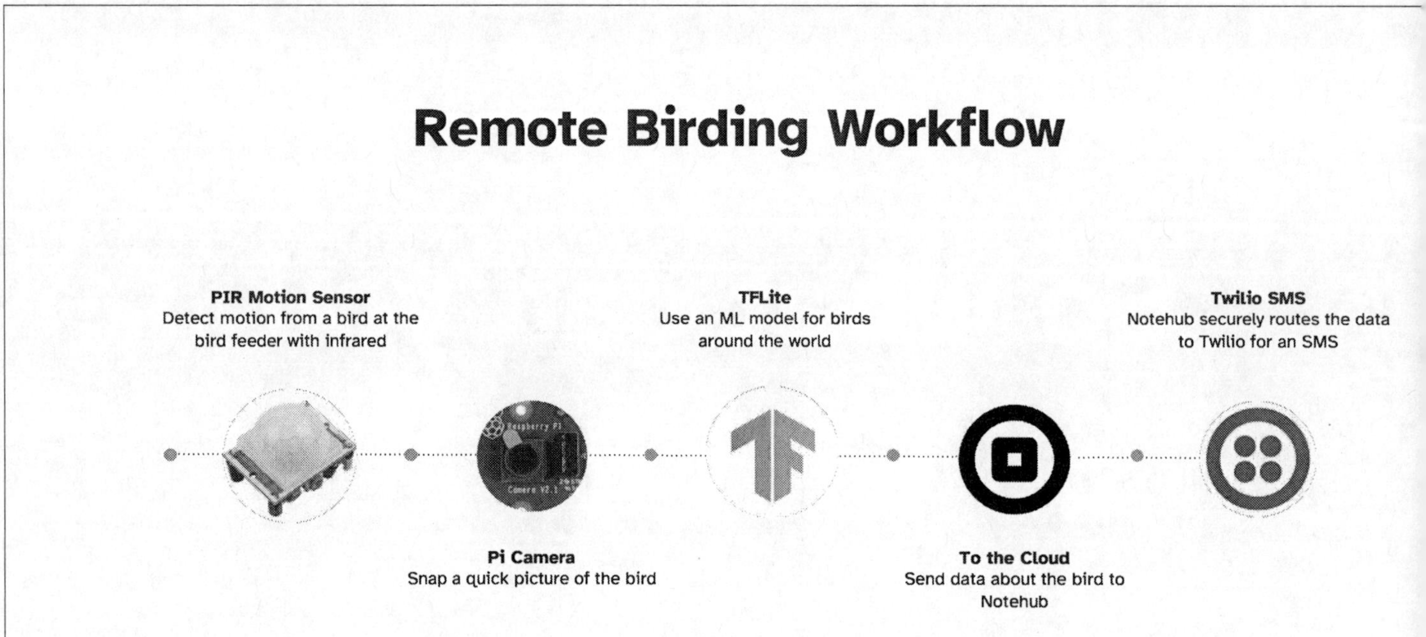
Remote Birding Workflow
PIR Motion Sensor
Detect motion from a bird at the bird feeder with infrared
Pi Camera
Snap a quick picture of the bird
TFLite
Use an ML model for birds around the world
To the Cloud
Send data about the bird to Notehub
Twilio SMS
Notehub securely routes the data to Twilio for an SMS

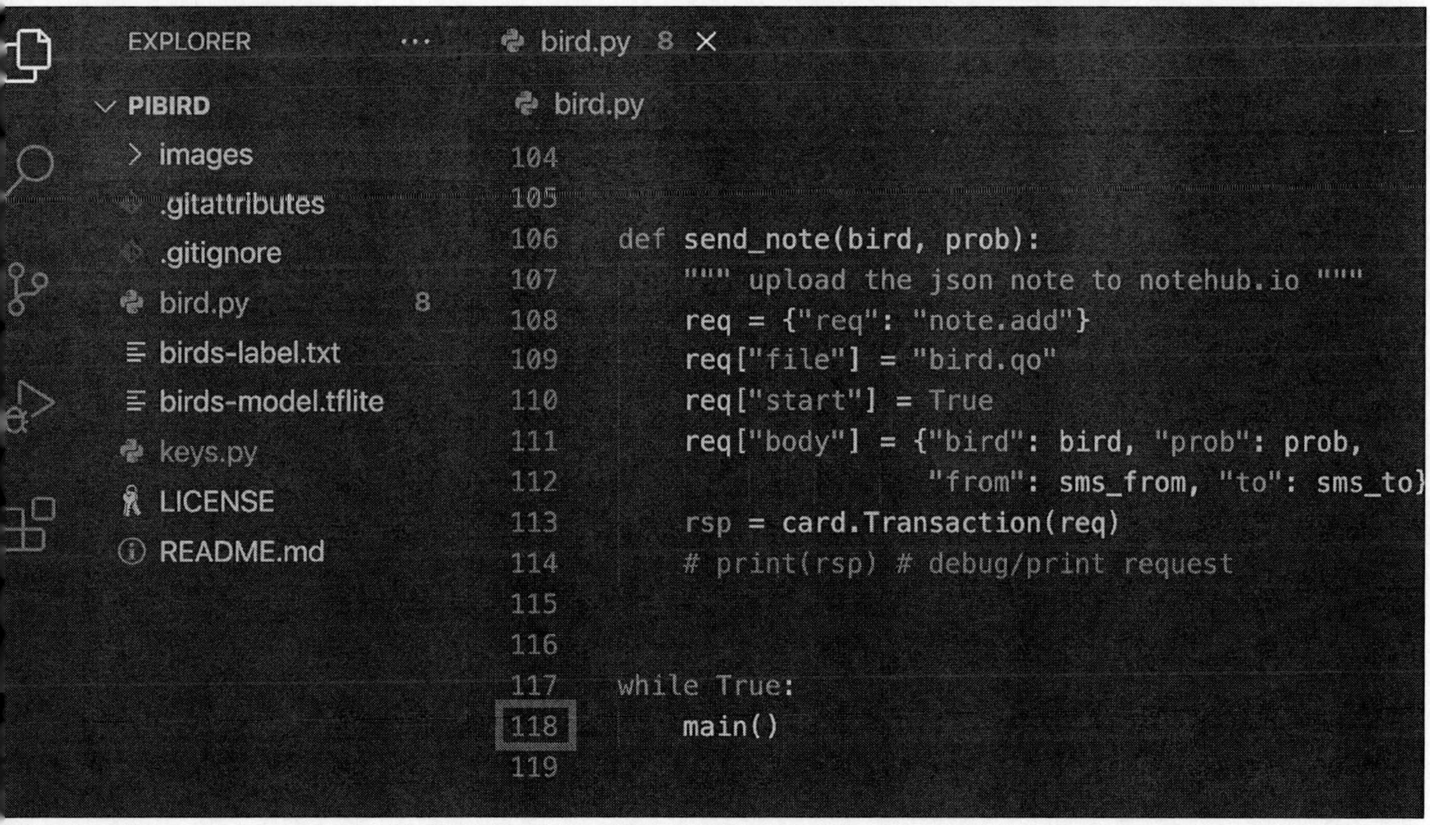
EXPLORER
bird.py 8
PIBIRD
images
.gitattributes
.gitignore
bird.py 8
birds-label.txt
birds-model.tflite
keys.py
LICENSE
README.md
bird.py
def send_note(bird, prob):
""" upload the json note to notehub.io """
req = {"req": "note.add"}
req["file"] = "bird.qo"
req["start"] = True
req["body"] = {"bird": bird, "prob": prob,
"from": sms_from, "to": sms_to}
rsp = card.Transaction(req)
# print(rsp) # debug/print request
while True:
main()

3:49
Edge
+1 (260) [redacted]
Text Message
Today 3:49 PM
Sent from your Twilio trial account - Bird spotted! Gallus gallus (Probability: 89.1%)
Text Message

Build a Portable
Speed Trap

Portable "Speed Trap"

- Uses **ML** to identify vehicles on the road
- Uses a **doppler radar sensor** to gather speed
- Uses a **Notecard** to relay aggregated data to cloud
- Uses a **cloud-based dashboard** for reporting

OmniPreSense
OPS243
NOTECARRIER-PI

ubidots
Devices
Data
Speed Trap
Jul 06 2021 11:14 - Jul 06 2021 12:14
Deployed Location
Madison
Leaflet
Average Recorded Speed
35.45
0
100
Frequency of Speeding
0.50
Fastest Speed
Maximum (07/06/2021 11:14 - 07/06/2021 12:14)
54.00
Last Updated: 07/06/2021 12:13
Speed Limit
Last value
30.00
Last Updated: 07/06/2021 12:13

Thermal Image Anomaly Detection

NOTECARRIER-PI

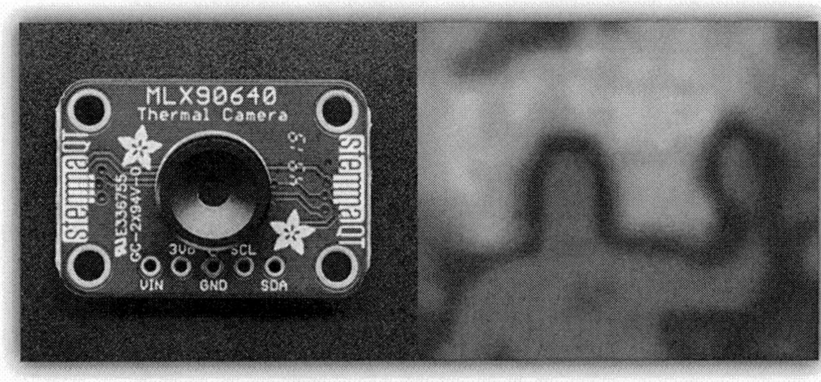
MLX90640
Thermal Camera
SCL
VIN
GND
SDA

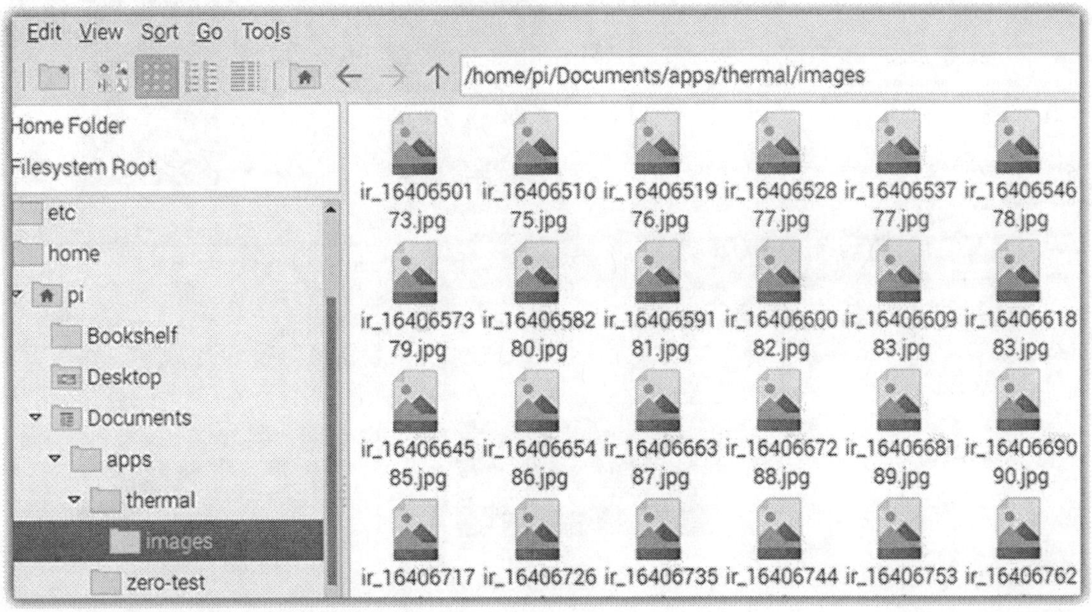
Edit View Sort Go Tools
/home/pi/Documents/apps/thermal/images
Home Folder
Filesystem Root
etc
home
pi
Bookshelf
Desktop
Documents
apps
thermal
images
zero-test
ir_1640650173.jpg
ir_1640651075.jpg
ir_1640651976.jpg
ir_1640652877.jpg
ir_1640653777.jpg
ir_1640654678.jpg
ir_1640657379.jpg
ir_1640658280.jpg
ir_1640659181.jpg
ir_1640660082.jpg
ir_1640660983.jpg
ir_1640661883.jpg
ir_1640664585.jpg
ir_1640665486.jpg
ir_1640666387.jpg
ir_1640667288.jpg
ir_1640668189.jpg
ir_1640669090.jpg
ir_16406717
ir_16406726
ir_16406735
ir_16406744
ir_16406753
ir_16406762

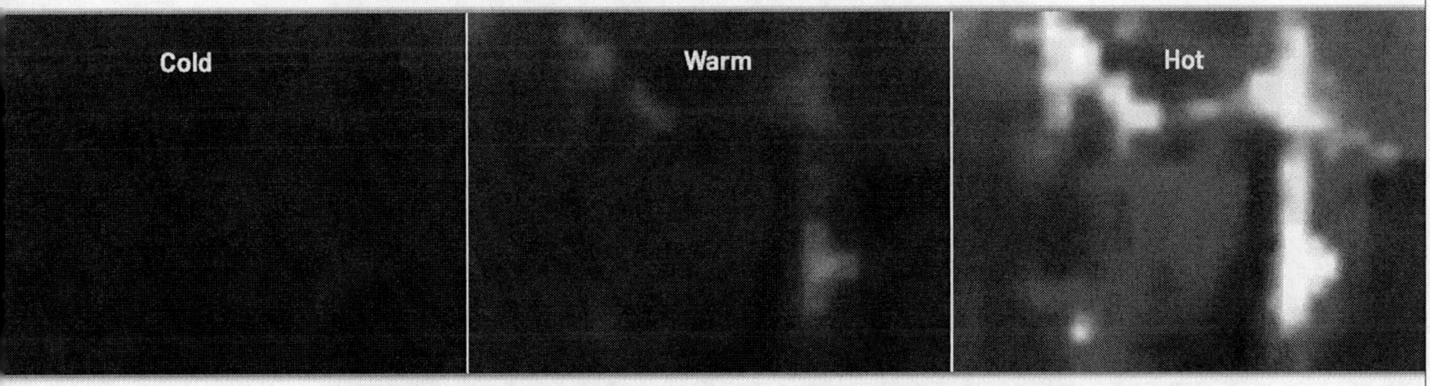
Cold
Warm
Hot

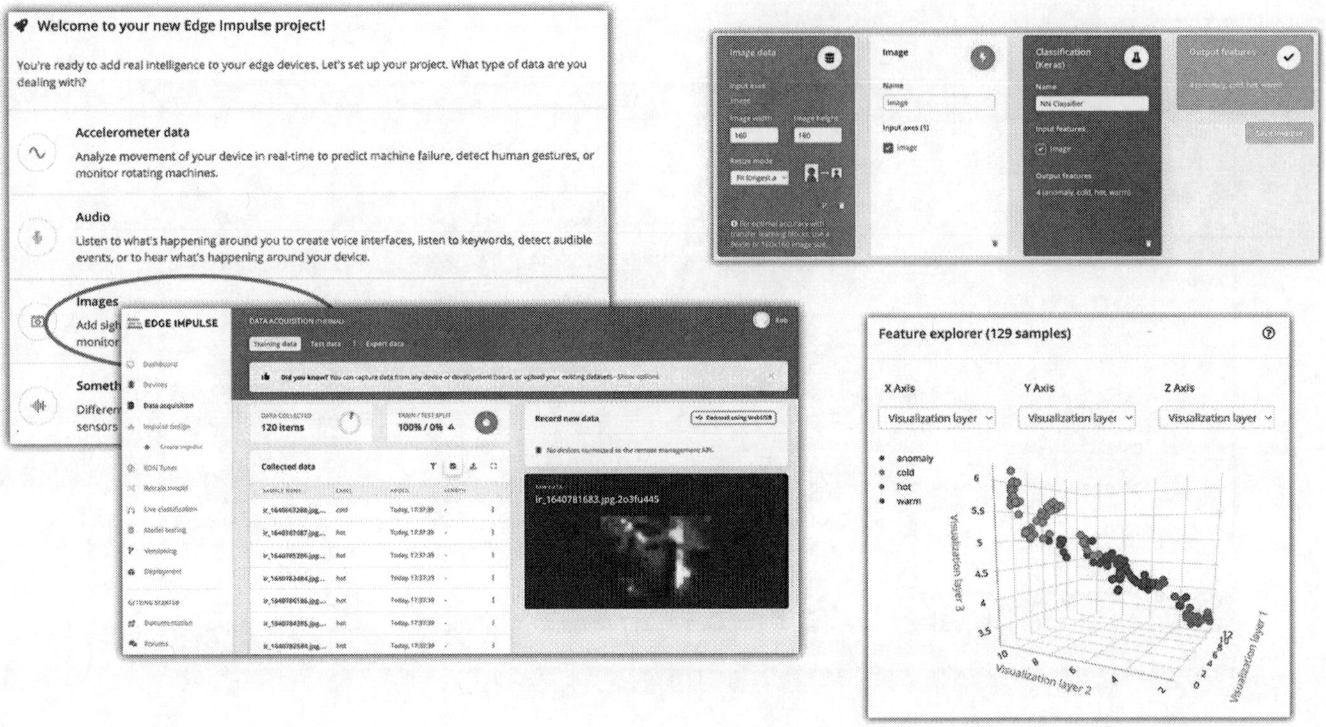
Welcome to your new Edge Impulse project!
You're ready to add real intelligence to your edge devices. Let's set up your project. What type of data are you dealing with?
Accelerometer data
Analyze movement of your device in real-time to predict machine failure, detect human gestures, or monitor rotating machines.
Audio
Listen to what's happening around you to create voice interfaces, listen to keywords, detect audible events, or to hear what's happening around your device.
Images
EDGE IMPULSE
120 items
100% / 0%
Collected data
Record new data
ir_1640781683.jpg.2o3fu445
Image data
Image
Classification (Keras)
Output features
Feature explorer (129 samples)
X Axis
Y Axis
Z Axis
Visualization layer
anomaly
cold
hot
warm
Visualization layer 1
Visualization layer 2
Visualization layer 3

ubidots twilio

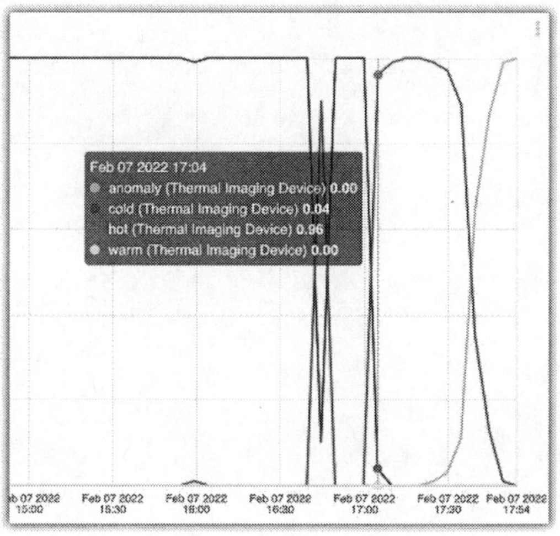

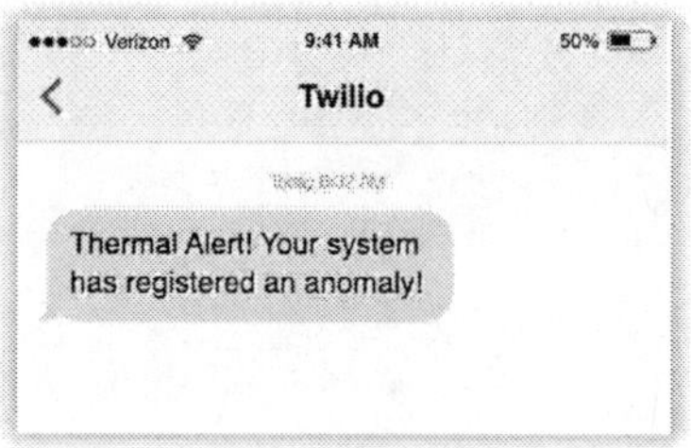


```
# initialize variables for Edge Impulse
runner = None
dir_path = os.path.dirname(os.path.realpath(__file__))
modelfile = os.path.join(dir_path, "modelfile.eim")

# initialize the Blues Wireless Notecard (blues.io)
productUID = keys.PRODUCT_UID
port = I2C("/dev/i2c-1")
nCard = notecard.OpenI2C(port, 0, 0)

# associate Notecard with a project on Notehub.io
hub.set(nCard, product=productUID, mode="periodic", outbound=30, inbound=720)

def main():

    print('MODEL: ' + modelfile)

    with ImageImpulseRunner(modelfile) as runner:
        try:
            model_info = runner.init()
            print('Loaded runner
                  model_info['pro
            labels = model_info['

            # grab image from the
            filename = thermal.ta
            img = cv2.imread("images/" + filename)

            features, cropped = runner.get_features_from_image(img)
            res = runner.classify(features)

            if "classification" in res["result"].keys():
                            note_body = {}
                for label in labels:
                    score = res['result']['classification'][label]
                    print('%s: %.2f\t' % (label, score), end='')
                    note_body[label] = round(score, 4)

                note.add(nCard,
                        file="thermal.qo",
                        body=note_body)


while True:
    main()
    time.sleep(60 * 5)
```

hackster.io/blues-wireless

blues
Break Time

blues
Lab #3: TinyML
bit.ly/blues-ml

EMBEDDED RUST
FOR C PROGRAMMERS
BENINGO
EMBEDDED GROUP
Presented by: JACOB BENINGO
EMBEDDED
SOFTWARE ACADEMY

BENINGO
EMBEDDED GROUP
Simplifying Concepts, Delivering Success℠
6
THE SPEAKER
Jacob Beningo
Beningo Embedded Group
CEO & Founder
Focus: Embedded Software Consulting and Training
Specializes in the design of real-time, microcontroller based embedded software.
Embedded Software Design
MicroPython Projects
Reusable Firmware Development
Blogs for Embedded.com, DesignNews.com, etc, focused on embedded system design techniques and challenges.
Visit www.beningo.com to learn more ...
©2023 Beningo Embedded Group. All Rights Reserved.

0

Session Goals

"Without a defined path, every path is aimless"

\- Unknown

SESSION GOALS

A few simple take-a-ways

- How Rust fits into the industry
- Containerizing the Rust Environment
- The Peripheral Access Crate (PAC)
- Creating your first blinky LED program
- Rust language fundamentals

OBJECTIVE

Learn about Rust for embedded.

Demo: Blinky LED

SESSION GOALS

Download the Materials

Slides, Lab and Solutions can be downloaded from:

- https://mailchi.mp/beningo/rust

1 Embedded Programming Languages

"You can't allow tradition to get in the way of innovation. There's a need to respect the past, but it's a mistake to revere your past."

- Bob Iger

EMBEDDED PROGRAMMING LANGUAGES

General Language Popularity

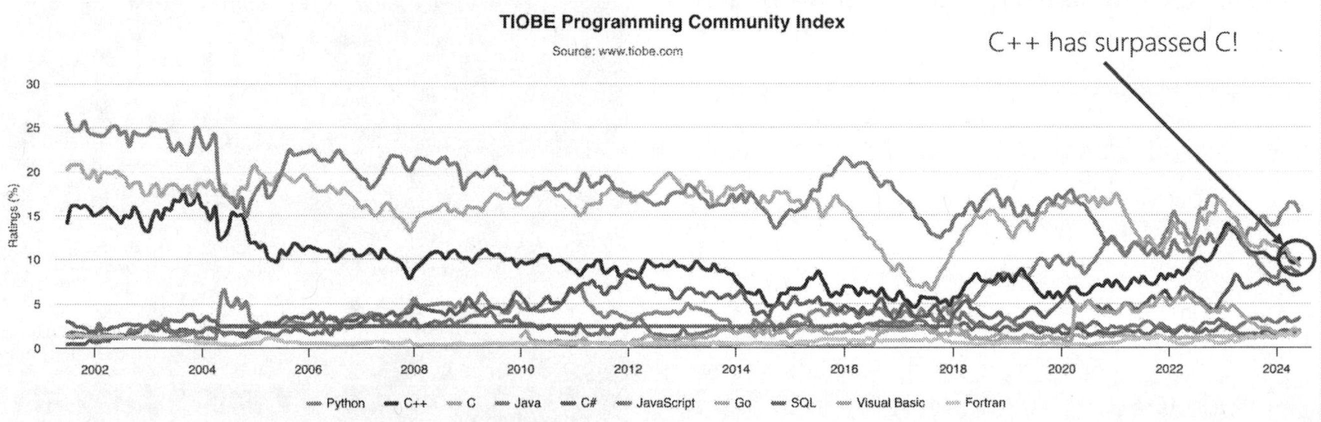

EMBEDDED PROGRAMMING LANGUAGES

Embedded Software Languages

Most Popular Embedded

- C (60 - 70%)
- C++ (20% - 25%)
- Python (<5%)
- Assembly
- Other

Note: 13-14% of Rust Developers are developing bare-metal embedded systems! Source

Jun 2024	Jun 2023	Change	Programming Language	Ratings	Change
1	1		Python	15.39%	+2.93%
2	3	^	C++	10.03%	-1.33%
3	2	⌄	C	9.23%	-3.14%
4	4		Java	8.40%	-2.88%
5	5		C#	6.65%	-0.06%
6	7	^	JavaScript	3.32%	+0.51%
7	14	⇈	Go	1.93%	+0.93%
8	9	^	SQL	1.75%	+0.28%
9	6	⌄	Visual Basic	1.66%	-1.67%
13	10	⌄	Assembly language	1.26%	-0.03%
17	20	^	Rust	1.17%	+0.26%

EMBEDDED PROGRAMMING LANGUAGES

What is Rust?

Rust is a modern systems programming language focused on safety, speed, and concurrency.

- Developed by Mozilla Research, with the first stable release in 2015
- Employs a rich type system and ownership model to guarantee memory and thread safety
- Uses a unique system of ownership with rules that the compiler checks at compile time to achieve memory safety without garbage collection
- Advanced features like ownership, types, and borrowing prevent data races at compile time
- Strives for performance equal to C in terms of speed and control over system resources
- Rust's build system and package manager make it easy to manage dependencies through crates and Cargo

Can still leverage existing C code and libraries!

2 Rust in Embedded Systems

BENINGO EMBEDDED GROUP

RUST IN EMBEDDED SYSTEMS

Why choose Rust for Embedded?

Advantages:

- Memory Safety
- Concurrency Safety
- Zero Overhead Abstractions
- Cross-Platform Development
- Modern Tooling
- Growing ecosystem
- Deterministic resource cleanup
- Compile-time error checking
- Interoperability

Disadvantages:

- Steep learning curve
- Smaller talent pool
- Limited library support for some targets
- Longer compile times
- Evolving language and ecosystem
- Verbose error handling
- Limited support for very low-level dev
- Lack of IDE support similar to C/C++
- Cross compilation complexity

BENINGO EMBEDDED GROUP

RUST IN EMBEDDED SYSTEMS

Language Mapping

Ownership and borrowing: Critical to safety. Similar to C++ concepts like smart pointers, references, move semantics etc.

Generics: C++ templates

No inheritance: Only uses composition.

Traits: behave like abstract classes and interfaces. Provides polymorphism..

Cargo: Built-in package manager and build system tool(s)

Attributes: think preprocessor directives

Unsafe: allows unsafe libraries and other language code to be executed.

Build Types: standard builds included in the language: release, debug, and test.

RUST IN EMBEDDED SYSTEMS

Memory Safety - A C Example

```c
#include <stdio.h>
#include <stdint.h>

int main (void){
    printf ("Hello, world!\n");
    printf ("Let's overflow the buffer!\r\n");

    uint32_t array[5] = {0, 0, 0, 0, 0,};

    for(int index = 0; index < 6; index++) {
      printf("Index %d: %d\r\n", index, array[index]);
    }

    return 0;
}
```

Buffer Overflows

A buffer overflow is a type of software vulnerability that occurs when more data is written to a buffer in memory than the buffer can store. This can cause the data stored in adjacent memory locations to be overwritten, leading to unintended and potentially harmful consequences.

Buffer overflows can cause crashes, corrupt data, or even allow attackers to execute arbitrary code on the system.

RUST IN EMBEDDED SYSTEMS

Memory Safety - A Rust Example

```rust
fn main() {
  println!("Hello World!");
  println!("Let's overflow the buffer!");

  let array: [u32; 5] = [0;5];

  for index in 0..array.len() + 1 {
    println!("Index {}: {} ", index, array[index])
  }
}
```

Buffer Overflow Detection

- **Bounds Checking**: Data can never be written outside a buffer's boundaries
- **Ownership and Borrowing**: Prevents use-after-free and double-free bugs.
- **Safe Rust**: Language subset that makes it easier to write memory safe code.
- **Mutability**: by default, variables are not mutable and must be declared so.

RUST IN EMBEDDED SYSTEMS

Running the Applications

C Example

```
Hello, world!
Let's overflow the buffer!
Index 0: 0
Index 1: 0
Index 2: 0
Index 3: 0
Index 4: 0
Index 5: 1
```

Rust Example

```
beningo@Jacobs-MacBook-Pro buffer_overrun % cargo run
   Compiling buffer_overrun v0.1.0 (/Users/beningo/rust/buffer_overrun)
    Finished dev [unoptimized + debuginfo] target(s) in 0.39s
     Running `target/debug/buffer_overrun`
Hello World!
Let's overflow the buffer!
Index 0: 0
Index 1: 0
Index 2: 0
Index 3: 0
Index 4: 0
thread 'main' panicked at 'index out of bounds: the len is 5 but the index is 5', src/main.rs:8:42
note: run with `RUST_BACKTRACE=1` environment variable to display a backtrace
beningo@Jacobs-MacBook-Pro buffer_overrun %
```


3 The Rust Toolchain

THE RUST TOOLCHAIN

What is needed to build Rust applications?

- **Rustup** is a command-line tool for managing Rust versions and associated tools. It simplifies installing and managing different versions of Rust and associated toolchains.
- **Cargo** is the Rust package manager. It handles dependencies, compiles packages, runs tests and generates documentation.
- **Rustc** is the Rust compiler, which converts Rust code into executable binaries.

https://www.rust-lang.org/learn/get-started

THE RUST TOOLCHAIN

Rust Toolchain Overview

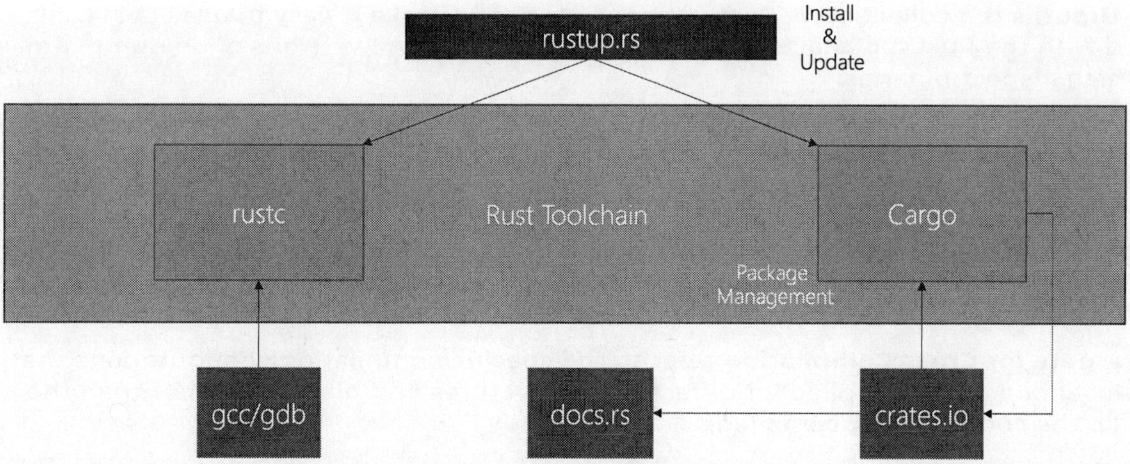

THE RUST TOOLCHAIN

Rustup

Visit https://rustup.rs/

- Follow install instructions

```
beningo@Jacobs-MacBook-Pro ~ % rustc -V
rustc 1.65.0 (897e37553 2022-11-02)
beningo@Jacobs-MacBook-Pro ~ %
```

To install Rust, if you are running Unix,
run the following in your terminal, then follow the onscreen instructions.

```
$ curl --proto '=https' --tlsv1.2 -sSf https://sh.rustup.rs | sh
```

If you are running Windows 64-bit,
download and run
rustup-init.exe
then follow the onscreen instructions.

If you are running Windows 32-bit,
download and run
rustup-init.exe
then follow the onscreen instructions.

THE RUST TOOLCHAIN

What is needed to build Embedded Rust applications?

- **Cargo-Binutils** is a collection of Cargo subcommands to make it easy to use LLVM tools shipped with the Rust toolchain. These tools include the LLVM versions of objdump, nm, and size, which inspect binaries.
- **LLVM Tools** are a collection of modular and reusable compiler and toolchain technologies.
- **Cargo-Generate** is a developer tool to help you get up and running quickly with a new Rust project by leveraging a pre-existing git repository as a template.
- **GNU Arm Toolchain is a cross-compilation toolchain** for ARM Cortex-M processors. It includes the GCC compiler and other necessary tools to compile code for ARM-based microcontrollers.
- **Rust Targets for Cross Compilation** refer to the specific compilation configurations that allow Rust code to be compiled for different architectures and platforms other than the one on which the code is being compiled.

BENINGO
EMBEDDED GROUP

Simplifying Concepts, Delivering Success℠ | 25

4 Containerizing Rust

BENINGO
EMBEDDED GROUP

Simplifying Concepts, Delivering Success℠ | 26

CONTAINERIZING RUST

Docker Containers

A **container** is a standard unit of software that packages up code and all its dependencies, so the application runs quickly and reliably from one computing environment to another.

A **Docker container** image is a lightweight, standalone, executable package of software that includes everything needed to run an application: code, runtime, system tools, system libraries and settings.

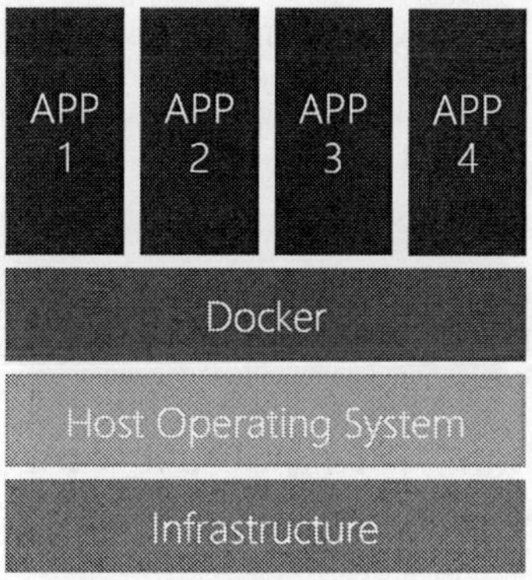

CONTAINERIZING RUST

Benefits of Containers

1. **Consistent Environment**: Containers provide a consistent development environment across all stages of the embedded software lifecycle, from development to testing to deployment. This reduces the "it works on my machine" problem.
2. **Isolation**: Containers isolate the build environment from the host system, ensuring that dependencies and configurations do not clash with the developer's environment or with other projects.
3. **Dependency Control**: By using containers, you can precisely control and version the dependencies and tools required for your build, ensuring that every build uses the exact same set of tools and libraries
4. **Portability**: Since containers package an application with all of its dependencies, the containerized build system can easily be moved between different machines, different CI/CD systems, or even different cloud providers without needing any changes.
5. **CI/CD Integration**: Containers integrate well with continuous integration and continuous deployment (CI/CD) pipelines, allowing you to create reproducible builds and automate the testing and deployment of embedded software.

DOCKER CONTAINERS

Docker Architecture

Client – Docker API and command interface.

Daemon – listens for API requests and manages Docker objects.

Images – ready-to-use templates with instructions for creating a container.

Container – A runnable instance of an image.

Registry – stores Docker images.

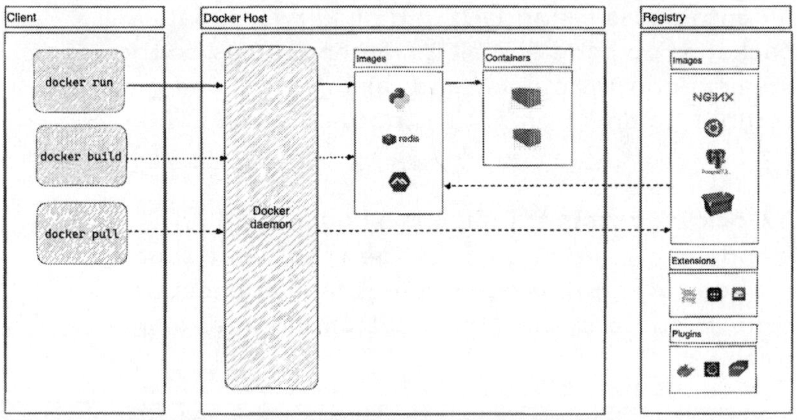

CONTAINERIZING RUST

Container Demo

GOING FURTHER

Lab #1 – Containerize Rust

In this lab, you'll get your Rust environment containerized:

- Create a Dockerfile
- Build an image
- Verify the rust toolchain
- Create a Hello World! application.

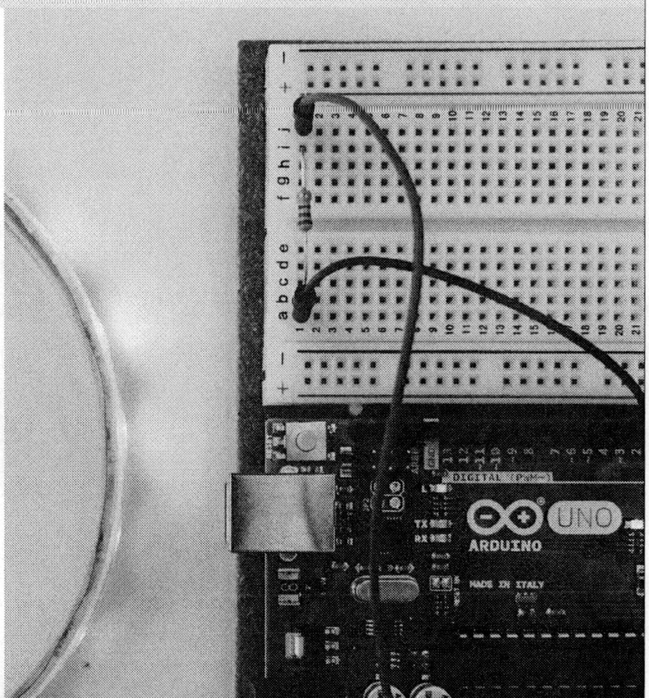

5 The Peripheral Access Crate (PAC)

CRATES

Overview

- A crate is a compilation unit in Rust.
- Rust treats each *.rs file as a crate file.
- There are several types of crates for embedded developers.

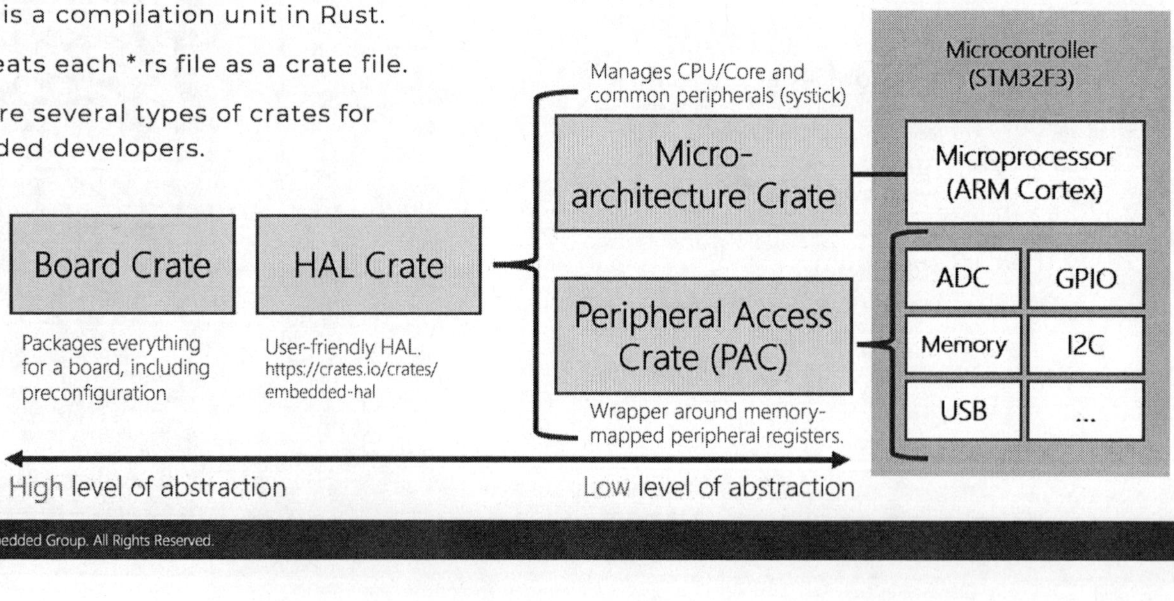

THE PERIPHERAL ACCESS CRATE (PAC)

Defined

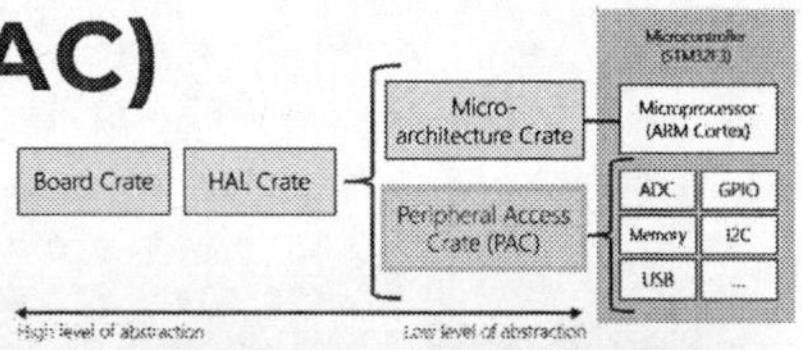

What is the PAC?

- PAC stands for Peripheral Access Crate.
- Provides direct, low-level access to a microcontroller's peripherals.
- Auto-generated from the microcontroller's SVD (System View Description) files, ensuring accuracy and completeness.

Key Features

- Type Safety: Utilizes Rust's type system to prevent common bugs (e.g., invalid register access).
- Memory Safety: Ensures safe access to peripheral registers, mitigating risks of memory corruption.
- Concurrency Safety: Facilitates safe sharing of peripherals between tasks in concurrent environments.

```
#![no_std]
#![no_main]

use panic_halt as _; // panic handler

use cortex_m_rt::entry;
use tm4c123x;

#[entry]
pub fn init() -> (Delay, Leds) {
    let cp = cortex_m::Peripherals::take().unwrap();
    let p = tm4c123x::Peripherals::take().unwrap();

    let pwm = p.PWM0;
    pwm.ctl.write(|w| w.globalsync0().clear_bit());
    // Mode = 1 => Count up/down mode
    pwm._2_ctl.write(|w| w.enable().set_bit().mode().set_bit());
    pwm._2_gena.write(|w| w.actcmpau().zero().actcmpad().one());
    // 528 cycles (264 up and down) = 4 loops per video line (2112 cycles)
    pwm._2_load.write(|w| unsafe { w.load().bits(263) });
    pwm._2_cmpa.write(|w| unsafe { w.compa().bits(64) });
    pwm.enable.write(|w| w.pwm4en().set_bit());
}
```


THE PERIPHERAL ACCESS CRATE (PAC)

How it works

How PACs Work:

- Each PAC corresponds to a specific microcontroller or family, encapsulating all peripheral definitions.
- Developers interact with hardware registers directly, using strongly-typed Rust structs and enums.
- Provides the foundation for higher-level abstractions, like HALs (Hardware Abstraction Layers).

Benefits:

- Accuracy: Reflects the microcontroller's hardware design accurately, enabling precise control over hardware features.
- Efficiency: Low overhead, direct manipulation of hardware registers without intermediate abstractions.
- Flexibility: Allows for advanced techniques and optimizations specific to the hardware's capabilities.

Use Cases:

- Custom driver development for peripherals not covered by existing libraries.
- High-performance, low-level embedded applications requiring fine-grained hardware control.
- Learning and teaching purposes, providing insights into microcontroller architecture and peripheral programming.

BENINGO
EMBEDDED GROUP

Simplifying Concepts, Delivering Success℠ | 35

6 Creating a PAC with svd2rust

BENINGO
EMBEDDED GROUP

Simplifying Concepts, Delivering Success℠ | 36

THE PERIPHERAL ACCESS CRATE (PAC)

Peripheral Access Crates

svd2rust is a command-line tool in the Rust embedded ecosystem designed to generate Rust Peripheral Access Crates (PACs) from System View Description (SVD) files.

SVD files are XML documents that describe the hardware peripherals of a microcontroller, including registers and their bitfields, in a standardized format.

Key Features:

- Code generation
- Documentation
- Zero-Run-Time Cost Abstractions

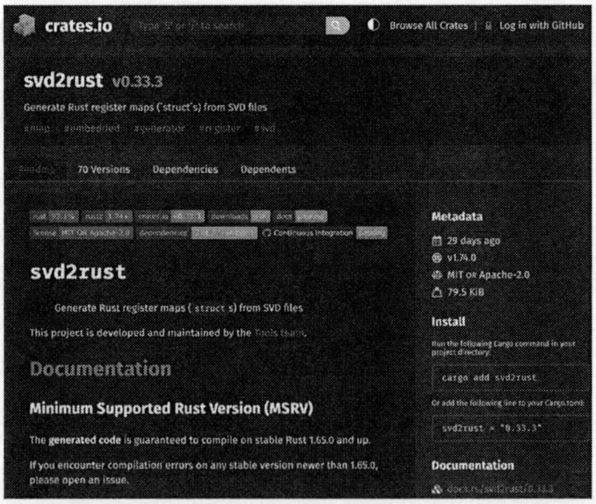

CREATING A PAC WITH SVD2RUST

The STM32U575 Nucleo Board

A feature-rich development tool designed for IoT applications, leveraging the power of the STM32U575ZI-Q microcontroller.

- Equipped with an ARM Cortex-M33 core that operates at up to 160 MHz with 2 MB of Flash memory and 784 KB of SRAM.
- Includes Red, Green, and Blue user LEDs, USB, Arduino Headers, user push button, and more.

CREATING A PAC WITH SVD2RUST

Running svd2rust

Update Rust:

```
rustup update
```

Install the tool:

```
cargo install svd2rust
```

Create a new library project:

```
cargo new stm32u575_pac --lib
```

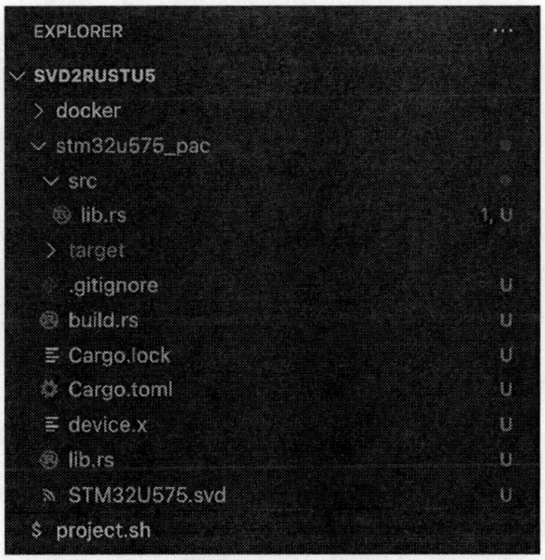

CREATING A PAC WITH SVD2RUST

Getting your SVD file

- SVD Files are available from Silicon Vendor
- Place the SVD into your project directory
- Run the tool

  svd2rust –i <device>.svd

```
root@0a9ee1908b65:/home/app/stm32u575_pac# svd2rust -i STM32U575.svd
[INFO  svd2rust] Parsing device from SVD file
[INFO  svd2rust] Rendering device
```

STM32U575.SVD Download

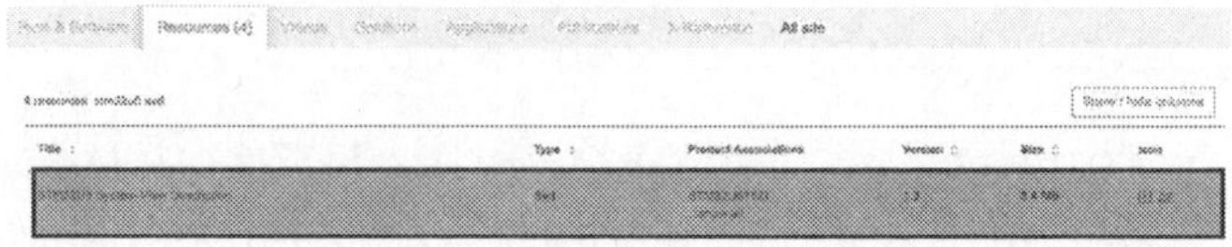

https://www.st.com/content/ccc/resource/technical/ecad_models_and_symbols/svd/group0/a5/b3/ec/b4/9b/42/43/f0/STM32U5_svd/files/STM32U5_svd.zip/jcr:content/translations/en.STM32U5_svd.zip

CREATING A PAC WITH SVD2RUST

Understanding svd2rust output

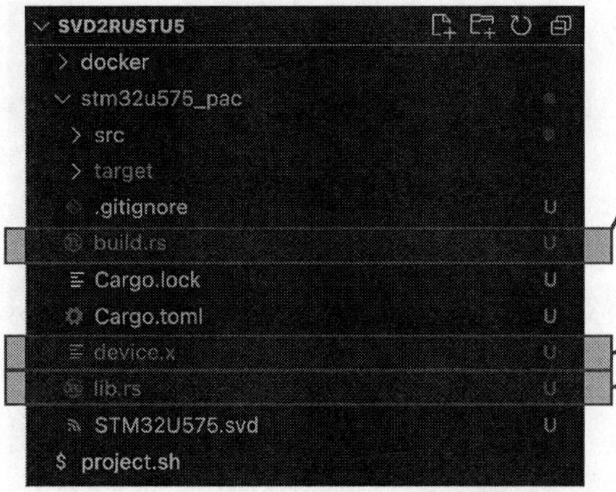

Build script

- Conditional compilation
- Device.x handling
- Linker configuration
- Build dependency tracking

Linker fragment for interrupts

Peripheral Implementation

- Not “clean”, or easily readable

CREATING A PAC WITH SVD2RUST

Separate and Format Modules

Install form (if you don't have it already)

```
cargo install form
```

Remove src

```
rm -rf src
```

Split lib.rs into separate modules

```
form -i lib.rs -o src/ && rm lib.rs
```

Format to be human readable and "clean"

```
cargo fmt
```

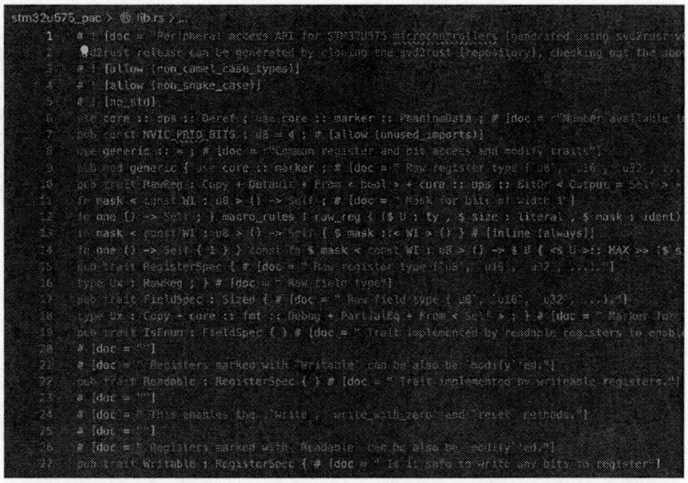

CREATING A PAC WITH SVD2RUST

Add dependencies to the toml

Add to TOML file:

[dependencies]

critical-section = { version = "1.1.2", optional = true }

cortex-m = "0.7.7"

cortex-m-rt = { version = "0.7.3", optional = true }

vcell = "0.1.3"

[features]

rt = ["cortex-m-rt/device"]

- Provides a mechanism for creating critical sections within your code, allowing you to prevent race conditions and ensure data consistency when accessing shared resources from multiple contexts, such as interrupt service routines (ISRs) and the main program.
- Offers low-level access to core ARM Cortex-M functionality, such as registers and instructions specific to these microcontrollers
- Provides runtime support for ARM Cortex-M microcontrollers, including startup code, linker scripts, and definitions for the interrupt vector table.
- Offers volatile cell types, enabling safe read and write operations to memory-mapped peripheral registers.
- This feature flag is typically used to conditionally compile parts of the application that require runtime support, such as startup code and interrupt handling.

Check Rust Documentation for latest version #'s

BENINGO EMBEDDED GROUP

Simplifying Concepts, Delivering Success℠ | 43

CREATING A PAC WITH SVD2RUST

Build the crate

Build the crate:

```
cargo build -r
```

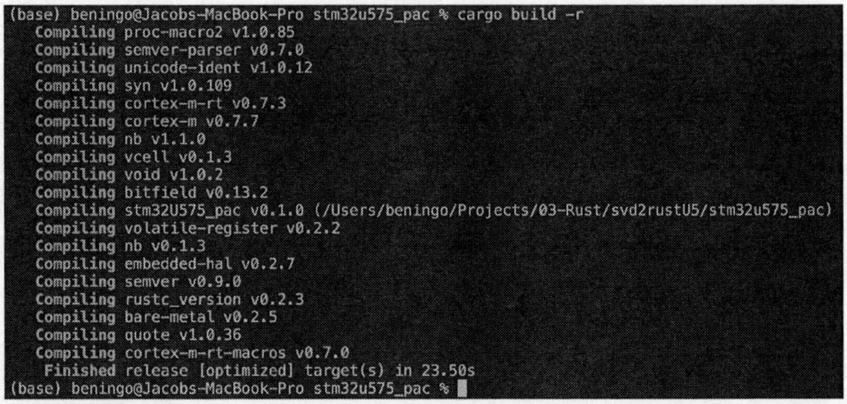

BENINGO EMBEDDED GROUP

Simplifying Concepts, Delivering Success℠ | 44

7 Embedded Rust Applications

EMBEDDED RUST APPLICATIONS

Creating a New Project

Embedded Applications are special:

- Linker files
- Target core support
- Semi-hosting / ITM
- Debug scripts
- SVD files
- Constrained memory environments
- etc

```
beningo@Jacobs-MacBook-Pro rust % cargo generate --git https://github.com/rust-embedded/cortex-m-quickstart
   Project Name: stm32f3_hello
   Renaming project called `stm32f3_hello` to `stm32f3-hello`...
   Destination: /Users/beningo/rust/stm32f3-hello ...
   project-name: stm32f3-hello ...
   Generating template ...
[ 1/25]   Done: .cargo/config.toml
[ 2/25]   Done: .cargo
[ 3/25]   Done: .gitignore
[ 4/25]   Done: .vscode/README.md
[ 5/25]   Done: .vscode/extensions.json
[ 6/25]   Done: .vscode/launch.json
[ 7/25]   Done: .vscode/tasks.json
[ 8/25]   Done: .vscode
[ 9/25]   Done: Cargo.toml
[10/25]   Done: README.md
[11/25]   Done: build.rs
[12/25]   Done: examples/allocator.rs
[13/25]   Done: examples/crash.rs
[14/25]   Done: examples/device.rs
[15/25]   Done: examples/exception.rs
[16/25]   Done: examples/hello.rs
[17/25]   Done: examples/itm.rs
[18/25]   Done: examples/panic.rs
[19/25]   Done: examples/test_on_host.rs
[20/25]   Done: examples
[21/25]   Done: memory.x
[22/25]   Done: openocd.cfg
[23/25]   Done: openocd.gdb
[24/25]   Done: src/main.rs
[25/25]   Done: src
   Moving generated files into: `/Users/beningo/rust/stm32f3-hello`...
   Initializing a fresh Git repository
   Done! New project created /Users/beningo/rust/stm32f3-hello
beningo@Jacobs-MacBook-Pro rust %
```


BENINGO
EMBEDDED GROUP

EMBEDDED RUST APPLICATIONS

main.rs

Don't link to the standard crate!

Define how panics are handled

Don't want to link to nightly

Divergent Function. Only process running on target hardware

Define the entry function into application

```rust
#![no_std]
#![no_main]

// pick a panicking behavior
use panic_halt as _; // you can put a breakpoint on `rust_begin_unwind` to catch panics
// use panic_abort as _; // requires nightly
// use panic_itm as _; // logs messages over ITM; requires ITM support
// use panic_semihosting as _; // logs messages to the host stderr; requires a debugger

use cortex_m::asm;
use cortex_m_rt::entry;

#[entry]
fn main() -> ! {
    asm::nop(); // To not have main optimize to abort in release mode, remove when you add code

    loop {
        // your code goes here
    }
}
```

EMBEDDED RUST APPLICATIONS

std vs. no_std

feature	no_std	std
heap (dynamic memory)	*	✓
collections (Vec, BTreeMap, etc)	**	✓
stack overflow protection	✘	✓
runs init code before main	✘	✓
libstd available	✘	✓
libcore available	✓	✓
writing firmware, kernel, or bootloader code	✓	✘

* Only if you use the `alloc` crate and use a suitable allocator like alloc-cortex-m.

** Only if you use the `collections` crate and configure a global default allocator.

** HashMap and HashSet are not available due to a lack of a secure random number generator.

EMBEDDED RUST APPLICATIONS

Target Configuration

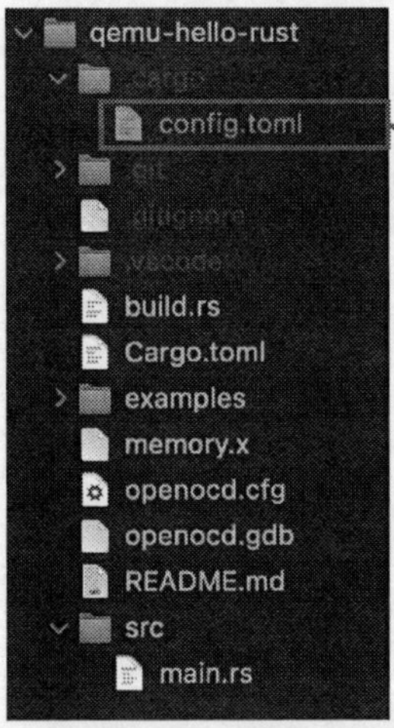


```
[target.thumbv7m-none-eabi]
# uncomment this to make `cargo run` execute programs on QEMU
# runner = "qemu-system-arm -cpu cortex-m3 -machine lm3s6965evb -nographic -semihosting-config enable=on,target=native -kernel"

[target.'cfg(all(target_arch = "arm", target_os = "none"))']
# uncomment ONE of these three option to make `cargo run` start a GDB session
# which option to pick depends on your system
# runner = "arm-none-eabi-gdb -q -x openocd.gdb"
# runner = "gdb-multiarch -q -x openocd.gdb"
# runner = "gdb -q -x openocd.gdb"

rustflags = [
  # This is needed if your flash or ram addresses are not aligned to 0x10000 in memory.x
  # See https://github.com/rust-embedded/cortex-m-quickstart/pull/95
  "-C", "link-arg=--nmagic",

  # LLD (shipped with the Rust toolchain) is used as the default linker
  "-C", "link-arg=-Tlink.x",

  # if you run into problems with LLD switch to the GNU linker by commenting out
  # this line
  # "-C", "linker=arm-none-eabi-ld",

  # if you need to link to pre-compiled C libraries provided by a C toolchain
  # use GCC as the linker by commenting out both lines above and then
  # uncommenting the three lines below
  # "-C", "linker=arm-none-eabi-gcc",
  # "-C", "link-arg=-Wl,-Tlink.x",
  # "-C", "link-arg=-nostartfiles",
]

[build]
# Pick ONE of these compilation targets
# target = "thumbv6m-none-eabi"        # Cortex-M0 and Cortex-M0+
# target = "thumbv7m-none-eabi"        # Cortex-M3
target = "thumbv7em-none-eabi"         # Cortex-M4 and Cortex-M7 (no FPU)
# target = "thumbv7em-none-eabihf"     # Cortex-M4F and Cortex-M7F (with FPU)
# target = "thumbv8m.base-none-eabi"   # Cortex-M23
# target = "thumbv8m.main-none-eabi"   # Cortex-M33 (no FPU)
# target = "thumbv8m.main-none-eabihf" # Cortex-M33 (with FPU)
```

EMBEDDED RUST APPLICATIONS

Compiling an Application

Compile the application for a Cortex-M33

- rustup target add thumbv8m.main-none-eabihf
- cargo build

Use the following to verify the elf file is arm

- cargo readobj --bin blinky -- --file-headers

```
root@20d054703a23:/home/app/blinky# cargo build
   Compiling semver-parser v0.7.0
   Compiling proc-macro2 v1.0.86
   Compiling cortex-m v0.7.7
   Compiling unicode-ident v1.0.12
   Compiling nb v1.1.0
   Compiling syn v1.0.109
   Compiling cortex-m-rt v0.7.3
   Compiling void v1.0.2
   Compiling vcell v0.1.3
   Compiling bitfield v0.13.2
   Compiling critical-section v1.1.2
   Compiling cortex-m-semihosting v0.3.7
   Compiling stm32u575_pac v0.1.0 (/home/app/stm32u575_pac)
   Compiling blinky v0.1.0 (/home/app/blinky)
   Compiling panic-halt v0.2.0
   Compiling nb v0.1.3
   Compiling semver v0.9.0
   Compiling volatile-register v0.2.2
   Compiling embedded-hal v0.2.7
   Compiling rustc_version v0.2.3
   Compiling bare-metal v0.2.5
   Compiling quote v1.0.36
   Compiling cortex-m-rt-macros v0.7.0
    Finished `dev` profile [unoptimized + debuginfo] target(s) in 45.23s
root@20d054703a23:/home/app/blinky# 
```


EMBEDDED RUST APPLICATIONS

Reading an Object File

```
root@20d054703a23:/home/app/blinky# cargo readobj --bin blinky -- --file-headers
    Finished `dev` profile [unoptimized + debuginfo] target(s) in 0.37s
ELF Header:
  Magic:   7f 45 4c 46 01 01 01 00 00 00 00 00 00 00 00 00
  Class:                             ELF32
  Data:                              2's complement, little endian
  Version:                           1 (current)
  OS/ABI:                            UNIX - System V
  ABI Version:                       0
  Type:                              EXEC (Executable file)
  Machine:                           ARM
  Version:                           0x1
  Entry point address:               0x8000259
  Start of program headers:          52 (bytes into file)
  Start of section headers:          910444 (bytes into file)
  Flags:                             0x5000400
  Size of this header:               52 (bytes)
  Size of program headers:           32 (bytes)
  Number of program headers:         5
  Size of section headers:           40 (bytes)
  Number of section headers:         23
  Section header string table index: 21
root@20d054703a23:/home/app/blinky# 
```

EMBEDDED RUST APPLICATIONS

Size Info and Objdump

```
root@20d054703a23:/home/app/blinky# cargo size --bin blinky --release -- -A
   Compiling cortex-m v0.7.7
   Compiling proc-macro2 v1.0.86
   Compiling syn v1.0.109
   Compiling cortex-m-rt v0.7.3
   Compiling bare-metal v0.2.5
   Compiling cortex-m-semihosting v0.3.7
   Compiling stm32u575_pac v0.1.0 (/home/app/stm32u575_pac)
   Compiling blinky v0.1.0 (/home/app/blinky)
   Compiling quote v1.0.36
   Compiling cortex-m-rt-macros v0.7.0
    Finished `release` profile [optimized + debuginfo] target(s) in 23.69s
blinky  :
section              size        addr
.vector_table         600   0x8000000
.text                 600   0x8000258
.rodata                16   0x80004b0
.data                   0  0x20000000
.gnu.sgstubs            0   0x80004c0
.bss                   12  0x20000000
.uninit                 0  0x2000000c
.debug_loc           1104         0x0
.debug_abbrev        2210         0x0
.debug_info         26266         0x0
.debug_aranges        672         0x0
.debug_ranges        1656         0x0
.debug_str          21546         0x0
.comment               64         0x0
.ARM.attributes        58         0x0
.debug_frame          992         0x0
.debug_line          4668         0x0
.debug_pubnames       803         0x0
.debug_pubtypes        71         0x0
Total               61338
```

```
root@376d134fd775:/home/app/blinky# cargo objdump --bin blinky --release -- --disassemble --no-show-raw-insn --print-imm-he
    Finished `release` profile [optimized + debuginfo] target(s) in 0.50s

blinky: file format elf32-littlearm

Disassembly of section .text:

08000258 <__stext>:
 8000258:       bl      0x800047e <__pre_init>  @ imm = #0x222
 800025c:       ldr     r0, [pc, #0x38]         @ 0x8000298 <__stext+0x40>
 800025e:       ldr     r1, [pc, #0x3c]         @ 0x800029c <__stext+0x44>
 8000260:       movs    r2, #0x0
 8000262:       cmp     r1, r0
 8000264:       beq     0x800026a <__stext+0x12> @ imm = #0x2
 8000266:       stm     r0!, {r2}
 8000268:       b       0x8000262 <__stext+0xa> @ imm = #-0xa
 800026a:       ldr     r0, [pc, #0x34]         @ 0x80002a0 <__stext+0x48>
 800026c:       ldr     r1, [pc, #0x34]         @ 0x80002a4 <__stext+0x4c>
 800026e:       ldr     r2, [pc, #0x38]         @ 0x80002a8 <__stext+0x50>
 8000270:       cmp     r1, r0
 8000272:       beq     0x800027a <__stext+0x22> @ imm = #0x4
 8000274:       ldm     r2!, {r3}
 8000276:       stm     r0!, {r3}
 8000278:       b       0x8000270 <__stext+0x18> @ imm = #-0xc
 800027a:       ldr     r0, [pc, #0x30]         @ 0x80002ac <__stext+0x54>
 800027c:       mov.w   r1, #0xf00000
 8000280:       ldr     r2, [r0]
 8000282:       orr.w   r2, r2, r1
 8000286:       str     r2, [r0]
```


EMBEDDED RUST APPLICATIONS

Launch Configuration

Things to update:

- Executable target
- Device
- Config Files
- Svd File
- SWO Configuration

```
{} launch.json U ×
.vscode > {} launch.json > [ ] configurations > {} 1
    "configurations": [
        {
            /* Configuration for the STM32U575 Nucleo board */
            "type": "cortex-debug",
            "request": "launch",
            "name": "Debug (OpenOCD)",
            "servertype": "openocd",
            "cwd": "${workspaceRoot}",
            "preLaunchTask": "Cargo Build (debug)",
            "runToEntryPoint": "main",
            "executable": "./target/thumbv8m.main-none-eabihf/debug/blinky",
            /* Run `cargo build --example itm` and uncomment this line to run itm example */
            // "executable": "./target/thumbv7em-none-eabihf/debug/examples/itm",
            "device": "STM32U575ZIT",
            "configFiles": [
                "interface/stlink-v2-1.cfg",
                "target/stm32u5x.cfg"
            ],
            "svdFile": "${workspaceRoot}/.vscode/stmu575.svd",
            "swoConfig": {
                "enabled": true,
                "cpuFrequency": 8000000,
                "swoFrequency": 2000000,
                "source": "probe",
                "decoders": [
                    { "type": "console", "label": "ITM", "port": 0 }
                ]
            }
        }
    ]
}
```

8 Embedded Rust Blinky Application Example

EMBEDDED RUST BLINKY APPLICATION EXAMPLE

Hello Blinky!

- Use the peripheral pac
- Initialize the clock
- Initialize the GPIO connected to an LED
- Loop and toggle

```
#![no_std]
#![no_main]

use cortex_m_rt::entry;
use panic_halt as _;
use stm32l475_pac::Peripherals;

#[entry]
fn main() -> ! {
    let dp = Peripherals::take().unwrap();

    // Enable clock for GPIOA
    dp.RCC.ahb2enr.modify(|_, w| w.gpioaen().set_bit());

    // Set PA5 as output
    dp.GPIOA.moder.modify(|_, w| w.moder5().bits(0b01));

    // Assuming LED is active high and connected to PA5
    loop {
        // Set PA5 high
        dp.GPIOA.bsrr.write(|w| w.bs5().set_bit());
        // Delay
        delay(4_000_000); // Rough approximation for 500 ms at 8 MHz SysClk

        // Set PA5 low
        dp.GPIOA.bsrr.write(|w| w.br5().set_bit());
        // Delay
        delay(4_000_000); // Rough approximation for 500 ms
    }
}
```

BENINGO
EMBEDDED GROUP

Simplifying Concepts, Delivering Success℠ | 55

EMBEDDED RUST BLINKY APPLICATION EXAMPLE

Hello Blinky!

DEMO

BENINGO
EMBEDDED GROUP

Simplifying Concepts, Delivering Success℠ | 56

GOING FURTHER

Lab #2 – Hello Blinky!

In this lab, you'll create a hello blinky application for the STM32U575 Nucleo Board:

- Create an embedded project form a template
- Configure the template
- Write the blinky application
- Configure and run the blinky application

BENINGO
EMBEDDED GROUP

9 Next Steps

BENINGO
EMBEDDED GROUP

GOING FURTHER

https://shorturl.at/Sssip
Save $100 (33%) using RUSTWS24

To go deeper into Rust with Jacob Beningo, here are some additional resources you may find helpful:

- C to Rust Workshop
- Embedded Software Training
- Consulting and Coaching Services
- Jacob's Blog
- Jacob's Newsletter

Jacob@Beningo.com

www.beningo.com

THANK YOU
Let's Stay Connected
JacobBeningo
Jacob_Beningo
beningoembedded
BENINGO
EMBEDDED GROUP
www.beningo.com
Jacob@beningo.com
EMBEDDED
SOFTWARE ACADEMY
BY BENINGO

Sensors Converge

Key considerations in designing low-power sensors for IoT sustainability to succeed

Amit Purohit

June 24–26, 2024 | Santa Clara, CA

#SensorsConverge

AGENDA

1) Rise of Secure Edge
2) Sensors Proliferation
3) Why Low-Power Designs are Critical
4) Technology Drivers
5) Key Considerations in System Solutions
6) Low Power Sensors for Effective Power Management
7) Mission Profiles
8) Maximizing Value for Customers
9) Summary

#SensorsConverge

Sensors Converge

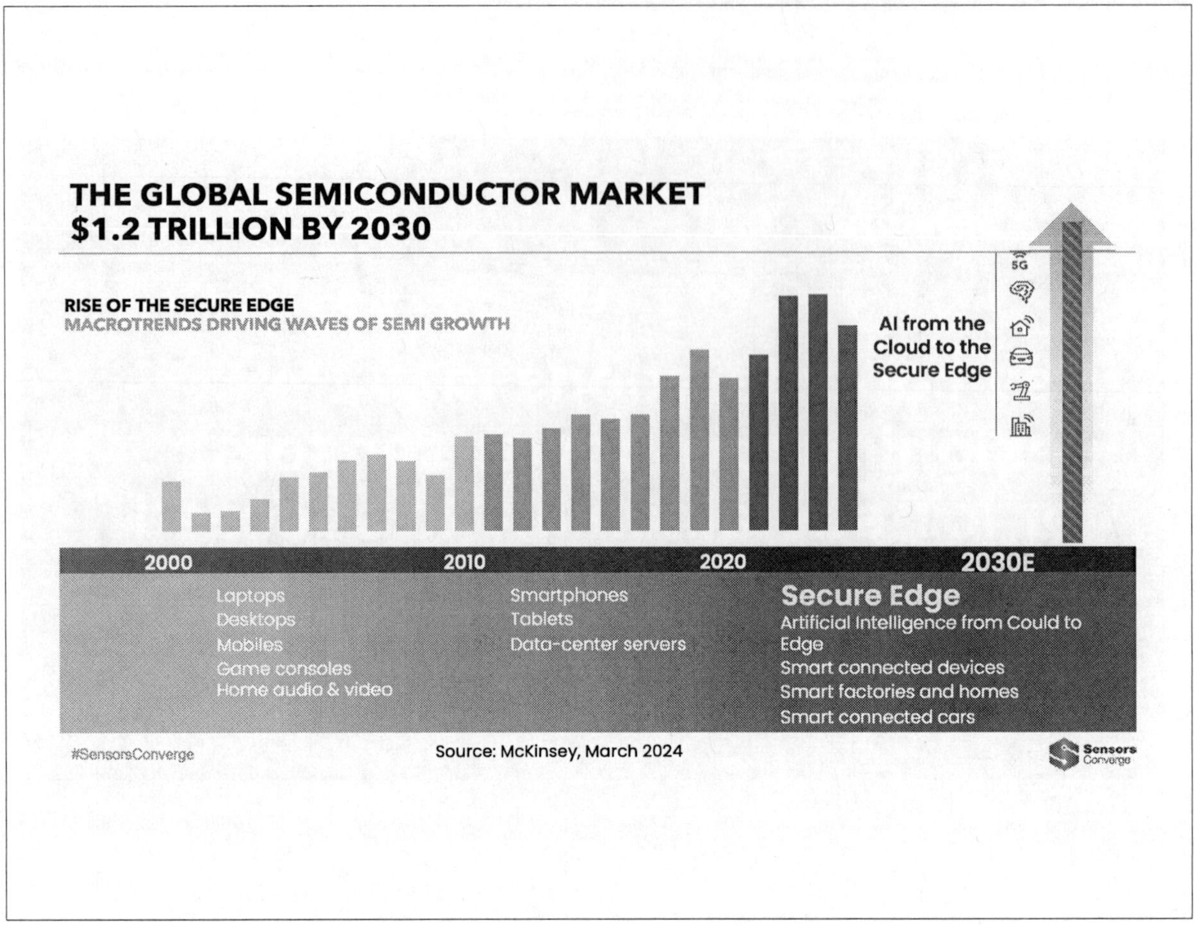
THE GLOBAL SEMICONDUCTOR MARKET
$1.2 TRILLION BY 2030
RISE OF THE SECURE EDGE
MACROTRENDS DRIVING WAVES OF SEMI GROWTH
AI from the Cloud to the Secure Edge
5G
2000
2010
2020
2030E
Laptops
Desktops
Mobiles
Game consoles
Home audio & video
Smartphones
Tablets
Data-center servers
Secure Edge
Artificial Intelligence from Could to Edge
Smart connected devices
Smart factories and homes
Smart connected cars
#SensorsConverge
Source: McKinsey, March 2024
Sensors Converge

SENSORS PROLIFERATION
The broad portfolio of sensing technologies combined with computing & connectivity enabling transformation across a range of IoT/Industrial/Medical applications.
SMART HOME
HOME AUTOMATION
SMART APPLIANCES
INDOOR LOCALIZATION
HOME CONTROL & SECURITY
SMART HEALTH
TELEHEALTH
HEALTHCARE
WEARABLES
HEALTH MONITORS
SMART CITIES
TAMPER/THEFT DETECTION
SMART RETAIL
SMART TRANSIT
SMART UTILITIES
SMART ACCESS
SMART FACTORIES
INDUSTRY 4.0
FACTORY AUTOMATION
SMART LOGISTICS
PREDICTIVE MAINTENANCE
AUTO NON-SAFETY
SECURITY AND CONVENIENCE
KEY-FOB
NAVIGATION
Sensors not only driving multiple use-cases but also enabling effective power consumption in edge devices
#SensorsConverge
Sensors Converge

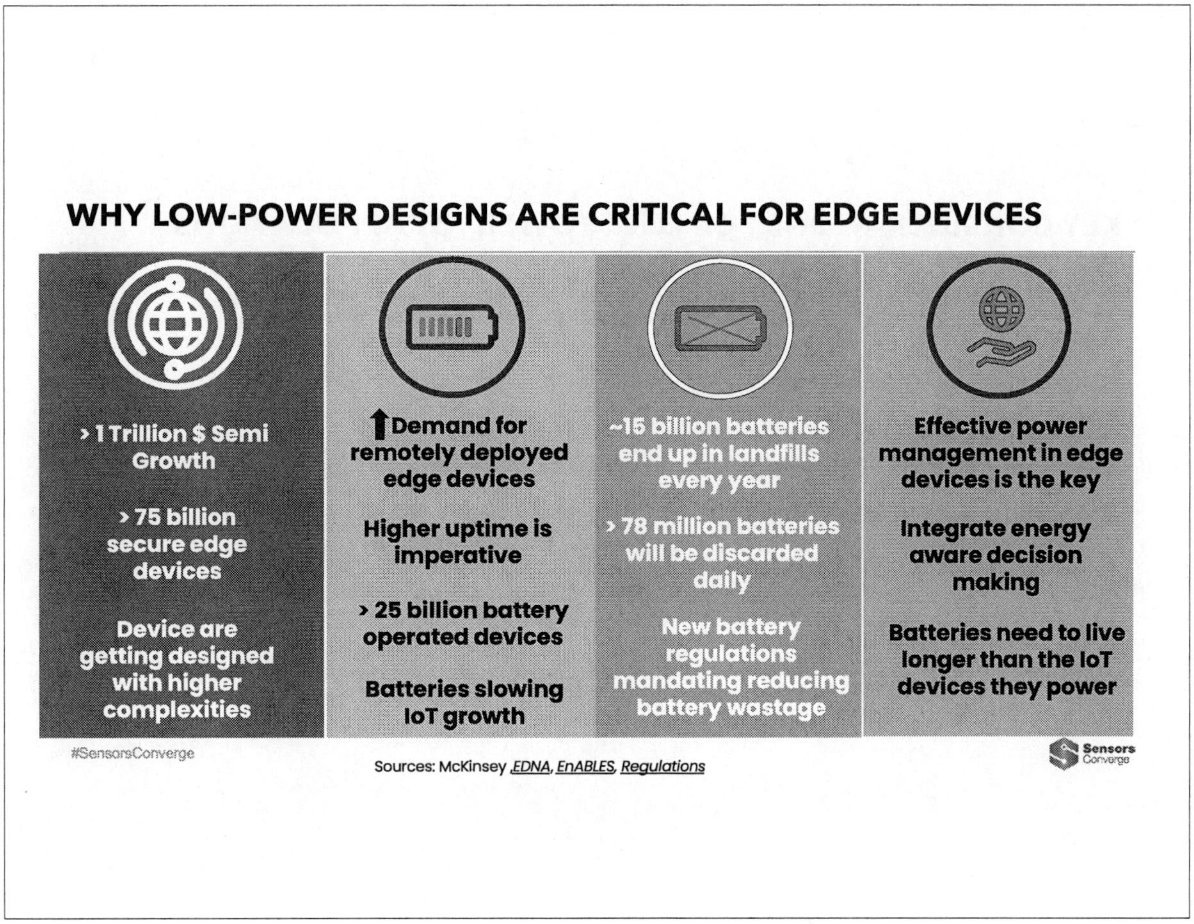
WHY LOW-POWER DESIGNS ARE CRITICAL FOR EDGE DEVICES
> 1 Trillion $ Semi Growth
> 75 billion secure edge devices
Device are getting designed with higher complexities
Demand for remotely deployed edge devices
Higher uptime is imperative
> 25 billion battery operated devices
Batteries slowing IoT growth
~15 billion batteries end up in landfills every year
> 78 million batteries will be discarded daily
New battery regulations mandating reducing battery wastage
Effective power management in edge devices is the key
Integrate energy aware decision making
Batteries need to live longer than the IoT devices they power
#SensorsConverge
Sources: McKinsey ,EDNA, EnABLES, Regulations
Sensors Converge

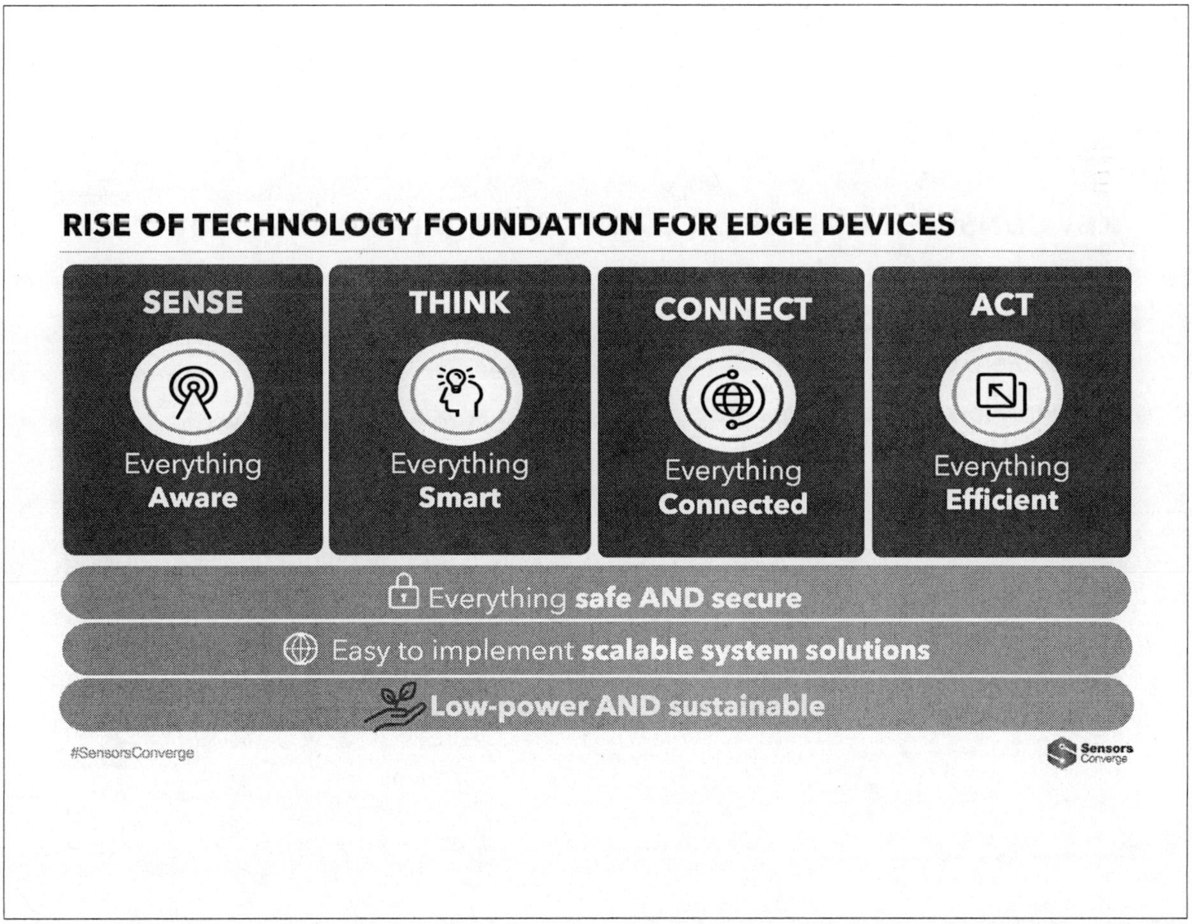
RISE OF TECHNOLOGY FOUNDATION FOR EDGE DEVICES
SENSE
Everything Aware
THINK
Everything Smart
CONNECT
Everything Connected
ACT
Everything Efficient
Everything safe AND secure
Easy to implement scalable system solutions
Low-power AND sustainable
#SensorsConverge
Sensors Converge

KEY CONSIDERATIONS FOR LOW-POWER IOT APPLICATIONS

Low-Power Operation:

- ❑ Integrated PMU
- ❑ Reduced power modes
  - Sleep, Deep-Sleep, Power Down, Deep-Power Down modes
- ❑ Configurable wake-up options
- ❑ Low-power consumption (nAmp to uAmp)
- ❑ Quick wake-up time (transition to active mode)

Embedded Functions:

- ❑ Fully configurable, completely autonomous solution
- ❑ Programmable state machine & thresholds
- ❑ Reduces bandwidth, latency and computational requirements
- ❑ Interrupt mode
- ❑ No complex algorithm, low-code, low-memory

#SensorsConverge

Sensors Converge

KEY CONSIDERATIONS FOR LOW-POWER IOT APPLICATIONS

Autonomous Operation:

- ❑ Use LPTIMER to define autonomous operations.
- ❑ Identify low-power modes that allow LPTIMER functionality without compromising on power.
- ❑ Define Auto-sleep feature, allowing to migrate to power save/sleep mode.
- ❑ Programmable state machine & counters.
- ❑ Provide ease of configurability.

Power Profiling:

- ❑ Identify target applications and use-cases.
- ❑ Measure active and power save/sleep power consumption.
- ❑ Define mission profiles.
- ❑ Define energy aware decision making.
- ❑ Identify value-add of low-power sensing to trigger power save modes.

#SensorsConverge

Sensors Converge

SENSORS FOR EFFECTIVE SYSTEM POWER MANAGEMENT

- Battery operated IoT devices with wireless connectivity (NFC, BLE, UWB, SigFox, LoRaWAN, WiFi etc.) generally have MCUs (ARM Cortex M0+ or M4 or M33 based) that support low power save modes.
- Depending on end use-case, wireless connectivity can consume between 40-70% of the total power consumption of such devices.
- Value-add of having low-power wake up sensor in such devices:
  - Ultra-low power wakeup on motion/magnetic field change : wake up MCU from ultra-low power mode.
  - Reduce the wireless RX/TX time for meaningful data transmission ex: motion anomalies.
  - Depending on acceptable lag in connection restoration for the use-case, significant power saving can be achieved if wireless connection

#SensorsConverge

Low Power Sensors can help increase battery lifetime by 8x – 252x, refer to next slides.

Sensors Converge

MISSION PROFILE STUDIES

- Sensors features and use-cases are getting integrated into many system solutions enabling IoT/Industrial/Medical, automotive non-safety applications.
- In next few slides, we will be covering mission profile studies performed to demonstrate low-power wake up sensors value-add to such system solutions.

Disclaimer: The power consumption numbers for assumed mission profile use-cases only give approximate values to ONLY describe motion sensor value-add in designing power optimized solutions. The actual power consumption might vary based on use-case.

NTAG Smart Sensor

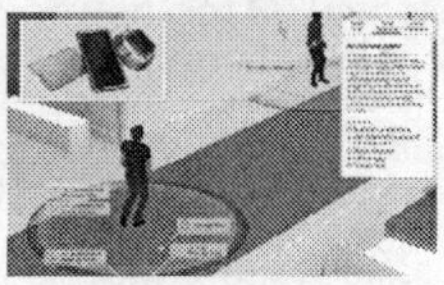

UWB Smart Sensing Tags

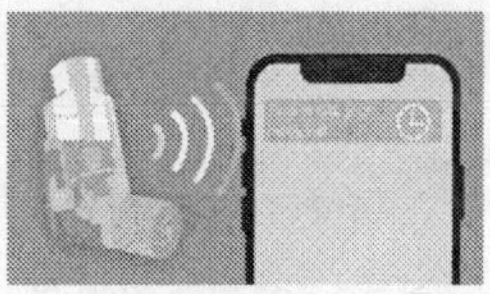

BLE Smart Sensing Inhaler

Sigfox Asset Tracker

#SensorsConverge

Sensors Converge

MISSION PROFILE 1: NTAG SMART SENSOR TAG

Application: A battery-operated condition monitoring data logger device using NFC, RAIN RFID and motion sensors.

Assumptions: Device wakes-up every 10 mins and takes temperature, motion sensor reading. Store anomaly events (if any) to EEPROM.

- ❑ Assuming the device need to only wake-up when there is an anomaly detected and log the event to EEPROM.

Sensor Value-Add: Such an NFC based battery-operated date logger devices can consume more power for unnecessary periodic wake-up operation.

- ❑ Low-power motion wakeup accelerometer addition to such devices can save overall power consumption of the device by avoiding periodic wake-up.
- ❑ Adding a low-power accelerometer can help design power optimized solution, for the assumed mission profile it can increase battery lifetime by: ~ >8x.

#SensorsConverge

Sensors Converge

MISSION PROFILE 2: UWB SENSOR TAG/WEARABLE

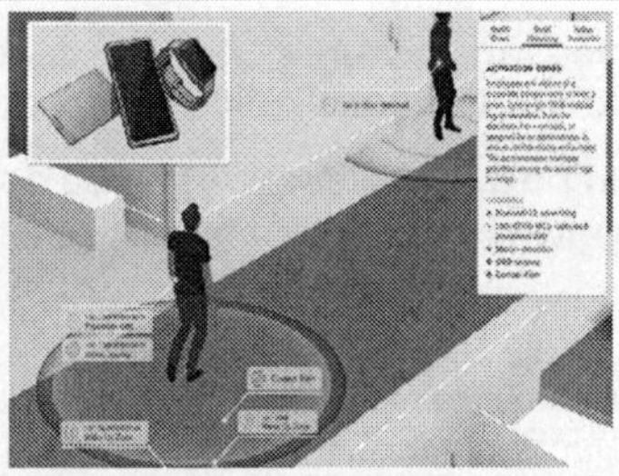

Application: Smart devices for post-covid safer workplaces. A smart tag or wearable for employees to practice social distancing to contribute towards safer workplaces in the times of COVID-19.

Assumptions: Every employee spends 8 hours at workplace wearing safe workplace wearable/tag.

- ❑ ~6 hours sitting (no motion - safe mode)
- ❑ ~2 hours at other workplace locations showing motion (risk mode).

Sensor Value-Add: Such a battery operated safe-workplace UWB tag or wearable solution can be extremely power hungry and hence associated battery usage can be considerably high.

- ❑ Low-power motion wakeup accelerometer in addition to a UWB tag or wearable can save power consumption and help in managing connection priorities of connected UWB tags/wearables.
- ❑ Adding a low-power accelerometer can help enable a power optimized solution – for the assumed mission profile it can increase battery lifetime by: ~ >20x.

#SensorsConverge

Sensors Converge

MISSION PROFILE 3: SMART SENSING INHALER

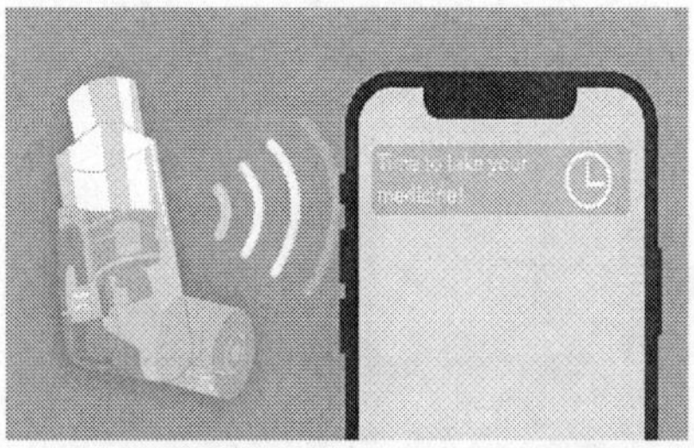

Application: Smart devices for patient care. A smart sensing inhaler provides precision patient breathing detection using tidal breathing with bio-compatible pressure sensor and assures proper inhaler position for automatic dispensation of prescribed dosage.

Assumptions:
- ❑ Patient uses inhaler 2-3 times a day for ~10 mins each time
- ❑ Rest of the day inhaler device is inactive or idle.

Sensor Value-Add: Such a battery operated BLE Inhaler solution can be extremely power hungry and hence associated battery usage can be considerably high.

- ❑ Low-power motion wakeup accelerometer addition to such devices can save power consumption overall power consumption of the device by detecting no motion to put device is deep sleep state and wakes up the device when patient picks up the device (showing motion).
- ❑ Adding a low-power accelerometer can help design power optimized solution, for the assumed mission profile it can increase battery lifetime by: ~ >10x.
- ❑ Adding an ultra-low power magnetic switch at the inhaler lid with magnet, can help totally disable battery connection. If BLE connection latency is allowed, then significant power saving can be achieved

#SensorsConverge

Sensors Converge

MISSION PROFILE 4: SUBGHZ ASSET TRACKER

Application: A Low-cost asset tracker with real-time outdoor Geo-localization using GPS receiver & SigFox triangulation schemes with low-power accelerometer, temperature sensor for monitoring/tracking logistics

Assumptions: Device wakes-up every 10 mins and send uplink message consisting of GPS coordinates, motion events and keep alive message (every SigFox message takes 6 seconds).
- ❑ Assuming the tracker need to only send uplink message when there is an anomaly detected and 1 message to keep alive the connection per day.

Source: https://partners.sigfox.com/products/chipfox-gps-tracker-heavy-duty

Sensor Value-Add: Such a battery operated SigFox tracker solution can be power hungry and hence associated battery usage can be high.

- ❑ Low-power motion wakeup accelerometer addition to such devices can save overall power consumption of the device by reducing the periodic SigFox transmission to only transmit when there is anomaly detected.
- ❑ Adding a low-power accelerometer can help design power optimized solution, for the assumed mission profile it can increase battery lifetime by: ~ 16x.

#SensorsConverge

Sensors Converge

BIKE GARAGE POC STUDY: UWB KEY FOB

Scenario 1: Default consumption	
Power mode	Average measured currents (A)
Low power	0
Active mode	0.01447
BLE connected	0.0135
UWB ranging	0.0155
Power mode	Power mode duration (s)
Low power	0
Active	86366
BLE connected	4
UWB ranging	30
Power mode	Probability
P(Low power)	0
P(Active)	0.999606481
P(BLE Connected)	4.62963E-05
P(UWB Ranging)	0.000347222
Power mode	Total current consumption(A)
Low power	0
Active	0.014464306
BLE connected	0.000000625
UWB ranging	5.38194E-06
Total	0.014470313
Results	
Battery lifetime (h)	15.20354149
Battery lifetime (d)	0.633480895

Scenario 2: Optimized consumption	
Power mode	Average measured currents (A)
Low power	0.00001347
Active mode	0.00102
BLE connected	0.0035
UWB ranging	0.007
Power mode	Power mode duration (s)
Low power	82766
Active	3600
BLE connected	4
UWB ranging	30
Power mode	Probability
P(Low power)	0.957939815
P(Active)	0.041666667
P(BLE Connected)	4.62963E-05
P(UWB Ranging)	0.000347222
Power mode	Total current consumption(A)
Low power	1.29034E-05
Active	0.0000425
BLE connected	1.62037E-07
UWB ranging	2.43056E-06
Total	5.7996E-05
Results	
Battery lifetime (h)	3793.362319
Battery lifetime (d)	158.0567633

Power consumption estimation
Power consumption analysis

- To estimate the battery lifetime of the UWB Tag, the following constraints are assumed:

Day (s)	86400	Seconds in a day: 24x60x60
CR2032 capacity (mAh)	220	
Number of trips	2	
Average trip duration (s)	3600	Tag attached to Bike: 30 minute ride home to office
Bike Garage entry duration (s)	15	Time duration for garage access
BLE connection duration (s)	2	
UWB session duration (s)	15	

Movement detected for 2 x (30min + 15 sec)

Battery lifetime is increased by a factor of **252x**, from **0.63 days** to **158 days**

#SensorsConverge

Brighter Together

TRANSFORMATIONAL VALUE:

- Drive true system value for our customers
- Integral roadmap and co-development
- Ease-of-use enablement
- Use-case focus, system-level solutions

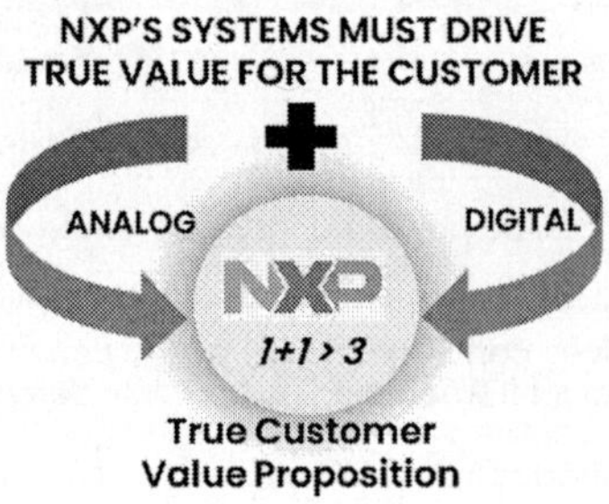

#SensorsConverge

TRANSFORMING FROM COMPONENTS TO SYSTEMS

LEVERAGE FULL POTENTIAL OF NXP'S PORTFOLIO & CAPABILITIES

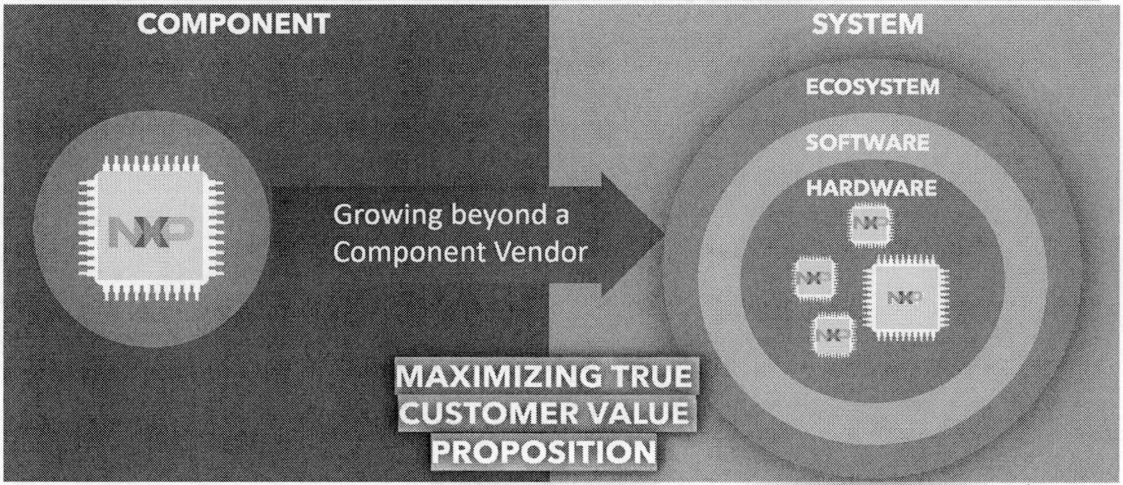

#SensorsConverge

Sensors Converge

SUMMARY

- ❑ Need to change our ways of working: Think about optimizing power consumption from the outset, in the early product design phase.
- ❑ IoT edge devices growth will be restricted if nothing is done to improve battery lifetime or uptime for these devices.
- ❑ We need to solve this problem collaboratively; we can only achieve better future together.
- ❑ We need to focus on use-case, system selling to drive true customer value.
- ❑ Identifying end use-cases, applications can help design better power optimized system solutions.

#SensorsConverge

Sensors Converge

Sensors Converge

Q & A

#SensorsConverge

Innovation...
from 1901 to 2000

A Very Busy Farmer

A Tailor of the Latest Fashion

Electric Scrubbing

Aerial Firemen

A Whale-Bus

Aviation Police

The future cannot be predicted,
but futures can be invented.
— Dennis Gabor, 1971 Nobel prize in physics

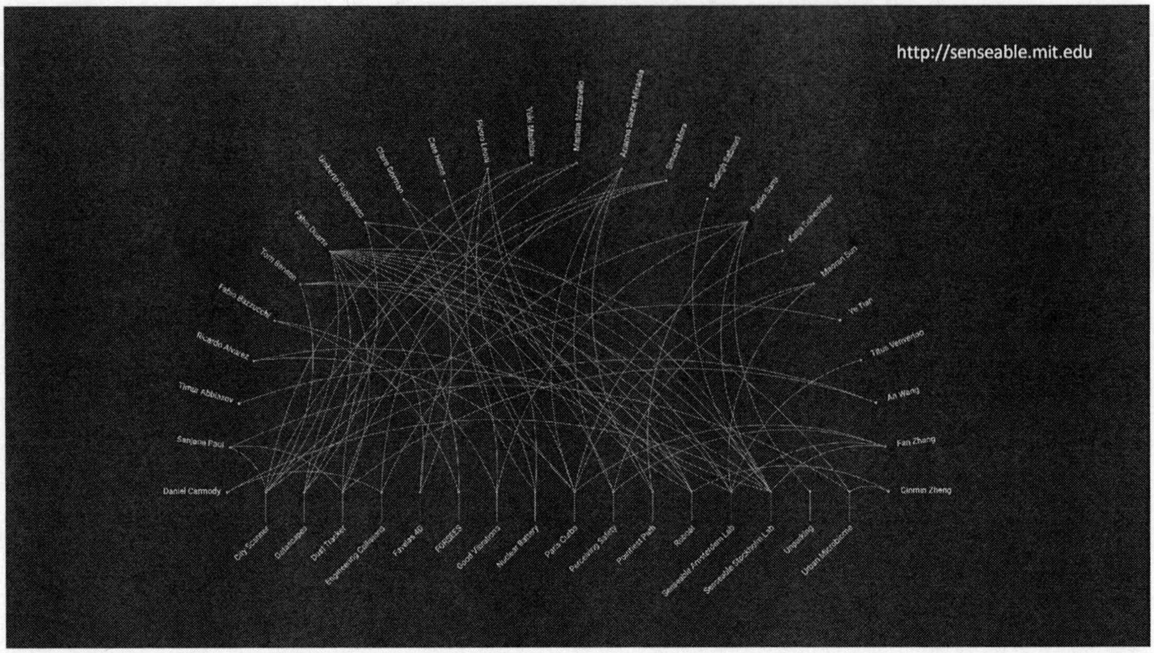
http://senseable.mit.edu
Tom Benson
Ricardo Alvarez
Timur Abbiasov
Sanjana Paul
Daniel Carmody
Ye Tian
Titus Venverloo
An Wang
Fan Zhang
City Scanner
Dust Tracker
Favelas 4D
FORCES
Good Vibrations
Nuclear Battery
Perceiving Safety
Senseable Amsterdam Lab
Senseable Stockholm Lab
Urban Microbiome

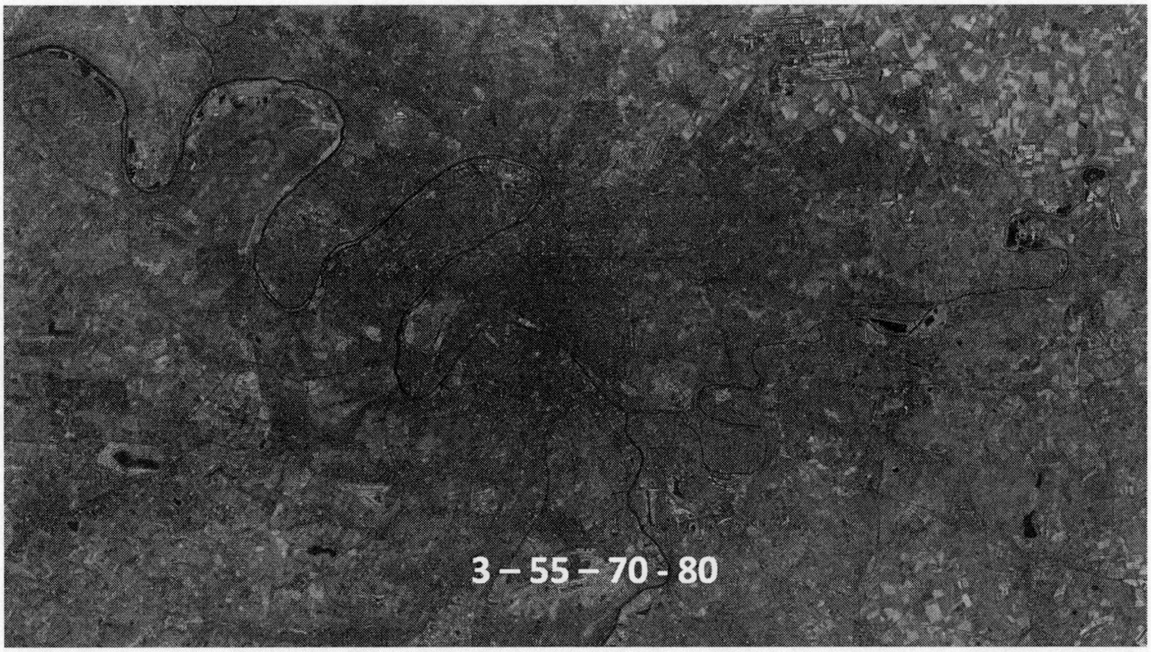
3 – 55 – 70 - 80

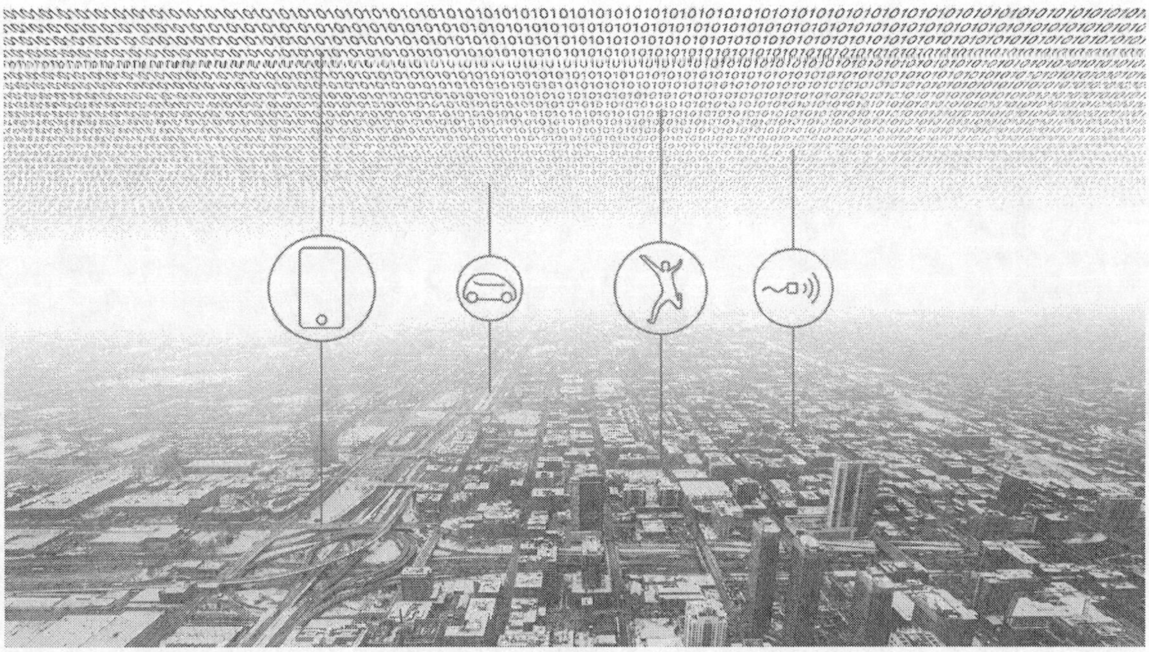

Projects

senseable city lab.

Trash Track

WASTE, INVESTIGATION TOOL

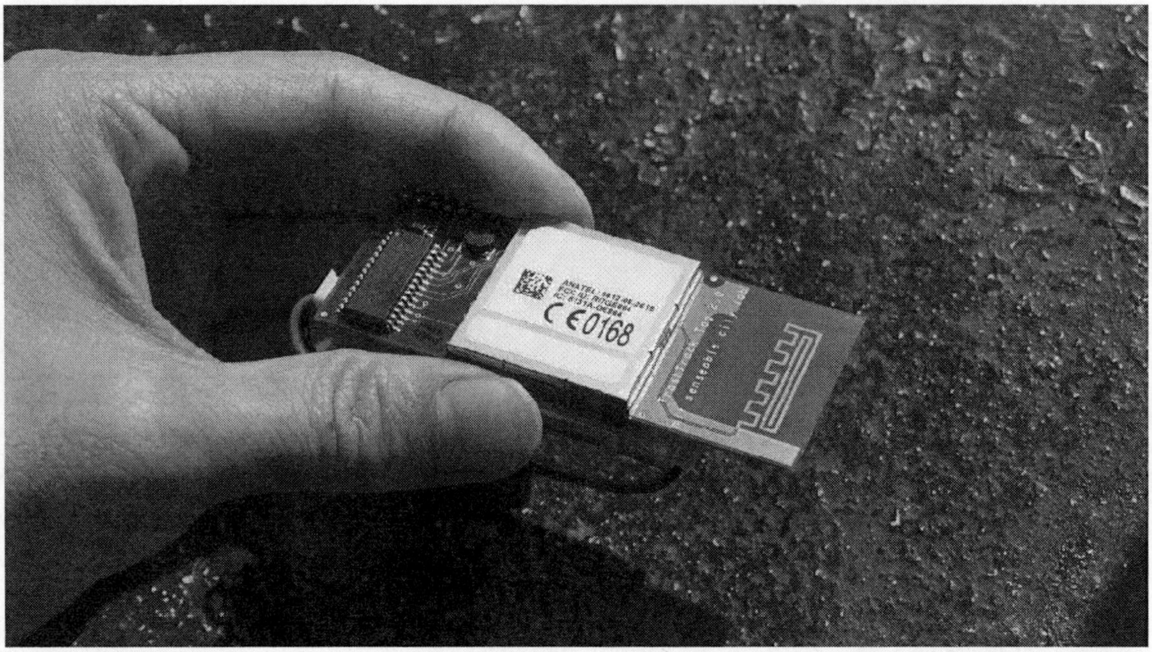
CE0168

Trash | Track

Underworlds

HEALTH, ROBOTICS

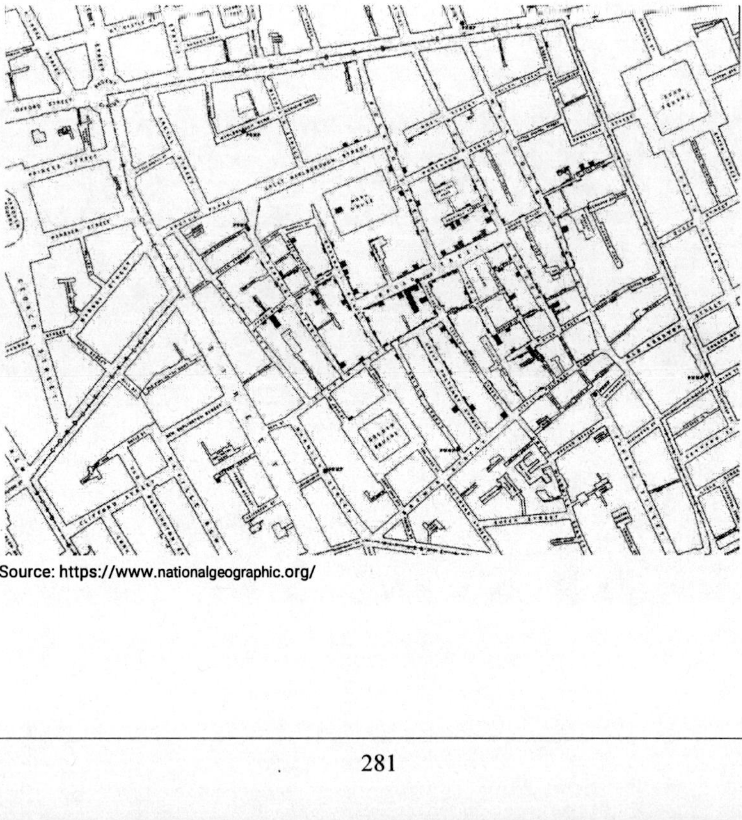

Source: https://www.nationalgeographic.org/

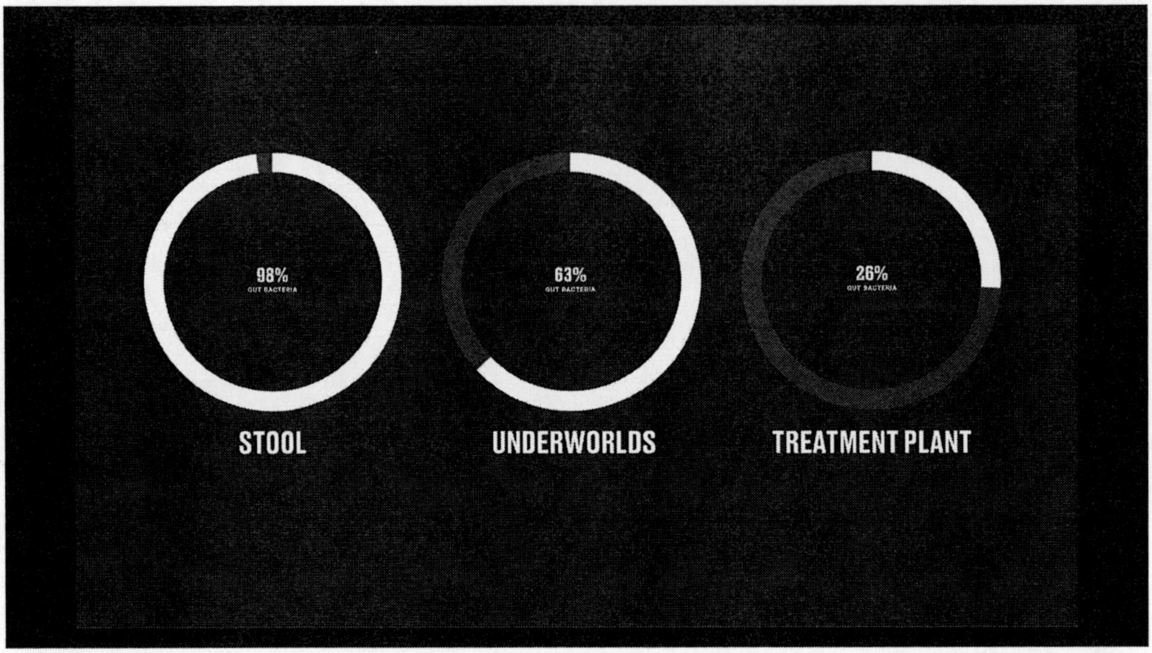
98%
GUT BACTERIA
63%
GUT BACTERIA
26%
GUT BACTERIA
STOOL
UNDERWORLDS
TREATMENT PLANT

City Scanner
ENVIRONMENT

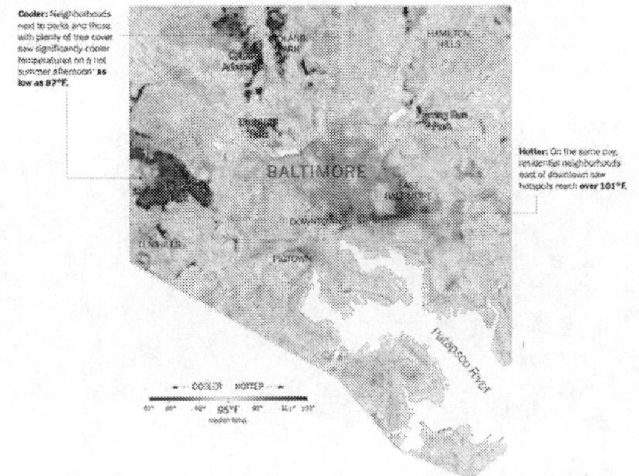

Nadja Popovich and Christopher Flavelle
The New York Times

How many sensors do we need to cover a city?

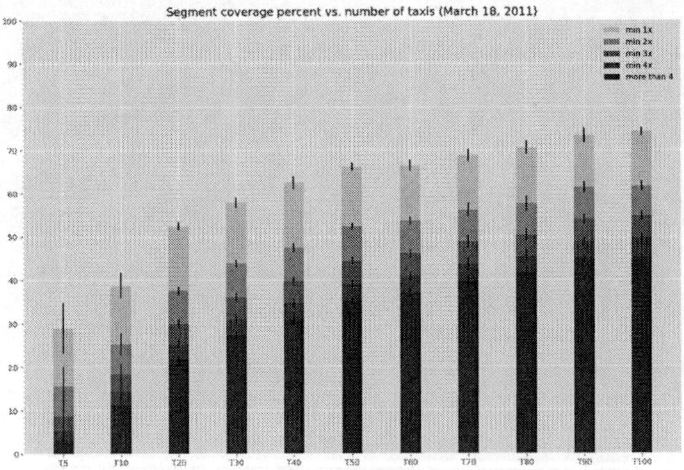

Flatburn

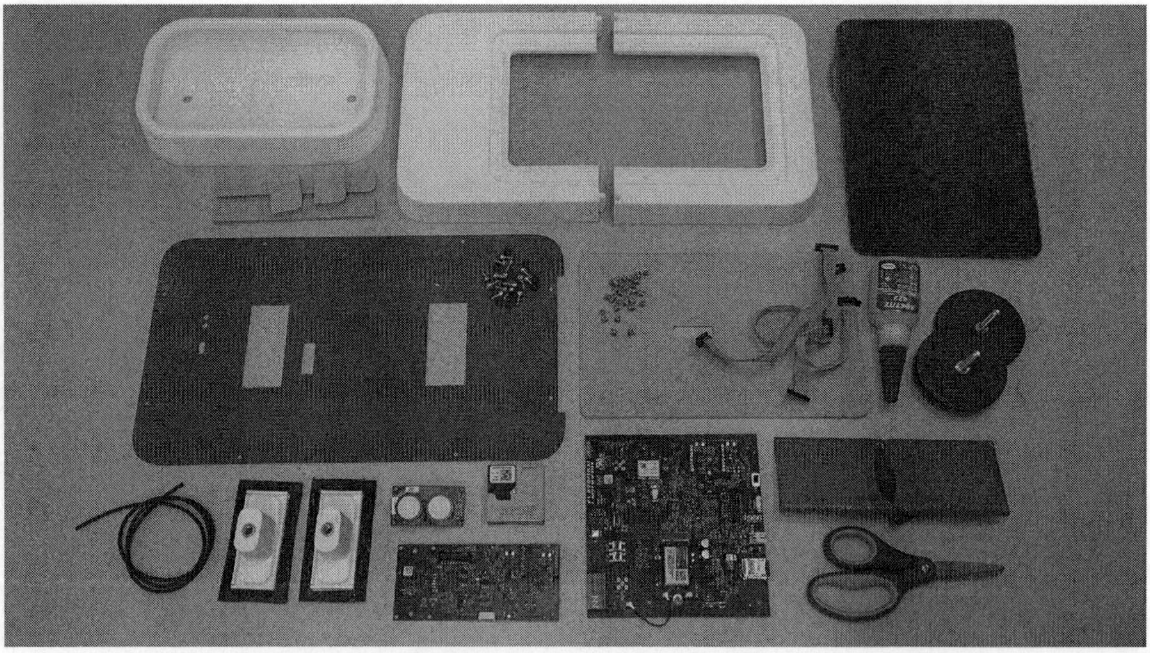

PILOT STUDIES

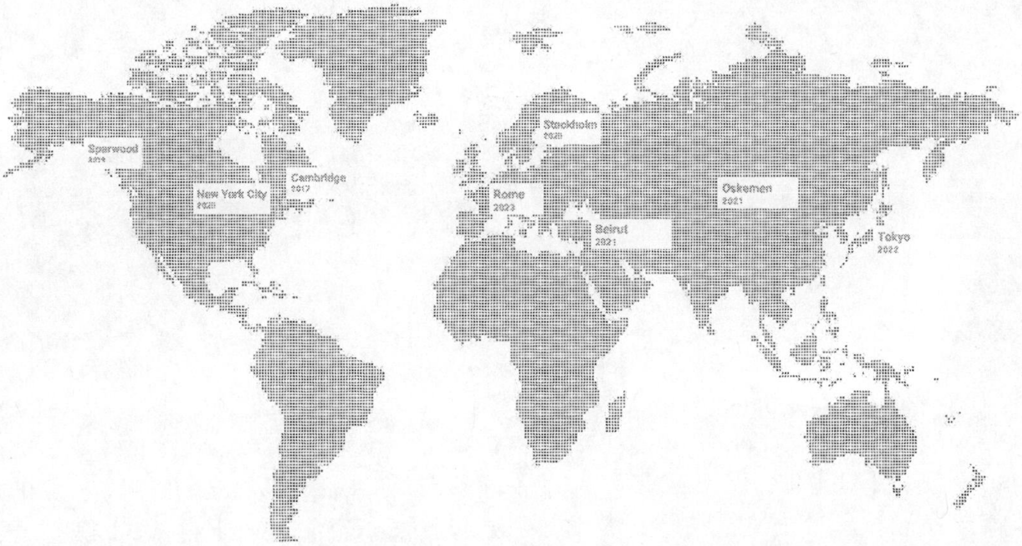

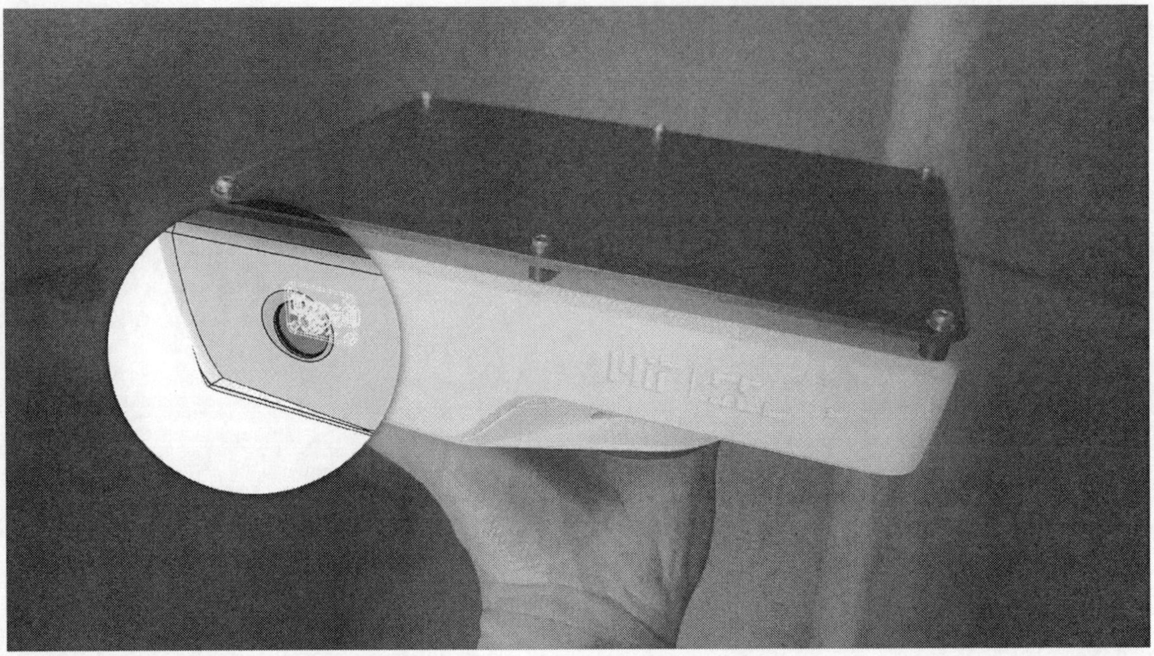

UTDELNING
UTAN
UTSLÄPP

senseable
city lab.

Instagram
@Senseable_City_Lab

Facebook
@SenseableCity

Twitter
@SenseableCity

Simone Mora
moras@mit.edu

LEHIGH UNIVERSITY | SESHADRI LAB | mHEAL

Wearable Sensors and Generative AI for Clinical Decision Making

Dhruv R. Seshadri, PhD
Assistant Professor
P.C. Rossin College of Engineering and Applied Science
Dept of Bioengineering, Lehigh University, Bethlehem, PA, USA

Sensors Converge
Santa Clara, CA, USA, June 25th, 2024

www.seshadrilab.com

What's Your Why?

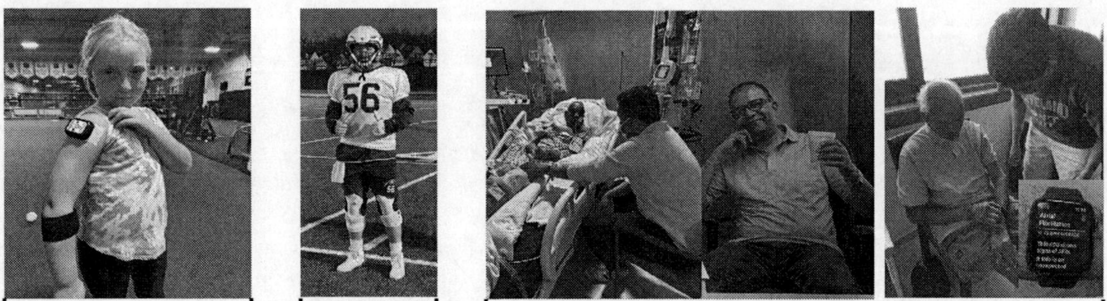

Aim 1 | Aim 2 | Aim 3

Develop, validate, and commercialize medical devices that addresses the most critical areas in medicine

Thrust 1: Use sports medicine to collect baseline data (healthy athletes, musculoskeletal/physiological modeling)

Thrust 2: Use return to play progressions to understand nuances in biomechanics and physiology

Thrust 3: Translate learnings for disease monitoring or treatment leveraging learnings from thrusts 1 and 2

2

Wearable Sensors and Artificial Intelligence

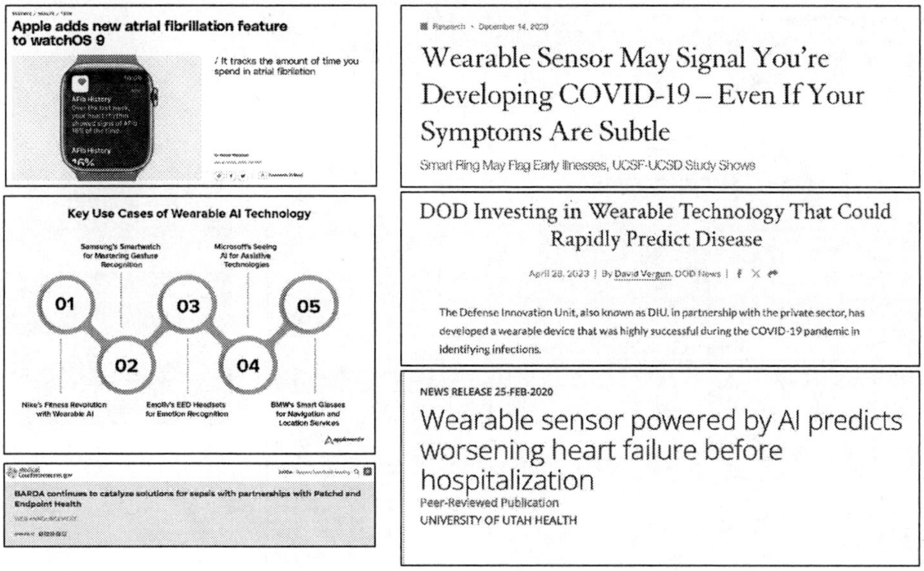

3

AI-powered Electronic Skin for Health and Performance

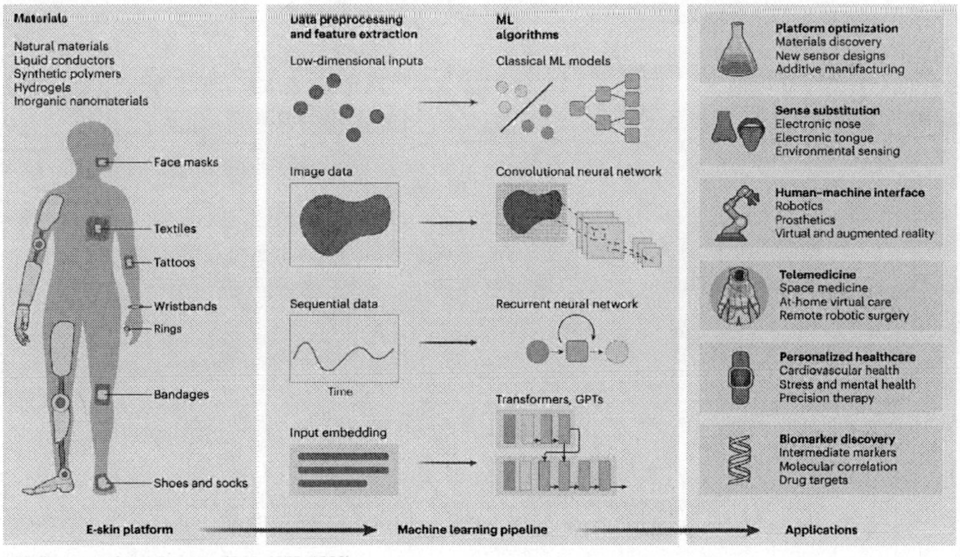

Nature Machine Intelligence **volume 5**, *pages 1344–1355 (2023)*

4

mobile Health Engineering and Analytics Laboratory (mHEAL)

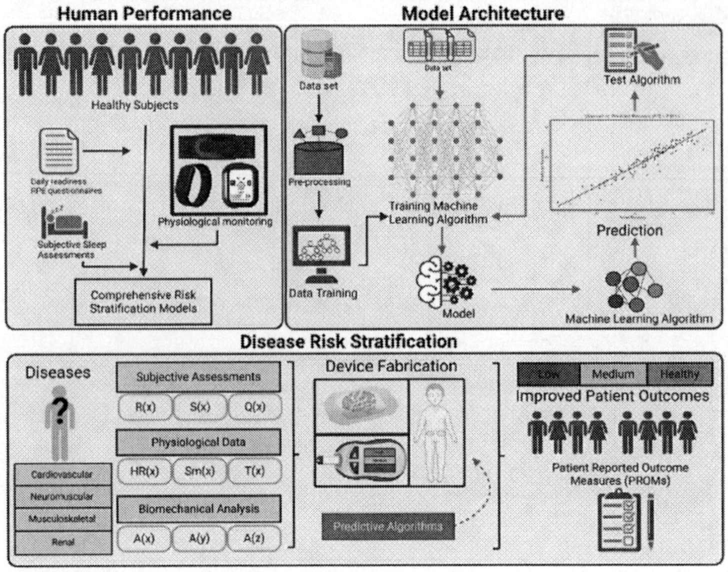

Thrust 1: Human Performance

Thrust 2: Disease Monitoring

Thrust 3: Smart Biomaterials

5

Pathway to Translate Data for Clinical Applications

Identifying Question and Technology → Assessing Efficacy → Normative Data and Visualization → Clinical Applications

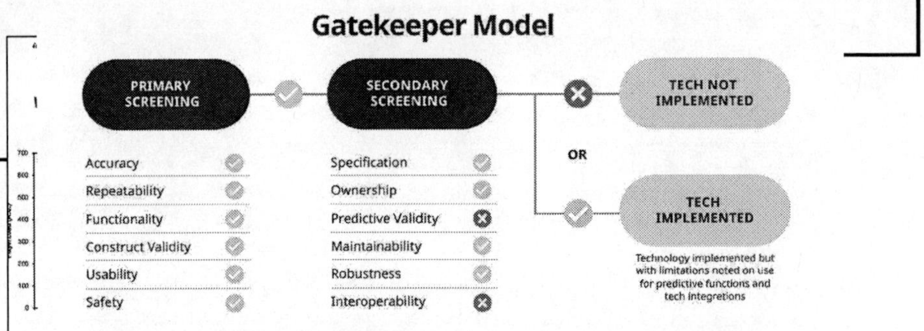

Figure 5. Example of gatekeeper model example applied to a sports tech device or metric where the user decides whether the technology is not implemented, or implemented with limitations on specific functionalities

Journal of Sports Science (2024)

6

Does FDA Clearance Suggest a Technology is Ready for Patients?

Q1: How accurate was the AW4 at detecting AF when AF was detected on telemetry?

	Detecting Atrial Fibrillation								
	N	TP	TN	FP	FN	PPV	NPV	Sensitivity	Specificity
AW notification	292	34	202	0	56	100	78	38	100
AW PDF Interpretation	292	84	202	0	6	100	97	93	100

Seshadri et al. ***Circulation.*** *2020;141:702–703*

Cleveland Clinic study: Apple Watch lags behind physicians in AFib detection

Andrea Park - Wednesday, February 26th, 2020 Print I Email

https://www.beckershospitalreview.com/healthcare-information-technology/cleveland-clinic-study-apple-watch-lags-behind-physicians-in-afib-detection.html

Q2: How accurate was the Omron Heartguide Smartwatch at detecting BP compared to arterial line?

Modality	Device	FDA Cleared
PPG	Valencell	No
Pulse Arterial Time	Fitbit	No
Oscillometry	Omron Heartguide	Yes

	BP Agreement with Arterial pulse line	
Device	r_c	95% CL
Diastolic BP	.49	(.38, .59)
Systolic BP	.43	(36, .50)

Sensors *(In Review)*

Validation of wearable technology is needed before application in patients

7

Uncovering the Mystery Behind Black Box Metrics

Study 1: Comparison of "Recovery" Metrics

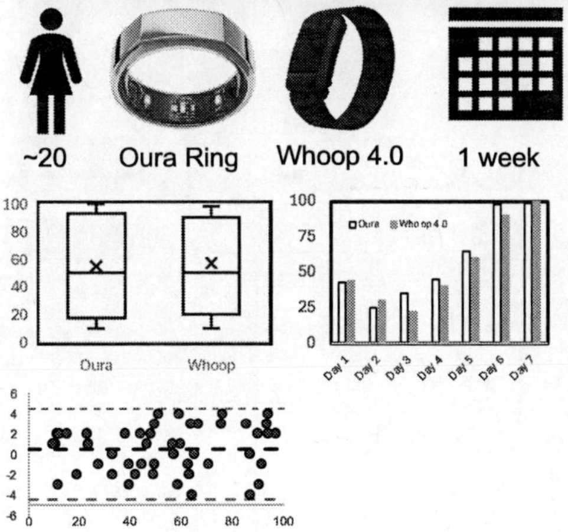

Study 2: Assessing Efficacy of Metrics

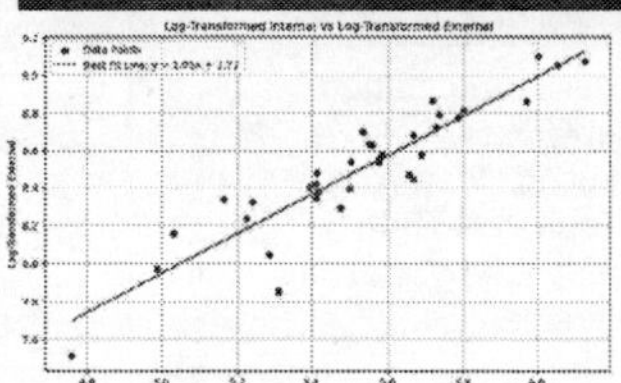

$$TEi = \frac{External}{Internal^X}$$

X = Slope of Log Transform

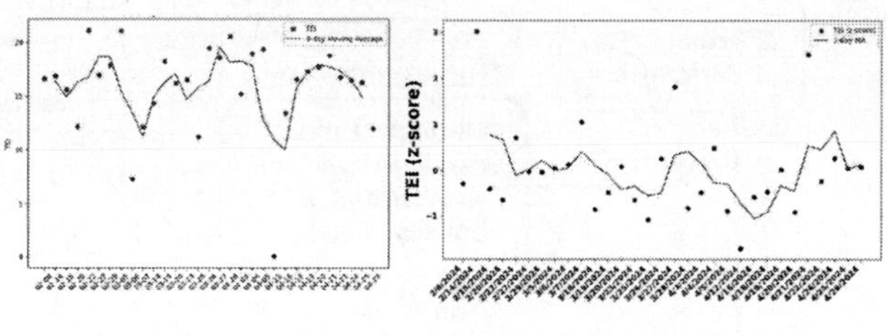

8

Wearable Technology Data to Develop Risk Stratification Analytics

1. Do healthcare devices add value to the clinical problem at hand?
2. What does baseline data look like in healthy individuals?
3. What does data look like in compromised individuals (e.g. patients)?
4. Are the trends predictive? Can models be generated?
5. Which variables are correlative towards providing clinical insight?

9

Developing Risk Stratification Analytics

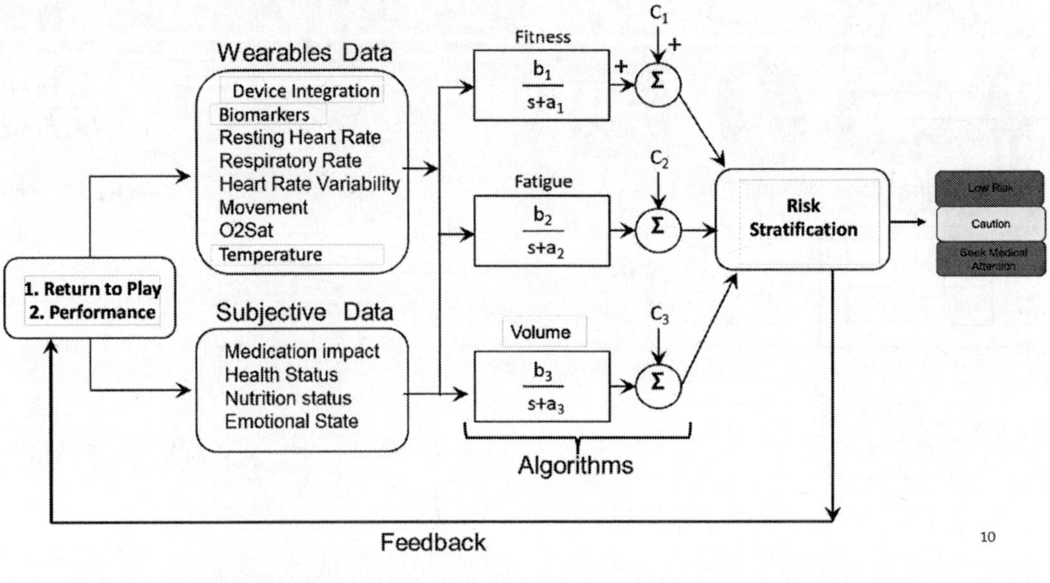

10

Wearable Technology for Women's Health

- **Disparity in funding** across male and female collegiate athletics
- Female athletes are **2-8x more likely** for ACL tears than male counterparts

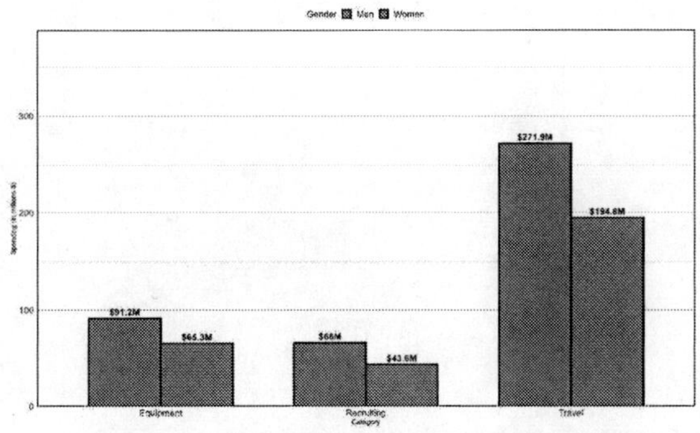

1) PLoS One. 2023; 18(1): e0280800. PMCID: PMC9879429
Published online 2023 Jan 26. doi: 10.1371/journal.pone.0280800 PMID: 36701354

Effects of the menstrual cycle phase on anterior cruciate ligament neuromuscular and biomechanical injury risk surrogates in eumenorrheic and naturally menstruating women: A systematic review

2)

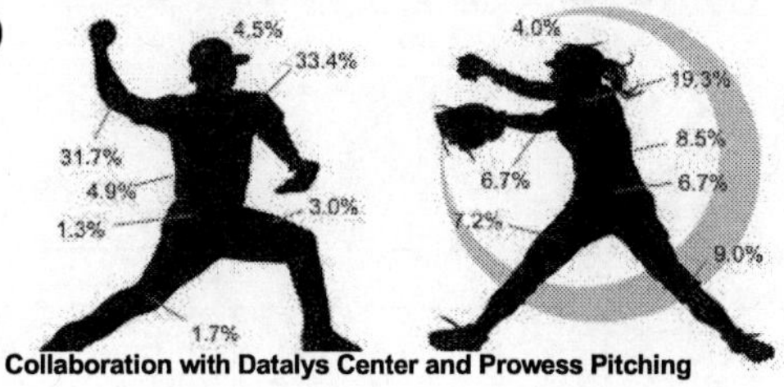

Collaboration with Datalys Center and Prowess Pitching

Women's health remains an understudied area despite the increased injury risks faced by this population. Further research and funding is needed and lacking

International Journal of Exercise Science: Conference Proceedings: Vol. 15: Iss. 4, Article 31 (2024)
European Congress of Sports Science (Accepted, 2024)
Scientific Reports, British Journal of Sports Medicine (In Review)

11

Recovery and Performance Division I Female Soccer

- Quantify movement biomechanics and cardiovascular workload in trainings and matches using wearables
- Retrospectively analyzing all data from 2020-2023 (2023-2024 season team utilized WHOOP)
- Starting Spring 2024 with pre-season heading into Fall 2024 season: WHOOP, Beyond Pulse, Surveys

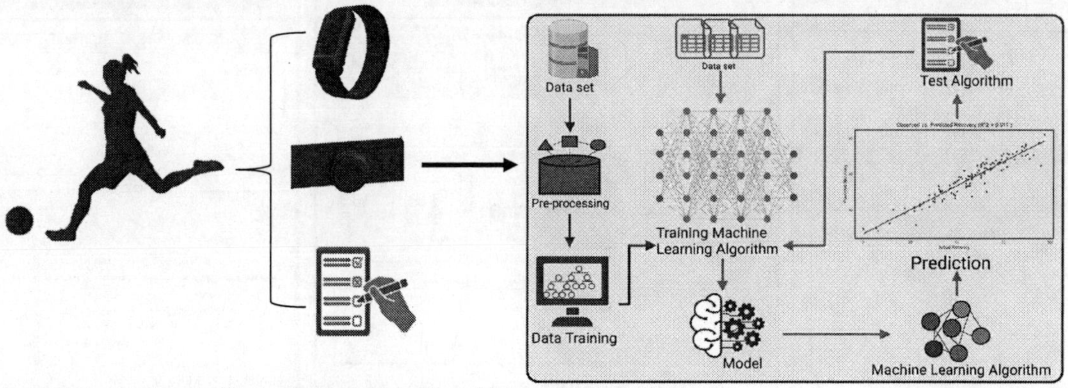

International Journal of Exercise Science: Conference Proceedings: Vol. 15: Iss. 4, Article 31 (2024)
European Congress of Sports Science (Accepted, 2024)
Scientific Reports, British Journal of Sports Medicine (In Review)

12

Recovery and Performance Division I Female Soccer

- WHOOP data across 14 athletes from August 1st, 2023 to January 31, 2024 (full season; 16,913 data points)
- Correlation among physiological and recovery-based parameters

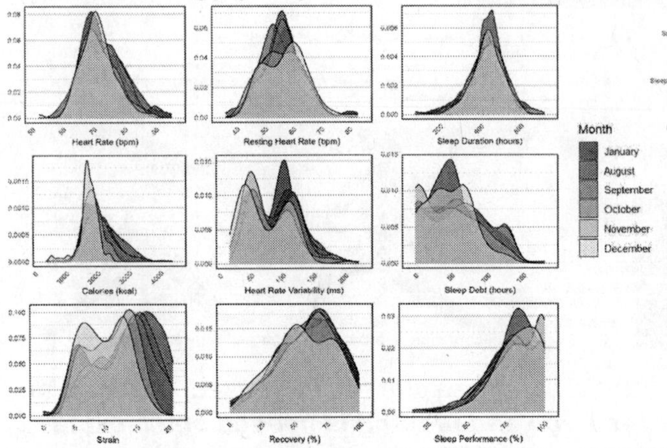

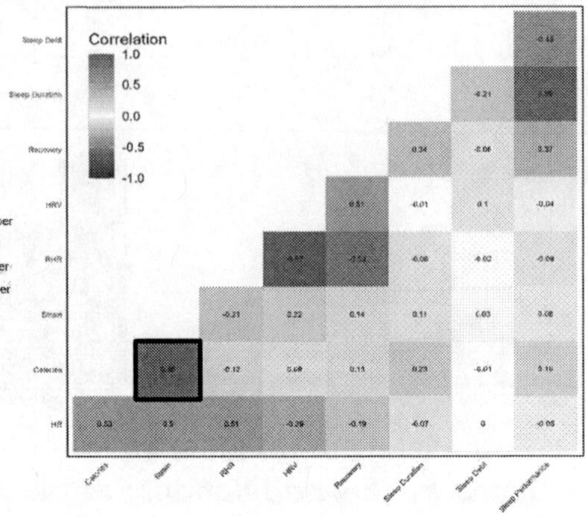

International Journal of Exercise Science: Conference Proceedings: Vol. 15: Iss. 4, Article 31 (2024)
European Congress of Sports Science (Accepted, 2024)
Scientific Reports, British Journal of Sports Medicine (In Review)

13

Modeling Trends for AI Performance and Rehabilitation Models

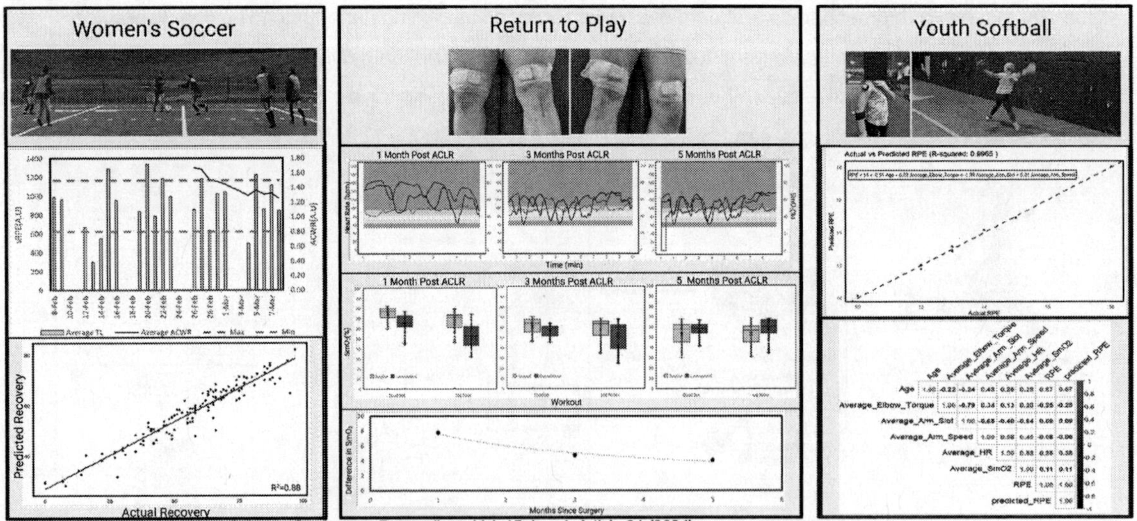

International Journal of Exercise Science: Conference Proceedings: Vol. 15: Iss. 4, Article 31 (2024)
European Congress of Sports Science (Accepted, 2024)
Scientific Reports, British Journal of Sports Medicine (In Review)

14

Wearable Technology and AI for Digital Therapeutics

Data Analytics Capability

For novel digital endpoints development and implementation

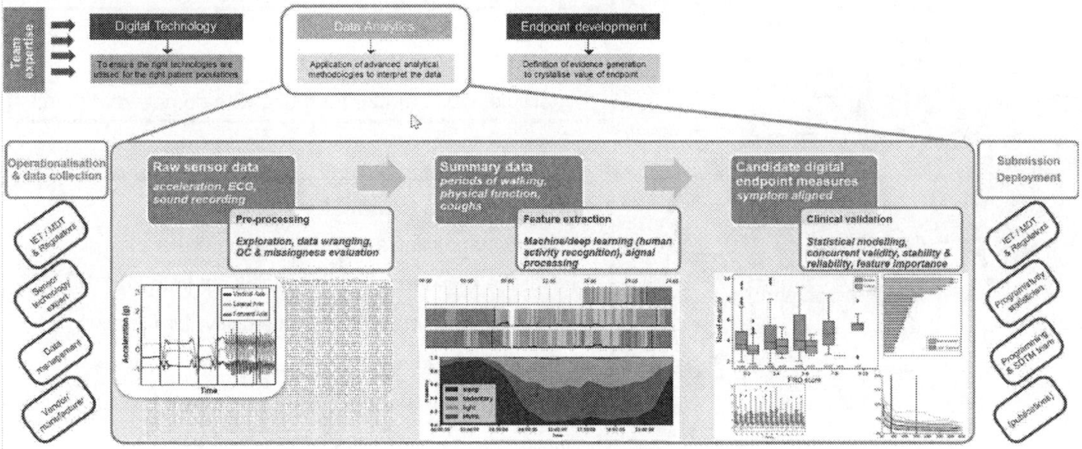

15

Digital Health and Therapeutics for Decentralized Clinical Trials

- Atopic Dermatitis (**13% of children and 5% of adults worldwide**) adversely affects sleep quality
- Itch evaluated through **subjective surveys/grading scales**; gold standard: **direct visualization** w/video
- Wearables may facilitate **behavior modifying strategies**, providing **therapeutic benefit with minimal risk**
- Patients with AD (73 patient nights), **sensitivity of 93%** and **specificity of 100%**

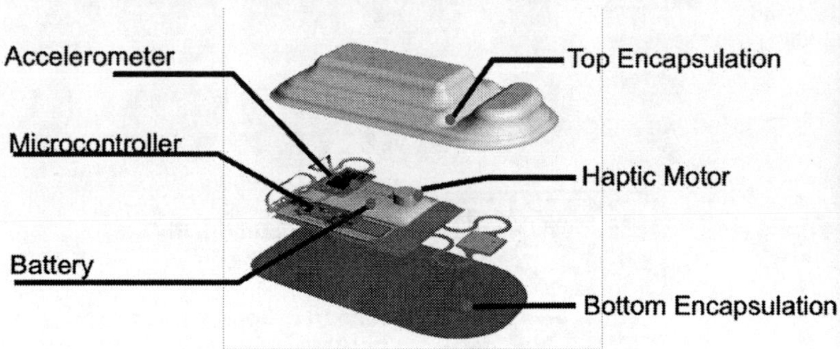

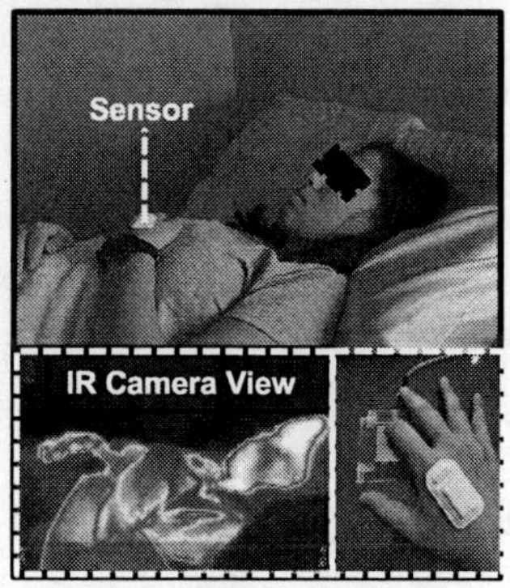

16

Journal American Academy of Dermatology (2022)

Closing Thoughts

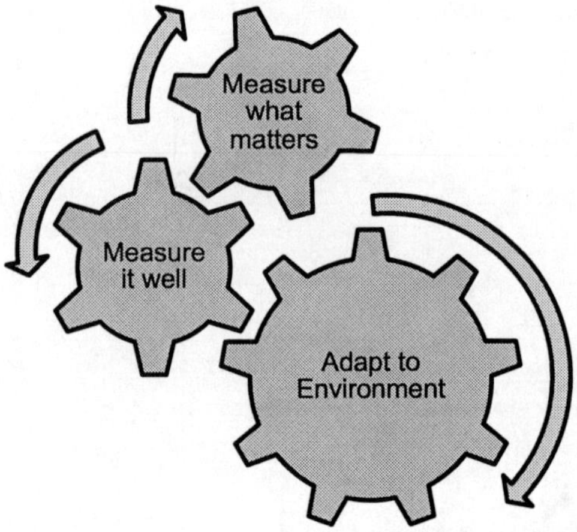

Drugs don't matter if patients do not take them

↓

Wearables don't matter for those who do not wear them

From Academia to Industry and Back

1) Understand clinical need and standard of care
2) Get the engineers into the clinic/field from Day 1
3) Little things matter! (UI/UX, usability, form factor)
4) Clinical design reviews start once MVP is ready
5) Engage early & often (FDA--letter of intent/Qsub)

17

Collaborators and Team at Lehigh University

LEHIGH

CASE WESTERN RESERVE UNIVERSITY

SPIRE FUEL YOUR PASSION

NEMOURS CHILDREN'S HEALTH

Atrium Health

Cleveland Clinic

University Hospitals

CLEVELAND BROWNS

IIT PALAKKAD

Technische Universität Braunschweig

GHENT UNIVERSITY

Prowess Pitching

सी-डैक CDAC

Meet the team! We are actively hiring and opened our doors in August 2023!

Dhruv R. Seshadri, PhD
dhs223@lehigh.edu

Seshadri Laboratory webpage:
http://seshadrilab.com/

18

ANALOG DEVICES

FROM POINT OF CARE TO POINT OF NEED

Leveraging advanced sensing technologies to enhance monitoring performance in connected medical devices

MAHDI SADEGHI
PRODUCT MARKETING
MEMS TECHNOLOGY GROUP

analog.com

Chronic Disease Prevalence

129M, 40%
of the US, with at least 1 major Chronic Disease
42% with 2 or more
12% have 5 or more

50% leading causes of death in the US
are, or are strongly associated with, preventable and treatable chronic diseases

Prevalence has increased steadily
By 2050, people over 50 y.o. increases by 60%, 50 y.o. with chronic disease will double by 2050

90% Of the annual **$4.1T**
health care expenditure is attributed to managing & treating chronic diseases and mental health conditions

Chronic Disease Prevalence in the US: Sociodemographic and Geographic Variations by Zip Code Tabulation Area (cdc.gov)
Projecting the chronic disease burden among the adult population in the United States using a multi-state population model - PMC (nih.gov)

Point of Care vs. Point of Need Health Care Benefits

Insight to Physicians

- Predictive vs. reactive care
- Timely intervention due to availability of information

Patients

- Personalized care based on personalized data
- Access and convenience
- Flexibility of use

Financial Advantages

- Cost efficiency, avoiding complications
- Intervention at the right time
- Scalability

Connected Medical Devices

Over the Counter Connected Gadgets (e.g. fitness trackers, smart watches)

- Continuous informative motivational data
- Lifestyle management, health consciousness

Prescription Medical Devices

- Clinical grade data, continuous accessible monitoring
- Disease management (Cardiac Monitoring Devices, CGM, Wearables Patches, etc.)

Diagnostic/Procedure Augmentation

- Assists physicians in procedures and/or diagnosis, computer vision, MRI, etc.

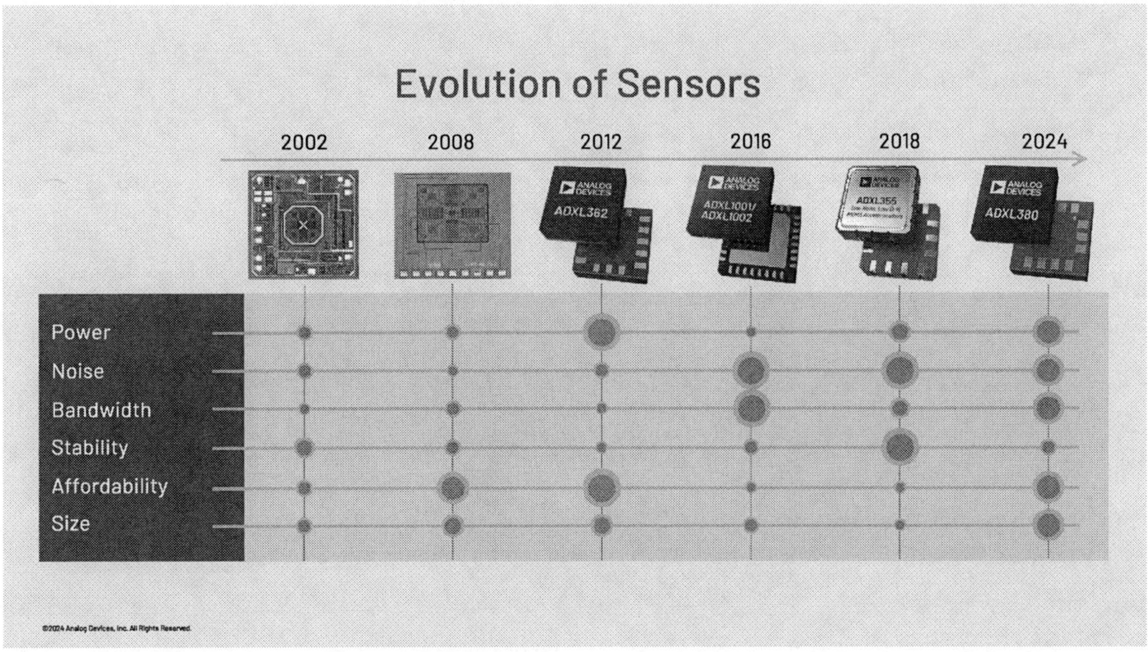
Evolution of Sensors
2002
2008
2012
2016
2018
2024
ANALOG DEVICES
ADXL362
ADXL1001/
ADXL1002
ADXL355
ADXL380
Power
Noise
Bandwidth
Stability
Affordability
Size
©2024 Analog Devices, Inc. All Rights Reserved.

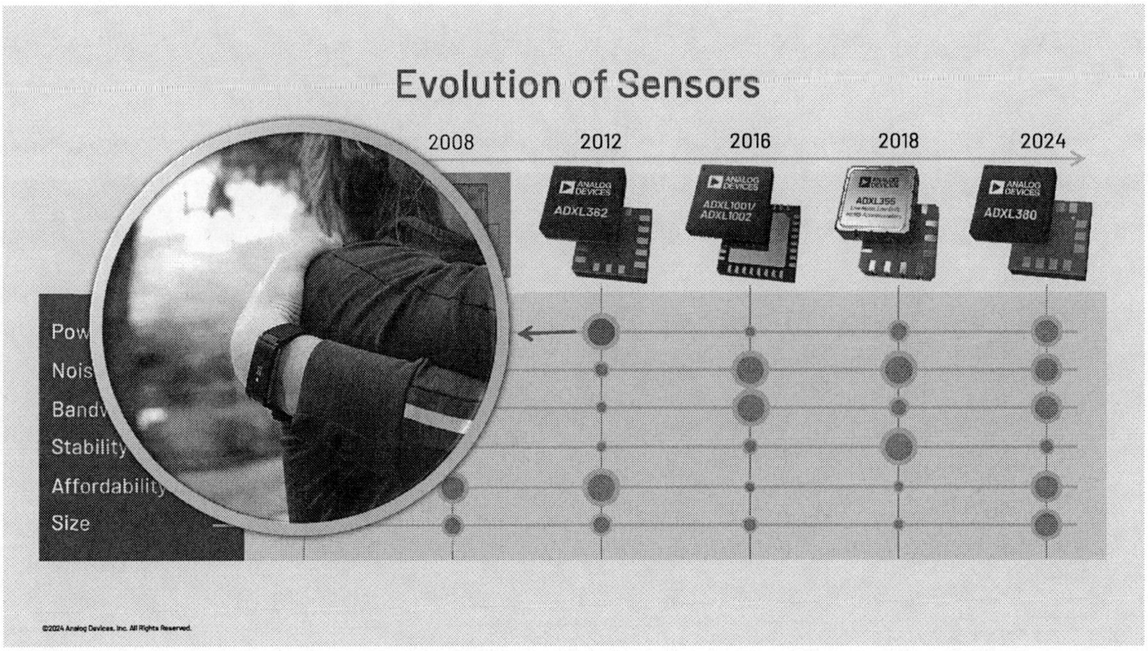
Evolution of Sensors
2008
2012
2016
2018
2024
ANALOG DEVICES
ADXL362
ADXL1001/
ADXL1002
ADXL355
ADXL380
Stability
Size
©2024 Analog Devices, Inc. All Rights Reserved.

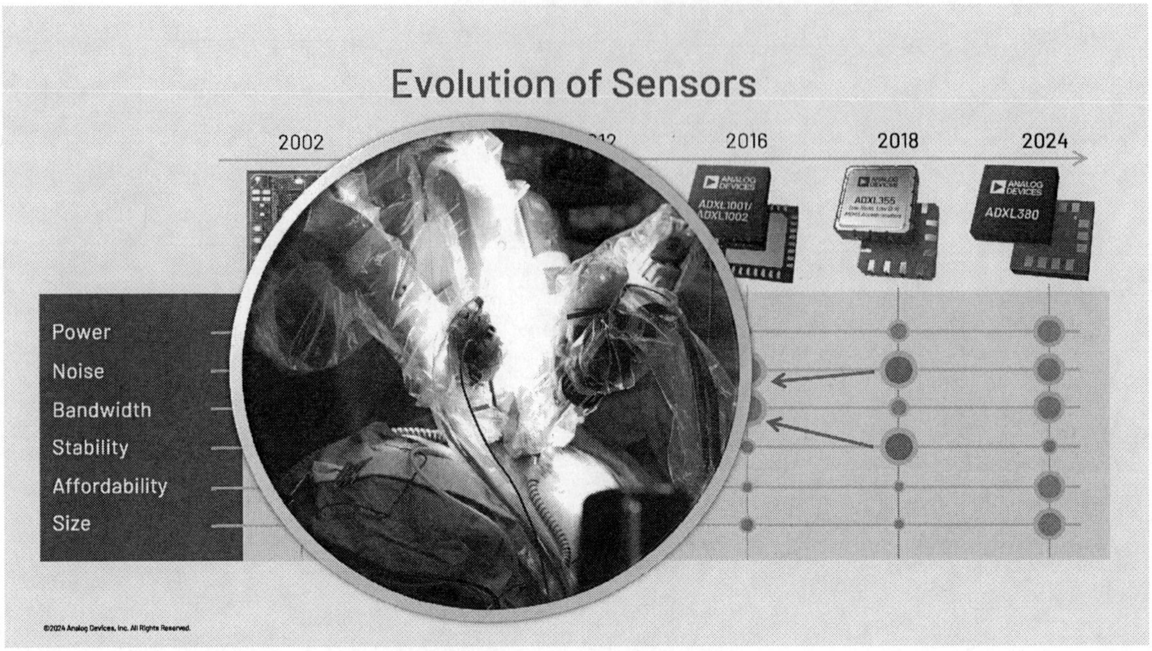
Evolution of Sensors
2002
2016
2018
2024
ADXL1001/
ADXL1002
ADXL355
ADXL380
Power
Noise
Bandwidth
Stability
Affordability
Size
©2024 Analog Devices, Inc. All Rights Reserved.

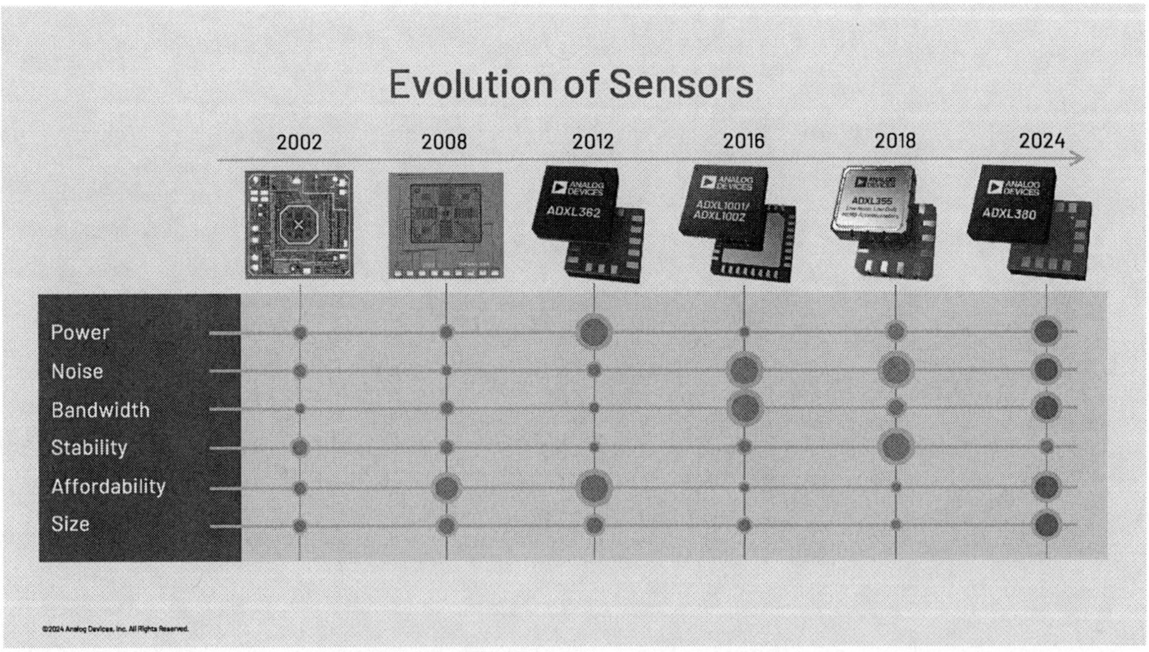
Evolution of Sensors
2002
2008
2012
2016
2018
2024
ADXL362
ADXL1001/
ADXL1002
ADXL355
ADXL380
Power
Noise
Bandwidth
Stability
Affordability
Size
©2024 Analog Devices, Inc. All Rights Reserved.

Examples of Chronic Disease: CVD, COPD

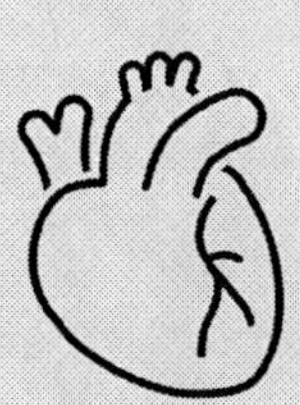

Every 45 Sec a person dies from cardiovascular disease (CVD) in the US

CVD is the leading cause of death globally according to the WHO with

17.9 million deaths per year

Chronic obstructive pulmonary disease (COPD) is the third leading cause of death worldwide.

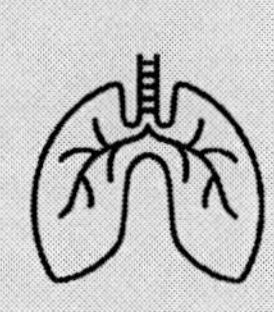

Cardiovascular diseases (who.int)

Multi-parameter VSM System for Heart & Lung Auscultation

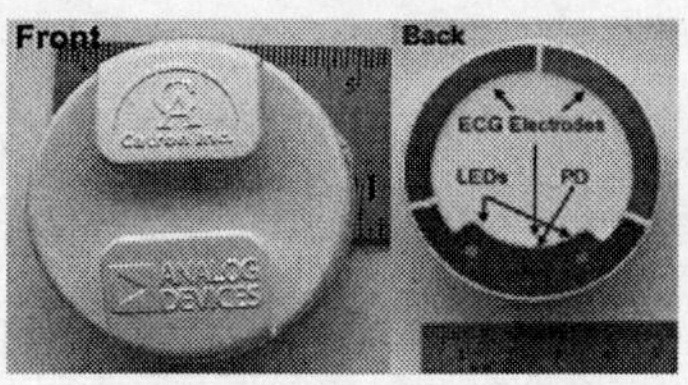

"... the chest patch is enabled through an ultra-low-noise, wide-bandwidth, and low-power; offering a new level of performance and power consumption ... that is enabling for wireless edge sensing applications."

"Cardiopulmonary Auscultation System Enabled By A Novel Beyond-resonance Sensing Accelerometer," A Solid-State Sensors, Actuators and Microsystems Workshop, June 2024.

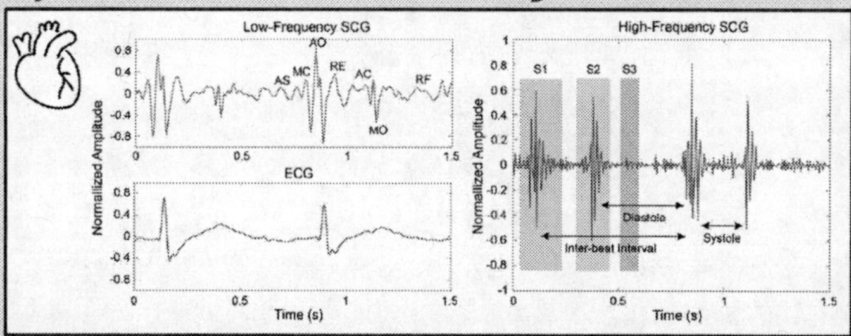

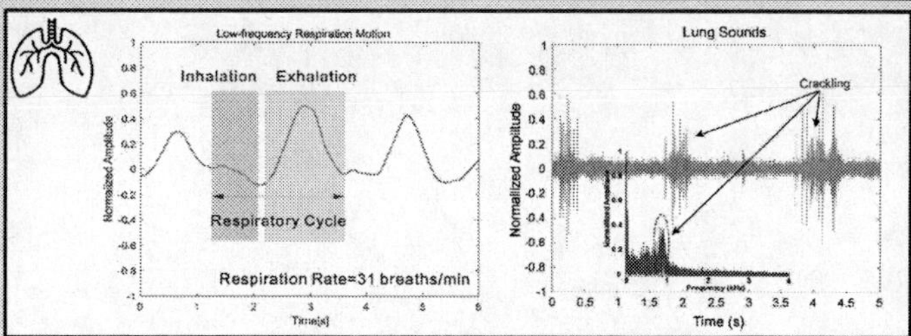

For More Information,
Complete Our Inquiry Form
ANALOG
DEVICES
AHEAD OF WHAT'S POSSIBLE™
©2024 Analog Devices, Inc. All Rights Reserved.

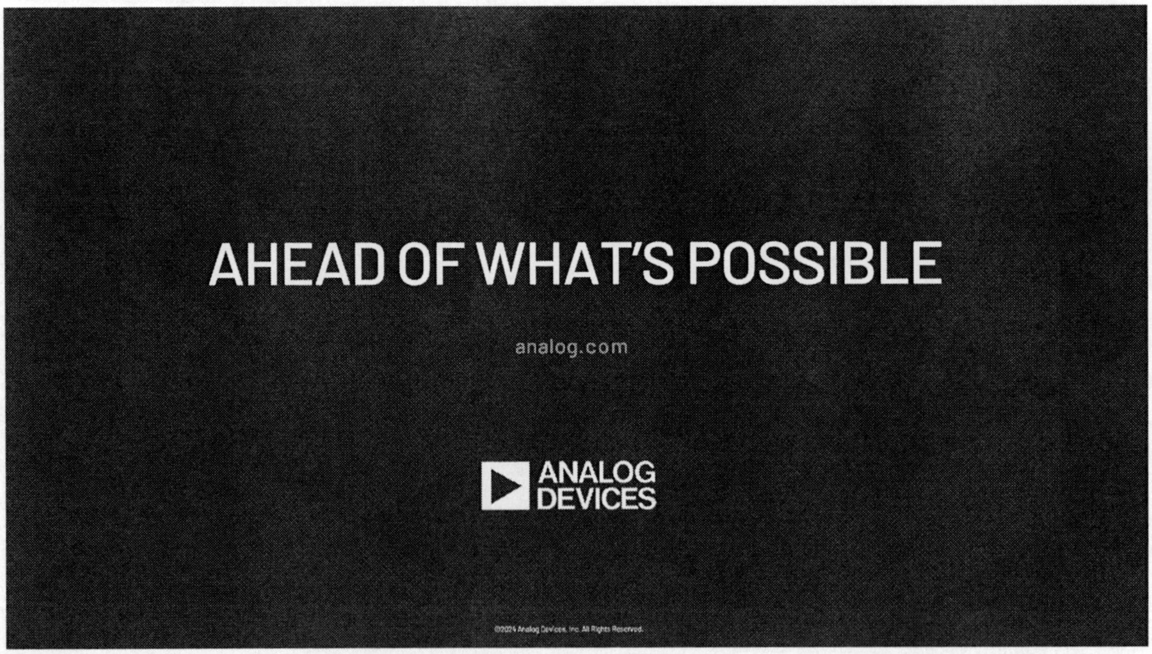
AHEAD OF WHAT'S POSSIBLE
analog.com
ANALOG
DEVICES
©2024 Analog Devices, Inc. All Rights Reserved.

Sensors Converge

IOT and Security:
What You Need to Know

June 24–26, 2024 | Santa Clara, CA

Steve Kapp, Principal / Chief Innovation Officer
nFocal Inc • skapp@nfocal.com nFocal

#SensorsConverge

Agenda

- Whirlwind Tour in 15 Minutes
  - The *What*
  - The *Why*
  - The *Who*
  - The *How*
  - The *When*
- Where to Start
- Guard Against
- Key Takeaways
- Questions

For more details, see the full presentation here

SCAN ME

#SensorsConverge

Sensors Converge

The Landscape

The What
- Establish trust
- Recognize attacks
- Protect yourself
- Minimize loss
- Minimize investments

The Why
- Health/safety/welfare
- Financial/personal
- Intellectual property
- Contractual
- Malware/ransomware

The Who
- Your product/device
- Bad actors
- Your company's IT
- Your customer's IT / OT
- Good actors
- Industry consortiums

The How
- Encrypt
- Authenticate
- Authorize
- Log & audit
- Patch & upgrade

The When
- Yesterday!!!

Sensors Converge

Where Do You Start?

Understand your desired device operations
- What should it do?
- What can it do?
- What should it not do?
- What *must* it not do?

Evaluate risks and threats
- Cyber (networking)
- Local (HMI / serial)
- Physical (motion / sensing / actuating)
- Human authority (levels / overrides)

Mitigate by architecting solutions
- Physical / electronic / cryptographic / process

#SensorsConverge

Sensors Converge

But Be Careful ///

There is often no upside – only a very, very bad downsides

Guard against:

- Not considering the full lifecycle
- Over-architecting complex solutions
- Making assumptions

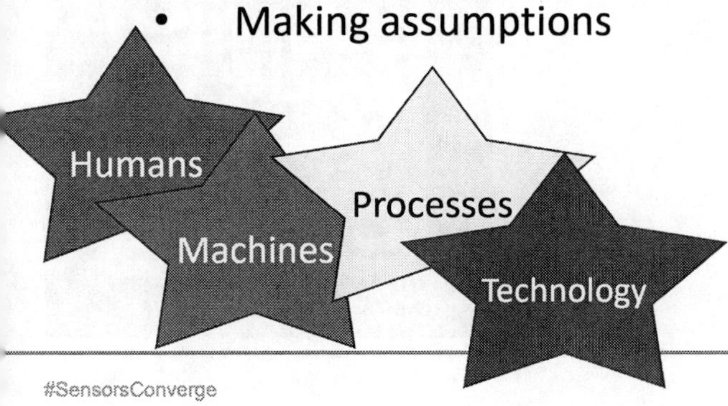

Avoid this

#SensorsConverge

Sensors Converge

Key Takeaways

- First know your needs / requirements
- Know your deployed environment
  - Threats
  - Risks
  - Costs
- Be as simple as possible, but no simpler
- Document everything
  - Include failure/attack modes & assumptions
- Test extensively
  - Including internal interfaces

#SensorsConverge

Sensors Converge

Thanks for Coming!

I'm always happy to answer questions; contact me at:

Steve Kapp, skapp@nfocal.com

For more details

SCAN ME

#SensorsConverge

Sensors Converge

Voice Unleashed:
Transforming IoT with Autonomous, Battery-Powered Recognition

Chris Rogers, SensiML CEO/Founder
Claudio Filho, Sr. FAE Manager

June 25, 2024

Quick Introduction

Pioneer in AutoML Developer **Software for tinyML Applications**

- Software tools that create ultra-compact ML sensor models
  - Model size as small as 5kB
  - Suitable for 64-bit MPUs down to 8-bit MCUs
  - Deep learning NNs, classic ML, feature transforms, regression models
- Broad ecosystem of supported hardware platforms
- Incorporated in 2017 from former Intel Curie/Quark ML tools team
- Offering SaaS dev tool suite, turnkey models, and custom engineering services
- Full ML workflow from dataset creation to model testing and integration
- Suitable for ML novices and data science experts alike
- **Just Announced: SensiML Open Source AutoML (sensiml.org)**

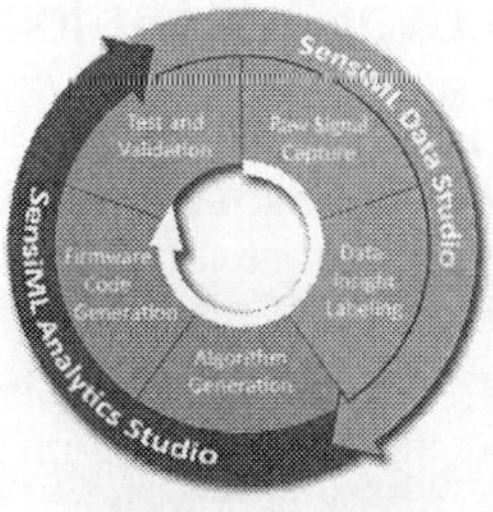

Supporting smart ML sensing for these leading embedded hardware platforms

Audio Wake Word Detection

- Audio Wake Word Detection Use Cases:
  - NLP query triggering ("Hey Google")
  - Hands-Free UI Voice Command
  - Emerging: Speaker ID / Authentication
- Common Device Categories
  - Wall-powered Smart Home Hubs
  - Smartphone Voice Assistant Apps
  - Car Infotainment Systems
  - TV Remote Controls
  - Wearables
  - IoT Enabled Devices and Sensors

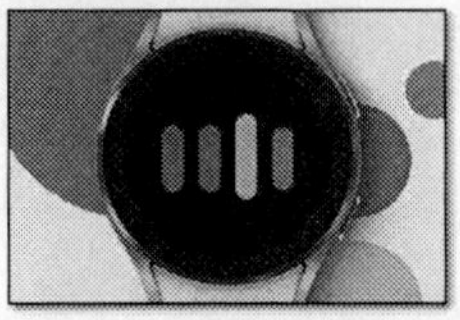

SensiML

Novel But Difficult Use Cases for Battery-Powered Always-On Voice

- **Find lost TV remote by voice:** Requires voice activation on remote control without pressing a button to trigger
- **Silence unreachable smoke alarm:** Requires always-on voice with 5-10 year life expectancy
- **Voice-triggered IoT smart lock:** Requires autonomy, highly accurate voice ID, and battery power
- **Wearable virtual coaching:** Requires autonomous voice UI on small form factor battery device

SensiML

Maximum Component Power Consumption

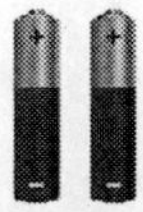
Two AAA Batteries

Component	Active	Power	Battery Life (days) 1000 mAh BAT @ 80%
Microphone (Analog MEMS)	150 µA @ 1.8V	270 µW	222 days
MCU (Cortex-M33)	1068 µA @ 38MHz clock	1922 µW	30 days
Radio (BLE)	4400 µA @ 1Mbps Rx 19100 µA @ 10 dBm Tx	21150 µW	2.8 days
Total		**23760 µW**	**2.5 days**

Contrived worst-case example to illustrate relative power draws and where to focus

5

A More Realistic Scenario: Always-on Hands-Free TV Remote Control

- Microphone always listening, no button press to trigger (that's cheating)
- 2 AAA batteries, 1 year life expectancy requirement
- BLE radio streaming used to convey:
  - Button press commands
  - 5 second voice query streams following wake word trigger
- Real-world acoustic environment
  - TV background noise
  - Household background noise
- High user performance expectations
  - False positive triggers unacceptable (near zero FPs)
  - Wake word misses must be low (>95% recognition accuracy)
  - Speaker independent, no pre-training

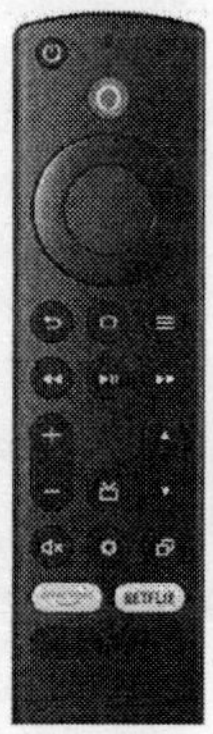

6

Optimized Always Listening R/C Pipeline and Duty Cycle Assumptions

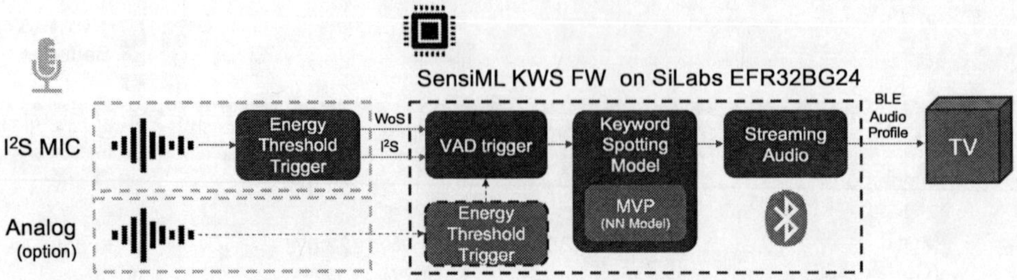

Operation Duty Cycle	90%	10% (5-10 msec @ 78MHz)	2.5% (~25 msec @ 78MHz)	50 / day x 5 secs / stream
I2S Mic	Sleep Mode	Low Pwr Mode	Low Pwr Mode	Low Pwr Mode
EFR32BG24 (Core)	Standby	Normal (78 MHz)	Normal (78 MHz)	Normal (78 MHz)
EFR32BG24 (Radio)	Sleep	Connected Idle	Connected Idle	BLE Stream

Assumptions:

- System Energy capacity: 2AAA cells = 1000mAh or 2 AA cells = 2500 mAh, 2.5VDC

SensiML

 7

Benefits of the SiLabs MVP ML Hardware Accelerator

- Dedicated ML computing subsystem next to the CPU: Matrix Vector Processor (MVP)
- Optimized MVP to accelerate ML inferencing with a lot of processing power offloading the CPU
- Up to 8x faster inferencing over Cortex-M (see below perf. benchmark)
- Up to 6x lower power for inferencing (see below perf. benchmark)
- Dedicated OPNs for MVP accelerated parts → EFR32MG24B[2]… or [3]

Performance data with ML hardware accelerator vs. pure SW on CortexM*

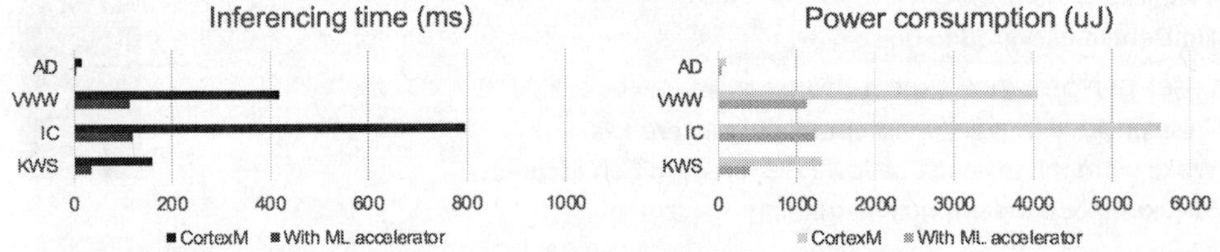

*Standardized performance benchmark validated by independent benchmarking body **MLCommons.org**. Published in MLPerf Tiny v1.0. Results are for inferencing only (not for the complete application). You can refer to MLCommons as validated results-

ML Commons

8 SILICON LABS

Energy Consumption Breakdown

- **Energy estimate over 1 day period**
  - 50 KWS events / day
  - False wakeups – 4.16hrs / day
- **Software VAD Implementation**
  - VAD requires 0.5s of audio
- **Option 1 – Analog Mic**
  - Duty cycled audio capture
- **Option 2 – I²S Mic with AAD**
  - Acoustic Activity Detection (AAD) triggers MCU wakeup

		Option 1: Analog Mic + Op-Amp	Option 2: I2S Mic (Built-in AAD)
Energy Consumption per Day (uJ)	AAD / Sleep	3.08	32.08
	KWS Audio	179.17	303.52
	VAD	41.27	2.99
	KWS	416.95	209.52
	Audio after KWS	2.44	5.03
	BLE	0.04	0.04

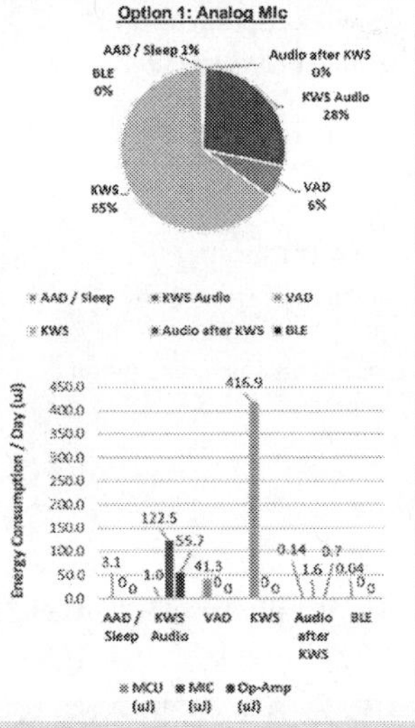

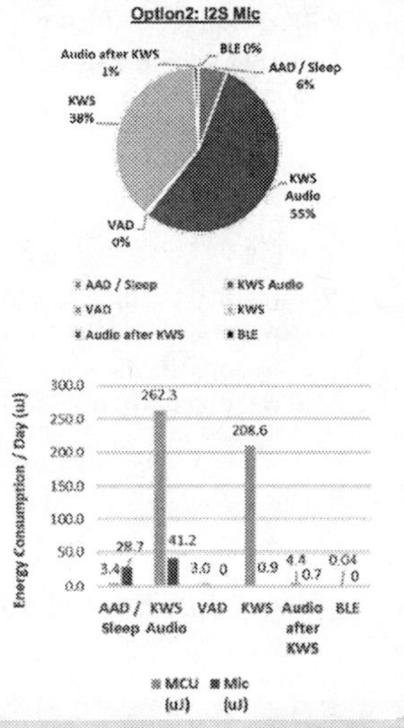

SILICON LABS

Average Current Consumption Comparison

		Option 1: Analog Mic	Option 2: I²S Mic
State 1 (VAD)	---	0.072 mA	0.022 mA [1]
			0.54 mA [2]
State 2 (KWS) [3]	Running on just MCU	2.597 mA	2.597 mA
	Running on MVP Accelerator [4]	~ 0.65 mA	~ 0.65 mA
State 3 (Audio Transmit)	Capture and Transmit audio	0.25 mA	0.55 mA

[1] In a silence room (no voice)
[2] In a noisy room (no voice)
[3] Execution time of the KWS model is ~70ms
[4] MVP reduces current consumption by 400%

SILICON LABS

Results

With assumed 4 hours/day of false wakeup duration

- For either microphone type, VAD power consumption amounts to 6%
- 93% of overall energy consumed to capture audio to perform KWS and by the KWS algorithm

Battery life vs False wakeup duration tradeoff

- When false wakeup is low, AAD in I2S mic significantly improves battery life performance
- Both options achieve same battery life performance when false wakeup duration / day = 6 hours

		Battery Life (Years)	
		Option 1: Analog Mic	**Option 2:** I^2S Mic
False Wakeup Duration / Day (Hours)	1	2.14 yrs.	3.74 yrs.
	2	1.67 yrs.	2.26 yrs.
	4	1.16 yrs.	1.26 yrs.
	6	0.9 yrs.	0.9 yrs.
	8	0.72 yrs.	0.67 yrs.

For typical ambient noise levels, one year battery life IS achievable

SensiML

11

Current Voice Solutions Can Deliver Accuracy in Toughest Settings

- SensiML AutoML pipeline for performance optimized edge inferencing
- Silicon Labs power-efficient radio SoCs with ML accelerator technology
- SensiML + Silicon Labs solution combines SW and HW optimizations
- Other audio processing pipelines available but not covered due to time:
  - Speaker identification
  - Acoustic event recognition
  - Audio anomaly detection
- Stop by the SensiML booth (#1333) to discuss further with our team

SensiML

12

Thank You!

SensiML

13

How Open RAN Empowers IoT Deployment & Enablement

Azita Arvani
Former CEO Rakuten Symphony NA,
Board Member, and Entrepreneur

Evolving Digital Transformation

- Digital Transformation
- Business Transformation
- Industry Transformation

Catalyzing Digital Transformation

Digital Transformation enabled by:

- Cloud
- Internet of Things
- Next Generation Communications
- Artificial Intelligence

Internet of Things

- Component-level monitoring & management
- Rich data sources for AI
- High-Density IoT leveraging 5G
- Precision digital twins

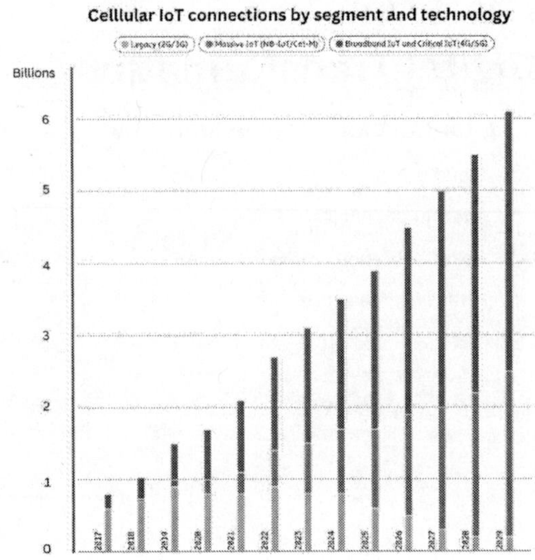

Internet of Things

- Cellular IoT
- Doubling in 5 years
- Cellular offers: broadband, low latency, reliability, and density

Source: Ericsson Mobility Report

Arvani Group Inc. 2024

Open RAN Networks:

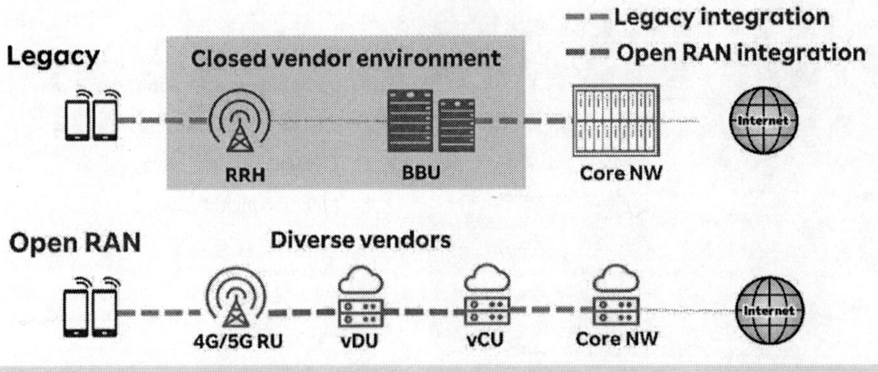

Comparison of conventional RAN and Open RAN technology

Source: Rakuten Symphony

Arvani Group Inc. 2024

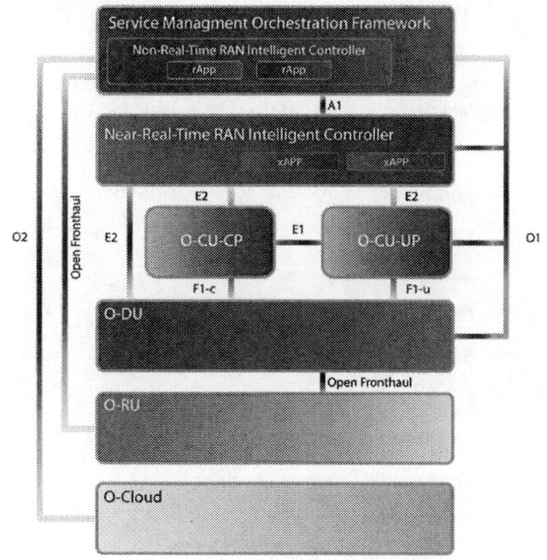

Open RAN Benefits

- Intelligent & Programmable
- Cost Efficient
- Vendor diversity
- Scalability
- Faster innovation
- Automation and Manageability

Source: ORAN Alliance

Arvani Group Inc. 2024

Integrated Communications & Computation Layers

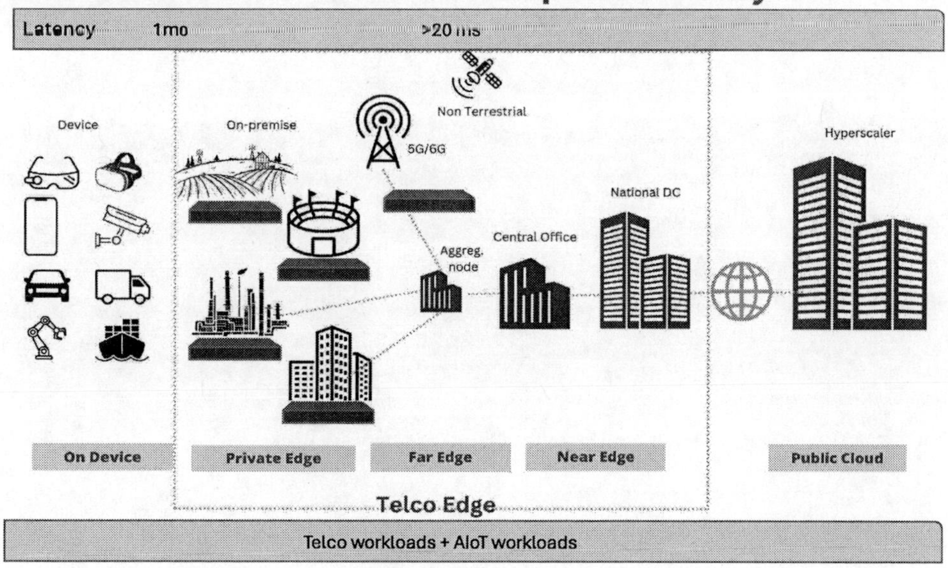

Reference: GSMA

Arvani Group Inc. 2024

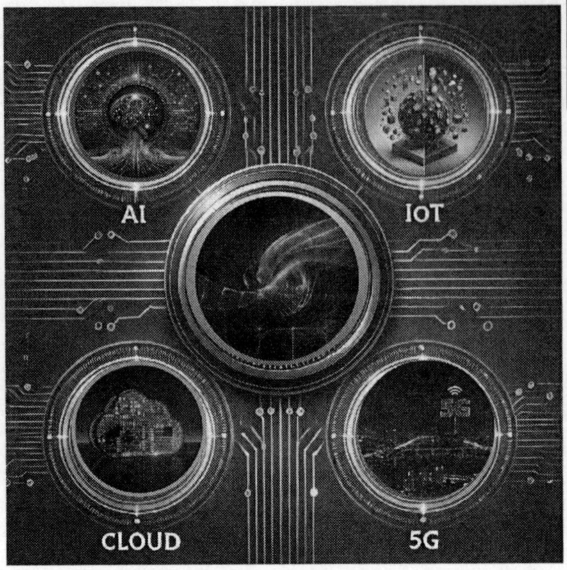

Summary

Open RAN creates powerful synergies across four key digital transformation catalysts to enhance:

- Low latency
- Autonomy
- Edge cloud
- Power efficiency
- Compute efficiency
- Better RoI
- Flexibility
- Safety and privacy
- Configurability & management

Arvani Group Inc. 2024

7

Sensors Converge

Wireless Sensor Modeling and Analyzing for 5G/6G Applications

June 24–26, 2024 | Santa Clara, CA

#SensorsConverge

Agenda

- Introduction
- Evolution of wireless design to 6G
- 5G/6G, Wi-Fi perspective
- AI/ML for wireless sensing
- Wireless sensing/detection example
- Summary

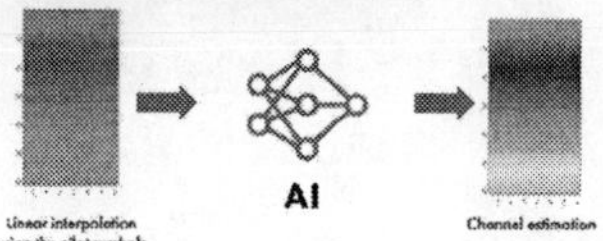

#SensorsConverge

Sensors Converge

What is 6G?

- 6G: next generation mobile wireless communication system
- Built on the strength of 5G
- Envisioned to provide ubiquitous and sustainable connectivity
- Expected to become available in early 2030s
- Research is underway. Various industry and academic consortiums researching and proposing technologies

#SensorsConverge

Sensors Converge

6G Use Cases

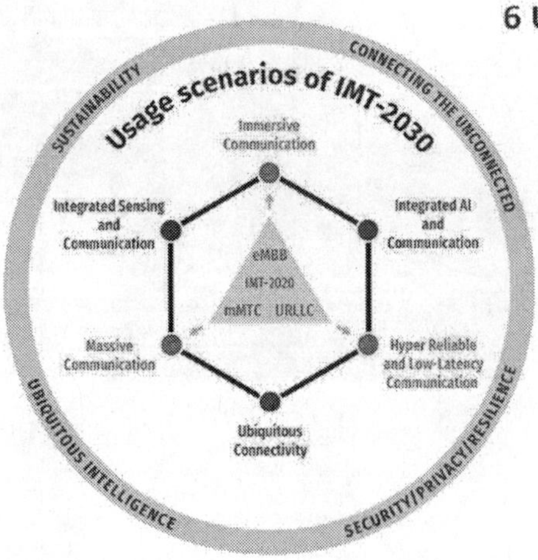

6 Usage scenarios

Extension from IMT-2020 (5G)

- eMBB ➡ Immersive Communication
- mMTC ➡ Massive Communication
- URLLC ➡ HRLLC (Hyper Reliable & Low-Latency Communication)

New

- Ubiquitous Connectivity
- Integrated AI and Communication
- Integrated Sensing and Communication

#SensorsConverge

Sensors Converge

Possible 6G New Applications and Use Cases

Fixed mobile and broadband evolution

Extended reality

Real time robot command and control

Wireless sensor fusion

Digital twin

Holograms

#SensorsConverge

Sensors Converge

6G Timeline

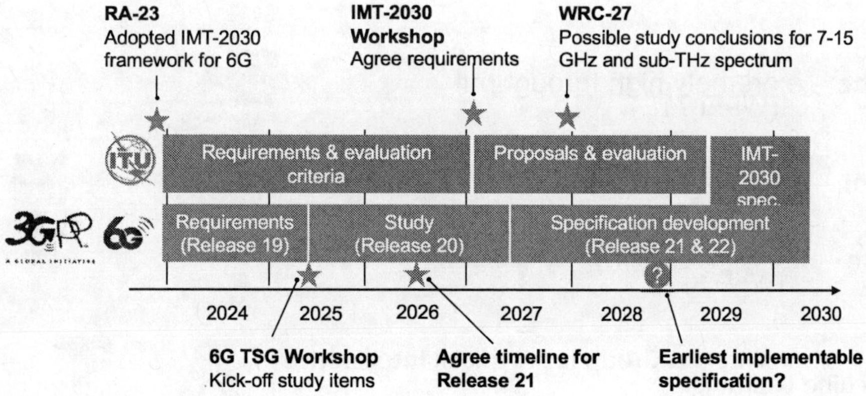

#SensorsConverge

ITU timeline: https://www.itu.int/dms_pub/itu-r/oth/0a/06/R0A060000C80001PDFE.pdf

3GPP timeline based on info in https://atis.org/wp-content/uploads/2024/04/3GPP-Webinar-Slides_04.03.24.pdf

Sensors Converge

6G and Future Wireless – Enabling Technologies

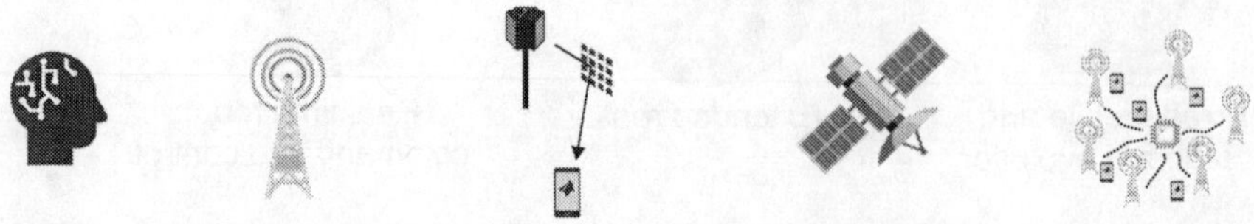

#SensorsConverge

Sensors Converge

Emerging WLAN standards

- **802.11be** – extremely high throughput (Wi-Fi 7)
- **802.11bf** – wireless sensing
- 802.11bn - ultra high reliability (Wi-Fi 8)
- **TG-AIML** - Topic Interest Group for Artificial Intelligence and Machine Learning

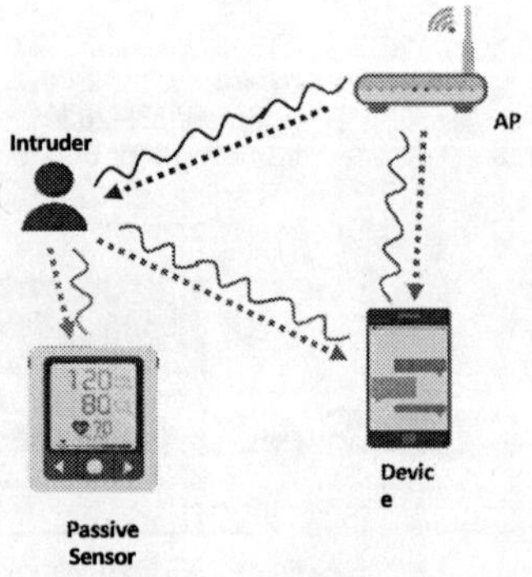

Leverage AI/ML

#SensorsConverge

Sensors Converge

Artificial Intelligence (AI)

MOTIVATIONS FOR AI IN WIRELESS

- Success of AI in other application areas (image processing, NLP)
- Hardware and computation power advancements

→ Improve performance using data-driven vs model-based approaches

→ Reduce algorithm complexity

→ Facilitate joint optimization of network and device operations

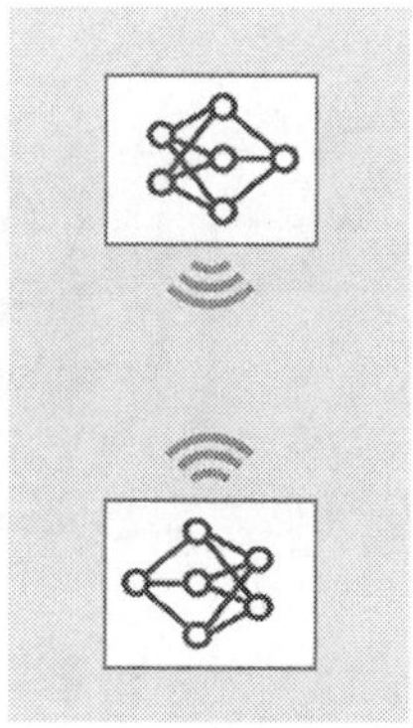

#SensorsConverge

Sensors Converge

Workflow of AI-driven Wireless System Design

Data Preparation	AI Modeling	Simulation & Test	Deployment
Data cleansing and preparation	Model design and tuning	Integration with complex systems	Embedded devices
Human insight	Hardware accelerated training	System simulation	Enterprise systems
Simulation-generated data	Interoperability	System verification and validation	Edge, cloud, desktop

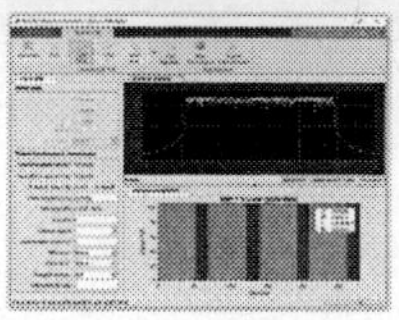

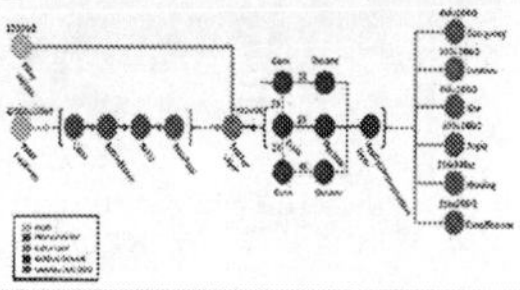

10 #SensorsConverge

Sensors Converge

Reinforcement Learning

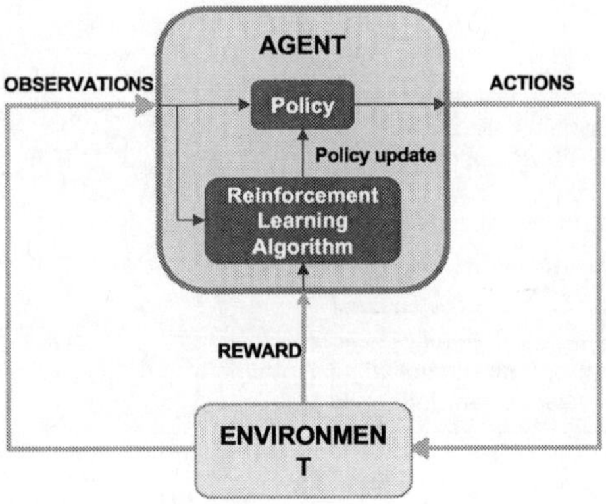

- Vehicle's computer... **(agent)**
- is reading sensor measurements from LIDAR, cameras,... **(observations)**
- that represent road conditions, vehicle position,... **(environment)**
- and generates steering, braking, throttle commands,... **(action)**
- based on an internal state-to-action mapping... **(policy)**
- that tries to optimize, e.g., lap time & fuel efficiency... **(reward)**.

- The policy is updated through repeated trial-and-error by a **reinforcement learning algorithm**

#SensorsConverge

AI for 6G – How MATLAB can Help

Ready-to-use AI Workflows for Wireless

CSI Feedback with Autoencoders

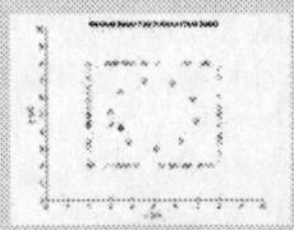

Neural Networks for Beam Selection

Neural Networks for Digital Predistortion

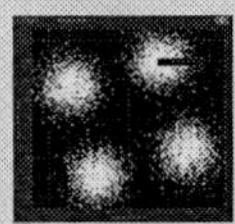

E2E Comms Systems with Autoencoders

Interoperate and Exchange Models with Python and other Frameworks

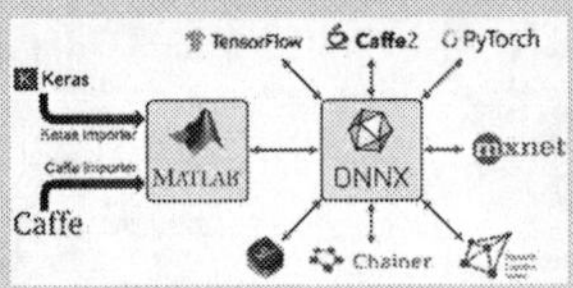

Capture Over the Air Signals to Train AI Models

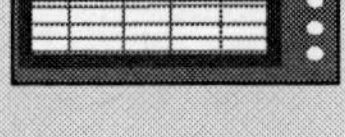

Test and Measurement Devices

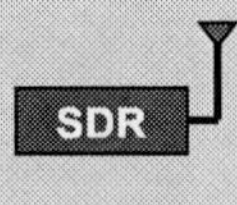

Software-Defined Radios

#SensorsConverge

Augment Existing Data or Synthesize Data

Data Preparation

- Data cleansing and preparation
- Human insight
- Simulation-generated data
- HW connection Over-the-Air Signal

Wireless Waveform Generator app to create, impair, visualize, and export modulated waveforms

- Interactive waveform generation
- Arbitrary waveforms (OFDM, QAM, PSK)
- Standards-based (5G NR, LTE, WLAN)
- Add signal impairments
- Generate MATLAB script for reuse
- Custom waveforms

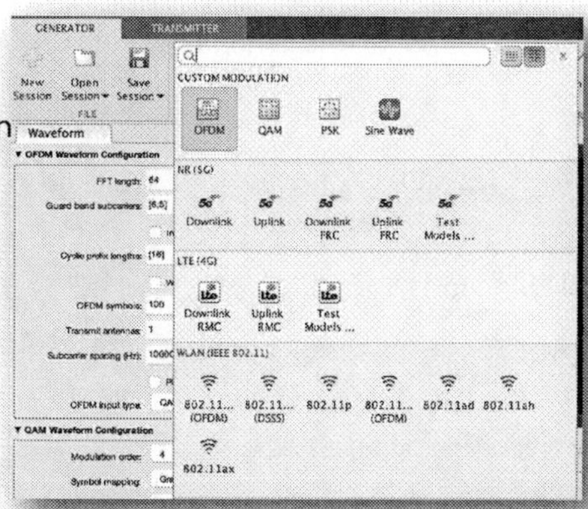

#SensorsConverge

Sensors Converge

Generate Waveforms

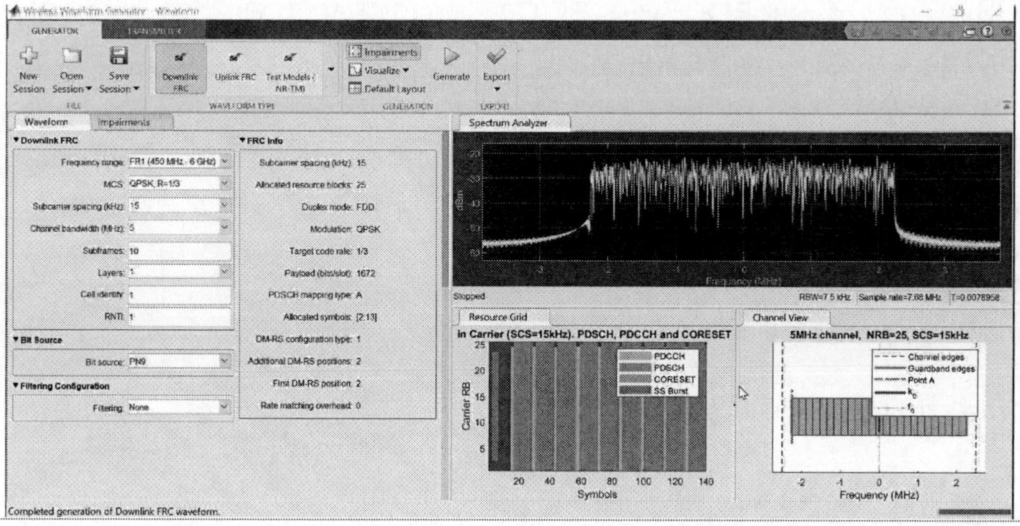

#SensorsConverge

Sensors Converge

802.11az Positioning and Localization Examples

"super-resolution" ranging

- Simulate ranging and positioning measurements with TGax channel and MUSIC algorithm

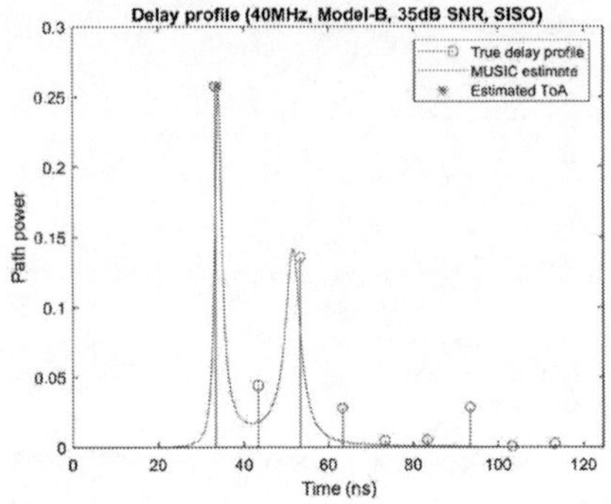

3D indoor positioning with fingerprinting and deep learning

- Train a convolutional neural network for localization and positioning with 802.11az data

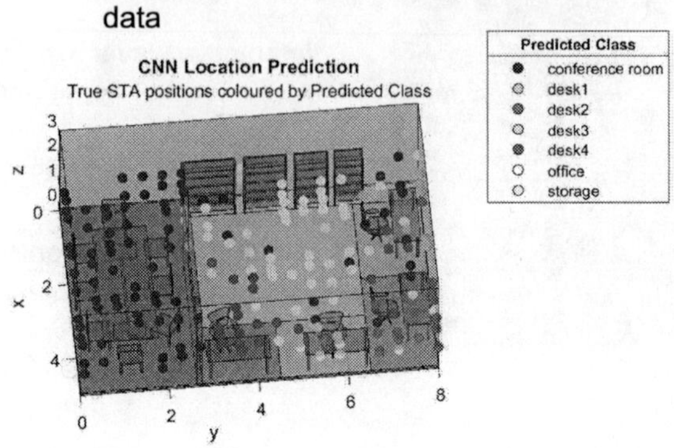

Detect Human Presence Using Wireless Sensing with Deep Learning

- Use Wi-Fi channel state information to detect the presence of people in a room
- Capture Wi-Fi beacon CSI with SDR and WLAN Toolbox with and without movement to create a data set
- Train a neural network to classify presence

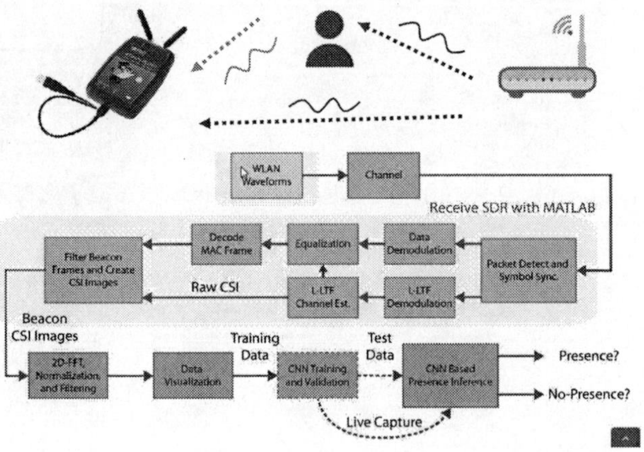

Training and Testing Wireless Sensing for Human Presence

Deep Convolutional Receiver

- Replace 5G receiver components with deep convolutional neural networks (CNNs) :
    - Channel Estimation
    - Channel Equalization
    - Layer Demapping
    - Symbol Demodulation
- Novel deep learning architecture support
- GPU/CPU parallelization support for training and inference stages.

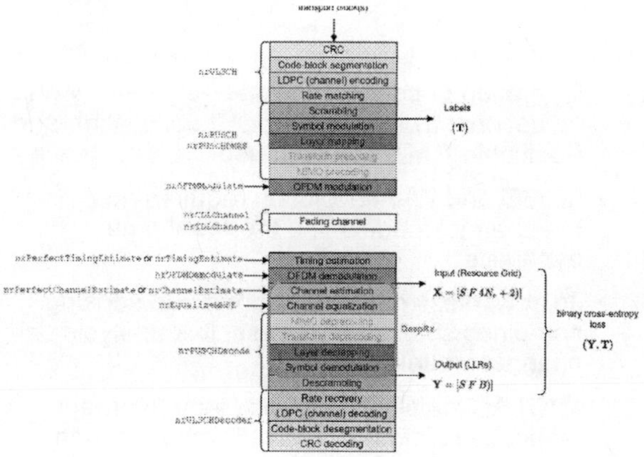

5G NR PDSCH Throughput Using Channel State Information Feedback

- Supports
  - RI-PMI-CQI
  - AI-based feedback
  - Perfect CSI

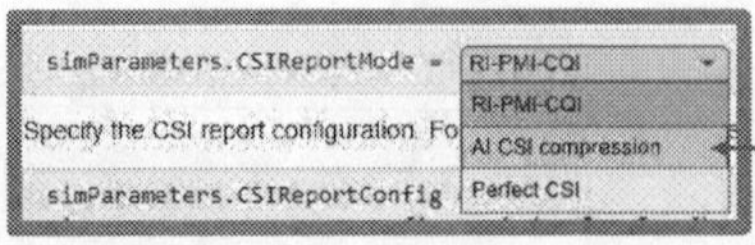

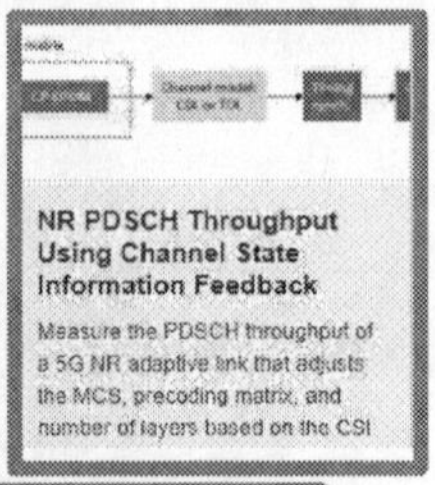

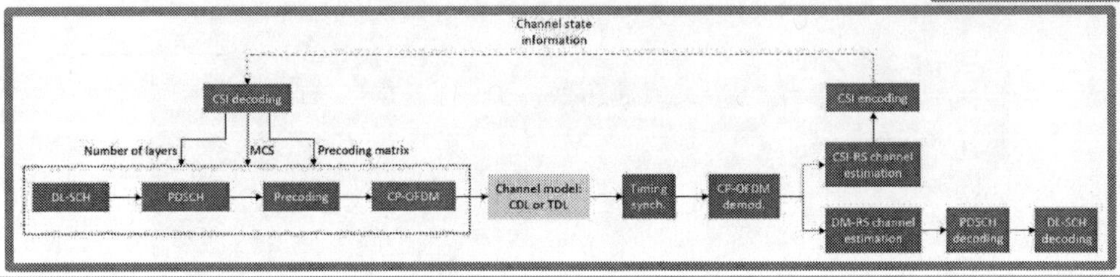

Summary

- Operation of sensor networks rely heavily on "situational awareness" and "Localization and Positioning" of sensors in use
- 5G/6G and Wi-Fi evolution requires modeling the channel models and their real-time dynamics
- Joint wireless communications and sensing combines spatial awareness, link analysis and channel modeling
- MATLAB tools in Deep and Reinforcement leaning can jointly optimize Digital, RF and Antenna parts of your sensor network design.

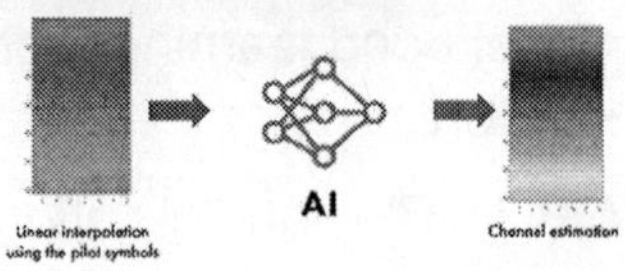

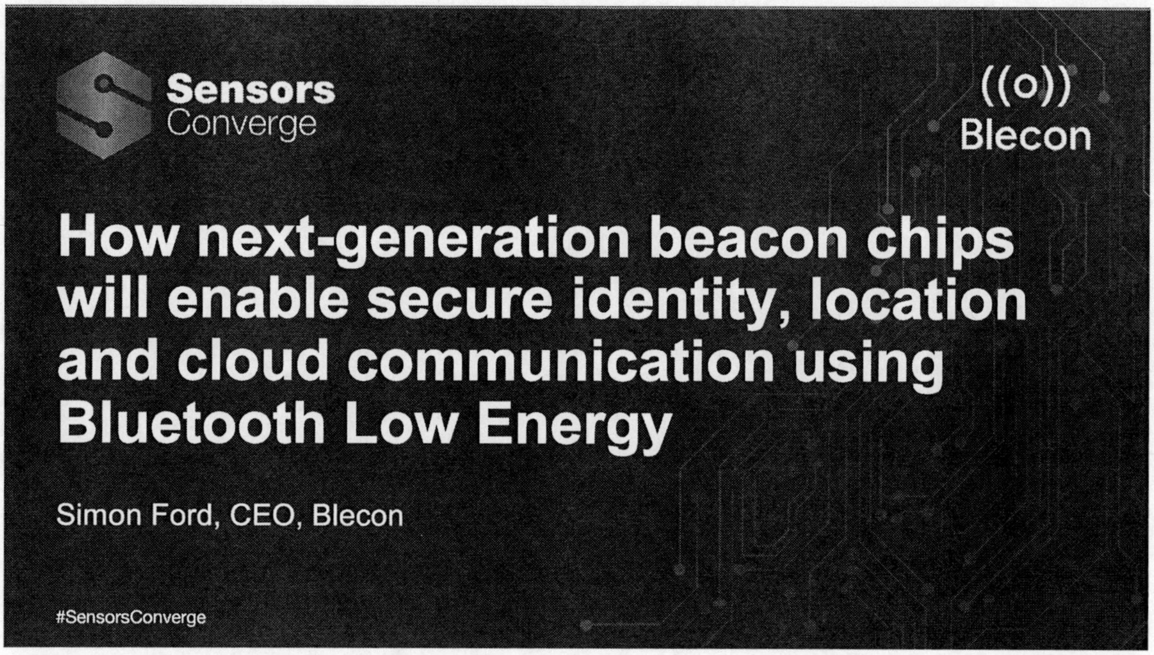
Sensors
Converge
((o))
Blecon
How next-generation beacon chips will enable secure identity, location and cloud communication using Bluetooth Low Energy
Simon Ford, CEO, Blecon
#SensorsConverge

Beacons were first used as a marketing tool
Bluetooth
Low Energy
iBeacon
Google
Eddystone
15:33
Monday, October 7
Starbucks
Hi Phil! You are near Starbucks Oxford st. Currently 50% off on your favorite drink: the Vanilla Latte!
#SensorsConverge
Sensors
Converge

Beacons now…

Low cost, low power devices that generate tracking & sensing data

Beacon market

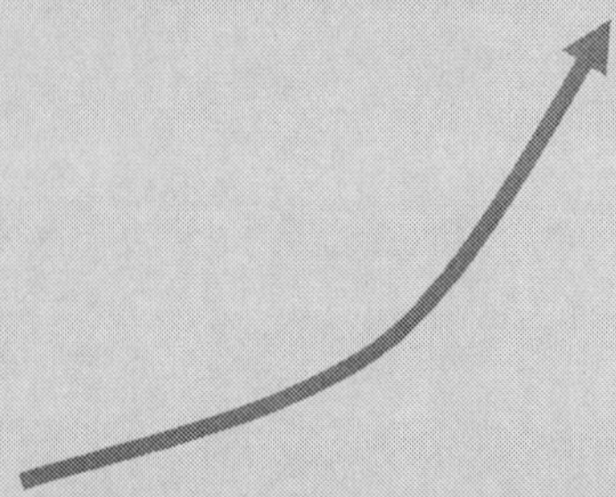

$1.3B (2018) **$31B** (2026) **$103B** (2030)

Source: Fortune Business Insights, Allied Market Research

#SensorsConverge Bluetooth Sensors Converge

Bluetooth Low Energy

First introduced in **Bluetooth 4.0**

Enabled a new class of **low cost, low power, medium range** wireless devices

Has **advertising** and **fast connections**

Global standard for single SKU

Now supported in **all phones & laptops**

Consumer enabled **huge economies of scale,** now being **exploited by industry**

Bluetooth Low Energy Device Unit Shipments

***>1B** in 2022*

***>3B** in 2026*

25% CAGR

Bluetooth®

#SensorsConverge Sensors Converge

Why companies choose Bluetooth vs. others

Need Proximity, Limited Data

High Power, IT Complexity

Bluetooth®

LoRa®

NB-IoT

LTE-M

Low Cost, Low Power, Medium Bandwidth, Global

Low Bandwidth, Regional

Already supported in many MCUs, Gateways & Smartphones/Laptops

High Cost, High Power

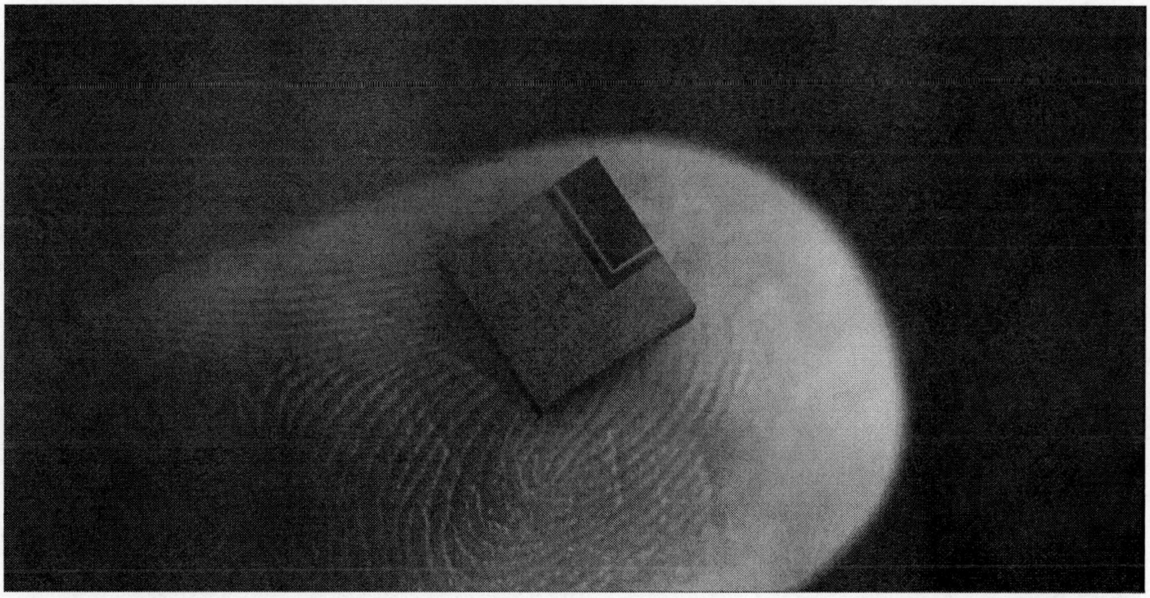

Bluetooth Low Energy Ecosystem

e.g. MCU Silicon Vendors:

NORDIC SEMICONDUCTOR · ST life.augmented · SILICON LABS · MICROCHIP · TEXAS INSTRUMENTS · infineon

Qualcomm · CYPRESS EMBEDDED IN TOMORROW · RENESAS · ESPRESSIF

Telink · GOODiX · NXP · TOSHIBA

nuvoTon · INPLAY · Atmosic™ · ONiO®

#SensorsConverge

7

Sensors Converge

Beacon Architecture

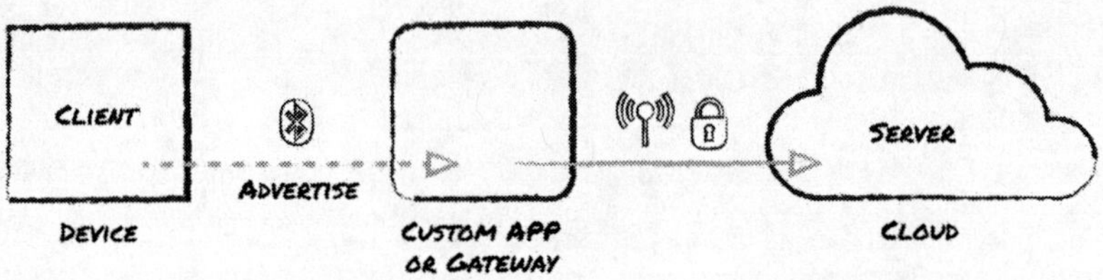

Limited Data ~ No Response ~ No Security

#SensorsConverge

Sensors Converge

Bluetooth Architecture

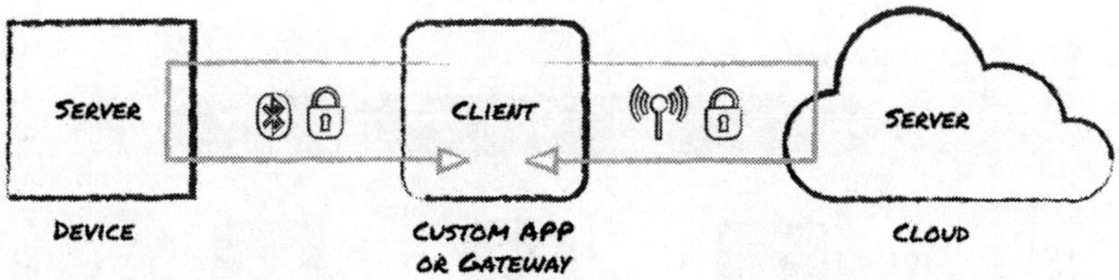

Device is a Server ~ Custom App/Gateway ~ Requires Pairing

#SensorsConverge

Sensors Converge

Required Architecture

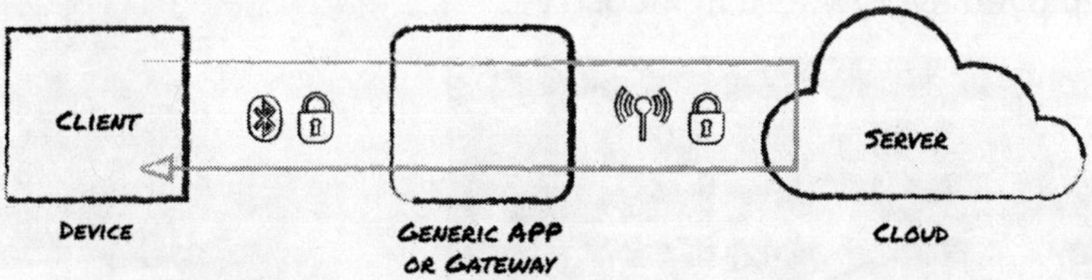

Device is a Client ~ Generic Hotspot ~ Secure E2E

#SensorsConverge

Sensors Converge

Enables IoT Connectivity network

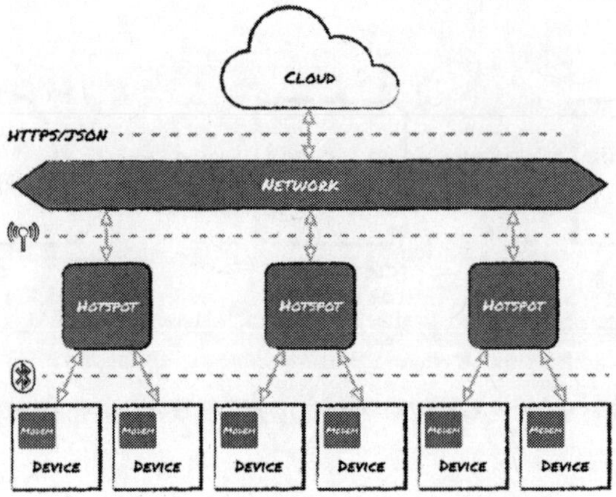

#SensorsConverge

Sensors Converge

Hotspots on the front line

Smartphones & tablets are now deployed everywhere in industry

Can be exploited as flexible hotspots

#SensorsConverge

Sensors Converge

Enables Device and Hotspot mobility

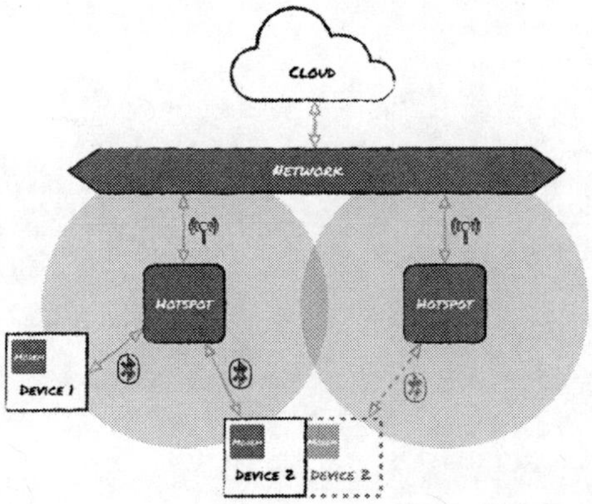

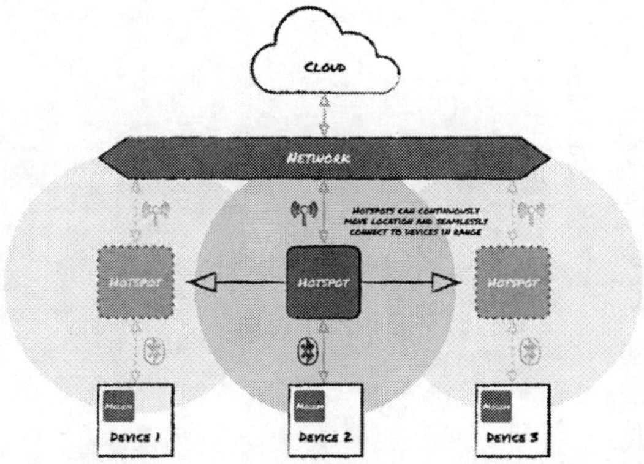

Bluetooth Low Energy for IoT Connectivity

Bluetooth Low Energy delivers low-cost, low-power connectivity and has achieved global adoption and unprecedented economies of scale.

Beacons and other industrial applications are driving it in to use cases beyond classic Personal Area Networking.

By combining the benefits of Bluetooth Low Energy with a wifi-like deployment model and cellular-like network model, companies are applying it for use as a low-cost, low-power IoT Connectivity.

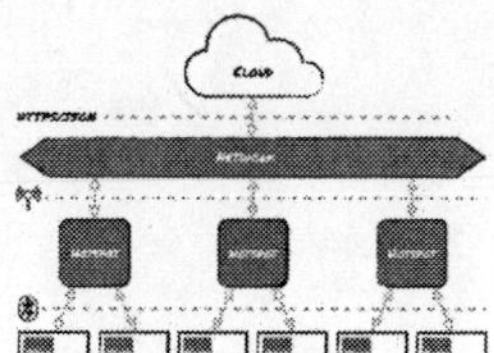

((o))
Blecon
http://blecon.net
#SensorsConverge
Sensors Converge

VERY

Using AI to Unlock your IoT Infrastructure

Presented by:
Daniel Fudge, Senior Director @ Very

verytechnology.com

VERY

Agenda

- **01** Why Build an IoT Infrastructure
- **02** How Very is Organized to Unlock this Value
- **03** High Level IoT Infrastructure
- **04** Pattern 1 - Low Power Telemetry & Control
- **05** Pattern 2 - Heavy AI Workloads

Visit **booth #802** to speak with the Very team

VERY

IoT Value Generation

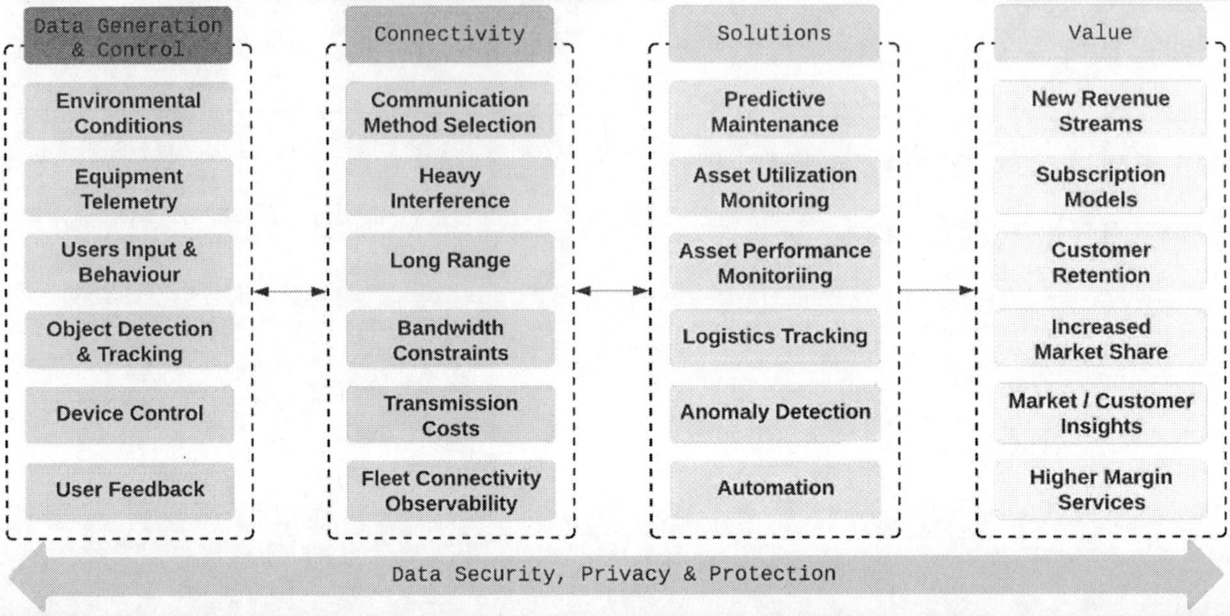

Visit **booth #802** to speak with the Very tean

VERY

Been there. Built that.

Unlock the full potential of IoT and accelerate business growth with:

IoT Product + Interface Design

Hardware + Firmware

Data Solutions + Machine Learning

IoT Software + Digital Infrastructure

End-to-End IoT Development

With Very, innovate, differentiate and deliver powerful IoT solutions that deliver undeniable business value

2011	4.9	425+
Founded	Clutch Rating	Projects Shipped

Visit **booth #802** to speak with the Very tear

VERY

Related AI Ecosystem

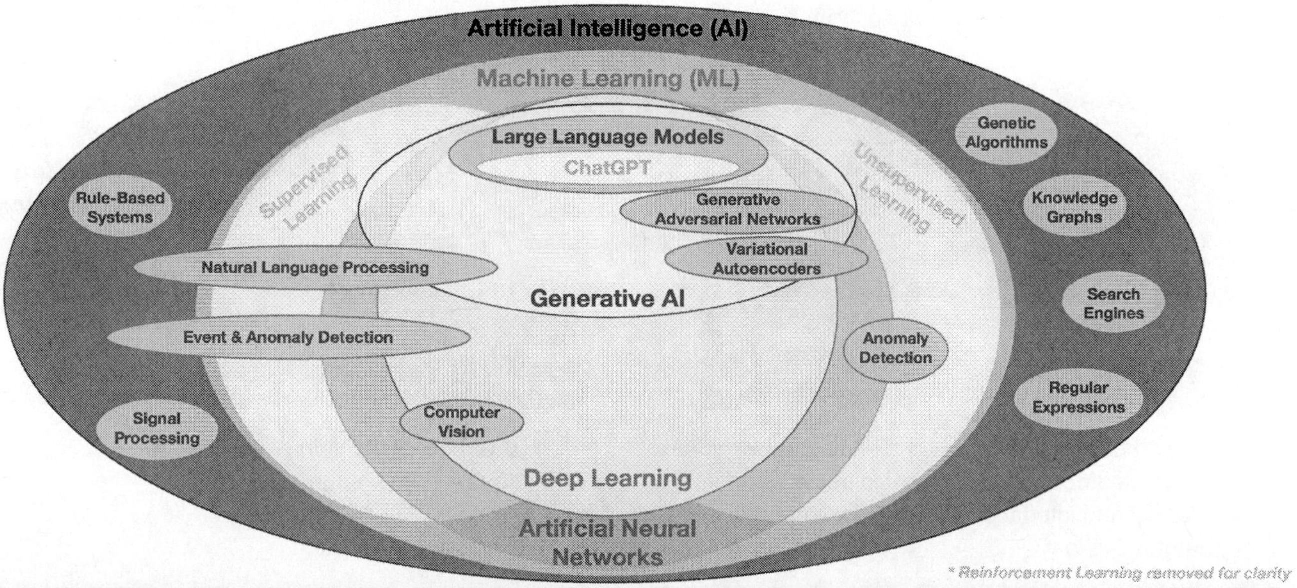

* Reinforcement Learning removed for clarity

Visit **booth #802** to speak with the Very team

VERY

High Level IoT Infrastructure

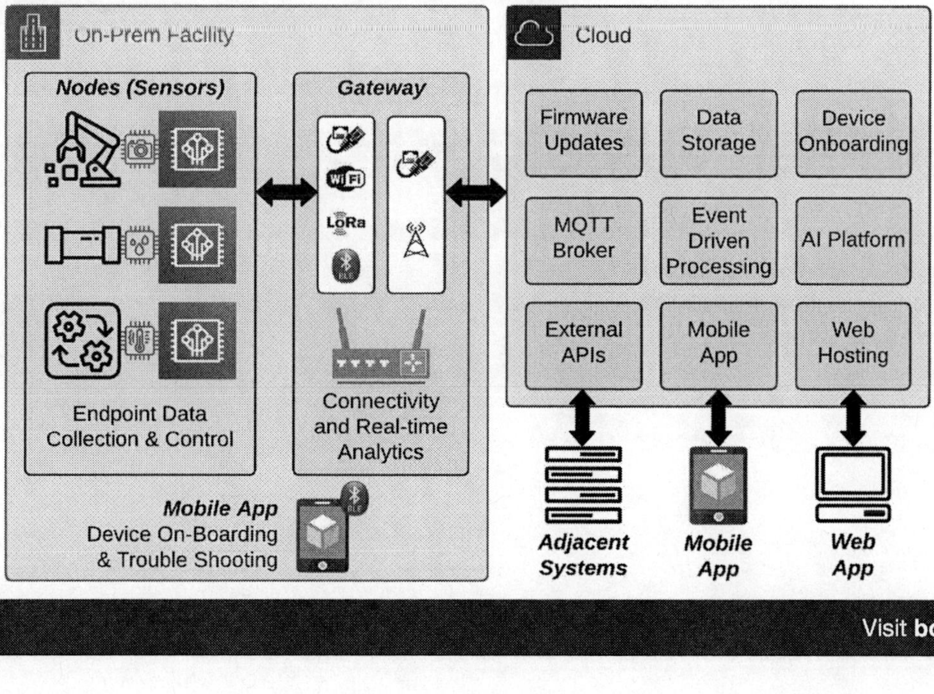

The cloud could be a **single system** or a **collection of cloud platforms.**

Visit **booth #802** to speak with the Very team

VERY

Custom IoT Platforms

Very's Proven IoT ToolKit

- Infrastructure as Code
- Automated deployment
- Well defined interfaces
- SaaS & Custom

Your Unique Opportunity

- Existing infrastructure
- Unique environments
- Digital maturity
- Strategic objectives

Your Optimized IoT Platform

- Full data & IP ownership
- Competitive advantage
- Scaled to fit
- Minimum dependencies

Rapidly deploy IoT Infrastructure ***tailored*** to convert ***physical device data*** into your most ***valuable asse***

Visit **booth #802** to speak with the Very tear

VERY

Pattern 1
Low Power Telemetry & Control

- → Battery powered nodes
- → Challenging node / gateway communication
- → Environmental monitoring and device telemetry
- → Localized event detection and control

VERY

Low Power Telemetry & Control

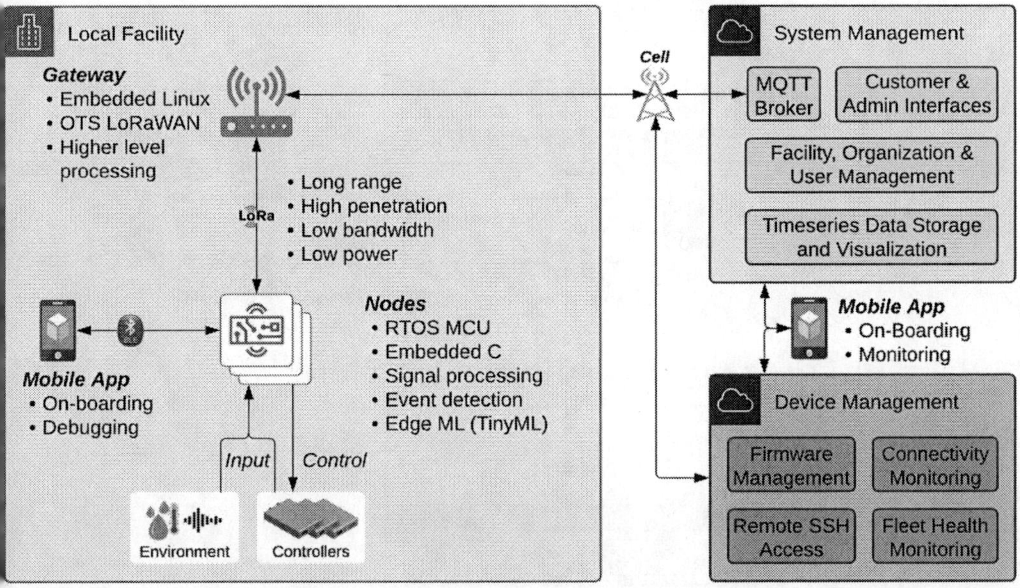

Key Edge Compute Advantages

- Reduced offline memory requirements
- Increased functionality in event of communication loss
- Reduced communication & cloud costs

Key Edge Compute Drivers

- BOM costs
- Battery life
- Bandwidth

Visit **booth #802** to speak with the Very team

VERY

Pattern 2 - Heavy AI Workloads

➔ Low latency
➔ Heavy data processing and larger machine learning models
➔ Heightened data security and privacy concerns

VERY

Heavy AI Workloads

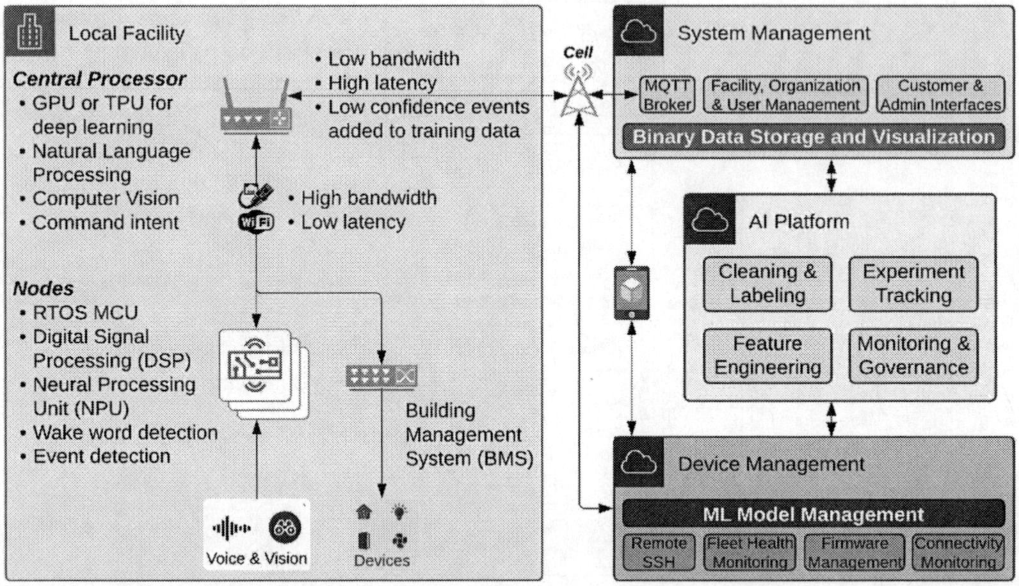

Key Edge Compute Advantage

- Greatly reduced communication & cloud cost
- Sub-second latency
- Full offline capability
- Privacy & Security

Key Edge Compute Drivers

- BOM costs
- Training data quality
- Full model pipeline maturity

Visit **booth #802** to speak with the Very tear

Questions?

Visit our team at **booth #802**

End-to-End IoT Development

*With Very, innovate, differentiate and deliver **powerful IoT solutions** that deliver undeniable business value.*

2011 Founded | **4.9** Clutch Rating | **425+** Projects Shipped

Daniel Fudge, Senior Director @ Very

daniel.f@verytechnology.com

linkedin.com/in/**daniel-fudge/**

VERY

Building IoT Value

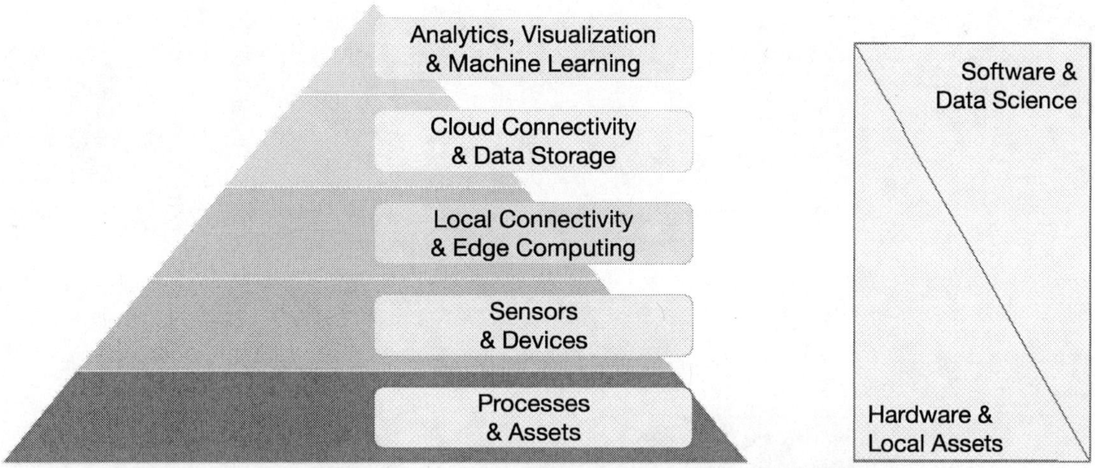

Visit **booth #802** to speak with the Very team

VERY

The Four Levels of Analytics

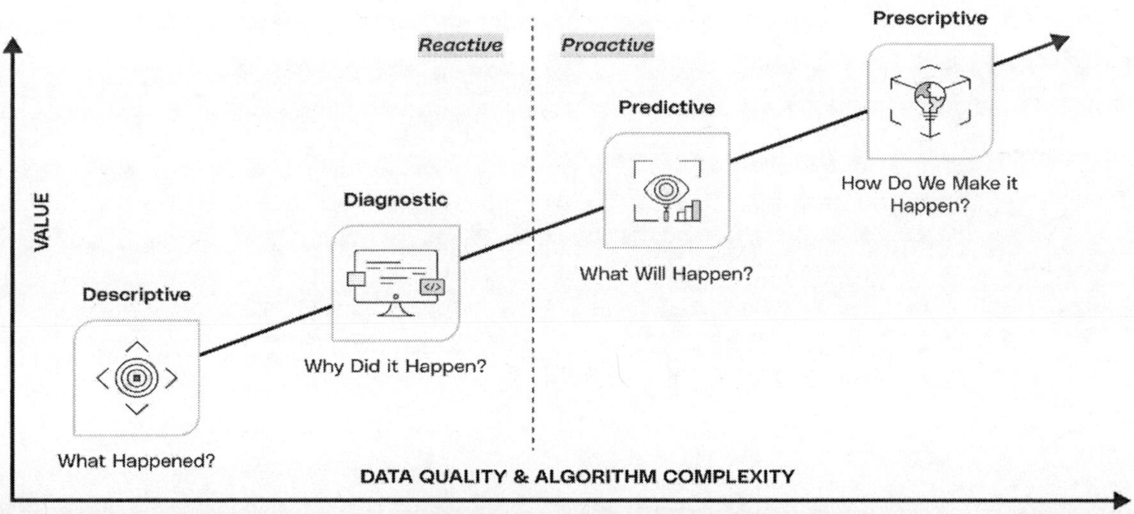

Visit **booth #802** to speak with the Very team

Related AI Ecosystem

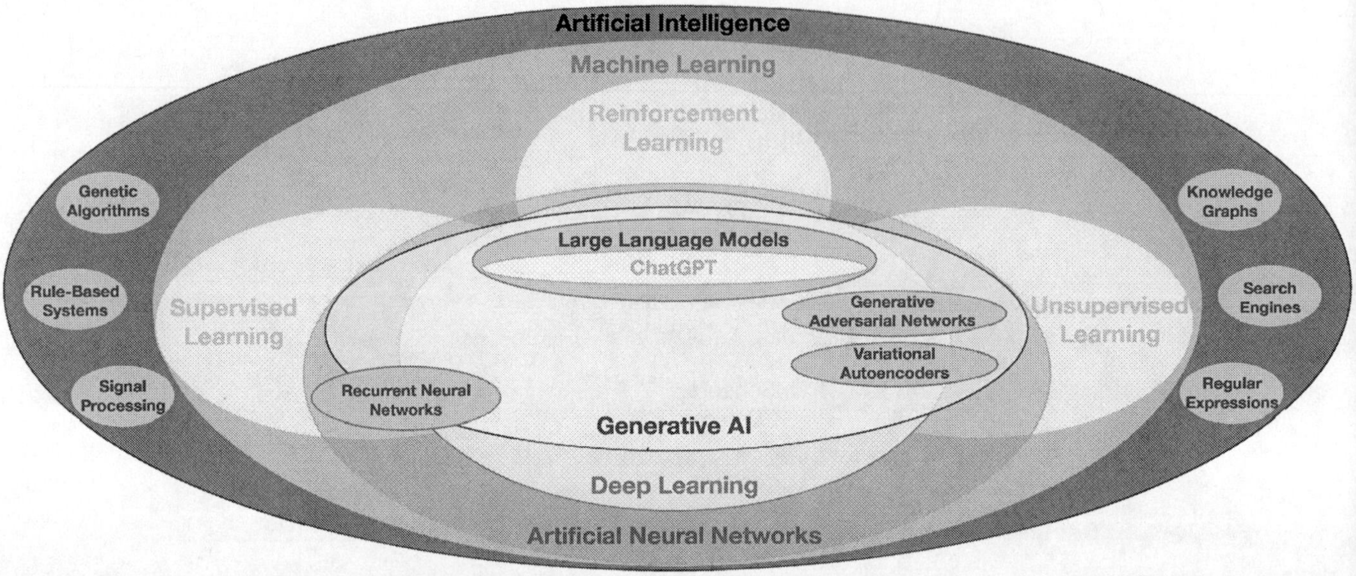

Visit **booth #802** to speak with the Very tean

Sensors Converge

June 24–26, 2024 | Santa Clara, CA

GE VERNOVA

Edge-based multi-gas sensors:

anticipated and unanticipated advantages over last-century sensor designs

Radislav A. Potyrailo
GE Vernova Advanced Research Center, Niskayuna, NY, USA
potyrailo@ge.com

Every century - solving practical challenges with creativity:

First "edge – based" chemical detectors…

1911 Coal MInes Act : canaries as detectors of carbon monoxide

Mine rescue workers, Pittsburgh , 1910 http://ae.msasafety.com/msa100
https://miningheritage.co.uk/pit-canaries-end-of-an-era/
https://www.macearchive.org/films/atv-today-26041971-underground-fire-desford-colliery

Worl War I: Gas scouts trained to warn on an incoming gas cloud

To R. A. Potyrailo from Archives of US Army Edgewood ChemBio Center

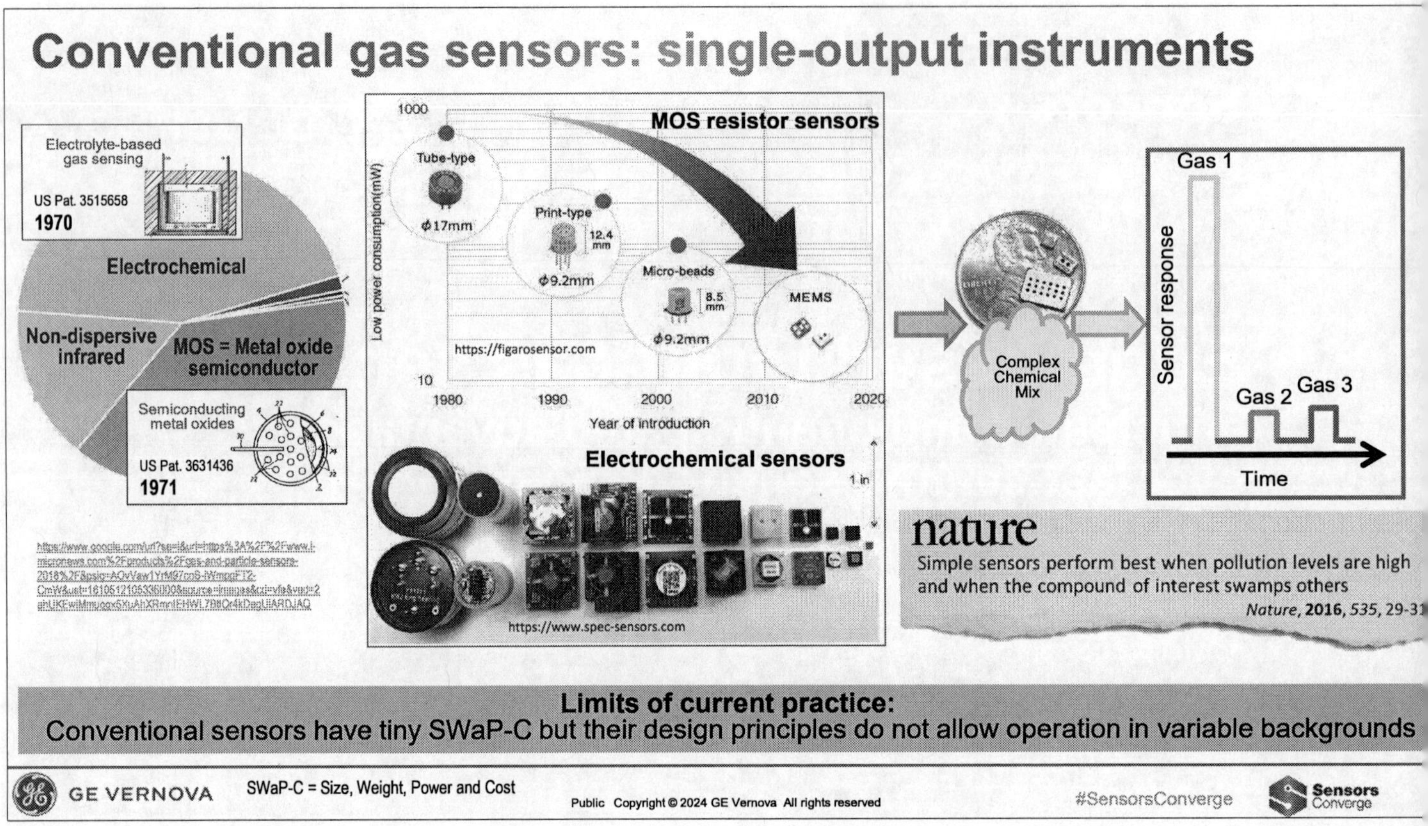
Conventional gas sensors: single-output instruments
Electrolyte-based gas sensing
US Pat. 3515658
1970
Electrochemical
Non-dispersive infrared
MOS = Metal oxide semiconductor
Semiconducting metal oxides
US Pat. 3631436
1971
MOS resistor sensors
Low power consumption(mW)
1000
10
Tube-type
ϕ17mm
Print-type
12.4 mm
ϕ9.2mm
Micro-beads
8.5 mm
ϕ9.2mm
MEMS
https://figarosensor.com
1980
1990
2000
2010
2020
Year of introduction
Electrochemical sensors
1 in
https://www.spec-sensors.com
Complex Chemical Mix
Gas 1
Gas 2
Gas 3
Sensor response
Time
nature
Simple sensors perform best when pollution levels are high and when the compound of interest swamps others
Nature, 2016, 535, 29-31
Limits of current practice:
Conventional sensors have tiny SWaP-C but their design principles do not allow operation in variable backgrounds
GE VERNOVA
SWaP-C = Size, Weight, Power and Cost
Public Copyright © 2024 GE Vernova All rights reserved
#SensorsConverge
Sensors Converge

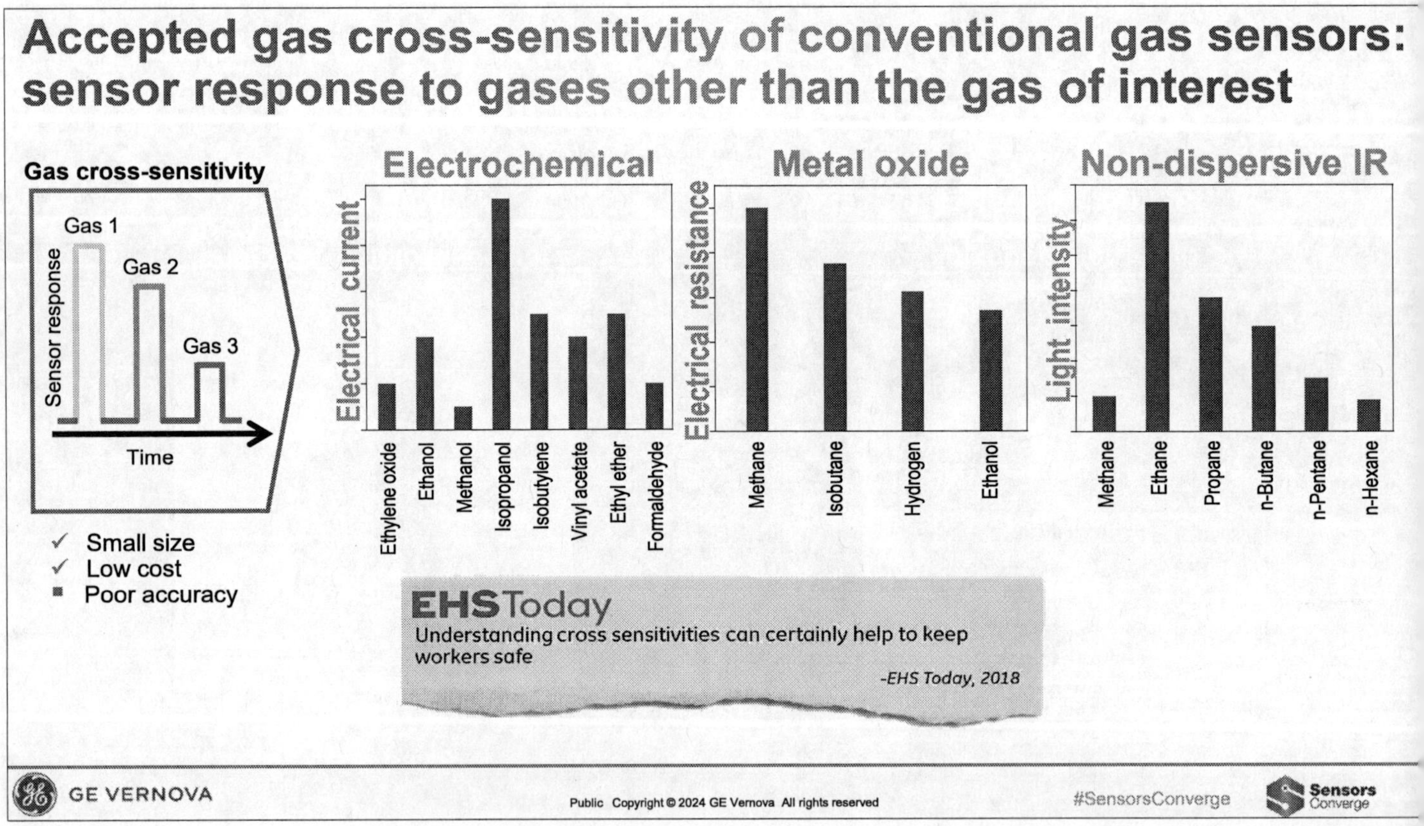
Accepted gas cross-sensitivity of conventional gas sensors: sensor response to gases other than the gas of interest
Gas cross-sensitivity
Gas 1
Gas 2
Gas 3
Sensor response
Time
✓ Small size
✓ Low cost
▪ Poor accuracy
Electrochemical
Electrical current
Ethylene oxide
Ethanol
Methanol
Isopropanol
Isobutylene
Vinyl acetate
Ethyl ether
Formaldehyde
Metal oxide
Electrical resistance
Methane
Isobutane
Hydrogen
Ethanol
Non-dispersive IR
Light intensity
Methane
Ethane
Propane
n-Butane
n-Pentane
n-Hexane
EHSToday
Understanding cross sensitivities can certainly help to keep workers safe
-EHS Today, 2018
GE VERNOVA
Public Copyright © 2024 GE Vernova All rights reserved
#SensorsConverge
Sensors Converge

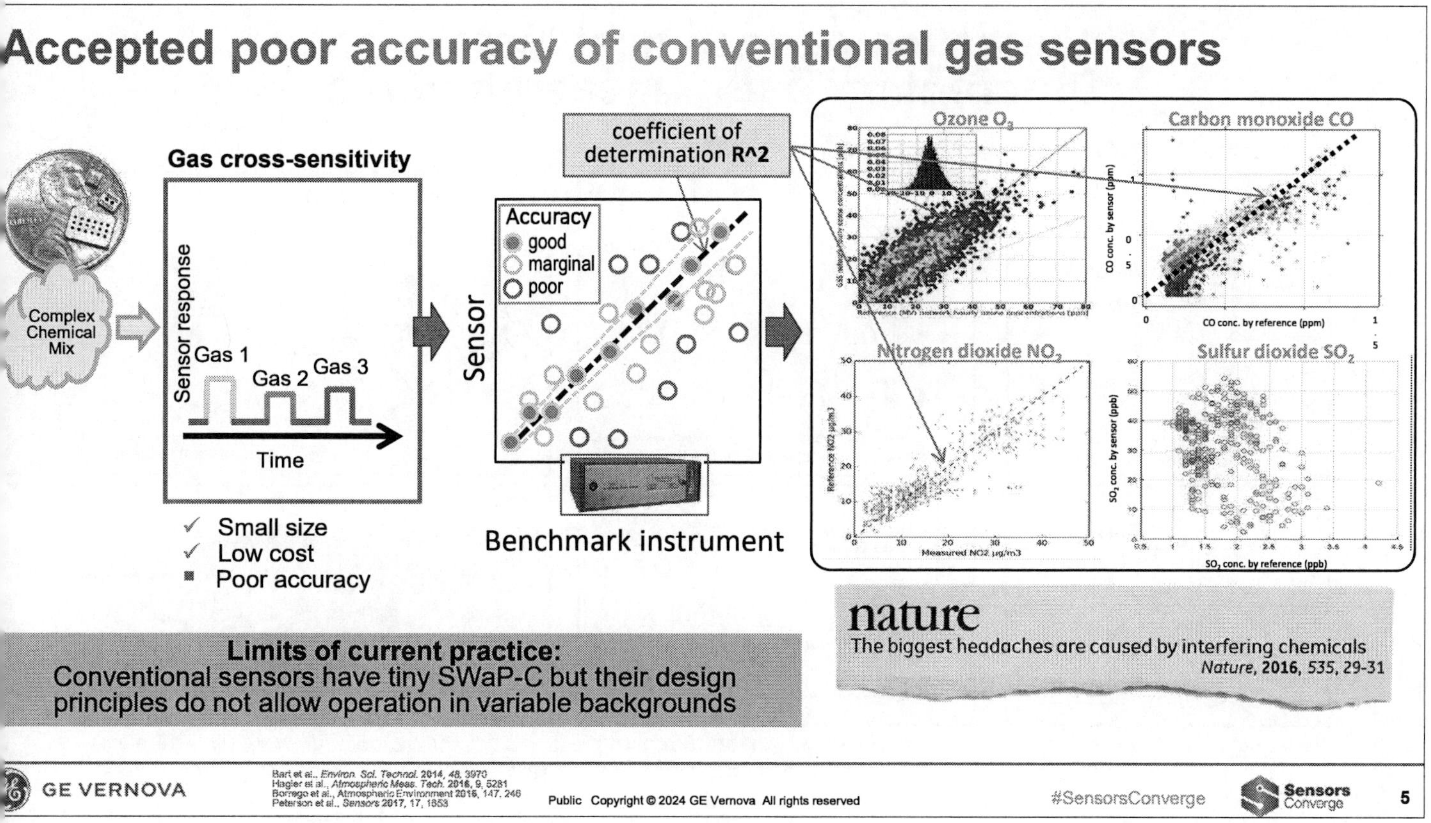
Accepted poor accuracy of conventional gas sensors
Gas cross-sensitivity
Complex Chemical Mix
Sensor response
Gas 1
Gas 2
Gas 3
Time
✓ Small size
✓ Low cost
■ Poor accuracy
coefficient of determination R^2
Accuracy
good
marginal
poor
Sensor
Benchmark instrument
Ozone O_3
Carbon monoxide CO
Nitrogen dioxide NO_2
Sulfur dioxide SO_2
CO conc. by sensor (ppm)
CO conc. by reference (ppm)
Measured NO2 µg/m3
SO_2 conc. by sensor (ppb)
SO_2 conc. by reference (ppb)
nature
The biggest headaches are caused by interfering chemicals
Nature, **2016**, *535*, 29-31
Limits of current practice:
Conventional sensors have tiny SWaP-C but their design principles do not allow operation in variable backgrounds
GE VERNOVA
Bart et al., *Environ. Sci. Technol.* 2014, 48, 3970
Hagler et al., *Atmospheric Meas. Tech.* 2016, 9, 5281
Borrego et al., Atmospheric Environment 2016, 147, 246
Peterson et al., *Sensors* 2017, 17, 1653
Public Copyright © 2024 GE Vernova All rights reserved
#SensorsConverge
Sensors Converge
5

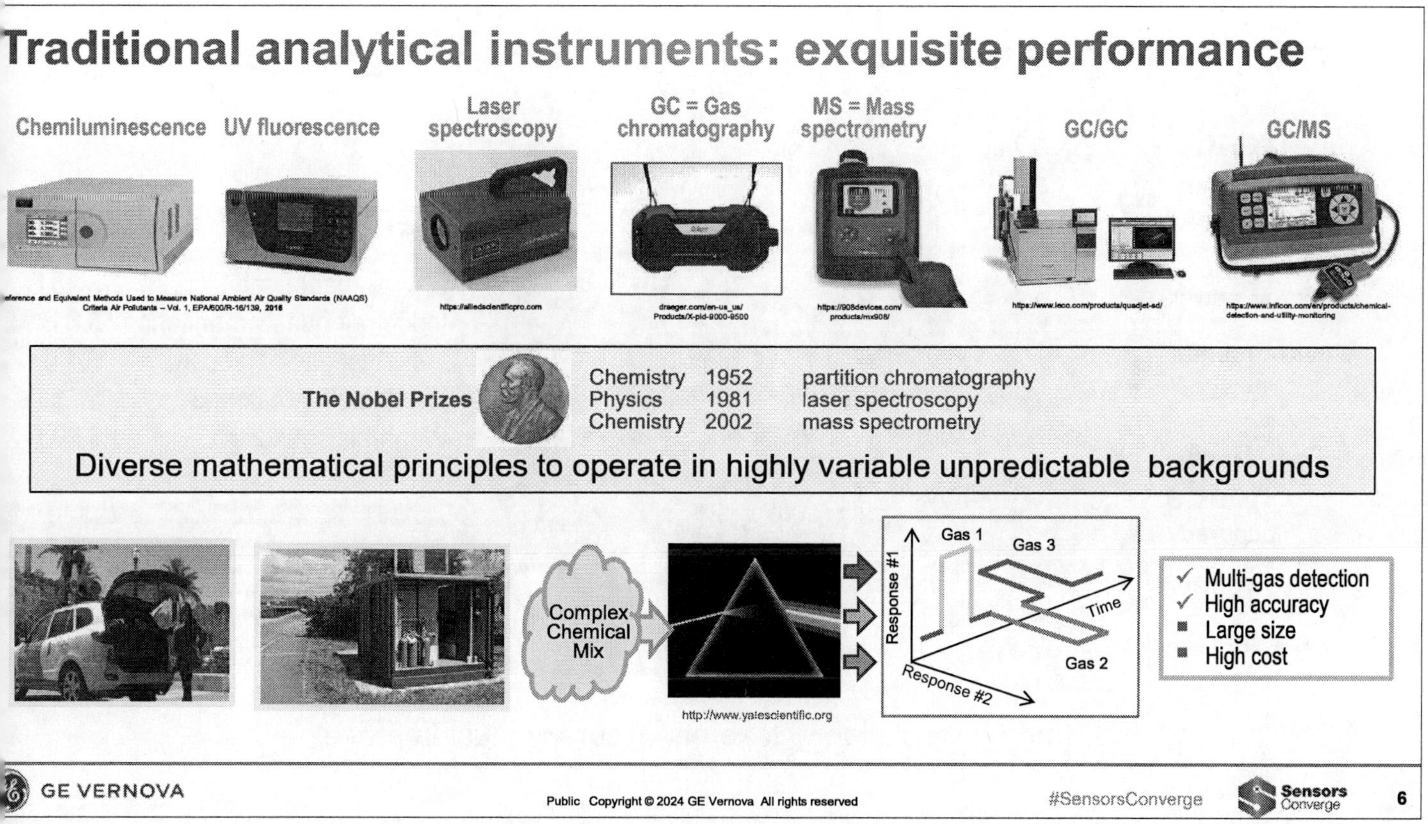
Traditional analytical instruments: exquisite performance
Chemiluminescence
UV fluorescence
Laser spectroscopy
GC = Gas chromatography
MS = Mass spectrometry
GC/GC
GC/MS
Reference and Equivalent Methods Used to Measure National Ambient Air Quality Standards (NAAQS) Criteria Air Pollutants – Vol. 1, EPA/600/R-16/139, 2016
https://alliedscientificpro.com
draeger.com/en-us_us/Products/X-pid-9000-9500
https://908devices.com/products/mx908/
https://www.leco.com/products/quadjet-sd/
https://www.inficon.com/en/products/chemical-detection-and-utility-monitoring
The Nobel Prizes
Chemistry 1952 partition chromatography
Physics 1981 laser spectroscopy
Chemistry 2002 mass spectrometry
Diverse mathematical principles to operate in highly variable unpredictable backgrounds
Complex Chemical Mix
http://www.yalescientific.org
Response #1
Response #2
Time
Gas 1
Gas 2
Gas 3
✓ Multi-gas detection
✓ High accuracy
■ Large size
■ High cost
GE VERNOVA
Public Copyright © 2024 GE Vernova All rights reserved
#SensorsConverge
Sensors Converge
6

Mathematics of analytical instruments: Different orders of measurements

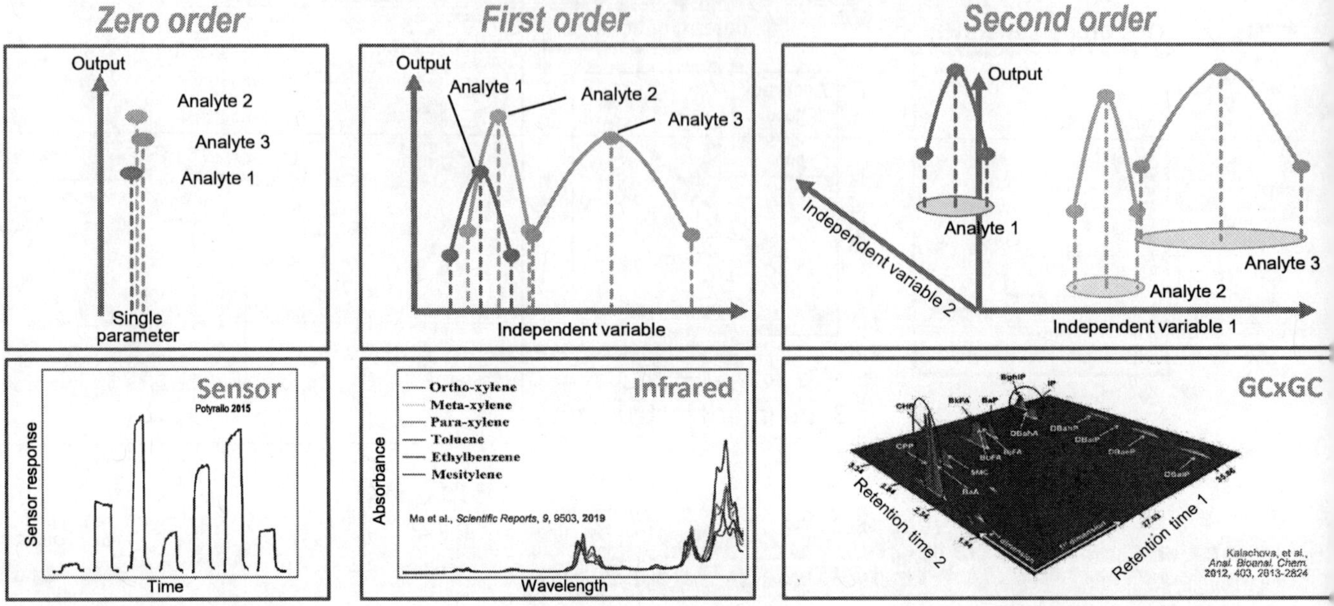

No rejection of interferences | Rejection of known interferences | Rejection of unknown interferences

Trends, requirements, and opportunities for gas sensors

Trends

Industrial safety
accuracy

Health / Fitness
accuracy, power

Environmental
accuracy

Top three needs

accuracy
cost
power

Potyrailo, *IEEE Sensors* **2023**

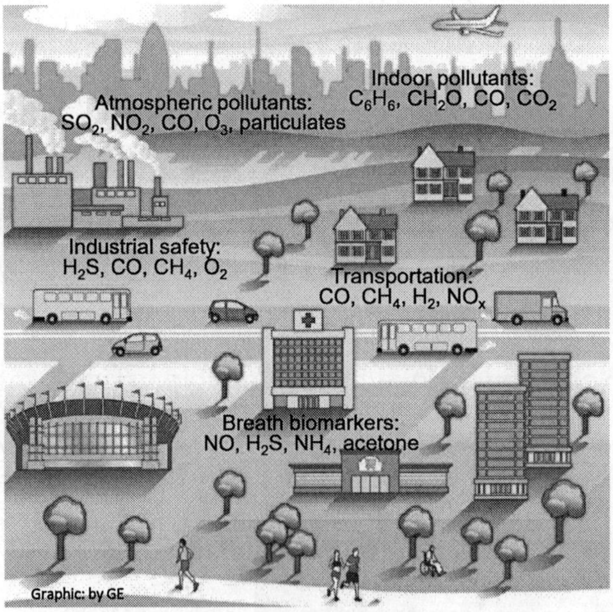

Global market drivers

Environmental monitoring	\$ 18 B
Indoor air quality monitoring	\$ 8 B
Industrial gas detection	\$ 4 B
Health self-monitoring	\$ 15 B
Wearable sensors	\$ 20 B

https://www.globenewswire.com/en/news-release/2023/01/26/2595862/0/en/Environmental-Monitori Market-Size-worth-17-9-billion-by-2026-Exclusive-Report-by-MarketsandMarkets.html

https://www.researchandmarkets.com/reports/4805488/indoor-air-quality-monitors-global-strategic?gclid=Cj0KCQjw2v-gBhC1ARIsAOQdKY0o1osIJrqIK8727nPIZXr4CX-eMNSGOZLSb2tsdeial7QY8nbjbLgaAvGTEALw_wcB

https://www.grandviewresearch.com/industry-analysis/gas-detection-equipment-market

https://www.prnewswire.com/news-releases/health-self-monitoring-technologies-and-global-markets 300102733.html

https://www.mordorintelligence.com/industry-reports/global-wearable-sensors-market

"For the revolution to take off, accuracy must improve"

Mathematics of traditional analytical instruments
→ to gas sensors with edge analytics

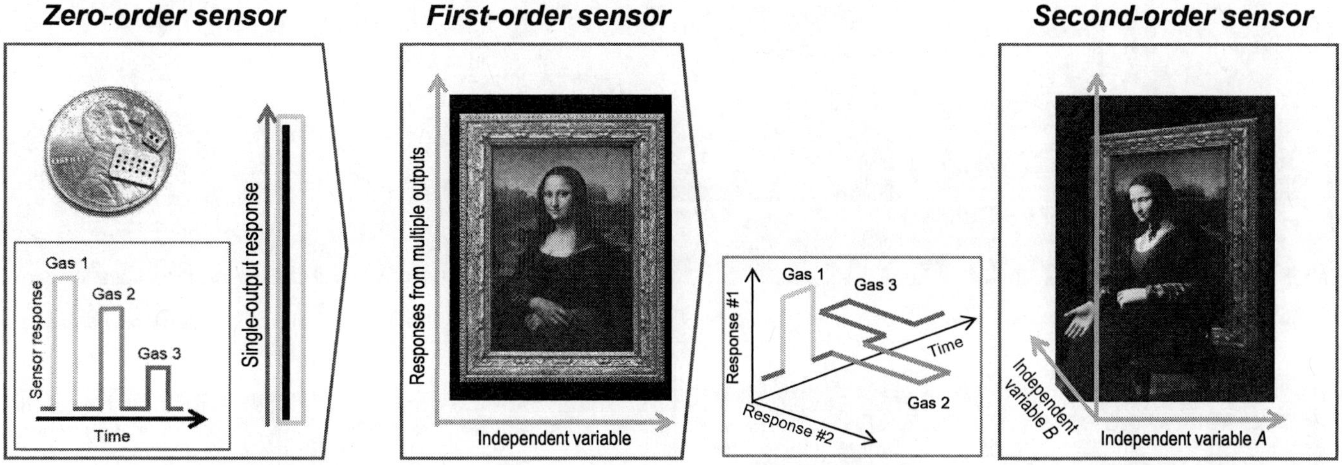

Applying innovative sensor-excitation methodologies coupled with edge analytics to deliver sensors with exquisite performance on par with traditional analytical instruments

Our industrial R&D goal:
Develop sensors with new capabilities, transition for commercialization

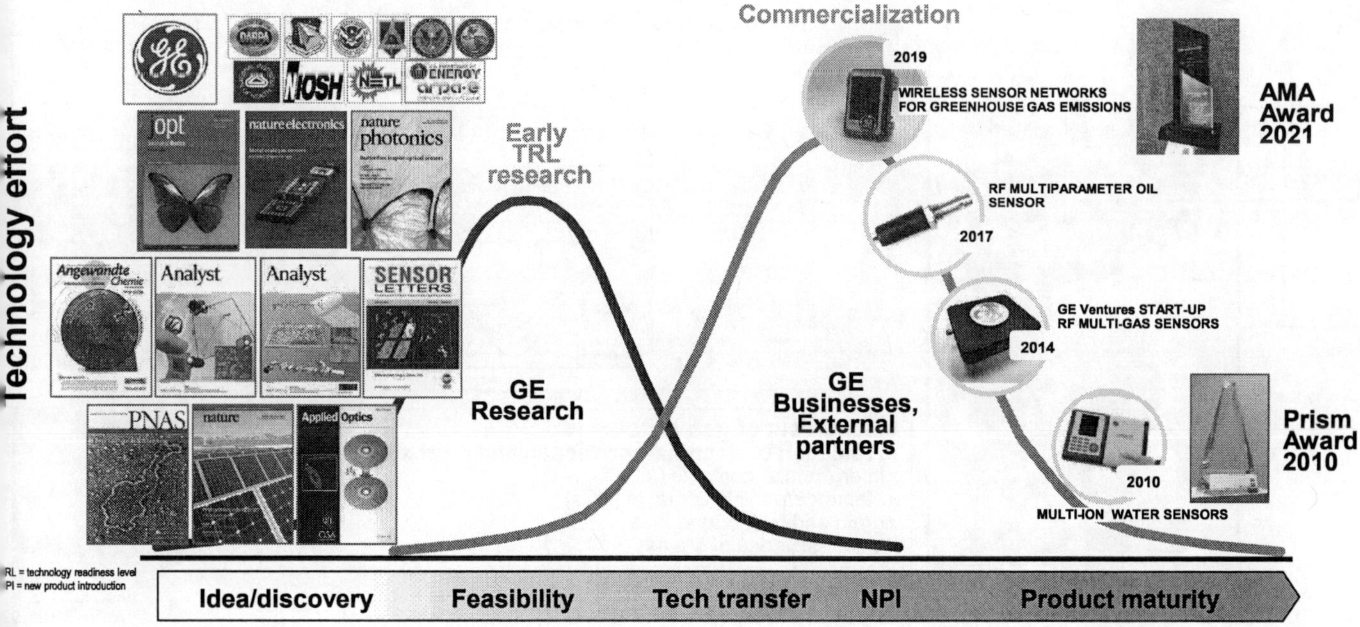

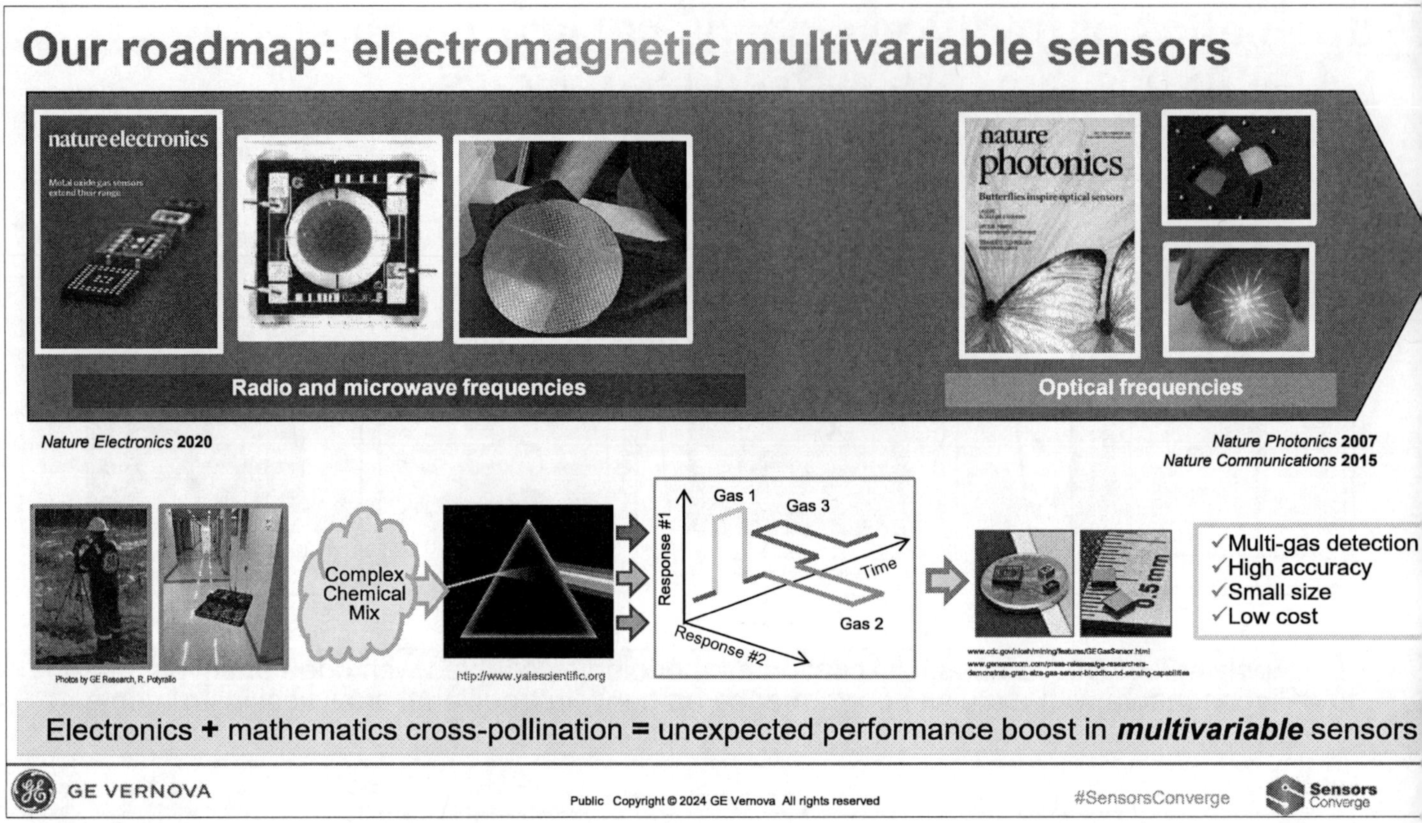
Our roadmap: electromagnetic multivariable sensors
nature electronics
nature photonics
Butterflies inspire optical sensors
Radio and microwave frequencies
Optical frequencies
Nature Electronics 2020
Nature Photonics 2007
Nature Communications 2015
Photos by GE Research, R. Potyrailo
Complex Chemical Mix
http://www.yalescientific.org
Gas 1
Gas 3
Gas 2
Response #1
Response #2
Time
0.5mm
✓Multi-gas detection
✓High accuracy
✓Small size
✓Low cost
Electronics + mathematics cross-pollination = unexpected performance boost in multivariable sensors
GE VERNOVA
Public Copyright © 2024 GE Vernova All rights reserved
#SensorsConverge
Sensors Converge

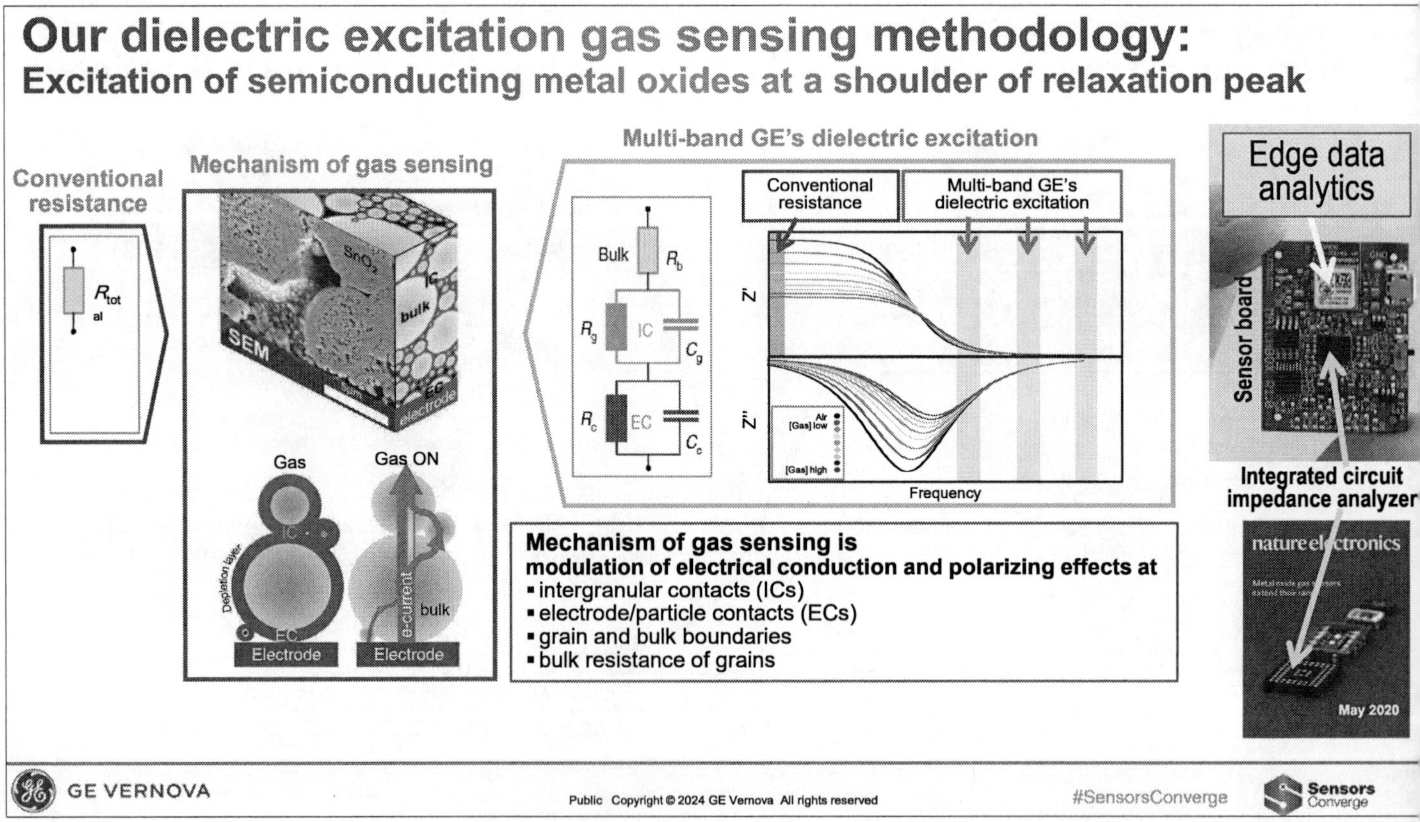
Our dielectric excitation gas sensing methodology:
Excitation of semiconducting metal oxides at a shoulder of relaxation peak
Conventional resistance
Mechanism of gas sensing
Multi-band GE's dielectric excitation
Edge data analytics
R_{total}
SnO_2
IC
bulk
SEM
EC
electrode
Gas
Gas ON
Depletion layer
e-current
Electrode
Electrode
Bulk
R_b
R_g
C_g
R_c
C_c
Conventional resistance
Multi-band GE's dielectric excitation
Z'
Z''
Air
[Gas] low
[Gas] high
Frequency
Sensor board
Integrated circuit impedance analyzer
nature electronics
May 2020
Mechanism of gas sensing is
modulation of electrical conduction and polarizing effects at
▪ intergranular contacts (ICs)
▪ electrode/particle contacts (ECs)
▪ grain and bulk boundaries
▪ bulk resistance of grains
GE VERNOVA
Public Copyright © 2024 GE Vernova All rights reserved
#SensorsConverge
Sensors Converge

Technology validated for monitoring of CH_4 greenhouse gas; launched product in 2019

2015 – 2018

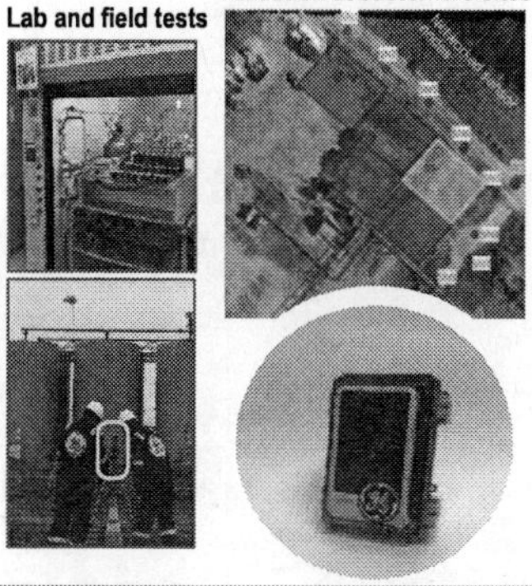

Product launch 2019

2019 +
Commercial Success Stories

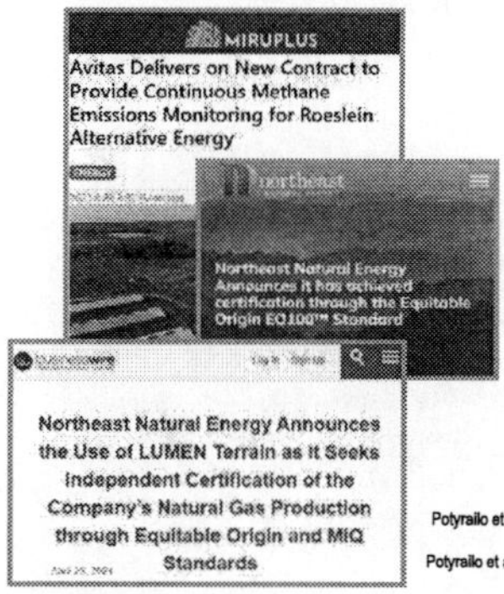

2020 – 2021

Scientific + industrial validation

Potyrailo et al., Extraordinary performance of semiconducting metal oxide gas sensors using dielectric excitation, *Nature Electronics* **2020** May 11:1-0

Potyrailo et al., Numerous granted US Patents on multivariable gas sensing, see **USPTO.gov**

- ✓ Linear gas response (coeff. of determination $R^2 > 0.99$)
- ✓ Broad range of gas detection (six decades of conc.)
- ✓ Improved limit of detection (50-fold vs. chemiresistors)
- ✓ Insensitivity to ambient temperature (-25 … + 50 °C)
- ✓ Baseline self-correction using high-frequency response
- ✓ Multi-gas detection by multi-frequency readout

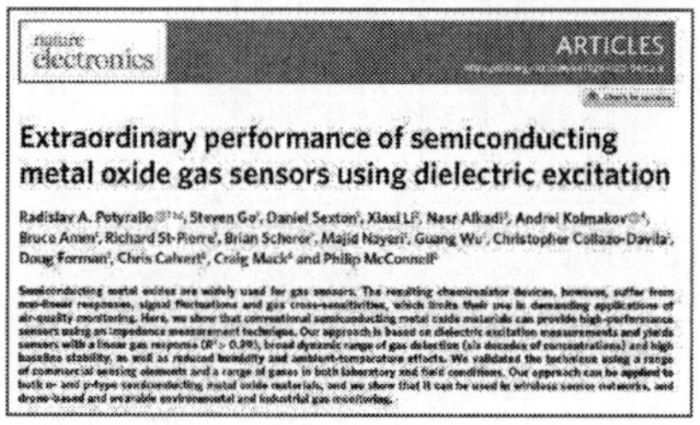

Miniaturization

SWaP-C = Size, Weight, Power and Cost

ASIC = application-specific integrated circuit

Size = 22×30×43 cm^3
Weight = 14 kg
Power = 160 W
Cost = $ 20,000

Size = 1×5×6 mm^3
Weight = 0.05 g
Power = 50 mW
Cost = $ 6

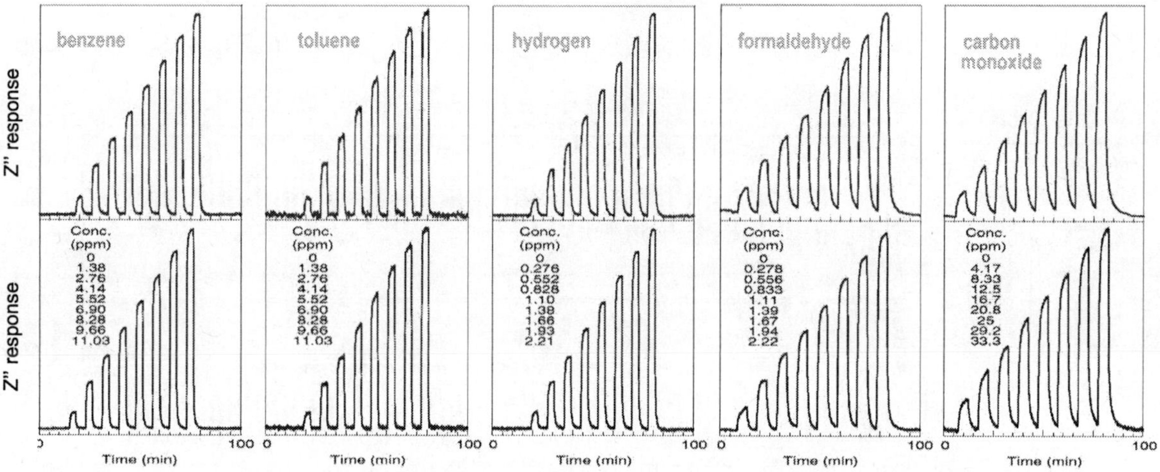

Same performance of ASIC vs. desktop analyzer, with tremendous SWaP-C advantage

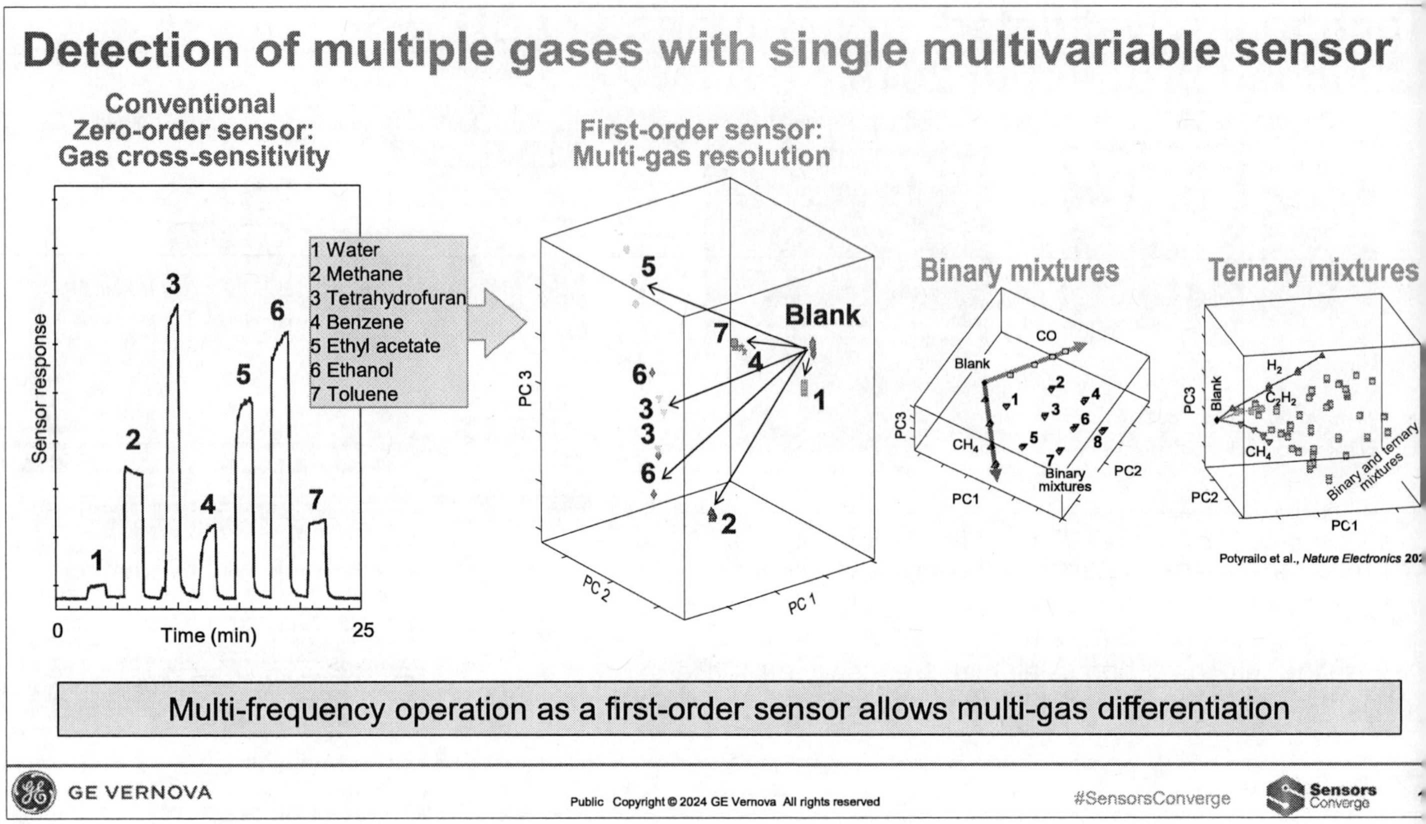
Detection of multiple gases with single multivariable sensor
Conventional
Zero-order sensor:
Gas cross-sensitivity
Sensor response
Time (min)
0
25
1 Water
2 Methane
3 Tetrahydrofuran
4 Benzene
5 Ethyl acetate
6 Ethanol
7 Toluene
First-order sensor:
Multi-gas resolution
Blank
PC 1
PC 2
PC 3
Binary mixtures
Ternary mixtures
Binary
mixtures
CO
CH_4
H_2
C_2H_2
Binary and ternary mixtures
Potyrailo et al., *Nature Electronics* 20
Multi-frequency operation as a first-order sensor allows multi-gas differentiation
GE VERNOVA
Public Copyright © 2024 GE Vernova All rights reserved
#SensorsConverge
Sensors Converge

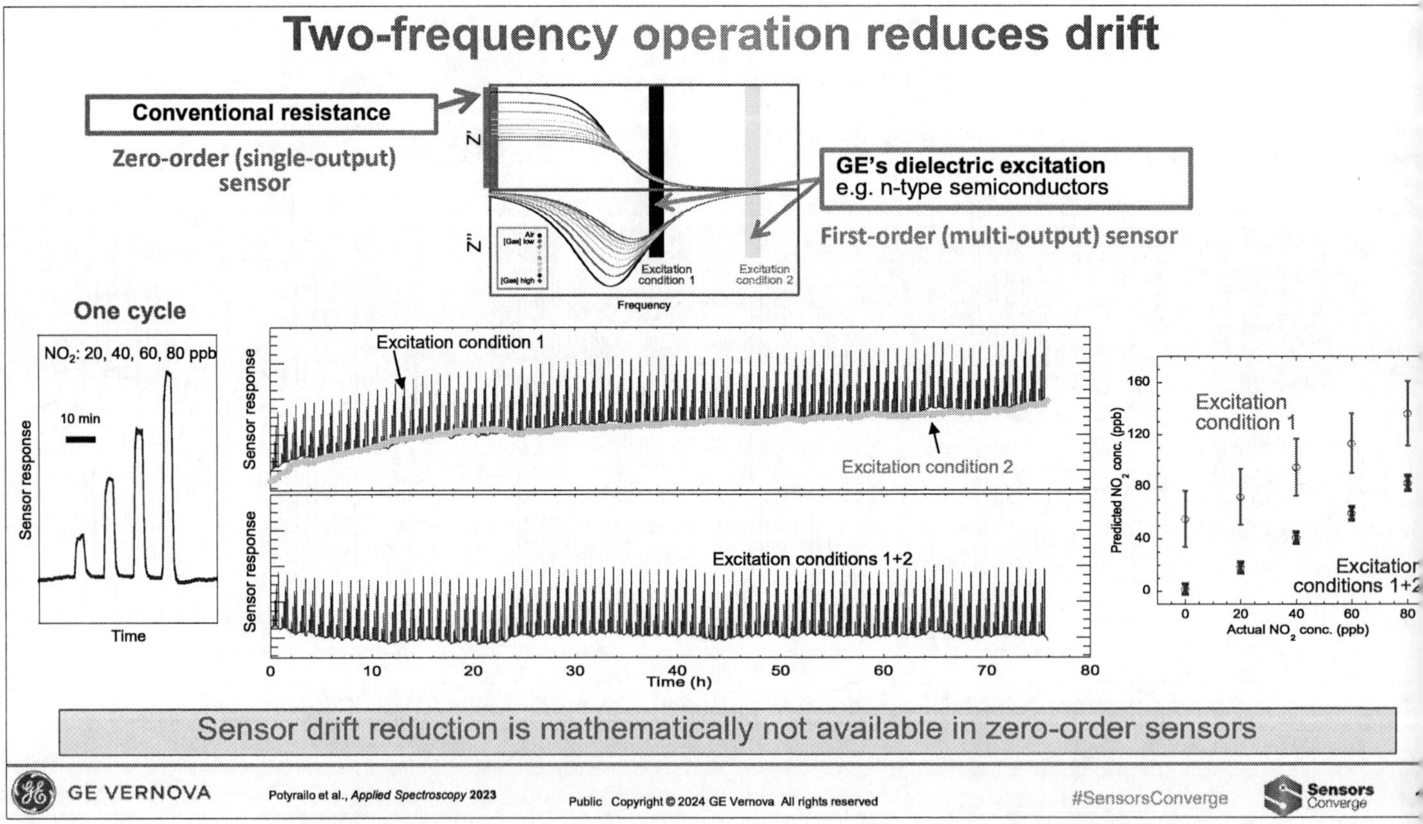
Two-frequency operation reduces drift
Conventional resistance
Zero-order (single-output)
sensor
GE's dielectric excitation
e.g. n-type semiconductors
First-order (multi-output) sensor
Z'
Z''
Excitation
condition 1
Excitation
condition 2
Frequency
One cycle
NO_2: 20, 40, 60, 80 ppb
10 min
Sensor response
Time
Excitation condition 1
Excitation condition 2
Excitation conditions 1+2
Time (h)
Predicted NO_2 conc. (ppb)
Actual NO_2 conc. (ppb)
Sensor drift reduction is mathematically not available in zero-order sensors
GE VERNOVA
Potyrailo et al., *Applied Spectroscopy* 2023
Public Copyright © 2024 GE Vernova All rights reserved
#SensorsConverge
Sensors Converge

Multi-frequency operation reduces drift and noise

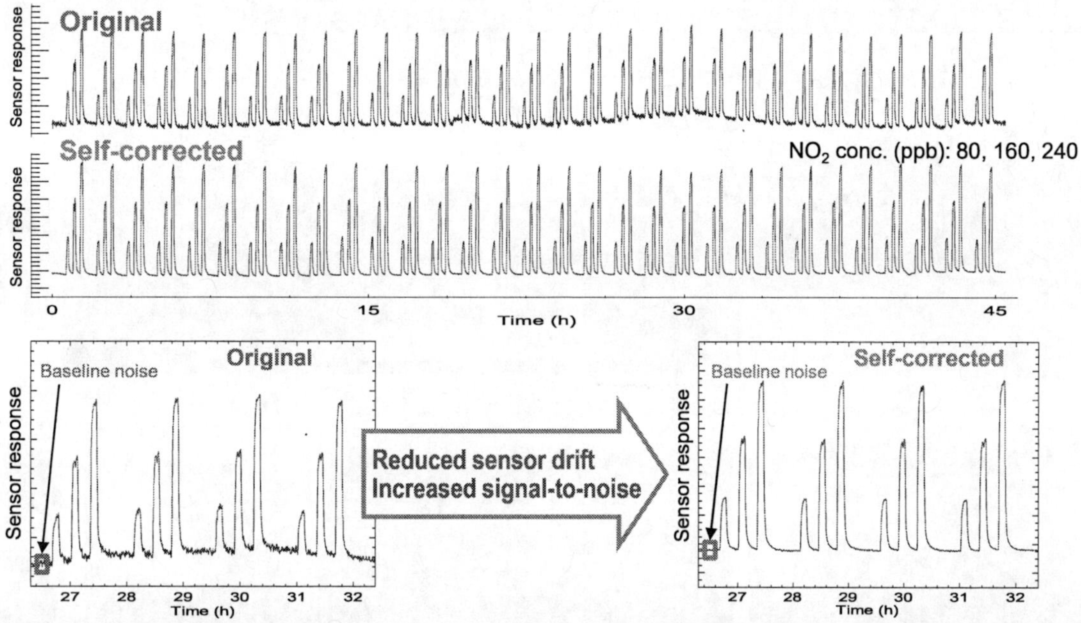

Sensor drift and noise reduction is mathematically not available in single-output sensors

Multi-frequency operation eliminates effects of temperature

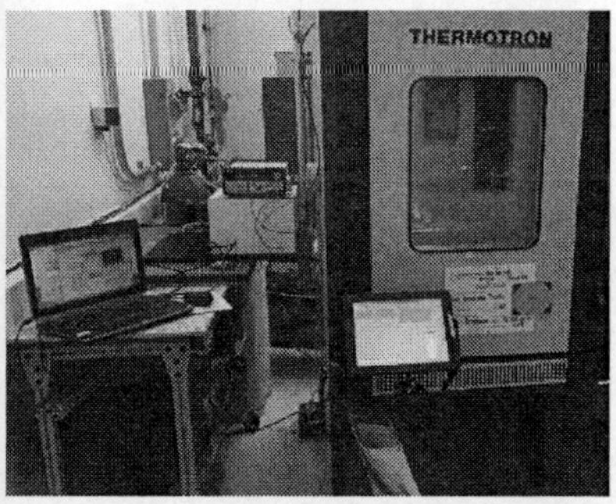

Ambient temp., °C
50, 25, 0, -25

Methane conc. (ppm)
0, 50, 100, 150, 200, 250

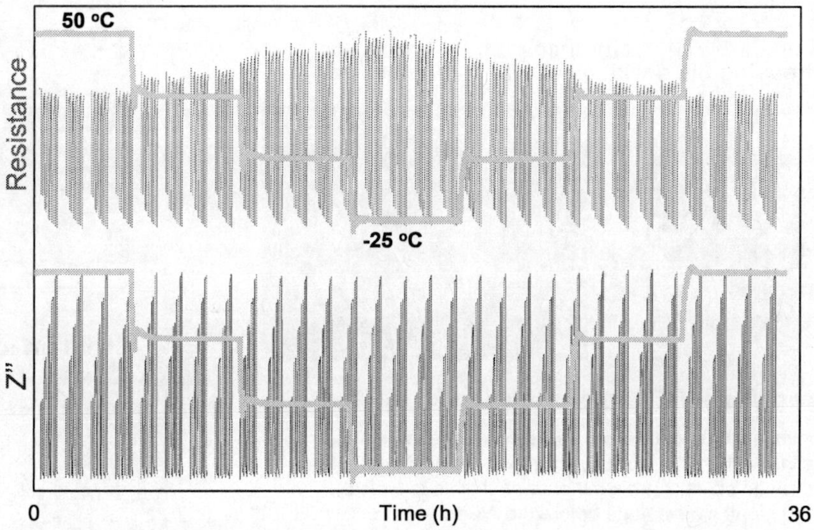

System design for all-weather applications

Field validated and delivered to diverse customers wearable prototypes for multi-gas analysis

Three gases: industrial safety project 2019 - 2021

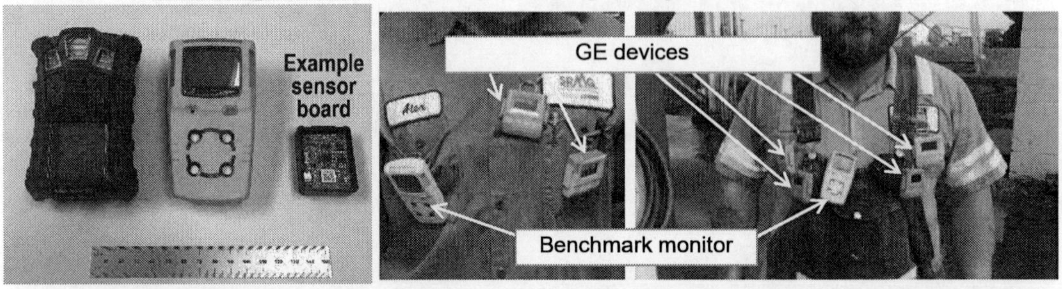

20+ gases: homeland security project 2021 – current

GE VERNOVA

#SensorsConverge

Sensors Converge

Detection, differentiation, localization of multi-gas leaks in gas-insulated equipment (GIE)

arpa·e CHANGING WHAT'S POSSIBLE

GIE: assembly of circuit breakers, switches, etc. in a housing filled with electrical insulating gas

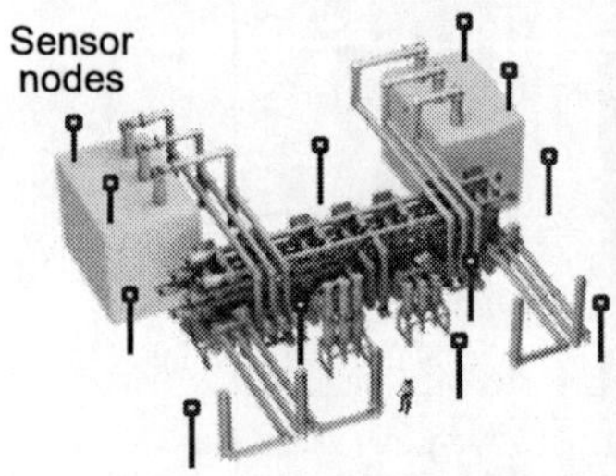

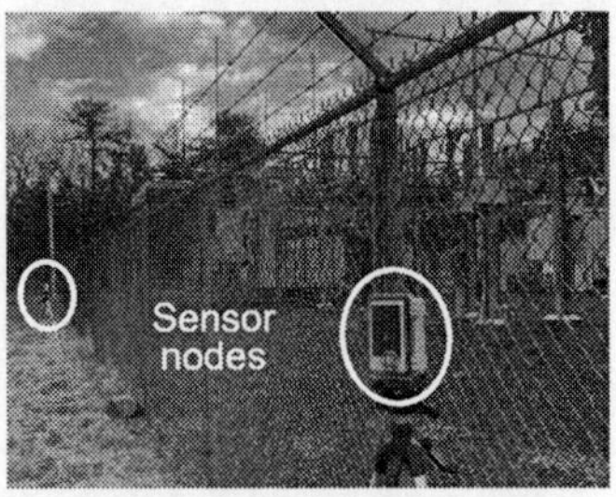

140-ft stand-off leak detection field test

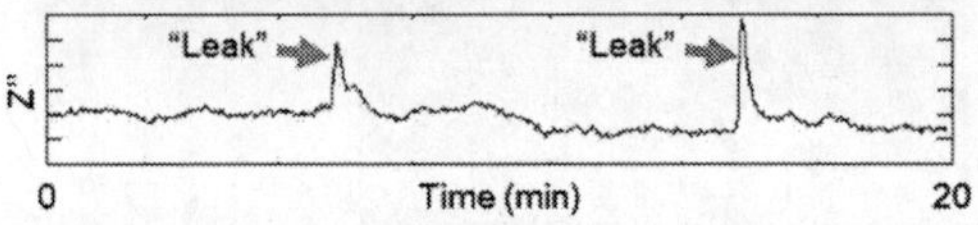

Stand-off localization of multi-gas leaks

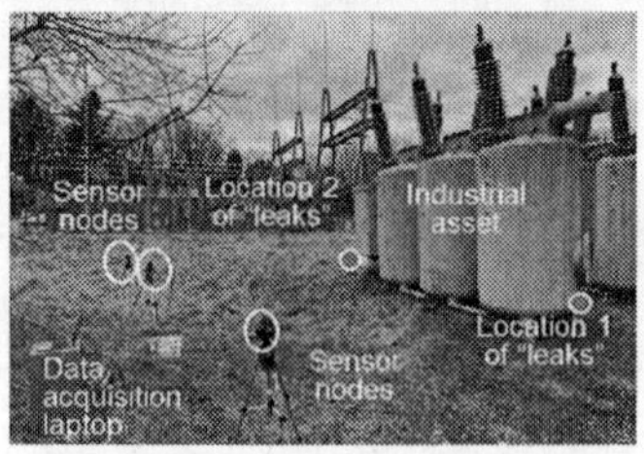

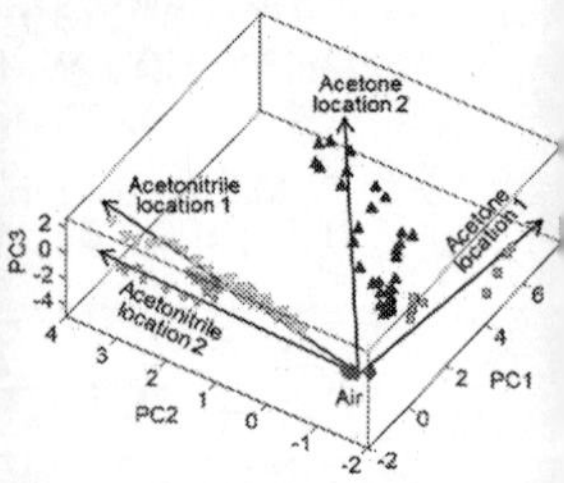

Key benefits of GE Vernova solution for utilities

- ✓ Detects minor leaks, 100-1000x more sensitive vs. pressure sensors
- ✓ Detects minor leaks, 10-100x more sensitive vs. handheld detectors
- ✓ Detects broad range of leaks (from minor or negligible to typical)
- ✓ Can provide 2-6 months advantage before the Alarm 1
- ✓ Unattended localization of minor and typical multi-gas leaks for prognostics
- ✓ Can detect and identify gas-decomposition products for prognostics
- ✓ Monitors legacy and new generation GIE without modifications

GE VERNOVA

#SensorsConverge

Sensors Converge

Reduced false alarms with edge-based GE Vernova algorithms

Ideal confusion matrix =
only zeros in non-diagonal cells

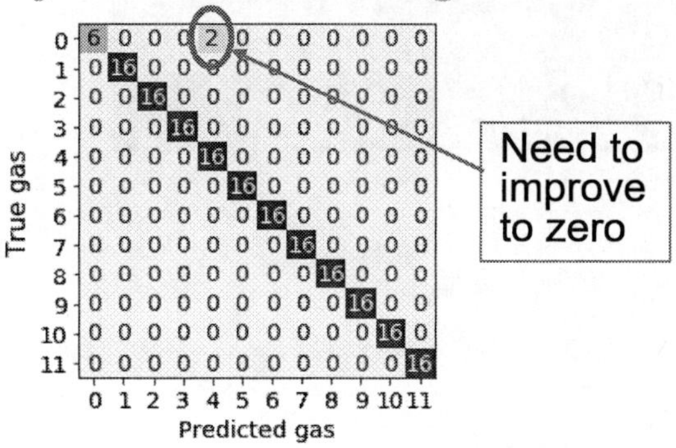

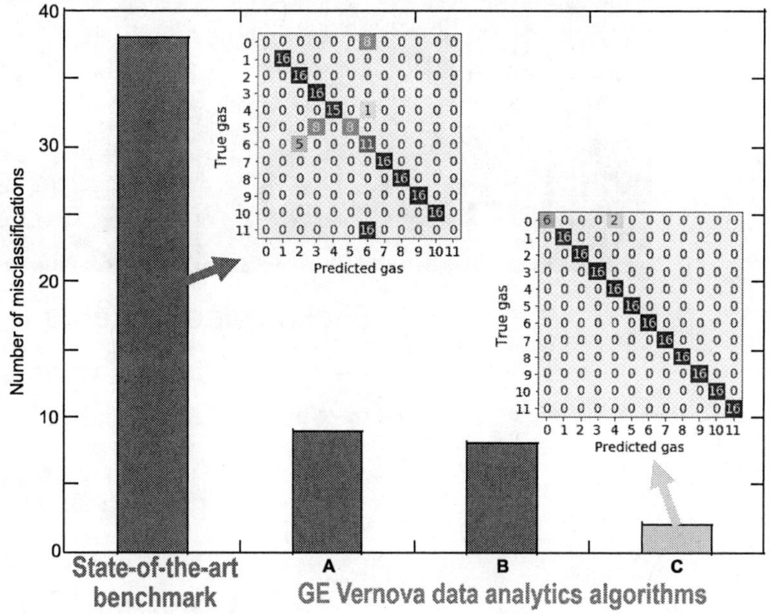

Conclusions

Benefits of multivariable sensors versus single-output sensors

- **Expected** multi-gas detection
- **Unexpected** (1) increased signal-to-noise, (2) reduced temperature effect, (3) reduced drift effect

Individual multivariable sensors with edge data analytics

- **Unexpected** boosting data analytics accuracy (correlated responses in multivariable sensor)
- **Unexpected** reducing data analytics demands for (1) computing and (2) electrical power

Mathematics of traditional analytical instruments → to gas sensors with edge analytics

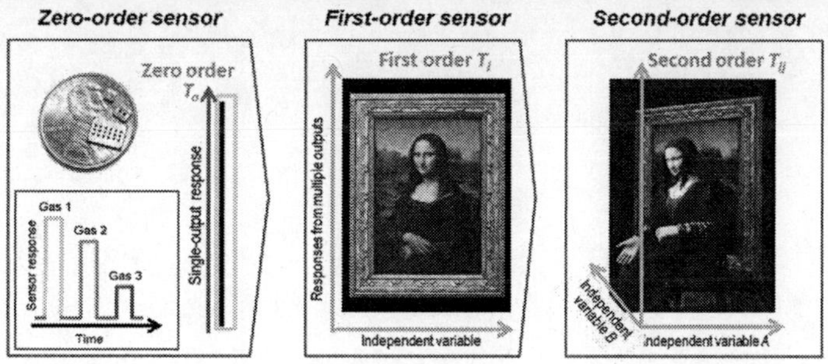

Thank you !

Acknowledgements

potyrailo@ge.com

GE VERNOVA

#SensorsConverge

Sensors Converge

Sensors
Converge

A year in Review: Exploring the Evolving Landscape of Sensors, Semiconductors and the Electronics Industry

June 25th 2024 | Santa Clara, CA

Aditya Dayal, Ph.D.

Head of AI and Data Science
Lendlease Digital

Lendlease Corporation

Our global business

More than
60
Years of experience

$48b
Funds under management

$33b
Assets under management

$121b
Development pipeline

$9.6b
Construction backlog revenue

We help shape cities and create communities

Aditya Dayal Sensors Converge

Commercial real estate market is in turmoil…

- **Hybrid working** and **omnichannel retail** are redefining the very purpose and use of commercial real estate
- **High inflation, interest rates** and **vacancies** are driving imperatives to cut costs and increase efficiency
- **ESG** and **sustainability** objectives are now playing a much larger role in real estate decision making

Demand for sensors and software technology

Podium Property Insights: sensors and technology

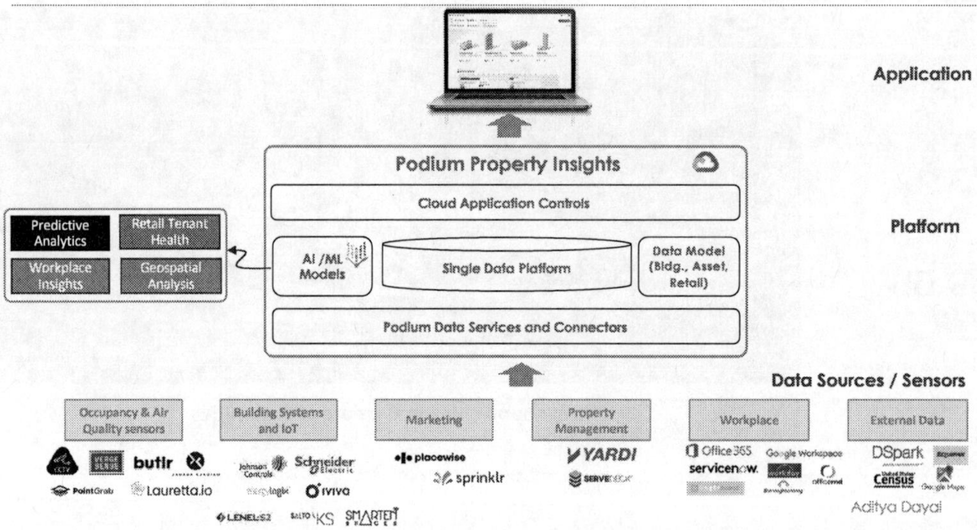

Aditya Dayal

Sensors Converge

Smart buildings software: 8% CAGR

Supports $75B Real Estate and Workplace market

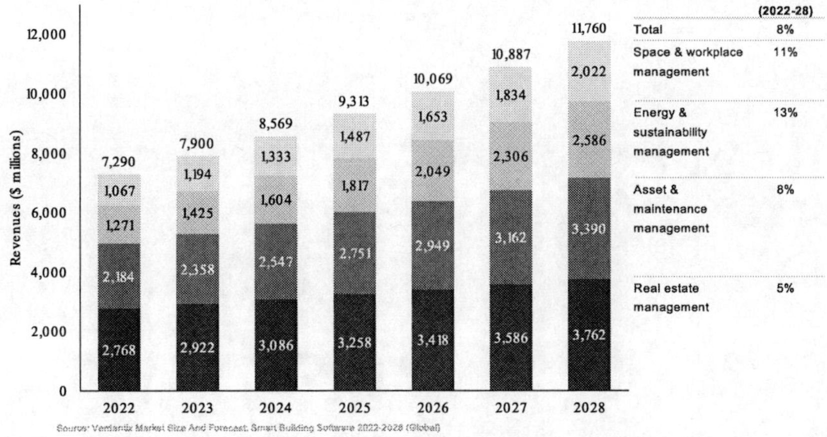

Aditya Dayal

Sensors Converge

Future Trends: Data Center Power Demand

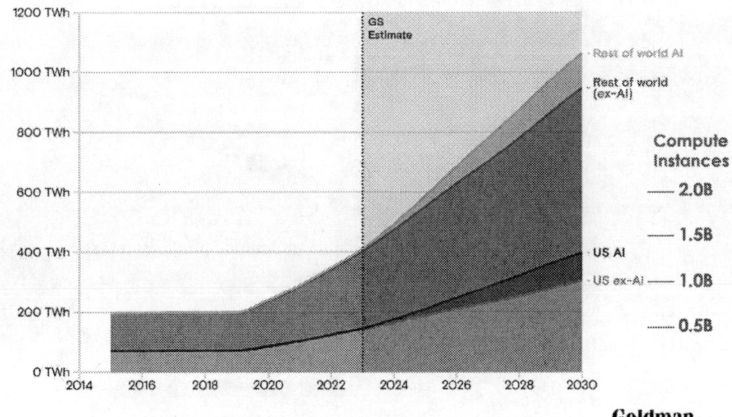

Source: Masanet et al. (2020), Cisco, IEA, Goldman Sachs Research

Goldman Sachs

Aditya Dayal

Sensors Converge

Sensors Converge

CAN-MD®: Sensing Evolved

June 24–26, 2024 | Santa Clara, CA

Dytran by HBK HOTTINGER BRÜEL & KJÆR

#SensorsConverge

Agenda

01	Introduction to CAN-MD®
02	Applications and Benefits
03	Developer Kits and Software
04	Future Product Line Developments

#SensorsConverge

UNRESTRICTED

Sensors Converge

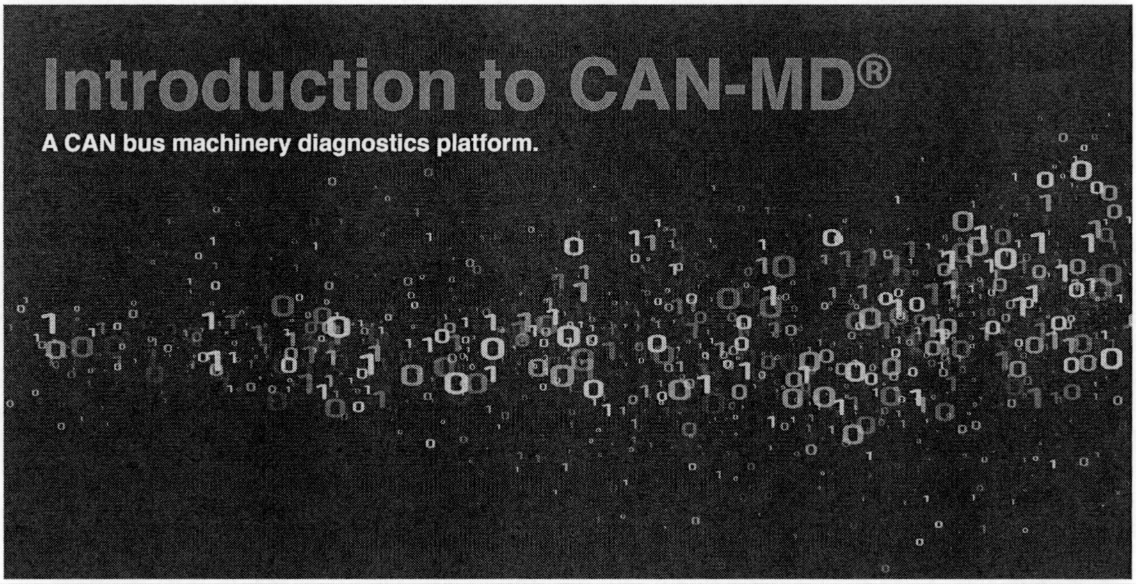

#SensorsConverge

UNRESTRICTED

Sensors Converge

Sensing Evolved

CAN-MD® is a **digital sensor platform** that processes raw analog data *inside each sensor* on the machine, enabling a bussed architecture that **delivers actionable results**, not just raw data!

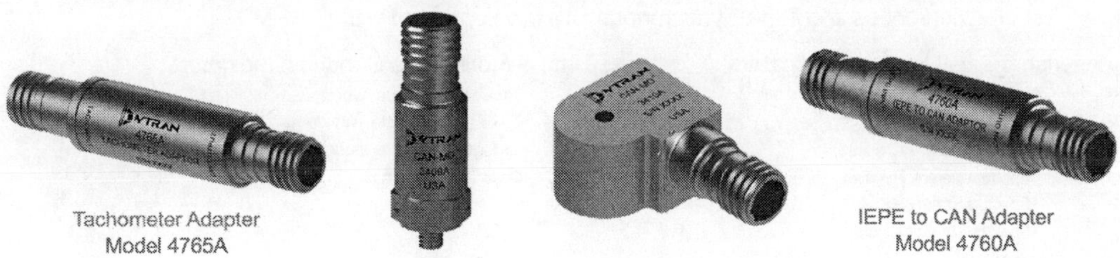

Tachometer Adapter
Model 4765A

Sensor
Model 3409A

Sensor
Model 3410A

IEPE to CAN Adapter
Model 4760A

#SensorsConverge

UNRESTRICTED

Sensors Converge

Key Concepts

- A Condition Indicator (CI) is the result of the processed data that is provided as an output on the data bus.
- No longer is a complicated central DSP system needed to process the raw data from analog accelerometers.
- In order to perform their duties, the sensors need to know some setup information.
- Each sensor can boot up and start collecting and processing CIs automatically. These CIs can later be filtered with additional information to classify "operating mode" dependent results.
- Up to 31 Sensors can reside on a single CAN Network.
- The sensors themselves process the data!

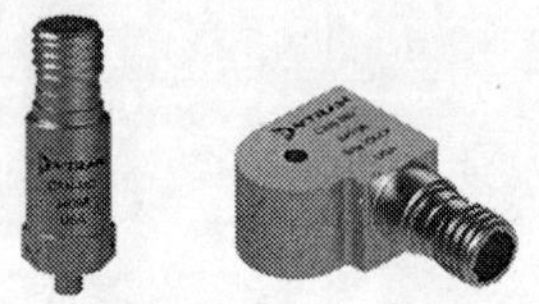

CAN-MD® Condition Indicators

- A Condition Indicator (CI) is the result of the processed data that is provided as an output on the data bus
- Sensor configurations are stored in sensor memory with up to 63 acquisitions and 127 CI's that can generate and output results to the bus.
- Simple CI's return a single processed value to be trended over time.
- Complex CI's return an array of values for further analysis and review.
- Both Asynchronous and Time Synchronous CI's are supported with CAN-MD®.

Asynchronous Condition Indicators:

- RMS
- Skew
- Spectral Peak – Absolute
- Spectral Peak – Relative
- Spectral Energy – Absolute
- Spectral Energy – Relative
- Spectrum – FFT
- Time Domain

Time Synchronous Condition Indicators:

- Time Synchronous Average
- Order Domain Data Waveform
- Order Domain, Amplitude
- Order Domain, Phase

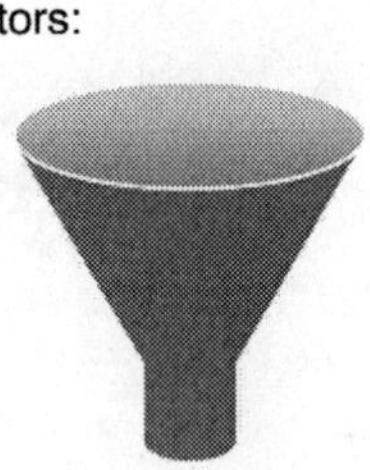

CAN-MD® Sensor Network

- CAN-MD® distributes data processing across the entire network rather than through one central processor.
- Each sensor has its own address, and the setup configuration is stored at the sensor level rather than on a central processor.
- Up to 31 CAN-MD® sensors can be connected to a single CAN channel.

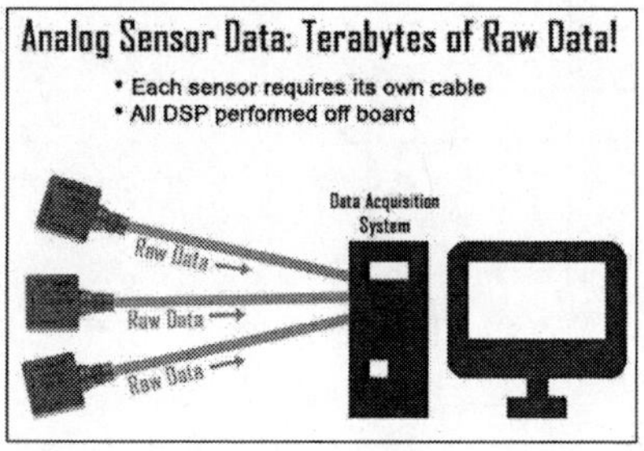

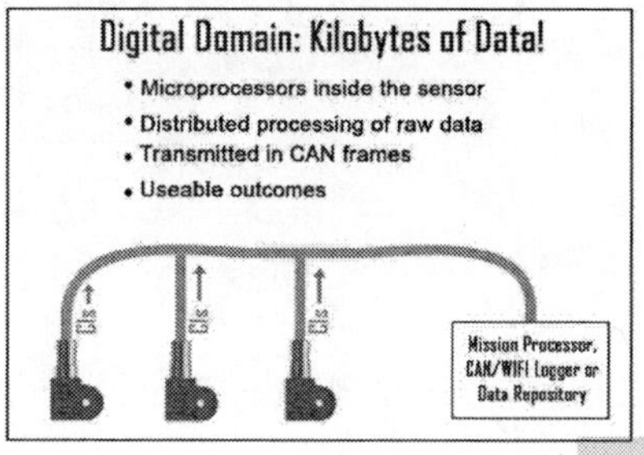

CAN-MD® Sensor Specifications

Parameter	Value	Parameter	Value
Mating Connector	D38999/26WA35SN	Sealing	Hermetic
Input range:	+/-500g	Housing	300 Series SS
Bandwidth:	1 to 15,500 Hz	Temp - Operating	-45°C to 121°C
Noise Floor:	0.015 G rms	Ground Isolation	10 MΩ, min
Resolution:	16 bit	Current Draw	<65 mA
Sampling rates:	1,600 to 52,000 SPS	Input Power:	10-30 VDC
Sampling blocks:	500-60,000	Internal clock	20MHz
Bus Specification	CAN 2.0b	Max # Nodes	31
Bus Speed	500 Kbps	CAN Protocol	CAN-MD®

CAN-MD® Sensor Architecture

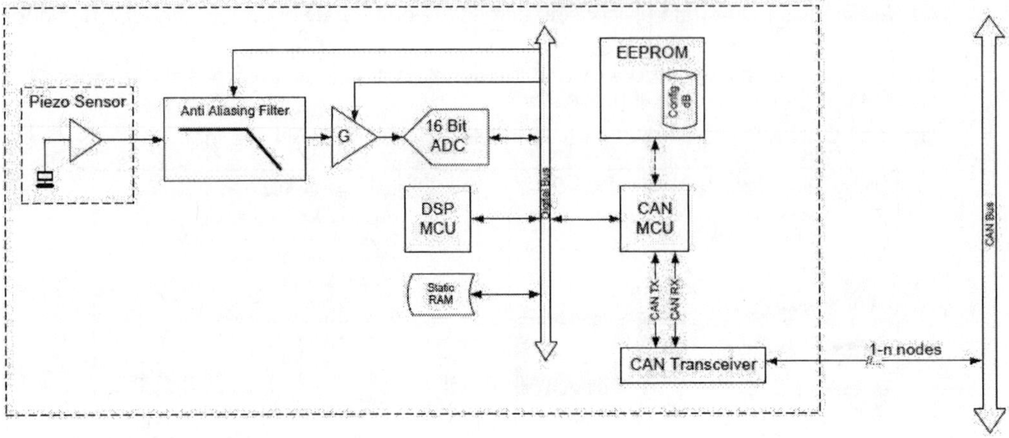

CAN-MD® Measurement Structure

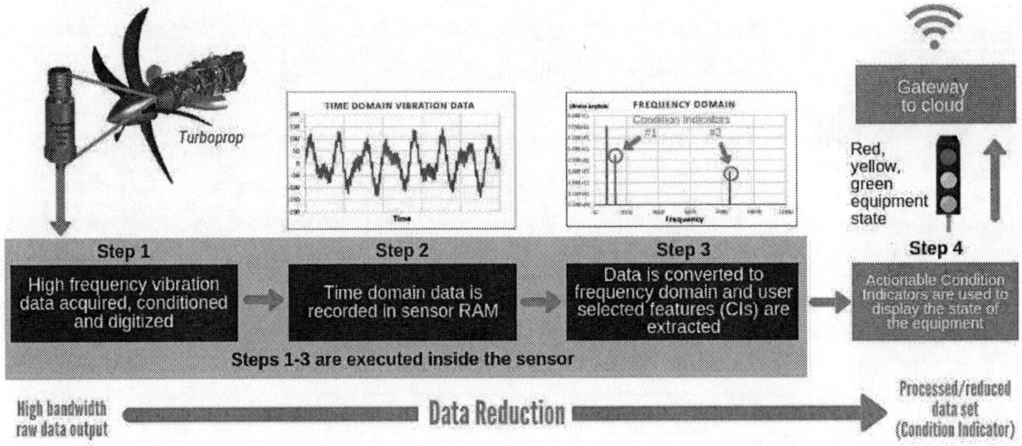

Applications and Benefits

CAN-MD® has been deployed in a variety of monitoring application to meet customers needs for a next generation digital monitoring solution.

#SensorsConverge

UNRESTRICTED

Sensors Converge

CAN-MD® Benefits: Aircraft HUMS

- Reduced system cost by removing centralized flight HUM acquisition processor for cost effective installation on light helicopters and fixed wing aircraft.
- Reduction of cable weight and increased ease of installation based on bus-based architecture.
- Data reduction with CAN-MD® Condition Indicators allow for real time telemetry for fleet monitoring.
- Available Interface Control Documents for integration with existing CAN supported avionics hardware.

#SensorsConverge

UNRESTRICTED

Sensors Converge

CAN-MD® Benefits: Industrial Condition Based Monitoring

- Cost effective solution to connect multiple CAN bus monitoring networks to Internet protocols using commercially available hardware.
- CI calculation at the sensor reduced the bandwidth and storage requirements of cloud monitoring solutions.
- Interface Control Documents allow CAN-MD® to be programed to communicate with commercially available CAN controllers, loggers and bridges for data transmission and feedback to networked machinery.

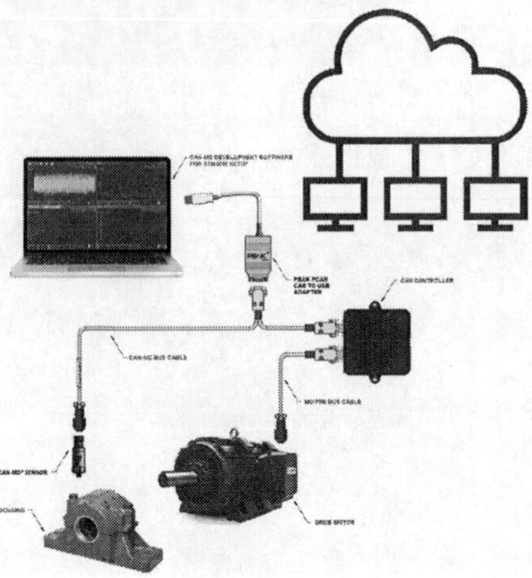

Developer Kits and Software

Developer kits offer a convenient solution to get started with CAN-MD®.

CAN-MD® Developer Kits

- Dytran offers CAN-MD® developer kits which include all the hardware necessary to setup a CAN-MD® network.
- The developer kits can be used as a turnkey system ready for application use or as an integration tool for development.
- The developer kits are configurable to match the customer needs for sensor count, synchronous or asynchronous measurements, data logging and software preferences.
- Dytran offers Interface Control Documents with CAN-MD® developer kits for users to unlock the potential of CAN-MD® by communicating directly with other CAN bus assets or send data remotely to the cloud.

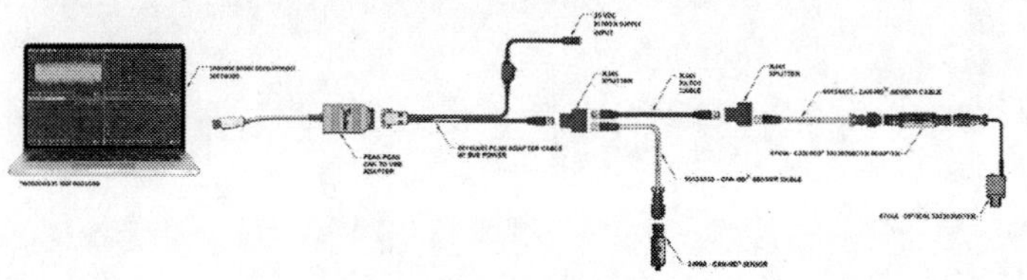

CAN-MD® Laboratory PC Software

- LabView based software for us on Windows PC
- Configure sensor Acquisitions and Condition Indicators
- View live data from the CAN-MD® sensors
- Load and plot saved data from the PC
- Communicates with COTS PCAN USB Adapter

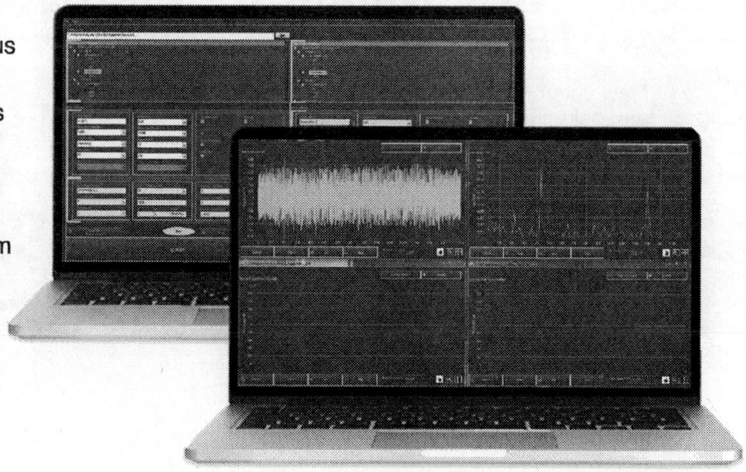

Future Developments

To meet the challenges of tomorrow, Dytran continues to develop innovative capabilities for the CAN-MD® product line.

#SensorsConverge

UNRESTRICTED

Sensors Converge

CAN-MD® Miniature Piezoelectric Sensor

Model 3495A2

- New version of existing CAN-MD® piezoelectric sensor
- Reduced size and weight from standard 3410A
- Updated board stack to include Sandbox functionality
- Sandbox demodulation algorithm has been developed to run in this unit for bearing analysis

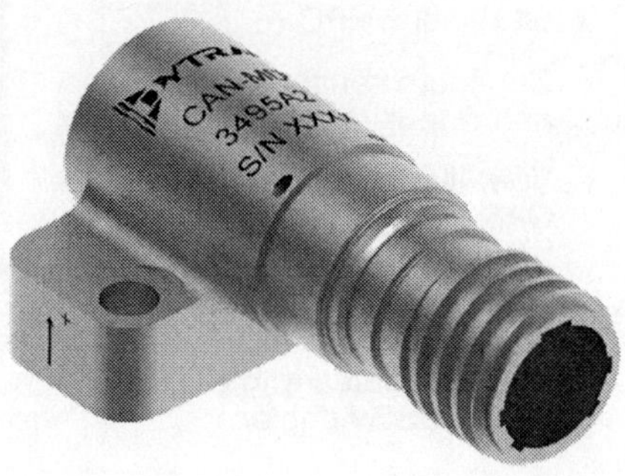

#SensorsConverge

UNRESTRICTED

Sensors Converge

CAN-MD® Triaxial MEMS Accelerometer

Model 3763A1

- VC MEMS for DC response
- Triaxial output from single CAN node
- Programable axis orientation
- CAN-MD® Sandbox functionality
- Thru-hole mount with anti-rotation pin
- Compact package: 1in x 0.8in x 0.8in
- Hermetically sealed housing
- Integral cable terminating to flying leads

CAN-MD® Charge to CAN Adapter

Model 4785A

- New CAN-MD® adapter to add smart sensor capabilities to single ended charge mode sensors.
- Utilizing existing CAN-MD® board stacks.
- 10-32 connection for use with standard low noise cables or connection to hardline cables.

WANT MORE INFO?

Dytran.com

canmd@dytran.com

818-700-7818

#SensorsConverge

UNRESTRICTED

Sensors Converge

Dytran by

HBK

HOTTINGER BRÜEL & KJÆR

THANK YOU!

#SensorsConverge

UNRESTRICTED

Sensors Converge

Promex

Microelectronics Assembly Technologies

Design Considerations for Building Heterogeneously Integrated Sensor Devices

Presented By: David Fromm, PhD
Chief Operating Officer, Promex Industries
Santa Clara, CA
***Date:** June 25, 2024*
dfromm@promex-ind.com
www.promex-ind.com

Promex
Microelectronics Assembly Technologies

Agenda

- Introduction to Heterogeneous Integration & Promex
- Why Heterogeneous Integration is becoming prevalent in devices containing sensors and/or actuators
- Sensor-containing device case study
- A modernized product development paradigm for modern integrated devices

https://promex-ind.com 2

What is Heterogeneous Integration?

Promex
Microelectronics Assembly Technologies

One integrated device built using many different kinds of parts

- A term recently coined in the semiconductor industry – several working definitions
- HI co-packages parts made using multiple technologies with conventional CMOS parts to increase functionality via integration
- Which parts can be combined with CMOS and qualify as "heterogeneous integration" is not well defined; hence, many combinations are subjectively labeled as such
- Promex considers HI to be a combination of microelectronics **and** something else:
  - Mechanical components/functionality
  - Optical components/functionality
  - Sensors
  - Actuators
  - Chemistry
- Major increases in microelectronic device functionality and miniaturization can be achieved by integrating parts made with multiple technologies

https://promex-ind.com 3

Sensor Integration in Modern Electronics

Promex
Microelectronics Assembly Technologies

Technological advances in components → Greater accessibility of components → Technological advances in integration and device functionality = Democratization of Technology

- Today's sensor/actuator devices: Sensor, On-board Computing, Supporting Electronics, Connectivity & Cloud (often with a battery)

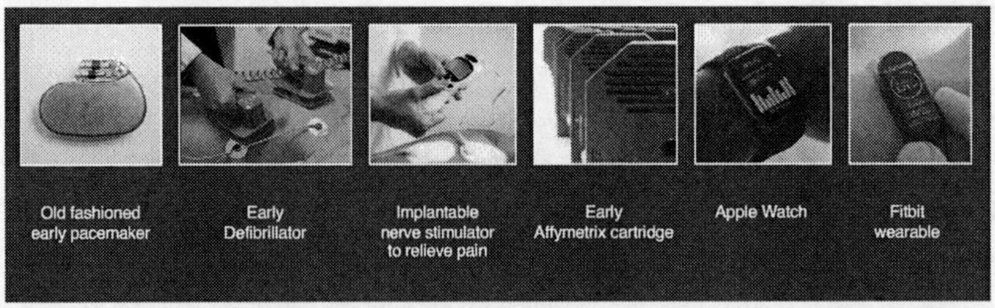

- We work with innovators to develop a manufacturing process that allows us to combine electronics and non-electronics in devices with minimized form factors

https://promex-ind.com 4

Anatomy of Modern HI Sensor Devices

Promex
Microelectronics Assembly Technologies

- Modern devices: transitioned from off-the-shelf to component-level integrations
  - Higher capability, smaller form factor, decreased costs, lower power consumption
  - New central design elements: Component selection/availability, assembly process, assembly materials

Legacy Device Design Elements	Modern Device Design Elements
Skeleton: Mechanical parts (sheet metal, injection molded, machined)	Flat carrier substrate: Provides structure & electrical interconnections between components (laminate PCB, flex circuit, alternative substrates – glass, ceramic)
Computer motherboard (on- or off-board)	Onboard computer chips (often purpose-built) w/ connectivity
Discrete analog electronics on PCB(s)	Integrated, co-packaged microelectronics components
Specialized actuators/sensors (low fidelity)	Miniaturized custom actuators/sensors (high fidelity)
External housing	Integrated housing
Assembly: Screws, bolts, wires	Assembly: Solder, specialized adhesives & bonding processes
Manufacturing processes: Traditional assembly tools/lines	Manufacturing processes: Microelectronics assembly tools/lines

- How device is assembled often directly impacts final function!

https://promex-ind.com 5

Case Study: Lab-on-a-Chip Sensor

Promex
Microelectronics Assembly Technologies

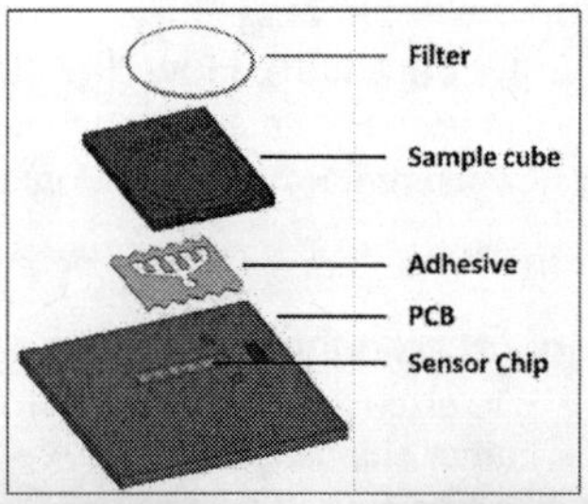

- Purpose: Ultra-sensitive and highly specific detection of a specific molecule, DNA sequence or cell - the **"target"**
  - **Target(s) present = Positive**
  - **Target(s) absent = Negative**
  - **Control(s) = Sample OK**
- Challenge: High accuracy detection in a reliable, fast manner
- Typical Device Anatomy: Consumable + Instrument
  - Filter: Sample purification
  - Microfluidics: Sample concentration (mL → µL)
  - Detection: Sample enhancement for observation

https://promex-ind.com 6

Common Issues Building HI Devices

Promex
Microelectronics Assembly Technologies

- Changes to one design element often negatively impact other design elements

Added Functionality	Unique Component	Resulting Manufacturing and Assembly Issues
Gather an image and analyze it	Image sensors, data processors, high-speed IO	Must be particle free. May require GB/s communication via RF or optical fiber (special interconnection design/assembly)
Spectrometer	Optical filters on glass	Robotic vision cannot see part. Zero defects tolerated
Detect specific proteins, or DNA sequences	Chemistry on a surface	Must be kept dry, below 40C, controlled/protected from UV & visible light exposure
Micro gyroscope, valve, lever, etc.	MEMS device	Very sensitive to touch. ESD sensitive
Ultrasonic Image	Ultrasonic source/detectors	Must be kept below 50C once ultrasonic element integrated
High data rates >100 Mbs	Optical fibers	Submicron assembly tolerances
Control kilowatts of power	Power devices	High electrical and thermal conductivity required
Flexible device	Flex circuitry	Assembly of parts on a substrate that is not rigid

https://promex-ind.com 7

A Modern Development Cycle for HI Devices

Promex
Microelectronics Assembly Technologies

- A new paradigm: <u>How</u> device is assembled often directly impacts final function!
  - Traditional Product Development Cycle: Get a design to work, then build your assembly line
  - Concurrent Product Development Cycle: Must co-design product and assembly processes!

- How should this be done?
  - Bite-sized test builds (coupons)
  - Larger sample sizes
  - Careful metrology & (sub) system measurements
  - Link function to low-level requirements & specs

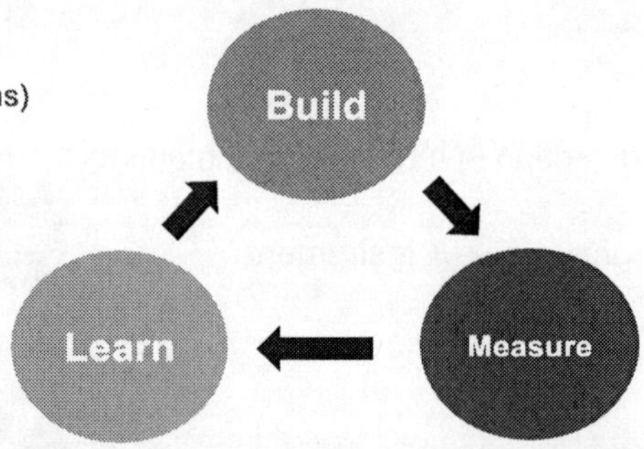

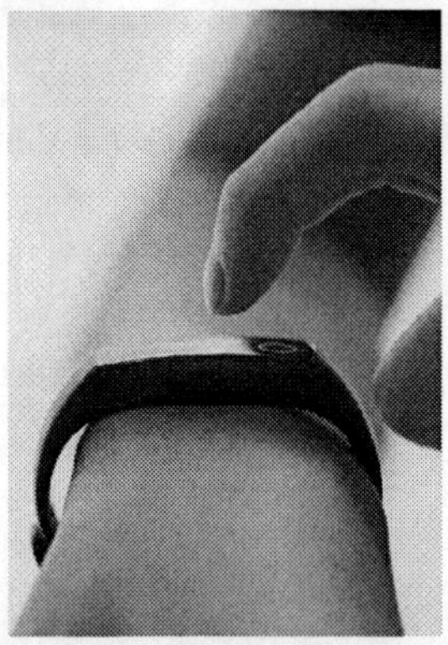

https://promex-ind.com 8

Taking Ideas From Concept to Production

Promex
Microelectronics Assembly Technologies

- <u>Phase Gate Overview</u>: Formal phases define manufacturing maturity
  - Build sizes increase, build predictability/cadence improves, cost per unit decreases
  - Processes & docs iterated & improved upon from previous learnings & customer performance feedback

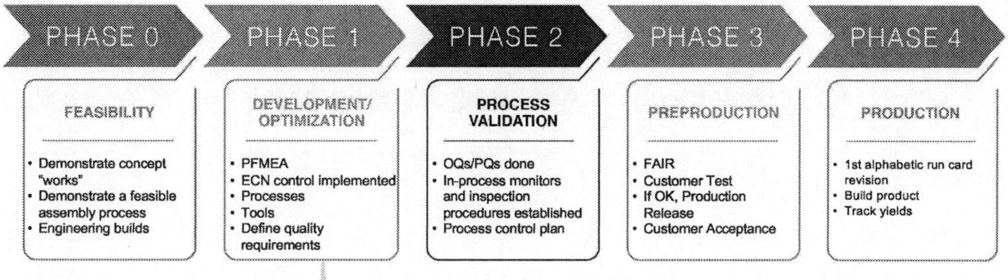

The bulk of the technical and engineering work is done in Phase 1. Processes are defined and requirements detailed.

Summary

Promex
Microelectronics Assembly Technologies

- Promex considers Heterogeneous integration (HI) as the combination of microelectronics with non-electronic content – mechanical, optical, actuators, chemistries, or sensors – in a single assembly
- Building HI devices involves numerous design and manufacturing factors that must be taken into consideration
  - Many design elements impact others, requiring careful decision-making
- Concurrent development of manufacturing processes is required for HI devices
  - *How* device is assembled impacts *what* the device is and *how* it performs

Thank you.

Promex

Microelectronics Assembly Technologies

Promex Industries Inc • 3075 Oakmead Village Dr • Santa Clara, CA 95051
www.Promex-ind.com
Tel: +1.408.496.0222
Email: Sales@promex-ind.com

Confidential 11

ENABLING HEALTHY AIR IN EVERY HOME

Next Generation Miniaturized CO2 Gas Sensors

Dr. Kaitlin Howell, Product Manager at Sensirion

SENSIRION

OUTLINE

PART 1	Healthy Indoor Air
PART 2	Stakeholders and CO_2 Sensing Technologies
PART 3	STCC4: Technology and Potential
PART 4	The Future is Bright

SENSIRION

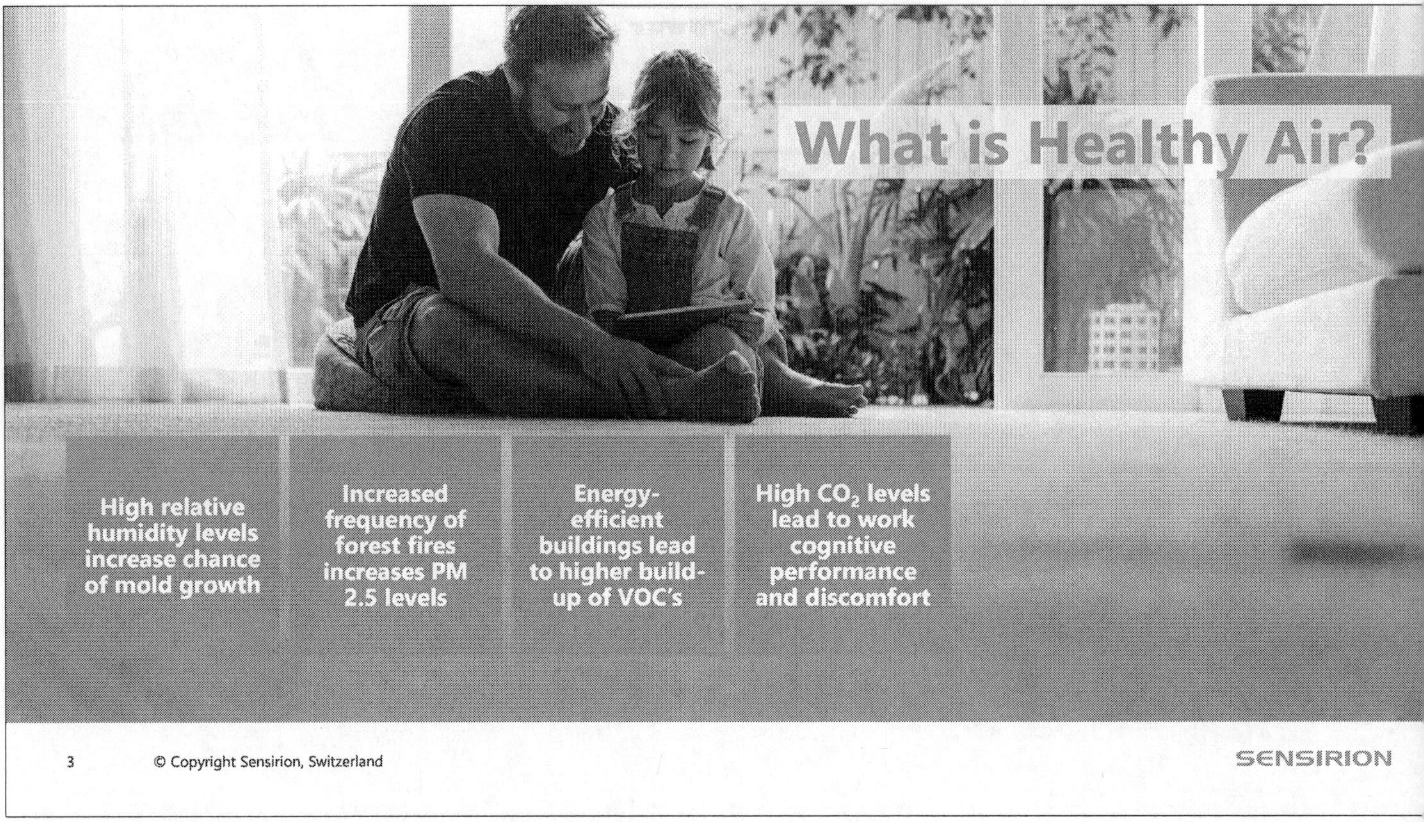
What is Healthy Air?
High relative humidity levels increase chance of mold growth
Increased frequency of forest fires increases PM 2.5 levels
Energy-efficient buildings lead to higher build-up of VOC's
High CO_2 levels lead to work cognitive performance and discomfort
3
© Copyright Sensirion, Switzerland
SENSIRION

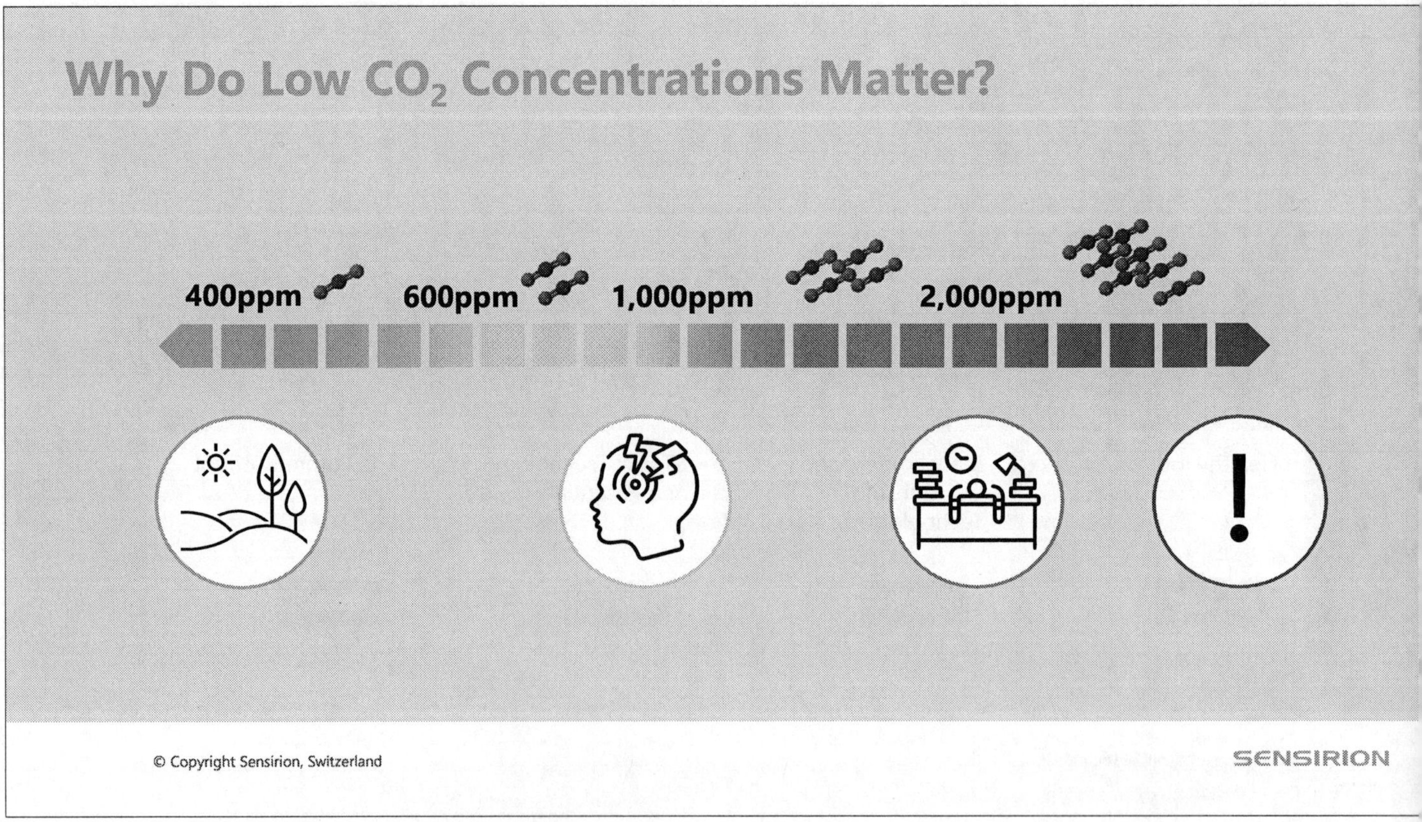
Why Do Low CO_2 Concentrations Matter?
400ppm
600ppm
1,000ppm
2,000ppm
© Copyright Sensirion, Switzerland
SENSIRION

Who Is Impacted By Indoor CO_2 Levels?

SENSIRION

Different Technologies for Measuring CO_2

NDIR

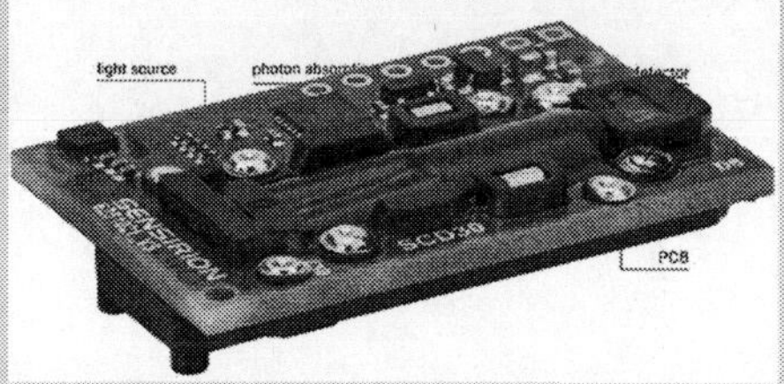

Photoacoustic NDIR

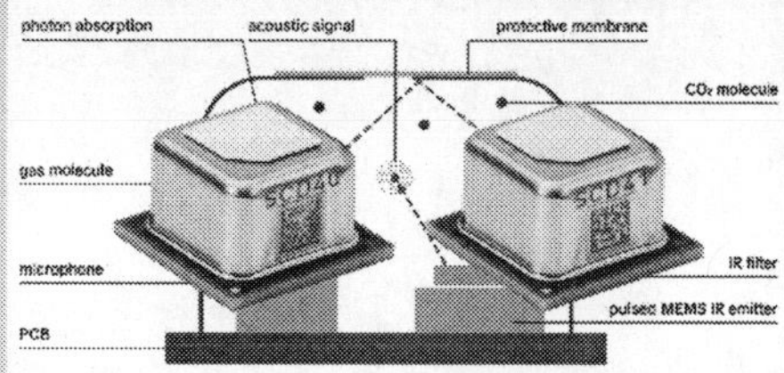

Thermal Conductivity

SENSIRION

STCC4

Minimal Size.
Maximize the Potential.

Striking the right balance between performance, size, power consumption and price. Optimized for indoor air quality applications from monitors to appliances and thermostats.

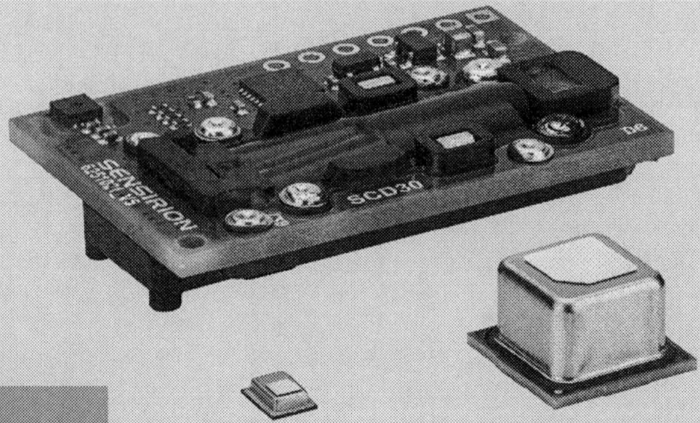

50x smaller than SCD4x	**±(100ppm+10%)** accuracy	**850 mA** average current consumption
	Cost efficiency compared to optical sensors	

SENSIRION

STCC4 CO_2 Sensing in Action

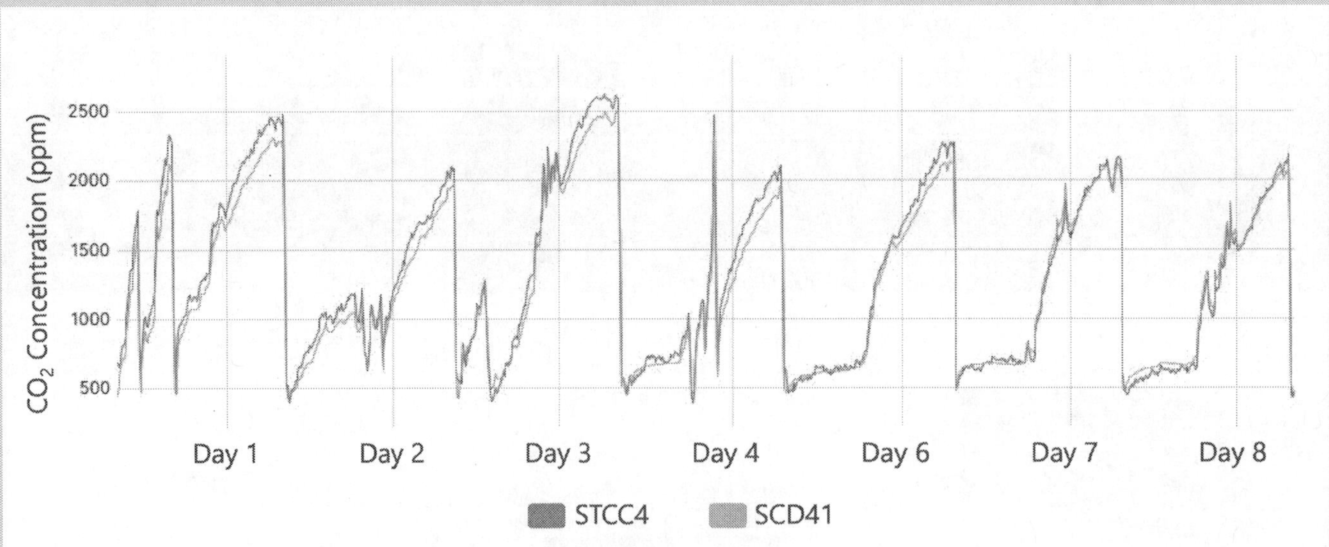

SENSIRION

Thermal Conductivity for CO_2 Sensing

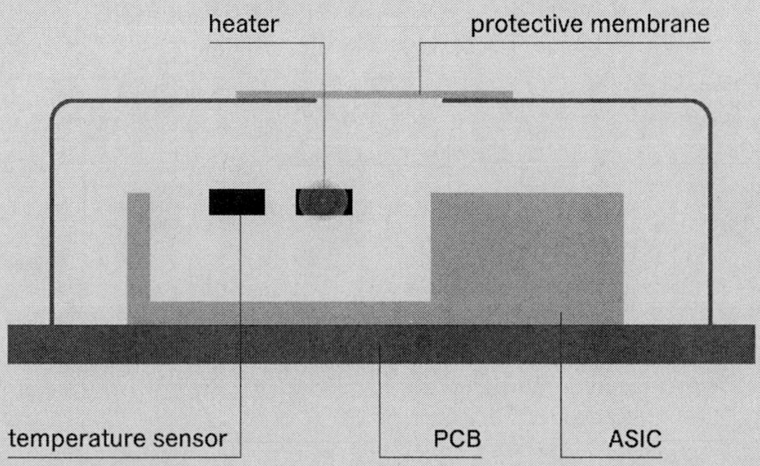

1. MEMS heater heats up gas in cavity of sensor
2. Heat in air conducts outward from heater
3. MEMS temperature sensor detects heat transferred through air

→ Measure thermal conductivity

SENSIRION

From Thermal Conductivity to CO_2 Concentration

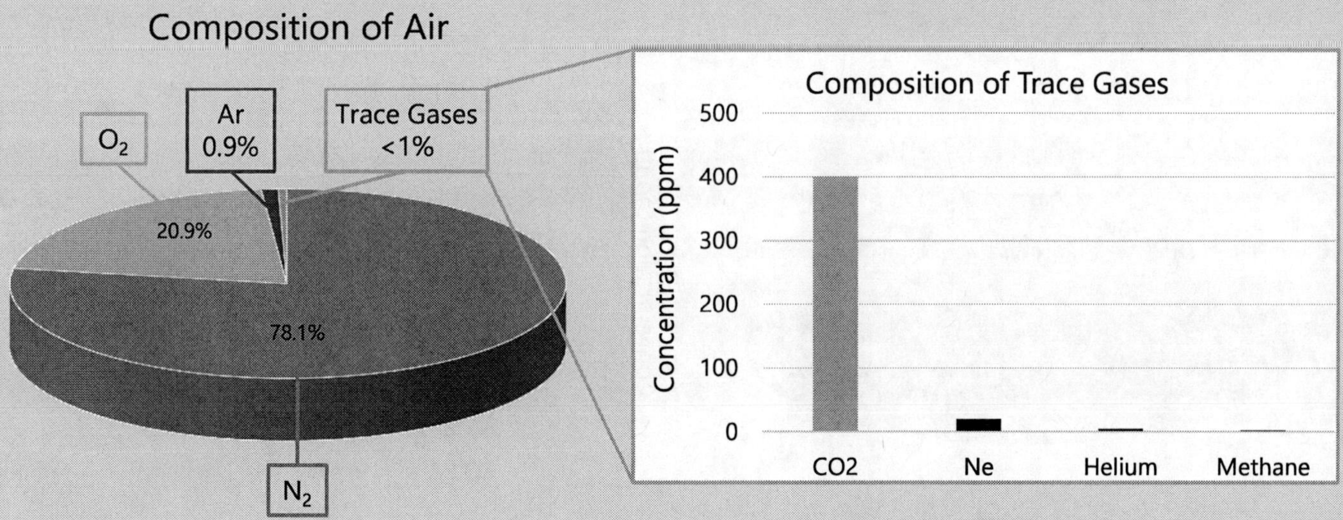

SENSIRION

From Thermal Conductivity to CO_2 Concentration

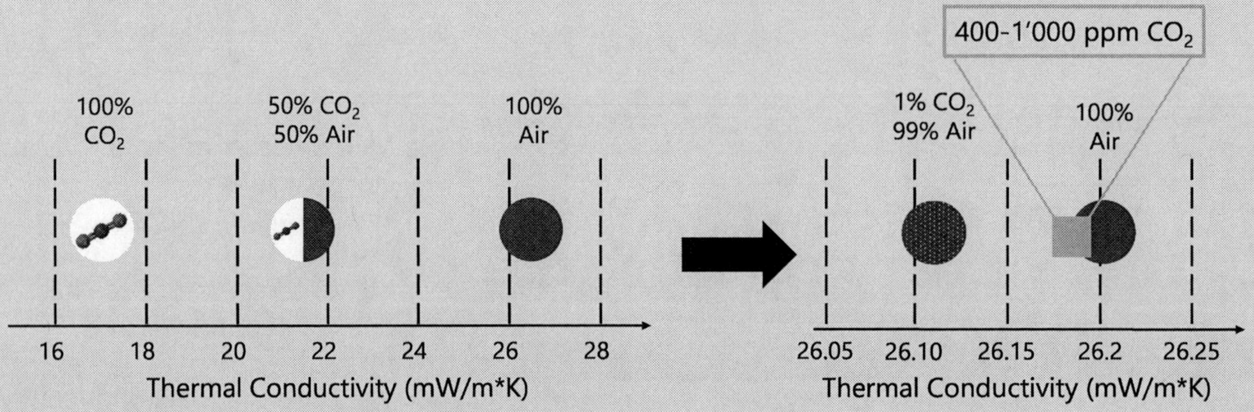

SENSIRION

From Thermal Conductivity to CO_2 Concentration

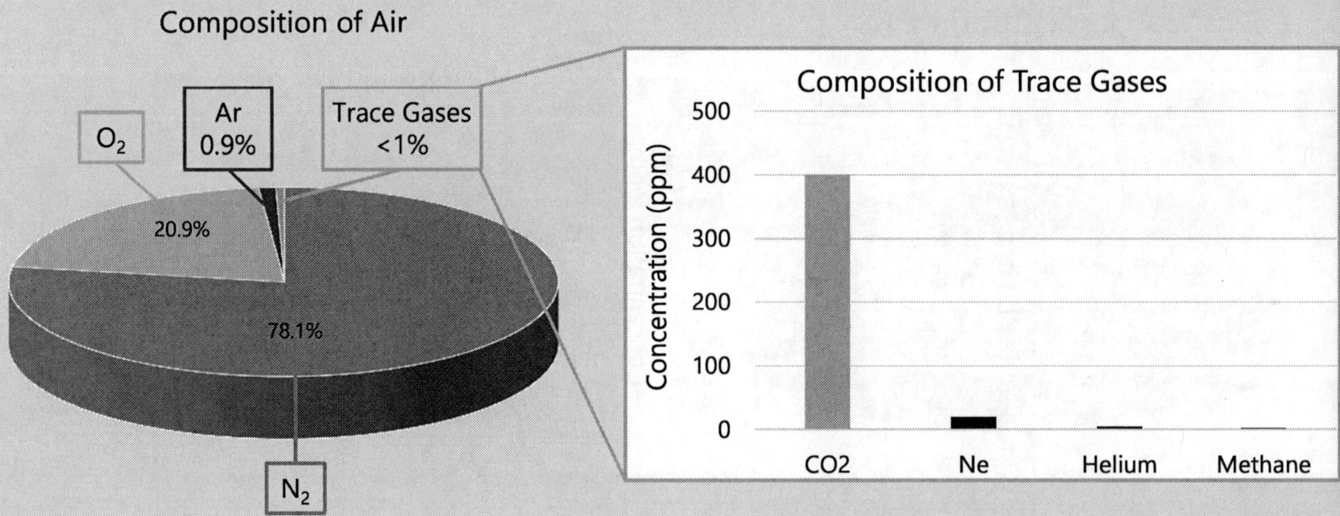

SENSIRION

STCC4 Key Features and Applications

CO_2 Sensors: Looking Beyond

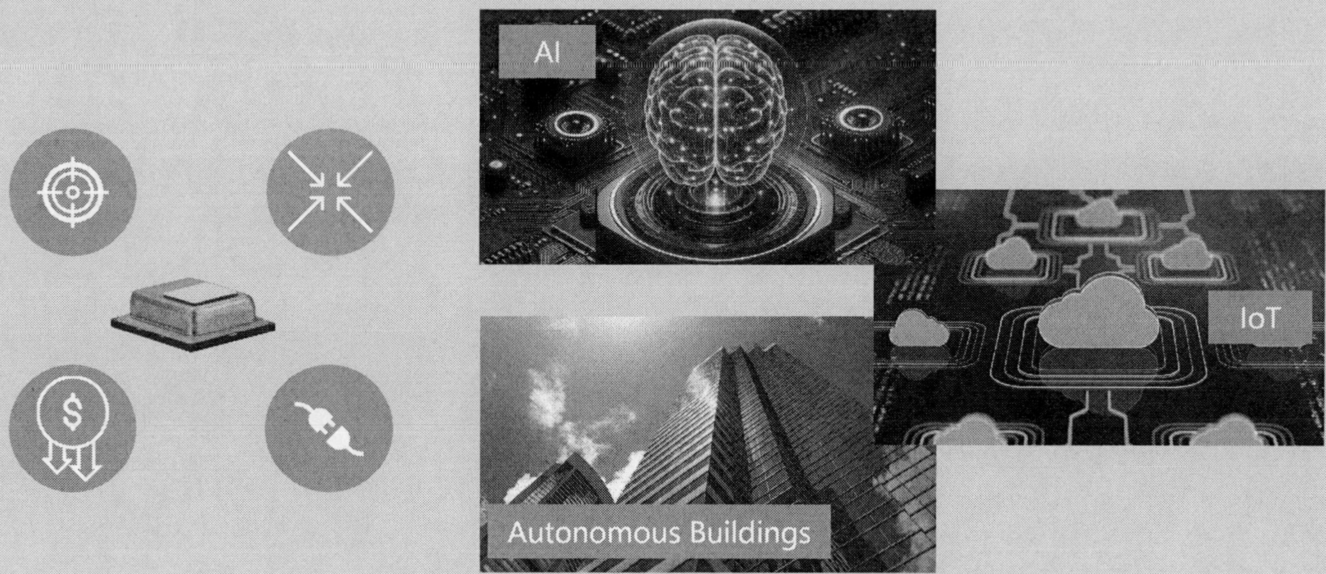

The Future is Bright

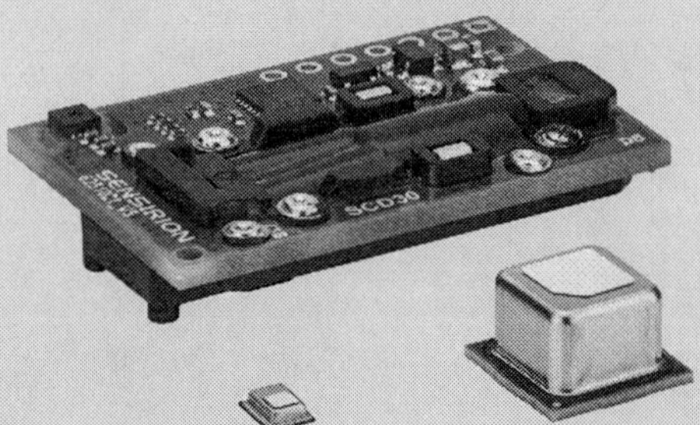

SENSIRION

SENSIRION

THE 2023 MEMS INDUSTRY COMMERCIALIZATION REPORT CARD: OPPORTUNITIES AND CHALLENGES

Sensors Converge 2024

Santa Clara Convention Center

June 25, 2024

Roger H. Grace
President, Roger Grace Associates

rgrace@rgrace.com
www.rgrace.com

ROGER GRACE ASSOCIATES
MARKETING COUNSEL

Janusz Bryzek Ph.D. R.I.P.

- Janusz passed on November 2022 and was considered a true visionary and entrepreneur having created 11 MEMS companies (NovaSensor to Exo Imaging) over his 40-year career
- Bestowed the Sensors Converge "Industry Impact Award"
- Abundant Nexus Conference honoring Janusz was held on April 24, 2024, to a sellout crowd of approximately 150 attendees at the Silicon Valley Computer History Museum
- Janusz was my close friend and colleague for over 40 years
- Cheers to you Janusz from your MEMS family…R.I.P.

ROGER GRACE ASSOCIATES
MARKETING COUNSEL

ROGER GRACE ASSOCIATES

- Founded in 1982
- Offices in Bonita Springs, Florida and San Francisco, California
- Over 40 Years of experience in the MEMS/Nano industry…an industry pioneer
- International clientele of companies, laboratories and governments
- Specializing in sensors, semiconductors, MEMS/MST, Nanotechnology, capital equipment
- Focus on:
  - custom market research
  - strategic marketing
  - due diligence analysis / merger and acquisition support
  - strategic marketing communications
    - company and product positioning
    - new product introduction
    - branding
    - promotion
  - business development
  - distribution channel development
- For more information…www.rgrace.com; rgrace@rgrace.com

ROGER GRACE ASSOCIATES
MARKETING COUNSEL

ROGER GRACE BACKGROUND

- Education: BSEE, MSEE (Raytheon Graduate Fellow) Northeastern University, Boston, MA; MBA Program, University of California Berkeley
- Design Engineer / Project Engineer with specialty in microwave and RF, 13 years…Raytheon, Avco Missile Systems, Ford Aerospace
- Applications Engineer, RF semiconductors, 3 years, Avantek/HP
- Marketing Manager, MEMS, 3 years ,Foxboro ICT
- Marketing Consultant, MEMS, Sensors and Semiconductors, 40+years
- Guest Lecturer, University of California Berkeley, 1990-2003
- Engineering Alumni Engineer of the Year, 2004, Northeastern University
- Co-Founder, Past President and VP Americas of Micro and Nanotechnology Commercialization Education Foundation (MANCEF)
- Published over 50 papers and articles on MEMS/Sensors
- Organized and Chaired over 40 technical sessions worldwide on MEMS/Sensors
- Board membership…Florida MEP, University of Michigan WIMSS, Northeastern University High Rate Nanomanufacturing Center, Sensors , MEPTEC
- Organizing committee includes Transducers 2009,COMS, Smart Systems Integration (EU), Advanced Microsystems for Automotive Applications (EU), IRISS(EU), IWLPC
- Citizenship…US / Portugal

ROGER GRACE ASSOCIATES
MARKETING COUNSEL

TECHNOLOGY COMMERCIALIZATION* PROCESS MODEL

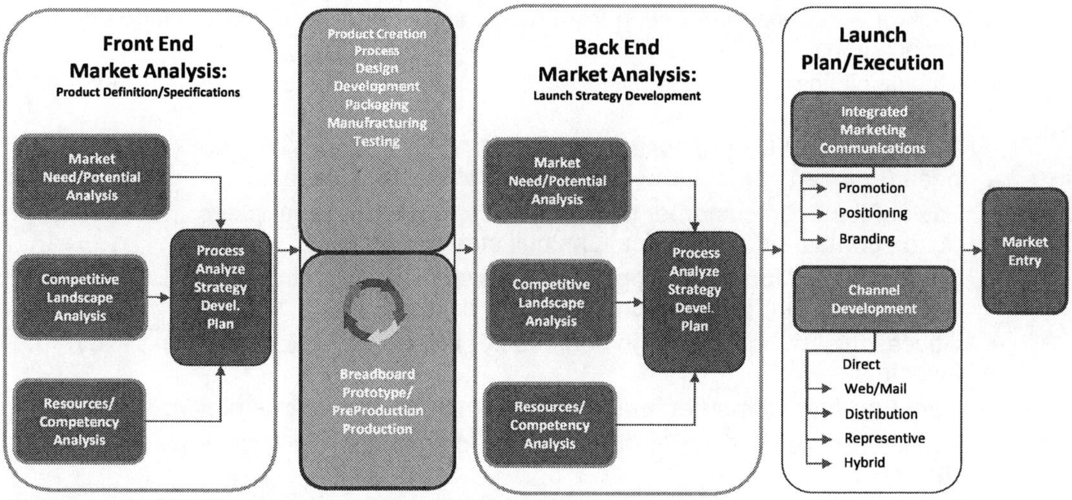

*Def: Process or cycle of introducing a new product or production method to the market

Roger Grace Associates supports its clients in front and back-end market analysis as well as in the product launch plan and execution

ROGER GRACE ASSOCIATES
MARKETING COUNSEL

OUTLINE

- Situational Analysis
- Market Research Background
- Market Research Mythology
- Results
- Responses to Chip Act
- Responses to Post-Covid
- Summary/Call to Action/Recommendations
- References
- For more information
- Appendix : Verbatims

ROGER GRACE ASSOCIATES
MARKETING COUNSEL

BARRIERS TO COMMERCIALIZATION SITUATIONAL ANALYSIS

- Lack of well defined direction from roadmaps, industry standards, industry associations
- Multidisciplinary knowledge is required…materials, electronic design, mechanical design
- Packaging and testing costs typically at 70% of total value…however focus has been (and continues to be) on devices not systems solutions
- Lack of focus on customer needs…technology-centric suppliers…technology push versus market / applications pull strategy
- Lack of capital formation opportunities, risk averse investors; low IPO opportunity because of small sales volume levels of companies
- Successive “bubble busts” in sensors i.e. biomems, optical telecom...wary investors
- Very fragmented market, many small companies, few large players
- Limited “success stories” of MEMS/MST companies e.g. Invensense, SiTime (IPOs)
- However…new market opportunities for large volume applications have emerged in Automotive; Consumer e.g. mobile phones; Point-of-Care Diagnostics; Wearables; Environmental/Infrastructure Monitoring; Internet of Things (IoT)

ROGER GRACE ASSOCIATES
MARKETING COUNSEL

MEMS COMMERCIALIZATION TIMETABLE

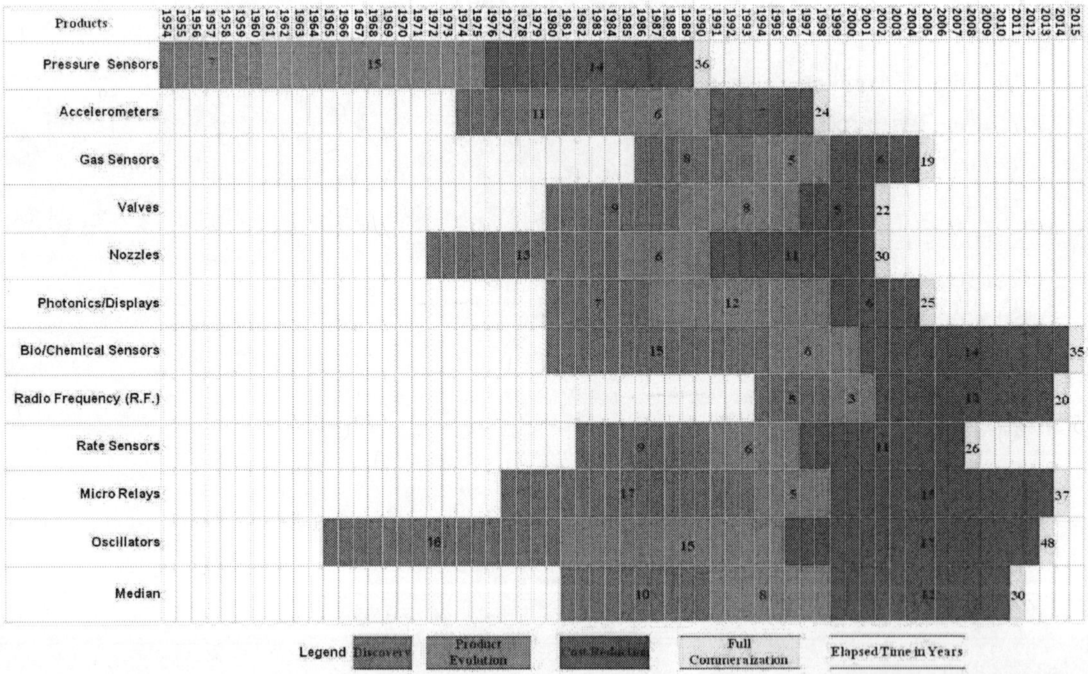

ROGER GRACE ASSOCIATES
MARKETING COUNSEL

SENSOR PRODUCT LIFE CYCLES

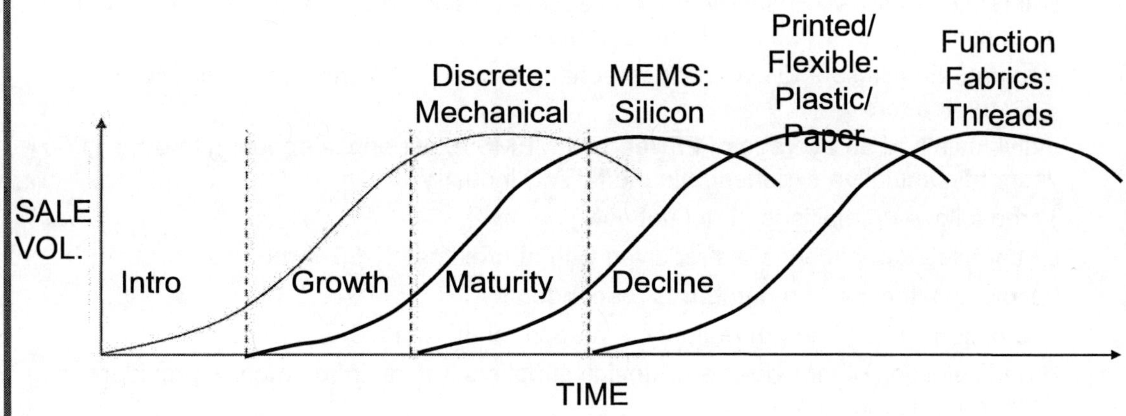

ROGER GRACE ASSOCIATES MARKETING COUNSEL

DOES THE MEMS INDUSTRY COMMERCIALZATION REPORT CARD MATTER?

- Initiated in 1998 during Hilton Head Conference
- 25th. continuous year in its reporting
- Determination of 14 critical success factors established after investigation of various other industries (9 initial and 5 added over time)
- Everyone loves grades…people can easily relate…e.g. NY Department of Health grades restaurants regarding their cleanliness, Michelin Restaurant Stars, AAA Diamonds, Amazon, Yelp etc.
- Study Objective: monitor and report on the "health" of the MEMS industry in hopes of creating and influencing positive change…not only by conducting the research but by "evangelizing" via presentations and articles…and especially learning from past performance [1]
- Added motivation was to determine:
  - the possible continuing effects of COVID on the grades into 2023 and how earlier problems were mitigated/overcome,
  - the possible impact of the CHIPS act…especially on the subject Established Infrastructure
  - the influence and relevance of the meteoric growth of Artificial Intelligence on MEMS and MEMS-based systems

ROGER GRACE ASSOCIATES MARKETING COUNSEL

MARKET RESEARCH METHOLOGY

- "Delphi"/"Mass Observation" hybrid approach used…not statistically significant i.e. non-projectable…however constitutes the opinions and rationale (via verbatim comments) of MEMS industry thought leaders (average experience 25 plus years) amounting to over 1,000 aggregated person-years of experience
- Personal Emails sent to over 120 personally known and highly respected MEMS industry leaders
- Individuals had an average of 25 years of MEMS experiences equating to over 1,000 years of cumulative experience in the MEMS industry
- Three follow- up mailings. (I did not vote)
- 54 completed questionnaires received with approximately 50 verbatims
- Follow up telecons with numerous respondents
- International in scope with majority of respondents from US and Europe
- Broad selection of interviewees…device suppliers, users, infrastructure providers (little-to-no academics)
- Incentive of $100 Amazon gift card (random drawing from submissions)

ROGER GRACE ASSOCIATES
MARKETING COUNSEL

2023 MEMS INDUSTRY COMMERCIALIZATION REPORT CARD

SUBJECT / YEAR	1998	1999	2000	2001	2002	2003	2004	5005	2006	2007	2008	2009	2010	2011	2012	2013	2014	2015	2016	2017	2018	2019	2020	2021	2022	2023	Δ
R&D	A	A	A	A	A	A-	A-	A-	A-	A-	B+	B	B	B+	B	B	B	B	B+	A-	A-	B+	B	B-	B	B	0
Marketing	C-	C	C+	C+	C+	C	C	C+	C+	C+	C+	C	C	C+	C+	B-	B-	B	B	B	B	B-	B-	C+	B-	B-	0
Market Research	C	B-	B-	B-	B	B	B+	B-	B	B	B	B+	A-	B	B-	B-	B-	C+	C+	B-	B-	B-	C+	C	C+	C+	0
Design For Manufacturing	C+	B-	B	B	B	B	B	C+	B-	B	B+	A-	A-	B+	B-	B	B+	A-	A-	A-	B+	B	B	B-	B	B	0
Established Infrastructure	C+	B	B+	A	A	A	A	A-	A-	A-	B+	B+	A-	A-	A-	A-	A-	A-	A-	A-	A-	A-	B+	B-	B	B+	1
Management Expertise	C	C	C+	C+	C+	C+	C+	B-	B-	B	B	B	B	B	B	B	B	B	B	B	B	B	B	B-	B-	B	1
Venture Capital Attraction	C	B-	B+	A	C	C-	C	C+	C+	C	C-	D	D+	D+	D+	D+	D+	D	D	D+	C-	C-	C	C-	B-	C+	-1
Creation Of Wealth	C	B-	B+	A	C	C-	C-	C-	C-	C	C-	D+	C-	C+	C+	C+	B-	C+	C+	C+	C+	C+	C+	C	C+	C+	0
Profitability	C-	C-	C-	C-	C-	C-	C-	C	C+	C	C-	D+	D	C-	C	C+	C+	C	C-	C-	C	C	C+	C	C	C	0
Industry Roadmap		B-	B	B+	A-	A	A	B	B-	C+	C-	C-	C	C	C	C+	B-	C+	C	C-	C	C	C	C	C	C+	1
Industry Association				B	B+	B+	B+	B	B	B+	B	B	A-	B+	B+	B+	B+	B+	A-	B+	B-	B-	B-	C+	B	B	0
Standards					C	B-	B-	B-	C+	C	C	C	C+	C	C	C+	B-	C+	C-	C-	C-	C	C	C-	C	C	0
Employment						C	C	C+	C+	C+	C	C-	C	C+	C+	C+	B-	B-	B	B	B	B	B	B-	B-	B-	0
Cluster Development						B	B+	B+	B	B-	C+	C+	C+	C	C+	C+	B-	C+	B-	C+	C+	C+	C+	C	C+	C+	0
Overall Grade	C+	B-	B	B	B-	B-	B	B	B-	B-	C+	C+	B-	B-	B-	B-	B	B-	B-	B-	B-	B-	B-	C+	B-	B-	0

ROGER GRACE ASSOCIATES
MARKETING COUNSEL

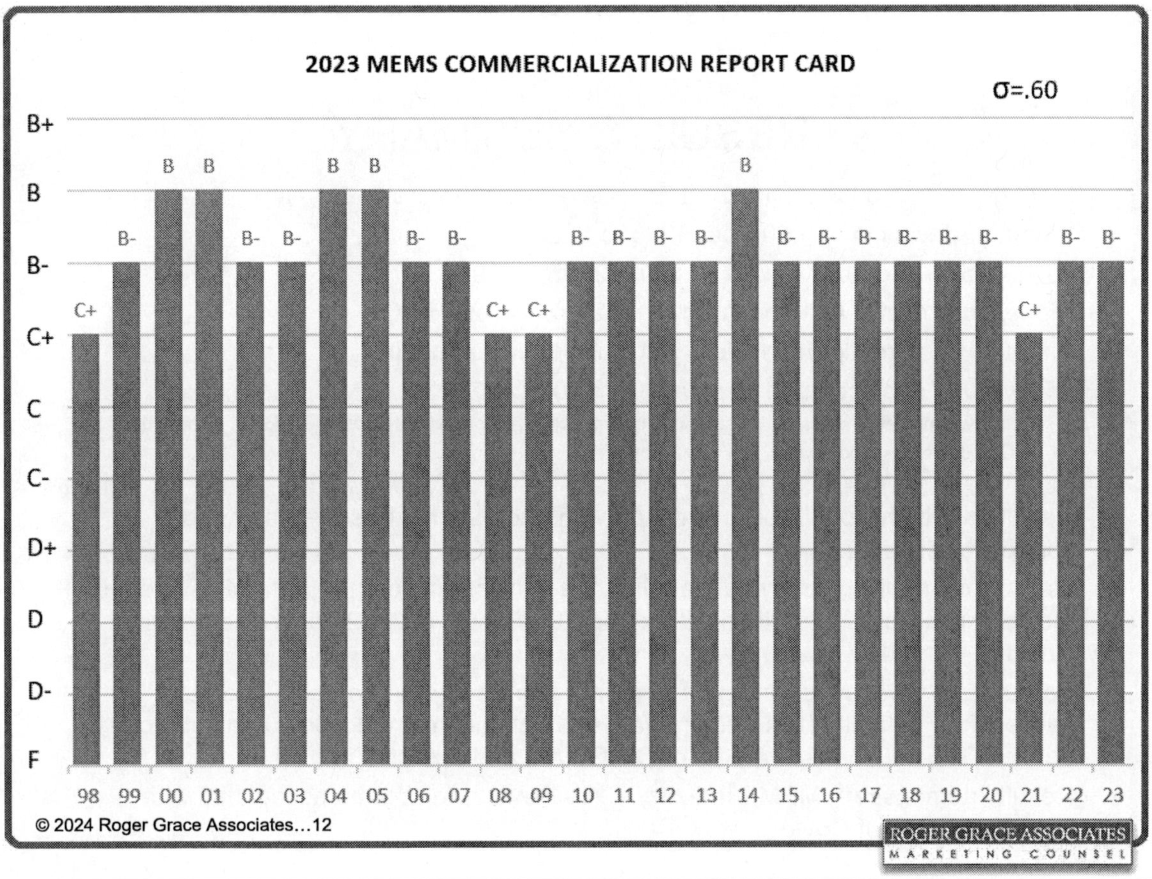

STANDARD DEVIATIONS OF GRADES

• INDUSTRY ASSOCIATION	1.63
• VC ATTRACTION	1.61
• MARKET RESEARCH	1.55
• CREATION OF WEALTH	1.46
• PROFITABILITY	1.43
• R&D	1.38
• EMPLOYMENT	1.37
• STANDARDS	1.36
• INDUSTRY ROADMAP	1.36
• MARKETING	1.35
• MANAGEMENT EXPERTISE	1.31
• CLUSTER DEVELOPMENT	1.27
• ESTAB. INFRASTRUCTURE	1.22
• DESIGN FOR MFG.	0.96

- Results are for all 14 subjects and from the grades of the 54 respondents for the year 2023

ROGER GRACE ASSOCIATES
MARKETING COUNSEL

RESULTS SUMMARY

- 2023 grade improved maintained its B- level from the previous year
- Standard deviation of 0.60 from 1998 to 2023
- Lowest overall grade was C+ in 1998, 2008, 2009
- Highest grade of B attained in 2020, 2021, 2024, 2025,2014
- A total of 72 verbatims provided…all included in Appendix
- Overview of subject grade changes from 2022 to 2023:
  - Three improved one grade…Established Infrastructure, Management Expertise, Industry Roadmap
  - One decreased one grade…V.C. Attraction
  - Ten were unaffected…
- Results are highly positively correlated with international business and social economics situation
- Maturity of MEMS industry validated by the consistency of the grade of B- in eight of the last nine reporting periods with a departure to C+ in 2012 as a direct result of Covid
- Verbatims provided respondent's personal approach(es)/strategies used to successfully mitigate the limited negative effects of continued Covid on subjects during 2023…outlook on impact of CHIPS Act and potential impact on A.I.
- Results demonstrate MEMS industry's resilience to problems associated with lingering effects of Covid

ROGER GRACE ASSOCIATES
MARKETING COUNSEL

SUMMARY IMPLICATIONS OF COVID ON GRADES

INTRODUCTION

As can be seen in the verbatim slides provided in Appendix, none of the 14 grades have been significantly negatively affected by the ongoing effects of Covid during 2023. The many insightful verbatims provided by the respondents addressed several of these issues from their personal perspectives

GRADE SUMMARY EFFECTS

- Established Infrastructure …decreased two points in the 2021 Report Card to B- increased one grade to B in 2022 and another grade to B+ in 2023 thus showing that the industry is resilient and has significantly recovered
- R & D….work at home negatively affected progress in the previous Report Card became a work-around
- Established Infrastructure…where supply chains were severely challenged and under-performed in the previous Report Card bounced back using work-arounds and inventory strategies
- VC Attraction… decrease one grade from 2022 demonstrating that VCs are significantly shunning MEMS investments and favoring A.I. startups
- Six of the respondents provided inputs with Covid mentions (see appendix)

ROGER GRACE ASSOCIATES
MARKETING COUNSEL

SUMMARY / ANALYSIS / CALL TO ACTION / RECOMMENDATIONS

- Adoption of a marketing / applications pull vs. technology push strategy
- Adopt new media strategies including social media, webinars, email to keep/develop new customers…lessons learned from Covid [4].
- Continue to develop manufacturing / packaging solutions that can help differentiate the product from a price / feature / performance perspective…packaging and testing will continue to be "king"
- Be aware of new technologies e.g. printed and functional fabrics to potentially replace MEMS in certain applications
- Embrace system solutions/integrated products vs. component approach e.g. (pMUT) to maximize value and encourage investments (Exo Imaging which recently obtained its Series C funding of $220M US.)…N.B. The "S" in MEMS is for systems!
- Accept the fact that obtaining VC funding for MEMS will continue to be a big struggle. It declined from B- in 2022 to C+ in 2023. Other technologies e.g. A.I. are preferred. Better routes include angels, industrial partnering and buy-outs need to be pursued judiciously.

ROGER GRACE ASSOCIATES
MARKETING COUNSEL

SUMMARY / ANALYSIS / CALL TO ACTION / RECOMMENDATIONS (cont.)

- Final aggregated grade for 2022 was B- which it maintained from 2022. The B- grade existed for the prior six years and was recently reported in Fierce Electronics [1].
- Limited and unremarkable positive increase in grades:
  - Standard deviation=0.60 from 1998 to 2023
  - Three subjects increased one grade…Established Infrastructure, Management Expertise, Industry Roadmap
  - One subject decreased one grade…VC Attraction
  - 10 were unchanged
- Report Card grades accurately reflect the economic trends e.g. 2001, 2008
- 54 respondents provided 72 verbatims with all appearing in the Final Report Appendix
- Continue to create significant awareness as to the unique solution benefits of MEMS based system solutions (MBSS)…add value
- Understand customer / market needs vis-à-vis rigorous market research
- Define and establish defensible product differentiation
- MEMS continues to be a "go-to" technology for the measurement of many parameters and in many applications
- Those who forget the past are condemned to relive it [5]. Embrace the lessons to be learned from the results of the Report Card and especially the verbatims.

ROGER GRACE ASSOCIATES
MARKETING COUNSEL

REFERENCES

- [1] R. Grace; 2020 MEMS Industry Commercialization Report Card; Fierce Electronics; July 21, 2023; www.rgrace.com.
- [2] R. Grace; Industry Insiders Share Their Sensors/MEMS Industry Forecasts for 2022, Including the Impact of Covid ;Fierce Electronics; January 18, 2022; www.rgrace.com.
- [3] R. Grace; Forecast 2022 for Sensors/MEMS: Focus on the Impact of Covid-19 on the Commercialization Process Global Supply Chain; NASA Tech Briefs; June 2022; www.rgrace.com.
- [4] R. Grace; Marketing in a Recession: How to Survive; Sensors Daily; April 8, 2020; www.rgrace.com.
- [5] G. Santayana, Reason in the Common Sense, 1905.

ROGER GRACE ASSOCIATES
MARKETING COUNSEL

CHIPS ACT VERBATIMS

- Investments forthcoming from CHIPS act and new TIP directorate at NSF
- With the Chips and Science Act of 2022, it is expected that employment in the MEMS industry will increase.
- With the Chips and Science Act of 2022, and increased funding in the DoD, MEMS is an enabling technology that will be a part of several industry roadmaps, from Automotive, to Aerospace, Electronics.
- Has improved primarily due to DoD, SEMI MEMS & Sensors Industry Group, Sensors Converge participants, and CHIPS Act language.
- Thanks to the CHIPS Act, MEMS foundries are starting to think more strategically, forming alliances, focusing on workforce development – everything that is needed to further grow our industry. CHIPS has been a great shot in the arm for MEMS, even though we are not likely to get the big bucks like cutting edge semiconductor fabs. And hasn't it been amazing that the NYTimes and Wall Street Journal are suddenly writing articles about key topics like foundry access, advanced packaging and workforce training?! The MEMS industry needs to capitalize on its moment in the national spotlight.

ROGER GRACE ASSOCIATES
MARKETING COUNSEL

POST-COVID VERBATIMS

- The tight capacity seen at the end of COVID has eased due to economic uncertainty. Despite the economic uncertainty, employment opportunities remain abundant.
- I really don't have a lot of significant movement in any given category. The country has moved out of Covid into a period of high inflation (with accompanying rising interest rates to try curb inflation) and uncertainty about the economy in general. In addition, the complete incompetence of the current administration on at all levels after two years of chaos has left many in this country and abroad wondering what is the future of the US as a world leader in anything. Not a good scenario for any high tech field. Therefore, a lowering of the grade.
- The big players are doing well to very well. While Corona has hampered the overall development of the industry, it also initiated new activities in healthcare products. In particular, many start-ups developed new diagnostic tools for fast PCR as an example but also for other applications. How many of these newcomers will survive after Corona is more or less over, remains to be seen.
- Covid has created a large surplus of inventory with many customers around the world. This will definitely solve the supply chain problem as growth starts to normalize.
- Pandemic complicated teamwork and this still felt in 2022. In many instances Expenditures for R&D is the first victim in budget reductions

ROGER GRACE ASSOCIATES
MARKETING COUNSEL

ARTIFICIAL INTELLIGENCE VERBATIMS

- (Marketing will be enhanced) Especially using new technologies, like Artificial Intelligence

ROGER GRACE ASSOCIATES
MARKETING COUNSEL

SUMMARY OF VERBATIMS BY SUBJECT

R&D	13
VC ATTRACTION	12
EMPLOYMENT	10
INDUSTRY ROADMAP	7
ESTAB. INFRASTRUCTURE	6
MARKETING	5
STANDARDS	3
PROFITABILITY	3
CLUSTER DEVELOPMENT	3
DESIGN FOR MFG.	3
INDUSTRY ASSOCIATION	3
MARKET RESEARCH	2
CREATION OF WEALTH	2
MANAGEMENT EXPERTISE	0

- A total of 72 verbatim responses were received (Ref: Appendix)
- Most popular subject for responses:
  - R&D
  - VC Attraction
  - Employment
- Least popular responses
  - Market Research
  - Creation of Wealth
  - Management Expertise

ROGER GRACE ASSOCIATES
MARKETING COUNSEL

FOR MORE INFORMATION

- A copy of the article on the 2023 MEMS Industry Commercialization Report Card Study summarizing its results will be published in Fierce Sensors/Fierce Electronics and will be available on the Roger Grace
- A complimentary copy of this Final Report (including all 72 verbatims) also appears on the Roger Grace Associates website www.rgrace.com.

ROGER GRACE ASSOCIATES
MARKETING COUNSEL

Since this was a shortened presentation due to time constraints…

the entire presentation will be available to attendees by kindly requesting it via email to me at …rgrace@rgrace.com

Please visit the Roger Grace Associates Booth #308 at Sensors Converge 2024

ROGER GRACE ASSOCIATES
MARKETING COUNSEL

HAMAMATSU
PHOTON IS OUR BUSINESS

The Future of IR Point Detectors: Smaller, Scalable, No Cooling

Gary Spingarn
Product Manager – Infrared Devices

Sensors Converge 6/25/24

About Me

HAMAMATSU
PHOTON IS OUR BUSINESS

HAMAMATSU
PHOTON IS OUR BUSINESS

Index

- Use Cases
- Initial Technical Concepts
- NIR/SWIR Development – "Long" InGaAs
- MIR Development – Stable and Uncooled
- Summary

 3

Why Point Detectors?

HAMAMATSU
PHOTON IS OUR BUSINESS

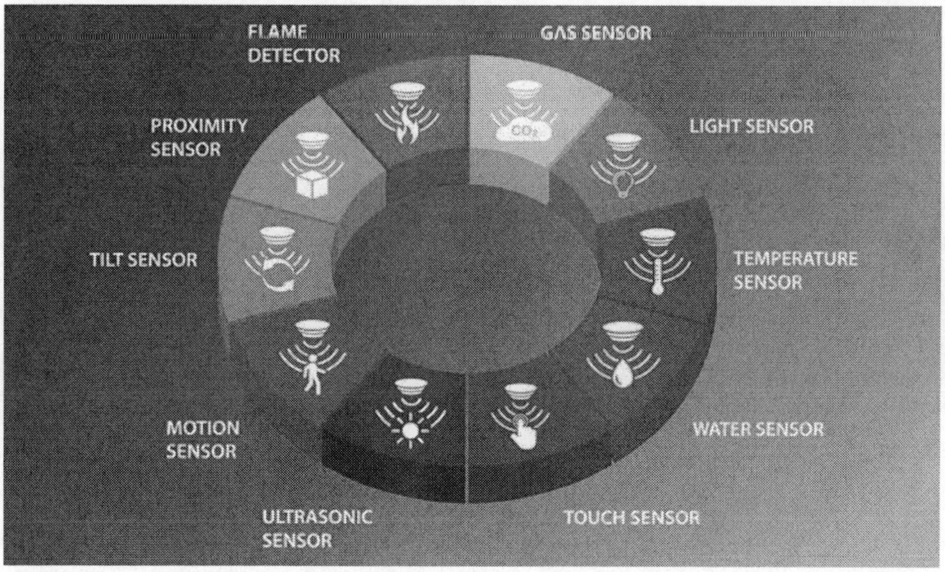

 4

Why Point Detectors?

HAMAMATSU
PHOTON IS OUR BUSINESS

Industrial process control
Process control with real-time measurement of industrial gas.

Flue gas monitor
Analysis of SOx and NOx in gases emitted from factories and the like.

Portable gas sensor
Gas leak detection at factories and other work sites.

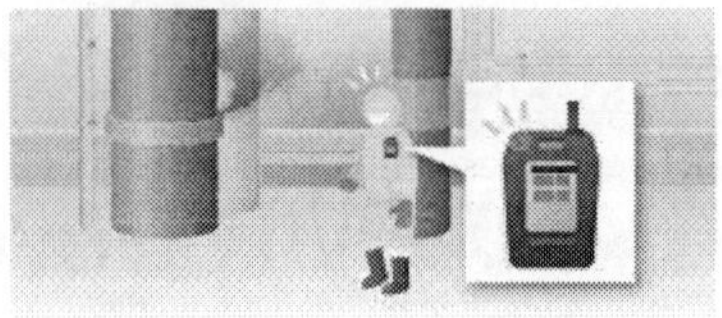

Vehicle exhaust gas measurement
Real-time monitoring of vehicle exhaust gas

Air quality monitoring
Analysis of pollutant gases in the atmosphere

IR Electromagnetic Spectrum

HAMAMATSU
PHOTON IS OUR BUSINESS

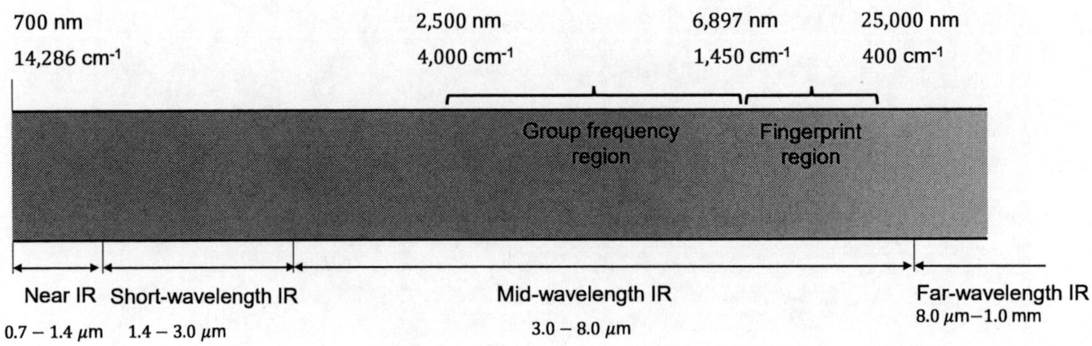

Types of IR detectors: Thermal Sensors

HAMAMATSU
PHOTON IS OUR BUSINESS

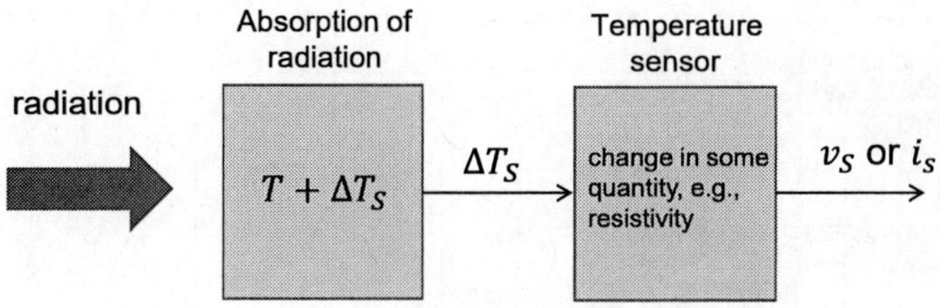

Thermal sensors experience a temperature change due to absorption of radiation. The change in temperature is converted to electrical signal.

 7

Types of IR detectors: Photon Sensors

HAMAMATSU
PHOTON IS OUR BUSINESS

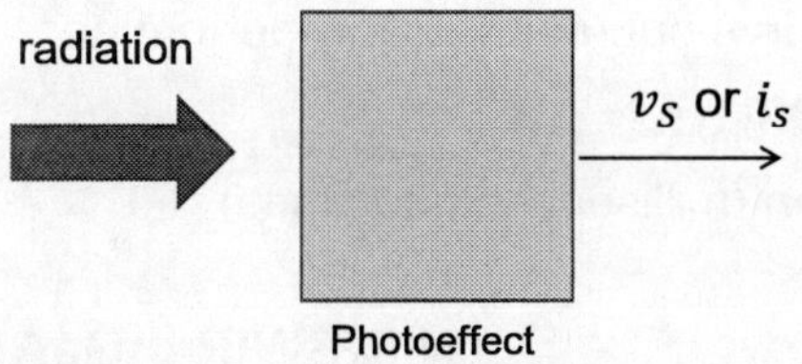

In a photon detector, the interaction of photons with charge carriers in the detector leads directly to the formation of the electrical signal. A photodiode and avalanche photodiode are two well-known examples of photon detectors.

 8

Spectral Response Range of Infrared Detectors

HAMAMATSU
PHOTON IS OUR BUSINESS

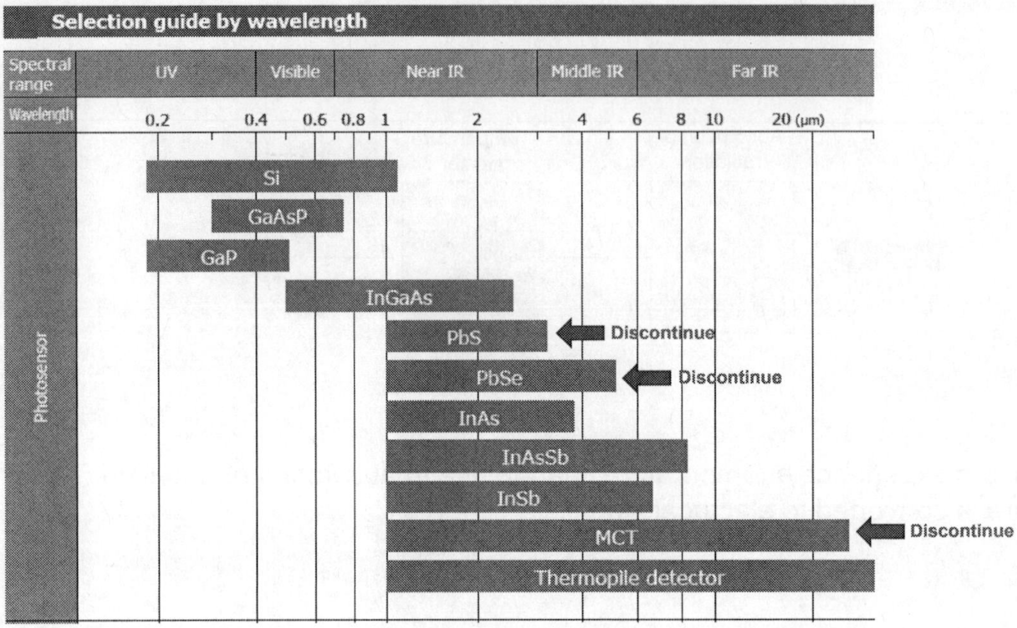

Comparison

HAMAMATSU
PHOTON IS OUR BUSINESS

Thermal Detector

- Lower cost and versatile
- Consistent sensitivity curve but relatively low performance versus photonic detectors
- Very slow by comparison (millisecond rise times)

MIR InAsSb Detectors

- RoHS compliant, consistent manufacturing yields, high linearity
- Versatile wavelength coverage, cutoff at 14 microns
- **High noise floor, high temp variance**

NIR/SWIR InGaAs Detectors

- Industry standard for this wavelength region
- Detectors and image sensors
- Sensitivity changes with ambient temperature, can be contribute noise
- **Standard cutoff is 1700nm**

Historically, IR photodetectors are associated with higher cost and cooling….

Cooling

HAMAMATSU
PHOTON IS OUR BUSINESS

Thermoelectric Cooling

Cryogenic cooling

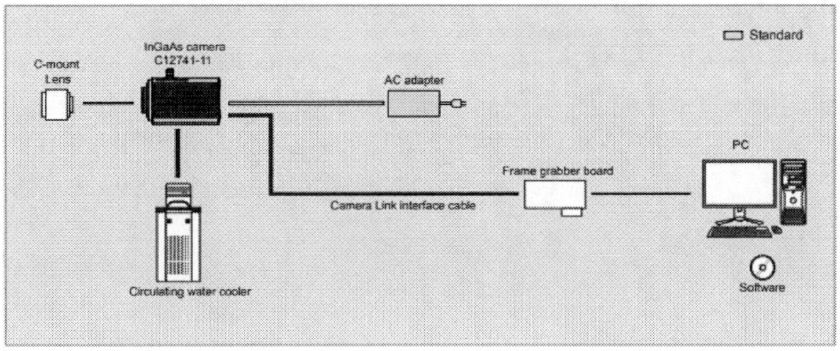

 11

HAMAMATSU
PHOTON IS OUR BUSINESS

InGaAs for NIR/SWIR

 12

InGaAs Structure - FI V.S. BT

■ Front-Illuminated type

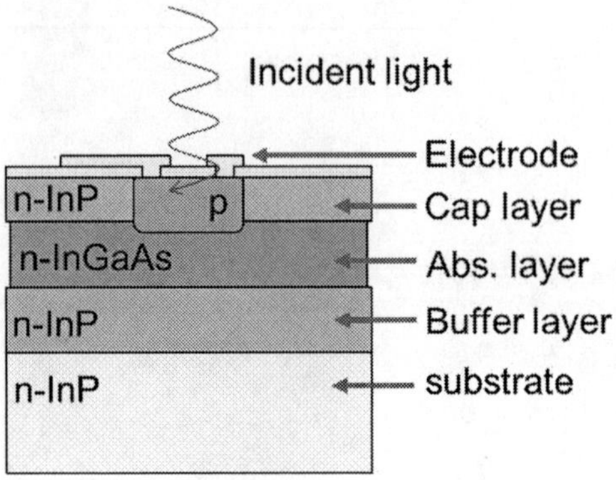

High Q.E.
Higher cost

■ Back-Illuminated type

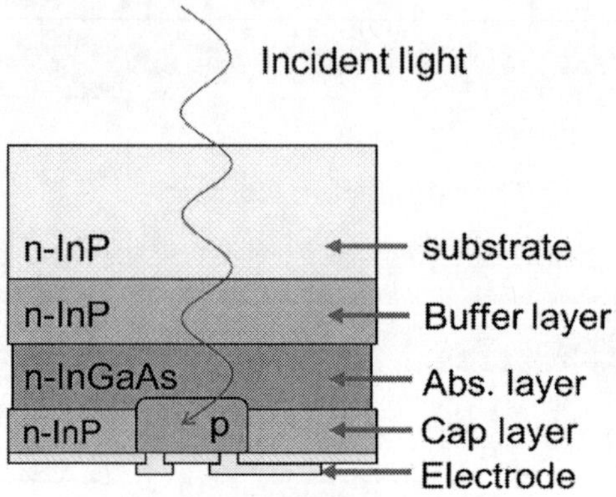

Lower Q.E.
Less cost

Extended V.S. Standard InGaAs

Standard InGaAs

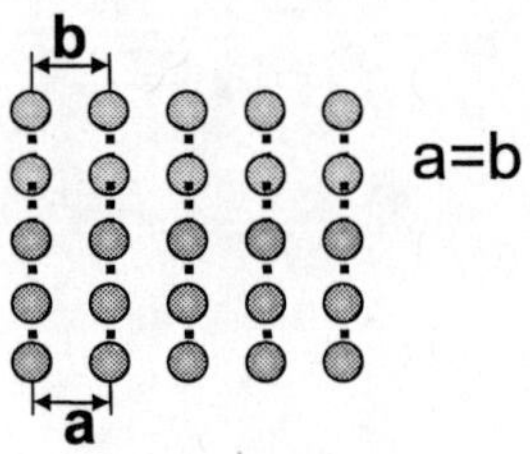

Matched lattice

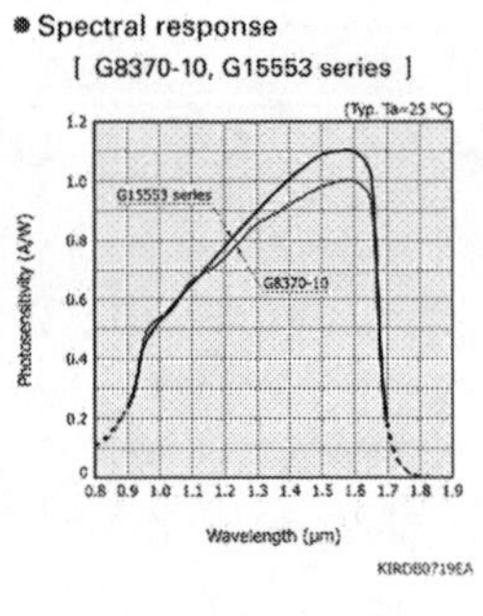

Cutoff = 1.7um

"Long" InGaAs

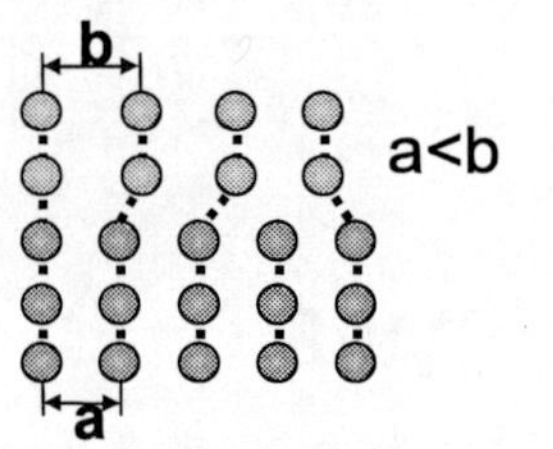

Unmatched lattice

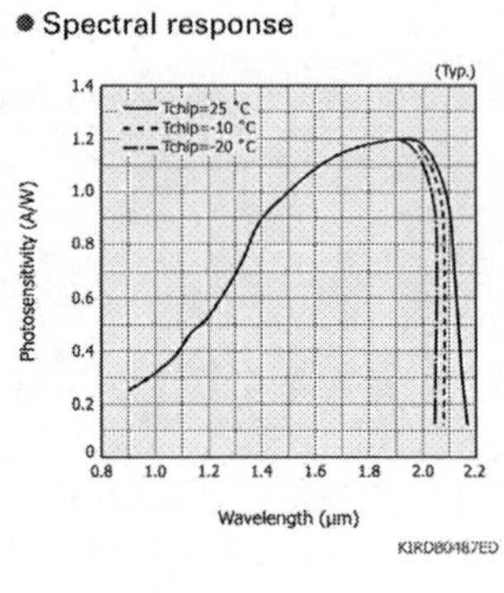

Cutoff 1.8um ~ 2.2um

- **Standard InGaAs has a cutoff wavelength of 1.7um, extended InGaAs cutoff wavelength could be up to 2.6um.**
- **Extended InGaAs requires high quality wafer with reduce of thin film quality for production plus cooling.**
- **"Long" InGaAs extends to a crucial region with manageable impact on yield and noise floor**

Example: G12181 Series

HAMAMATSU
PHOTON IS OUR BUSINESS

- Cooling improves performance but not necessary
- Covers the critical ~1650nm region
- Temperature Stable
- High response

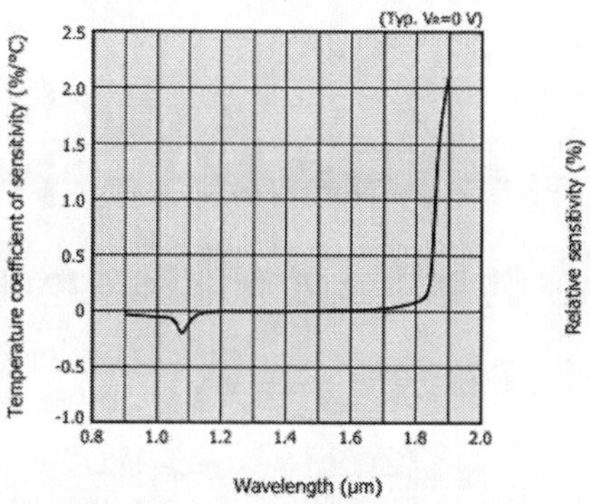

Type no.	Measurement Condition / Element temperature Tchip (°C)	Cutoff frequency fc VR=0 V RL=50 Ω		Terminal capacitance Ct VR=0 V f=1 MHz		Shunt resistance Rsh VR=10 mV		Detectivity D* λ=λp		Noize equivalent power NEP λ=λp	
		Min. (MHz)	Typ. (MHz)	Typ. (pF)	Max. (pF)	Min. (MΩ)	Typ. (MΩ)	Min. (cm·Hz$^{1/2}$/W)	Typ. (cm·Hz$^{1/2}$/W)	Typ. (W/Hz$^{1/2}$)	Max. (W/Hz$^{1/2}$)
G12181-003K	25	40	90	25	50	10	50	3×10^{11}	1×10^{12}	2×10^{-14}	5×10^{-14}
G12181-005K		15	35	70	150	4	20			3×10^{-14}	8.5×10^{-14}
G12181-010K		5	10	230	500	1	5			6×10^{-14}	2×10^{-13}
G12181-020K		1.2	2.5	1000	2000	0.2	1			1.5×10^{-13}	4×10^{-13}
G12181-030K		1	1.5	2000	3000	0.1	0.5			2×10^{-13}	5×10^{-13}

HAMAMATSU
PHOTON IS OUR BUSINESS

InAsSb for MIR

Multi-stage InAsSb Detectors

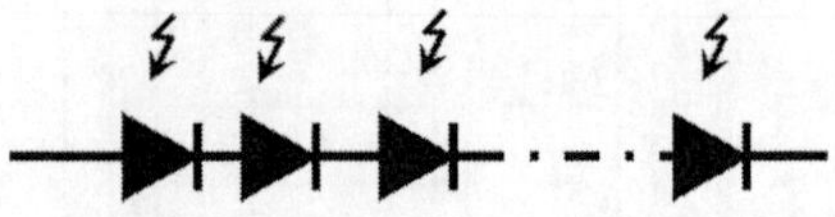

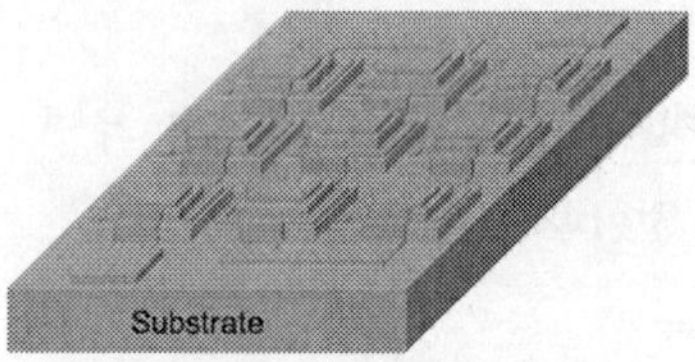

Structure of Multi-stage element PD

·Equivalent circuit

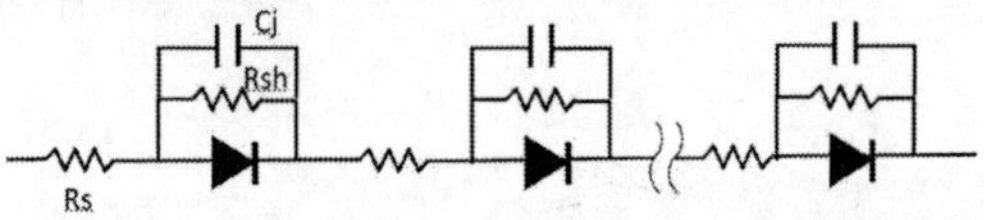

- **High shunt resistance, low photocurrent shuffles noise characteristics**
- **Same or better SNR than single active area**
- **NEP, D* definitions still apply**

 1

Back Illuminated Sensors

- **Improvement of temperature dependency**

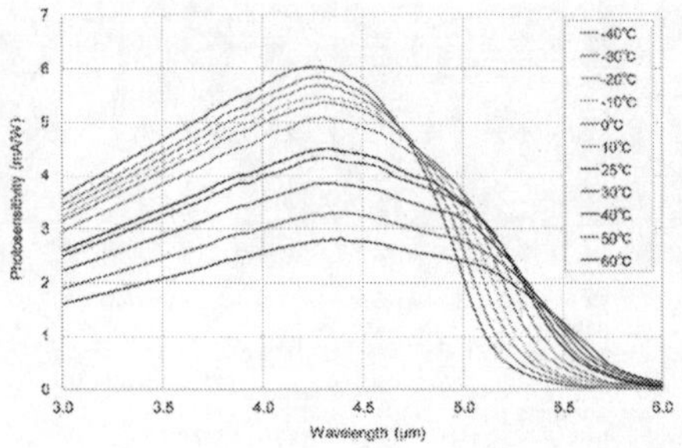

FI PD

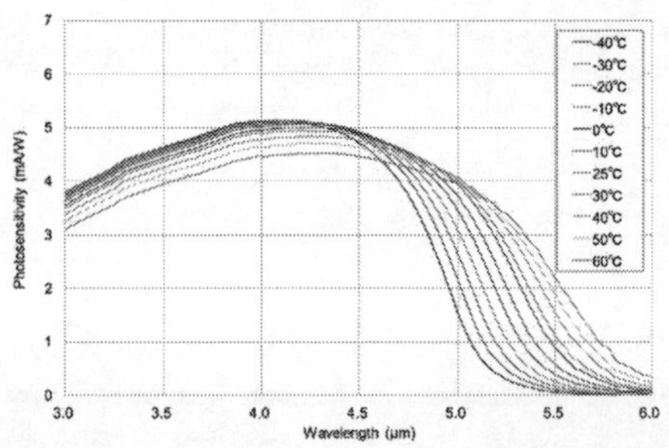

BI PD

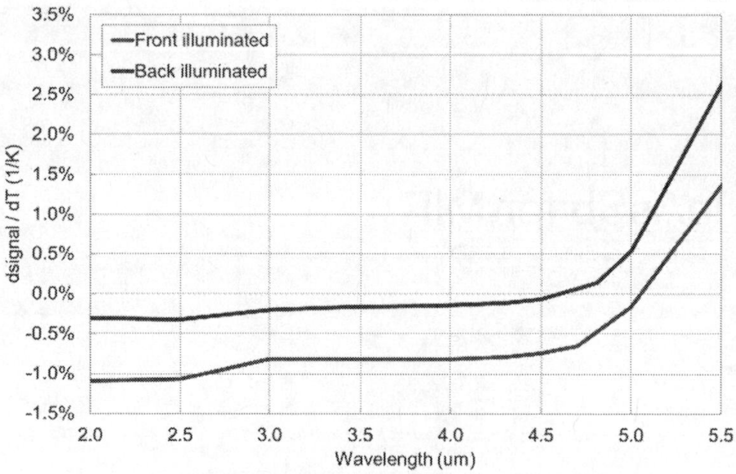

Temperature coefficient of sensitivity

-0.9%/°C ⇒ -0.1%/°C

 1

InAsSb Photovoltaic Detectors Lineup – P1661x Series

- With BPF (3.3μm, 3.9μm, 4.26μm)
- 2ch with BPF (3.3μm+3.9μm, 4.26μm+3.9μm)
- Standard Si w/ AR coating available as well

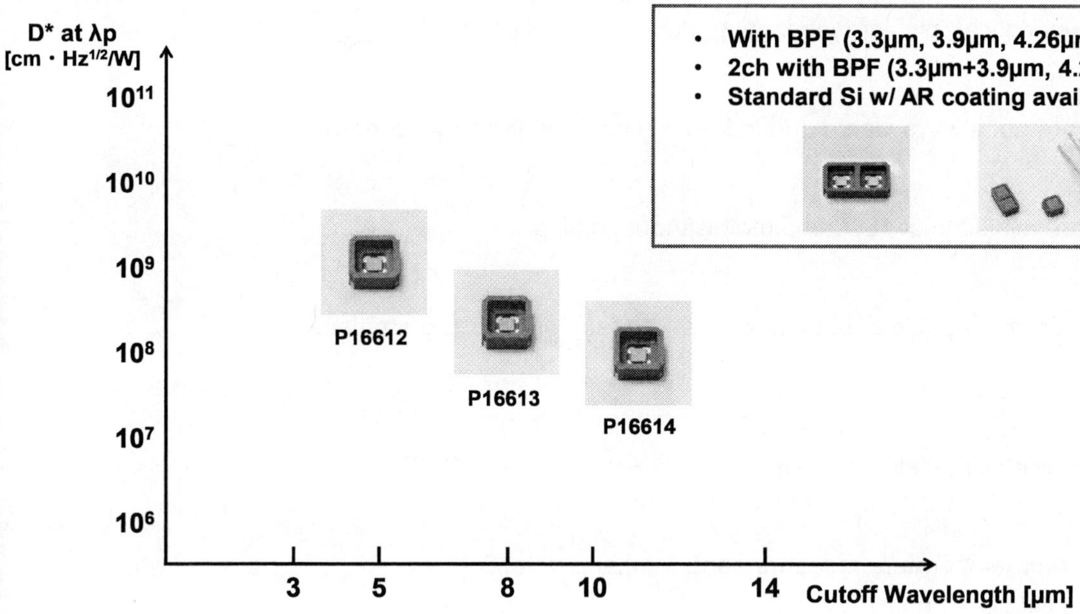

 19

HAMAMATSU
PHOTON IS OUR BUSINESS

P1661x series

- 5, 8, 11 micron bands w/ BI technology
- Stable room temperature operation, surface mount devices
- High shunt (kΩ+ range)
- Heavily scales with volume

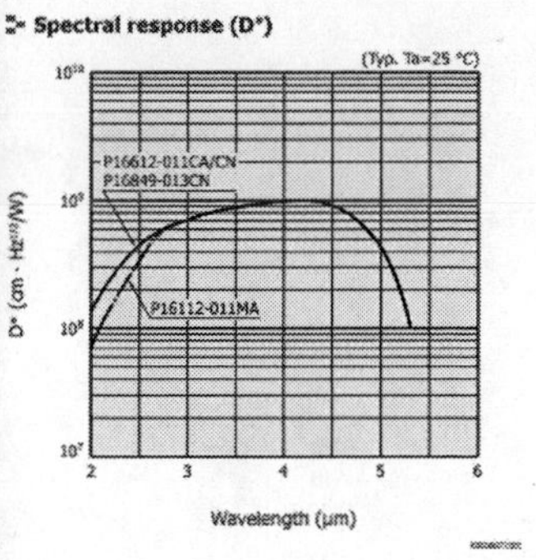

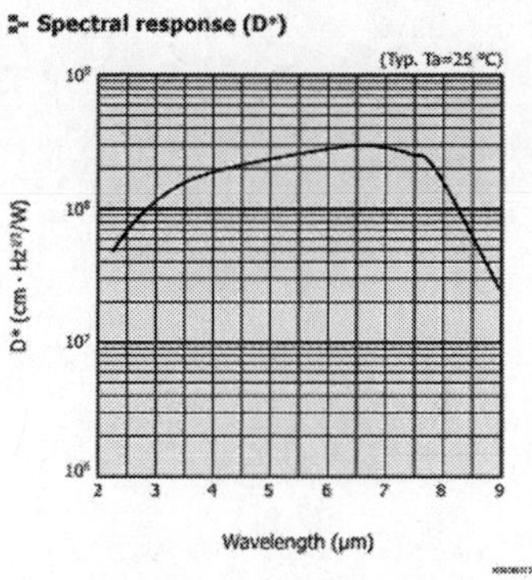

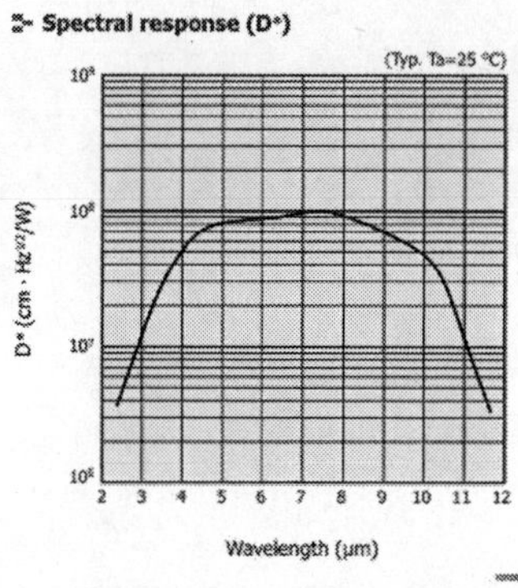

 20

Summary

HAMAMATSU
PHOTON IS OUR BUSINESS

- Point detectors play a critical role across many markets and applications
- Thermal detectors are not always viable due to lower sensitivity and slow response
- InGaAs detectors are available at 1800nm cutoff without cooling
- InAsSb MIR detectors are capable of high stability in the face of changing ambient conditions
- No cooling means lower cost, ability to scale
- Exciting possibilities for temperature measurement, methane detection, spectroscopy…..the list goes on

HAMAMATSU
PHOTON IS OUR BUSINESS

www.hamamatsu.com

Sensors Converge

Energy Harvesting - Kinetic Solutions

June 24–26, 2024 | Santa Clara, CA

#SensorsConverge

Understanding Energy versus Power

Power is the time *rate* at which work (energy) is done.

In this case, the drops per second representing water flow is Power (drops/sec).
In Electrical terms – Joules/sec = Watt = POWER

Energy represents a *finite amount* of work done.

In this case, the number of finite drops represent Energy.
In Electrical terms – Joules = Energy.

#SensorsConverge

Sensors Converge

Industry Challenges with Finite Energy

- Commercial IC Industry focuses for Ultra Low Power with Strategy of powering up then going into periodic deep sleep. Low duty cycle promotes long battery Life.
- Logical design evolution in commercial ICs must drive Ultra-low Energy, not just power centric initiatives.
  - Start-up energy is crucial – many existing commercial ICs are not optimized for low energy start-up but focus on a single start-up event with sleep mode and periodic wake-up for life.
- Next Generation Products will support Low Energy start-up
  - Focus on minimizing start-up energy and initialization code, crystal oscillator start-up, etc...

Reimagining Power: Energy and the Utility of milliJoules

- Advances in Kinetic Energy Generators and highly-efficient energy conversion circuitry yield small form factor (scalable) devices capable of delivering 3+ mJ of net energy to an application.
- Energy = Volts (V) x Current (A) x Time (s); with fixed energy, you have a finite amount of time for application execution.
  - 3 mJ = 1.8V x 10mA x **167ms**
  - 3 mJ = 3.0V x 10mA x **100ms**
- Any combination of Voltage x Current x Time = 3mJ can be delivered.

So, what can we do with 3mJ of energy?

3mJ Kinetic Application Example

Industrial 22mm Industrial Switch

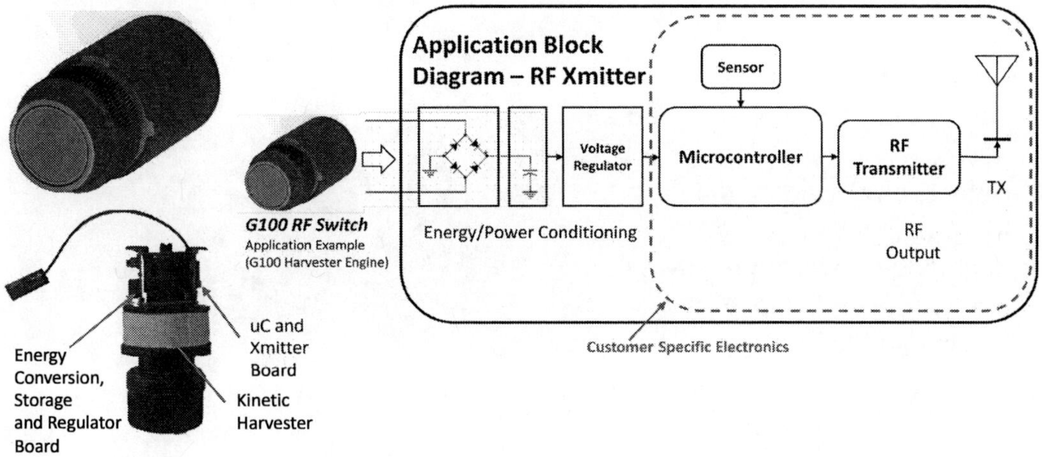

3mJ Kinetic Application Example

iOS User Interface

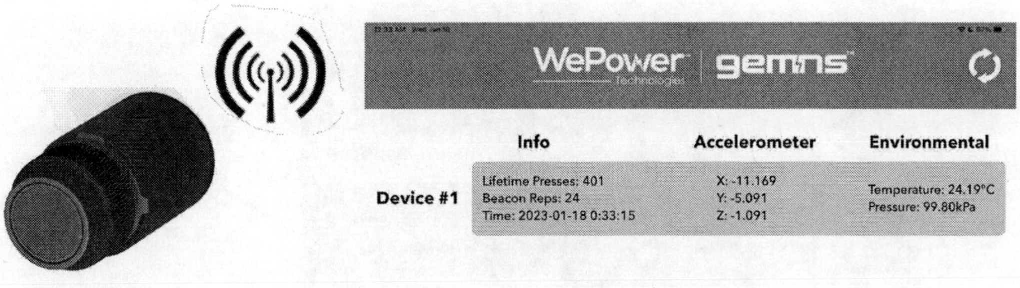

iOS Application Receiver

Wireless Liquid Leak Detector Application

- Integrated Kinetic Harvester, Energy Conversion Board, and RF Radio.
- Detects any liquid media.
- Ideal Energy Source – no degradation over time, always ready, 100% reliable, easily "rechargeable" energy.

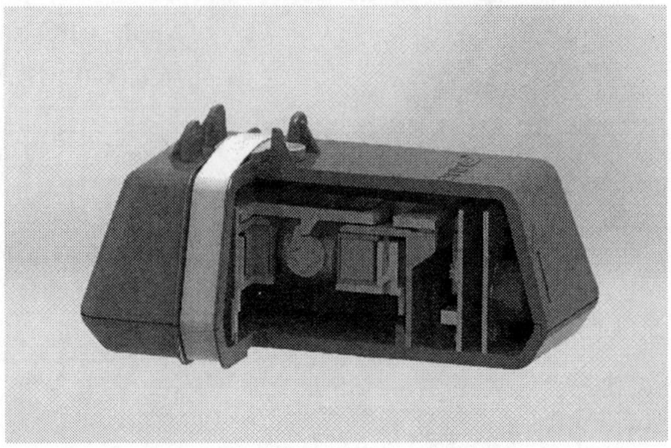

Kinetic Evaluation/Development Hardware

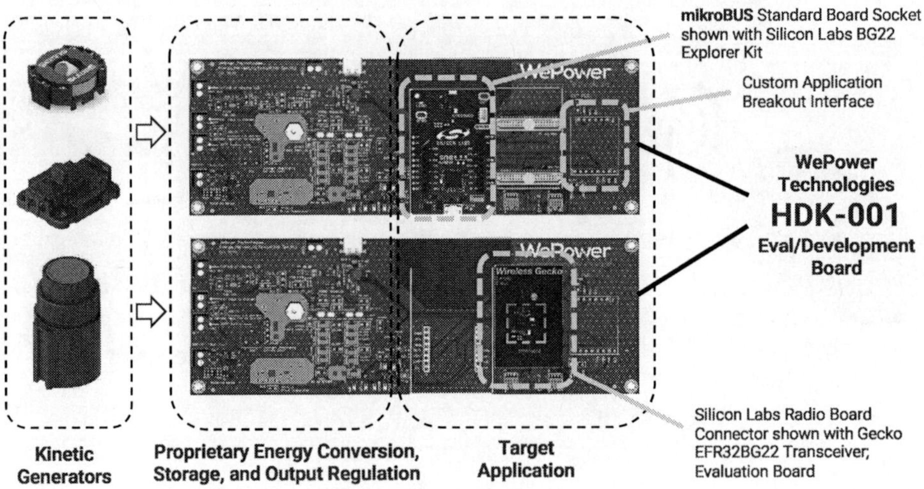

Kinetic Harvesting Applications
Endless Possibilities

#SensorsConverge

Sensors Converge

Kinetic Harvesting Benefits

- No Batteries – no hazardous chemicals for disposal.
- Energy Generator Service-free, Maintenance-free for life of Product.
- Remote Location placement.
- Wireless operation – drastic reduction in wiring and integration costs.
- Software Configuration with unique IDs.
- Scalable Technologies.
- Reliable and Realizable Technology available today.

#SensorsConverge

Sensors Converge

Sensors Converge

Solar Energy Harvesting for Maintenance Free Sensor Deployment

June 24–26, 2024 | Santa Clara, CA

#SensorsConverge

What is Energy Harvesting?

- What Is Energy Harvesting? Is It Really Free Energy??
- What Types of Energy can be Harvested? **Light,** Motion/Vibration, Electrodynamic/Magnetic, Heat, Electromagnetic

Example of Outdoor EH System

Electronics

Solar Panel

Charge Controller, Battery

Example of Indoor EH System

Storage Element

EH PMIC

Solar Panel

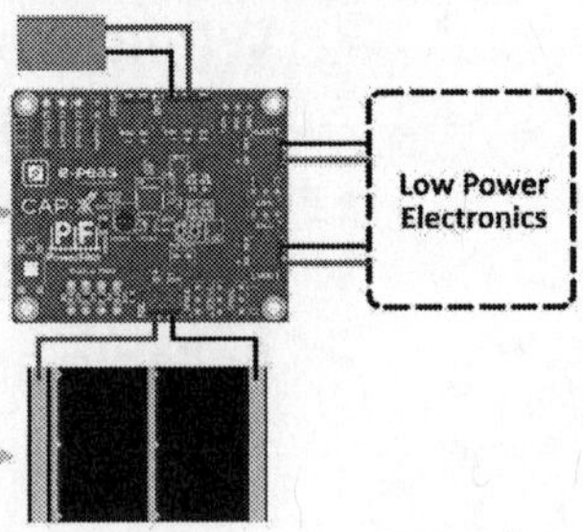

#SensorsConverge

1

Sensors Converge

What are the Benefits?

- Enables large, long term, and remote sensor deployments collecting large data sets in many markets
  - Agriculture
  - Retail
  - Transportation
  - Industrial

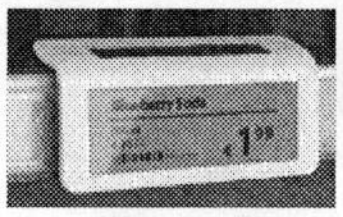

Shelf Labels
https://www.epishine.com/industries/retail

Specialty Gas Monitoring

Soil Conditions

Remote Camera System

Livestock Health
Allflex Livestock Monitoring | Merck Animal Health USA (merck-animal-health-usa.com)

Transportation Refrigeration/ Telematics Unit

#SensorsConverge

Sensors Converge

What are the Costs? – Coin Cell vs Indoor Solar Panel

- Cost of indoor solar energy harvesting
  - Solar panel cost \$1-\$5
  - Energy harvesting electronics cost \$3-\$5
- Cost of ownership for battery powered system

Time to Change Battery (minutes)	15
Cost of Battery	\$0.20
Hourly wage of Employee Performing Battery Change	\$16.00
Battery Change Interval (years)	3
Device Lifetime (years)	10
Price of Solar Energy Harvesting System	\$7.00

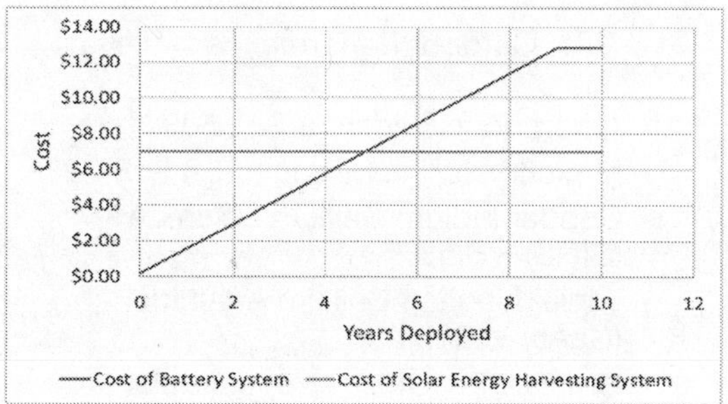

- Array of 20,000 sensors installed in a facility requires a full time employee just to replace batteries
- Cost of grid wired installation- \$6-8 per foot (2022 Electrical Work Pricing Guide | Cost Calculator & Prices List (homeguide.com))
- Significant quantity of battery waste generated without solar

#SensorsConverge

Sensors Converge

What are the Costs? – Transportation Telematics

- Cost of transportation solar \$3.30 to \$10 per watt including charge controllers and cabling
- Costs of drawing from starter battery without solar
  - Jump starts – \$150 each
  - No start on refer – Lost Load
  - Idling diesel engine – 1 gal/hr
- Benefits of adding solar
  - Increased battery lifetime for lead acid batteries from 2yr to 5-7yr
  - Improved up time for telematics system
  - Reduced maintenance costs
  - Vehicle readiness
  - Payback in 1-3 years depending on vehicle usage

Indoor vs Outdoor – Which Technology is Best?

Outdoor Performance

- Amorphous Silicon (a-Si) ~6%
- Monocrystalline Silicon (c-Si) ~18-22%
- Copper Indium Gallium Selenide (CIGS) ~ 8.5%
- Triple Junction Gallium Arsenide (GaAs) ~30%
- Organic PV (OPV) – Not suitable

Indoor Performance

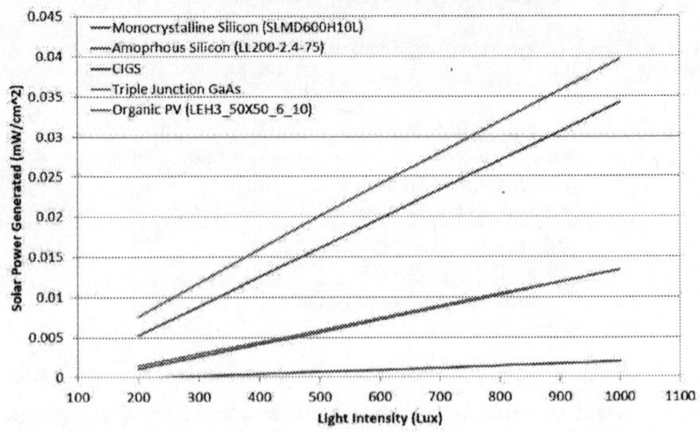

Getting Started

Development kits are a great way to start!

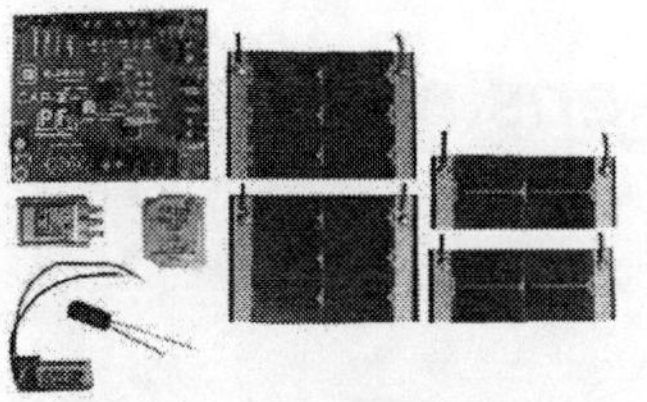

DEV-EPEAS-CAPXX
https://www.powerfilmsolar.com/products/development-kits/solar-development-kit-with-e-peas-pmic-cap-xx-supercapacitors

EK01LEH3_6
https://se.farnell.com/en-SE/epishine/ek01leh3-6/eval-kit-light-energy-harvesting/dp/3771691

EVSLB-EHEP02A
https://nichiconbattery.com/product/designtool/

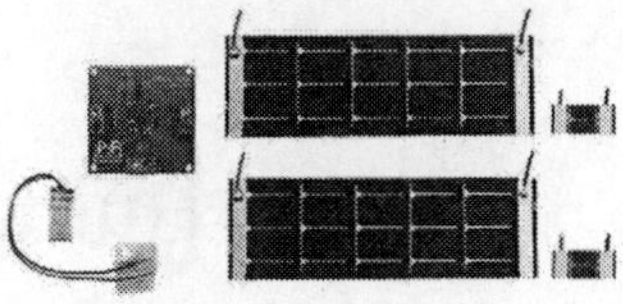

DEV-BASIC
https://www.powerfilmsolar.com/products/development-kits/solar-development-kit

Questions? Visit PowerFilm at booth 424

#SensorsConverge

Sensors Converge

Sensors Converge | June 24-26, 2024 Santa Clara, CA

Low-power capacitive sensing technology for Human Body sensing applications

Gary Johnson
gary.johnson@microdul.com

MICRODUL
Customized Swiss Microelectronics

Contents

- Microdul - introduction
- Human Body Detection – Capacitance sensing
- EU-2020 Project AMANDA Example
- Low power ASIC for electronic temperature monitoring for wound care
- InPlay Inc & Microdul collaboration Temp sensing Bluetooth beacon
- Links & contact

06-26-2024

MICRODUL
Customized Swiss Microelectronics

Introduction to Microdul

- Microdul was founded in 1991 by management buy out of Faselec AG (Philips Semiconductors Hybrid Department) Zurich
- 98 Employees, 26% development,

  32 with university education (9 doctor degrees, 15 master degrees, 8 bachelor degrees)
- Turnover 65% medical, 35% industrial
- Three Product Lines:
  - Modules From schematic to module
  - Semiconductors From idea to ASIC (nA, nW)
  - Thick-film Printing on ceramic substrates
- ISO 9001: 2015 and ISO 13485: 2016
  - Microdul is ISO13485 certified since 2003

MICRODUL
Customized Swiss Microelectronics

Introduction to Microdul Semiconductors

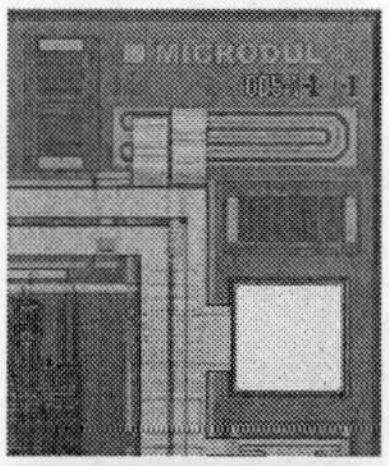

Business models

- ASICs
- Standard products

Value proposition

- Custom ASIC product development and supply
- Ultra low-power analog/mixed-signal design (nA, nW)
- Industrialisation including test, logistics, quality and supply
- Packaging portfolio including plastic package, die delivery, flip-chip or chip-scale packaging.
- Support over product life-cycle.
- Extensive experience with capacitive sensing, temperature sensing and monitoring, 32kHz timing (RTC) and power management.

MICRODUL
Customized Swiss Microelectronics

Value of Body detection for Medical device

- Patient compliance improves outcomes
  - Patients can be reminded to use or wear device
- Clinician decisions improved with patient usage dada
  - AI data tools require accurate data to be useful
- System energy use management
  - Smaller battery and device
    - Lowers cost
  - Less frequent or shorter recharge times
    - Increases compliance

MICRODUL
Customized Swiss Microelectronics

Low-Power Human Body Detector (HBD) application example

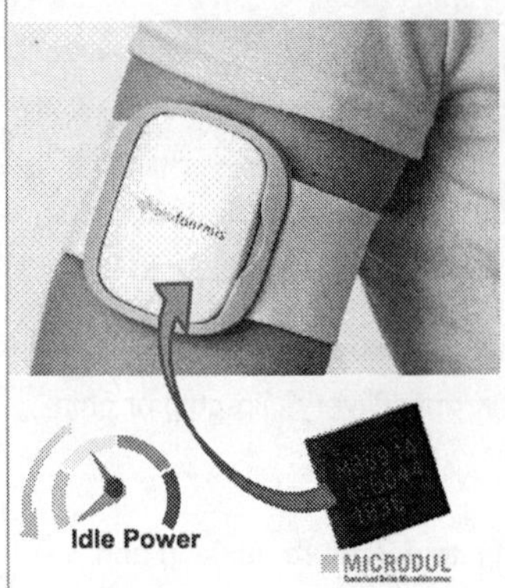

Capacitive sensor in fF range

- Idle current 50nA
- Average current for 2 measurements/s in switch mode typ. 725nA (1 channel, no noise filter)
- Two capacitive sensor channels
- Meter (measures capacitance) or switch mode (compares capacitance)
- Sensor capacitance range 0-1.6pF
- Voltage range 1.8-4.5V
- Active current during measurement typ. 11µA
- Temperature range -40° to 85°C
- I²C interface or standalone operation
- No external components required
- Available in QFN16 or chip-scale package
- Video: https://youtu.be/FGz2HWKBLwE

MICRODUL
Customized Swiss Microelectronics

Principle of low-power HBD

- SA is driven and SB receives
- There is a capacitance CS between SA and SB
- An electric field is present between SA and SB
- When a finger touches the cover, the field lines are interrupted and the observed value of CS will change

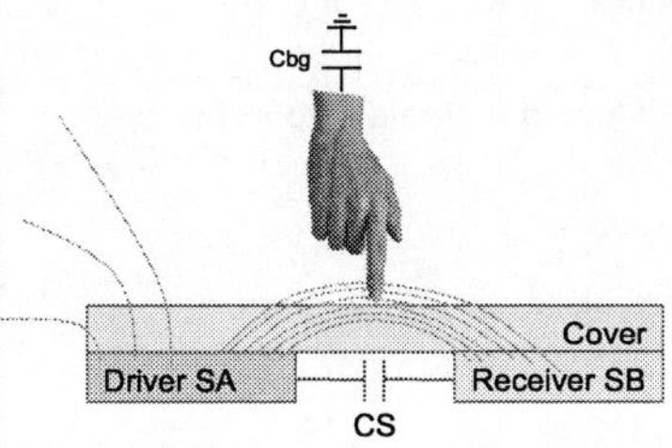

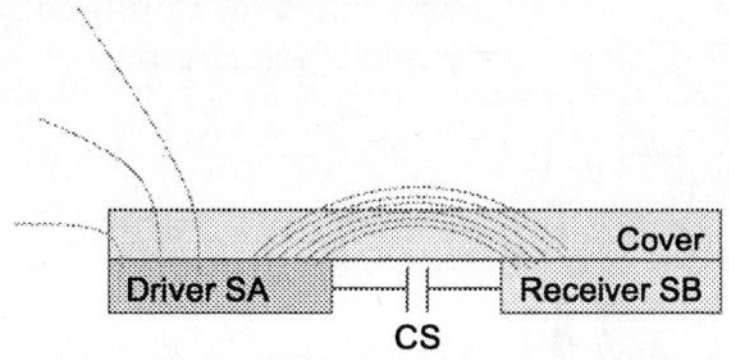

Principle of low-power HBD

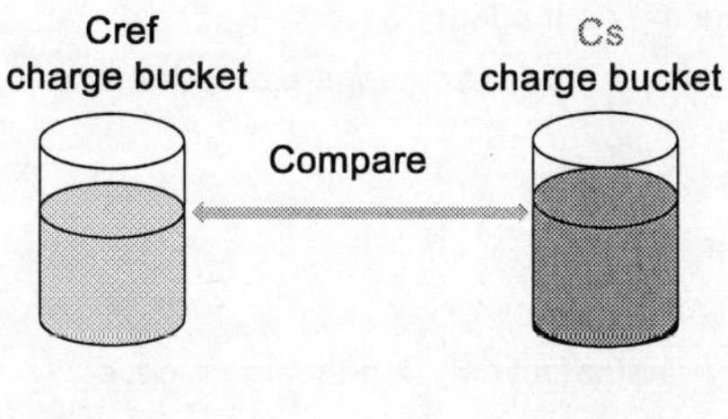

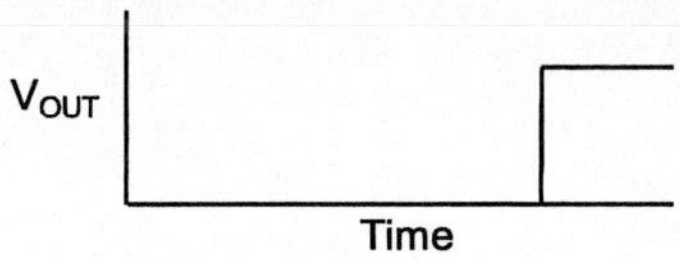

- The principle is to compare charge.
- We can visualise a reference (Cref) capacitor bucket that holds a reference charge determined by a DAC voltage that can be set by the user.
- We can visualise a sampling (Cs) capacitor bucket that holds the sampled charge.
- When the MS8891A is in switch mode, a fixed charge on Cref is compared to the charge on Cs.
- In measurement mode the charge in the reference (Cref) capacitor bucket is varied in a successive approximation.

HBD sensor electrodes

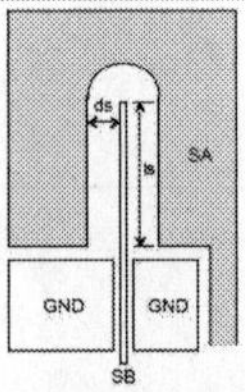

Distance ds [mm]	Length ls [mm]	Approx. sensor capacitance [fF]
2.5	4	160
1.6	4	220
0.6	4	320

- Two electrodes SA (driver) and SB (receiver)
- SA typically surrounds SB
- Different shapes possible, some examples are shown to the left. The table shows some examples of electrode capacitance as a result of the geometry.
- SB is shielded from other dynamic signals using a shield (ground or any other static signal)

HBD characteristics

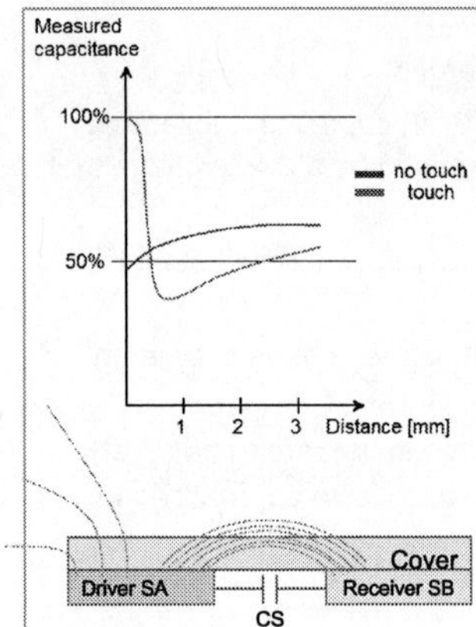

- Very low power (0.72-1.5μA depending on modes)
- Can measure the capacitance (measure mode) or compare to a threshold (switch mode)
- Digital 8-bit output value
- Is suitable for head/body detection
- Tolerant to supply noise
- Touch can increase, or decrease, or not affect CS, depending on cover thickness (see diagram left).

Block diagram

Basic functionality

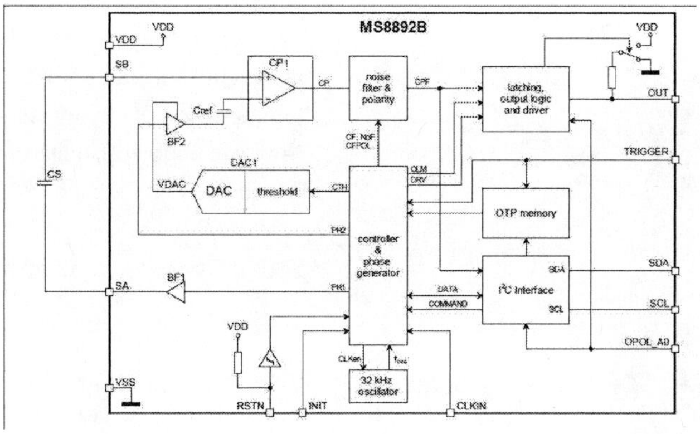

MICRODUL
Customized Swiss Microelectronics

EU-2020 Project AMANDA

AMANDA
The world in your hands

AutonoMous self powered miniAturized iNtelligent sensor for environmental sensing anD asset tracking in smArt IoT environments

AMANDA

- Autonomous, connected sensor card
- Ultra-low-power, ultra long life – 10 years
- Solid state battery, no battery change required
- Small and thin (3mm thickness)
- Multi-sensor (see next slide)

Microdul

- MS8892 Ultra-low-power capacitive sensor 65nA used for wake-up
- MS1089 Ultra-low-power temperature sensor with "zero" standby current

Use Cases

- Environment monitoring and reporting (comfort monitoring, fire monitoring)
- Assets tracking and occupancy monitoring (parking lot, asset access & localization)
- Mitigating the effects of the current pandemic (vaccine monitoring, crowd counting)

This project has received funding from the European Union's Horizon 2020 Research and innovation programme under Grant Agreement n°825464

MICRODUL
Customized Swiss Microelectronics

AMANDA, save power, wake-up with MS8892

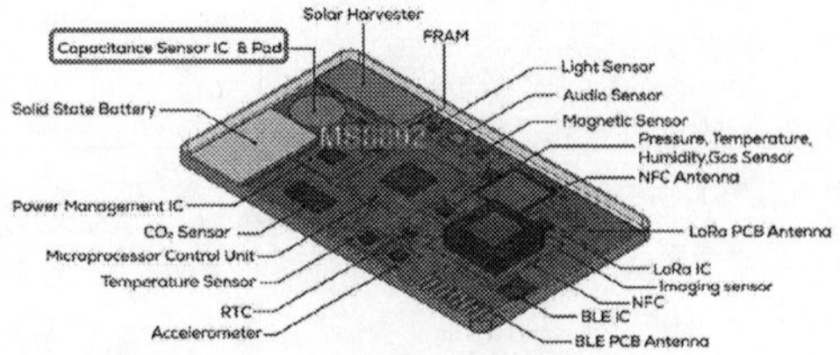

Small

QFN 3x3mm

CSP 1.52 x 1.03mm

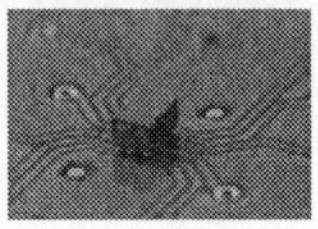

MS8892

- 65nA external clock, 725nA internal clock
- Capacitance measurement or switch mode
- Compensation of factory tolerances possible
- Measures up to 1pF, voltage range 1.8-4.5V
- Autonomous operation or I²C with MCU

MS8892 Cap-Sensor Current

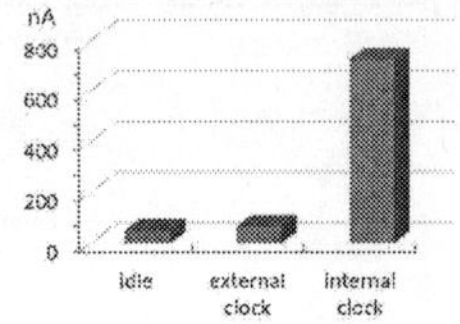

06-26-2024

MICRODUL
Customized Swiss Microelectronics

AMANDA, save power, wake-up with MS8892

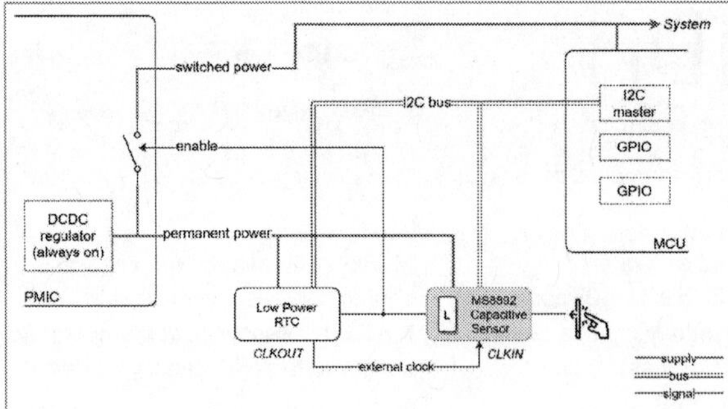

- The permanent power, from the PMIC to the RTC and the capacitive sensor is always on.
- The MCU and rest of system are supplied by a switched power supply.
- System power is switched on when there is an alarm from the RTC or a touch event at the capacitive sensor.
- The power state is latched (L) in the MS8892.
- The RTC enable and the MS8892 enable are low active, open drain types.
- Either the RTC or the MS8892 can cause the power state (L) to be switched to power-on.
- The MCU switches off (its) power via I²C or GPIO
- When the system is powered down, I = ~300nA.

06-26-2024

MICRODUL
Customized Swiss Microelectronics

AMANDA, temperature sensor with “zero” standby current MS1089

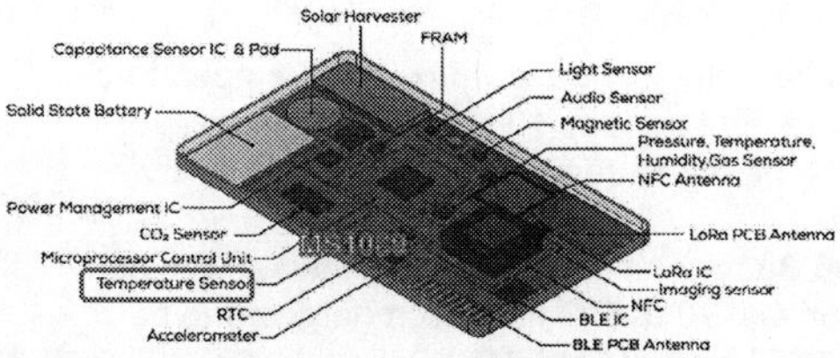

MS1089

- “Zero standby” (~5nA) current in sleep mode
- Average 27nA at one measurement per minute
- 70μA peak current during measurement
- Supply range 1.8V – 3.6V
- ±0.3°C from 10°C to 50°C, -40°C to 85° range
- Suitable for autonomous systems

Small

CSP 1.17 x 1.095mm

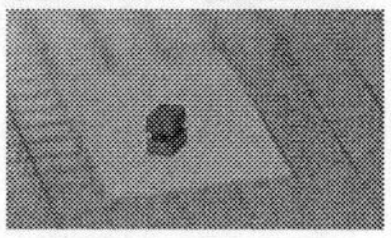

MS1089 “Zero” Standby current

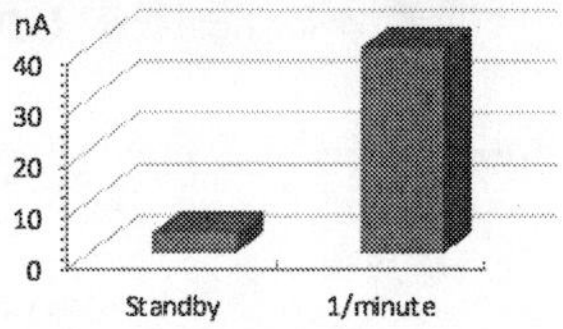

MICRODUL
Customized Swiss Microelectronics

Semiconductors – Innovation Study Temperature Monitor with a Blue-Tooth Beacon

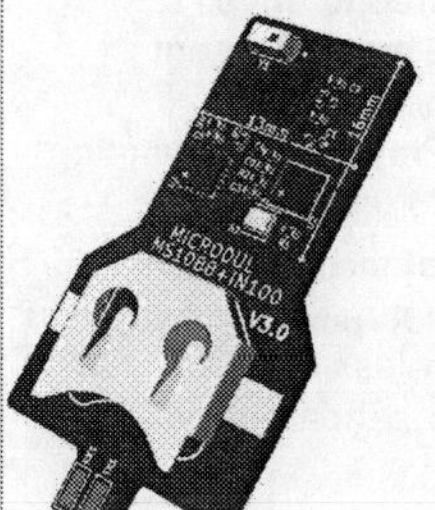

What?

- MS1088 temperature sensor
- IN100 NanoBeacon BTLE (Bluetooth Low Energy) transmitter
- RF antenna with matching circuit
- 26MHz XTAL (for RF Tx)
- I2C external resistors (not mounted)
- POR circuit for IN100 (RC timing on the enable)
- Lithium coin cell battery (3.0V, CR1216, CR1220 or CR1225 for this specific demoboard)

MICRODUL
Customized Swiss Microelectronics

Semiconductors – Innovation Study
Temperature Monitor with a Blue-Tooth Beacon

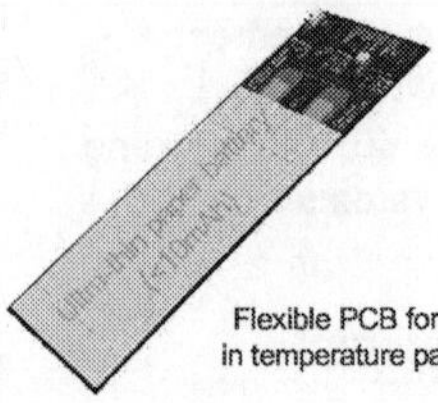

Flexible PCB for use in temperature patches

Why?

- Targeting the RF Tagging market with an ultra low power RF temperature sensor (~1uA for 1min measurement period). 10mAh battery capacity enables operation for >1year (one measurement & transmission every 60sec; i.e. >520'000 cycles).
- Targeting the wireless Human Body Temperature Sensor market with our ultra accurate MS1089 sensor with ±0.025°C resolution (targeted to be compliant with both the ISO80601 and ATSM E1112).
- Space-efficient power source (coin cell, paper battery ultra-cap).
- Low external component count (C's + quartz). Possible to implement in any rigid form PCB and Flexible PCB.

MICRODUL
Customized Swiss Microelectronics

Semiconductors – Innovation Study
Temperature Monitor with a Blue-Tooth Beacon

MICRODUL
Customized Swiss Microelectronics

INPLAY

- **InPlay Inc**, in collaboration with **Microdul AG**, is delighted to unveil a reference design for a medical-grade body temperature measurement wireless system. This ambitious endeavor harnesses the power of Microdul's MS108x-series temperature sensors and InPlay's award-winning IN100 NanoBeacon™ SoC integrated with Bluetooth 5.3 technology
- **Microdul** and **InPlay** showcased a live demonstration of the reference design at the Wireless IoT Tomorrow 2023 show in Wiesbaden, Germany, in October 2023. Attendees witnessed the remarkable wireless body temperature monitoring solution that aims to redefine healthcare monitoring systems firsthand.
- **Microdul** and **InPlay** are looking forward to forging ahead on the healthcare sector's digital transformation journey, offering avant-garde solutions that promise to elevate patient care and operational efficiency.

MICRODUL
Customized Swiss Microelectronics

Introducing Microdul / Inplay Flexible Wireless Disposable Temperature Patch

A combination between Microdul's MS1088 high accuracy temperature sensor and the InPlay IN100 BLE beacon:

- Measurement accuracy +- 0.3 C
- Low power
- 10 mAh battery enables >1 year lifetime at 1 minute transmission and measurement interval
- Total thickness below 3 mm

Applications:

- Wireless sensor tags
- Human body temperature
- Wearables
- Environment temperature monitoring and HVAC
- Battery Management
- Thermostat controls
- Power-Supply Monitoring

>Beacon
- Bluetooth 5.3 compliant

>Memory
- 4KB SRAM, 4Kb OTP memory

>RF performance
- Bluetooth SIG compliant 2.4GHz band
- Tx power, up to +5dBm, w/ programmable output power

>Power Consumption
- 2.3uA @ 10s interval, 900nA @ 1min

>Security
Authentication of Beacon ID and Privacy of adv. Payload

>Peripheral Interface
- UART
- I2C
- 11-bit ADC, 100Ksps, up to 3 channels
- Integrated ultra-low leakage load switch

>Reduced eBOM
- 1 Crystal and 2 caps, 50 Ohm antenna pin(No RF matching)

>Wide Operating Voltage Range
- 1.1 - 3.6V input- works with 1.5v disposable batteries

>Package
- WLCSP, 1.1x2.0mmx0.35mm, DFN8, QFN18

InPlay Technologies

Thanks!

Contact

Microdul AG
Grubenstrasse 9
CH-8045 Zürich

www.microdul.com
Gary.johnson@@microdul.com

+1-651—323-0510

06-26-2024

Sensors Converge

Reducing time-to-market for digital sensors

The benefits of a combined Lab and Fab test system

June 24–26, 2024 | Santa Clara, CA

#SensorsConverge

Table of contents

Digital sensor design & production cycle

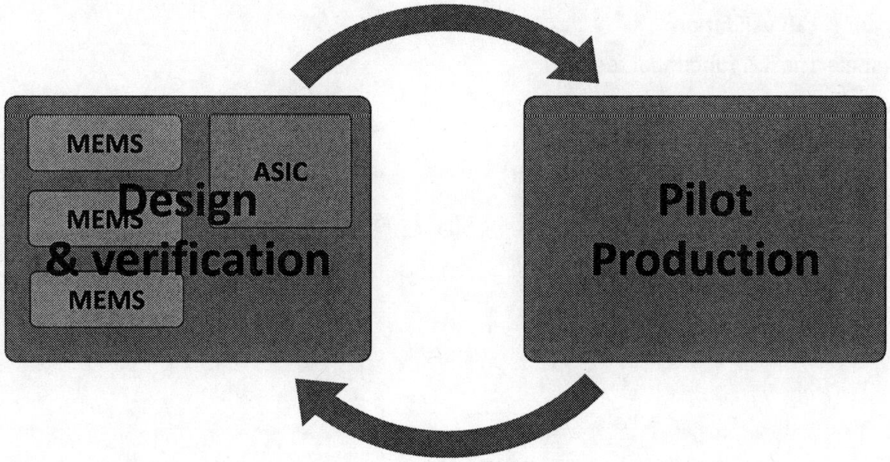

Pilot production - getting first packaged & tested parts

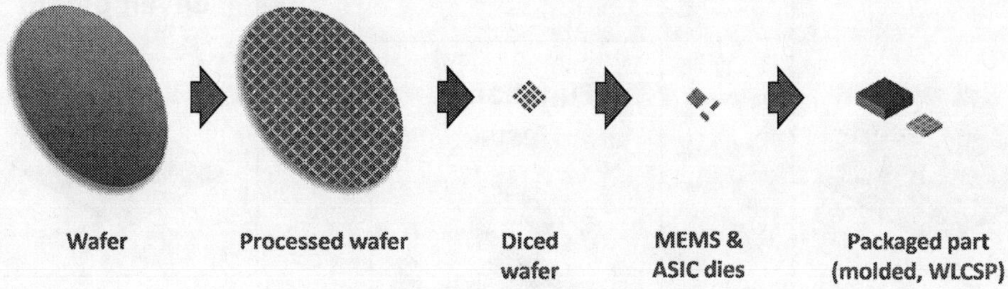

Functional validation of first packaged parts in the Lab

1st bring-up & Lab validation:

- Do first electrical & functional tests
- Characterize the sensor and gather first key parameters (used for preliminary DS)
- Further develop & optimize SW (low layer)
- Provide (alpha) silicon to key customers

Sensor carrier board

#SensorsConverge | The benefits of a combined Lab and Fab test system | 6/25/2024 | Sensors Converge

Lab validation setups for different tests

Electrical Tests

Functional Tests

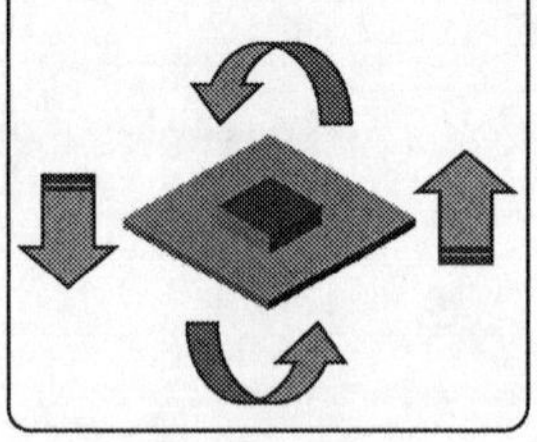

Software development

#SensorsConverge | The benefits of a combined Lab and Fab test system | 6/25/2024 | Sensors Converge

Functional validation of first packaged parts in the Lab

Lab setups are often designed to get quick first hand info about the sensor

- Sensor is applied on different "carriers" to accommodate specific tests (sockets etc.)
- Some sensor IDM's have developed **standard "carriers"** to simplify Lab work
- These carriers can also become evaluation or shuttle boards for end customers

Functional validation of first packaged parts in the Lab

Lab setups used to apply controlled environmental conditions to validate functions

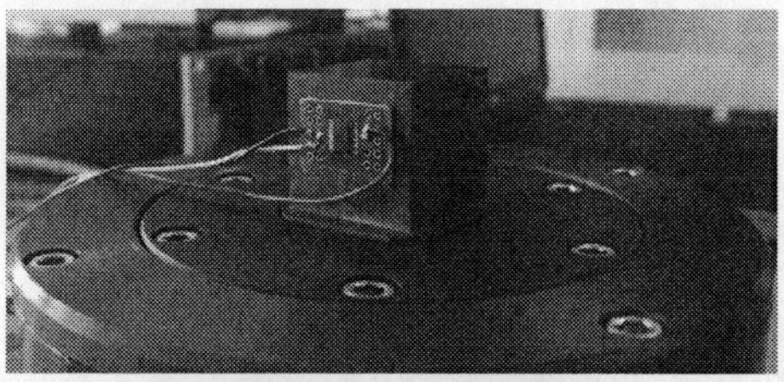

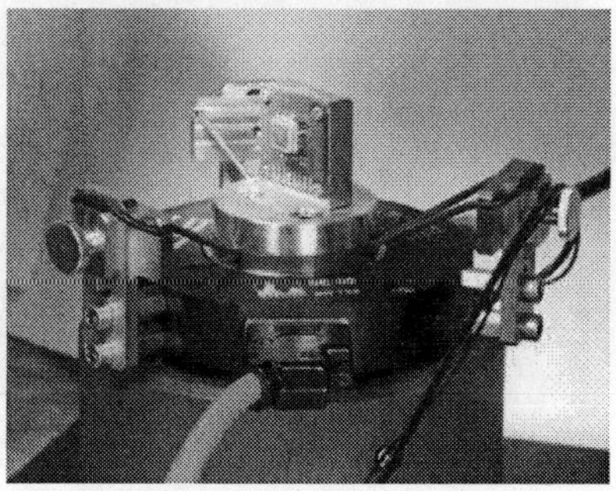

Functional validation of first packaged parts in the Lab

But what is used to communicate with the sensor during Lab testing ?

Developer setup based on standard sensor shuttle and 3rd party MCU Evaluation board

* image source: https://community.bosch-sensortec.com/t5/MEMS-sensors-forum/BMI055-Shuttle-Board-I2C-connection/td-p/25955

#SensorsConverge The benefits of a combined Lab and Fab test system 6/25/2024 Sensors Converge

Functional validation of first packaged parts in the Lab

But what is used to communicate with the sensor during Lab testing ?

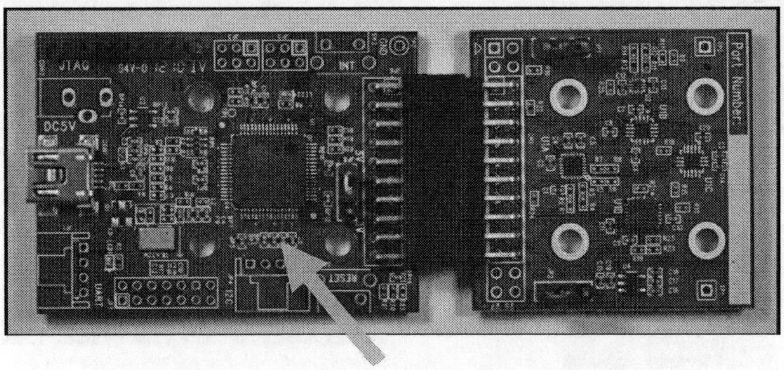

Standard MCU host board developed by sensor IDM

#SensorsConverge The benefits of a combined Lab and Fab test system 6/25/2024 Sensors Converge

What is always required to test sensors in the Lab ?

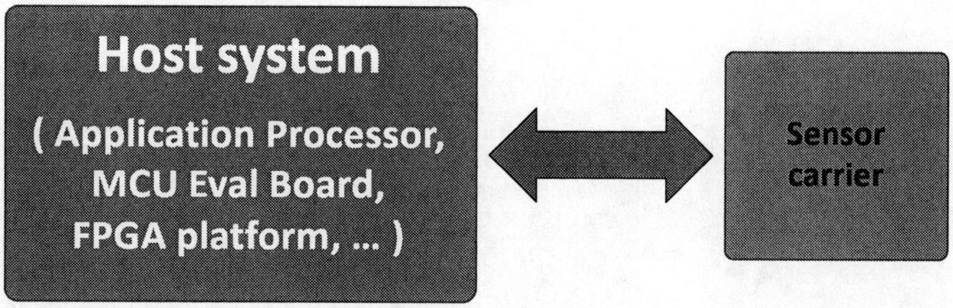

Simplified Lab setups with standard host systems

Standardized Host (test) system

- Support for different digital sensor interfaces & protocols
- Allows addition of new digital sensor protocols
- Integrated supply, measurement & test capabilities
- Allows development of standard test procedures for different sensor derivatives
- Allows easy connection of different sensor carrier boards/shuttles/sockets

Standardized System Level Test solution for the Lab

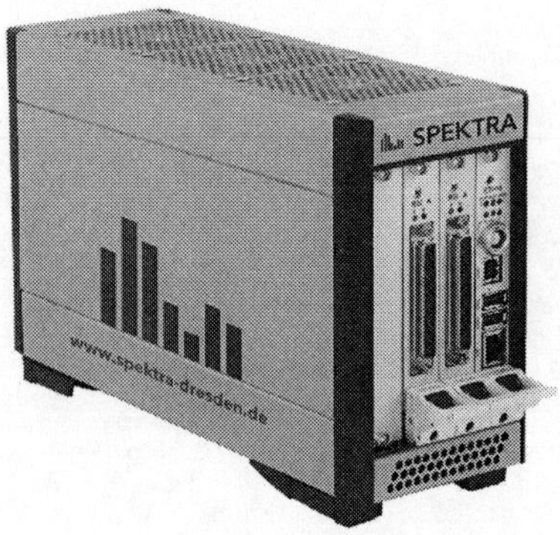

- Integrated DVM with pin multiplexer
- Multiple PMU for DUT supply & measurement
- Support for wide range of digital sensor protocols (SPI, I2C, CAN, JTAG, PSI5, LIN, RS232, SENT, ZACwire, mipi I3C®, TDM, PDM, …
- Digital Pin driver to adjust logic levels
- Freely configurable IO concept
- Timing measurement capabilities
- Simplified TCP/IP control interface
- Fast real-time testing capabilities
- Built-in self-calibration

➢ **Fast & flexible Lab test of up to 8 DUT**

Final Test solution for the Fab

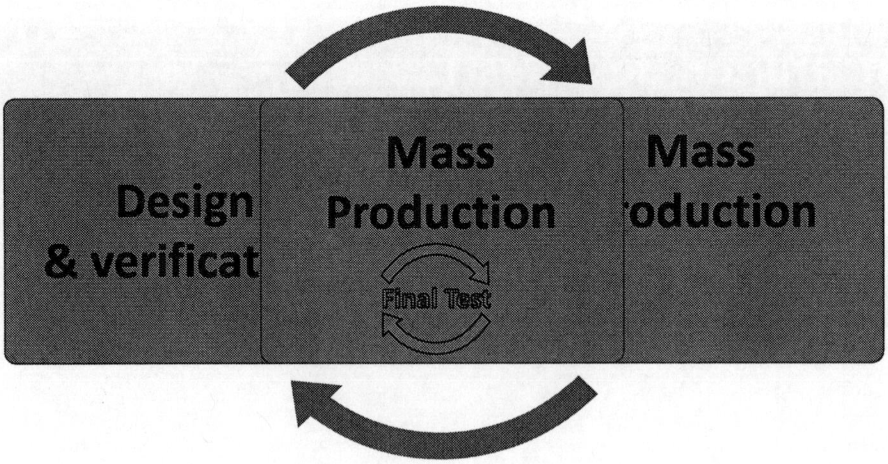

Final Test solution for the Fab

- **Automated Handling (Loading, Unloading, Binning etc.) of large number of sensors**
- **Sensor stimulus by automation system (rotation table, pressure chamber, etc.)**
- **All test steps optimized to increase UPH (units per hour)**
- **Device specific „carriers" like customized socket boards, connectors, cables**
- **Large final test systems for MEMS sensors primarily used by IDM's & OSAT's**

➢ **Final test „host" systems mostly realized by expensive ATE equipment**
➢ **They need specially developed test programs**
➢ **Test iterations require new Lab test development & new final test programs**
➢ **High cost when test scaling is required to increase production output**

Reuse of Lab System Level Test solution also for the Fab

Benefits of reusing Lab test system also for Final Test

- Reuse tests already developed during Lab testing
- Use optimized real-time test capabilities
- Better system knowledge transfer from development team to final test team
- Fast test iteration cycles as Fab test issues can easier be replicated by Lab validation
- Simpler test devlopment for device derivatives
- Easy to scale to accomodate higher demand
- Test cost reduction due to standardized components for Lab and Fab setups

➢ **Significant faster Time-to-Market !!**
➢ **Significant lower cost for FT**

#SensorsConverge | The benefits of a combined Lab and Fab test system | 6/25/2024 | Sensors Converge

Thank you

Booth #1441
www.spektra-dresden.com

SPEKTRA
Ready for TESTelligence!

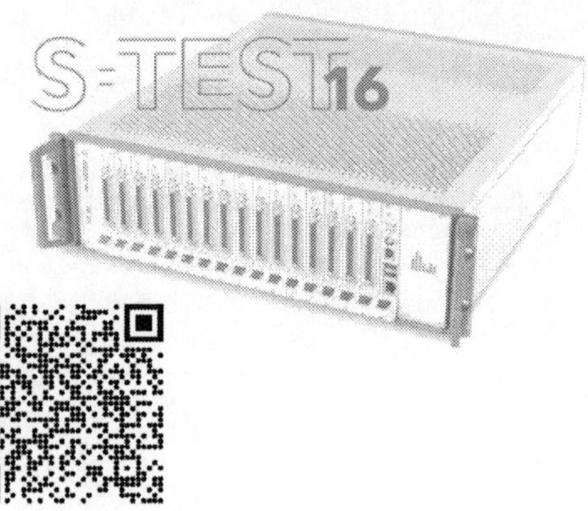

More info:

#SensorsConverge | The benefits of a combined Lab and Fab test system | 6/25/2024 | Sensors Converge

Sensors Converge

Interoperability Testing Methods of Smart Sensors in IoT/IIoT Applications

June 24–26, 2024 | Santa Clara, CA

Dr. Eugene Song
Electronics Engineer

IoT Devices and Infrastructures Group
Smart Connected System Division (SCSD)
Communications Technology Laboratory (CTL)
National Institute of Standards and Technology (NIST)

#SensorsConverge

Interoperability Testing Methods of Smart Sensors in IoT/IIoT Applications

Agenda

1. **Sensors Are Used Everywhere**
2. **Interoperability Challenges for Smart Sensors in IoT/IIoT**
3. **How to Overcome Interoperability Challenges**
4. **Interoperability Testing Methods of Standard-based Smart Sensors**
5. **Interoperability Test Cases of Smart Sensors**
6. **Key Takeaways**

#SensorsConverge

Sensors Converge

1. Sensors Are Used Everywhere

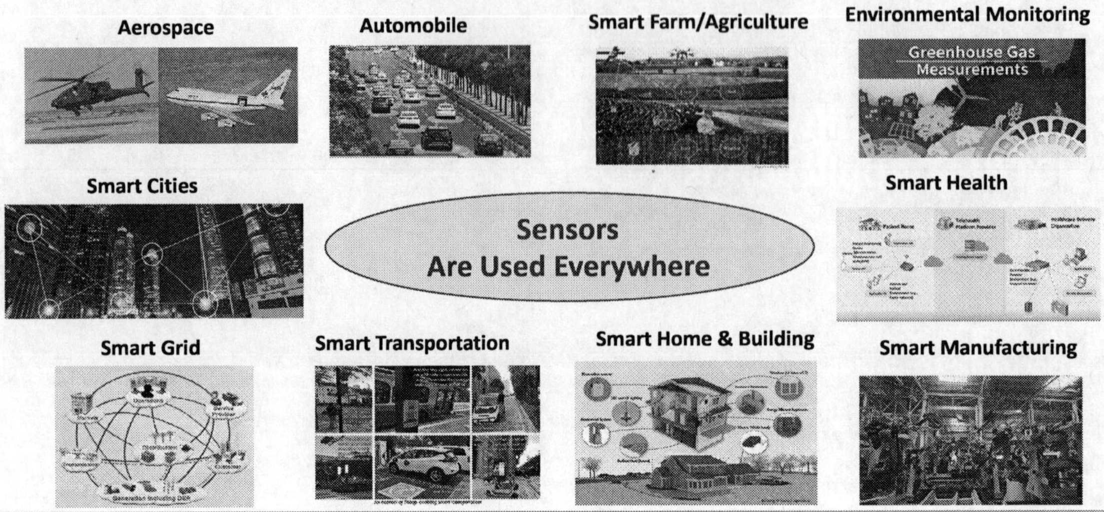

#SensorsConverge

Sensors Converge

2. Interoperability Challenges of Smart Sensors in IoT/IIoT Applications

What is A Smart Sensor?

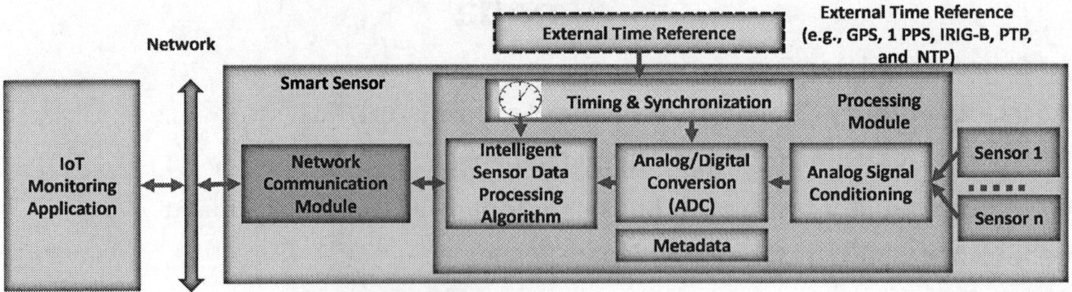

Smart Sensor Capabilities:

- Sensing
- Signal/Data Processing & Conversion
- Time & Synchronization
- Metadata
- Network Communication

#SensorsConverge

Sensors Converge

2. Interoperability Challenges of Smart Sensors in IoT/IIoT Applications (Cont'd)

Interoperability challenges between IoT application and sensor network gateway (<u>network Level</u>):

- Diverse wireline or wireless connectivity (e.g., LTE/5G/Ethernet/Internet,...)
- Diverse proprietary or standardized protocols (TCP/UDP, MQTT, HTTP, Web Service, ...)

➢ Message payload contents and formats are **<u>vendor-dependent – not interoperable among different vendor products.</u>**

Interoperability challenges between sensors and senser network gateway (<u>sensor Level</u>):

- Wireline or wireless connectivity and protocols (e.g., LoRaWAN, NB-IoT, WiFi, BlueTooth, and ZigBee, ...)
- Diverse proprietary or standardized protocols (e.g., TCP/UDP)

➢ Message payload contents and formats are **<u>vendor-dependent – not interoperable among different vendor products.</u>**

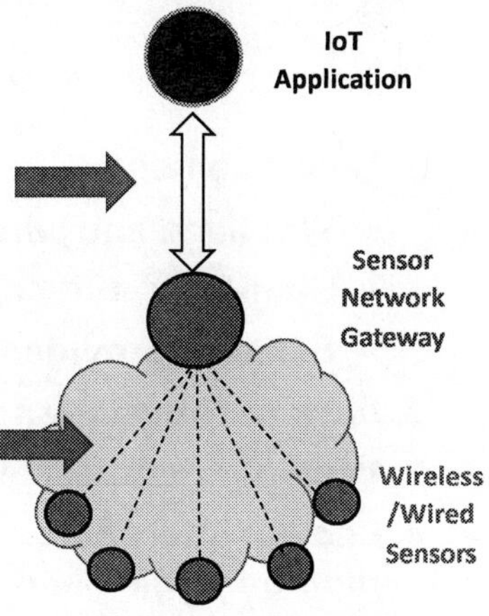

IoT Sensor Network

2. Interoperability Challenges of Smart Sensors in IoT/IIoT Applications (Cont'd)

Interoperability challenges in sensor network gateway (network Level):

- Wireline or wireless connectivity (e.g., LTE/5G/Ethernet/Internet)
- Diverse propitiatory or standardized protocols (TCP/UDP, MQTT, HTTP, Web Service, ...)

➢ Message payload contents and formats are **standardized** (e.g., **<u>P1451.0 network service messages)</u>** - help to achieve network level interoperability.

Interoperability Challenges in sensors and actuators (sensor Level):

- Wireline or wireless Connectivity (e. g. LoRa WAN, NB-IoT, WiFi, Bluetooth, and ZigBee ...)
- Diverse propitiatory or standardized protocols (e.g., TCP/UDP)

➢ Message payload contents and formats are **standardized** (e.g., **<u>P1451.0 sensor service messages)</u>** - help to achieve sensor level interoperability.

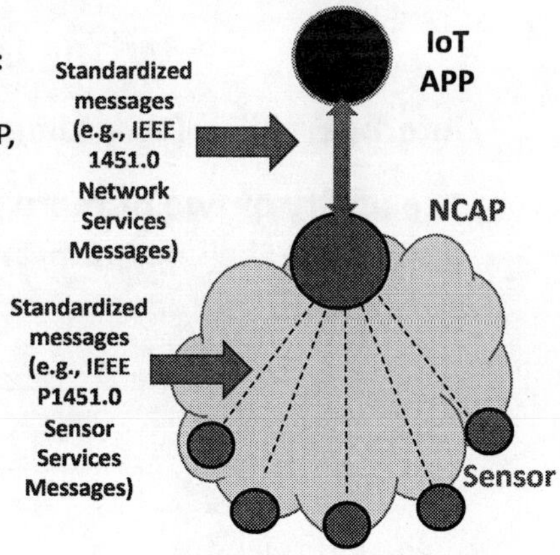

IEEE 1451-based Sensor Network

2. Interoperability Challenges of Smart Sensors in IoT/IIoT Applications (Cont'd)

Summary of Interoperability Challenges of Smart Sensors

1. **Heterogeneity:**
   - **Wirelines and wireless connectivity**
   - **Standards and communication protocols**
   - **Sensors provided by diverse vendors and manufacturers**
2. **Lack of robust standards and standards harmonization**
3. **Lack of interoperability test and plugfest**
4. **Lack of interoperability modeling, measurement & assessment methodologies and software tools**

3. How to Overcome Interoperability Challenges

What Is Interoperability?

Interoperability (according to IEEE):

The ability of two or more systems or components to exchange information and to use the information that has been exchanged.

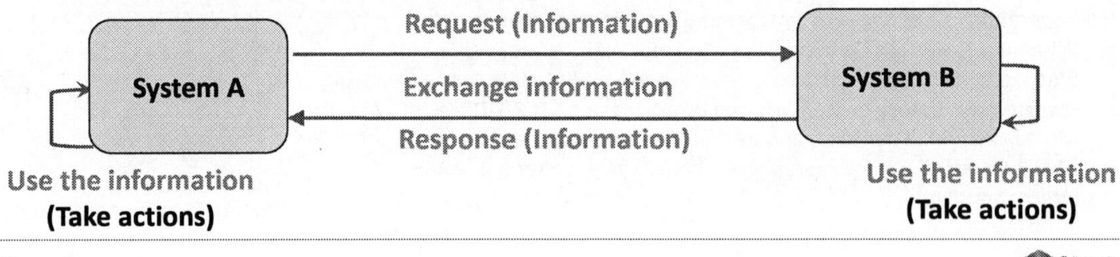

3. How to Overcome Interoperability Challenges (Cont'd)

Interoperability of Smart Sensor and Its Client (extended for M&A) :

The ability of smart sensor and its client to exchange information and to use the information that has been exchanged <u>through standard communication protocols to achieve the specific functions or goals.</u>

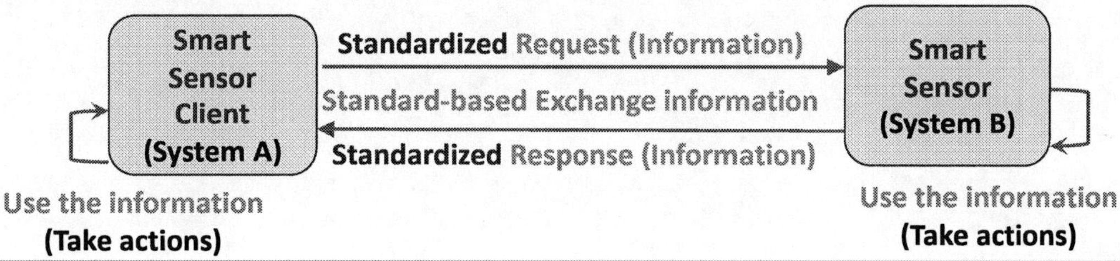

3. How to Overcome Interoperability Challenges (Cont'd)

What Is Interoperability Testing?

- **Interoperability testing is a process to verify if two or more systems (implementations of the standard in SW, HW, SW & HW) can be <u>interoperate</u> based on the standard.**

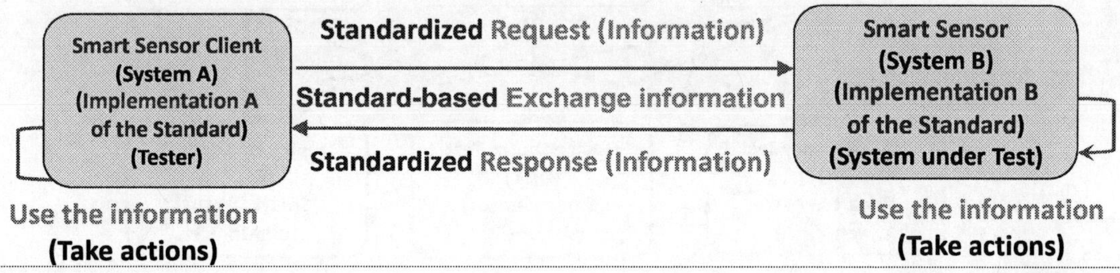

4. Interoperability Testing Methods of Standard-based Smart Sensors

4.1 Device-to-Device (D2D) Testing Method

4.2 Hardware-In-the-Loop (HIL) Simulation-based Testing Method

#SensorsConverge

Sensors Converge

4. Interoperability Testing Methods of Standard-based Smart Sensors (Cont'd)

4.1 Device-to-Device (D2D) Testing Method of Smart Sensors

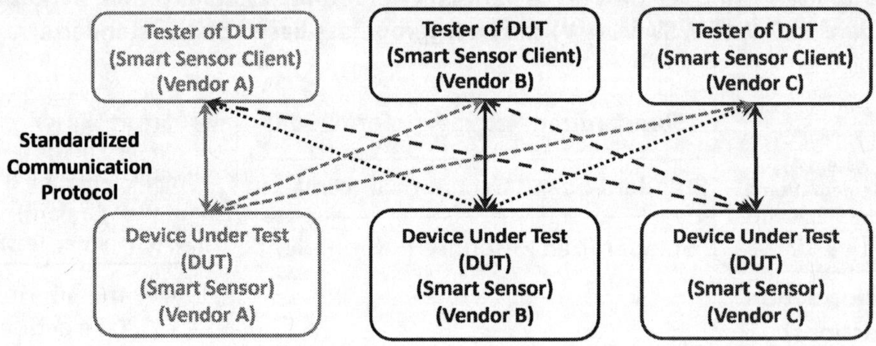

#SensorsConverge

Sensors Converge

4. Interoperability Testing Methods of Standard-based Smart Sensors (Cont'd)

4.1 Device-to-Device (D2D) Testing Method of Smart Sensors

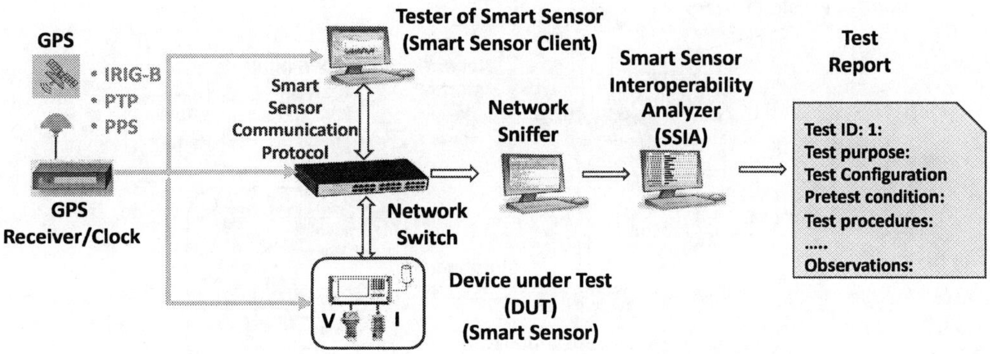

#SensorsConverge

4. Interoperability Testing Methods of Standard-based Smart Sensors (Cont'd)

4.2 Hardware-In-the-loop (HIL) Simulation-based Testing Method of Smart Sensors

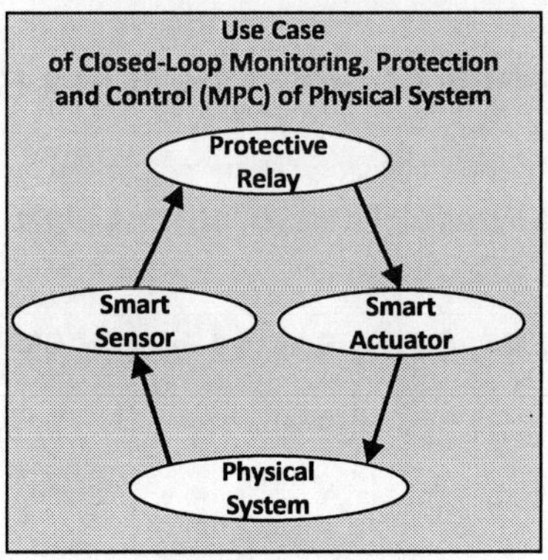

MPC Simulation

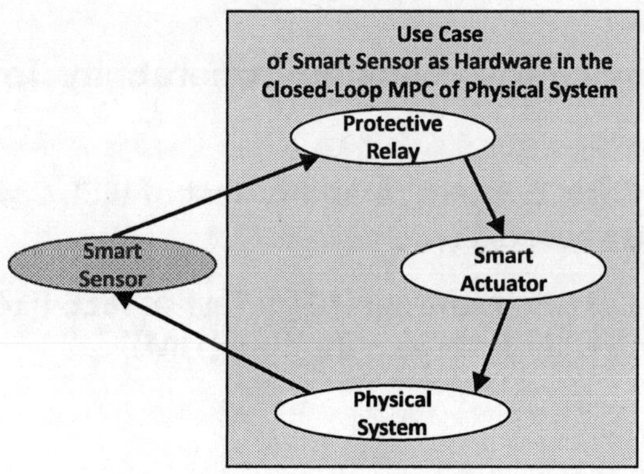

Smart Sensor (as Hardware) in MPC Simulation

#SensorsConverge

4. Interoperability Testing Methods of Standard-based Smart Sensors (Cont'd)

4.2 Hardware-in-the-loop (HIL) Simulation-based Testing Method

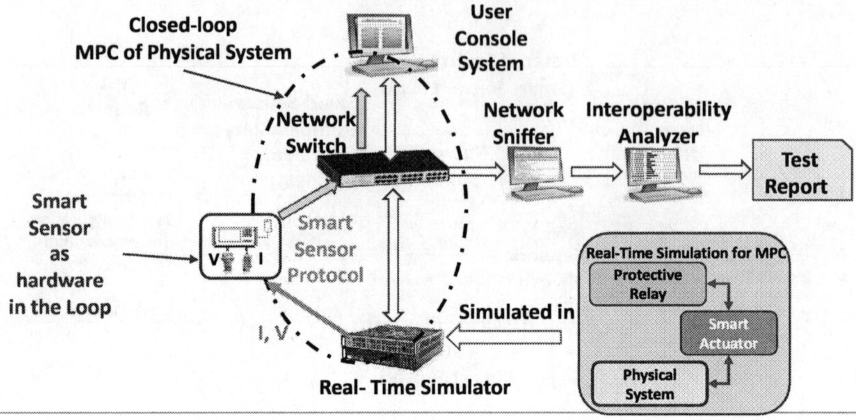

#SensorsConverge

5. Interoperability Test Cases of Smart Sensors

5.1 Device-to-Device Interoperability Test Cases of Smart Sensors (SS)

- **Test Case 1: Interoperability Test of IEEE C37.118 Phasor Measurement Unit (PMU)-based SS**
- **Test Case 2: Interoperability Test of IEEE P1451.0 & 1451.5-802.11-based SS (Transducer Interface module (TIM))**

#SensorsConverge

5.1 Device-to-Device Interoperability Test Cases

Test Case 1: Interoperability Test of IEEE C37.118 PMU-based Smart Sensors

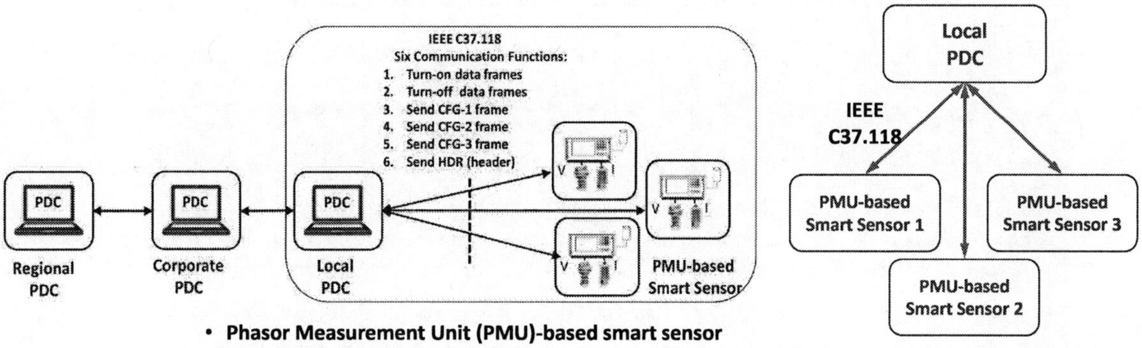

- **Phasor Measurement Unit (PMU)-based smart sensor**
- **Phasor Data Concentrator (PDC)**

5.1 Device-to-Device Interoperability Test Cases (Cont'd)

Test Case 1: Interoperability Test of IEEE C37.118 PMU-based Smart Sensors

Eight Commercial PMU-based Smart Sensors (SS)

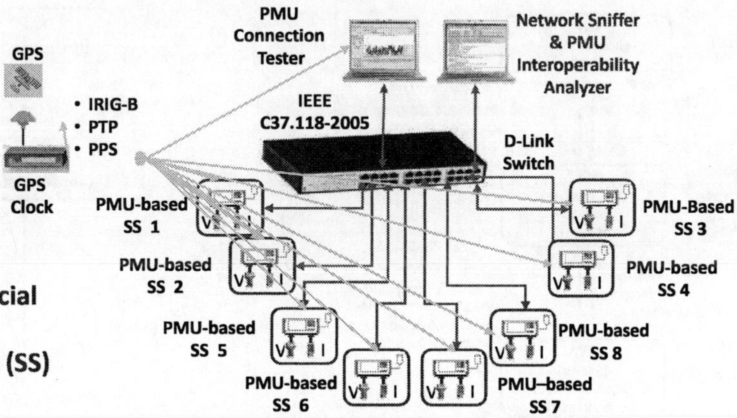

Source: *Eugene Y. Song; Gerald J. FitzPatrick, Interoperability test for IEEE C37.118 standard-based phasor measurement units (PMUs), https://ieeexplore.ieee.org/document/7781240.*

5.1 Device-to-Device Interoperability Test Cases (Cont'd)

Test Case 1: Interoperability Test of IEEE C37.118 PMU-based Smart Sensors

Interoperability Test case		PMU 1 (TCP)	PMU 2 (TCP)	PMU 3 (TCP)	PMU 4 (TCP)	PMU 5 (UDP)	PMU 6 (TCP)	PMU 7 (TCP)	PMU 8 (TCP)
Turn Off	Procedures	P	P	P	P	P	P	P	P
	Command	P	P	P	P	P	P	P	P
	Response	P	P	P	P	P	P	P	P
Turn On	Procedures	P	P	P	P	P	P	P	P
	Command	P	P	P	P	P	P	P	P
	Response	P	P	P	P	P	P	P	P
Header	Procedures	P	P	P	P	P	F	P	P
	Command	P	P	P	P	P	P	P	P
	Response	P	P	P	P	P	F	P	P
CFG-1	Procedures	P	P	P	P	P	P	P	P
	Command	P	P	P	P	P	P	P	P
	Response	P	P	P	P	P	P	P	P
CFG-2	Procedures	P	P	P	P	P	P	P	P
	Command	P	P	P	P	P	P	P	P
	Response	P	P	P	P	P	P	P	P
Overall		P	P	P	P	P	P(80%)	P	P

#SensorsConverge

Source: *Eugene Y. Song; Gerald J. FitzPatrick, Interoperability test for IEEE C37.118 standard-based phasor measurement units (PMUs), https://ieeexplore.ieee.org/document/7781240.*

Sensors Converge

5.1 Device-to-Device Interoperability Test Cases (Cont'd)

Test Case 2: Interoperability Test of IEEE P1451.0 and 1451.5-802.11-based Smart Sensor (TIM/WTIM)

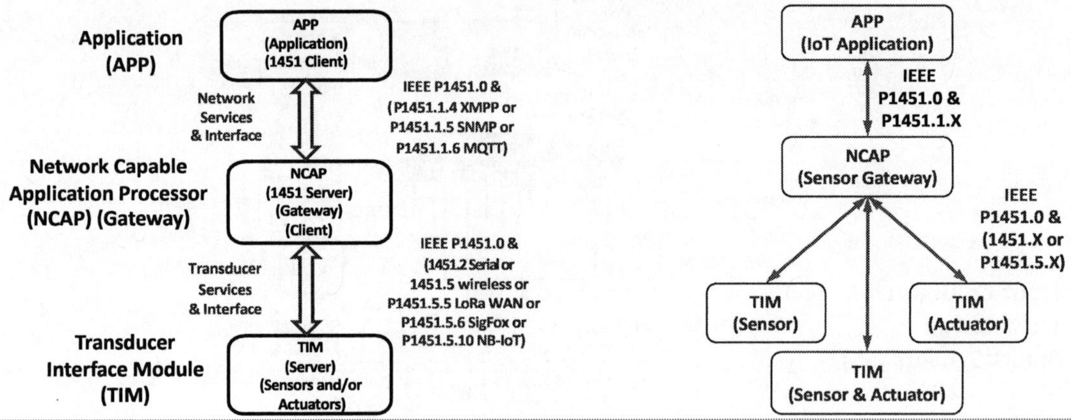

#SensorsConverge

Source: *Eugene Y. Song; Kang B. Lee; Fred Proctor, Testing system for IEEE 1451.5–802.11 standard-based wireless sensors, https://ieeexplore.ieee.org/document/6860865*

Sensors Converge

5.1 Device-to-Device Interoperability Test Cases (Cont'd)

Test Case 2: Interoperability Test of IEEE 1451.0 and 1451.5 802.11-based Smart Sensor (TIM/WTIM)

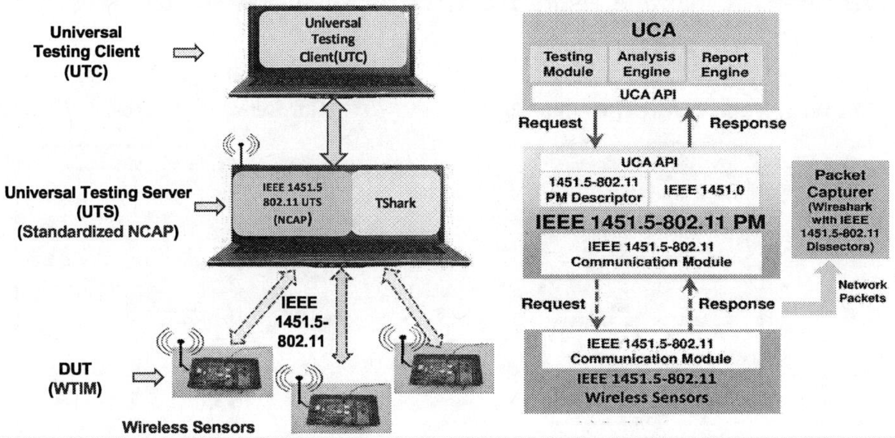

#SensorsConverge

Source: *Eugene Y. Song; Kang B. Lee; Fred Proctor, Testing system for IEEE 1451.5–802.11 standard-based wireless sensors, https://ieeexplore.ieee.org/document/6860865*

Sensors Converge

5.1 Device-to-Device Interoperability Test Cases (Cont'd)

Test Case 2: Interoperability Test of IEEE 1451.0 and 1451.5-802.11-based Smart Sensor (TIM/WTIM)

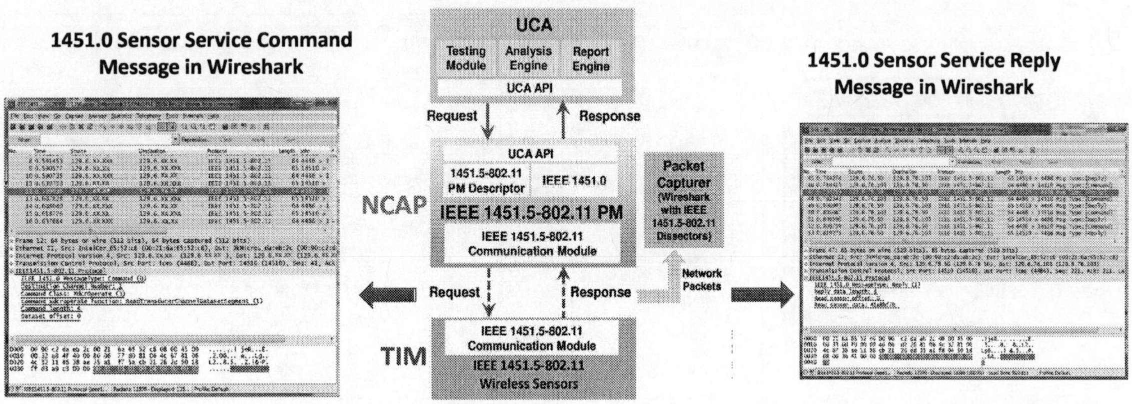

#SensorsConverge

Source: *Eugene Y. Song; Kang B. Lee; Fred Proctor, Testing system for IEEE 1451.5–802.11 standard-based wireless sensors, https://ieeexplore.ieee.org/document/6860865*

Sensors Converge

5.2 HIL Simulation-based Interoperability Test Case of Smart Sensors

Test Case: HIL Interoperability Test of IEC 61850-9-2 Merging Unit (MU)-based Smart Sensors

Use Case of Closed-Loop Monitoring, Protection and Control (MPC) of EPG

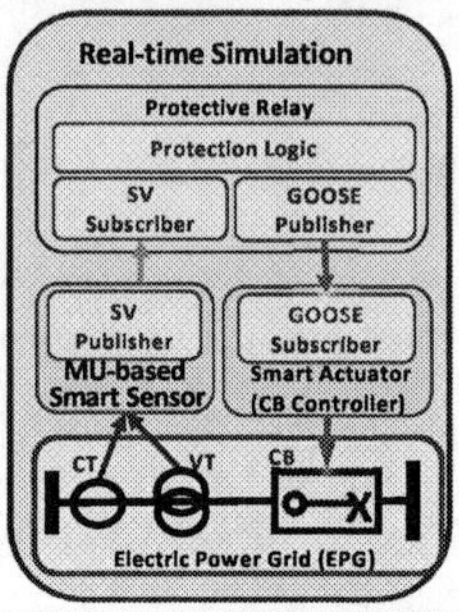

Use Case of MU-based smart sensor as Hardware in Closed-Loop MPC of EPG

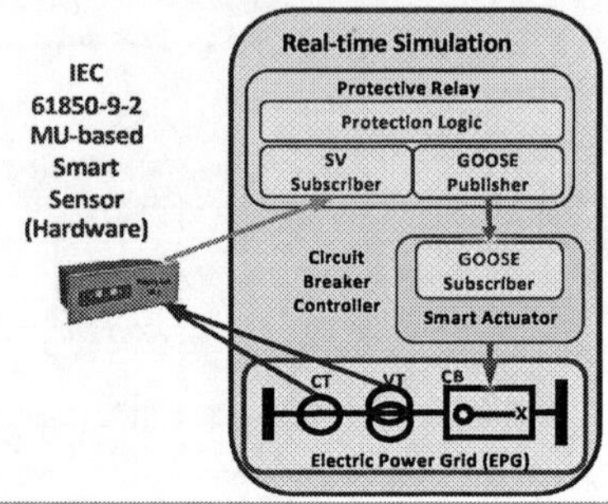

- **SV-Sampled Values**
- **GOOSE-Generic Object-Oriented Substation/System Events**

5.2 HIL Simulation-based interoperability Test Case of Smart Sensors (Cont'd)

Test Case: HIL Interoperability Test of IEC 61850-9-2 Merging Unit (MU)-based Smart Sensors

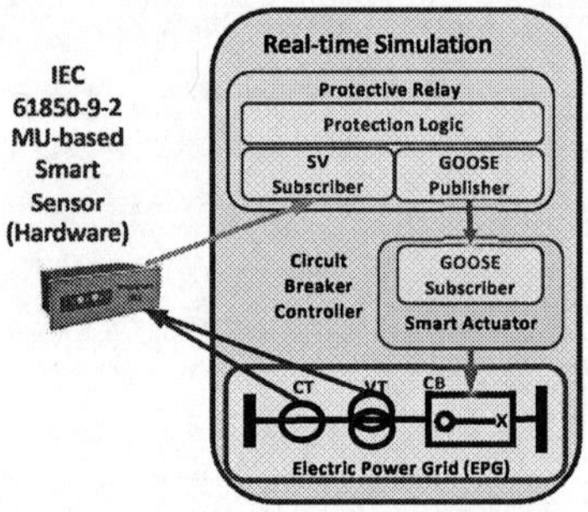

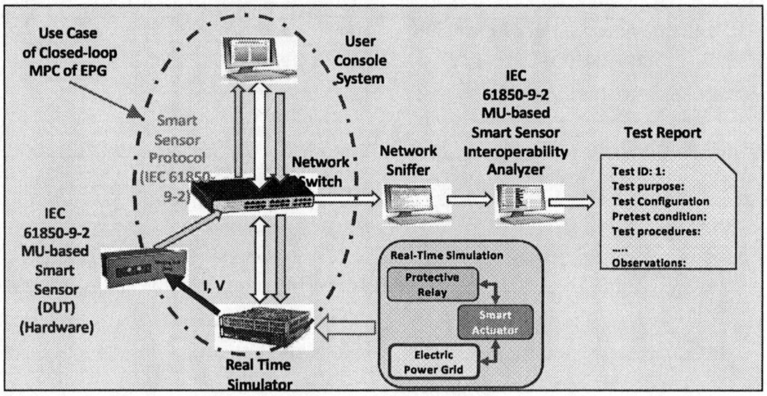

Source: *Eugene Song and Kang Lee, Hardware-In-The-Loop (HIL) Simulation-based Interoperability Testing Method of Smart Sensors in Smart Grids, 2024 ICPS 7th IEEE International Conference on Industrial Cyber-Physical Systems (ICPS), May 12-15, 2024, St. Louis, MO, USA.*

5.2 HIL Simulation-based interoperability Test Case of Smart Sensors (Cont'd)

Test Case: HIL Interoperability Test of IEC 61850-9-2 Merging Unit (MU)-based Smart Sensors

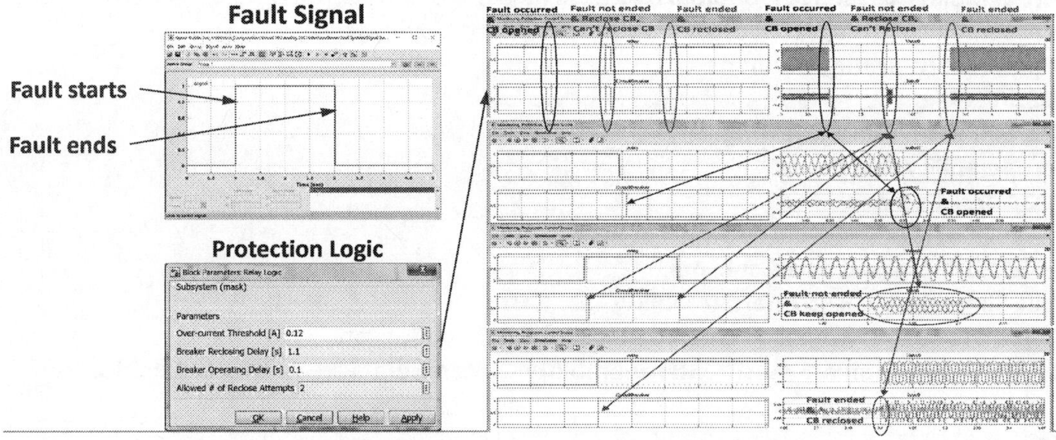

Source: *Eugene Song and Kang Lee, Hardware-In-The-Loop (HIL) Simulation-based Interoperability Testing Method of Smart Sensors in Smart Grids, 2024 ICPS 7th IEEE International Conference on Industrial Cyber-Physical Systems (ICPS), May 12-15, 2024, St. Louis, MO, USA.*

5.2 HIL Simulation-based interoperability Test Case of Smart Sensors (Cont'd)

Test Case: HIL Interoperability Test of IEC 61850-9-2 Merging Unit (MU)-based Smart Sensors

IEC 61851-8-1 GOOSE messages are used to <u>open (false)</u> **or** <u>close (true)</u> the circuit breaker to protect power grid

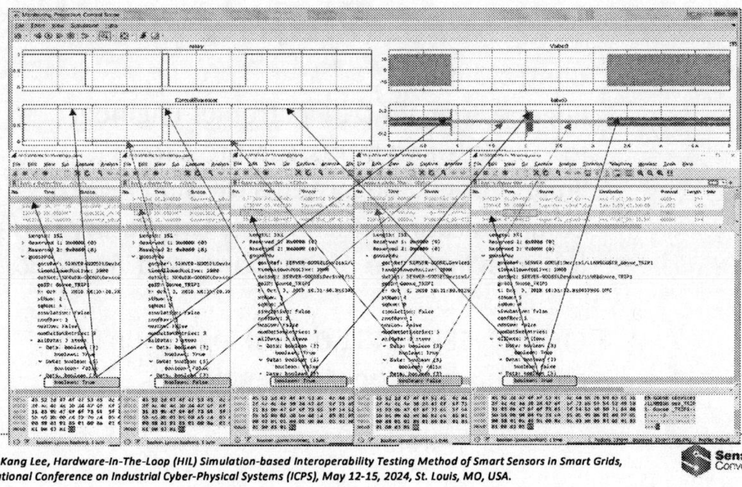

- True → false → true → false → true
- Close → open → reclose → reopen → reclose

Source: *Eugene Song and Kang Lee, Hardware-In-The-Loop (HIL) Simulation-based Interoperability Testing Method of Smart Sensors in Smart Grids, 2024 ICPS 7th IEEE International Conference on Industrial Cyber-Physical Systems (ICPS), May 12-15, 2024, St. Louis, MO, USA.*

6. Key Takeaways

1. Interoperability Challenges for Smart Sensors in IoT/IIoT
2. Interoperability Testing to Overcome Interoperability Challenges
3. Interoperability Testing methods
   - D2D Testing
   - HIL Simulation-based Testing
4. Interoperability Test Cases:
   - D2D Test Cases:
     - IEEE C37.118 PMU-based Smart Sensors
     - IEEE 1451-based smart sensors
   - HIL Simulation-based Interoperability Test Case:
     - IEC 61850-9-2 MU-based smart sensor for MPC applications
5. Solution to assure smart sensor interoperability – Interoperability Testing & Certification

#SensorsConverge

Sensors Converge

Questions?

Thank you!!!

Contact Info:
Eugene Song Ph.D., Electronics Engineer
IoT Devices and Infrastructure Group
Smart Connected Systems Division (SCSD)
Communications Technology Laboratory (CTL)
National Institute of Standards and Technology (NIST)

Chair of IEEE P1451.0 Working Group (WG)
email: eugene.song@nist.gov

#SensorsConverge

Sensors Converge

AUTHOR INDEX

Questex Media Group, Inc.
275 Grove Street, Suite 2-130
Newton, Massachusetts 02466
USA

ISBN 979-8-3313-0065-4

CURRAN ASSOCIATES INC.
proceedings.com